"For nearly a century, only a handful of scholars have published manuals for the exegesis of the Hebrew Bible. *How to Understand and Apply the Old Testament* surpasses all previous works with its biblical-theological orientation, purposeful organization, depth of analytical guidance, clarity of explanation, illustrative examples, and direction regarding interpretive implications. DeRouchie walks the aspiring exegete and expositor through the steps of a text-focused, genre-aware, and context-sensitive methodology. No matter what one's theological views might be on any particular text, this volume gives users superb guidance for interpreting the Old Testament. I commend it to every teacher and student of Hebrew exegesis as the best textbook available."

—**William D. Barrick**, Retired Professor of Old Testament, The Master's Seminary; Old Testament Editor, Evangelical Commentary on the Old Testament

"This book is an invaluable resource for anyone serious about preaching and teaching the Old Testament in a way consistent with our Lord's words (Luke 24:25–27, 44–49). From genre classification to the biblical, systematic, and practical theological implications of expositing the Old Testament, DeRouchie works through every step necessary for establishing a Christ-centered (biblical-theological) exegetical methodology; the examples provided throughout are extremely helpful. This is the book I longed for as a student and pastor and am now excited to be using in several of my courses (Hebrew Syntax, Hebrew Prose, Hebrew Poetry, Old Testament Biblical Theology) as I train the next generation of international pastors and church-planters to preach Christ rightly from all of Scripture for the glory of Christ's name among the nations."

—**Derek D. Bass**, Assistant Professor of Old Testament Language and Literature, Tyndale Theological Seminary, The Netherlands

"DeRouchie's latest offering provides exegetical and theological tools for how to read and apply the Old Testament in a way that is centered on Christ, while having controls to ensure that we are reading out of the text what the authors intended rather than reading into the text our own ideas. Two contributions stand out. The first is the extended discussion of various genres, explaining the literary conventions that are required for responsible interpretation and showing how each genre contributes to the Bible's coherent message, which centers its hope in the coming Messiah. The second is the thorough explanation of the method of discourse analysis that DeRouchie developed in his doctoral dissertation. The analysis begins with building a text hierarchy, which in turn supplies an objective basis for tracing the literary argument in a way that shows how each part of the text contributes to the author's main point. The argument diagram then provides the basis for an exegetical outline that allows one to preach a text, confident that one is teaching what the author intended. DeRouchie's book is a sure-footed guide to Old Testament interpretation and proclamation."

—**John C. Beckman**, Assistant Professor of Old Testament, Bethlehem College & Seminary

"Not only is this the best road map to interpreting the Hebrew Bible that I know of, it also strengthens faith, motivates study, and exalts the Messiah. DeRouchie has carefully designed this book to serve both the reader who knows biblical Hebrew and the one who doesn't. DeRouchie models excellent scholarship propelled by a passion for the Lord, and this book will provide the reader with the tools to study, apply, and teach the Scriptures for the good of the church and the glory of God."

—**Todd Bolen**, Associate Professor of Biblical Studies, The Master's College

"*How to Understand and Apply the Old Testament* is not just another introduction to Bible interpretation. This is hinted at by the subtitle, *Twelve Steps from Exegesis to Theology.* Readers—no, users—of this book will discover something of Jason DeRouchie's passion for the good news as it is in Jesus that all his classroom students regularly observe as he provides tested and proven step-by-step procedures on progressing from simply reading the Old Testament Scriptures to deepening and enriching belief in Jesus Christ. Yes, indeed, this book features the Old Testament, but it focuses on the Lord Jesus Christ because DeRouchie correctly argues that from its beginning to its climax, the whole Old Testament is about the coming Messiah. He is rightly convinced that the Old Testament is Christian Scripture because it finds its true and proper culmination and fulfillment only in Jesus of Nazareth. I heartily commend this book. May it be instrumental in the formation of belief in Christ Jesus for many."

—**Ardel B. Caneday**, Professor of New Testament and Greek, University of Northwestern—St. Paul

"DeRouchie brings both scholarly expertise and mission experience into the service of helping us see the Old Testament as *Christian* Scripture. Here is faithful interpretation of the Word of God in accord with its own historical setting and in harmony with its redemptive context. Such a whole-Bible perspective will help enable Bible interpreters to identify the particular concerns of Old Testament writers and to celebrate the continuities of their words with New Testament revelations of our Redeemer. As a result, believers will be enriched in their ability to apply the Old Testament to their lives in ways that nurture hope in the gospel and that fuel zeal for the glory of Christ."

—**Bryan Chapell**, Pastor, Grace Presbyterian Church, Peoria, IL

"Just looking over the table of contents gave me an adrenaline surge. I wish I'd had this book when I was teaching Old Testament, and I now envy the professors and students who use the book. Its content does not disappoint. Every sentence conveys the result of careful thought. DeRouchie is a scholar who knows the theological discourse regarding biblical interpretation and is thus well equipped to introduce students to it. But his work does more than orient the student's head; DeRouchie also aims at producing the heart of a faithful interpreter of God's Word. I applaud his commitment to 'the distinct nature of Scripture as God's unique Word' against some (even evangelicals) who fail to distinguish the Bible as such. Thus he differentiates biblical narrative from 'myth.' As he says, 'We cannot deny the reality of an event that the biblical authors believed to be historical and still say that we affirm Scripture's authority.' I also applaud DeRouchie's belief that Old Testament interpretation cannot end until we have discerned how each book points to Christ. The book is abundantly sprinkled with excellent instructive charts. In addition to being friendly to the reader (with chapter previews, reviews, and study questions), this book does not sidestep difficult issues but includes many footnotes pointing them out and suggesting helpful thoughts and resources. It is also full of insights regarding many biblical texts, such as Proverbs 22:6 (over three pages) and 1 Samuel 13:14 (four pages). Students who know Hebrew will be especially excited by many sections in the book that discuss issues arising in the study of the Hebrew Bible. I will be returning to this book often."

—**E. Ray Clendenen**, Senior Editor of Bible and Reference Publishing, B&H Publishing Group

"In this monument of industry, Jason DeRouchie has appropriated insights from discourse linguistics to lay out for students the essential questions and methods for responsible study of the Hebrew Bible as Christian Scripture. And the overview of all the tools and resources—what a treasure trove! You don't have to agree with every exegetical decision he makes to be grateful to him for his tireless work and to use this as a tool for learning and teaching the art of exegesis. Thank you, Dr. DeRouchie!"

—**C. John ("Jack") Collins**, Professor of Old Testament, Covenant Theological Seminary

"DeRouchie's *How to Understand and Apply the Old Testament* is a veritable treasure trove for anyone interested in academically rigorous, God-glorifying, Christ-savoring Old Testament interpretation. His book is not just a book on hermeneutics; it is a biblical theology of how we should read our Bibles. His volume runs the gamut from highly detailed work, on such topics as word studies and the relationship between clauses, to grander, big-picture ideas, encompassing the Bible's overall narrative. This book is must reading for anyone who is hungry to dig into the riches of the Old Testament."

—**John C. Crutchfield**, Professor of Bible, Columbia International University

"DeRouchie writes with rigor, clarity, and passion. He details the extraordinary amount of work that is involved in seeking to understand the meaning of the biblical text—and yet at the same time the extraordinary importance of getting that meaning, for the exegetical payoff is out of this world. He moves us from the individual tree (exegesis) to the larger forest (theology) and then to the breathtaking, worship-inspiring view of the whole (doxology). He gives many examples and illustrations throughout the book that will help the student understand. I can sense that he wants us to 'get' the Bible so that the Bible can 'get' us."

—**Stephen G. Dempster**, Professor of Religious Studies, Crandall University, Moncton, New Brunswick, Canada

"This book is an excellent resource with many strengths. It has tracks for those who do and do not know Hebrew and includes study questions, a glossary, and extensive bibliographical aids. As a textbook this work targets a specific theological audience, but its cutting-edge application of discourse analysis makes it a valuable reference work for all Hebrew-informed interpreters. It is set forth in a clear step-by-step format with helpful illustrations. Methodologically, it correctly works from the largest literary-linguistic unit to the smallest; then it progresses contextually from the smallest unit to larger spheres of literary, historical, cultural, and theological contexts; and most importantly, it continues on to guided reflection for the purposes of biblical theology, systematic theology, and practical application—all with a strong Christocentric focus."

—**Rodney K. Duke**, Professor of Religion, Appalachian State University

"Once again DeRouchie has evidenced his special gift in combining the precision of a scholar, the organization of a teacher, and the heart of a pastor in his new textbook, *How to Understand and Apply the Old Testament*. Writing in three concurrent tracks for beginning, intermediate, and advanced students, he develops a clear trajectory from exegesis to theology, providing discussion informed by recent scholarship, clear biblical examples, and abundant resources for further study. This, then, is a manual that invites rereading at increasing levels of insight and precision. For students of the Old Testament, DeRouchie's work will likely become the standard for the next generation."

—**Daniel J. Estes**, Distinguished Professor of Old Testament, Cedarville University

"This book is a marriage of hermeneutical theory and practice, of doctrinal and ethical theology. Dr. Jason DeRouchie has done an outstanding job of writing a step-by-step guide to studying the Old Testament that is both comprehensive and balanced. Jason is a man of scholarship and godliness. In this work he shares his expertise and faith to help readers interpret God's Word accurately and apply it more appropriately. Each chapter offers options for reading depending on one's ability and interest in studying the text in the original language. This approach makes it ideal for many classroom settings. From students to experienced preachers and teachers, people who want to know God better through the Scriptures will gain much from this careful study."

—**Lee M. Fields**, Professor of Bible, Mid-Atlantic Christian University

"Too many American Christians either have given up altogether on understanding the Old Testament or have accepted shallow, even unbiblical readings. But Jesus didn't! In *How to Understand and Apply the Old Testament*, Dr. DeRouchie has given the church a great gift. These pages are packed with lucid, enlightening, and inspiring examples of exegesis done well—and done in ways that drive us to godly theology. Dr. DeRouchie's methods will bless you and, above all, lead you to see Christ more clearly and love him more dearly. Highly recommended!"

—**William Fullilove**, Assistant Professor of Old Testament, Reformed Theological Seminary

"Students of God's Word from all walks of life will benefit from *How to Understand and Apply the Old Testament*. Reflecting on my travels and work overseas, I can't help but think of how much less doctrinal error and how much more peace in Christ we would enjoy if we took theology as seriously and cheerfully as DeRouchie. One of the key components of this volume's usefulness is its three tracks for target audiences. As a busy mom, I don't have time to read every page, but as a wannabe Hebrew student, I do want to grow in my understanding. The chapter-by-chapter 'trail guides' really helped me maximize my time in the book. Use and enjoy this volume in your personal studies, discipleship, and parenting."

—**Gloria Furman**, Cross-Cultural Worker

"Textbooks on biblical hermeneutics generally come in two varieties: Either they are theoretical, describing the philosophical underpinnings of an interpretive method and meant primarily for the academy, or they are practical, giving instruction in how to go about interpretation and meant primarily for pastors, Bible teachers, and students. DeRouchie's text is of the second variety, and it fulfills its purposes admirably. But DeRouchie also fills a significant gap among textbooks: he gives a clear and informed presentation of how the tools provided by Hebrew linguistics and discourse analysis enable readers to better understand the Hebrew Scriptures. So this is not just another book on how to read the Bible; it is a major resource for all who seek to seriously engage with the biblical text."

—**Duane A. Garrett**, John R. Sampey Professor of Old Testament Interpretation, Professor of Biblical Theology, The Southern Baptist Theological Seminary

"Magisterial in depth and scope, DeRouchie's guide to biblical interpretation (exegesis and theology) of the Old Testament is an excellent beginning to a new truly Christian *Literarkritik*, which moves us away from the dead ends of the Enlightenment's placing of critical human reason as the highest criterion for determining truth."

—**Peter J. Gentry**, Donald L. Williams Professor of Old Testament Interpretation, The Southern Baptist Theological Seminary

"DeRouchie's *How to Understand and Apply the Old Testament* is a guidebook for those who want to seriously pursue God in the Old Testament Scriptures. DeRouchie leads his readers through a twelve-stage interpretive process that takes them from the text of the Old Testament Scriptures to a Christ-centered application of those Scriptures to themselves, the church, and the world. This book is user-friendly, and its pages are filled with applications of Scripture that will draw the student into the deep and thorough study of the Old Testament that the book teaches and models. If you are serious about loving God with all your heart, mind, and strength, then this is the book for you. Its contents will feed and challenge your heart and mind. And if you are going to master everything in this book, it will require all the strength the Lord gives you."

—**W. Edward Glenny**, Professor of New Testament and Greek, University of Northwestern—St. Paul

"Busy pastors and Bible teachers often see the various disciplines that structured their theological education recede into the distance because of the demands on their time. If only someone would provide them with a basic yet comprehensive handbook to serve as a reference resource and means of revision when needed! Jason DeRouchie has done exactly that. He sets out the logical stages in dealing with the exegesis of the biblical text in a way that can be negotiated even by readers who have no formal theological training. But for the student or pastor, this is a wonderful aid to teaching and preaching. The progression of the twelve steps from text to application highlights the care needed to arrive at a sound biblical theology and trustworthy doctrinal statements. The final stage of practical theology places the whole process into the pastoral ministry to God's people. I consider this the crowning achievement of the book. All the toil in language and exegesis, moving through biblical and systematic theology, brings its copious rewards in the way the text is applied so that we, the readers, as well as our hearers, can truly discern the very Word of God to us in the Bible."

—**Graeme Goldsworthy**, Former Lecturer in Old Testament, Biblical Theology, and Hermeneutics, Moore Theological College, Sydney, Australia

"As one who loves and teaches exegesis of Old Testament texts, I view Jason DeRouchie's volume *How to Understand and Apply the Old Testament* as nothing less than a gold mine! As with any other exegesis 'how-to' book, each of us will have this or that quibble. Regardless, DeRouchie has given professors, pastors, and students a treasure trove of solid procedure, great examples, and helpful insights. Besides providing a thorough explanation of his twelve steps, he provides clear examples, threading the same passages for the various steps (along with some new ones). On top of all that, his abundant provision of resources to aid the exegete for each step is a great asset. I look forward to using the book and recommending it to my students and alumni."

—**Michael A. Grisanti**, Lead Professor of Old Testament and Director of the Th.M. Program, The Master's Seminary

"People often ask me how they can grow in understanding the Bible when seminary is not an option. *How to Understand and Apply the Old Testament* provides exactly what those of us who don't know Hebrew and Greek need to take a huge step forward in our learning. This book not only provides instruction on using the tools such as genre, grammar, and context, but also demonstrates clearly and effectively how to use these tools."

—**Nancy Guthrie**, Bible Teacher; Author, *Seeing Jesus in the Old Testament* Bible study series

"This is the most thoughtful and well-developed guidebook on how to do exegesis that I have encountered. While it is designed for a student of the Old Testament who has or is acquiring Hebrew skills, it is organized so that anyone who desires to study the Old Testament seriously can use it. The steps are not only clearly defined but also excellently modeled through the exegesis of several key passages. The result is a book that is packed with rich nuggets of expositional insight embedded in a matrix of solid exegetical 'how-to' and thus an invaluable reference tool."

—**Michael A. Harbin**, Professor of Biblical Studies and Chair of the Department of Biblical Studies, Christian Educational Ministries, and Philosophy, Taylor University

"DeRouchie has written a true gem—the many facets of a seminary education are encapsulated in this single volume! It will serve to encourage and guide serious Bible students seeking to understand the message of the Scriptures of Jesus and apply it to their contemporary settings. The book is plainly written with clear steps and adroit examples that model how one should study, do, and teach, following the ancient model of Ezra the scribe."

—**Chip Hardy**, Assistant Professor of Old Testament and Semitic Languages, Southeastern Baptist Theological Seminary

"DeRouchie's *How to Understand and Apply the Old Testament* is perhaps the most comprehensive and complete practical guide to Old Testament hermeneutics and exegesis available today. This is an outstanding work, and I heartily recommend it to all who teach Old Testament exegesis."

—**J. Daniel Hays**, Professor of Biblical Studies, Ouachita Baptist University

"DeRouchie offers a twelve-step process for Old Testament exegesis that goes beyond exegesis proper to include biblical, systematic, and practical theology. From the beginning, DeRouchie's confessional commitments are clear and central to the task. He provides an excellent ten-point argument for the importance of the Old Testament for Christians—not least of which is the fact that it was the only Scriptures of Jesus and the earliest church. DeRouchie presents an insightful introduction to the genres of the Old Testament (i.e., historical narrative, prophecy and law, psalms, and proverbs) with principles for interpreting each (chapter 1). His explanations of clause and text grammar (chapter 5) and argument diagramming (chapter 6)—with several examples—are particularly helpful. Notably, DeRouchie regularly discusses the New Testament authors' interpretation of the Old Testament. He begins each chapter with 'trail guides' and then carries images through the rest of the book to aid in faster navigation of the material for readers who feel less adroit with Old Testament Hebrew. One strength of this book, besides illustrating the exegetical steps with a variety of biblical examples, is that the reader can follow DeRouchie's treatment of one particular model passage—Exodus 19:4–6—through all twelve steps of the process. If you are looking for an integrative introduction to Old Testament exegesis that is aimed at worshipful application of God's Word, this volume is worthy of your consideration."

—**Douglas S. Huffman**, Professor and Associate Dean of Biblical and Theological Studies, Talbot School of Theology, Biola University

"DeRouchie has provided an excellent resource in his *How to Understand and Apply the Old Testament: Twelve Steps from Exegesis to Theology*. His explanations are clear and easy to follow, and they provide genuine helps in the process of preaching and teaching the Old Testament text. It encourages leaders to teach from the Old Testament in a day when such a practice of teaching is hard to find."

—**Walter C. Kaiser Jr.**, President Emeritus, Gordon-Conwell Theological Seminary

"*How to Understand and Apply the Old Testament* takes seriously the testimony of Scripture—that the Old Testament is *Christian Scripture*, and as such, it ought to be preached and taught in the church today. Anyone wanting to grapple with how to interpret and apply the Old Testament will find this volume immensely helpful. It is scholarly, rich in theological and exegetical insight, and attentive to Hebrew grammar and syntax, yet the step-by-step approach to the interpretive task means that it is accessible for pastors and Bible teachers alike. You will want to have this volume in your library!"

—**Carol M. Kaminski**, Professor of Old Testament, Gordon-Conwell Theological Seminary

"This book is late. I wish I'd had it about fifteen years ago, because so much here would have helped me. This isn't just a book about the Old Testament. DeRouchie never acts as though the Old Testament were the only testament, for he celebrates the gospel event page after page. Because of this, *How to Understand and Apply the Old Testament* will impact your understanding of the New Testament. It is clear that DeRouchie knows the mechanics of the Old Testament. But far more than that, it is clear that he knows the God of the Old Testament. And he wants his readers to join him in worship. I can't wait to get this into the hands of the people with whom I work."

—**Tom Kelby**, President, Hands to the Plow Ministries; President, Alliance for Renewal Churches

"There can often be confusion for Christians in seeing the relevance of the Old Testament for modern-day living. DeRouchie systematically overcomes these obstacles and demonstrates both the need to study 'Jesus' Bible' and the joy that awaits Christians who do. DeRouchie's work is a thorough and sure guide in how to understand and apply the truths contained in the Old Testament. It also serves as a great reminder that biblical interpretation is the necessary ground for sound doctrine and practical Christian living. May many take up this book and be exhorted to engage the text of Scripture so as to love our great God—the Sovereign, Savior, and Satisfier."

—**Jeremy M. Kimble**, Assistant Professor of Theological Studies, Cedarville University

"DeRouchie has produced a masterpiece of a guide to interpreting the Old Testament Scriptures. He has written it so that beginning, intermediate, and advanced students may grow in their understanding of the message of the divinely inspired text.

I enthusiastically recommend this book for everyone who desires to interpret the Old Testament faithfully."

—**Tremper Longman III**, Robert H. Gundry Professor of Biblical Studies, Westmont College

"Here is a comprehensive handbook that I readily endorse as a remedy to the problem of widespread ignorance of the Old Testament. Pedagogically sensitive, DeRouchie provides well-outlined steps, numerous creative charts, and ample documentation, together with resources and a glossary. DeRouchie has admirable control of all sections of the Old Testament, and is clearly conversant with current scholarship. Sections in which the author leans hard on the Hebrew language (of great help to seminarians) need not be offputting for the average reader, given his many helps along the way. Definitely evangelical and conservative, DeRouchie writes with spiritual warmth. I salute his passion for sound Bible interpretation that will yield understanding and result in godly behavior to the praise of God, the Author of Scripture and of salvation."

—**Elmer A. Martens**, President Emeritus and Professor Emeritus of Old Testament, Fresno Pacific University Biblical Seminary

"*How to Understand and Apply the Old Testament* is rightly titled, for it is more than an ordinary introduction. It's a thorough, complete presentation of how Christian readers interpret the Old Testament correctly and effectively. DeRouchie's treatment recognizes that proper interpretation takes account of the whole-Bible canonical perspective and that interpretation is deficient without practical application for Christian life. It is must reading for anyone—with or without knowledge of Hebrew—who wants more out of his or her study of the Scriptures."

—**Kenneth A. Mathews**, Professor of Divinity—Old Testament, Beeson Divinity School

"When reading DeRouchie's *How to Understand and Apply the Old Testament*, two words come to mind: *comprehensive* and *accessible* (think: Grant Osborne meets Fee and Stuart). DeRouchie's passion for the Old Testament and love for Christ come through on virtually every page. This book is a reliable guide for interpreting the Old Testament that is balanced with both light and heat."

—**Benjamin L. Merkle**, Professor of New Testament and Greek, Southeastern Baptist Theological Seminary

"Conversationally engaging; literarily transparent; materially comprehensive; pedagogically superb; academically sound, precise, and informed—all this and more. In over fifty-two years of teaching in the classrooms of higher education, I have seen nothing comparable to this magnificent work by DeRouchie—destined to be the classic in its field."

—**Eugene H. Merrill**, Distinguished Professor Emeritus of Old Testament Studies, Dallas Theological Seminary

"This book (and its companion volume) does the church a great service. It is a rare and precious thing to combine the rigor of the academy with the passion of the preacher, but DeRouchie does just that. Rather than separate how to exegete and interpret the Old Testament from how to preach and apply it, this volume manages to bring both together in a way that is massively helpful and enormously enriching. I am confident that this handbook will prove to be a rich resource for generations of God's people who want to take studying the Bible seriously."

—**J. Gary Millar**, Principal and Lecturer in Old Testament, Biblical Theology, and Preaching, Queensland Theological College, Brisbane, Queensland, Australia

"Jason DeRouchie has given us a comprehensive and readable orientation to reading, interpreting, and applying the Old Testament. He covers all the relevant issues and offers a sensible and balanced approach to controversial ones. Especially noteworthy is the way he illustrates key principles and issues through careful and detailed exegesis of texts."

—**Douglas J. Moo**, Wessner Chair of Biblical Studies, Wheaton College; Chair, NIV Committee on Bible Translation

"What sets DeRouchie's text apart is his intentional cultivation of a method of interpretation that aims at the heart. His clarity is surpassed only by his conviction that the Scripture is worthy of dedicated study because it testifies to the supremacy of Christ. DeRouchie guides the reader through a wise and skillful exegetical approach to the Old Testament and does not shy away from tackling some important questions of application in the life of the church. While some evangelical scholars might hold to a different point of view on a particular application, he surely succeeds in equipping students of the Bible to 'rightly handl[e] the word of truth' (2 Tim. 2:15)."

—**Christine Palmer**, Adjunct Professor of Old Testament, Gordon-Conwell Theological Seminary

"In *How to Understand and Apply the Old Testament: Twelve Steps from Exegesis to Theology*, Jason DeRouchie reveals his great love for God, Scripture, and the church. He combines a clear and inductive presentation with key insights developed over many years of teaching. His contagious enthusiasm for the text empowers Christians to study and appreciate the Old Testament. He invites us to see that the Old Testament reveals the character of God, anticipates Christ, and clarifies how love for God and neighbor can be lived and applied today."

—**David Palmer**, Adjunct Professor of New Testament, Gordon-Conwell Theological Seminary; Senior Pastor, Kenwood Baptist Church, Cincinnati

"I think Jason DeRouchie would be happy if I said that this book is designed to move us from revelation through rigor to rapture—from the sacred Word of God, through the serious work of reading, to the satisfaction of knowing and enjoying God. There is no getting around the hard work of reading for holy wonder of worship. So DeRouchie spares no effort to make the rigors of careful reading plain. For many folks, the Old Testament is a foreign land. Oh, how good it is to have a native with you when you travel to an unfamiliar place. With his help, dozens of strange things begin to make sense. You even start to feel at home. I recommend this book if you have a wanderlust for exploring ancient treasures. There are many, and they are great. DeRouchie will show you how to find them."

—**John Piper**, Founder and Teacher, Desiring God; Chancellor and Professor of Biblical Exegesis, Bethlehem College & Seminary

"When I think back to my own student days of learning to exegete the Hebrew Scriptures, how I wish this resource had existed! DeRouchie is a sure and clear guide to studying the Old Testament with faithfulness and rigor—all with the goal of thinking and preaching rightly about God. Highly recommended!"

—**Robert L. Plummer**, Professor of New Testament Interpretation, The Southern Baptist Theological Seminary

"In *How to Understand and Apply the Old Testament,* Dr. DeRouchie has produced a thorough, comprehensive, and erudite introduction to the principles and objectives of exegesis and to the essential steps and component disciplines that are involved in the process. His style of writing and organization of the material is inviting, engaging, clear, and easy to follow. The foundation for this study is the author's unwavering conviction that the biblical writings (Old and New Testaments) are the Word of God, that they are authoritative for Christian living (accurate, infallible, and inerrant), that they are relevant to life and living in today's world, and that they are altogether sufficient for living in the presence of God. Delightfully, this study is infused throughout with a manifest love, reverence, and deep appreciation for God's Word. There is also sustained emphasis on the glory of God and the good of his people as the ultimate objectives of the exegetical process, from establishing the text to proclaiming and applying its truths. This study is persuasive in making the case that proficiency with the biblical languages or even a measure of exposure to either of them will enhance the prospects for realizing these two main objectives of biblical exegesis. In my many years of teaching the various levels of Hebrew language and exegesis, I would have enthusiastically used Jason DeRouchie's text in the noble responsibility of training men and women for the ministry of God's precious Scriptures."

—**Gary D. Pratico**, Retired Senior Professor of Old Testament, Gordon-Conwell Theological Seminary

"DeRouchie's book *How to Understand and Apply the Old Testament* is a wonderful resource for both pastors and teachers. The book takes readers through all the steps needed for interpretation and application, and it is beautifully clear in providing guidance for readers. Numerous examples keep the book from being too abstract. DeRouchie teaches a method that interpreters can actually use! Finally, the book stands out because of its theological stance. In other words, here is a book on Old Testament interpretation that is deeply informed by both biblical and systematic theology. A most helpful resource. I commend it enthusiastically."

—**Thomas R. Schreiner**, James Buchanan Harrison Professor of New Testament Interpretation and Associate Dean, The Southern Baptist Theological Seminary; Cochair, CSB Translation Oversight Committee

"Jason DeRouchie has organized vast quantities of useful information into a comprehensive and practical handbook, covering the entire process of interpretation from textual criticism to systematic theology. Discussions of theory and principle are avoided in favor of copious worked examples, reams of sensible advice, and well-considered models for theological and Christological interpretation. Students with some Hebrew will derive the most benefit from this book, but it would make a valuable resource for any beginning theological student, as well as for preachers seeking to deepen and enrich their engagement with the biblical text."

—**Andrew Shead**, Head of Department of Old Testament and Hebrew and Lecturer in Hebrew and Old Testament, Moore Theological College, Sydney, Australia

"This fascinating study teaches and demonstrates to readers (especially those who know Hebrew) how to systematically and accurately use the important exegetical tools available to us to comprehend and communicate the full theological message of the Old Testament. DeRouchie richly illustrates how this is possible by (1) taking into consideration the genre characteristics that influence the meaning and function of each different type of literature; (2) illustrating how to outline various Hebrew passages into a hierarchy of clausal dependency (using both a text hierarchy and arcing or bracketing) in order to bring out the persuasive contribution that each clause makes to support the central message; (3) securing the textual accuracy of a passage by critically evaluating various manuscript traditions; (4) preparing an outline based on the hierarchy of clauses in a passage in order to bring out the development of the theological purpose; (5) showing how to do word studies of key Hebrew terms; and (6) guiding the use of historical and literary context in order to ground the message in its original setting. But DeRouchie is not satisfied with just understanding the genre, words, structure, and context of a text! He cogently argues that it is necessary to press on for a wider synthetic biblical and theological examination that identifies the organic connections between passages throughout the Old and New Testaments, particularly those that relate to aspects of salvation history and the hope of a coming messianic King and his kingdom. Then, having thoroughly considered what God was communicating, DeRouchie addresses in the last section of this impressive study the challenge of setting forth principles for modern Christians that will provide appropriate and powerful applications, so that the lasting value of the Old Testament is preserved for our generation. I highly recommend this admirable approach, for it will greatly enhance the results of anyone's biblical study."

—**Gary V. Smith**, Retired Professor of Christian Studies, Union University

"If there is a deficiency in the contemporary evangelical pulpit, it is the absence of consistent expositional preaching of the Old Testament Scriptures. Many pastors either have lost touch with the biblical Hebrew they learned in seminary or are intimidated by the demands placed on those who would venture into the interpretation of complex Old Testament texts. If that is you, or perhaps someone you know, rejoice with me to see the publication of DeRouchie's excellent treatment of the twelve steps essential for movement from exegesis to sound and substantive pastoral theology. The church has long awaited and greatly needed this volume. I highly recommend it."

—**Sam Storms**, Lead Pastor for Preaching and Vision, Bridgeway Church, Oklahoma City; President, Enjoying God Ministries

"DeRouchie has put together a wonderfully comprehensive guide to the methodologies that allow us to see what the Old Testament is actually saying, so that we can rightly use the Old Testament for God's glory. His book teems with user-friendly explanations, smart charts, diagrams, lists, judicious bibliographical pointers, and patient, step-by-step guidance through even the toughest sorts of interpretational challenges. Anybody—from beginner to seasoned interpreter—can learn a lot from this book."

—**Douglas Stuart**, Professor of Old Testament, Gordon-Conwell Theological Seminary

"This volume faces the challenge of understanding and applying the Old Testament as Christian Scripture. This has been a tricky and (sometimes) contentious endeavor in the history of the church. DeRouchie faces the challenge head-on with clarity and provides a constructive and thoroughly Christian proposal. There is much to learn from his approach, and I suspect that many will embrace it."

—**Heath A. Thomas**, Dean, Herschel H. Hobbs College of Theology & Ministry, Professor of Old Testament, and Associate Vice President for Church Relations, Oklahoma Baptist University

"This ain't your mama's inductive Bible study method! This book is a practical and scholarly outworking of Ezra 7:9–10: 'Ezra had set his heart to *study* the Law of the LORD, and to *do* it and to *teach* his statutes and rules in Israel.' With his *TOCMA* method (*Text, Observation, Context, Meaning, Application*), DeRouchie provides both Bible student and Bible teacher with a one-stop resource for engaging and grasping the Old Testament. It is unusual in its balance of depth of scholarship and practicality—of academic rigor and precision to details, concepts, and terminology—yet it is written in a winsome, passionate, even pious style. The book includes topics covered in other good resources (e.g., how to identify genre, how to do a word study, how to trace a text's argument, discussion of historical and literary contexts). But this book also incorporates advanced and specialized topics usually reserved for separate journals and books—such as Hebrew text linguistics and the interaction between exegesis and theological disciplines (biblical theology, systematic theology, and practical theology).

Throughout, DeRouchie expresses sensitivity to evangelical concerns (e.g., biblical authority, genre and historicity, Christological reading of the Old Testament). The book also includes all the practical items that make it a teacher's best friend: the inclusion of many examples of applying hermeneutical principles to specific texts; study questions in each section of the book; huge lists of resources; and a thorough glossary of technical terms. I will personally use this book in my own scholarship and adopt it as a required textbook in several introductory and advanced courses."

—**Kenneth J. Turner**, Associate Professor of Biblical Studies, Toccoa Falls College

"Like few others, DeRouchie understands that the path to orthodox theology and true worship is driven by one's encounter with the incarnate Word as presented in the written Word (Luke 24:44; John 5:39; Rom. 1:1–3). Thus, no amount of rigor is spared in leading students of the Bible from the science of analytical, exegetical analysis into the art of theological and practical application, which then culminates in the satisfaction of worship. Especially helpful are the sections on "Literary Units and Text Hierarchy" and then "Clause and Text Grammar." This volume not only will become a standard course textbook, but will also serve as a lifelong resource for those called to study and faithfully proclaim the good news of the gospel of Jesus Christ from the Old Testament. If you are hungry to devour Scripture (Ezek. 3:1–3), then 'rise,' take this book, and 'eat' (Acts 10:13)."

—**Miles V. Van Pelt**, Alan Belcher Professor of Old Testament and Biblical Languages, Director of the Summer Institute for Biblical Languages, and Academic Dean, Reformed Theological Seminary, Jackson

"Jason DeRouchie has accomplished something unusual—a guide to interpreting the Old Testament that emphasizes reading the Old Testament as Christian Scripture while giving thorough attention to the original historical and literary context. He faithfully guides readers though the maze of interpretive issues beginning with the foundational aspects of genre and context, and then working all the way up to theology and application. Students often ask me for resources for digging into the Old Testament, and now I know what to recommend first. DeRouchie writes with a scholar's touch and a pastor's heart, and his love for God's Word fills every page. He doesn't just talk *about* the Bible; he shows us how to open its treasures for ourselves."

—**Brian J. Vickers**, Professor of New Testament Interpretation and Biblical Theology, The Southern Baptist Theological Seminary; Assistant Editor, *The Southern Baptist Journal of Theology*

"DeRouchie is committed to reading the Old Testament as *Christian* Scripture, and in this volume he guides biblical interpreters in how best to grasp a passage's makeup, shape, placement, meaning, and application. His interpretive approach leaves few stones unturned, and he even gives helpful guidance to Christians in how to relate to Old Testament laws and promises and how to faithfully preach Christ and the gospel from the Old Testament. *How to Understand and Apply the Old Testament* is an up-to-date, accessible, and theologically rich guide to faithful biblical interpretation, and I heartily recommend it."

—**Bruce K. Waltke**, Professor Emeritus of Biblical Studies, Regent College, Vancouver; Distinguished Professor Emeritus of Old Testament, Knox Theological Seminary

"This book lays out a clear and creative way to explain the steps in exegeting a passage. Its comprehensive twelve-step plan skillfully introduces readers to the basics of understanding an Old Testament passage—beginning with determining what the text says and going all the way to applying it. This volume is accessible and well organized, and will be helpful for students and laypeople alike."

—**Paul D. Wegner**, Professor of Old Testament Studies and Director of Academic Graduate Studies Program, Gateway Seminary

"It is rare to find in one book everything you need to learn how to rightly interpret and wisely apply God's Word to our lives, yet this is such a work! In addition, many Christians struggle with how to understand the Old Testament and apply it to their lives today, but this work removes the fog and makes the Old Testament come alive for Christians. Whether you have been studying God's Word for years or you are a novice, *How to Understand and Apply the Old Testament* is a must-read. One will learn how to move rightly from the biblical texts in all their instruction, authority, and beauty to their proper theological application in our lives viewed in light of the glorious work of our Lord Jesus Christ. I know of no book that better puts all the pieces together and so wonderfully teaches the reader how to move from exegesis to theology, and that practically helps us become better readers of the Old Testament. Jason DeRouchie has given us a real gift, and I highly recommend this work for anyone who is serious about the study of Scripture and desirous of seeing God's Word proclaimed, taught, and obeyed in the church."

—**Stephen J. Wellum**, Professor of Christian Theology, The Southern Baptist Theological Seminary; Editor, *The Southern Baptist Journal of Theology*

"Rather than being simply another 'how-to' manual for doing Old Testament exegesis well, this book delivers much more besides. It includes a penetrating analysis of several Old Testament books and key Old Testament texts, as well as detailed discussion of how biblical, systematic, and practical theology inform our understanding and application of the Old Testament in a Christian context. Reflecting a deep respect for the Old Testament as inspired Scripture, DeRouchie helpfully uncovers various pitfalls that must be avoided by the sure-footed interpreter, and consistently demonstrates how his proposed 'Twelve Steps from Exegesis to Theology' will help elucidate the divinely intended meaning and message. While the benefits of learning biblical Hebrew are clearly illustrated in a number of sections, this book is a must-read for everyone who wants a better grasp of how the Old Testament should be read and taught as Christian Scripture."

—**Paul R. Williamson**, Senior Lecturer in Old Testament, Hebrew, and Aramaic, Moore Theological College, Sydney, Australia

"This book is an outstanding accomplishment. It reflects years of careful and faithful investigation of that older half of our Bible that too often seems foreign to the rest of us. Every preacher will want to read this resource carefully and repeatedly because it is an invaluable guide toward a responsible, informed handling of the Old Testament Scriptures."

—**Fred G. Zaspel**, Pastor, Reformed Baptist Church, Franconia, Pennsylvania; Executive Editor, *Books at a Glance*; Associate Professor of Christian Theology, The Southern Baptist Theological Seminary

HOW TO UNDERSTAND AND APPLY THE OLD TESTAMENT

HOW TO UNDERSTAND AND APPLY THE OLD TESTAMENT

TWELVE STEPS FROM EXEGESIS TO THEOLOGY

Jason S. DeRouchie

P U B L I S H I N G
P.O. BOX 817 • PHILLIPSBURG • NEW JERSEY 08865-0817

Italics within Scripture quotations indicate emphasis added.

Printed in the United States of America

ISBN: 978-1-62995-245-1 (casebound)
ISBN: 978-1-62995-246-8 (ePub)
ISBN: 978-1-62995-247-5 (Mobi)

Library of Congress Cataloging-in-Publication Data

Names: DeRouchie, Jason Shane, 1973- author.
Title: How to understand and apply the Old Testament : twelve steps from exegesis to theology / Jason S. DeRouchie.
Description: Phillipsburg : P&R Publishing, 2017. | Includes bibliographical references and index.
Identifiers: LCCN 2016047347| ISBN 9781629952451 (casebound) | ISBN 9781629952468 (epub) | ISBN 9781629952475 (mobi)
Subjects: LCSH: Bible. Old Testament--Hermeneutics. | Bible. Old Testament--Criticism, interpretation, etc.
Classification: LCC BS476 .D47 2017 | DDC 221.601--dc23
LC record available at https://lccn.loc.gov/2016047347

To my beloved children—
Janie, Ruthie, Isaac, Ezra, Joey, and Joy.
May the Scripture on which this book focuses
increasingly help you to set your hope in God
and not to forget his works
but to keep his commandments (Ps. 78:7),
all for the glory of Christ.

CONTENTS

FIGURES

ANALYTICAL OUTLINE

FOREWORD

I HAVE A confession to make: by default, I am suspicious of books with titles like *Ten Ways to Something-or-Other* and *Five Steps to Overcome This or That*. So what shall I make of a book titled *How to Understand and Apply the Old Testament: Twelve Steps from Exegesis to Theology*? It sounds painfully mechanical, and good readers know full well that good reading cannot be broken down into a small number of "steps." Such titles may reflect robust marketing strategy, but hype should not be confused with subtlety and rigor. Right?

Well, *usually* right. This outstanding book is the exception. Jason DeRouchie tackles an amazing range of material, and does so in an orderly fashion that never feels boxy or merely theoretical. Partly this is because he provides many, many concrete examples of Old Testament exegesis; partly it is because his work, while rigorous, never fails to arouse wonder and worship. This book doubtless demands the hard work of intellectual discipline, but it is more than an intellectual exercise.

Part of the reason for the book's length turns on the fact that DeRouchie writes at a beginning level, an intermediate level, and an advanced level (the latter requiring a reasonable grasp of Hebrew), with all the sections of the book clearly marked. Many of the book's features make it an admirable textbook; its biblical indexes will be worth consulting by anyone preaching or teaching from the Old Testament, to check out whether DeRouchie has something to say on any particular passage. He provides penetrating structural analysis of several Old Testament books, and probing exegesis of many passages.

The heart of this textbook, however, is its competent and up-to-date treatment of the elements that go into faithful exegesis: competent comprehension of literary genres, accurate treatment of clausal dependence on which so much structural analysis depends, text-critical decisions that must be made, word studies (both how to do them and how not to do them), and careful study of the historical and literary contexts in which any particular passage is embedded. Most of these elements, of course, are nowadays grouped under discourse analysis. But DeRouchie is not satisfied to stop there: he leads his readers to think through how to read Old Testament passages in a canonical context. Discourse analysis is wedded to biblical theology. Moving from Old Testament exegesis in an Old Testament matrix to an Old Testament exegesis in the context of the Christian Bible opens up a plethora of challenges. DeRouchie avoids the common mistakes and reductionisms, but still wants to remind his readers that the Old Testament books constituted the only Bible that Jesus had—and what he did with it has binding authority on those who confess him as Lord. And having gone so far, DeRouchie then reflects on what appropriate application looks like to contemporary Christians reading their Bibles.

All of this is packaged in twelve steps, complete with useful charts, symbols, thoughtful discussion questions, and other guides to make this an extraordinarily useful and reliable textbook. What this volume does *not* bother with is treatment of the so-called new (now aging) hermeneutic: the omission is a wise one.

It is a pleasure and a privilege to commend this book.

D. A. Carson
Research Professor of New Testament
Trinity Evangelical Divinity School

PREFACE

An Overview of the Book

This year, 2017, marks the five hundredth anniversary of Martin Luther's posting of his Ninety-five Theses (October 31, 1517)—the spark that enflamed a global Reformation that is still alive and advancing today. The book you are now reading falls within and builds on this great gospel tradition, celebrating *sola Scriptura*—that Scripture *alone* stands as our highest authority in all matters of doctrine and practice.

Jesus loved the Old Testament. Indeed, it was his only Bible, and he believed that it pointed to him. I wrote this book to help believers better study, practice, and teach the Old Testament as *Christian* Scripture. I view God's inerrant Word as bearing highest authority in our lives, and I want Christians everywhere to interpret all of the Bible with care, celebrating the continuities between the Testaments while recognizing that Christ changes so much. I want to help Christians understand and apply the Old Testament in a way that nurtures hope in the gospel and that magnifies our Messiah in faithful ways.

This book targets both laypeople who don't know Hebrew and students studying the Old Testament in the original languages. This book is for anyone who wants to learn how to observe carefully, understand accurately, evaluate fairly, feel appropriately, act rightly, and express faithfully God's revealed Word, especially as embodied in the Old Testament. Through this book you will:

- Learn a twelve-step process for doing exegesis and theology;
- See numerous illustrations from Scripture that model the various interpretive steps;
- Consider how new covenant believers are to appropriate the Old Testament as Christian Scripture; and
- Celebrate the centrality of Christ and the hope of the gospel from the initial three-fourths of our Bible.

Two of the distinctive contributions of this book are its focus on discourse analysis (tracking an author's flow of thought) and biblical theology (considering how Scripture fits together and points to Christ). Some of the practical questions that I will seek to answer include:

- What are Christians to do with Old Testament laws? Do any of Moses' requirements still serve as guides for our pursuit of Christ?
- How should Christians consider Old Testament promises, especially those related to physical provision and protection? Can we really sing, "Every promise in the Book is mine"?[1]
- How does the Old Testament point to Christ and the hope of the gospel? How could Paul, who preached from the Old Testament, say, "I decided to know nothing among you except Jesus Christ and him crucified" (1 Cor. 2:2)?

I originally drafted this book in preparation for a course titled Old Testament Exegesis that I taught for Logos Mobile Ed in a studio at the Faithlife headquarters in Bellingham, Washington, in summer 2015. My colleague Andy Naselli taught the companion New Testament Exegesis course, and both are available at https://www.logos.com/product/117883/mobile-ed-biblical-exegesis-bundle. At the end of that process, John Hughes and the P&R Publishing team invited Andy and me to publish counterpart volumes, which are fraternal twins in every way—conceptually, structurally, theologically, and pedagogically.

A Guide to Using the Book

Every level in the study of God's Word includes beauties to discover and challenges to overcome. Recognizing that not every interpreter is the same, I have written this book with three tracks.

Easy

Moderate

Challenging

Level 1—Easy makes up most of the book and is for all readers. For *beginning interpreters*, this track may be the only one you will take, since it includes no exposure to biblical Hebrew. It will, however, still contain numerous exegetical and theological paths and vistas that will instruct, awe, inspire, and motivate.

1. The Sensational Nightingales, "Every Promise in the Book Is Mine," *Let Us Encourage You* (Malco Records, 2005; orig. 1957).

Level 2—Moderate is also for all readers and does not require a knowledge of biblical Hebrew. It does, however, interact with the original language where beneficial for *intermediate interpreters*. I always translate the Hebrew and try to instruct clearly. Here you will gain exposure to some of the benefits of Hebrew exegesis and will learn how even those without Hebrew can profit greatly from important interpretive tools.

Level 3—Challenging is specialized for more *advanced interpreters* who know or are learning biblical Hebrew. These sections likely include technical discussions that will substantially benefit only those with some awareness of the original language and who will use their Hebrew Bibles for study.

Throughout the book I use the three symbols above to identify the difficulty level of each section or subsection. Decide what path you want to travel, and follow my lead. At the head of every chapter I also include a "Trail Guide" that will remind you where you are in the journey from exegesis to theology and that will give you a quick overview of the paths you are about to tread.

Even if you don't know Hebrew, I encourage you to work through all Level 2—Moderate material, for the exegetical and theological payoff will be rich and the discussions should not be beyond your grasp. If you choose this path, just remember that all Level 1 material is also for you. For those who are studying or have studied Hebrew, *every part* of this book is for you, and my hope is that it will remind, clarify, and instruct, leading you into more focused, richer engagement with God and the biblical text.

At the end of every chapter I include "Key Words and Concepts," "Questions for Further Reflection," and "Resources for Further Study." I hope these additions will benefit personal study, small-group discussions, and classroom use. The back of the book also includes a full glossary of the key terms, along with The KINGDOM Bible Reading Plan, a selected bibliography, the Index of Scripture, and the Index of Subjects and Names.

As we set out on our journey into biblical interpretation, may God the Father, by his Spirit, stir your affections for Christ and awaken your mind to think deeply. May you increase your skill at handling the whole Bible for the glory of God and the good of his church among the nations.

Jason S. DeRouchie
Bethlehem College & Seminary
Minneapolis, Minnesota

ACKNOWLEDGMENTS

MANY INDIVIDUALS HAVE influenced the shaping of this book and my own journey in learning to understand, apply, and communicate the greatest Book. Though I may forget some folks, I will limit my thanks to seven groups:

First, I shaped the foundations of my interpretive approach during my B.A. and M.Div., the latter of which I completed nearly two decades ago. I took my initial two years of Greek study at Taylor University under the direction of Bill Heth. He modeled for me a zeal for God and his Word and gave me an initial framework for asking good questions and tracking an author's flow of thought. During my season at Gordon-Conwell Theological Seminary, key figures such as Greg Beale, Scott Hafemann, Gordon Hugenberger, Gary Pratico, and Doug Stuart helped me hone my skill at original language exegesis and theology. Aware readers will see the distinctive influence of Beale and Stuart in my own exegetical and theological method.[1] I am deeply grateful for their faithful approach to Scripture as God's authoritative and inerrant Word.

Second, my doctoral studies at The Southern Baptist Theological Seminary found me under the able care of both Dan Block and Peter Gentry. Their rigorous method of biblical interpretation matched by a deep-seated commitment to Christ and his church has forever shaped me. Block's entire ministry is dedicated to hearing the message of Scripture through careful literary analysis.[2] I hope the present book models this kind of attentiveness. Hours of dialogue with Gentry helped concretize my early approach

1. See especially G. K. Beale, *A New Testament Biblical Theology: The Unfolding of the Old Testament in the New* (Grand Rapids: Baker Academic, 2011); Beale, *Handbook on the New Testament Use of the Old Testament: Exegesis and Interpretation* (Grand Rapids: Baker Academic, 2012); Douglas Stuart, *Old Testament Exegesis: A Handbook for Students and Pastors*, 4th ed. (Louisville: Westminster John Knox, 2009); Gordon D. Fee and Douglas Stuart, *How to Read the Bible for All Its Worth*, 4th ed. (Grand Rapids: Zondervan, 2014).

2. See, for example, Daniel I. Block, *The Book of Ezekiel: Chapters 1–24* and *The Book of Ezekiel: Chapters 25–48*, NICOT (Grand Rapids: Eerdmans, 1997); Block, *Judges, Ruth: An Exegetical and Theological Exposition of Holy Scripture*, NAC 6 (Nashville: Broadman & Holman, 1999); Block, *Deuteronomy*, NIVAC (Grand Rapids: Zondervan, 2012).

to Hebrew discourse analysis, and since then I have greatly benefited from his own wrestlings with whole-Bible theology from the bottom up.[3] To these I add a note of thanks to Tom Schreiner, whose discussion of tracing Paul's argument[4] served as an impetus in my choosing to devote my doctoral dissertation to tracing Moses' argument in Deuteronomy. Schreiner's own pastoral disposition and his approach to Paul and the Law have influenced me greatly.[5]

Third, during the summer of 2005, a brief lunch with John Piper and Justin Taylor set my life on a fresh trajectory of discovery and zeal, which has resulted in over a decade-long quest to learn how to faithfully make much of Christ and the gospel from the Old Testament. I feel as though I am only beginning, but being a part of both Bethlehem Baptist Church and, since 2009, the faculty of Bethlehem College & Seminary has helped to fuel this passion and has added to it a commitment to lead others in treasuring and proclaiming the glory of God in Christ by his Spirit among the nations. I thank my administration for empowering me to write and enabling me to teach in such a context and with such a goal. I love my school's theology, team, and strategy.

Fourth, my gratitude for Miles Van Pelt, Jason Meyer, and Andy Naselli deserves special comment. During my doctoral studies, numerous conversations with Van Pelt fanned my biblical-theological flames, especially with respect to how Scripture's frame is God's kingdom, form is covenantal, and fulcrum is Christ. Van Pelt's own thoughts are now captured in the introduction of *A Biblical-Theological Introduction to the Old Testament: The Gospel Promised*,[6] and the informed reader will see many parallels in our approaches. I am very thankful for our continued friendship and for the way his godliness pushes me closer to the Lord. Before taking on the role of Pastor for Preaching and Vision at Bethlehem Baptist Church, Meyer served full-time as New Testament professor at Bethlehem College & Seminary, spurring me to deeper levels of holiness and increasing my celebration of God's covenantal purposes throughout all of Scripture. My life and teaching are better because of my time with him.[7] Naselli and I get to commute for about three hours per week, and our families are deeply entwined. My time with him fuels both godliness and joy in my life. He is constantly helping me think theologically, and I especially love coteaching a fourth-year graduate course with him on biblical theology.

3. See especially Peter J. Gentry and Stephen J. Wellum, *Kingdom through Covenant: A Biblical-Theological Understanding of the Covenants* (Wheaton, IL: Crossway, 2012); Gentry and Wellum, *God's Kingdom through God's Covenants: A Concise Biblical Theology* (Wheaton, IL: Crossway, 2015).

4. Thomas R. Schreiner, *Interpreting the Pauline Epistles*, 2nd ed. (Grand Rapids: Baker Academic, 2011), 97–124.

5. See, most recently, Thomas R. Schreiner, *40 Questions about Christians and Biblical Law*, 40 Questions (Grand Rapids: Kregel, 2010); cf. Schreiner, *The Law and Its Fulfillment: A Pauline Theology of Law* (Grand Rapids: Baker Academic, 1998).

6. Miles V. Van Pelt, ed., *A Biblical-Theological Introduction to the Old Testament: The Gospel Promised* (Wheaton, IL: Crossway, 2016), 23–42.

7. See Jason C. Meyer, *The End of the Law: Mosaic Covenant in Pauline Theology*, NSBT 7 (Nashville: Broadman & Holman, 2009); Meyer, *Preaching: A Biblical Theology* (Wheaton, IL: Crossway, 2013).

I am so grateful for our partnership in the gospel at Bethlehem. Be sure to check out his companion volume to this one titled *How to Understand and Apply the New Testament*.[8]

Fifth, my thanks extend to many folks who made this particular volume possible. John Hughes and the P&R Publishing team accepted the project and have offered solid, Christ-honoring support from beginning to end. I am so grateful for Karen Magnuson's careful copyediting and Thomas Shumaker's painstaking typesetting! My thanks go out to Scott Jamison, Danny Francis, and Don Straka, all of whom offered solid suggestions on how to improve the manuscript. The latter two also helped prepare the "Key Words and Concepts" lists, the "Questions for Further Reflection," and the glossary. I also thank my colleague John Beckman for test-using the volume in his intermediate Hebrew course, and the thirty-five Bethlehem Seminary students from the 2016 spring semester who offered helpful feedback. I offer a special note of thanks to Andy Hubert of Biblearc (www.Biblearc.com) for his labors in finalizing the arcs and brackets and to my former student and freelance graphic designer Joel Dougherty, who generated most of the images and icons used in this volume. I believe his creativity and attention to detail have helped me communicate better. Finally, I say "thanks" to my student Ryan Eagy, who also stepped in to finalize some images.

Sixth, I thank the Lord for my faithful wife, Teresa, who stands on earth as my biggest advocate, best help, and truest friend. She is a model of wisdom, balance, and God-dependence. She treasures Christ, steadies and complements me, and enthusiastically supports the research-writing-teaching-shepherding ministry to which God has called me. She also delights in guiding our six children and in making our "Apple Tree Farm" a place of family rest and ministry fruitfulness. I am so grateful to her.

Seventh, I praise the Lord for my six children, to whom I dedicate this book. Each of them is a treasure, and each has encouraged and shaped this Daddy in various ways toward Christlikeness and careful Bible-reading. I love them all dearly, and I pray that the principles and guidelines I set forth in this book—many of which have been taught and modeled in our home—can help them to better see and savor the beauty of God in the face of Christ as disclosed in the pages of Scripture.

8. Andrew David Naselli, *How to Understand and Apply the New Testament: Twelve Steps from Exegesis to Theology* (Phillipsburg, NJ: P&R Publishing, 2017).

ABBREVIATIONS

AB	Anchor Bible
ABD	*The Anchor Bible Dictionary*, ed. David Noel Freedman, 6 vols. (New York: Doubleday, 1992)
ANET	*Ancient Near Eastern Texts Relating to the Old Testament*, ed. James B. Pritchard, 3rd ed. (Princeton, NJ: Princeton University Press, 1969)
ApOTC	Apollos Old Testament Commentary
ASOR	American Schools of Oriental Research
ASV	Authorized Standard Version
BA	*Biblical Archaeologist*
BBE	Bible in Basic English
BBR	*Bulletin of Biblical Research*
BDB	Francis Brown, S. R. Driver, and Charles A. Briggs, *The New Brown-Driver-Briggs Hebrew and English Lexicon*
BECNT	Baker Exegetical Commentary on the New Testament
BETL	Bibliotheca Ephemeridum Theologicarum Lovaniensium
BHQ	*Biblia Hebraica Quinta*, ed. Adrian Schenker et al. (Stuttgart: Deutsche Bibelgesellschaft, 2004–)
BHS	*Biblia Hebraica Stuttgartensia*, ed. Karl Elliger et al., 5th rev. ed. (Stuttgart: Deutsche Bibelgesellschaft, 1983)
Bib	*Biblica*
BSac	*Bibliotheca Sacra*
CBQ	*Catholic Biblical Quarterly*

CDCH	*The Concise Dictionary of Classical Hebrew*, ed. David J. A. Clines (Sheffield, UK: Sheffield Phoenix, 2009)
CEB	Contemporary English Bible
CEBA	Contemporary English Bible with Apocrypha
COS	*The Context of Scripture*, ed. William W. Hallo and K. Lawson Younger Jr., 3 vols. (Leiden: Brill, 1997–2002)
CSB	Christian Standard Bible
CurBR	*Currents in Biblical Research*
CurBS	*Currents in Research: Biblical Studies*
DBCI	*Dictionary of Biblical Criticism and Interpretation*, ed. Stanley E. Porter (London: Routledge, 2007)
DBSJ	*Detroit Baptist Seminary Journal*
DCH	*The Dictionary of Classical Hebrew*, ed. David J. A. Clines, 9 vols. (Sheffield, UK: Sheffield Phoenix, 1993–2014)
DJD	Discoveries in the Judaean Desert
DJG	*Dictionary of Jesus and the Gospels*, ed. Joel B. Green and Scot McKnight (Downers Grove, IL: InterVarsity Press, 1992)
DLNT	*Dictionary of the Later New Testament and Its Developments*, ed. Ralph P. Martin and Peter H. Davids (Downers Grove, IL: InterVarsity Press, 1997)
DNTB	*Dictionary of New Testament Background*, ed. Craig A. Evans and Stanley E. Porter (Downers Grove, IL: InterVarsity Press, 2000)
DOT:P	*Dictionary of the Old Testament: Pentateuch*, ed. T. Desmond Alexander and David W. Baker (Downers Grove, IL: InterVarsity Press, 2003)
DOT:WPW	*Dictionary of the Old Testament: Wisdom, Poetry, and Writings*, ed. Tremper Longman III and Peter Enns (Downers Grove, IL: InterVarsity Press, 2008)
DSS	Dead Sea Scrolls
DTIB	*Dictionary for Theological Interpretation of the Bible*, ed. Kevin J. Vanhoozer (Grand Rapids: Baker Academic, 2005)
EDBT	*Evangelical Dictionary of Biblical Theology*, ed. Walter A. Elwell (Grand Rapids: Baker, 1996)
EDT	*Evangelical Dictionary of Theology*, ed. Walter A. Elwell, 2nd ed. (Grand Rapids: Baker Academic, 2001)
EJ	*Evangelical Journal*
ESV	English Standard Version
ExpTim	*Expository Times*

GKC	*Gesenius' Hebrew Grammar*, ed. E. Kautzch, trans. A. E. Cowley, 2nd ed. (Oxford: Clarendon, 1910)
GNB	Good News Bible
GTJ	*Grace Theological Journal*
HALOT	*The Hebrew and Aramaic Lexicon of the Old Testament: Study Edition*, ed. Ludwig Koehler, Walter Baumgartner, and Johann Jakob Stamm, trans. M. E. J. Richardson, 2 vols. (Leiden: Brill, 2001)
HBCE	The Hebrew Bible: A Critical Edition
HCSB	Holman Christian Standard Bible
HS	*Hebrew Studies*
HSM	Harvard Semitic Monographs
HUCA	*Hebrew Union College Annual*
IBHS	*An Introduction to Biblical Hebrew Syntax*, by Bruce K. Waltke and M. O'Connor (Winona Lake, IN: Eisenbrauns, 1990)
Int	*Interpretation*
ISBE	*International Standard Bible Encyclopedia*, ed. Geoffrey W. Bromiley, 4 vols. (Grand Rapids: Zondervan, 1979–88)
JAAS	*Journal of Asia Adventist Seminary*
JAOS	*Journal of the American Oriental Society*
JBL	*Journal of Biblical Literature*
JBLMS	Journal of Biblical Literature Monograph Series
JBMW	*Journal for Biblical Manhood and Womanhood*
JDFM	*Journal of Discipleship and Family Ministry*
JETS	*Journal of the Evangelical Theological Society*
JMT	*Journal of Ministry and Theology*
JNSL	*Journal of Northwest Semitic Languages*
JSNT	*Journal for the Study of the New Testament*
JSOT	*Journal for the Study of the Old Testament*
JSOTSup	Journal for the Study of the Old Testament Supplement Series
JSPHL	*Journal for the Study of Paul and His Letters*
KJV	King James Version
LSAWS	Linguistic Studies in Ancient West Semitic
LXX	Septuagint (the Greek Old Testament)

MCED	*Mounce's Complete Expository Dictionary of Old and New Testament Words*, ed. William D. Mounce (Grand Rapids: Zondervan, 2006)
Ms(s)	Manuscript(s)
MSG	The Message
MSJ	*The Master's Seminary Journal*
MT	Masoretic Text
NAB	New American Bible
NAC	New American Commentary
NASB	New American Standard Bible
NASU	New American Standard Updated
NCE	*New Catholic Encyclopedia*, ed. Thomas Carson, 2nd ed., 15 vols. (Washington, DC: Catholic University of America Press, 2003)
NDBT	*New Dictionary of Biblical Theology: Exploring the Unity and Diversity of Scripture*, ed. T. Desmond Alexander and Brian S. Rosner (Downers Grove, IL: InterVarsity Press, 2000)
NEB	New English Bible
NET Bible	New English Translation Bible
NETS	New English Translation of the Septuagint
NICNT	New International Commentary on the New Testament
NICOT	New International Commentary on the Old Testament
NIDB	*The New Interpreter's Dictionary of the Bible*, ed. Katharine Doob Sakenfeld, 5 vols. (Nashville: Abingdon, 2009)
NIDOTTE	*New International Dictionary of Old Testament Theology and Exegesis*, ed. Willem A. VanGemeren, 5 vols. (Grand Rapids: Zondervan, 1997)
NIV	New International Version
NIVAC	NIV Application Commentary
NJB	New Jerusalem Bible
NKJV	New King James Version
NLT	New Living Translation
NRSV	New Revised Standard Version
NSBT	New Studies in Biblical Theology
OTL	Old Testament Library
RBén	*Revue bénédictine*
RBTR	*The Reformed Baptist Theological Review*

REB	Revised English Bible
RevQ	*Revue de Qumrân*
RSV	Revised Standard Version
SBET	*Scottish Bulletin of Evangelical Theology*
SBJT	*Southern Baptist Journal of Theology*
SBL	Society of Biblical Literature
SBLDS	Society of Biblical Literature Dissertation Series
SBLSS	Society of Biblical Literature Semeia Studies
SBTS	Sources for Biblical and Theological Study
SIL	Summer Institute for Linguistics, International
SOTBT	Studies in Old Testament Biblical Theology
TDOT	*Theological Dictionary of the Old Testament*, ed. G. Johannes Botterweck and Helmer Ringgren, trans. John T. Willis et al., 15 vols. (Grand Rapids: Eerdmans, 1974–2006)
TJ	*Trinity Journal*
TLB	The Living Bible
TLOT	*Theological Lexicon of the Old Testament*, ed. Ernst Jenni and Clause Westermann, trans. Mark E. Biddle, 3 vols. (Peabody, MA: Hendrickson, 1997)
TNTC	Tyndale New Testament Commentaries
TWOT	*Theological Wordbook of the Old Testament*, ed. R. Laird Harris, Gleason L. Archer Jr., and Bruce K. Waltke. 2 vols. (Chicago: Moody Press, 1980)
TynBul	*Tyndale Bulletin*
UBS	United Bible Societies Greek New Testament
UCSD	University of California, San Diego
VTSup	Supplements to *Vetus Testamentum*
WEB	World English Bible
WTJ	*Westminster Theological Journal*
WUNT	Wissenschaftliche Untersuchungen zum Neuen Testament
YLT	Young's Literal Translation
ZAH	*Zeitschrift für Althebräistik*
ZEB	*The Zondervan Encyclopedia of the Bible*, ed. Merrill C. Tenney and Moisés Silva, 2nd ed., 5 vols. (Grand Rapids: Zondervan, 2009)
ZECOT	Zondervan Exegetical Commentary on the Old Testament

INTRODUCTION

A JOURNEY OF DISCOVERY AND ENCOUNTER

"The good hand of his God was on him. For Ezra had set his heart to study the Law of the Lord, and to do it and to teach his statutes and rules in Israel." (Ezra 7:9–10)

Basic Overview

The Interpretive Task

Ten Reasons That the Old Testament Is Important for Christians

The Benefits of Hebrew Exegesis

Overview of the Interpretive Process: TOCMA

Fig. 0.1. Trail Guide to Introduction

WE ARE ABOUT to embark on a journey of discovery and divine encounter. Beauty abounds at every turn, and the goal is to worship the living God in the face of Jesus Christ. What we call the Old Testament was the only Bible that Jesus had. Books such as Genesis and Deuteronomy, Isaiah and Psalms guided his life and ministry as the Jewish Messiah. It was these "Scriptures" that Jesus identified as God's Word (Mark 7:13; 12:36), considered to be authoritative (Matt. 4:3–4, 7, 10; 23:1–3), and called people to know and believe in order to guard against doctrinal error and, even worse, hell (Mark 12:24; Luke 16:28–31; 24:25; John 5:46–47). Jesus was convinced that what is now the initial three-fourths of our Christian Bible "cannot be broken" (John 10:35).[1] He was also certain that the Old Testament bore witness about him (Luke 24:27, 46;

1. Unless otherwise noted, all English translations within the *body* text of the book are from the ESV® Bible (The Holy Bible, English Standard Version®), copyright © 2001 by Crossway, a publishing ministry of Good News Publishers. Used by permission. All rights reserved. Unless otherwise noted, all English translations *within examples* are the author's own.

John 5:39, 46), that it would be completely fulfilled (Matt. 5:17–18; Luke 24:44), and that it called for repentance and forgiveness of sins to be proclaimed in his name to all nations (Luke 24:47). I love the Old Testament because of the way it portrays God's character and actions and serves as a witness to the majesty of our Messiah. The Old Testament is the initial three-fourths of God's special revelation to us, and I want you to interpret the Old Testament rightly because there is no higher need for mankind than to see and celebrate the Sovereign, Savior, and Satisfier disclosed in its pages.

The Interpretive Task

This book is designed to guide Christians in interpreting the Old Testament. The process of ***biblical interpretation*** includes both exegesis and theology. The former focuses mostly on analysis, whereas the latter addresses synthesis and significance.[2]

Our English term ***exegesis*** is a transliteration of the Greek noun ἐξήγησις (ἐκ "from, out of" + ἄγω "to bring, move [something]"), meaning an "account, description, narration." Narrowly defined, exegesis of Scripture is the personal discovery of what the biblical authors intended their texts to mean.[3] Texts convey meaning; they do not produce it. Rather, following God's leading, the biblical authors purposely wrote the words they did with specific sense and purpose. "Men spoke from God as they were carried along by the Holy Spirit" (2 Peter 1:21). We have to carefully read what the Lord through his human servants gives us in Scripture. Exegesis is about discovering what is there, which includes both the specific meaning that the authors convey and its implications—those inferences in a text of which the authors may or may not have been unaware but that legitimately fall within the principle or pattern of meaning that they willed.[4]

2. For these distinctions, see Andrew David Naselli, "D. A. Carson's Theological Method," *SBET* 29, 2 (2011): 256–72; cf. D. A. Carson, "Unity and Diversity in the New Testament: The Possibility of Systematic Theology," in *Scripture and Truth*, ed. D. A. Carson and J. D. Woodbridge (Grand Rapids: Zondervan, 1983), 65–95, 368–75, repr. in D. A. Carson, *Collected Writings on Scripture*, comp. Andrew David Naselli (Wheaton, IL: Crossway, 2010), 111–49; Carson, "The Role of Exegesis in Systematic Theology," in *Doing Theology in Today's World: Essays in Honor of Kenneth S. Kantzer*, ed. John D. Woodbridge and Thomas Edward McComiskey (Grand Rapids: Zondervan, 1991), 39–76; Carson, "Systematic Theology and Biblical Theology," *NDBT* 89–104.

3. The term ἐξήγησις shows up in one Greek manuscript of Judges 7:15: "As soon as Gideon heard *the telling* [i.e., the *narration*, τὴν ἐξήγησιν] of the dream and its interpretation, he worshiped." This context associates exegesis with the mere description of the dream, which stands distinct from the assessment of the dream's meaning. Today, exegesis of written material usually implies some level of interpretation, but the stress is still significant that exegesis is about carefully reading what is there in the biblical text.

4. For more on this, see Robert H. Stein, *A Basic Guide to Interpreting the Bible: Playing by the Rules*, 2nd ed. (Grand Rapids: Baker Academic, 2011), 30–38; Stein, "The Benefits of an Author-Oriented Approach to Hermeneutics," *JETS* 44, 3 (2001): 451–66; G. K. Beale, "The Cognitive Peripheral Vision of the Biblical Authors," *WTJ* 76, 2 (2014):

The English term ***theology*** comes from the Latin *theologia*, which derives from a combination of the Greek nouns θεός ("God") and λόγος ("a formal accounting, reckoning"). In short, theology is a "reasoning or study of God." Because Scripture is *God's* Word for all time and because every biblical passage has a broader context (historical, literary, and biblical), exegesis (narrowly defined) naturally moves us into various theological disciplines:

- Biblical theology considers how God's Word connects together and climaxes in Christ.
- Systematic theology examines what the Bible teaches about certain theological topics.
- Practical theology details the proper Christian response to the Bible's truths.

Biblical interpretation is not complete until it gives rise to application through a life of worship. Exegesis moves to theology, and the whole process is to result in a personal encounter with the living God disclosed in Scripture. Doxology—the practice of glorifying or praising God—should color *all* biblical study.

In this book, chapters 1–9 cover the basics of exegesis, whereas chapters 10–12 address theology. Here are a number of foundational presuppositions that guide my approach to biblical interpretation.

1. Biblical interpretation necessitates that we view Scripture as God's Word.

The only way to truly arrive at what the biblical authors intended is to believe (as they did) that they were reading and writing God's very Word (Isa. 8:20; 1 Cor. 2:13; 14:37). This requires a submissive disposition to Scripture's authority. We must be willing to let our understanding and application of truth be conformed to the Bible's declarations, all in accordance with God's revealed intention. The Bible is ***special revelation***—God's disclosure of himself and his will in a way that we can understand (1 Cor. 14:37; 2 Tim. 3:16; 2 Peter 1:20–21). The very words, and not just the ideas, are God-inspired (Matt. 5:17–18; 1 Cor. 2:13; 2 Tim. 3:16–17). And the "words of the Lord are pure" (Ps. 12:6); his "law is true" (Ps. 119:142); "every one of [his] righteous rules endures forever" (Ps. 119:160); and his "commandments are right" (Ps. 119:172). Jesus said, "Scripture cannot be broken" (John 10:35), and Paul said that this is so because "all Scripture is breathed out by God" (2 Tim. 3:16). Indeed, as Peter said, "No prophecy was ever produced by the will of man, but men spoke from God as they were carried along by the Holy Spirit" (2 Peter 1:21).

The implication of these truths is that Scripture is both authoritative and accurate in all it declares. In order to stress that the Bible's assertions are both reliable and unerring, the church has historically stated that (a) in matters of *faith* (doctrine) and *practice* (ethics), Scripture's teaching is ***infallible***—a sure and safe guide, and that (b) in matters

263–93, esp. 266–70; cf. G. K. Beale and Benjamin L. Gladd, *Hidden but Now Revealed: A Biblical Theology of Divine Mystery* (Downers Grove, IL: InterVarsity Press, 2014), 340–64, esp. 344–47.

of *fact* (whether history, chronology, geography, science, or the like), Scripture's claims are ***inerrant***—entirely true and trustworthy.[5] Both terms mean something comparable but address different spheres, and both are rightly understood only in relation to what the authors, led by the Spirit, intended to convey by their texts (for more on this, see "History, Myth, and the Biblical Narratives" in chapter 1). The key for us is that the Bible will never lead us astray and should bear highest influence in our lives.

2. Biblical interpretation assumes that Scripture's truths are knowable.

Proper understanding of Scripture assumes that the Bible is, by nature, clear in what it teaches. In short, truth can be known. Peter recognized that "there are some things in [Paul's letters] that are hard to understand," but he went on to say that it is "the ignorant and unstable" who "twist" these words "to their own destruction, as they do the other Scriptures" (2 Peter 3:16). The psalmists were convinced that God's Word enlightens our path and imparts understanding (Ps. 119:105, 130). Paul wrote his words plainly (2 Cor. 1:13) and called others to "think over" what he said, trusting that "the Lord will give you understanding in everything" (2 Tim. 2:7). I will comment further on Scripture's clarity in "Shared Assumptions and the Bible's Clarity" in chapter 8.

3. Biblical interpretation requires that we respond appropriately.

The process of biblical interpretation is not complete once we have discovered what God has spoken. We must then move on to recognize that his Word is "profitable for teaching, for reproof, for correction, and for training in righteousness" (2 Tim. 3:16). We must grasp not only the biblical author's intended meaning (which is possible for nonbelievers) but also his intended effect (possible only for believers, Rom. 8:7–8; 1 Cor. 2:14). We thus pray ***IOUS***: "*Incline* [our] heart[s] to your testimonies" (Ps. 119:36); "*Open* [our] eyes that [we] may behold wondrous things out of your law" (119:18); "*Unite* [our] heart[s] to fear your name" (86:11); and "*Satisfy* us in the morning with your steadfast love, that we may rejoice and be glad all our days" (90:14).[6]

John Piper has helpfully captured the sixfold process of education:[7]

- *Observe* carefully;
- *Understand* rightly;
- *Evaluate* fairly;
- *Feel* appropriately;

5. The "Chicago Statement on Biblical Inerrancy" (1978) states: "*Infallible* signifies the quality of neither misleading nor being misled and so safeguards in categorical terms the truth that Holy Scripture is a sure, safe, and reliable rule and guide in all matters. Similarly, *inerrant* signifies the quality of being free from falsehood or mistake and so safeguards the truth that Holy Scripture is entirely true and trustworthy in all its assertions. We affirm that canonical Scripture should always be interpreted on the basis that it is infallible and inerrant" (http://www.bible-researcher.com/chicago1.html).

6. John Piper, *When I Don't Desire God: How to Fight for Joy* (Wheaton, IL: Crossway, 2004), 151.

7. John Piper, *Think: The Life of the Mind and the Love of God* (Wheaton, IL: Crossway, 2010), 191–98. Piper actually applies the same process to both general revelation (God's world) and special revelation (God's Word).

- *Apply* wisely;
- *Express* articulately and boldly.

These are the necessary habits of the heart and mind needed for rightly grasping all truth in God's Book.

4. Biblical interpretation that culminates in application demands God-dependence.[8]

The process of moving from study to practice is something that only God can enable, and he does so only through Jesus. In 1 Corinthians 2:14, Paul writes, "The natural person does not accept the things of the Spirit of God, for they are folly to him, and he is not able to understand them because they are spiritually discerned." By "understand" here, Paul means "embrace, affirm, align with, delight in, apply." Only in Christ is the veil of hardness toward God's Word taken away (2 Cor. 3:14), but in Christ, the Word becomes near us, in our mouth and in our heart (Rom. 10:8). The biblical authors' ultimate intent included a transformed life, the foundation of which is a personal encounter with the living God. This will not be experienced apart from the Lord's help.

This book describes a process of Old Testament interpretation that is intended for the glory of God and the good of his people. Putting the Bible under a microscope (careful study) should always result in finding ourselves under its microscope, as Scripture changes us more into Christ's likeness. We engage in exegesis and theology in order to encounter God. We approach humbly and dependently and never with manipulation or force. Biblical interpretation should create servants, not kings.

To this end, I invite you to pray the following words to the Lord:

> You have said, O Lord, "But this is the one to whom I will look: he who is humble and contrite in spirit and trembles at my word" (Isa. 66:2). I want you to look toward me, Father, so overcome my pride, arrest my affections, and move me to revere you rightly. May I approach the Bible with a heart ready to conform, a heart awed by the fact that you have spoken in a way that I can understand, and a heart hungry to receive. Enable this book to guide me well, and help me to learn how to study, how to live out, and how to proclaim your Word with care, humility, and confidence. In the name of King Jesus, I pray. Amen.

8. For more on this theme, see John Piper, *Reading the Bible Supernaturally: Seeing and Savoring the Glory of God in Scripture* (Wheaton, IL: Crossway, 2017).

Ten Reasons That the Old Testament Is Important for Christians

If Christians are part of the new covenant, why should we seek to understand and apply the Old Testament? While I will develop my response in chapter 12, I will give ten reasons here why the first word in the phrase ***Old** Testament* must not mean "unimportant or insignificant to Christians."

1. The Old Testament was Jesus' only Scripture and makes up three-fourths (75.55 percent) of our Bible.

If space says anything, the Old Testament matters to God, who gave us his Word in a Book. In fact, it was his first special revelation, which set a foundation for the fulfillment that we find in Jesus in the New Testament. The Old Testament was the only Bible of Jesus and the earliest church (e.g., Matt. 5:17; Luke 24:44; Acts 24:14; 2 Tim. 3:15), and it is a major part of our Scriptures.

2. The Old Testament substantially influences our understanding of key biblical teachings.

By the end of the Law (Genesis–Deuteronomy), the Bible has already described or alluded to all five of the major covenants that guide Scripture's plot structure (Adamic-Noahic, Abrahamic, Mosaic, Davidic, and new). The rest of the Old Testament then builds on this portrait in detail. Accordingly, the Old Testament narrative builds anticipation for a better king, a blessed people, and a broader land. The Old Testament creates the problem and includes promises that the New Testament answers and fulfills. We need the Old Testament to fully understand God's work in history.

Furthermore, some doctrines of Scripture are best understood only from the Old Testament. For example, is there a more worldview-shaping text than Genesis 1:1–2:3? Where else can we go other than the Old Testament to rightly understand sacred space and the temple? Is there a more explicit declaration of YHWH's incomparability than Isaiah 40,[9] or a more succinct expression of substitutionary atonement than Isaiah 53? Where should we go to know what Paul means by "psalms and hymns and spiritual songs" (Eph. 5:19; Col. 3:16)? All of these are principally derived from our understanding of the Old Testament.

9. *YHWH*, sometimes rendered with vowels as *Yahweh*, is the personal name by which the one true God identified himself and that the seers, sages, and songwriters employed in worship and preaching. YHWH is both the Creator of all things and Israel's covenant Lord. Most modern translations represent the name through large and small capitals: LORD. The name is related to the verb of being and likely means "he causes to be"; that is, the Lord alone is the only uncaused being from whom, through whom, and to whom are all things.

Finally, the New Testament worldview and teachings are built on the framework supplied in the Old Testament. In the New Testament we find literally hundreds of Old Testament quotations, allusions, and echoes, none of which we will fully grasp apart from saturating ourselves in Jesus' Bible.

3. We meet the same God in both Testaments.

Note how the book of Hebrews begins: "Long ago, at many times and in many ways, God spoke to our fathers by the prophets, but in these last days he has spoken to us by his Son" (Heb. 1:1–2). The very God who spoke through the Old Testament prophets speaks through Jesus!

Now, you may ask, "But isn't the Old Testament's God one of wrath and burden, whereas the God of the New Testament is about grace and freedom?" Let's consider some texts, first from the Old Testament and then from the New.

Perhaps the most foundational Old Testament statement of YHWH's character and action is Exodus 34:6: "The LORD, the LORD, a God merciful and gracious, slow to anger, and abounding in steadfast love and faithfulness." The Old Testament then reasserts this truth numerous times in order to clarify why it is that God continued to pardon and preserve a wayward people: "But the LORD was gracious to them and had compassion on them, and he turned toward them, because of his covenant with Abraham, Isaac, and Jacob, and would not destroy them, nor has he cast them from his presence until now" (2 Kings 13:23). "For if you return to the LORD, your brothers and your children will find compassion with their captors and return to this land. For the LORD your God is gracious and merciful and will not turn away his face from you, if you return to him" (2 Chron. 30:9). "Many years you bore with them and warned them by your Spirit through your prophets. Yet they would not give ear. Therefore you gave them into the hand of the peoples of the lands. Nevertheless, in your great mercies you did not make an end of them or forsake them, for you are a gracious and merciful God" (Neh. 9:30–31). Thus God's grace fills the Old Testament, just as it does the New.

Furthermore, in the New Testament, Jesus speaks about hell more than anyone else. He declares, "Do not fear those who kill the body but cannot kill the soul. Rather fear him who can destroy both soul and body in hell" (Matt. 10:28). Similarly, "Whoever causes one of these little ones who believe in me to sin, it would be better for him to have a great millstone fastened around his neck and to be drowned in the depth of the sea" (18:6). Paul, quoting Deuteronomy 32:35, asserted, "Beloved, never avenge yourselves, but leave it to the wrath of God, for it is written, 'Vengeance is mine, I will repay, says the Lord'" (Rom. 12:19). And the author of Hebrews said, "For if we go on sinning deliberately after receiving the knowledge of the truth, there no longer remains a sacrifice for sins, but a fearful expectation of judgment, and a fury of fire that will consume the adversaries" (Heb. 10:26–27). Thus God is just as wrathful in the New Testament as he is in the Old.

Certainly there are numerous expressions of YHWH's righteous anger in the Old Testament, just as there are massive manifestations of blood-bought mercy in the

New Testament. What is important is to recognize that *we meet the same God in the Old Testament as we do in the New.* In the whole Bible we meet a God who is faithful to his promises both to bless and to curse. He takes both sin and repentance seriously, and so should we!

4. The Old Testament announces the very "good news/gospel" we enjoy.

The gospel is this—that the reigning God saves and satisfies believing sinners through Christ Jesus' life, death, and resurrection. Paul states that "the Scripture, foreseeing that God would justify the Gentiles by faith, preached *the gospel* beforehand to Abraham, saying, 'In you shall all the nations be blessed'" (Gal. 3:8). Abraham was already aware of the message of global salvation that we now enjoy. Similarly, in the opening of Romans, Paul stresses that the Lord "promised beforehand through his prophets in the holy Scriptures" (i.e., the Old Testament Prophets) the very powerful "gospel of God . . . concerning his Son" that the apostle preached and in which we now rest (Rom. 1:1–3, 16). Key among these prophets was Isaiah, who anticipated the day when YHWH's royal servant (the Messiah) and the many servants identified with him would herald comforting "good news" to the poor and broken—news that the saving God reigns through his anointed royal deliverer (Isa. 61:1; cf. 40:9–11; 52:7–10; Luke 4:16–21). Reading the Old Testament, therefore, is one of God's given ways for us to better grasp and delight in the gospel (see also Heb. 4:2).

5. Both the old and new covenants call for love, and we can learn much about love from the Old Testament.

Within the old covenant, love was *what* the Lord called Israel to do (Deut. 6:5; 10:19); all the other commandments simply clarified *how* to do it. This was part of Jesus' point when he stressed that all the Old Testament hangs on the call to love God and neighbor: "You shall love the Lord your God with all your heart and with all your soul and with all your mind. This is the great and first commandment. And a second is like it: You shall love your neighbor as yourself. On these two commandments depend all the Law and the Prophets" (Matt. 22:37–40). Christ emphasized, "Whatever you wish that others would do to you, do also to them, for this is the Law and the Prophets" (7:12). Similarly, Paul noted, "The whole law is fulfilled in one word: 'You shall love your neighbor as yourself'" (Gal. 5:14; cf. Rom. 13:8, 10). As with old covenant Israel, the Lord calls Christians to lives characterized by love. But he now gives *all* members of the new covenant the ability to do what he commands. As Moses himself asserted, the very reason why God promised to circumcise hearts in the new covenant age was "so that you will love the Lord your God with all your heart and with all your soul" (Deut. 30:6). Moses also said that those enjoying this divine work in this future day would "obey the voice of the Lord and keep all his commandments that I command you today" (30:8). Moses' old covenant law called for life-encompassing love, and Christians today, looking through the lens of Christ, can gain clarity from the Old Testament on the wide-ranging impact of love in all of life.

6. Jesus came not to destroy the Law and the Prophets but to fulfill them.

Far from setting aside the Old Testament, Jesus stressed that he had come to fulfill it, and in the process he highlighted the lasting relevance of the Old Testament's teaching for Christians: "Do not think that I have come to abolish the Law or the Prophets; I have not come to abolish them but to fulfill them. For truly, I say to you, until heaven and earth pass away, not an iota, not a dot, will pass from the Law until all is accomplished. Therefore whoever relaxes one of the least of these commandments and teaches others to do the same will be called least in the kingdom of heaven, but whoever does them and teaches them will be called great in the kingdom of heaven" (Matt. 5:17–19). In chapters 10 and 12 we'll further consider the significance of this text, but what is important to note here is that while the age of the old covenant has come to an end (Rom. 6:14–15; 1 Cor. 9:20–21; Gal. 5:18; cf. Luke 16:16), the Old Testament itself maintains lasting relevance for us in the way it displays the character of God (e.g., Rom. 7:12), points to the excellencies of Christ, and portrays for us the scope of love in all its facets (Matt. 22:37–40).

7. Jesus said that all the Old Testament points to him.

After his first encounter with Jesus, Philip announced to Nathanael, "We have found him of whom Moses in the Law and also the prophets wrote" (John 1:45). Do you want to see and savor Jesus as much as you can? We find him in the Old Testament. As Jesus himself said, "You search the Scriptures because you think that in them you have eternal life; and it is they that bear witness about me" (John 5:39; cf. 5:46–47). "And beginning with Moses and all the Prophets, he interpreted to them in all the Scriptures the things concerning himself" (Luke 24:27). After his resurrection, proclaiming the gospel of God's kingdom (Acts 1:3), Jesus opened the minds of his disciples "to understand the Scriptures, and said to them, 'Thus it is written, that the Christ should suffer and on the third day rise from the dead, and that repentance and forgiveness of sins should be proclaimed in his name to all nations, beginning from Jerusalem'" (Luke 24:45–47). A proper "understanding" of the Old Testament will lead one to hear in it a message of the Messiah and the mission that his life would generate. Similarly, Paul taught "nothing but what the prophets and Moses said would come to pass: that the Christ must suffer and that, by being the first to rise from the dead, he would proclaim light both to our people and to the Gentiles" (Acts 26:22–23). As an Old Testament preacher, Paul could declare, "I decided to know nothing among you except Jesus Christ and him crucified" (1 Cor. 2:2). If you want to know Jesus more fully, read the Old Testament!

8. Failing to declare "the whole counsel of God" can put us in danger before the Lord.

Paul was a herald of the good news of God's kingdom in Christ (e.g., Acts 19:8; 20:25; 28:30–31), which he preached from the law of Moses and the Prophets—the Old Testament (28:23; cf. 26:22–23). In Acts 20:26–27 he testified to the Ephesian elders, "I am innocent of the blood of all, for I did not shrink from declaring to you the whole counsel of God." The "***whole counsel of God***" refers to the entirety of God's purposes in salvation history as revealed in Scripture. Had the apostle failed to make known the Lord's redemptive plan of blessing overcoming curse in the person of Jesus, he would have stood accountable before God for any future doctrinal or moral error that the Ephesian church carried out (cf. Ezek. 33:1–6; Acts 18:6). With the New Testament, Scripture is complete, and we now have in whole "the faith that was once for all delivered to the saints" (Jude 3). This "faith," however, is rightly understood only within the framework of "the whole counsel of God." So may we be people who guard ourselves from bloodguilt by making much of the Old Testament in relation to Christ.

9. The New Testament authors stressed that God gave the Old Testament for Christians.

Paul was convinced that the divinely inspired Old Testament authors wrote *for* New Testament believers, living on this side of the death and resurrection of Christ: "For whatever was written in former days was written *for our instruction*, that through endurance and through the encouragement of the Scriptures we might have hope" (Rom. 15:4; cf. 4:23–24). "Now these things happened to [the Israelites] as an example, but they were written down *for our instruction*, on whom the end of the ages has come" (1 Cor. 10:11).[10] Accordingly, the apostle emphasized to Timothy, who had been raised on the Old Testament by his Jewish mother and grandmother (Acts 16:1; 2 Tim. 1:5), that the *"sacred writings"* of his upbringing "are able to make you wise for salvation through faith in Christ Jesus" (2 Tim. 3:15). People today can get saved from God's wrath and from the enslavement of sin by reading the Old Testament through the lens of Christ!

This is why Paul says in the very next verse, "All Scripture is . . . profitable for teaching, for reproof, for correction, and for training in righteousness, that the man of God may be complete, equipped for every good work" (3:16–17). New covenant believers can correct and reprove straying brothers and sisters *from the Old Testament* when read in relation to Christ, for in it we find many "profitable" things (Acts 20:20)—a "gospel of the grace of God" (20:24)—that call for "repentance toward God" and "faith in our Lord Jesus Christ" (20:21). Based on this fact, New Testament authors regularly used the Old Testament as the basis for Christian exhortation, assuming its relevance for Christians (e.g., 1 Cor. 9:8–12; Eph. 6:2–3; 1 Tim. 5:18; 1 Peter 1:14–16). Because we are now part of the new covenant and not the old, natural questions arise regarding how exactly the Christian should relate to specific old covenant instruction. We will address these matters in chapter 12. Nevertheless, the point stands that the Old Testament, while not written *to* Christians, was still written *for* us.

10. Paul commands church leaders to preach the Old Testament.

The last of my ten reasons why the Old Testament still matters for Christians builds on the fact that Paul was referring to the Old Testament when he spoke of the "sacred writings" that are able to make a person "wise for salvation" and the "Scripture" that is

10. In chapter 12 under the section "God Gave the Old Testament to Instruct Christians," we'll see that the Old Testament prophets themselves anticipated that this would be the case.

"breathed out by God and profitable" (2 Tim. 3:15–16). Knowing this colors our understanding of his following charge to Timothy: "Preach the word; be ready in season and out of season; reprove, rebuke, and exhort, with complete patience and teaching. For the time is coming when people will not endure sound teaching, but having itching ears they will accumulate for themselves teachers to suit their own passion, and will turn away from listening to the truth and wander off into myths" (4:2–4). For the apostle, Christian preachers such as Timothy needed to preach the Old Testament in order to guard the church from apostasy. While we now have the New Testament, we can, and indeed must, appropriate the Old Testament as Jesus and his apostles did for the good of God's church.

The Benefits of Hebrew Exegesis

You do not have to know Hebrew to profit much from this book. Indeed, every chapter contains solid information for guiding English-only Old Testament interpretation. Nevertheless, God gave us most of the Old Testament in Hebrew, and because of this a lot of material in the first half of the book (chaps. 2–7) clarifies the process of *Hebrew* exegesis. If you do not know Hebrew, I encourage you to keep reading this section, for I believe that it can move you to appreciate and pray for those who do. If you are not interested in hearing some of the benefits of Hebrew exegesis, feel free to jump ahead to the next section.

For most of my academic ministry career, the priest-scribe Ezra's approach to Scripture has highly influenced my biblical interpretation. "The good hand of his God was on him. For Ezra had set his heart to *study* the Law of the LORD, and to *do* it and to *teach* his statutes and rules in Israel" (Ezra 7:9–10).

STUDY DO TEACH God's Word: This was the order of Ezra's resolve. Study shaped by careful observation, right understanding, and fair evaluation is to give rise to practice—feeling appropriately about the truth that is seen and then acting accordingly. Only after we have studied and practiced are we ready to teach. If we teach without having studied, we replace God's words with our own; we become the authority instead of the Lord. If we teach without having practiced, we are nothing more than hypocrites. I want to consider why we need men and women in every generation who can approach the Old Testament using biblical Hebrew, and I want to consider the answer in light of Ezra's resolve.[11]

11. For more pastoral reflection on Ezra 7:10, see Jason S. DeRouchie, "A Life Centered on Torah (Ezra 7:10)," in *Basics of Biblical Hebrew: Grammar*, by Gary D. Pratico and Miles V. Van Pelt, 2nd ed. (Grand Rapids: Zondervan, 2007), 249–50.

While every believer must seek to know God, not everyone needs to know the biblical languages. Indeed, the Lord has graciously made his Word translatable so that those "from every tribe and language and people and nation" may hear of and believe in the Savior (Rev. 5:9; cf. Neh. 8:7–8; Acts 2:6). With this, grasping the fundamentals of Hebrew and Greek neither ensures correct interpretation of Scripture nor removes all interpretive challenges. It does not automatically make one a good exegete of texts or an articulate, winsome proclaimer of God's truth. Linguistic skill also does not necessarily result in deeper levels of holiness or in greater knowledge of God. Without question, *the most important skill for interpreting Scripture* is to read, read, and read the biblical text carefully and God-dependently and to consider what it says about God's character, actions, and purposes and how it points to Christ.

Nevertheless, we need some in the church in every generation who can skillfully use the biblical languages. Why? I have four reasons.[12] As I give an overview of these, if you don't know Hebrew (yet), keep in mind what I say in the previous paragraph and let any inkling of discouragement turn into gratefulness to God for raising up some who can study, practice, and teach from this framework.

1. The biblical languages give us direct access to God's written Word.

Original-language exegesis exalts Jesus by affirming God's decision to give us his Word in a Book, written first in Hebrew, Aramaic, and Greek. In his wisdom and for the benefit of every generation of humankind, God chose to preserve and guard in a Book his authoritative, clear, necessary, and sufficient Word. Jesus highlights the significance of this fact when he declares that he prophetically fulfills all Old Testament hopes: "Do not think that I have come to abolish the Law or the Prophets; I have not come to abolish them but to fulfill them. For truly, I say to you, until heaven and earth pass away, not an iota, not a dot, will pass from the Law until all is accomplished" (Matt. 5:17–18). The very details of the biblical text (every iota and every dot) bear lasting significance and point to the person and work of Christ. So we align ourselves with God's wisdom and participate in his passion to exalt his Son when we take the biblical languages seriously in the study of his Book. This is the first reason why we do *Hebrew* exegesis.

2. The biblical languages help us study God's Word.

Using Hebrew and Greek can give us greater certainty that we have grasped the meaning of God's Book. Knowing the biblical languages can also help us observe more accurately, understand more clearly, evaluate more fairly, and interpret more confidently the inspired details of the biblical text. Without Hebrew and Greek, ministers are:

- Required to trust someone else's translation (many of which are excellent, but which are translations/interpretations nonetheless);

12. What follows is a condensed version of the main points in Jason S. DeRouchie, "The Profit of Employing the Biblical Languages: Scriptural and Historical Reflections," *Themelios* 37, 1 (2012): 32–50.

- Left without help when translations differ;
- Forced to rely heavily on what others say in commentaries and other tools without accurate comprehension or fair evaluation; and
- Compelled to miss numerous discourse features that are not easily conveyed through translation.

Knowing the languages neither makes an interpreter always right nor sets all interpretive challenges aside. Nevertheless, by using the biblical languages we remove hindrances to understanding and take away many occasions for mistakes. Furthermore, knowing Hebrew and Greek enables interpreters to more accurately track an author's flow of thought through which the Bible's message is revealed.

3. The biblical languages help us practice God's Word.

Employing Hebrew and Greek can assist in developing Christian maturity that validates our witness in the world. Scripture is clear that a true encounter with God's Word will alter the way we live, shaping servants instead of kings and nurturing Christ-exalting humility rather than pride. Sadly, practicing the Word is too often forgotten, thus hindering the spread of the gospel in the world.

Now, because our knowing the Lord and living for him develops only in the context of the Word and because Bible study is best done through the original languages, Hebrew and Greek can serve as God's instruments to develop holiness, which enhances the church's mission. Original-language exegesis can help clarify what feelings the Lord wants us to have and what actions he wants us to take. And along with opening fresh doors of discovery into the biblical text, the arduous task of learning, keeping, and using the languages itself provides many opportunities for growth in character, discipline, boldness, and joy. Hypocrisy hinders kingdom expansion, but biblically grounded study accompanied by a virtuous life substantiates the gospel and promotes mission, leading to worship.

4. The biblical languages help us teach God's Word.

Original-language exegesis fuels a fresh and bold expression and defense of the truth in preaching and teaching. Saturated study of Scripture through Hebrew and Greek provides a sustained opportunity for personal discovery, freshness, and insight, all of which can enhance our teaching. Moreover, the languages provide a powerful means for judging and defending biblical truth. The church needs earnest contenders for the faith, those who are "able to give instruction in sound doctrine and also to rebuke those who contradict it" (Titus 1:9). The biblical languages sharpen our teaching and preaching to make it as pointed, accurate, and penetrating as possible.

In summary, for the Christian minister who is charged to proclaim God's truth with accuracy and to preserve the gospel's purity with integrity, the biblical languages help in one's study, practice, and teaching of the Word. Properly using the languages opens doors of biblical discovery that would otherwise remain locked and provides interpreters with accountability that they would otherwise not have. Ministers who know Hebrew and Greek not only can feed themselves but will also be able to gain a level of biblical discernment that will allow them to respond in an informed way to new translations, new theological perspectives, and other changing trends in church and culture.

In light of the above, I offer the following action steps to readers of all vocational callings:

- ***Seminary professors and administrators.*** Fight to make exegeting the Word in the original languages the core of every curriculum that is designed to train vocational ministers of God's Book.
- ***Church shepherds and shepherds-in-training.*** Seek to become God-dependent, rigorous thinkers who study, practice, and teach the Word—in that order!
- ***Other congregational leaders.*** Give your ministers who are called to preach and teach time to study, and help your congregations see this as a priority.
- ***Young-adult leaders and college professors.*** Encourage those sensing a call to vocational ministry of God's Word to become thoroughly equipped for the task.
- ***Everyone.*** Seek as much as possible to be a first-hander when interpreting God's Word, guard yourself from false teaching, hold your leaders accountable, and pray to our glorious God for the preservation of the gospel, for our leaders, and for the churches and schools training them.

Now let's discover how to understand and apply the Old Testament.

Overview of the Interpretive Process: TOCMA

This book employs a twelve-step process to guide the move from exegesis to theology and from personal study to practice and then instruction. While this guidebook considers each stage independently, the interpretive process is more like a spiral by which we continually revisit various interpretive stopping points in our up-road climb to biblical faithfulness.

For the sake of easy recollection, I have tagged the whole process ***TOCMA***, which stands for *Text, Observation, Context, Meaning, Application*. Each of the twelve stages falls within one of these overarching categories.

Part 1: TEXT—"What is the makeup of the passage?"

1. **Genre:** Determine the literary form, subject matter, and function of the passage, compare it to similar genres, and consider the implications for interpretation.
2. **Literary units and text hierarchy:** Determine the limits and basic structure of the passage.
3. **Text criticism:** Establish the passage's original wording.
4. **Translation:** Translate the text and compare other translations.

Part 2: OBSERVATION—"How is the passage communicated?"

5. **Clause and text grammar:** Assess the makeup and relationship of words, phrases, clauses, and larger text units.
6. **Argument-tracing:** Finish tracing the literary argument and create a message-driven outline that is tied to the passage's main point.
7. **Word and concept studies:** Clarify the meaning of key words, phrases, and concepts.

Part 3: CONTEXT—"Where does the passage fit?"

8. **Historical context:** Understand the historical situation from which the author composed the text and identify any historical details that the author mentions or assumes.
9. **Literary context:** Comprehend the role that the passage plays in the whole book.

Part 4: MEANING—"What does the passage mean?"

10. **Biblical theology:** Consider how your passage connects to the Bible's overall flow and message and points to Christ.
11. **Systematic theology:** Discern how your passage theologically coheres with the whole Bible, assessing key doctrines especially in direct relation to the gospel.

Part 5: APPLICATION—"Why does the passage matter?"

12. **Practical theology:** Apply the text to yourself, the church, and the world, stressing the centrality of Christ and the hope of the gospel.

Come with me now on a journey of discovery and skill development. Chapters 1–9 focus especially on the process of exegesis, whereas chapters 10–12 address theology. God-honoring worship is both the fuel and the goal of every stage of biblical interpretation. So may your study result in practice and overflow in teaching that is filled with praise and proclamation—all for the glory of Christ and the good of his church among the nations.

Key Words and Concepts

Biblical interpretation
Exegesis
Theology
Special revelation
Infallible and inerrant
IOUS
Whole counsel of God
Study → do → teach!
TOCMA

Questions for Further Reflection

1. Describe the connection between exegesis and theology. What is the danger of doing theology apart from exegesis or exegesis apart from theology?
2. What are DeRouchie's four presuppositions that guide his study of the Bible?
3. What is the risk if you do not hold each of these presuppositions?
4. What is the ultimate goal of biblical interpretation?
5. Which of the ten reasons why the Old Testament is important for Christians most moved your soul? Which one most compels you to study the Old Testament?
6. In what ways does knowing Hebrew benefit and not benefit the process of biblical exegesis?

Resources for Further Study[13]

Baker, David W., and Bill T. Arnold. *The Face of Old Testament Studies: A Survey of Contemporary Approaches*. Grand Rapids: Baker Academic, 2004.

Carson, D. A. "Approaching the Bible." In *New Bible Commentary: 21st Century Edition*, edited by D. A. Carson, R. T. France, J. A. Motyer, and G. J. Wenham, 1–19. 4th ed. Downers Grove, IL: InterVarsity Press, 1994.

———, ed. *The Enduring Authority of the Christian Scriptures*. Grand Rapids: Eerdmans, 2016.

———. *Exegetical Fallacies*. 2nd ed. Grand Rapids: Baker Academic, 1996.

Chisholm, Robert B., Jr. *From Exegesis to Exposition: A Practical Guide to Using Biblical Hebrew*. Grand Rapids: Baker Academic, 1999.

13. In each chapter, I have included "Resources for Further Study" that I believe will serve the student of Scripture in various ways. Not all the books listed are unified in their theological perspectives or interpretive approaches, so the reader needs to carefully evaluate all claims up against the Bible, which supplies the highest authority for the Christian. I have preceded with a star those resources that I believe to be the most important or best. A plain black star (★) marks resources that are intended for all readers, whereas a white star within a black circle (✪) highlights those that are designed for more advanced readers and that may also contain Hebrew. I thank my friend and colleague Andy Naselli for his help in shaping these bibliographies.

DeRouchie, Jason S. "The Profit of Employing the Biblical Languages: Scriptural and Historical Reflections." *Themelios* 37, 1 (2012): 32–50.

Dockery, David S., Kenneth A. Mathews, and Robert B. Sloan, eds. *Foundations for Biblical Interpretation: A Complete Library of Tools and Resources*. Nashville: Broadman & Holman, 1994.

Duvall, J. Scott, and J. Daniel Hays. *Grasping God's Word: A Hands-On Approach to Reading, Interpreting, and Applying the Bible*. 3rd ed. Grand Rapids: Zondervan, 2012.

Dyer, John. *Best Commentaries: Reviews and Ratings of Biblical, Theological, and Practical Christian Works*. http://www.bestcommentaries.com/.

Evans, John F. *A Guide to Biblical Commentaries and Reference Works*. 10th ed. Grand Rapids: Zondervan, 2016.

Glynn, John. *Commentary and Reference Survey: A Comprehensive Guide to Biblical and Theological Resources*. Grand Rapids: Kregel, 2007.

Goldsworthy, Graeme. *Gospel-Centered Hermeneutics: Foundations and Principles of Evangelical Biblical Interpretation*. Downers Grove, IL: InterVarsity Press, 2006.

Grudem, Wayne A., C. John Collins, and Thomas R. Schreiner, eds. *Understanding the Big Picture of the Bible: A Guide to Reading the Bible Well*. Wheaton, IL: Crossway, 2012.

Guthrie, George H. *Read the Bible for Life: Your Guide to Understanding and Living God's Word*. Nashville: Broadman & Holman, 2011.

InterVarsity Press dictionaries on the Old Testament:

- Alexander, T. Desmond, and David W. Baker, eds. *Dictionary of the Old Testament: Pentateuch*. Downers Grove, IL: InterVarsity Press, 2003.
- Arnold, Bill T., and H. G. M. Williamson, eds. *Dictionary of the Old Testament: Historical Books* Downers Grove, IL: InterVarsity Press, 2005.
- Boda, Mark J., and J. Gordon McConville, eds. *Dictionary of the Old Testament: Prophets*. Downers Grove, IL: InterVarsity Press, 2012.
- Longman, Tremper, III, and Peter Enns, eds. *Dictionary of the Old Testament: Wisdom, Poetry, and Writings*. Downers Grove, IL: InterVarsity Press, 2008.

Kaiser, Walter C., Jr. *Toward an Exegetical Theology: Biblical Exegesis for Preaching and Teaching* Grand Rapids: Baker Academic, 1981.

Kaiser, Walter C., Jr., and Moisés Silva. *Introduction to Biblical Hermeneutics: The Search for Meaning*. 2nd ed. Grand Rapids: Zondervan, 2007.

Köstenberger, Andreas J., and Richard D. Patterson. *For the Love of God's Word: An Introduction to Biblical Interpretation*. Grand Rapids: Kregel, 2015.

———. *Invitation to Biblical Interpretation: Exploring the Hermeneutical Triad of History, Literature, and Theology*. Grand Rapids: Kregel, 2011.

Longman, Tremper, III. *Old Testament Commentary Survey*. 5th ed. Grand Rapids: Zondervan, 2013.

McCartney, Dan, and Charles Clayton. *Let the Reader Understand: A Guide to Interpreting and Applying the Bible*. 2nd ed. Phillipsburg, NJ: P&R Publishing, 2002.

Naselli, Andrew David. "D. A. Carson's Theological Method." *SBET* 29, 2 (2011): 245–74.

Osborne, Grant R. *The Hermeneutical Spiral: A Comprehensive Introduction to Biblical Interpretation*. 2nd ed. Downers Grove, IL: InterVarsity Press, 2006.

Piper, John. *Reading the Bible Supernaturally: Seeing and Savoring the Glory of God in Scripture* Wheaton, IL: Crossway, 2017.

★ Plummer, Robert L. *40 Questions about Interpreting the Bible*. 40 Questions. Grand Rapids: Kregel, 2010.

Poythress, Vern S. *Reading the Word of God in the Presence of God: A Handbook for Biblical Interpretation*. Wheaton, IL: Crossway, 2016.

Soulen, Richard N., and R. Kendall Soulen. *Handbook of Biblical Criticism*. 4th ed. Louisville: Westminster John Knox, 2011.

✪ Stuart, Douglas. *Old Testament Exegesis: A Handbook for Students and Pastors*. 4th ed. Louisville: Westminster John Knox, 2009.

PART 1

TEXT—"WHAT IS THE MAKEUP OF THE PASSAGE?"

1

GENRE

Goal: Determine the literary form, subject matter, and function of the passage, compare it to similar genres, and consider the implications for interpretation.

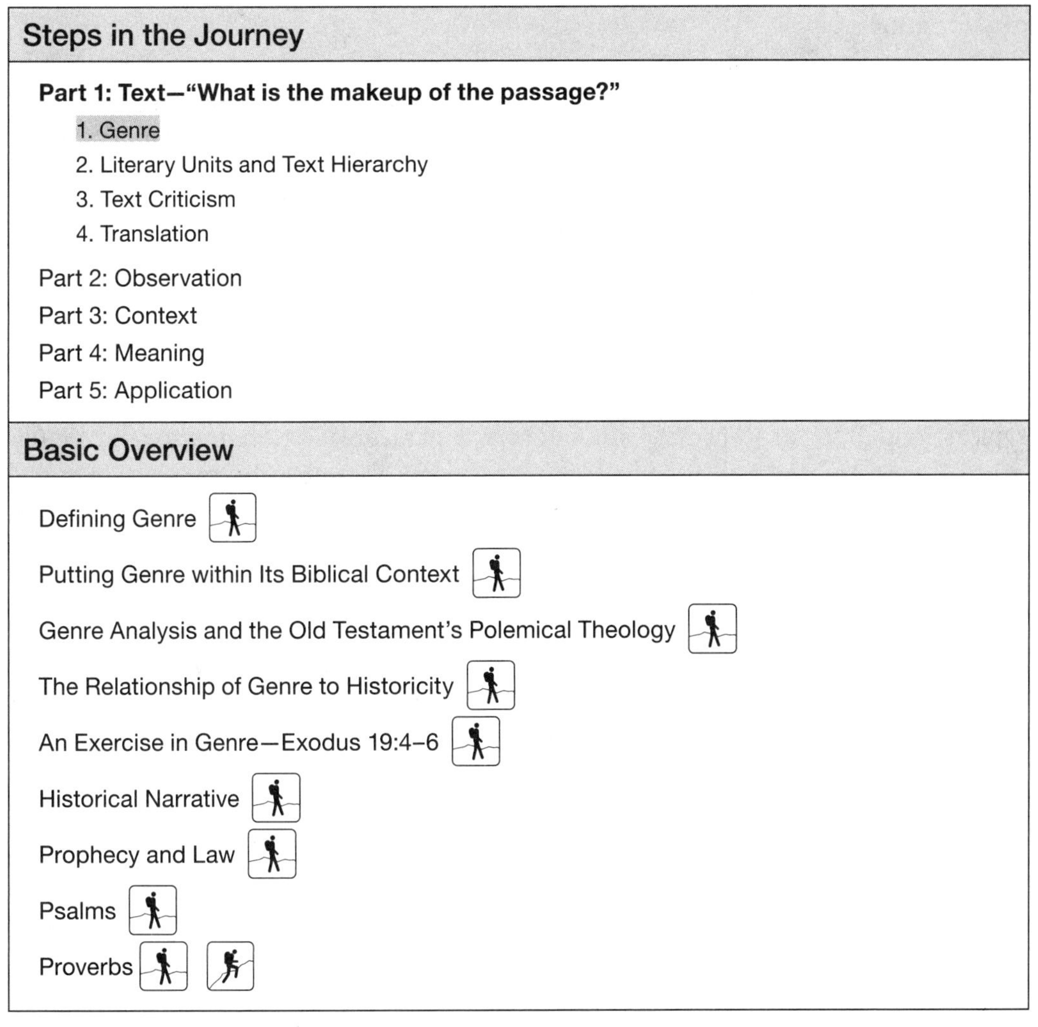

Steps in the Journey

Part 1: Text—"What is the makeup of the passage?"

1. Genre
2. Literary Units and Text Hierarchy
3. Text Criticism
4. Translation

Part 2: Observation
Part 3: Context
Part 4: Meaning
Part 5: Application

Basic Overview

Defining Genre
Putting Genre within Its Biblical Context
Genre Analysis and the Old Testament's Polemical Theology
The Relationship of Genre to Historicity
An Exercise in Genre—Exodus 19:4–6
Historical Narrative
Prophecy and Law
Psalms
Proverbs

Fig. 1.1. Trail Guide to Chapter 1

Defining Genre

My oldest daughter is a master of "genre" analysis. I see it most after her daily trip to the mailbox, as she pushes aside the bills and advertisements to select the letters from friends or family. With every new piece of literary composition, we almost always identify genre. We decide (consciously or unconsciously, rightly or wrongly) whether a text is a research paper or poem, a factual history or a fairy tale. We look for clues in format, presentation, introductory or closing statements, and content. We seek the author's signals as to whether something is satire, fiction, or nonfiction.

These markers point to a document's genre. ***Genre*** refers to an identifiable category of literary composition that usually demands its own exegetical rules. Accordingly, a misunderstanding of a work's genre can lead to skewed interpretation. Our decisions at this point will color the rest of the exegetical process. This first chapter is one of the longest chapters of the book, and the overview will set trajectories for the remaining eleven steps of interpretation. Every reader will benefit from this material, despite your level of exposure to biblical Hebrew.

Genre analysis is concerned not only with grammatical makeup but also with the patterns, content, and function in context. It examines the shape, subject matter, and purpose of a particular unit. It asks whether these elements are defined enough and typical enough for us to classify and interpret a passage as belonging to a particular genre. If the form, content, and function are sufficiently comparable to other texts, and if we can establish definite criteria for identifying the pattern's occurrence, the unit may be said to belong to a given genre. Knowing the genre of a text helps us know what types of questions we should ask of the material. Assigning the wrong genre to a text can lead our biblical interpretation astray.

We discern a text's genre by carefully noting literary details and authorial comments that clarify how we should read it. Are we reading a blessing or curse, a court annal or exhortation, a doxology or genealogy, a proverb or prayerful petition, a love song or a lament, or any number of other possibilities?[1]

1. Genre analysis came to the fore in Old Testament studies in the early nineteenth century after the increased discovery of ancient Near Eastern texts that bear similarity to the Bible. Extrabiblical materials such as Sumerian king lists, Egyptian proverbs, Babylonian creation accounts and law codes, Hittite and Assyrian treaties, and Assyrian prophecies helped clarify how the Old Testament was both at home within and an affront to its culture. Immediately people felt led to compare and, less often, contrast the forms, content, and function of these outside texts with the Scriptures. Genre analysis was important to the comparative enterprise because texts needed to be similar in genre in order to provide legitimate comparison—laws to laws, proverbs to proverbs, prophecies to prophecies.

The sages, seers, singers, and sovereigns that God used to produce our Bible sometimes sought to convey information and to stir thoughts. Laws and historical narratives are mostly of this type. Through other genres they intended to affect and effect certain behaviors , beliefs, and feelings—to awaken emotions and to arouse affections. Here we would place most of the psalms and books such as Song of Songs. Some genres served to blend both of these purposes, such as much prophecy and some proverbs.

Every genre has its own interpretive rules. Some allow for high use of hyperbole and figurative language, but others do not. Signals in the text distinguish parables from history writing. Each demands a very different reading, but both can come to us in a similar form. The biblical authors picked different genres in order to communicate their intended truths in the most effective way. They consciously submitted themselves to the rules of a given genre, and they expected their readers to do the same. Grasping how the various genres work will help us better interpret Scripture.

Putting Genre within Its Biblical Context

The Jewish Bible that Jesus and the apostles used appears to have been structured differently from our English Bible. While the Jewish Scriptures are limited to the same thirty-nine books found in our English Old Testament, they pair some of the books into single volumes (e.g., 1–2 Samuel, 1–2 Kings, the Twelve Minor Prophets, Ezra-Nehemiah, 1–2 Chronicles)[2] and arrange the whole in a different order and in three main divisions: the Law (תּוֹרָה, *tôrâ*), the Prophets (נְבִיאִים, *nĕḇîʾîm*), and the Writings (or "the other Scriptures," כְּתוּבִים, *kĕṯûḇîm*).[3] Many refer to the Jewish arrangement as the ***TaNaK***, which is an acronym derived from the first Hebrew letters of each of the three major section titles. We see potential evidence of this three-part structure in Luke 24:44, when Jesus declared after his resurrection, "These are my words that I spoke to you while I was still with you, that everything written about me in the Law of Moses and the Prophets and the Psalms must be fulfilled." In most reckonings, Psalms is the first main book in the Writings (though prefaced by Ruth), and Jesus here seems to treat it as a title for the whole third division.

2. At least in the case of the books of Samuel, Kings, and Chronicles, the reason that these were later separated into two books appears to be merely pragmatic: the Hebrew Bible used only consonants, and when it was translated into Greek, which included vowels, the books got too long for single scrolls.

3. For examples of the threefold division outside the Bible, see the prologue to Ben Sira and 4QMMT C.10 in the DSS.

The biblical evidence also suggests that Jesus' Bible began with Genesis and ended with Chronicles. We see this in one of Jesus' confrontations with the Pharisees, in which he spoke of the martyrdom of the Old Testament prophets "from the blood of Abel to the blood of Zechariah" (Luke 11:51; cf. Matt. 23:35). This is not a simple "A to Z" statement, for Zechariah's name does not begin with the last letter of any biblical-language alphabet. Also, it is not strictly a chronological statement, for while Abel was clearly the first martyr (Gen. 4:4, 8), the Old Testament's last martyr with respect to time was Uriah the son of Shemaiah, who died during the reign of Jehoiakim (609–598 B.C.; see Jer. 26:20–23). Instead, Jesus appears to have been speaking canonically, mentioning the first and last martyr in his Bible's literary structure. Specifically, just as Genesis records Abel's murder, the end of Chronicles highlights a certain Zechariah who was killed in the temple court during the reign of Joash (835–796 B.C.; see 2 Chron. 24:20–21).

Stephen Dempster has observed how the Hebrew Old Testament's three-part structure distinguishes the "narrative" of God's redemptive story from the "commentary" sections and does so in a way that the former frames the latter.[4] The canonical arrangement I am following here is not that of the standard critical edition of the Hebrew Bible (i.e., the *Biblia Hebraica Stuttgartensia*, *BHS*) but is found in the most ancient listing of the Jewish canonical books in *Baba Bathra* 14b.[5] The guiding principles for the structure appear to be both literary and rational, in that the majority of the narrative books are chronological, whereas the commentary books are generally patterned longest to shortest.

As is evident in figure 1.2, the major prophets are out of chronological order (i.e., not Isaiah, Jeremiah, Ezekiel), Ruth is totally separated from its temporal context after Judges, Daniel is not among the Prophets, and Chronicles and Ezra-Nehemiah are

4. Stephen G. Dempster, *Dominion and Dynasty: A Biblical Theology of the Hebrew Bible*, NSBT 15 (Downers Grove, IL: InterVarsity Press, 2003), 45–51.

5. *Baba Bathra* 14b is a baraita, which is an ancient tradition found in the Babylonian Talmud (ca. A.D. 500) that dates from around the time of the Mishnah but was not included in it. Beckwith provides a complete evaluation of the textual data and posits that the arrangement of biblical books in *Baba Bathra* 14b most likely originated from a list drawn up by Judas Maccabaeus around 164 B.C. (see 2 Macc. 2:14–15) (Roger T. Beckwith, *The Old Testament Canon of the New Testament Church and Its Background in Early Judaism* [Grand Rapids: Eerdmans, 1985], 121–27, 152–53, 198). For a popular-level, succinct summary of Beckwith's conclusions, see his "The Canon of Scripture," *NDBT* 27–34. For more on the historical and theological priority of this structure above others, see Stephen G. Dempster, "An 'Extraordinary Fact': Torah and Temple and the Contours of the Hebrew Canon, Part 1," *TynBul* 48, 1 (1997): 23–56; Dempster, "An 'Extraordinary Fact': Torah and Temple and the Contours of the Hebrew Canon, Part 2," *TynBul* 48, 2 (1997): 191–218; Dempster, "From Many Texts to One: The Formation of the Hebrew Bible," in *The World of the Aramaeans 1: Biblical Studies in Honour of Paul-Eugène Dion*, ed. P. M. Michèle Daviau, John W. Wevers, and Michael Weigl (Sheffield, UK: Sheffield Academic, 2001), 19–56; Dempster, "The Place of Nehemiah in the Canon of Scripture: Wise Builder," *SBJT* 9, 3 (2005): 38–51; Dempster, "Canons on the Right and Canons on the Left: Finding a Resolution in the Canon Debate," *JETS* 52, 1 (2009): 47–77; Dempster, "Canon and Old Testament Interpretation," in *Hearing the Old Testament: Listening for God's Address*, ed. Craig G. Bartholomew and David J. H. Beldman (Grand Rapids: Eerdmans, 2012), 154–179; Dempster, "Ecclesiastes and the Canon," in *The Words of the Wise Are like Goads: Engaging Qoheleth in the 21st Century*, ed. Mark J. Boda, Tremper Longman III, and Christian G. Rata (Winona Lake, IN: Eisenbrauns, 2013), 389–402; Dempster, "A Wandering Moabite: Ruth—A Book in Search of a Canonical Home," in *The Shape of the Writings*, ed. Julius Steinberg and Timothy J. Stone, Siphrut: Literature and Theology of the Hebrew Scriptures 16 (Winona Lake, IN: Eisenbrauns, 2015), 87–118.

placed in reverse chronological order. The narrative runs chronologically from Genesis to Kings, pauses from Jeremiah to Lamentations, and then resumes from Daniel to Ezra-Nehemiah. Chronicles then recalls the story from Adam to Cyrus's decree that Israel can return. As for the commentary, the Latter Prophets structure the four books largest to smallest, and the Former Writings follow the same pattern, except that Ruth prefaces the Psalter and the longer Lamentations follows Song of Songs. The former shift places the Psalter in the context of Davidic hope, and the latter switch (1) allows Jeremiah's writings to frame the whole commentary unit, (2) allows Solomon's three volumes (Proverbs, Ecclesiastes, and Song of Songs) to remain together, and (3) lets Lamentations reorient the reader to the exilic context where Kings left off and where the narrative in Daniel resumes.

Law	Former & Latter Prophets		Former & Latter Writings	
Genesis Exodus Leviticus Numbers Deuteronomy	Joshua Judges 1–2 Samuel 1–2 Kings	Jeremiah Ezekiel Isaiah The Twelve	Ruth Psalms Job Proverbs Ecclesiastes Song of Songs Lamentations	Daniel Esther Ezra-Nehemiah 1–2 Chronicles
Narrative	**Narrative**	**Commentary**	**Commentary**	**Narrative**

Fig. 1.2. The Arrangement of the Hebrew Bible in *Baba Bathra* 14b

The *Law*, also called the *Pentateuch*, is the Bible's first five books, Genesis through Deuteronomy. This section is all narrative and is devoted to clarifying God's relationship with and purpose for Israel in the context of the world. Genesis provides a "kingdom prologue" that sets the stage for Israel's God-exalting task, which is then detailed in Exodus through Deuteronomy.

We then move to the *Prophets*, which contain two sections. The first in Joshua through Kings is a narrative history of Israel's covenant failure. The second in Jeremiah through the Twelve is a prophetic commentary on the people's rebellion that places their sin within the overall scope of God's redemptive plan. Whereas the Former Prophets focus on what happened in Israel's downward spiral from conquest through monarchy to exile, the Latter Prophets develop why the drama went the way it did.

Like the Prophets but in reverse order, the *Writings* include both commentary and narrative, but the Writings are dominated by a much more positive thrust. The commentary of the Former Writings in Ruth through Lamentations clarifies how those hoping in God's messianic kingdom were to live—that is, how they could maintain satisfaction in God amid life's pleasures and pains. Following Lamentations, which resituates us to the exilic context highlighted at the end of 2 Kings, the narrative resumes in Daniel and continues through Chronicles, detailing God's preservation of a remnant in exile, the people's initial restoration to the land, and the promise of complete kingdom realization. Because the story is unfinished at the end of Chronicles, the reader is pushed into the New Testament for fulfillment, which is ultimately realized in the person of Christ and his church.

For now, there are two significant points to make. First, because the Old Testament is framed by historical *narrative*, it is both right and necessary to read the entire Old Testament through the lens of God's history of redemption. This (true) story of salvation clarifies God's perspective on how the peoples and events of space and time relate to his kingdom purposes, which move from original creation to new creation, from the old, cursed world in Adam to the new, blessed world in Christ. As will be made clear, the main character in the redemptive drama is God, who stands supreme over all things and who graciously set Israel apart to serve as the channel through which he would overcome the world's plague of sin and replace it with the blessing of salvation ultimately through Christ.

Second, Jesus' Bible was more than narrative, for not only do the *narrative* portions themselves contain various genres such as laws (e.g., Ex. 20:1–17; Deut. 12–26), oracles (Num. 23–24), blessings and curses (Lev. 26; Deut. 28), songs (e.g., Ex. 15; Deut. 32), riddles (e.g., Judg. 14:14), parables (e.g., 2 Sam. 12:1–4), and apocalyptic visions (e.g., Dan. 7), but also the Old Testament includes the Latter Prophets and the Former Writings, two large groupings of highly poetic books that provide *commentary* on the story line of the narrative books that surround them (i.e., the Former Prophets and Latter Writings). So we will grasp Scripture's overarching message most clearly only when the history of redemption is read alongside the additional material and placed within the three-part structure. It is through this lens that Jesus and the apostles preached the good news of God's kingdom, manifest in a message of the Messiah and mission (Luke 24:44–47; Acts 26:22–23; 28:23).

As we consider the diversity of the Bible's genres, we must see them as only adding flavor to an overarching biblical unity with respect to both message and purpose.[6] Like its thirty-nine individual books (twenty-four by Jewish numbering), the Old Testament as a whole shows signs of intentional shaping toward a common goal—a quality testifying to the guiding hand of the supreme author.

6. For more on the overarching message and purpose of the Old Testament, see Dempster, *Dominion and Dynasty*; Jason S. DeRouchie, ed., *What the Old Testament Authors Really Cared About: A Survey of Jesus' Bible* (Grand Rapids: Kregel, 2013); and Miles V. Van Pelt, "Introduction," in *A Biblical-Theological Introduction to the Old Testament: The Gospel Promised*, ed. Miles V. Van Pelt (Wheaton, IL: Crossway, 2016), 23–42. It is noteworthy that the Narrative → Narrative → Commentary → Commentary → Narrative pattern is maintained in the structure of the New Testament canon in the form of the Gospels (N) → Acts (N) → Paul's Epistles and Hebrews (C) → General Epistles (C) → Revelation (N). Even if, as Trobisch has argued, the most ancient canonical arrangement placed the General Epistles before Paul's letters, the generic pattern of the whole remains parallel to that of the Old Testament (see David Trobisch, *The First Edition of the New Testament* [Oxford: Oxford University Press, 2000]; cf. C. E. Hill, "The New Testament Canon: Deconstructio ad Absurdum?," *JETS* 52, 1 [2009]: 101–19).

Genre Analysis and the Old Testament's Polemical Theology

Spirit-inspired priests, prophets, poets, and princes produced our Bible. And the language, culture, and situations of the time conditioned every line of every book. Yet all the while, God was the one guiding the shaping, keeping it as pure, true, and lasting as his character, not only with respect to issues of faith (doctrine) and practice (ethics) but also with reference to the facts (history, geography, science, etc.). The Bible grew up within history, but it also shapes history. It arose in the midst of culture but was intentionally designed to confront culture. No other ancient literature is like the Christian Scripture, for no other writing is God's Word. While we can legitimately engage in genre comparison, we must never treat the Bible as if it were wholly like any other book.

Many scholars today, even some who claim to be evangelicals, assert that the Bible's use of forms or genres that are common to the ancient world supports the belief that the biblical worldview, while monotheistic, often parallels and at times borrows with minimal discrimination the pre-enlightened religious ideas and rituals of ancient Israel's neighbors. Because the Bible is ancient literature, these scholars claim, we must interpret it like all other ancient literature. So if we know that ancient kings outside the Bible often fabricated history for the purpose of propaganda, to build up their own names, we should be open to read Israel's history in this same way. They say that because all predictive prophecy outside the Bible was written after the fact, we should be open to the possibility and perhaps even expect that the Bible's prophets did the same thing. They say that all ancient creation accounts witness prescientific understandings of reality, and that we therefore expect too much of Scripture when we look for scientifically factual data. All these statements appear to assume that the Bible is not unique literature. They fail to account for the distinct nature of Scripture as God's unique Word.

I agree with Old Testament Professor John Currid that when we affirm the Old Testament's historical reliability and assess not only similarities but also differences with comparative ancient accounts, we see that the Bible sets itself apart within its ancient environment. Just because the Bible uses genres such as history and law and prophecy and lament that were common in the ancient world does not mean that it uses them in the same way. In his book *Against the Gods*, Currid persuasively argues that the Bible's tendency is not to appropriate but to dispute and repudiate pagan myths, ideas, identities, and customs.[7] It does this by:

7. John D. Currid, *Against the Gods: The Polemical Theology of the Old Testament* (Wheaton, IL: Crossway, 2013).

- Establishing the authentic, original historical event that had been vulgarized and distorted through polytheism, magic, violence, and paganism; and
- Showing that what was myth in the ancient world had real and factual substance in Israel's time and history.

Let's consider for the moment the ancient suzerain-vassal treaty pattern, which finds parallels in the biblical text. In his Deuteronomy commentary titled *Treaty of the Great King*, Meredith Kline was one of the first to identify the way in which the Hittite treaty pattern parallels the book of Deuteronomy.[8]

Preamble	Deut. 1:1–5
Historical Prologue: Covenant History	1:6–4:49
Stipulations: Covenant Life	5:1–26:19
Sanctions: Covenant Ratification	27:1–30:20
Dynastic Disposition: Covenant Continuity	31:1–34:12

Fig. 1.3. The Treaty Structure of Deuteronomy

Many have tweaked Kline's initial proposal, but most recognize treaty parallels and believe that God is approaching Israel as the Great King in Deuteronomy (Deut. 33:5). At one level we can view YHWH as intentionally adopting and adapting international treaty patterns for his own purposes. But we can also see geopolitical treaties on earth as only fruits and reflections of a more prototypical covenantal relationship that God initiated with mankind in the garden of Eden. Not only this, what God started with humanity at creation itself is an overflow of his own eternal intra-Trinitarian covenantal agreement and decree, which are worked out through salvation history (Eph. 1:4–14). In using the treaty pattern with Israel, the Lord is not simply borrowing from the ancient world but is actually returning to his original covenantal approach with humanity and modeling for the world what true kingship should look like. All the kingdoms of mankind are but warped reflections of God's ultimate kingdom.

Scripture arose in an ancient context that was filled with perspectives, powers, and practices sometimes like but often unlike those of our Western world. Into this

8. Meredith G. Kline, *Treaty of the Great King—The Covenant Structure of Deuteronomy: Studies and Commentary* (Grand Rapids: Eerdmans, 1963; repr., Eugene, OR: Wipf & Stock, 2012); cf. George E. Mendenhall, "Covenant Forms in Israelite Tradition," *BA* 17 (1954): 50–76; Mendenhall, "The Suzerainty Treaty Structure: Thirty Years Later," in *Religion and Law: Biblical-Judaic and Islamic Perspectives*, ed. Edwin B. Firmage, Bernard G. Weiss, and John W. Welch (Winona Lake, IN: Eisenbrauns, 1990), 85–100.

environment the Old Testament stands as polemical theology, confronting false perceptions and activities.[9]

The Relationship of Genre to Historicity

Form alone does not clarify an account's historicity or factuality. For example, when King David heard the prophet Nathan's story of the robbed lamb, it appeared factual, but it shifted from a historical narrative of injustice to a narrative parable of injustice through the single statement "You are the man!" (2 Sam. 12:1–7). Narratives can express both history and fiction, and numerous other genres can supply the medium for history writing. Historical facts, for example, can appear both in narrative prose and in poetic song. While each genre has its own governing rules (e.g., poetry allows for more figurative language), the form itself has no bearing on the factuality of the account.

In order to get a sense for differences in genre and for how form does not influence historicity, let's consider a parallel historical account in Judges. In Judges 4 we read the great narrative record of the judgeship of Deborah and Barak, whom God raised up to confront the enemy Jabin, king of Canaan, who reigned in Hazor. The commander of Jabin's army was Sisera, and we are told in Judges 4:18–21 that as he fled from Deborah and Barak,

> [a woman named] Jael *came out* to meet Sisera *and said* to him, "Turn aside, my lord; turn aside to me; do not be afraid." *So he turned aside* to her into the tent, *and she covered him* with a rug. *And he said* to her, "Please give me a little water to drink, for I am thirsty." *So she opened* a skin of milk *and gave him a drink and covered him*. *And he said* to her, "Stand at the opening of the tent, and if any man comes and asks you, 'Is anyone here?' say, 'No.'" *But* Jael the wife of Heber *took* a tent peg, *and took* a hammer in her hand. *Then she went* softly to him *and drove* the peg into his temple *until it went down* into the ground while he was lying fast asleep from weariness. *So he died*.

The account is straight narrative, and all but one clause from the narrator's pen begins with the Hebrew storytelling *wayyiqtol* (*waw*-consecutive imperfect) verb (signaled by the italicized phrases).

9. I encourage you to check out Currid's book *Against the Gods*. It's loaded with examples and clearly written commentary that respects the nature of God's Word and that helps us grasp how much of the Old Testament was written to confront improper worldviews of the day.

Now, in a way that draws attention to the main point of the story, Judges 5 contains a retelling of the same event through the song of Deborah and Barak, but now the historical account is delivered in full-blown Hebrew poetry. Jael's part comes in 5:24–27. Note how the episode is now cast in a different genre:

24 Most blessed of women be Jael,
the wife of Heber the Kenite,
of tent-dwelling women most blessed.
25 He asked for water and she gave him milk;
she brought him curds in a noble's bowl.
26 She sent her hand to the tent peg
and her right hand to the workmen's mallet;
she struck Sisera;
she crushed his head;
she shattered and pierced his temple.
27 Between her feet
he sank, he fell, he lay still;
between her feet
he sank, he fell;
where he sank,
there he fell—dead.

The ESV's paragraphing signals that the translator recognized this text as poetry. The entire flow has a different feel from the narrative. It's rhythmic and paced, and not one *wayyiqtol* verb occurs in the entire passage. The song awakens emotion, passion, and praise. The entire piece moves us to sing with Deborah and Barak the final line of the song, "So may all your enemies perish, O LORD! But your friends be like the sun as he rises in his might" (Judg. 5:31).

We see a comparable contrast of genre in the story of the exodus in Exodus 14–15. In Exodus 14 we read the historical-narrative account in prose of YHWH's deliverance of Israel from Egypt; it is a detailed, step-by-step narration of the events as they played out in space and time. In Exodus 15, however, the same account is recast in song, filled with poetic images and figures of speech. Exodus 15:3–11 reads:

3 The LORD is a man of war;
the LORD is his name.

4 Pharaoh's chariots and his host he cast into the sea,
and his chosen officers were sunk in the Red Sea.
5 The floods covered them;
they went down into the depths like a stone.
6 Your right hand, O LORD, glorious in power,
your right hand, O LORD, shatters the enemy.
7 In the greatness of your majesty you overthrow your adversaries;
you send out your fury; it consumes them like stubble.

8 At the blast of your nostrils the waters piled up;
the floods stood up in a heap;
the deeps congealed in the heart of the sea.
9 The enemy said, "I will pursue, I will overtake,
I will divide the spoil, my desire shall have its fill of them.
I will draw my sword; my hand shall destroy them."
10 You blew with your wind; the sea covered them;
they sank like lead in the mighty waters.

11 Who is like you, O Lord, among the gods?
Who is like you, majestic in holiness,
awesome in glorious deeds, doing wonders?

In this poetic account we read things not seen in the narrative version. In the narrative we read only that "the Lord drove the sea back by a strong east wind" (Ex. 14:21), but in the song we read, "At the blast of your nostrils the waters piled up" (15:8). The imagery is akin to the force of Aslan's roar in *The Chronicles of Narnia*, and the repetition only adds to the emotive effect.

In the song we hear "likenings," similes: "They went down into the depths *like* a stone" (Ex. 15:5); "it consumes them *like* stubble" (15:7). In the narrative we read in 14:23, 28 that "the Egyptians pursued and went in after them. . . . The waters returned and covered the chariots and the horsemen; of all the host of Pharaoh that had followed them into the sea, not one of them remained." In contrast, the poem declares in 15:10, "You blew with your wind; the sea covered them; they sank *like* lead in the mighty waters." One portrayal delivers the facts; the other captures the emotive force that we should feel as we read the story. The use of similes contributes to the feeling of the poem.

Significantly, the historical narrative does not refrain from stressing YHWH as the great mover in the exodus. In the narrative at Exodus 14:25, the Egyptians recognize YHWH's strong hand, for they assert, "Let us flee from before Israel, for the Lord fights for them against the Egyptians." But in addition to this the poem rings out, "The Lord is a man of war, the Lord is his name. . . . Who is like you, O Lord, among the gods? Who is like you, majestic in holiness, awesome in glorious deeds, doing wonders?" (15:3, 11).

The change from historical narrative to poetic song in Exodus 14 and 15 does not alter the historical truthfulness of the account, but each genre portrays the history in different ways. The narrative simply unpacks a progression of temporally successive events in space and time. The song uses much more concrete imagery, figurative language, and poetic parallelism, but through these means it still proclaims the same story. Similarly, the changes in form between Judges 4 and 5 have no bearing on the text's historicity or factuality. Both accounts tell how Jael killed Sisera, but the poem intentionally moves us in a fresh way to praise the one who controls history.

The biblical authors can cast both history and fiction in various genres. In the rest of this chapter, I will lay down some basic guidelines for interpreting different biblical genres.

An Exercise in Genre—Exodus 19:4–6

This book offers numerous biblical examples to illustrate whatever point I am trying to make. At times I reuse some texts, relooking at them from fresh angles as we walk through the interpretive process. But I will look at one text at every one of the twelve steps from exegesis to theology. It is Exodus 19:4–6, perhaps the clearest, simplest snapshot of the revealed makeup of the old covenant that we have in Scripture.

When we consider the genre of Exodus 19:4–6, we immediately recognize two things. First, it is a speech of God recorded by his prophet, and therefore we can rightfully call it a *prophetic oracle*. More specifically, it is a messenger speech from God through Moses to the people, and it includes instruction mixed with implied exhortation. Second, the speech itself falls within a grand narrative that begins in Genesis and continues unbroken through the end of 2 Kings, only to be picked up again in Daniel and carried on to the end of 2 Chronicles (see "Putting Genre within Its Biblical Context" earlier in this chapter). The narrative relays the history of salvation that ultimately climaxes in Christ and the New Testament.

Thus we can tag the genre of Exodus 19:4–6 as a prophetic-messenger speech made up of instruction and implied exhortation. It is part of the historical narrative of Exodus, the Pentateuch, and the greater Old Testament.

Historical Narrative

The Distinctive Nature of Biblical Narrative

The Bible's historical narratives chronicle connected events in story format, usually in past time. Around 65 percent of Scripture is narrative—Genesis through Kings, Daniel through Chronicles, the Gospels and Acts, and even parts of Revelation. These books recount the true story of God's workings in history to make a people and a name for himself, ultimately through Jesus.

On the surface, biblical historical narrative resembles the factual historical reporting that we read today in a news account or a history book. As in contemporary historical writing, the Old Testament records a chronology of key persons, ages, places, powers, and events from creation to Israel's initial restoration from Babylon. But the Bible does so much more than simply register facts. It intentionally selects which facts to include and then shapes them from God's perspective and for God's purposes. Biblical historical narrative stands distinct in at least four ways.

1. Old Testament narratives commonly contain various subgenres within them.

The Bible's stories are often peppered with numerous subgenres, such as genealogies (e.g., Gen. 5; 11:10–26), deathbed blessings (e.g., Gen. 49; Deut. 33), songs (Ex. 15:1–18; Deut. 32:1–43), predictive prophecies (Num. 23–24), sermons (Deut. 5–26), and covenants (Josh. 24:1–28). You can find this incorporation in other ancient texts, but it is very pronounced in the Bible.

2. Old Testament narratives focus on God and anticipate the Christ.

As with all history writing, the Bible's narratives are selective and purposeful in their presentation. But in biblical narrative God is the key character and the key mover—his words and his deeds guide each story. This is true even in the book of Esther, where the narrator never mentions the Lord's name or title explicitly but where God's providential purposes are evident at every turn. With this, the Old Testament stories themselves offer God's perspective on history and disclose that his redemptive program for the world climaxes in Christ Jesus and his church. The Old Testament story creates longing for a better king, a blessed people, and a broader land—all of which God promises as the answer to the world's problem detailed in the Old Testament.

3. Old Testament narratives teach.

Because Scripture is God's revelation, biblical historical narratives are designed not simply to inform but also to instruct—they are sermons in story form. Scripture's narratives seek to convince us of God's revelatory message and of the need to repent, believe, and obey. God's purposes guided what stories the narrators told and where they placed their focus. We must read not simply to gain the facts but to hear the message that the authors intended. Regularly the narrators detail sins and failures without clarifying whether they are good or bad. Not all decisions and actions of biblical characters are normative for us. The narrators expect us to know our Bibles well enough to read the history of the covenant in light of the covenant—both the covenant instruction and promises and the character of the covenant Lord. In Scripture, people are examples for us to follow only insofar as they point us to the supremacy and worth of God.

4. Old Testament narratives often have intentions other than our own.

Because the narrators were ultimately preaching as they crafted their stories, they at times were not as concerned with including certain details that concern us. They spoke accurately, but matters such as strict chronology and sequencing were not always their interest. As much as we may want to know the name of the Pharaoh of the exodus, the Bible is silent, being intentionally more concerned with God's name—YHWH. It is the Chronicler's prerogative to pass quickly over Saul's reign to get us to David, to focus almost completely on the southern kingdom, and not to even mention David's affair with Bathsheba, all things that are approached differently in Samuel-Kings. Such selection does not call into question the accuracy of what is there. It simply guides us to see that the message of Samuel-Kings is different from that of Chronicles.

History, Myth, and the Biblical Narratives

Scripture is God's written Word, which means that the biblical text should stand as our highest authority. It also means that insofar as it aligns with the original wording, the Bible is an *infallible* rule and guide in its claims regarding faith (doctrine) and practice (ethics) and *inerrant* in its claims of fact (history, geology, chronology, science). With respect to Scripture's authority, in biblical narrative, as with every other genre, we must respect the biblical authors' intentions and the literary conventions under which they wrote. We must allow for partial reporting, paraphrasing, and summarizing and must not require the Bible to give definitive or exhaustive information on every topic. We must allow for phenomenological language, with which the authors describe a phenomenon as they observed it or experienced it, not necessarily how it scientifically occurred. And we must allow for the reporting of a speech without the endorsement of that speech's truthfulness; a biblical character may truly say something that is not true. These things stated, outside those passages that are explicitly treated as parables, the biblical narratives present themselves as accurate accounts of what happened in space and time, so we should approach them this way.

In contrast to this approach, in recent days there has been a resurgence of scholars—even among those claiming to be evangelicals—who prefer to call the biblical narratives "myths" or just "stories," by which they mean fictional accounts related to the supernatural that include profound truths but that do not supply us with actual facts of history. They assert that the biblical text alone is what is authoritative and what gives rise to our faith; faith grows out of the Bible's message, they say, and is not related to the historicity of the events addressed. I have eight responses.

1. As a genre, biblical narrative is not myth.

It is true that the biblical story line is thoroughly centered on the Lord—his deeds and his words overseeing and judging all events in space and time. But the inclusion of

God does not make the Bible myth. We have already noted that Old Testament narrative seeks to show that what was myth in the ancient world has real and factual substance in Israel's time and history. We must recognize that Scripture is focused on a very real world, with real persons, real places, and real times, and that the biblical authors believed God to be part of this real world. Mythical monsters and places are not part of the presentation. They are present in Scripture in other genres, such as apocalyptic (e.g., Dan. 7), but they are not found in biblical narrative. We do find a tree of life and a talking serpent (Gen. 3), even a talking donkey (Num. 22)! Yet these are no different from other intrusions of the miraculous in space and time that we can only describe as the intervention of God—things such as the angel of death passing through Egypt, forty years of daily manna in the wilderness, YHWH's fiery glory visibly settling in the temple, the widow's son being raised to life, and an ax head floating. The Bible presents itself as history, not myth, and indeed it calls us to guard ourselves from the latter (1 Tim. 1:3–4; 4:7; 2 Peter 1:16).

2. Priority lies with texts.

Far too often scholars assert, "Archaeology has proved such and such." But the social sciences (archaeology, anthropology, sociology, etc.) deal only with general features of societies and cultures, and pots don't talk. Texts alone clarify specific events and individuals, and this places a priority on Scripture as an ancient textual witness.

3. Historicity and authority go hand in hand.

Because the Bible is God's revelation (2 Tim. 3:16), its historicity and authority are intimately united. We cannot deny the reality of an event that the biblical authors believed to be historical and still say that we affirm Scripture's authority. Moreover, we must recognize that the Bible is *not* like any other book, for it alone is special revelation. Thus, the level to which we affirm its claims is the level to which we submit ourselves to God himself.

4. The mention of the divine or of supernatural events does not mean that they are unhistorical.

Since the late 1800s, historical criticism has asserted that a belief in God is unscientific and that any claims to the intrusion of the supernatural are unverifiable and therefore unhistorical. In their attempt to gain greater objectivity, however, historical critics have increased subjectivity, limiting the possibilities to only that which their worldviews allow. Rather than being initially skeptical about Scripture's truth claims (= ***principle of criticism***), scholars should engage in a thoughtful appraisal of the evidence in keeping with its source. Rather than limiting what can qualify as "history" to present human experience (= ***principle of analogy***), they should judge historical plausibility by the reasonableness of arguments made for belief in occurrences with which the historians may themselves have no personal connection. Rather than limiting potential historical causation to natural forces or human agency (= ***principle of***

correlation), they should broaden causation to include all *personal* forces (such as God) and not limit it to just natural or material forces.[10]

With these, atheistic biblical historians should at least give the same level of credence to the biblical witness that historians working in areas other than Scripture give to their source data. When historians engage extrabiblical texts that mention the supernatural, even those who do not affirm such a possibility read the testimonies as religious encoding that in no way calls into question the viability of the other facts. For example, scholars do not question Sennacherib's firsthand account of his conquest of the Levant even though it is loaded with theological perspective and propagandistic bias.[11] Why, then, should scholars question the historical claims of the same events in 2 Kings 18:13–19:37? Similarly, as noted by ancient historian Edwin Yamauchi, Herodotus's belief in the "Delphic Oracles" does not disqualify him as an accurate source for Greek history, nor does Joan of Arc's unverifiable divine call to action move scholars to doubt that she roused her countrymen to push English forces out of France.[12]

5. Verifiability is not essential to make history.

We should not require extrabiblical confirmation in order to justify biblical claims, for there are just too many gaps in our knowledge of the past. For example, only in 1842 did we gain secondary attestation of the reign of Sargon II (Isa. 20:1).[13] Furthermore, as Yamauchi notes, it was not until 1932 that scholars identified the Babylonian exile of Jehoiachin on extrabiblical tablets (2 Kings 24:11–13), and only in 1961 and 1966, respectively, did archaeologists discover epigraphic attestation of Pontius Pilate (Luke 3:1; 23:1; Acts 4:27) and Felix the procurator (Acts 24).[14] The James Ossuary discovery in 2002 was the first extrabiblical source that directly mentioned the names of Jesus, his brother James, and their father Joseph.[15] No one can question that these findings accent the historicity of the biblical assertions, but the biblical figures did not all of a sudden become real when these texts were unearthed.

Furthermore, many of the events to which Scripture points are not the type to which we would expect material outside the Bible to refer. The patriarchs, for example, were relative "no-names" in the ancient world, so we should not anticipate finding "Abraham, Isaac, and Jacob" mentioned elsewhere. Nevertheless, the details of the

10. For these three responses, see William J. Abraham, *Divine Revelation and the Limits of Historical Criticism* (Oxford: Oxford University Press, 1982); cf. Craig S. Keener, *Miracles: The Credibility of the New Testament Accounts*, 2 vols. (Grand Rapids: Baker Academic, 2011).

11. See *ANET* 287–88; *COS* 2:300–305.

12. Edwin Yamauchi, "The Current State of Old Testament Historiography," in *Faith, Tradition, and History: Old Testament Historiography in Its Near Eastern Context*, ed. A. R. Millard, James K. Hoffmeier, and David W. Baker (Winona Lake, IN: Eisenbrauns, 1994), 27–28.

13. See *COS* 3:293.

14. Yamauchi, "The Current State of Old Testament Historiography," 26–27.

15. Some scholars do question the genuineness of the James Ossuary, but for a strong case for its authenticity, see Hershel Shanks and Ben Witherington III, *The Brother of Jesus: The Dramatic Story and Meaning of the First Archaeological Link to Jesus and His Family*, 2nd ed. (San Francisco: HarperOne, 2004).

patriarchal stories fit very nicely into the time period of which they propose to be a part.[16] Similarly, because so much ancient historiography was designed to make monarchs look good, we should not expect to find extrabiblical attestation of major imperial embarrassments such as YHWH's victory over Egypt at the exodus (Ex. 14–15) and his decimation of Sennacherib's army in the days of Hezekiah (2 Kings 19:35; Isa. 37:36). Still, there is substantial extrabiblical support for the veracity of both these biblical accounts.[17] Moreover, we should see the Bible's inclusion of both the victories and the failures/defeats of its key human characters as support for its own historical claims.

6. We should view the Bible's claims as innocent until proven guilty.

There is no evidence that Israel falsified or invented statements of fact, and this is highly unlikely due to the nature of the message and the judgment that the text itself places on false teachers (e.g., Deut. 13:1–5).[18] Furthermore, no other field of historical research practices a "guilty until proven innocent" approach, so why should this be done in biblical studies? As Craig Blomberg notes, historians should assume the factuality of the details in a work unless there is a good reason to believe otherwise.[19] K. A. Kitchen notes that in Egyptology, for example, the *Turin Papyrus of Kings*, dating to Egypt's Nineteenth Dynasty, lists seventy-six monarchs for the Fourteenth Dynasty, some five hundred years before, and although most of the rulers named are found only in this document, historians do not deny the existence of these kings.[20] Similarly, G. J. Renier notes that most of the works of Livy, the first books of Gregory of Tours's *A History of the Franks*, contain events known only from these sources, yet "since there is no other way of knowing the story they tell us, we must provisionally accept their version."[21]

7. God's revelation in history is the source, not the product, of biblical faith.

Biblical faith is grounded in God's revelation in history, and the significance of the biblical testimony stands or falls on whether or not the central events actually happened. If we view the central events as historical—creation, fall, flood, patriarchs, exodus, Sinai, wilderness, conquest, kingdoms, exile, initial restoration, Christ's death

16. See K. A. Kitchen, *On the Reliability of the Old Testament* (Grand Rapids: Eerdmans, 2003), 313–72.

17. On the exodus, see Charles F. Aling, *Egypt and Bible History: From Earliest Times to 1000 B.C.*, Baker Studies in Biblical Archaeology (Grand Rapids: Baker, 1981); John Bimson, *Redating the Exodus and Conquest*, 2nd ed., JSOTSup 5 (Sheffield, UK: Almond Press, 1981); James K. Hoffmeier, *Israel in Egypt: The Evidence for the Authenticity of the Exodus Tradition* (Oxford: Oxford University Press, 1996); Kitchen, *On the Reliability of the Old Testament*, 241–312; David Rohl, *Exodus: Myth or History?* (St. Louis Park, MN: Thinking Man Media, 2015); Timothy P. Mahoney with Steven Law, *Patterns of Evidence: Exodus* (St. Louis Park, MN: Thinking Man Media, 2015). On Sennacherib's 701 B.C. siege of Jerusalem during the days of King Hezekiah, see William R. Gallagher, *Sennacherib's Campaign to Judah: New Studies*, Studies in the History and Culture of the Ancient Near East 18 (Leiden: Brill, 1999); Kitchen, *On the Reliability of the Old Testament*, 40–42, 50–51.

18. See Stuart Lasine, "Fiction, Falsehood, and Reality in Hebrew Scripture," *HS* 25 (1984): 25–40.

19. Craig L. Blomberg, *The Historical Reliability of the Gospels*, 2nd ed. (Downers Grove, IL: InterVarsity Press, 2007), 304.

20. K. A. Kitchen, *Ancient Orient and Old Testament* (Downers Grove, IL: InterVarsity Press, 1975), 30.

21. G. J. Renier, *History: Its Purpose and Method* (London: Allen and Unwin, 1950), 90–91. I was directed to this source in Blomberg, *The Historical Reliability of the Gospels*, 304.

and resurrection, the growth of the early church—then we ought to consider the other noncentral events as factually accurate as well.

Most professing evangelicals will affirm the necessity of Jesus' resurrection for our faith to stand (1 Cor. 15:14). Nevertheless, some of these same persons discount many of the Old Testament's historical claims, viewing them more as parables than as testimonies to God's acts in history. Sternberg once noted that when interpreters view the Bible's historical narratives as fiction, they change YHWH from "the lord of history into a creature of imagination, with the most disastrous results."[22] Many dangerous teachings are being propounded today.

For example, many want to affirm Jesus' historicity yet deny a historical Adam and fall. But they should ask themselves, "In what *Jesus* do I believe?" Is he the one who said that not simply the ideas but the very letters and words of Scripture matter and point to him (Matt. 5:18)? Is he the Jesus who was the Word made flesh, who was "in the beginning with God" and through whom "all things were made" (John 1:2–3)? Is he the Jesus whose human lineage stretches back to Adam (Luke 3:38) and who affirmed the historical reality both of God's creating male and female in the beginning as a paradigm for marriage (Matt. 19:4) and of the global rebellion in the days of Noah (Luke 17:26–27)? Is he the Jesus who declared that Scripture "cannot be broken" (John 10:35) and who Paul emphasized answers the sin problem produced by a historical Adam (Rom. 5:12–19; 1 Cor. 15:22, 45)? If the *Jesus* we affirm is not *this Jesus*, then we are in peril of losing the historical grounding of our faith.[23]

8. Taking the Bible on its own terms requires a Christian theistic rather than a non-Christian or atheistic approach to interpretation.

The Spirit of the triune God guided every word of the Bible (2 Tim. 3:16; 1 Peter 1:21). The whole of it is *Christian* Scripture, with all the Old Testament pointing to Christ and fully understood only in light of his coming (Luke 24:44–46; 2 Cor. 3:14) and all the New Testament built on his person and work (Eph. 2:20).[24] Every reader of Scripture has a worldview and approaches the Bible with certain assumptions about the nature of reality (i.e., faith claims). We take Scripture on its own terms, however, only when we approach it through the lens of Christian theism. When atheism or aberrant forms of theism guide one's hermeneutical system, one cannot expect to grasp Scripture's *intended* message.

In conclusion, I believe the biblical authors viewed their narratives as "history"—accurate accounts of what God was doing in space and time. A faithful interpretive approach to the biblical text requires us to take it on its own terms, affirming Scripture's claims in accordance with its revealed intentions.

22. Meir Sternberg, *The Poetics of Biblical Narrative: Ideological Literature and the Drama of Reading*, Indiana Studies in Biblical Literature (Bloomington, IN: Indiana University Press, 1985), 32.

23. For more on this, see Jason S. DeRouchie, review of *Genesis: History, Fiction, or Neither? Three Views on the Bible's Earliest Chapters*, ed. Charles Halton, *Themelios* 40, 3 (2015): 485–90; for an abridged version of this review, see http://www.thegospelcoalition.org/article/book-reviews-genesis-history-fiction-or-neither-three-views.

24. For more on the Old Testament as *Christian* Scripture, see chapters 10 and 12.

How to Interpret Old Testament Narrative

Narrative is one of the most difficult biblical genres to preach and teach well, because the message is usually more hidden and illustrated than explicit. Numerous named and unnamed characters, various levels of drama, and numerous speeches challenge the best of interpreters to discover a narrative's main point. Yet it can be found, and its clearest statement is usually located in a speech, which in turn provides the lens for understanding the rest of the story.

In this section I am going to highlight four guiding principles for interpreting biblical narrative. In the next section we will then apply these principles to a specific episode in the biblical story.

1. Distinguish the episode and its scenes.

Like many TV dramas, biblical narratives are made up of episodes shaped by scenes (for more on this, see "Basic Rules for Establishing Literary Units" in chapter 2). The sermonic message that stands behind a given story is bound up in the whole episode, and we can easily miss a story's main point if we make our focus too narrow, looking only at a scene. So after establishing that you are looking at a story, the next step in interpreting biblical narrative is to identify the narrative episode and its various scene divisions, remembering that verse and chapter divisions were not inspired. If we are preaching in 1 Samuel 17, we would want to preach the entire story of David's defeat of Goliath and not just cover David's encounter with his brother Eliab or his dialogue with Saul regarding armor and weapons. Only when we look at the whole story do we clearly recognize that it is ultimately *not* a story about David but that he is merely an instrument to point us to the true warrior in the episode. As David says to Goliath in the longest speech of the episode: "This day the Lord will deliver you into my hand . . . that all the earth may know that there is a God in Israel, and that all this assembly may know that the Lord saves not with sword and spear. For the battle is the Lord's, and he will give you into our hand" (1 Sam. 17:46–47).

2. Consider literary features and theological trajectories.

a. The Literary Context

As you focus in on your episode, you need to ask, "What leads up to the episode, and how does the episode itself begin and end?" You also need to look more broadly to consider whether the narrator elsewhere offers any clarity on how we are to read a given passage.

b. The Plot Development and Characterization

There are a number of questions to ask here: (i) What is the nature of the drama? What is the conflict or problem? How is it resolved? (ii) Is there repetition? If there is, it can often clarify issues of structure or draw attention to what is important. (iii) God is always the most important character, so what is he saying or doing, and how do his words or deeds relate to the covenant or give clarity to the various scenes of the episode? (iv) Who are the named and secondary human characters, and what relationship do they have with God? What are they saying and doing, and how do their words or actions relate to the covenant or give clarity to the various scenes of the episode? Remember that human characters are examples for us to follow only insofar as they point us to God.

c. Any Editorial Comments

At times the narrator himself will speak into a story, offering commentary and thus giving God's perspective on an event. Such comments are especially helpful to us in discerning the point of an episode, section, or book.

d. How the Narrative Anticipates the Work of Christ

Christ is the ultimate goal of all of the Bible's story, so it is fair and expected to ask of every narrative episode how it helps set the stage for Jesus' coming. It could come through a divine or human speech or action, human failure, or a related event or institution.

3. State in a single sentence the narrative episode's main idea.

Three features are noteworthy here: (a) The main idea will almost always tell us something about God and may also focus on how we are rightly to relate to him. (b) While at times modeled in the characters' actions, the main idea is usually stated explicitly in a speech (whether directly from God, his prophet, or another main human character). (c) The main idea should speak to any generation and should thus be worded to convey the timeless message of the narrative episode.

4. Draft an exegetical outline of the narrative episode.

We'll cover exegetical outlining in greater detail in chapter 6. Nevertheless, the central thrust of the task is to clarify in outline form how every scene and all the parts relate and contribute to the overarching main idea.

As with any other part of Scripture, the goal in working through biblical narrative is to grasp the author's intent for the account. Why did he include the details he did? What was he wanting to teach? Why did he write it that way? Robert Stein has proposed the following helpful exercise for getting at the "why" of biblical narrative. He suggests that we attempt to complete the following sentence:[25]

> I, the author of X-biblical book, have narrated to you this account of X-scenario because ___________.

25. Robert H. Stein, *A Basic Guide to Interpreting the Bible: Playing by the Rules*, 2nd ed. (Grand Rapids: Baker Academic, 2011), 157.

Through this simple exercise, we take good steps toward getting to God's sermon bound up in the story—his lasting message for us.

Note that the intention behind a story is different from the story itself. The subject matter is different from its purpose. In the next section we'll apply these principles to the story in 1 Kings 17 that introduces the ministry of the prophet Elijah and highlights his role as a validator of God's Word.

An Example of Interpreting Historical Narrative—1 Kings 17

I now want to apply the principles for interpreting historical narrative to the first account of Elijah the prophet in 1 Kings 17. The ESV opens chapter 17 this way: "Now Elijah the Tishbite, of Tishbe in Gilead, said to Ahab, 'As the LORD, the God of Israel, lives, before whom I stand, there shall be neither dew nor rain these years, except by my word.'" It's clear that the ESV translator thought chapter 17 marked a fresh beginning, for he translated the וְ ("and") of the initial *wayyiqtol* (*waw*-consecutive imperfect) as "Now." There are at least two good reasons to affirm this approach and to see a new episode beginning here. First, 17:1 is the first time we have met Elijah the prophet, and his words to King Ahab point the reader forward to anticipate a new drama related to lack of rain. Therefore, 1 Kings 17:1 marks the beginning of a new topic and with that a new episode. Second, the previous chapter ends by using a series of marked clauses to signal the completion of a discourse unit, which suggests that the *wayyiqtol* verb at the head of 17:1 indeed begins something new. Even though it continues on the narrative of King Ahab's reign, it is still a fresh episode in the story.

As we move beyond 1 Kings 17:1, we see a handful of scene divisions that appear to be intentionally tied together. Verse 2 reads, "And the word of the LORD came to him . . . ." In this unit God calls Elijah to go to a brook near the Jordan River where he can drink and where he will be miraculously fed by ravens. "I have commanded the ravens to feed you there," God says (17:4). And the Lord is faithful to his word, meets Elijah, and supplies. But then we read in verse 7, "And after a while the brook dried up, because there was no rain in the land."

First Kings 17:8 repeats, "Then the word of the LORD came to him . . . ." This repetition with verse 2 raises the possibility that the narrator is about to introduce a parallel account. God now calls Elijah to go outside the boundaries of Israel along the Mediterranean coast to Sidon, where we are told that God has now commanded a widow to feed him. The mention of a command and of food recalls the miraculous provision through the ravens and suggests that this new scene does indeed parallel the first.

Upon meeting the widow, Elijah requests both drink and food. This foreigner then vows before YHWH that she has but enough for herself and her son to have one more meal, and then they will die. At this we get the most extensive quotation in the episode and the only speech that includes a speech within a speech. These factors suggest that it likely has something to do with the main point of the text (1 Kings 17:13–14): "And Elijah said to her, 'Do not fear; go and do as you have said. But first make me a little cake of it and bring it to me, and afterward make something for yourself and your son. For thus says the Lord, the God of Israel, "The jar of flour shall not be spent, and the jug of oil shall not be empty, until the day that the Lord sends rain upon the earth."'" Just as God purposed the ravens to meet Elijah's need at the brook, so he purposed this widow to be the instrument through which he would sustain his prophet. And as his word had proved true at the Jordan, so his word would again prove true here. We are told that the widow did as Elijah said and that she and her household ate for many days. Thus we read in verse 16, "The jar of flour was not spent, neither did the jug of oil become empty, according to the word of the Lord that he spoke by Elijah."

This seems like a natural break in the story, for we have had two parallel scenes of God's declared word and his faithful fulfillment of his promise. But at this point the story continues, for we read in 1 Kings 17:17, "After this the son of the woman, the mistress of the house, became ill. And his illness was so severe that there was no breath left in him." God's word is powerful enough to supply bread, but is it powerful enough to awaken the dead? The woman asks Elijah, "What have you against me, O man of God? You have come to me to bring my sin to remembrance and to cause the death of my son!" (v. 18). At this Elijah took her son and pleaded with God for the boy's life, and the Lord listened to the prophet and revived the child. And when the woman saw her living son, she declared to Elijah, "Now I know that you are a man of God, and that the word of the Lord in your mouth is truth" (v. 24). The miraculous awakening of the boy validated the words of God through his prophet.

All these various scenes work together to contribute to the episode's message. In contrast, 1 Kings 18:1 moves in a new direction, recalling the initial promise of a drought: "After many days the word of the Lord came to Elijah, in the third year, saying, 'Go, show yourself to Ahab, and I will send rain upon the earth.'" Chapter 18 shifts the temporal context from immediately following the initial prophecy to three years later, which suggests that we have likely moved to a new episode. The tightness of the introductory statement and three scenes in chapter 17 suggests that the various units are part of a single episode, focusing significantly on the truthfulness of God's word and his willingness and ability to care for the needy in miraculous ways.

In light of the flow of the story and the content of key speeches, in figure 1.4 I offer a main idea and exegetical outline for the episode:

Main idea: Because God has proved his willingness and ability to provide for even unlikely believers by raising a non-Israelite widow's son from the dead, we should affirm that God's word through his prophets is true and authoritative.

I. The Setting to Affirm the Truth and Authority of God's Word: Lack of Rain at God's Word (v. 1)

II. Affirmation of the Truth and Authority of God's Word for an Israelite Prophet (vv. 2–7)

III. Affirmation of the Truth and Authority of God's Word for a Foreign Widow (vv. 8–24)

A. The experience of the truth and authority of God's word (vv. 8–16)

B. The validation of the truth and authority of God's word: God's willingness and ability to raise the widow's son from the dead (vv. 17–24)

Fig. 1.4. Main Idea and Exegetical Outline for 1 Kings 17

Upon seeing her boy, the woman declared, "Now I know that you are a man of God, and that the word of the LORD in your mouth is truth" (1 Kings 17:24). Because God is both willing and able to care for even the least, we should affirm that his word through his prophets is true and authoritative.

This introductory truth then guides our reading of all the remaining episodes in the section, all of which are governed by the reality of no rain. You likely remember the story of the clash between Elijah and the 450 prophets of Baal on Mount Carmel. That happens in 1 Kings 18, where the storm god Baal is called on to go head-to-head with YHWH: "If the LORD is God, follow him; but if Baal, then follow him. . . . You call upon the name of your god, and I will call upon the name of the LORD, and the God who answers by fire, he is God" (18:21, 24). Even with all the prophets ranting and raving, no fire came. Then Elijah prayed for God's miraculous intervention, that "it be known this day that you are God in Israel, and that I am your servant, and that I have done all these things at your word" (18:36). At this, YHWH's fire came, resulting in the people's turning back to the true God in worship (18:38–39). After this, God brought rain on the earth (18:41–46).

When someone is raised from the dead on our behalf, we should realize that God has the power and willingness to fulfill his promises. His Word is both true and authoritative. For the exiles first reading 1–2 Kings, this widow woman's final affirmation of YHWH's truth and authority would have given hope that their context of death could be overcome. What is more, for those of us who have identified by faith with the death and resurrection of Christ, our hope in God should be all the more realized. "Christ has been raised from the dead, the firstfruits of those who have fallen asleep. For as by a man came death, by a man has come also the resurrection of the dead. For as in Adam all die, so also in Christ shall all be made alive" (1 Cor. 15:20–21). The story in 1 Kings 17 points to the truth of the gospel and should heighten our hope in God's faithfulness both today and forever.

Prophecy and Law

The Distinctive Nature of YHWH-Prophecy

The next several sections address biblical prophecy. The Bible presents YHWH's ***prophets*** as ambassadors of the heavenly court (2 Kings 17:13; Jer. 23:21–22), individuals whom God commissioned for two key purposes: to *preach* for God to the people and to *pray* for the people to God.

As chief prayer warriors, the prophets regularly interceded to God on behalf of those who were needy and rebellious. God said that Abraham was such a prophet who would pray for Abimelech's life after he claimed Sarah (Gen. 20:7). Moses is the chief example of a prophetic intercessor, for he "stood in the breach before [God], to turn away his wrath from destroying [Israel]" (Ps. 106:23). Even when YHWH commanded him to not intercede (Ex. 32:9–10), Moses was unrelenting in his prophetic role (32:11–14), and the result was God's mercy (32:14; cf. Num. 14:11–20).[26] Similarly, Samuel said that he would sin if he failed to pray for Israel, along with teaching the people God's ways (1 Sam. 12:23). Both Elijah and the prophets of Baal "call upon the name" of their respective gods (1 Kings 18:24, 26, 36–37), and Naaman the Aramean expected Elisha to intercede on his behalf (2 Kings 5:8). Amos pleaded with YHWH two times to forgive Israel and to withhold his punishment against the northern kingdom, and the Lord relented (Amos 7:1–6). God expected the true prophets who bore his word to pray for his people's needs: "If they are prophets, and if the word of the Lord is with them, then let them intercede with the Lord of hosts" (Jer. 27:18). As with Moses, the Lord charged Jeremiah to act opposite of his prophetic role (7:16; cf. 11:14; 14:11–12). Nevertheless, the prophet did pray, and he later implored God to protect him in return for his having done so (18:20). YHWH told Ezekiel that he was seeking a man to "build up the wall and stand in the breach before me for the land, that I should not destroy it" (Ezek. 22:30), but none could be found.

26. Ironically, YHWH's command, "Let me alone, that I may destroy them" (Deut. 9:14; cf. Ex. 32:10), was actually the means that God used to call the prophet to pray. God gave instruction that would have been sin for Moses to obey, since prophets were supposed to stand in the breach on behalf of God's people. In the Deuteronomy recounting, Moses stresses how Israel's sin was a serious offense against God (Deut. 9:14, 16, 18). Nevertheless, God asks the prophet to do what he himself would promise never to do (4:30–31; 31:6). That Deuteronomy 9:14 uses the verb "leave alone" (Hiphil of רפה) instead of "cause rest" (Hiphil of 1-נוח) as found in Exodus 32:10 suggests that Moses in Deuteronomy is intentionally echoing the divine promise in Deuteronomy 4:31 ("He will not leave you [Hiphil of רפה] or destroy you") and highlighting that he understood YHWH's intent in calling him to get out of the way to be that he actually wanted him to intercede as the means for preserving his people.

Along with kneeling as intercessors, the prophets were mouthpieces, God's preachers, who authoritatively presented the revelation of God to his people. Sometimes they did this by *foretelling* future realities, but more often, it was through *forthtelling* God's words in order to direct human action in the present and to reorient their audiences to reality from YHWH's perspective (2 Kings 17:13; 2 Chron. 36:15–16; Isa. 44:26; Jer. 23:21–22; Hos. 12:9–10; Hag. 1:13; Zech. 7:11–12; Mal. 3:1). At times the divine word came to a prophet through a dream or vision (e.g., Num. 12:6–7; Isa. 6:1–13; Jer. 31:26; Zech. 2:1; Amos 8:1–3), but normally we are not told the mode of inspiration. Sometimes we hear of the Holy Spirit's involvement in inspiration (e.g., 1 Sam. 10:6, 10; 1 Kings 22:24; Neh. 9:30; Ezek. 11:5; Joel 2:28–29; Mic. 3:8; Zech. 7:12), and oracles are frequently preceded with the formulaic expression: "The word of the Lord came to me, saying . . ." (e.g., 2 Sam. 7:4; 1 Kings 21:28; Jer. 1:2; Ezek. 36:16; Hag. 1:3; Zech. 4:8). The divine revelations were usually spoken as sermons, but at times they were framed as parables or allegories (e.g., 2 Sam. 12:1–7; Isa. 5:1–7; Ezek. 16, 23). Other times the prophets dramatically performed their oracles, symbolically working out God's message (e.g., 1 Sam. 15:27–28; 1 Kings 11:29–37; 2 Kings 13:14–20; Jer. 13:1–11; Ezek. 4).

With reference to content, some oracles provided a divine answer to human questions (e.g., Gen. 15:2–5; 2 Sam. 2:1; Hab. 1–2), but most were divinely initiated responses to Israel's covenant fidelity (or lack of it) at a particular time in history. That is, as covenant enforcers, the prophets confronted Israel's sin, called the people back to their commitment to YHWH, and reminded them of the covenant curses and blessings, the promises of death and life, that YHWH had sworn to honor (Lev. 26; Deut. 4:25–31; 28; 30:1–10). The prophets pronounced oracles of warning or imminent punishment against individuals (e.g., 1 Sam. 13:13–14; 1 Kings 11:11–13) and nations (e.g., Isa. 17; Jer. 8:4–12; Ezek. 15; Amos 4:1–3; Mic. 3:7–12) that failed to live loyally in the covenant or to treat God and his people with respect. They also declared salvation and restoration oracles that predicted a day when God would renew his relationship with his people (e.g., Isa. 10:5–12:6; Jer. 31:31–34; Ezek. 36:16–32; Amos 9:13–15; Zech. 8:1–8).

Both Scripture (e.g., Num. 22–24; 1 Kings 18:20–40) and numerous extrabiblical texts uncovered throughout the ancient world tell us that many pagans were speaking oracles and that words from the gods were not restricted to biblical prophecy. Like YHWH, these pagan false deities demanded homage and declared judgments. They warned of danger and offered assurance in the face of peril. They foretold national destruction and promised kingdom renewal. But YHWH's prophecy was nevertheless distinct in at least three ways:

1. Among the gods of the ancient world, YHWH alone spoke in order to establish, maintain, and enforce a covenant relationship with a people.

As Moses testifies in Deuteronomy 4:7–8, "For what great nation is there that has a god so near to it as the Lord our God is to us, whenever we call upon him? And what great nation is there, that has statutes and rules so righteous as all this law that I set before you today?" True prophecy promotes sustained loyalty to YHWH alone, exposing iniquity and calling for repentance that leads to blessing (Deut. 13:2–3; Lam. 2:14).

2. Whereas many pagan oracles were ambiguous as to their intent and fulfillment, YHWH's charges and predictions were intentionally clear and accurate.

Moses asserts in Deuteronomy 18:22, "When a prophet speaks in the name of the Lord, if the word does not come to pass or come true, that is a word that the Lord has not spoken" (cf. 1 Kings 22:28; Isa. 44:7–8; Jer. 28:8–9; Lam. 2:14; Ezek. 33:33). All of YHWH's predictions come true.

3. YHWH's prophecy includes no sign of pagan practices and finds its confirmation in God's Word alone.

Isaiah 8:19–20 declares: "And when they say to you, 'Inquire of the mediums and the necromancers who chirp and mutter,' should not a people inquire of their God? Should they inquire of the dead on behalf of the living? To the teaching and to the testimony! If they will not speak according to this word, it is because they have no dawn." In YHWH-oracles a staunch monotheism confronts polytheistic idolatry. "You shall have no other gods before me" (Deut. 5:7; cf. vv. 8–10; 6:4–5; Ps. 115; Isa. 40:18–31). YHWH is a jealous God who demands total allegiance. His voice will be heard, and his Word must be heeded.

The Categories of Prophetic Speech

An ***oracle*** is any divine pronouncement through a prophet that directs human action in the present or foretells future events. Prophetic oracles in Scripture are usually made up of one or more of the following speech types: ***indictment***, ***instruction***, ***warning/punishment***, and ***hope/salvation***.

1. Indictment	Statement of the offense *(Specification of covenant stipulations violated)*
2. Instruction	Clarification of the expected response *(Call to heed covenant stipulations)*
3. Warning/Punishment	Declaration of the punishment to be carried out *(Warning or promise of covenant curse)*
4. Hope/Salvation	Affirmation of future hope or deliverance *(Promise of covenant-restoration blessings)*

Fig. 1.5. Categories of Prophetic Speech

1. Indictment

A chief role of the prophet was to confront the covenantal violations of God's people. "I am filled with power, with the Spirit of the Lord, and with justice and might, to declare to Jacob his transgression and to Israel his sin" (Mic. 3:8 ; cf. Isa. 58:1). Often, the prophets identified the people's specific covenant violations. Micah, for example, declared: "Hear this, you heads of the house of Jacob and rulers of the house of Israel, who detest justice and make crooked all that is straight, who build Zion with blood and Jerusalem with iniquity. Its heads give judgment for a bribe; its priests teach for a price; its prophets practice divination for money; yet they lean on the Lord and say, 'Is not the Lord in the midst of us? No disaster shall come upon us'" (3:9–11). Similarly, Zephaniah proclaimed, "Woe to her who is rebellious and defiled, the oppressing city! She listens to no voice; she accepts no correction. She does not trust in the Lord; she does not draw near to her God. Her officials within her are roaring lions; her judges are evening wolves that leave nothing till the morning. Her prophets are fickle, treacherous men; her priests profane what is holy; they do violence to the law" (Zeph. 3:1–4).

2. Instruction

Instruction appears when the prophet guides the people in the way they should go, often recalling Moses' specific commands in the Law: "The Lord warned Israel and Judah by every prophet and every seer, saying, 'Turn from your evil ways and keep my commandments and my statutes, in accordance with all the Law that I commanded your fathers" (2 Kings 17:13). Thus, Micah wrote, "He has told you, O man, what is good; and what does the Lord require of you but to do justice, and to love kindness, and to walk humbly with your God?" (Mic. 6:8). And Zephaniah pleaded, "Seek the Lord, all you humble of the land, who do his just commands; seek righteousness; seek humility; perhaps you may be hidden on the day of the anger of the Lord" (Zeph. 2:3).

3. Warning/Punishment

When it comes to declarations of punishment and salvation, it is very important to recognize the close tie between Moses and the later prophets such as Isaiah, Obadiah, and Haggai. When the Latter Prophets spoke words of warning and words of hope, they were directly building on the covenant curses and restoration blessings that Moses spoke in Leviticus 26 and Deuteronomy 27–32. A close look at these texts reveals at least ten original blessings, twenty-seven different curses, and ten restoration blessings that would be enjoyed after the curse was overcome. Figure 1.6 gives an overview of all of these.

Blessings	
1. YHWH's presence / favor / loyalty (Lev. 26:11–12) 2. Confirmation of the covenant (Lev. 26:9) 3. Be a holy people to YHWH (Deut. 28:9) 4. Rains in season (Lev. 26:4; Deut. 28:12) 5. Abounding prosperity and productivity: a. General (Deut. 28:12); b. Fruit of the womb (Lev. 26:9; Deut. 28:4, 11); c. Fruit of the livestock (Deut. 28:4, 11); d. Fruit of the ground (Lev. 26:4–5, 10; Deut. 28:4, 8, 11)	6. General and unspecified (Deut. 28:2, 6, 8, 12–13) 7. Peace and security in the land with no fear: a. General (Lev. 26:5–6); b. From harmful animals (Lev. 26:6); c. From enemies (Lev. 26:6) 8. Victory over enemies (Lev. 26:7–8; Deut. 28:7) 9. Freedom from slavery (Lev. 26:13) 10. Global influence and witness (Deut. 28:1, 10, 12)
Curses	
1. Anger and rejection from YHWH (Lev. 26:17, 24, 28, 41; Deut. 4:24–25; 29:20, 24, 27–28; 31:17–18, 29; 32:16, 19–22, 30) 2. Rejection and destruction of the cult (Lev. 26:31) 3. War and its ravages: a. General (Lev. 26:17, 25, 33, 37; Deut. 28:25, 49, 52; 32:23–24, 30, 41–42); b. Siege (Lev. 26:25–26, 29; Deut. 28:52–53, 55, 57) 4. Fear, terror, and horror (Lev. 26:16–17, 36–37; Deut. 28:66–67; 32:25) 5. Occupation and oppression by enemies and aliens (Lev. 26:16–17, 32; Deut. 28:31, 33, 43–44, 48, 68; 32:21) 6. Agricultural disaster and nonproductivity: a. General (Lev. 26:20; Deut. 28:17–18, 22, 40; 29:23); b. Drought (Lev. 26:19; Deut. 28:22–24); c. Crop pests (Deut. 28:38–42) 7. Starvation / famine (Lev. 26:26, 29, 45; Deut. 28:53–56; 32:24)	8. Illness, pestilence, and contamination (Lev. 26:16; Deut. 28:21–22, 27–28, 35, 59–61; 29:22; 32:24, 39) 9. Desolation: a. Of holy places (Lev. 26:31); b. Of cities and towns (Lev. 26:31, 33); c. Of the land (Lev. 26:32–35, 43; Deut. 28:51; 29:23) 10. Destruction by fire (Deut. 28:24; 32:22) 11. Harm from wild animals (Lev. 26:22; Deut. 32:24) 12. Decimation and infertility: a. Of family (Lev. 26:22; Deut. 28:18, 59); b. Of cattle (Lev. 26:22; Deut. 28:18, 51); c. Of population generally (Lev. 26:22, 36; Deut. 4:27; 28:62; 32:36) 13. Exile and captivity: a. Of the people (Lev. 26:33–34, 36, 38–39, 41, 44; Deut. 4:27; 28:36–37, 41, 63–64, 68; 29:28; 30:4; 32:26); b. Of the king (Deut. 28:36)

Fig. 1.6. Mosaic Covenant Blessings, Curses, and Restoration Blessings

Curses	
14. Forced idolatry in exile (Deut. 4:28; 28:36, 64) 15. Futility (Lev. 26:16, 20; Deut. 28:20, 29–31, 33, 38–41) 16. Dishonor and degradation (Lev. 26:19; Deut. 28:20, 25, 37, 43–44, 68) 17. Loss of possessions and impoverishment (Deut. 28:31) 18. Loss of family (Deut. 28:30, 32, 41; 32:25) 19. Helplessness and stumbling (Lev. 26:36–37; Deut. 28:29, 32; 32:35–36; 38–39) 20. Psychological afflictions (Deut. 28:20, 28, 34, 65–67) 21. Lack of peace and rest (Deut. 28:65)	22. Denial of burial (Deut. 28:26) 23. Becoming like the cities of the plain (Deut. 29:23) 24. Death and destruction (Lev. 26:36, 39; Deut. 4:26; 28:20–22, 44, 48, 51, 61; 29:20; 30:15, 18–19; 31:17; 32:25–26, 35, 39, 42) 25. General and unspecified (Deut. 4:30; 28:20, 24, 45, 59, 61, 63; 29:19, 21–22; 31:17, 21, 29; 32:23, 35) 26. General punishment, curse, and vengeance (Lev. 26:41, 43; Deut. 28:16, 20–21, 27; 30:19; 32:35, 41, 43) 27. Multiple punishments (Lev. 26:18, 21, 24, 28)
Restoration Blessings	
1. Renewal of YHWH's presence, favor, and loyalty (Lev. 26:42, 45; Deut. 4:29, 31; 30:3, 9) 2. Renewal of the covenant (Lev. 26:42, 44–45; Deut. 4:31) 3. Restoration of true worship and ability to be faithful (Deut. 4:30; 30:6, 8) 4. Population increase (Deut. 30:5, 9) 5. Agricultural bounty (Lev. 26:42; Deut. 30:9)	6. Restoration of general prosperity, well-being, and wealth (Deut. 30:3, 5, 9; 32:39) 7. Return from exile and repossession of the land (Deut. 30:3–5) 8. Reunification (Deut. 30:3–4) 9. Power over enemies and aliens (Deut. 30:7) 10. Freedom and restoration from death and destruction (Lev. 26:44; Deut. 30:6; 32:39)
All references are from Leviticus 26, Deuteronomy 4; 28–32. No single prophetic book, except perhaps Isaiah, mentions all categories. The lists of "Curses" and "Restoration Blessings" are adapted from pp. 1259–60 in "Malachi" by Douglas Stuart in *The Minor Prophets: An Exegetical and Expository Commentary*, edited by Thomas Edward McComiskey, copyright ©1998 by Thomas Edward McComiskey. Used by permission of Baker. www.bakerpublishinggroup.com.	

Fig. 1.6. Mosaic Covenant Blessings, Curses, and Restoration Blessings (cont.)

With respect to oracles of punishment, Daniel prays, "All Israel has transgressed your law and turned aside, refusing to obey your voice. And the curse and oath that are written in the Law of Moses the servant of God have been poured out upon us, because we have sinned against him" (Dan. 9:11). Prophetic oracles of warning/punishment are words of warning or of imminent punishment against those who have failed to live loyally to the covenant or who have failed to treat God and his people with respect—whether individuals (e.g., 1 Sam. 13:13–14; 1 Kings 11:11–13) or nations (e.g., Isa. 17; Jer. 8:4–12; Ezek. 15; Amos 4:1–3; Mic. 3:7–12). These oracles specify the outworking of the covenant curses detailed in Leviticus 26 and Deuteronomy 4, 27–28. One example comes in Ezekiel 21:14–17:

> As for you, son of man, prophesy. Clap your hands and let the sword come down twice, yes, three times, the sword for those to be slain. It is the sword for the great slaughter, which surrounds them, that their hearts may melt, and many stumble. At all their gates I have given the glittering sword. Ah, it is made like lightning; it is taken up for slaughter. Cut sharply to the right; set yourself to the left, wherever your face is directed. I also will clap my hands, and I will satisfy my fury; I the Lord have spoken.

Echoed here is the Mosaic curse of exile and captivity, listed as curse #13 in figure 1.6. As YHWH warned through Moses: "And I will scatter you among the nations, and I will unsheathe the sword after you, and your land shall be a desolation, and your cities shall be a waste" (Lev. 26:33).

4. Hope/Salvation

Statements of hope/salvation unpack the restoration blessings that YHWH promises in Leviticus 26 and Deuteronomy 4, 30, along with the more specific dynastic promises to David (2 Sam. 7:12–16). The words of comfort predict a day when God, after punishing his people with exile and death, would renew his relationship with his people (e.g., Isa. 10:5–12:6; Jer. 31:31–34; Ezek. 36:16–32; Amos 9:13–15). Consider, for example, Zechariah 8:2–3, 7–8:

> Thus says the Lord of hosts: I am jealous for Zion with great jealousy, and I am jealous for her with great wrath. Thus says the Lord: I have returned to Zion and will dwell in the midst of Jerusalem, and Jerusalem shall be called the faithful city, and the mountain of the Lord of hosts, the holy mountain. . . . Thus says the Lord of hosts: Behold, I will save my people from the east country and from the west country, and I will bring them to dwell in the midst of Jerusalem. And they shall be my people, and I will be their God, in faithfulness and in righteousness.

In the backdrop here are a number of Mosaic restoration blessings listed in figure 1.6: #1, renewal of YHWH's presence, favor, and loyalty; #2, renewal of the covenant; #7, return from exile and repossession of the land. The Lord first proclaimed these promises through Moses, and now he is reasserting their coming fulfillment through his postexilic prophet.

As you work your way through the oracles in books such as Deuteronomy and the Latter Prophets, consider what kind of prophetic speech you are reading. If you are in one of the Latter Prophets and read pronouncements of indictment or instruction, consider which if any of Moses' commands may be on the mind of the preacher. If you read declarations of punishment or salvation, look back at Leviticus 26 and Deuteronomy 4, 27–30 to consider which of the blessings, curses, or restoration blessings the prophet is anticipating. Also, always keep in mind the Davidic covenant promises that made more specific the kingdom hopes of a royal deliverer and new covenant Mediator that Moses initially proclaimed (e.g., Gen. 3:15; 22:17b–18; 49:8–10; Num. 24:17–19; Deut. 18:15–18 with 34:10–12). God's prophets were covenant enforcers, and we have to read their words in light of the Mosaic and Davidic covenants, among others. They had their Bibles open when they were preaching, and so should we.

Law as Covenant Stipulation

Before laying out some principles for interpreting Old Testament prophecy, I want to detail further the specific shape of biblical law, which controlled the context for prophetic preaching. God gave his law in the framework of covenant relationship, with the various statutes and judgments supplying the stipulations of the covenant. I noted how the classical prophets such as Jeremiah, Zephaniah, and Malachi were covenant enforcers, speaking with their Bibles open to Moses' words. Moses himself was the greatest of all Old Testament prophets, supplying both the content and pattern for most Old Testament proclamation.

Moses' laws come to us in two forms, which scholars have tagged as *apodictic* and *casuistic*. ***Apodictic laws*** are those that are base principles stated in such a way that there is no qualification or exception. In contrast, ***casuistic laws*** are always situational, related to specific circumstances. Casuistic laws are often applications of apodictic laws.

Apodictic	Casuistic
Ex. 20:3. You shall have no other gods before me. Ex. 20:16. You shall never bear false witness against your neighbor.	Ex. 21:28. If a bull gores a man or a woman to death, the bull must be stoned to death, and its meat must not be eaten. But the owner of the bull will not be held responsible. Ex. 22:26–27. If you take your neighbor's cloak as a pledge, return it to him by sunset, because his cloak is the only covering he has for his body. What else will he sleep in? When he cries out to me, I will hear, for I am compassionate.
Unconditional and imperative, usually beginning with a volitional verb	Conditional and declarative, usually beginning with "if" or "when"
Second person	Usually third person
General: without qualification or exception	Specific: based on actual situations, often with motive or exception clauses
Often in negative form	Usually in positive form
Adapted from Daniel I. Block, "Reading the Decalogue from Right to Left: The Ten Principles of Covenant Relationship in the Hebrew Bible," in *How I Love Your Torah, O LORD! Studies in the Book of Deuteronomy* (Eugene, OR: Cascade, 2011), 31.	

Fig. 1.7. Formal Distinctions in Old Testament Law

Along with identifying these formal distinctions, it is helpful to recognize the different types of laws based on their variations in content. Figure 1.8 provides an overview of five different types of laws found in the Old Testament: ***criminal***, ***civil***, ***family***, ***cultic/ceremonial***, and ***compassion***.

Criminal Laws
Laws governing crimes or offenses that put the welfare of the whole community at risk; the offended party is the state or national community, and therefore the punishment is on behalf of the whole community in the name of the highest state authority, which in Israel meant YHWH.
Kidnapping (Ex. 21:16; Deut. 24:7) **Sustained insubordination to parents** (Ex. 21:15, 17; Deut. 21:18–21) **Homicide/premeditated or avoidable murder** (Ex. 21:14; Num. 35:16–21, 30–31; Deut. 19:11–13) **Religious malpractice:** a. Sabbath-breaking (Ex. 31:14–15; 35:2; cf. Num. 15:32–36) b. False prophecy (Deut. 13:1–5; 18:20) c. Idolatry (Ex. 22:20; Lev. 19:4; Deut. 13:1–18; 17:2–7) d. Child sacrifice (Lev. 20:1–5) e. Witchcraft (Ex. 22:18; Lev. 19:26, 31; 20:27) f. Blasphemy (Lev. 24:14–23) **Sexual offenses:** a. Adultery when married or engaged (Lev. 20:10; Deut. 22:22–24; cf. Gen. 38:24) b. Concealed premarital unchastity (Deut. 22:20–21) c. Rape of an engaged girl (Deut. 22:25) d. Prostitution of a priest's daughter (Lev. 21:9) e. Incest (Lev. 20:11–12, 14) f. Homosexuality (Lev. 20:13) g. Bestiality (Ex. 22:19; Lev. 20:15–16) **False witness in a capital case** (Deut. 19:16–21) Note: Nearly all the commands and prohibitions in the Decalogue are considered criminal offenses.
Civil Laws
Laws governing private disputes between citizens or organizations in which the public authorities are appealed to for judgment or called on to intervene; the offended party is not the state or national community.
Non-premeditated killing: a. Accidental death (Ex. 21:13; Num. 35:9–15; Deut. 19:1–13) b. Death due to self-defense (Ex. 22:2–3)

Fig. 1.8. Types of Old Testament Laws by Content

Civil Laws

Assault:

a. Human against human (Ex. 21:18–19, 22)

b. Animal against human (Ex. 21:28–32)

c. Animal against animal (Ex. 21:33–36)

Breaches of trust:

a. Theft (Ex. 22:1–4, 7–9, 12; Lev. 19:11, 13)

b. Destruction of property (Ex. 22:5–6, 14)

Falsehood as a witness:

a. In noncapital case (Ex. 23:1–3)

b. In commerce/trade (Lev. 19:35–36)

Limited family issues:

a. Premarital unchastity between consenting adults, whether real (Ex. 22:16–17; Lev. 19:20–22; Deut. 22:28–29) or potential (Deut. 22:13–21)

b. Postdivorce situations (Deut. 24:1–3)

c. The mistreatment of slaves (Ex. 21:20–21, 26–27)

d. The handling of runaway slaves (Deut. 23:15–16)

e. Failure to accept levirate marriage duties (Deut. 25:7–10)

Family Laws

Noncivil, domestic laws governing the Israelite household.

Levirate marriage (Deut. 25:5–6)

Inheritance (Deut. 21:15–16)

Jubilee and the redemption of land and persons (Lev. 25)

Family discipleship (Deut. 6:6–9, 20–25; 11:18–21)

Respect of and obedience to parents (Ex. 20:12; Lev. 19:3; Deut. 5:16)

Turning a daughter into a prostitute (Lev. 19:29)

Slavery, including limits of service, inheritance, and protection (Ex. 21:2–11; Deut. 15:1–23)

Maintaining gender distinctions (Deut. 22:5)

Fig. 1.8. Types of Old Testament Laws by Content (cont.)

Cultic/Ceremonial Laws
Laws governing the visible forms and rituals of Israel's religious life.

Sacrifice:

a. Altar and sacrifices (Ex. 20:24–26)

b. Offering of firstfruits (Ex. 22:29–30; 23:19)

c. Sacrifices:

- General guidelines (Ex. 23:18; 29:38–46; Lev. 1–7; 19:5–8)
- Day of Atonement (Lev. 16)
- Location (Lev. 17:1–9; Deut. 12)

Sacred calendar:

a. Weekly Sabbaths (Ex. 20:8–11; 23:12; 31:12–17; 35:1–3; Lev. 19:3, 30; Deut. 5:12–15)

b. Sabbatical year (Ex. 23:10–11; Lev. 25:3–7; Deut. 15:1–6)

c. Feasts and sacred days (Ex. 23:14–19; 34:22–23; Lev. 23:9–22; Deut. 16:1–17)

d. Jubilee (Lev. 25:8–55)

Sacred symbolism and distinction:

a. Tabernacle (Ex. 25–30)

b. Priesthood:

- Garments (Ex. 28)
- Consecration (Ex. 29:1–37; Lev. 8)
- Administration of sacrifices (Ex. 29:38–46; Lev. 6–7)

c. Ritual purity (clean/unclean):

- Food laws (Lev. 11:2–47; 20:24–26; Deut. 14:4–20) and the eating of blood (Lev. 17:10–16; 19:26)
- Childbirth (Lev. 12)
- Leprosy (Lev. 13–14)
- Bodily discharges (Lev. 15)

d. Distinction from the pagan nations:

- Interbreeding/mixing of cattle, seeds, garments (Lev. 19:19; Deut. 22:9–11)
- Trimming of sideburns, cutting of body, tattoos (Lev. 19:27–28; Deut. 14:1)

Fig. 1.8. Types of Old Testament Laws by Content (cont.)

Compassion Laws
"Laws" dealing with charity, justice, and mercy toward others. These are not exactly the kinds of laws that can be enforced in court, but God knows the heart.
Protection and care of others: a. The sojourner (Ex. 22:21; 23:9; Lev. 19:9–10, 33–34; Deut. 14:28–29; 24:19–22) b. The widow and orphan (Ex. 22:22–24; Deut. 14:28–29; 24:19–22) c. The poor (Ex. 22:25–27; 23:6; Lev. 19:9–10; Deut. 15:7–11; 24:10–13, 19–22) d. One's neighbor (Deut. 19:13, 16–18) e. The disabled (Lev. 19:14; Deut. 27:18) f. The Levite (Deut. 14:28–29) g. The released slave (Deut. 15:12–15) h. The hired servant (Deut. 24:14–15) **Justice and impartiality** (Ex. 23:7–8; Lev. 19:15; Deut. 24:17–18; 27:19, 25) **Honor of the elderly** (Lev. 19:32) **Return of an enemy or brother's lost goods** (Ex. 22:4; Deut. 22:1–3) **Help of an enemy or brother in need** (Ex. 23:5; Deut. 22:4) **Excusal from war:** a. For a new homeowner (Deut. 20:5) b. For a new business owner (Deut. 20:6) c. For a newly married man (Deut. 20:7; 24:5) **Marriage to foreign widows of war** (Deut. 20:10–14) **Preservation of means for food for future generations** (Deut. 20:6–7; 25:4) **Building safe homes** (Deut. 20:8) **Respect for others' means of sustenance** (Deut. 23:24–25; 24:6)
Prepared by both Jason S. DeRouchie and Kenneth J. Turner. Originally published in DeRouchie, ed., *What the Old Testament Authors Really Cared About*, 466–67. Used by permission. The examples are only illustrative. The five main categories are taken from Christopher J. H. Wright, *Old Testament Ethics for the People of God* (Downers Grove, IL: InterVarsity Press, 2004), 288–301, which he adapted from Anthony Phillips, *Ancient Israel's Criminal Law: A New Approach to the Decalogue* (New York: Schocken Books, 1970), 2, 13.

Fig. 1.8. Types of Old Testament Laws by Content (cont.)

As you read through books such as Exodus, Leviticus, and Deuteronomy, keep your eyes open to the different forms and types of laws, and as you work through the Old Testament's narratives, prophecies, and wisdom sayings, consider how they relate to Moses' original covenantal instruction. We'll consider how Christians are to relate to old covenant laws in chapter 12, which focuses on practical theology.

Guidelines for Interpreting Old Testament Prophecy

As you work your way through biblical prophecy, keep in mind the following five principles.[27]

1. Guard against interpretive fallacies. So many people approach Old Testament prophecy in the wrong way.

a. *Ancient-Modern Nation Confusion*: Attempting to link Old Testament prophecy with particular current political regimes. Not only is the modern, secular state of Israel different from the Israel of the Bible, the linking of unspecified Old Testament prophecies with particular contemporary events or peoples is extremely difficult, if not impossible. Even when the prophets foretell future events, they are still preaching sermons, and their purpose is to awaken fresh levels of covenant loyalty in the present in the light of God's supremacy over all. Even if we can't yet identify all images exactly, the prophets are clear enough in telling us that YHWH is in charge of history and will make all things right.

b. *Genre Confusion*: Assuming that the interpretational rules for one genre apply to another. Because literature varies so much, the interpreter must be guided by the dual authors' intent, distinguishing literal statements from figures of speech, symbolism, and metaphor, all of which are frequent in the Prophets.

c. *Spiritualizing*: Removing a statement from the historical truth to which it speaks in order to make a "deeper" or "spiritual" application that is absent from the context.

d. *Personalizing*: Assuming that a text could apply to you or your group in a way that it does not apply to anyone else.

e. *Allegorizing*: Assuming that components of a passage have meaning only as symbols of Christian truths. Usually this approach does not consider at all the intent of the biblical author.

f. *Universalizing*: Treating something unique or uncommon as though it applied to everyone equally.

g. *Moralizing*: Assuming that principles for living can be derived from every biblical passage. Some texts tell us not how to live but whom we should live for.

27. The first four were adapted from a course handout from Douglas Stuart, Gordon-Conwell Theological Seminary, 1999.

h. Exemplarizing: Assuming that because the Bible records an action, it is always an example for us to follow. For example, we would be wrong to conclude from the fact that David committed sexual immorality with Bathsheba that we are justified in doing the same.

i. Superficial Christologizing or Typologizing: Asserting that some person, event, or institution points to Christ without exegetical or theological warrant. We want to find Christ, but only how God intends him to be found.

2. Think in terms of oracles.

Nearly all prophetic teaching is in the form of oracles, self-contained verbal revelations from God, often beginning, "Thus says the LORD." The prophets appear to have spoken or sung the oracles publicly in order to call people to loyalty or to explain what God was doing in history and why.

We must carefully identify the beginning and end of an oracle and be sure that we understand its characteristic terminology, structure, and speech types. We must patiently analyze the oracle's historical, literary, and biblical context, grasping its place in history, the book, and the canon. We must also diligently scrutinize its form, structure and flow, and important words.

Most prophetic oracles fall between strict prose and poetry, and all employ multiple figures of speech. Some are visionary, and therefore we must carefully identify their symbolism for modern audiences unused to such imagery. We must faithfully interpret all oracles within the biblical-theological matrix of all of Scripture. People need to know the "big picture" if they are to orient their lives properly. They need to hear us teach the Prophets accurately.

3. Pay attention to history.

All fifteen Old Testament classical prophets preached during a monumental 340-year period (770–433 B.C.) during which Israel and Judah were reduced from independent nations to a single, pitiful, remnant state (Judah), one tiny district in the huge Persian Empire. Why? It was because their long history of disobedience to God's Mosaic covenant required the unleashing of its curses.

This was an era of dramatic change, and God's prophets clarified for Israel and the world why history was playing out the way it was and how this history fit within God's overall kingdom-building plan culminating in Christ. Were God's ancient promises of Israel's greatness void? Was there any hope for the promised future kingdom? Would the era of curse be supplanted by restoration blessing? Prophetic preaching is significantly about historical developments, and no interpretation of its message that ignores historical context can hope to be accurate.

Figure 1.9 gives an overview of the main world powers and the three main periods for the classical prophets. Note how the arrangement of the Prophets in the Bible is not chronological. This suggests that theology rather than chronology played the decisive factor in ordering the biblical Prophets.

<table>
<tr><th>Power & Prophetic Period</th><th>Israel</th><th>Judah</th><th>Canonical Order</th></tr>
<tr><td>Assyria (870–626 B.C.)
————
8th–early 7th century</td><td>Jonah (ca. 770)
Amos (ca. 760)
Hosea (ca. 760–730)</td><td>Isaiah (ca. 740–700)
Micah (ca. 737–690)
Nahum (ca. 650)</td><td rowspan="3">Jeremiah
Ezekiel
Isaiah
The Twelve
Hosea
Joel
Amos
Obadiah
Jonah
Micah
Nahum
Habakkuk
Zephaniah
Haggai
Zechariah
Malachi</td></tr>
<tr><td>Babylon (626–539 B.C.)
————
Late 7th–early 6th century</td><td></td><td>Habakkuk (ca. 630)
Jeremiah (ca. 627–580)
Zephaniah (ca. 622)
Joel (ca. 600?)
Obadiah (ca. 586?)
Ezekiel (ca. 593–570)
[in Babylon]</td></tr>
<tr><td>Persia (539–323 B.C.)
————
Late 6th–5th century</td><td></td><td>Haggai (ca. 520)
Zechariah (ca. 520–518)
Malachi (ca. 433)</td></tr>
<tr><td colspan="4">The canonical order is taken from Baba Bathra 14b (see “Putting Genre within Its Biblical Context” above). Most of the dates for the prophets are taken from John H. Walton, Chronological and Background Charts of the Old Testament, 2nd ed. (Grand Rapids: Zondervan, 1994), 52.</td></tr>
</table>

Fig. 1.9. The Chronology of the Classical Prophets

4. Remember the covenants and the canon.

YHWH's prophets were enforcers and ambassadors of the various covenants that God had made with those on earth. They also predicted the coming new covenant, which would fulfill in different ways all previous divine-human covenants.

Without question, the Mosaic covenant bore the greatest influence on prophetic preaching (Ex. 19–Deut. 33). It guided the prophets' indictments and instructions toward Israel and also supplied a framework for the blessings, curses, and restoration blessings they pronounced (see Lev. 26; Deut. 4, 27–32).

The first era of temporary blessing was prosperous life in the Promised Land, which culminated in the reigns of David and Solomon. Then, as a result of covenant-breaking, YHWH divided the monarchy and brought the curse of foreign oppression and exile, first against the northern kingdom of Israel and then against the southern kingdom of Judah. Reflecting on the Assyrian conquest of Samaria and the north in

723 B.C., the author of Kings asserted, "This occurred because the people of Israel had sinned against the LORD their God . . . . They would not listen, but were stubborn, as their fathers had been, who did not believe in the LORD their God. They despised his statutes and his covenant that he made with their fathers and the warnings that he gave them" (2 Kings 17:7, 14–15). The devastation of the north was then followed by Babylon's progressive oppression and exile of the southern kingdom of Judah (605, 597, 586 B.C.), climaxing in the destruction of Jerusalem with its temple in 586 B.C.

While YHWH promised through Moses this future desolation (Deut. 4:25–28; 31:16–17, 26–29), curse would not be his final word: "When you are in tribulation, and all these things come upon you in the latter days, you will return to the LORD your God and obey his voice. For the LORD your God is a merciful God" (4:30–31). The era of restoration blessing is the new creational age of the new covenant inaugurated in Christ's first coming. God would bring it about by *his* mercy alone and in order to restore honor to *his* name: "It is not for your sake, O house of Israel, that I am about to act, but for the sake of my holy name, which you have profaned among the nations to which you came" (Ezek. 36:22).

YHWH's vow to supply David with an eternal kingdom and throne (2 Sam. 7:12–16) gives focus to the Mosaic restoration promises by identifying that the promised seed of the woman and of Abraham (Gen. 3:15; 22:17b–18) would not only be in the line of Judah (Gen. 49:8–10) but also be in the line of David. The Major and Minor Prophets regularly build on these promises, fusing the Abrahamic, Mosaic, and Davidic covenant hopes into one (e.g., Isa. 9:7; 55:3; Jer. 23:5; 30:9; Ezek. 34:23; 37:24–25; Hos. 3:5; Amos 9:11; Zech. 13:1).

Because the Mosaic and new covenants operate as stage 1 and stage 2 of the Abrahamic covenant (see "An Example of Text Grammar—Genesis 12:1–3" in chapter 5 and the discussion of "Covenant" under "The Historical Context of Exodus 19:4–6" in chapter 8), the Prophets also put hope in the promises that God had made to the patriarchs (e.g., Isa. 29:22; 41:8; 51:2; Jer. 33:25–26; Mic. 7:20). These included both the assertion that "him who dishonors you I will curse" and the promise that "in you all the families of the earth shall be blessed" (Gen. 12:3). Such statements, along with the fact that all the world stands as part of the Adamic-Noahic covenants (see Gen. 9:9–11; Isa. 24:4–6; Zech. 11:10; cf. Isa. 43:27; Hos. 6:7), supply the backdrop for the numerous oracles toward the foreign nations (e.g., Isa. 13–23; Jer. 46–51; Ezek. 25–32; Obad. 1–21; Zeph. 2:5–15). In these, YHWH, the covenant Lord of creation, declares that he will both punish and reconcile on a global scale (Zeph. 3:8–10).

In anticipating the days of worldwide kingdom restoration, the Prophets in part predict the present age of the church, our own "last days," initiated by Christ's death and resurrection (Acts 2:17; Heb. 1:1–2). They also anticipate a consummated fulfillment in the age to come in which the blessings are not only greater than those of the first era but eternal for those who know God's redemption (Eph. 1:3, 13–14; 1 Peter 1:3–5) (see "Old Testament Promises and the Christian" in chapter 12).

The prophets were *not* first and foremost innovators; they were reminders and enforcers. They preached from their Scriptures, and we will understand them properly only by reading their books in this light.

We must be ever questioning how their message fits within the whole of the Christian canon. The Major and Minor Prophets make up the Latter Prophets, which occur after the Former Prophets. This structure allows Joshua-Kings to tell us *what* happened in the covenant history and Jeremiah-Malachi to describe *why* it happened the way it did. We must also consider the significance of the fact that the arrangement of the Latter Prophets in Scripture appears substantially driven by theological rather than chronological purposes. For example, even though Jonah is likely the earliest of the first-millennial writing prophets, the book of Jonah is placed fifth in the Book of the Twelve. We should ask, therefore, whether Obadiah's preceding Jonah is to influence our reading of Jonah.[28] Furthermore, we should always be asking how later prophetic voices in the Old and New Testaments pick up or relate to the message we are reading. We must read the Prophets within their canonical placement and in light of the Adamic-Noahic, Abrahamic, Mosaic, Davidic, and new covenants.

5. See and savor Christ and the gospel.

The New Testament is clear that the Old Testament prophets looked with anticipation for the days of the promised Messiah. For example, Jesus said, "Your father Abraham rejoiced that he would see my day. He saw it and was glad" (John 8:56; cf. Matt. 13:17). Furthermore, the prophets "searched and inquired carefully, inquiring what person or time the Spirit of Christ in them was indicating when he predicted the sufferings of Christ and the subsequent glories" (1 Peter 1:10–11).

Following his resurrection, Jesus asserted, "'O foolish ones, and slow of heart to believe all that the *prophets* have spoken! Was it not necessary that the Christ should suffer these things and enter into his glory?' And beginning with Moses and *all the Prophets*, he interpreted to them in all the Scriptures the things concerning himself" (Luke 24:25–27). We also read, "He opened their minds to understand the Scriptures, and said to them, 'Thus it is written, that the Christ should suffer and on the third day rise from the dead, and that repentance and forgiveness of sins should be proclaimed in his name to all nations, beginning from Jerusalem'" (24:45–47).

Many other New Testament voices stress that *every prophet* anticipated both Christ's tribulations and the triumph that would follow. In Peter's words, "But what God foretold by the mouth of *all the prophets*, that his Christ would suffer, he thus fulfilled. . . . Moses said, 'The Lord God will raise up for you a prophet like me from your brothers. . . .' And all the prophets who have spoken, from Samuel and those who came after him, also proclaimed these days" (Acts 3:18, 22, 24). And again, "to him all the prophets bear witness that everyone who believes in him receives forgiveness of sins through his name" (10:43). Later Paul also asserts, "I stand here testifying both to small

28. It is likely that the one who stitched the Twelve together believed that the pride of Edom against Israel that God condemns in Obadiah stood as a mirror of the pride of Jonah against Nineveh. Jonah represents the nation of Israel, and just as YHWH confronted Edom's pride, he will confront Israel's.

and great, saying nothing but what the prophets and Moses said would come to pass: that the Christ must suffer and that, by being the first to rise from the dead, he would proclaim light both to our people and to the Gentiles" (26:22–23).

The Old Testament prophets anticipated the Messiah's suffering and the mission it would spark. Because all the prophets point to Jesus, our interpretation of the prophetic books cannot end until we have discerned how each announces the Christ. This does not mean that every passage will point to the Messiah in the same way, but Jesus' gospel work can and should be magnified from every prophetic text. Only in this way do the Prophets take their place as Christian Scripture. As you read the Prophets, seek to see and savor Christ and the gospel (see the section with a similar title in chapter 12).

Psalms

A Christian Approach to the Psalms

The book of Psalms contains some of the most familiar and well-loved parts of the Bible. By seeing only the initial words of the following verses, many readers can probably recite the entire passages by heart: "Blessed is the man who walks not in the counsel of the wicked, nor stands in the way of sinners, nor sits in the seat of scoffers; but his delight is in the law of the LORD, and on his law he meditates day and night" (Ps. 1:1–2). "O LORD, our Lord, how majestic is your name in all the earth" (8:1[H2]).[29] "The LORD is my shepherd; I shall not want. He makes me lie down in green pastures. He leads me beside still waters. He restores my soul" (23:1–3).

Jesus loved the Psalter and often used it to defend his messiahship or to give voice to his pain. For example, in his dialogue with the chief priests and elders, Jesus identified himself as the suffering king of Psalm 118:22–23 when he questioned, "Have you never read in the Scriptures: 'The stone that the builders rejected has become the cornerstone; this was the Lord's doing, and it is marvelous in our eyes'?" (Matt. 21:42). Similarly, when engaging the Pharisees about the predicted Messiah and pushing them on their assertion that the Messiah was *David's* son, Jesus referred to Psalm 110:1, asking, "How is it then that David, in the Spirit, calls [the Christ] Lord, saying, 'The Lord said to my Lord, Sit at my right hand, until I put your enemies under your feet'?" (Matt. 22:43–44). Jesus saw Judas's betrayal predicted in the Psalter (Ps. 41:9[H10]; John 13:18), and in the garden of Gethsemane, Jesus appeared to allude to the words of the troubled king from Psalm 42:5–6[H6–7] (Matt. 26:38). At the cross he cried out,

29. The "H + number" in brackets refers to Hebrew verse numbers that differ from the English.

"My God, my God, why have you forsaken me?," identifying the cries of the king in Psalm 22:1[H2] with his own (Matt. 27:46). His last words before his death, "Father, into your hands I commit my spirit!" (Luke 23:46), declared as fulfilled the words of the king in Psalm 31:5[H6]. Jesus believed that the Psalms were about him, and it is from this context that he stressed after his resurrection that "everything written about me in the Law of Moses and the Prophets and *the Psalms* must be fulfilled" (Luke 24:44).

The apostles and New Testament authors, too, read the Psalms as supplying the laments, thanksgivings, and praises first of the Christ and then of all finding refuge in him (Ps. 2:12). They saw Jesus' substitutionary death at the cross as the culmination of the nations' and peoples' rage against YHWH and his anointed king (Ps. 2:1–2; Acts 4:25–28). They believed that the Psalter predicted the cross's graphic horror (Pss. 22:7[H8]; 109:25; Matt. 27:39), the taunting of the crowds (Ps. 22:8[H9]; Matt. 27:43), the dryness of Christ's mouth (Ps. 22:15[H16]; John 19:28; cf. Ps. 69:21[H22]), the preservation of his bones (Ps. 34:20[H21]; John 19:36), Judas's death (Pss. 69:25[H26]; 109:8; Acts 1:16, 20), and Jesus' greeting of his "brothers" after his resurrection (Ps. 22:22[H23]; Heb. 2:12; cf. Matt. 28:10; Rom. 8:29). They also believed that Jesus' bodily resurrection fulfilled the prophetic predictions that YHWH would preserve the anointed king's body through death (Ps. 16:10; Acts 2:24–32; 13:35–37) and would exalt him as his royal "begotten Son" (Ps. 2:7; see Acts 13:32–33; cf. Rom. 1:4). In the end, Jesus (Rev. 12:5; 19:15) and those identified with him (2:26–27) will use "a rod of iron" to break the rebellious, plotting peoples (Ps. 2:9).

As Bruce Waltke has noted, "The writers of the New Testament are not attempting to identify and limit the psalms that prefigure Christ but rather are assuming that the Psalter as a whole has Jesus Christ in view and that this should be the normative way of interpreting the psalms."[30] A Christian approach to the Psalms demands that we read the whole as messianic music, whether as songs "by Christ" or "about Christ."[31] And insofar as we identify ourselves with this Anointed One, his prayers become our prayers and his music our music.

Reading the Psalms as Messianic Music

It is important to recognize that the New Testament authors are not approaching the Psalms in a new way; they are simply following the pattern we see among the

30. Bruce K. Waltke, "A Canonical Process Approach to the Psalms," in *Tradition and Testament: Essays in Honor of Charles Lee Feinberg*, ed. John S. Feinberg and Paul D. Feinberg (Chicago: Moody Press, 1981), 7.

31. So Mark D. Futato, *Interpreting the Psalms: An Exegetical Handbook*, Handbooks for Old Testament Exegesis (Grand Rapids: Kregel, 2007), 174.

Prophets. For example, the prophet Zechariah alludes to Psalm 72 in a context saturated with messianic hope. Writing in a day when there was no Davidic king on the throne, Zechariah asserts in 9:9–10, "Rejoice greatly, O daughter of Zion! Shout aloud, O daughter of Jerusalem! Behold, your king is coming to you; righteous and having salvation is he, humble and mounted on a donkey, on a colt, the foal of a donkey. I will cut off the chariot from Ephraim and the war horse from Jerusalem; and the battle bow shall be cut off, and he shall speak peace to the nations; his rule shall *be from sea to sea, and from the River to the ends of the earth.*" John saw Jesus as fulfilling this text in his triumphal entry (John 12:14–16). The italicized portion parallels word for word Psalm 72:8, suggesting that Zechariah was reading this psalm as a prediction of the coming messianic king.

While the superscription of Psalm 72 attributes the prayer to Solomon, the body of the song has Israel's ruler praying in hope for someone greater than himself, whose kingship far exceeds that of any Old Testament king.[32] Psalm 72 is one of a host of ***royal psalms*** that display a portrait of an unparalleled coming deliverer (see Pss. 2, 18, 20, 21, 45, 72, 101, 110, 132, 144). Figure 1.10 summarizes the overall vision of this ruler in the Psalter's royal psalms.[33]

1.	He is not simply God's "son" (89:27[H28]) but his "begotten" son (2:7), who belongs to YHWH (89:18[H19]) and remains ever devoted to him (18:20–24[H21–25]; 21:1, 7[H2, 8]; cf. 63:1–8, 11[H2–9, 12]); he is seated at God's right hand (110:1) and is himself tagged both as "God" (45:6[H7]) and as David's "Lord" (110:1); he will experience joy in God's presence forever (21:6[H7]; cf. 16:11).
2.	He will receive YHWH's everlasting blessing (21:6[H7]; 45:2[H3]; cf. 72:17), fulfill the Davidic covenant promises (89:28–37[H29–38]; 132:11–12, 17–18), and be the heir of both the nations (2:8) and the Melchizedekian priesthood (110:1–4).
3.	The nations and peoples of the earth stand against him (2:1–3; 110:2), but he will overcome all of them (45:3–5[H4–6]; 89:22–23[H23–24]; 110:1, 5–7; 132:18) through tribulation unto triumph (18:37–50[H38–51]; 20:1–9[H2–10]; 21:1, 4[H2, 5]; 144:7–8, 11), and he will declare God's praises among them (18:49[H50]).

Fig. 1.10. The Portrait of the Messianic King in the Royal Psalms

32. We see the same pattern in Psalms 20–21, where the psalmist David prays on behalf of another—that YHWH would deliver his anointed king from his suffering (Ps. 20) and that God would be exalted for saving this king from death and establishing him with eternal days and blessing (Ps. 21). I suggest that the king for whom David prays is the one he later identifies as his "Lord" in Psalm 110:1 (cf. Matt. 22:41–46), whose personal pleas for God's help are then disclosed in laments such as Psalm 22 and whose personal deliverance is celebrated in Psalm 23. For the view that the preposition לְ ("to") + proper name (e.g., לְדָוִד "to David") designates authorship, see *GKC* § 129c; for an overview of the various proposals, see Uriel Simon, *Four Approaches to the Book of Psalms: From Saadiah Gaon to Abraham Ibn Izra*, trans. Lenn J. Schramm (Albany, NY: State University of New York Press, 1991), 179–82.

33. Some of this synthesis is adapted from J. Alec Motyer, *Look to the Rock: An Old Testament Background to Our Understanding of Christ* (Downers Grove, IL: InterVarsity Press, 1996), 23–38.

4.	By YHWH's act (2:6, 8; 18:31–36, 43, 46–50[H32–37, 44, 47–51]; 21:1–13[H2–14]; 110:1–2; 132:17–18), he will establish global rule (2:8–12; 45:17[H18]; 72:8–11; 89:25[H26]; 110:5–6; 132:18) based in Zion (2:6; 110:2; 132:13, 17).
5.	He will reign forever (21:4[H5]; 45:6[H7]; 72:5) in peace (72:7) and fruitfulness (72:3, 16), and he will rule in righteousness and justice (45:4, 6–7[H5, 7–8]; 72:2–3; 101:1–8), which will include befriending the poor and defeating the oppressor (72:2, 4, 12–14).
6.	Those finding refuge in him will be blessed (2:12; 72:17; 144:15), and under his rule, they will flourish (72:7) and enjoy abundance (72:3; 144:13–15), being both prosperous (72:3) and fruitful (72:16; 144:12).
7.	He will possess an everlasting name (72:17), be preeminent among men (45:2, 7[H3, 8]), and stand as the object of unending thanks (72:15).

Fig. 1.10. The Portrait of the Messianic King in the Royal Psalms (cont.)

Zechariah's messianic reading of Psalm 72 most likely aligns with its human author's original intent, for clearly these royal psalms speak of no normal, fleshly king. Looking beyond himself, the speaker in Psalm 72 envisioned the fulfillment of YHWH's royal ideal (Deut. 17:14–20) and his kingdom pledge to David (2 Sam. 7:12–16), which was itself built on the Lord's promises in the Law to raise up an evil-overcoming, blessing-securing, royal deliverer, whose reign would last forever (Gen. 3:14–15; 22:17b–18; 49:8–10; Num. 24:7–9, 17–19). With every new generation there was hope that the next monarch would be the chosen one, but each Judaean king proved that he was *not* the hoped-for Savior. Nevertheless, the community of faith continued to sing these psalms as a testament to his coming, and then the New Testament saints celebrated his arrival.

Zechariah does not appear to have been the first prophet to treat the Psalms messianically. Jeremiah, for example, seems to draw on Psalm 89 when he stresses in chapter 33 that the Davidic covenant is as firmly established as the day and night. In the psalm YHWH declares, "Once for all I have sworn by my holiness; I will not lie to David. His offspring shall endure forever, his throne as long as the sun before me. Like the moon it shall be established forever, a faithful witness in the skies" (Ps. 89:35–37[H36–38]). And Jeremiah states, "If you can break my covenant with the day and my covenant with the night, so that day and night will not come at their appointed time, then also my covenant with David my servant may be broken, so that he shall not have a son to reign on his throne" (Jer. 33:20–21; cf. 31:36–37).[34] Similarly, potentially

34. Along with 1–2 Samuel, Jeremiah witnesses major differences between the Masoretic Text (MT) and other texts and versions. In this instance, the LXX completely lacks Jeremiah 33:14–26, which does raise the possibility that the promises in this unit are not original to Jeremiah but arose later in the history of interpretation (so Emanuel Tov, *Textual Criticism of the Hebrew Bible*, 3rd ed. [Minneapolis: Fortress, 2011], 286–88). The Dead Sea Scroll 4QJerc does not preserve verses 16–20, and the size of the gap is too small to fit the entire text of the MT, so the scroll either included a shorter text at this point or had one or two words written above the line (so

declaring the fulfillment of YHWH's promise in Psalm 89:28[H29], "My steadfast love I will keep for [David] forever, and my covenant will stand firm for him," God declares to the faithful remnant through Isaiah, "I will make with you an everlasting covenant, my steadfast, sure love for David" (Isa. 55:3).[35] While YHWH's temporary punishment against the house of Judah made it appear that YHWH had forsaken his Davidic covenant promises (Ps. 89:38–46[H39–47]),[36] Psalm 89 testifies with later prophets that God would "not violate [his] covenant or alter the word that went forth from [his] lips" (89:34[H35]).[37]

Not only Isaiah, Jeremiah, and Zechariah, but David himself, at least in certain instances, was consciously looking beyond himself, predicting the work of the Christ when he wrote his poetry. While not evident in the ESV, an alternative reading of 2 Samuel 23:1 finds David's last words standing as a prophetic oracle *"concerning the Messiah of the God of Jacob."*[38] This is the reading retained in the Septuagint, and it was followed by early English translations such as Douay-Rheims (1610) and the YLT (1898). Regardless of how one renders this statement, the only other occurrences of the phrase "the utterance of the mighty man" (נְאֻם הַגֶּבֶר) are in Numbers 24:3, 15 and Proverbs 30:1, all of which introduce messianic oracles (see Num. 24:7, 17–19; Prov. 30:4).[39] Moreover, the content of David's "last words" clearly points beyond himself, speaking of one whose rule will bring forth light and new creation (2 Sam. 23:4) and who will overcome the man of worthlessness with an iron and wood spear (23:6–7), likely

---

Martin G. Abegg Jr., Peter Flint, and Eugene Ulrich, *The Dead Sea Scrolls Bible* [San Francisco: HarperSanFrancisco, 1999], 401). Significantly, the MT of Jeremiah speaks many times of the writing down of Jeremiah's words (e.g., Jer. 25:13; 30:2; 36:2, 28, 32; 45:1; 51:60, 63), and the book itself suggests multiple versions of various lengths coming from the prophet's own hand (see the shorter Babylonian edition in Jeremiah 51:59–64 versus Baruch's longer Egyptian edition in Jeremiah 36:32; 45:1–5 with 43:5–7). This may help explain the book's distinctive textual tradition, and it could mean that all known versions came from the prophet himself.

35. On these texts, see especially William C. Pohl IV, "A Messianic Reading of Psalm 89: A Canonical and Intertextual Study," *JETS* 58, 3 (2015): 522–25; cf. Knut M. Heim, "The (God-)forsaken King of Psalm 89: A Historical and Intertextual Enquiry," in *King and Messiah in Israel and the Ancient Near East: Proceedings of the Oxford Old Testament Seminar*, ed. John Day, JSOTSup 270 (Sheffield, UK: Sheffield Academic, 1998), 296–322. For a provocative alternative reading of Isaiah 55:3, see Peter J. Gentry, "Rethinking the 'Sure Mercies of David' in Isaiah 55:3," *WTJ* 62, 2 (2007): 279–304; Peter J. Gentry and Stephen J. Wellum, *Kingdom through Covenant: A Biblical-Theological Understanding of the Covenants* (Wheaton, IL: Crossway, 2012), 406–21. While less clear, two other texts from Isaiah and an additional one from Micah may be reading Psalm 72 as an eschatological text related to the end-times reign of God, which in context is recognized to come ultimately through his messianic figure (cf. Ps. 72:1–2 with Isa. 32:1; Ps. 72:9 with Mic. 7:17; Ps. 72:10 with Isa. 60:9, 11). For these and other potential links between the Psalms and the Latter Prophets, see Sue Gillingham, "From Liturgy to Prophecy: The Use of Psalmody in Second Temple Judaism," *CBQ* 64, 3 (2002): 471–76.

36. The dating of Psalm 89 is difficult, for (1) it is clearly written during a time when the Davidic kingdom promises appear to be in jeopardy (see Ps. 89:38–46[H39–47]), but (2) the attribution to "Ethan the Ezrahite" next to a similar attribution to "Heman the Ezrahite" in Psalm 88 seems to link Psalm 89 to the time of David and Solomon. Perhaps Ethan penned the text at an old age, soon after Solomon's death and just after the division of the empire in the days of Rehoboam (see esp. 1 Kings 4:31[H5:11]; cf. 1 Chron. 15:16–17, 19).

37. For this reading, see Pohl, "A Messianic Reading of Psalm 89," 507–25.

38. See Michael Rydelnik, *The Messianic Hope: Is the Hebrew Bible Really Messianic?*, NAC Studies in Bible and Theology 9 (Nashville: Broadman & Holman, 2010), 39–41.

39. For a discussion of the Numbers texts as messianic, see ibid., 38–39, 52–55.

echoing the imagery of Psalm 2:9, where God's royal Son will overcome the raging nations "with a rod of iron" (cf. Gen. 49:10; Num. 24:17; Rev. 12:5; 19:15).

More explicit are Peter's exegetical conclusions in Acts 2:30–31, where, in reflecting on the meaning of Psalm 16:8–11, the apostle asserts of David, "Being therefore a *prophet*, and *knowing* that God had sworn with an oath to him that he would set one of his descendants on his throne, *he foresaw and spoke* about the resurrection of the Christ." I will say more about this verse below, but what should be clear by now is that the New Testament authors, the Old Testament prophets, and David himself believed that the Psalms pointed ahead, portraying the sufferings of Christ and the subsequent glories (1 Peter 1:10–12). Insofar as we identify ourselves with this anointed king, his prayers become our prayers and his music our music.

The Variety of Psalm Subgenres

Psalms was the first book that Old Testament scholars assessed through the lens of genre, and this approach still dominates much Old Testament interpretation.[40] Eight of the most well-recognized psalm subgenres are:

- Lament psalms (including penitential and imprecatory psalms)
- Trust or confidence psalms
- Thanksgiving psalms
- Praise psalms or hymns (including enthronement psalms)
- Royal psalms
- Wisdom/Torah psalms
- Liturgy psalms
- Historical psalms

These categories are relatively self-explanatory and distinguished by their content. Knowing which psalms fit each category allows us to easily find words to express the prayers of our hearts. Figure 1.11 supplies one categorization of the Psalms by subgenre.

40. Two well-known, very helpful books that approach the Psalter by focusing on genre categories are Bernhard W. Anderson and Steven Bishop, *Out of the Depths: The Psalms Speak for Us Today*, 3rd ed. (Louisville: Westminster John Knox, 2000); and Gordon D. Fee and Douglas Stuart, *How to Read the Bible for All Its Worth*, 3rd ed. (Grand Rapids: Zondervan, 2003), 212–15.

Lament	3, 4, 5, 6, 7, 12, 13, 14 (= 53), 17, 22, 26, 27, 28, 35, 38, 39, 41, 42/43, 44, 51, 54, 55, 56, 57, 58, 59, 60, 61, 63, 64, 69, 70, 71, 74, 77, 79, 80, 82, 83, 85, 86, 88, 90, 94, 102, 106, 108, 109, 120, 123, 126, 130, 137, 140, 141, 142, 143 (Penitential Psalms = 6, 38, 51, 102, 130, 143; Imprecatory Psalms = 35, 55, 59, 69, 79, 109, 137)
Trust	11, 16, 23, 91, 121, 125, 129, 131
Thanksgiving	30, 66, 92, 107, 116, 118, 124, 138
Praise/Hymn	8, 29, 33, 46, 47, 48, 76, 84, 87, 93, 95, 96, 97, 98, 99, 100, 103, 104, 105, 111, 113, 114, 117, 122, 134, 135, 136, 145, 146, 147, 148, 149, 150 (Songs of Zion = 46, 48, 76, 84, 87; Enthronement of YHWH Psalms = 47, 93, 96, 97, 98, 99)
Royal	2, 18, 20, 21, 45, 72, 101, 110, 132, 144
Wisdom/Torah	1, 37, 49, 73, 112, 127, 128
Liturgy	15, 24 (cf. also 136)
Historical	78 (cf. also 105, 106, 107, 114)
Mixed	9/10, 19, 25, 31, 32, 34, 36, 40, 65, 89, 119
Unclear	50, 52, 62, 67, 68, 75, 81, 115, 133, 139
Prepared by John C. Crutchfield for *What the Old Testament Authors Really Cared About: A Survey of Jesus' Bible*, ed. Jason S. DeRouchie (Grand Rapids: Kregel, 2013), 342. Used by permission.	

Fig. 1.11. The Psalms by Subgenre

When David moved the ark of the Lord to Jerusalem, his delight in music matched by his passion for God moved him to commission the Levites as music ministers. He appointed leaders over harps and lyres, cymbals and trumpets, and he even appointed a vocal ensemble. Overall, he called these worship leaders "to invoke [i.e., appeal for help], to thank, and to praise the Lord" (1 Chron. 16:4). As we will see below, invocation is the essence of the psalms of *lament*, gratitude of the psalms of *thanksgiving*, and adoration of the psalms of *praise*. Furthermore, while most of the psalm genres listed above distinguish themselves by subject matter alone, the psalms of lament, thanksgiving, and praise are also marked by structural patterns. In light of David's directive, we may have biblical warrant for viewing all other psalm subgenres simply as types of these three main categories.

With this, the Chronicler asserted that the Levitical music leaders that David appointed (i.e., Asaph, Heman, and Jeduthun) were "seers" (1 Chron. 25:5; 2 Chron. 29:30; 35:15) who "prophesied under the direction of the king" "with lyres, with harps, and with cymbals . . . in thanksgiving and praise to the LORD" (1 Chron. 25:1–3). It was with their words and those of the "prophet" David (Acts 2:30; cf. 2 Sam. 23:2) that the faithful in Israel "sang praises with gladness" to the Lord (2 Chron. 29:30). Both the nature of the royal psalms and the fact that these leaders "prophesied under the direction of the king," whose life was shaped by the Davidic covenant kingdom promises (2 Sam. 7:12–16; 1 Chron. 17:11–14; 25:2), strongly suggest that we should understand this prophetic role to include foretelling (i.e., prediction) as well as forth-telling. We will now see that the New Testament authors read the various psalms in just this way.

Psalms of Lament, Trust, Thanksgiving, and Praise

By far the two most common psalm subgenres are laments and praises, and fitted between them in logical progression are trust psalms and thanksgivings. ***Psalms of lament*** are cries for help to God out of the midst of pain. ***Psalms of trust*** declare confidence in the Lord, yet still out of the midst of pain. ***Psalms of thanksgiving*** express gratitude for deliverance or provision after the pain. ***Psalms of praise*** are hymns that celebrate who YHWH is and what he has done, especially in relation to creation and redemption. Most psalm subgenres are distinguished only by their general subject matter, but psalms of lament, thanksgiving, and praise are also marked by structural patterns.

1. Psalms of Lament (APTRAP)

a. Address to God
b. Petitions, usually for being heard
c. Trouble described
d. Reason for why God should answer
e. Assurance declared (confidence or trust)
f. Praise or promise of sacrifice

One of the features highlighted in the royal psalms was that the Messiah's victory over evil and global reign would come only through great suffering (Pss. 18:37–50[H38–51]; 20:1–9[H2–10]; 144:7–8, 11). Similarly, Isaiah foretold that the royal servant's path to being "high and lifted up" (Isa. 52:13) would be as "a man of sorrows, and acquainted with grief" (53:3). Out of this perspective, the writer of Hebrews states, "In the days of his flesh, Jesus offered up prayers and supplications, with loud cries and tears, to him who was able to save him from death" (Heb. 5:7). The Gospel writers detail Christ's journey through tribulation unto triumph, and they note that Christ's prayers were often drawn directly from the psalms of lament.

As noted above, laments in ancient Israel often took on a specific form, often including six elements. For example, most of the pattern is evident in this lament from Psalm 6, in which the anointed king cries out as an innocent sufferer under the hand of God's punishment.

1	O LORD, rebuke me not in your anger	*Address to God*
2–4	Be gracious to me, O LORD, for I am languishing; heal me, O LORD, for my bones are troubled. My soul also is greatly troubled. . . . Turn, O LORD, deliver my life; save me for the sake of your steadfast love.	*Petitions and reasons for why God should answer*
6–7	I am weary with my moaning; every night I flood my bed with tears. . . . [My eye] grows weak because of all my foes.	*Trouble described*
8–10	Depart from me, all you workers of evil, for the LORD has heard the sound of my weeping. The LORD has heard my plea; the LORD accepts my prayer. All my enemies shall be ashamed	*Assurance declared*
NOTE: The missing element here is "praise or promise of sacrifice," but this feature is evident at the end of the lament in Psalm 7:17[H18] or in the midst of the lament in Psalm 27:6.		

Fig. 1.12. Psalm 6—A Psalm of Lament

Jesus prayed this psalm to God directly after his triumphal entry into Jerusalem, as his gaze became increasingly fixed on the path to death that he was about to tread. Drawing on Psalm 6:3–4[H4–5], he exclaimed, "Now is my soul troubled. And what shall I say? 'Father, save me from this hour'? But for this purpose I have come to this hour" (John 12:27). The anguish we hear reminds us of similar groanings he expressed in Gethsemane (Matt. 26:38–39, 44), associated with the lament in Psalm 42:5[H6]), and of his climactic cry from the cross, "My God, my God, why have you forsaken me?" (Matt. 27:46), which quotes from the lament in Psalm 22:1[H2]. Earlier in his ministry, Jesus drew from Psalm 6:8[H9] to describe what he will say to the wicked at the final judgment (Matt. 7:23). He also asserts that the world's hating him without cause was fulfilling exactly what had been predicted in the lament of Psalm 35:19 (John 15:25). In the first temple cleansing, he explains the distress of his soul by declaring, "Zeal for your house will consume me" (John 2:17), quoting from the lament in Psalm 69:9[H10].

Significantly, as "a disciple is not above his teacher, nor a servant above his master" (Matt. 10:24), anyone who wants to follow Christ must "deny himself and take up his cross and follow" him (16:24). "Through many tribulations we must enter the kingdom of God" (Acts 14:22). Thus, just as the king's journey through suffering becomes the journey of all finding refuge in him (Ps. 2:12), so, too, his prayers can become ours. Right after stressing that Christ suffered for God's sake and quoting the king's lament in Psalm 69:9[H10], "The reproaches of those who reproached you fell on me," Paul declares that "whatever was written in former days was written for our instruction, that through endurance and through the encouragement of the Scriptures we might have hope" (Rom. 15:3–4). While broadly speaking he means that all the Old Testament matters for Christians, most directly he means that the psalms of lament become the supplications of all who find refuge in Jesus. That is, the psalms that initially stood as the prayers of the Christ now become the songs of the saved. May we sing the laments in hope, confident that "those whom [God] foreknew he also predestined to be conformed to the image of his Son, in order that he might be the firstborn among many brothers" (Rom. 8:29; cf. Pss. 2:7; 22:22[H23]).

2. Psalms of Trust

Whereas laments focus on the problem, psalms of trust focus on the answer, but both are prayers grown out of a context of suffering. No special pattern is present in trust psalms, but all of them express confidence that God is both faithful and in charge.

The beloved Psalm 23 falls into this category. Placed after the lament of Psalm 22, which is loaded with predictions of Christ's suffering and exaltation (see "The Nature of Text Criticism and Psalm 22:16[H17]" in chapter 3) and which includes a vow to praise YHWH before his brothers for the divine rescue (22:22–24[H23–25]), we can read Psalm 23 first as Christ's testimony that YHWH is *his* Shepherd.[41] Then those of us who find refuge in him (2:12) can sing the same song of hope ourselves.

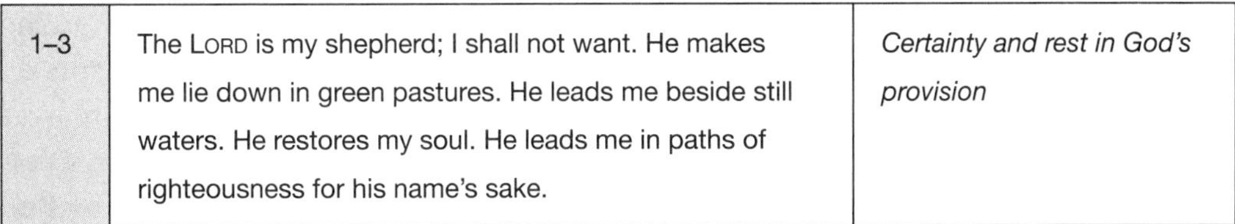

1–3	The LORD is my shepherd; I shall not want. He makes me lie down in green pastures. He leads me beside still waters. He restores my soul. He leads me in paths of righteousness for his name's sake.	*Certainty and rest in God's provision*

Fig. 1.13. Psalm 23—A Psalm of Trust

41. Douglas J. Green argues for the legitimacy of a messianic interpretation in "'The LORD Is Christ's Shepherd': Psalm 23 as Messianic Prophecy," in *Eyes to See, Ears to Hear: Essays in Memory of Alan Groves*, ed. Peter Enns, Douglas J. Green, and Michael B. Kelly (Phillipsburg, NJ: P&R Publishing, 2010), 33–46. Disappointingly, Green's approach separates the messianic reading of this psalm from its original historical context, claiming that David did not originally intend a messianic interpretation but that it is still legitimate in light of the way in which New Testament authors read the Psalms. In contrast, I want to stress that the messianic reading was indeed part of David's original historical intent, which also included the view that all finding refuge in the anointed king could in turn make his prayers their own; his words of trust become our words of trust. For an argument that Psalms 22–24 form a unit within the Psalter, see Nancy L. Declaissé-Walford, "An Intertextual Reading of Psalms 22, 23, and 24," in *The Book of Psalms: Composition and Reception*, ed. Peter W. Flint and Patrick D. Miller, VTSup 99 (Leiden: Brill, 2005), 139–52.

4–6	Even though I walk through the valley of the shadow of death, I will fear no evil, for you are with me; your rod and your staff, they comfort me. You prepare a table before me in the presence of my enemies; you anoint my head with oil; my cup overflows. Surely goodness and mercy shall follow me all the days of my life, and I shall dwell in the house of the LORD forever.	*Certainty and rest in God's protection*

Fig. 1.13. Psalm 23—A Psalm of Trust (cont.)

The New Testament draws on psalms of trust many times. One example is found in the account of Christ's death. Just before his final breath, Jesus drew verbatim from the declaration of trust in Psalm 31:5[H6], changing only the Greek future tense to present in order to stress that he was at that very moment fulfilling the king's vow from the psalm: "Father, into your hands I commit my spirit" (Luke 23:46).

Similarly, Luke notes that both Peter and Paul interpreted the testimony of trust in Psalm 16:8–11 as a direct prediction of Jesus' resurrection (Acts 2:25–32; 13:35–37). In order to clarify why "it was not possible" for the pangs of death to hold Jesus (Acts 2:24), Peter drew on the Greek version of Psalm 16:8–11 (= Ps. 15 LXX), saying, "David says *concerning him*, 'I saw the Lord always before me, for he is at my right hand that I may not be shaken; therefore my heart was glad, and my tongue rejoiced; my flesh also will dwell in hope. For you will not abandon my soul to Hades, or let your Holy One see corruption. You have made known to me the paths of life; you will make me full of gladness with your presence'" (Acts 2:25–28). At this, Peter then declares: "Brothers, I may say to you with confidence about the patriarch David that he both died and was buried, and his tomb is with us to this day. Being therefore a prophet, and knowing that God had sworn with an oath to him that he would set one of his descendants on his throne, he foresaw and spoke about the resurrection of the Christ, that he was not abandoned to Hades, nor did his flesh see corruption" (2:29–31). Peter says that David was a "prophet" who both "knew" of God's promise for an eternal kingdom and "foresaw" the resurrection of Christ (2:30–31; cf. 3:18, 24; 10:43). From 2 Samuel 7:12 we learn that David knew he would die, and the apostles stress that he "both died and was buried" (Acts 2:29) and that his body "saw corruption" (13:36). Thus, we cannot see the words of the king in Psalm 16 as referring to anything in David's life that perhaps in turn foreshadowed Christ's resurrection.[42] Rather, the apostles' exegesis of Psalm 16 led them to see it as a direct prediction.

42. A number of scholars hold this view, which we can tag as a *typological* reading of Psalm 16 (e.g., M. Rese, "Die Funktion der alttestamentlichen Zitate und Anspielungen in den Reden der Apostelgeschichte," in *Les Actes des Apôtres: Traditions, rédaction, théologie*, ed. J. Kremer et al., BETL 48 [Leuven: Leuven University Press, 1979], 76; Leonhard Goppelt, *Typos: The Typological Interpretation of the Old Testament in the New*, trans. Donald H. Madvig [Grand Rapids: Eerdmans, 1982], 122–23; James M. Hamilton Jr., personal correspondence). Yet we must ask with I. Howard Marshall, "Is it appropriate to use the term 'typological' of a statement that was not true of

3. Psalms of Thanksgiving (IMART)

a. Introduction of praise, addressed to God
b. Misery or trouble reported
c. Appeal for others to praise God
d. Rescue announced
e. Testimony of vow or praise

Gratitude to God should abound in the hearts of those he has saved, and we should often express our thanks in words. As figure 1.14 shows, the words of the king in Psalm 30 provide a good example of the pattern found in many thanksgiving psalms.

1	I will extol you, O LORD,	Introduction of praise, addressed to God
	for you have drawn me up and have not let my foes rejoice over me.	Misery or trouble reported
4	Sing praises to the LORD, O you his saints, and give thanks to his holy name.	Appeal for others to praise God
11–12	You have turned for me my mourning into dancing; you have loosed my sackcloth and clothed me with gladness, that my glory may sing your praise and not be silent.	Rescue announced
	O LORD, I will give thanks to you forever!	Testimony of vow or praise

Fig. 1.14. Psalm 30—A Psalm of Thanksgiving

The New Testament includes multiple links to psalms of thanksgiving. One of the favorites is Psalm 34. In 34:8[H9] the king appeals for his listeners to "taste and see that the LORD is good," and Peter says that if his readers have heeded this command, they should mature in godliness (1 Peter 2:2–3). Later, in order to motivate his audience to pursue obtaining blessing from God and to call them not to repay evil for evil, Peter draws on Psalm 34:12–16[H13–17]: "Whoever desires to love life and see good days, let him keep his tongue from evil and his lips from speaking deceit; let him turn away from evil and do good; let him seek peace and pursue it. For the eyes of the Lord are on

the 'type' himself?" (I. Howard Marshall, "Acts," in *Commentary on the New Testament Use of the Old Testament*, ed. G. K. Beale and D. A. Carson [Grand Rapids: Baker Academic, 2007], 538). As we will develop in chapter 10, *typology* refers to correspondences that God intended between earlier and later persons, events, or institutions, by which the earlier types are, at least in hindsight, recognized to predict the later antitypes. See especially Richard Davidson, *Typology in Scripture: A Study of Hermeneutical TUPOS Structures*, Andrews University Seminary Doctoral Dissertation Series 2 (Berrien Springs, MI: Andrews University, 1981).

the righteous, and his ears are open to their prayer. But the face of the Lord is against those who do evil" (1 Peter 3:9–12). Finally, in Psalm 34:20[H21] the king declares God to be his deliverer who has kept all his bones so that not one was broken—a prophecy that John declares is fulfilled in the way Jesus was crucified (John 19:36).

Another thanksgiving psalm that the New Testament authors frequently quote is Psalm 118, which shows up in many different contexts. For example, in order to clarify why Christians should be content, and as an inference from God's promise in Joshua 1:5 that the Lord will never leave or forsake us, the author of Hebrews quotes Psalm 118:6, declaring, "So we can confidently say, 'The Lord is my helper; I will not fear; what can man do to me?'" (Heb. 13:6). What was true for the psalmist continues to be true for all finding refuge in God. Drawing on Psalm 118:22–23, Jesus identified himself as "the stone that the builders rejected" who in turn would "become the cornerstone," and he said that all who spurned him would be crushed (Matt. 21:42–44). Peter stressed the same idea from Psalm 118 and added that the church is built on Christ, the cornerstone (1 Peter 2:4–8). In Psalm 118:25–26 the psalmist pleads for God to "save" and then declares blessed the one through whom YHWH will bring deliverance. These are the verses that the crowd drew from at Christ's triumphal entry, singing, "Hosanna to the Son of David! Blessed is he who comes in the name of the Lord! Hosanna in the highest!" (Matt. 21:9). Jesus also quoted them when he declared before his death that Jerusalem would not see him again until the city declared, "Blessed is he who comes in the name of the Lord" (23:39).

4. Psalms of Praise (SRS)

a. Summons to praise
b. Reason for praise
c. Summons to praise repeated

The shortest of all psalms, Psalm 117, provides a helpful overview of the basic parts of a hymn of praise.

1	Praise the LORD, all nations! Extol him, all peoples!	Summons to praise
2	For great is his steadfast love toward us, and the faithfulness of the LORD endures forever.	Reason for praise
	Praise the LORD!	Summons to praise repeated

Fig. 1.15. Psalm 117—A Psalm of Praise

The Lord is worthy of highest praise "from the heavens" (Ps. 148:1) unto "the earth" (148:7)—from the angels to the luminaries (148:2–3), from the mountaintops to the cedar trees (148:9), from "everything that has breath" (150:6). His anointed king (103:1–2), his people (118:2), and indeed all the nations of the earth (117:1; 148:11–12) must "praise him for his mighty deeds" and "according to his excellent greatness" (150:2).

The Psalter witnesses a progressive movement from shadow to sunlight, from tribulation to triumph, and from lament to praise (fig. 1.16). Psalms 144 and 145 end the book's main body by celebrating YHWH as the steadfast love and fortress of his king (144:1–2, 9–11) and as the one who graciously and mercifully reigns over all (145:1, 8–9). Each of the initial four books ends with a doxology, calling people to look Godward (41:13[H14]; 72:18–19; 89:52[H53]; 106:48). And then the fifth book concludes the whole Psalter with five psalms that begin and end with the declaration, "Praise the Lord!" (146:1, 10; 147:1, 20; 148:1, 14; 149:1, 9; 150:1, 6).

	Book I	Book II	Book III	Book IV	Book V
Psalms of Praise	9	9	0	9	13
Psalms of Lament	19	7	7	5	4

Fig. 1.16. From Lament to Praise in the Psalter[43]

Building on the praises in Psalm 8, we recognize that the Christ to whom children cried for deliverance at the triumphal entry (Matt. 21:16; cf. Ps. 8:2[H3]), the Son of Man who became human, is the one under whom God has subjected all things (Eph. 1:22; cf. Ps. 8:4–6[H5–7]). Still, we wait for this subjection to become fully visible (1 Cor. 15:27; Heb. 2:6–8). With the early church (Acts 4:24), we put our hope in the one "who made heaven and earth, the sea, and all that is in them" (Ps. 146:6). Today we sing and kneel to the Lord (95:1, 6), nurturing believing hearts that treasure God's promises in order that we might enter the rest that will never end (95:7–11; Heb. 3:7–11; 4:3, 5–10). We trust not simply the giver of bread but the very one who is the Bread of Life (Ps. 105:40; John 6:31–33).

The ultimate goal of the Psalms was to generate praise to YHWH for his saving and satisfying reign through his anointed king. The Psalms supplied messianic music to the saints of old—music designed to nurture hope for the coming kingdom. As the church of Jesus Christ, living in the days of fulfillment (Luke 24:44), may we "let the word of Christ" dwell in our hearts as we sing "psalms and hymns and spiritual songs, with thankfulness . . . to God" (Col. 3:16; cf. Eph. 5:19). In doing so, we will engage in the task for which we were designed—to glorify the one from whom, through whom, and to whom are all things (Rom. 11:36). "Praise the Lord!"

43. Prepared by Jason S. DeRouchie and John C. Crutchfield. Taken from Jason S. DeRouchie, ed., *What the Old Testament Authors Really Cared About*, 348. Used with permission.

Guidelines for Interpreting the Psalms

The move from exegesis to theology is ultimately to result in doxology, and the book of Psalms provides us a perfect springboard to praising God. What are some principles to help guide proper interpretation of the Psalms?

1. Recall the problems and promises of salvation history and the placement of the Psalms within the flow of Jesus' Bible.

The book of Psalms marks a significant shift in the flow of Jesus' Bible. Unlike the Prophets, which focus on Israel's sin and the covenant curses and give only minor (though always evident) attention to the promise of restoration blessing, each book of the Writings is dominated by a message of kingdom hope in an all-wise, all-sovereign God, who is faithful to his own, even in the midst of pain. Jeremiah-Malachi recalled the new covenant promises and clearly anticipated the new creational kingdom for which Israel longed. The final three Prophets of the Twelve were also part of the initial restoration (Haggai, Zechariah, Malachi). Nevertheless, none of the Prophets claimed that the new creational kingdom had yet arrived in history. Instead, even after the initial return to the land, the Jews continued in rebellion (Hag. 1:9; Zech. 1:2–6; Mal. 1:6) and did not experience either the inner transformation or the messianic king or kingdom that God had promised (see Ezek. 36:22–36; 37:21–28). Into this darkness, the prelude of Ruth affirms the kingdom of YHWH's redeeming grace through the line of David, and then Psalms proclaims hope for all who celebrate God's reign and find refuge in his Anointed Son. Psalms pushes the reader's hope forward, calling him to follow the anointed king on his journey from dirge to doxology and through tribulation unto triumph. The Lord's promises to David remained, and the eternal king and kingdom would come.

2. Remember the Psalter's overall structure, message, and flow.

The Psalter is made up of five books that move from lament to praise and nurture hope in the future fulfillment of God's kingdom promises, ultimately through his Christ.[44] *Book I* (Pss. 1–41) and *Book II* (Pss. 42–72) form a unit that begins (Ps. 2) and ends (Ps. 72) with a glorious vision of the coming king.[45] The two books together introduce in recurring cycles this king's journey through tribulation unto triumph. *Book III* (Pss. 73–89) then laments the disgraceful, broken state of the Davidic dynasty,

44. John C. Crutchfield, "The Redactional Agenda of the Book of Psalms," *HUCA* 74 (2003): 21–47.

45. So too David C. Mitchell, *The Message of the Psalter: An Eschatological Programme in the Book of Psalms*, JSOTSup 252 (Sheffield, UK: Sheffield Academic, 1997), 243–53.

but Psalm 89 supplies hope "that YHWH's covenant loyalty will reverse this deplorable condition."[46]

Book IV (Pss. 90–106) opens by stressing YHWH's sovereign reign and by recalling his past forgiveness in order to heighten hope that he can do it again. In contrast to some contemporary perspectives,[47] the focus on YHWH's kingship in Book IV does not stand as a rejection of the human, Davidic line, but rather aligns with the original vision of Psalm 2, in which YHWH and his anointed king reign together, the latter standing as the former's earthly representative.[48]

Book V (Pss. 107–150) then builds on this vision of sovereignty and includes a heightened number of Davidic psalms (Pss. 138–145) in order to give hope that God's kingdom promises will indeed come to pass through his Messiah.[49] With imagery akin to 1 Samuel 2:10, 35 and Zechariah 6:13, Psalm 110 finds YHWH vowing to David's "Lord" that he is "a priest forever after the order of Melchizedek" (110:1, 4). If God here promises to keep his less-prominent oath regarding the priesthood of Melchizedek, we must believe that he will also keep his well-known oath regarding the Davidic throne—an oath that Psalm 89 highlights three times (89:3–4, 35–36, 49[H4–5, 36–37, 50]). This fact is then reaffirmed in Psalm 132:11–18 and celebrated in the reaffirmation of both Davidic kingship and YHWH's kingship in Psalms 144–145.[50] While those finalizing the Psalter recognized the failure of the Davidic house to meet the complete vision of kingship that YHWH had promised, they did not lose hope in God's commitment to raise up a deliverer who would establish God's worldwide kingdom on earth.

From beginning to end, the Psalter focuses heavily on the hostility of mankind against YHWH and his anointed and on YHWH's final triumph through his righteous king for all finding refuge in him. The general perspective of the righteous and the wicked is laid out in Book I, where there is only one true "righteous one," the anointed of God (e.g., Pss. 5:12[H13]; 7:9[H10]; 14:5; 34:19, 21[H20, 22]; 37:12, 16, 25, 32). He is the "blessed man" (1:1), against whom stand various enemies both near and far

46. Michael K. Snearly, "The Return of the King: Book V as a Witness to Messianic Hope in the Psalter," in *The Psalms: Language for All Seasons of the Soul*, ed. Andrew J. Schmutzer and David M. Howard (Chicago: Moody Press, 2014), 210.

47. See especially Gerald H. Wilson, *The Editing of the Hebrew Psalter*, SBLDS 76 (Chico, CA: Scholars Press, 1985), 209–28, esp. 212–14; Wilson, "The Use of Royal Psalms at the 'Seams' of the Hebrew Psalter," *JSOT* 11, 35 (1986): 85–94; Wilson, "The Shape of the Book of Psalms," *Int* 46, 1 (1992): 129–42; Wilson, "Shaping the Psalter: A Consideration of Editorial Linkage in the Book of Psalms," in *The Shape and Shaping of the Psalter*, ed. J. Clinton McCann, JSOTSup 159 (Sheffield, UK: JSOT Press, 1997), 72–82; Wilson, "King, Messiah, and the Reign of God: Revisiting the Royal Psalms and the Shape of the Psalter," in *The Book of Psalms: Composition and Reception*, ed. Peter W. Flint and Patrick D. Miller, VTSup 99 (Leiden: Brill, 2005), 391–406.

48. David M. Howard Jr., *The Structure of Psalms 93–100*, UCSD Biblical and Judaic Studies 5 (Winona Lake, IN: Eisenbrauns, 1997), 200–207; Howard, "Divine and Human Kingship as Organizing Motifs in the Psalter," in *The Psalms: Language for All Seasons of the Soul*, ed. Andrew J. Schmutzer and David M. Howard (Chicago: Moody Press, 2014), 205–6; Snearly, "The Return of the King," 210.

49. See especially Snearly, "The Return of the King," 207–15; cf. John C. Crutchfield, *Psalms in Their Context: An Interpretation of Psalms 107–118*, Paternoster Biblical Monographs (Eugene, OR: Wipf & Stock, 2015).

50. So Howard, "Divine and Human Kingship as Organizing Motifs in the Psalter," 206.

(e.g., 2:1–2; 3:1; 5:8[H9]; 6:8[H9]; 7:1, 6, 9[H2, 7, 10]). Others are tagged as "blessed" and "righteous" (e.g., 1:5–6; 32:11; 33:1; 34:15[H16]; 37:17, 29, 39), but they are only so because they find refuge in the righteous *one* (2:12).[51] Apart from this anointed king, "there is none who does good, not even one" (14:3; 53:3[H4]; cf. Rom. 3:12). In the end, "affliction will slay the wicked, and those who hate the righteous [one] will be condemned" (Ps. 34:21[H22]). YHWH's royal Son (2:7) will "break them with a rod of iron" (2:9). Therefore, the evildoers "are in great terror," knowing that "God is with the generation of the righteous [one]," who himself finds refuge in the Lord (14:5–6). A proper reading of the Psalms requires that we keep in mind the progressive movement through tribulation unto triumph and that we seek to find deeper refuge in the king, whom we now know today as Jesus.

3. Keep the Christ central.

The words of the Psalter are either about Christ or by Christ.[52] In it we hear the prayers of the Christ and the songs of the saved. I say "Christ" for two reasons: (a) The Greek term Χριστός ("Christ") is the translation of the Hebrew term מָשִׁיחַ ("Messiah/Anointed One") in texts such as Psalm 2:2. This monarch is the principal human figure in the Psalms—both in suffering and in triumph.[53] (b) The Psalms portray this hoped-for royal figure as the ideal king and human who embodies the hopes of the world (see "Reading the Psalms as Messianic Music" above). Accordingly, salvation history identifies this Savior-deliverer as Jesus of Nazareth, and the New Testament tags him as "the Christ" in light of the way in which books such as the Psalms spoke of him (e.g., Acts 4:26 [ESV footnote]; cf. Matt. 1:1; 16:16). The various laments, thanksgivings, and praises in the Psalter are either about the anointed king or by the anointed king, and they also become the music of all finding refuge in him (Ps. 2:12).

The Old Testament explicitly tags many of its psalm writers as "seers" (1 Chron. 25:5; 2 Chron. 29:30; 35:15) who "prophesied" and whose words became the praises of Israel (1 Chron. 25:1–3). Accordingly, Jesus, the New Testament authors, and the Old Testament prophets all read the Psalms as predictions of the Messiah (see "Reading the Psalms as Messianic Music" and "The Variety of Psalm Subgenres" above). Also, David, the author of about half the psalms, was himself a "prophet" (Acts 2:30; cf. 2 Sam. 23:2) and was mindful both of his desperate state and that his hopes were in the one he called his "Lord" (Ps. 110:1; cf. Matt. 22:41–46).[54] Building on God's kingdom promise

51. To see the distinction between the "righteous [one]" and "righteous [ones]," track the shifts between the singular and plural forms of צַדִּיק ("righteous") in Psalms 34 and 37.

52. Futato, *Interpreting the Psalms*, 174.

53. For more on this idea, see Waltke, "A Canonical Process Approach to the Psalms," 11–12; Patrick D. Miller, "The Beginning of the Psalter," in *The Shape and Shaping of the Psalter*, ed. J. Clinton McCann Jr., Library of Hebrew Bible/Old Testament Studies (Sheffield, UK: Sheffield Academic, 2000), 83–92.

54. In Psalm 14:7, David pleads for God to let salvation come out of Zion, the abode of the anointed king (cf. 2:6), and he does so by alluding to Moses' promise of second exodus from exile associated with the latter days' new covenant: "When the LORD restores the fortunes of his people, let Jacob rejoice" (cf. Deut. 30:3). We see a similar perspective in David's song of thanks from 1 Chronicles 16:35: "Save us, O God of our salvation, and gather and

to David in 2 Samuel 7:12–14, Peter stressed how David himself consciously predicted Christ's victory over death: "Being . . . a prophet, and knowing that God had sworn with an oath to him that he would set one of his descendants on his throne, he foresaw and spoke about the resurrection of the Christ" (Acts 2:30–31; cf. 2 Sam. 23:1–7). In these words we see in action what Peter elsewhere identified—that the Old Testament prophets "searched and inquired carefully" regarding "what person or time the Spirit of Christ in them was indicating when he predicted the sufferings of Christ and the subsequent glories" (1 Peter 1:10–11). Where would they search but in their Scriptures? Peter also stressed that *all* the prophets from Moses forward—which would include David—spoke of the sufferings of the Christ and the mission that they would generate (Acts 3:18–24; 10:43; cf. Luke 24:44–47; Acts 26:22–23). Keep Christ in mind as you interpret the Psalms.

4. Read the Psalms as poetry.

Even a casual reader of Scripture can identify that the Psalter reads differently from historical narrative, such as Judges. The distinction is that psalms are poetry, and our English Bibles usually identify the difference by using poetic lines, which results in more white space on the page (compare the shape of Judges 4 and 5 in the ESV).

Traditionally, scholars have distinguished prose from poetry by identifying poetic "indicators." Wilfred Watson supplies nineteen such features, differentiating "broad indicators" and "structural indicators":[55]

a. *Broad indicators*: presence of established line forms,[56] ellipsis (gapping), unusual vocabulary, conciseness (terseness), unusual word order,[57] archaisms, use of meter, regularity and symmetry.
b. *Structural indicators*: parallelism, word pairs, chiastic patterns, envelope figure (inclusio), breakup of stereotyped phrases, repetition, gender-matched parallelism, tricolon, rhyme and other sound patterns, absence or rarity of prose elements.[58]

---

deliver us from among the nations, that we may give thanks to your holy name, and glory in your praise" (= Ps. 106:47–48). While David brought the nation of Israel to the height of its glory, he himself viewed the nation as already being under curse in desperate need of the future salvation that Moses promised.

55. Wilfred G. E. Watson, *Classical Hebrew Poetry: A Guide to Its Technique*, JSOTSup 26 (Sheffield, UK: JSOT Press, 1984), 46–54.

56. Michael Patrick O'Connor argues that the principle to identify Hebrew poetry is in neither meter nor parallelism but by seeing whether a text follows the constraints of a poetic line, having from 0 to 3 predicators (e.g., a finite verb), from 1 to 4 constituents (i.e., a grammatical phrase such as a verb, a noun, a prepositional phrase, a construct chain), and from 2 to 5 units (i.e., a word, though not including small particles such as כִּי ["since, because, that, when"] or אִם ["if"] or prepositions such as אֶל ["to"]) (*Hebrew Verse Structure*, 2nd ed. [Winona Lake, IN: Eisenbrauns, 1997]). For a brief summary and critique of his work, see Duane A. Garrett and Jason S. DeRouchie, *A Modern Grammar for Biblical Hebrew* (Nashville: Broadman & Holman, 2009), 340–42.

57. Poetic texts employ verb-initial clauses at a rate equal to non-verb-initial clauses, in which the linear as opposed to segmented nature of prose gives rise to its being dominated by verb-initial, default clauses. Furthermore, poetry regularly precedes a verb by two or more constituents, whereas prose rarely does. For more on this, see Jason S. DeRouchie, "Deuteronomy as Didactic Poetry? A Critique of D. L. Christensen's View," *JAAS* 10, 1 (2007): 1–13.

58. Comparatively infrequent in poetry, the definite article (הַ), the definite direct object marker (אֶת־), and the relative particle אֲשֶׁר occur in high concentrations in prose. See Francis I. Andersen and A. Dean Forbes,

Recognizably, all these elements show up with less frequency in prose,[59] so most scholars today treat the distinction between prose and poetry as "more one of degree than kind."[60] Framing the relationship this way allows for various literary and linguistic features to occur in prose while emphasizing that a predominance of them signals poetry.

Naturally, reading literature that is on a higher register of style requires careful reading to identify the various levels of artistry that the author used to convey his message and to effect response. The songwriters sought to move their audiences to worship, to draw their readers into the prayers and praises in personal ways. They use concrete words, vivid images, wordplay, and rhythm in order to help us feel lament, truth, thanksgiving, and praise. Read the Psalms as poetry.

5. Account for the psalm titles.

Of the 150 psalms, all but 34 of them have some form of title (i.e., superscription) that includes notes about their performance, type, author, purpose, or historical origin.[61] The only title with all these parts is Psalm 60, which opens: "To the choirmaster: according to Shushan Eduth. A miktam of David; for instruction; when he strove with Aram-Naharaim and with Aram-Zobah, and when Joab on his return struck down twelve thousand of Edom in the Valley of Salt." We can distinguish the various parts of the title as follows:

a. *Expanded performance instructions* (P): "To the choirmaster: according to Shushan Eduth"
b. *Type of psalm* (T): "A miktam"
c. *Author* (A): "Of David"
d. *Purpose* (Pu): "For instruction"
e. *Historical origin* (H): "When he strove with Aram-Naharaim and with Aram-Zobah, and when Joab on his return struck down twelve thousand of Edom in the Valley of Salt"

Figure 1.17 (on page 81) provides an overview of the patterns and attributed authorship of titles throughout the Psalms, with shifts between white and gray signaling movement

"'Prose Particle' Counts of the Hebrew Bible," in *The Word of the Lord Shall Go Forth: Festschrift for David Noel Freedman*, ed. Carol L. Meyers and Michael Patrick O'Connor, ASOR Special Volume Series 1 (Winona Lake, IN: Eisenbrauns, 1983), 165–83.

59. So James L. Kugel, *The Idea of Biblical Poetry: Parallelism and Its History* (New Haven, CT: Yale University Press, 1981; repr., Baltimore: Johns Hopkins University Press, 1998), 59–95, esp. 85–87, 94–95.

60. Sue E. Gillingham, *The Poems and Psalms of the Hebrew Bible*, Oxford Bible Series (Oxford: Oxford University Press, 1994), 36. For a helpful overview of the scholarly discussion on distinguishing prose and poetry, see J. Kenneth Kuntz, "Biblical Hebrew Poetry in Recent Research, Part I," *CurBS* 6 (1998): 55–57; Kuntz, "Biblical Hebrew Poetry in Recent Research, Part II," *CurBS* 7 (1999): 44–47.

61. Following comparative data from the ancient Near East, the pattern in Habakkuk 3, and internal clues within the book of Psalms itself, Bruce Waltke argues that we should actually divide the present psalm superscripts into superscripts and subscripts, with the fifty-five musical notations including "to the musical director/choirmaster" going with the psalms that precede. He believes the superscripts relate to a psalm's composition and the subscripts to its performance. See Bruce K. Waltke, "Superscripts, Postscripts, or Both," *JBL* 110, 4 (1991): 583–96.

	SG	Title	Author		SG	Title	Author		SG	Title	Author
1	W		Anonymous	51	L	PTAH	**David**	101	R	TA	**David**
2	R		Anonymous	52	U	PTAH	**David**	102	L	TPu	Anonymous
3	L	TAH	**David**	53	L	PTA	**David**	103	P	A	**David**
4	L	PTA	**David**	54	L	PTAH	**David**	104	P		Anonymous
5	L	PTA	**David**	55	L	PTA	**David**	105	P		Anonymous
6	L	PTA	**David**	56	L	PTAH	**David**	106	L		Anonymous
7	L	TAH	**David**	57	L	PTAH	**David**	107	Th		Anonymous
8	P	PA	**David**	58	L	PTA	**David**	108	L	TTA	**David**
9	M	PTA	**David**	59	L	PTAH	**David**	109	L	PTA	**David**
10	M		Anonymous	60	L	PTAPuH	**David**	110	R	TA	**David**
11	T	PA	**David**	61	L	PA	**David**	111	P		Anonymous
12	L	PTA	**David**	62	U	PTA	**David**	112	W		Anonymous
13	L	PTA	**David**	63	L	TAH	**David**	113	P		Anonymous
14	L	PA	**David**	64	L	PTA	**David**	114	P		Anonymous
15	Lit	TA	**David**	65	M	PTAT	**David**	115	U		Anonymous
16	T	TA	**David**	66	Th	PTT	Anonymous	116	Th		Anonymous
17	L	TA	**David**	67	U	PTT	Anonymous	117	P		Anonymous
18	R	PTAH	**David**	68	U	PTAT	**David**	118	Th		Anonymous
19	M	PTA	**David**	69	L	PA	**David**	119	M		Anonymous
20	R	PTA	**David**	70	L	PAPu	**David**	120	L	TPu	Anonymous
21	R	PTA	**David**	71	L		Anonymous	121	T	TPu	Anonymous
22	L	PTA	**David**	72	R	A	Solomon	122	P	TPuA	**David**
23	T	TA	**David**	73	W	TA	Asaph	123	L	TPu	Anonymous
24	Lit	TA	**David**	74	L	TA	Asaph	124	Th	TPuA	**David**
25	M	A	**David**	75	U	PTAT	Asaph	125	T	TPu	Anonymous
26	L	A	**David**	76	P	PTAT	Asaph	126	L	TPu	Anonymous
27	L	A	**David**	77	L	PTA	Asaph	127	W	TPuA	Solomon
28	L	A	**David**	78	H	TA	Asaph	128	W	TPu	Anonymous
29	P	TA	**David**	79	L	TA	Asaph	129	T	TPu	Anonymous
30	Th	TATH	**David**	80	L	PTAT	Asaph	130	L	TPu	Anonymous
31	M	PTA	**David**	81	U	PA	Asaph	131	T	TPuA	**David**
32	M	TA	**David**	82	L	TA	Asaph	132	R	TPu	Anonymous
33	P		Anonymous	83	L	TTA	Asaph	133	U	TPuA	**David**
34	M	AH	David	84	P	PTA	Sons of Korah	134	P	TPu	Anonymous
35	L	A	David	85	L	PTA	Sons of Korah	135	P		Anonymous
36	M	PA	David	86	L	TA	**David**	136	P		Anonymous
37	W	A	David	87	P	TAT	Sons of Korah	137	L		Anonymous
38	L	TAPu	David	88	L	TTAPTA	Sons of Korah*	138	Th	A	**David**
39	L	PTA	David	89	M	TA	Ethan the Ezrahite	139	U	PTA	**David**
40	M	PTA	David	90	L	TA	Moses	140	L	PTA	**David**
41	L	PTA	David	91	T		Anonymous	141	L	TA	**David**
42	L	PTA	Sons of Korah	92	Th	TTPu	Anonymous	142	L	TAHT	**David**
43	L		Anonymous	93	P		Anonymous	143	L	TA	**David**
44	L	PTA	Sons of Korah	94	L		Anonymous	144	R	A	**David**
45	R	PTAT	Sons of Korah	95	P		Anonymous	145	P	TPuA	**David**
46	P	PAPT	Sons of Korah	96	P		Anonymous	146	P		Anonymous
47	P	PTA	Sons of Korah	97	P		Anonymous	147	P		Anonymous
48	P	TTA	Sons of Korah	98	P	T	Anonymous	148	P		Anonymous
49	W	PTA	Sons of Korah	99	P		Anonymous	149	P		Anonymous
50	U	TA	Asaph	100	P	TPu	Anonymous	150	P		Anonymous

*Psalm 88 is also attributed to Heman the Ezrahite.

***KEY for Subgenre* (SG)**: "L" Lament; "T" Trust; "Th" Thanksgiving; "P" Praise; "R" Royal; "W" Wisdom; "Lit" Liturgy; "H" Historical; "M" Mixed; "U" Unclear.

Key for Title: "P" Performance: "To the choirmaster"; "T" Type: "A Psalm"; "A" Author: "of X [Proper Name]"; "Pu" Purpose; "H" Historical Context; **Bold**: Something distinct or expanded.

Fig. 1.17. Patterns and Authorship in Psalm Titles

from one book to the next. Also included is a list of subgenres (SG) associated with each psalm. In the title pattern, elements marked in **bold** signal that there is something distinct or expanded from the most basic pattern of "To the choirmaster. A psalm of X [proper name]."

Nearly all scholars affirm the antiquity of the psalm titles. We know that the musical terms in the titles were ancient enough to have already fallen out of disuse by the third century B.C., for those who translated the Old Testament into Greek (i.e., the Septuagint) were already struggling to understand their meaning (a problem that we still have today). With this, we should not be surprised by David's explicit connection with nearly half the psalms, for the Old Testament regularly points to him as Israel's foremost music leader (e.g., 1 Sam. 16:14–23; 2 Sam. 22; Ps. 18; 2 Sam. 23:1–7; 1 Chron. 6:31; 15:16; 16:7; 25:1; 2 Chron. 29:30; Ezra 3:10; Neh. 12:24–47), and we know that the nation was singing music associated with him at a very early time (2 Chron. 29:30; Ps. 72:20; cf. 1 Chron. 16:7–37). Those in the New Testament period were clearly aware of the psalm titles, and both Jesus and Peter built arguments that hinged on Davidic authorship of certain psalms (Matt. 22:41–46 with Ps. 110:1; Acts 2:25–29 with Ps. 16:8–11).[62] In light of the above, we have good reason to trust the authenticity of the titles as part of Scripture, believing that they are accurate in their claims to both authorship and history.[63]

According to the titles, David authored each of the fourteen psalms that include a historical note. Of these, most show signs of lament (except Pss. 18, 30, 34), and all but Psalm 30 are either expressions of thanks or praise after deliverance (Pss. 18, 34) or cries of distress while running from enemies, experiencing betrayal, engaging in battle, or confessing sin (Pss. 3, 7, 51, 52, 54, 56, 57, 59, 60, 63, 142). God thus led David on his own journey of suffering in order to create a typological context from which to predict the ultimate sufferings of the Christ and the subsequent glories (1 Peter 1:11). The titles ground David's messianic predictions in history and help us to see David's life as pointing to the Christ's.

The psalm titles place the seventy-three Davidic psalms mostly in Books I, II, and V.[64] The higher frequency of Davidic psalms at the beginning and end allows the whole Psalter to bear a Davidic-messianic stamp. While the sins of the Davidic line called the kingdom hope into question, the editor(s) of the Psalter stressed from beginning to end that God would deliver Israel's king and those associated with him and that he would preserve both the king and his kingdom forever.

6. Use the Psalms' subgenres to enhance personal and corporate worship.

In the two previous sections, I gave overviews of a number of subgenres in the Psalms (e.g., psalms of lament, thanksgiving, praise). This kind of analysis has a number of benefits.

62. In two instances the New Testament authors tag as Davidic psalms those that are not signaled as such in the Hebrew text (Acts 4:25–26 with Ps. 2:1–2; Heb. 4:7 with Ps. 95:7–8), though the LXX marks both as psalms of David.

63. For an overview of the question with an argument for the superscriptions' authenticity and accuracy, see D. A. Brueggemann, "Psalms 4: Titles," *DOT:WPW* 614–15; Gordon J. Wenham, *The Psalter Reclaimed: Praying and Praising with the Psalms* (Wheaton, IL: Crossway, 2013), 86–90.

64. The Septuagint (LXX) expands the list of Davidic psalms by fourteen; see Brueggemann, "Psalms 4: Titles," 614.

a. Knowing the patterns of the subgenres helps our interpretive expectations.

Knowing the general patterns of the various categories of psalms can help us have proper expectations in our interpretation. It can also signal important departures from the norm, which can mark something significant.

b. Considering the subgenres helps us recognize Christ's humanness and helps motivate our perseverance in holiness.

The Psalms portray the anointed king as expressing every emotion that we ourselves feel and as finding vindication from God: anger and rage, fear and sorrow, faith amid danger, peace, gratitude, praise. The New Testament discloses that the Christ was "made like his brothers in every respect, so that he might become a merciful and faithful high priest in the service of God" (Heb. 2:17). He was "in every respect . . . tempted as we are, yet without sin" (Heb. 4:15; cf. Phil. 2:6–8). In the Psalms we get a unique taste of the inner passions and prayers of the anointed king. We hear the anguish of his laments, the joys of his thanksgivings, and the pleasures of his praise. And through these various expressions, we find help for our own journey through tribulation unto triumph. The different types of psalms help us in various ways to look "to Jesus" and to "consider him who endured from sinners such hostility against himself, so that you may not grow weary or fainthearted" (Heb. 12:2–3).

c. The different categories of psalms give words to our prayers for every season of life.

Sometimes we don't know how to pray. Knowing which psalms are laments, thanksgivings, or praises can help us in seasons of pain and pleasure to find words to express our hearts to God, whether individually or corporately. May the church increasingly become a people who sings the psalms as a means of identifying with Christ in his sufferings and victory.

While the benefits of subgenre analysis are real, I offer two important cautions. First, subgenre analysis tends to isolate the psalms from one another, losing any sense of canonical continuity within the Psalter as a whole. As noted above, the book of Psalms evidences intentionality in its structure and flow, and we can miss the beauty of this forest if we look only at the trees in isolation. Second, some psalms do not fit into single subgenre categories but appear to be more fluid mixtures of different subgenres. Heartfelt words to God so often combine praise and petition, thanksgiving and plea that we must be careful not to force a given psalm into a preconceived mold.

Proverbs

General Characteristics of Biblical Proverbs

The nature of this book allows me to touch on only a sample of the various Old Testament genres. The last that we are going to consider are the proverbs. A ***proverb*** is a succinct, memorable saying in common use that states a general truth or piece of advice. Cover over the right-hand column in figure 1.18, and go through each English proverb one by one to see how many you can complete. Tally your total on a piece of paper.

Lightning never strikes twice . . .	in the same place.
A chain is no stronger . . .	than its weakest link.
A leopard cannot . . .	change its spots.
A penny saved . . .	is a penny earned.
The bigger they are . . .	the harder they fall.
Actions speak . . .	louder than words.
No news . . .	is good news.
Don't bite off more . . .	than you can chew.
Don't change horses . . .	midstream.
Don't count your chickens . . .	before they're hatched.
Don't cry . . .	over spilled milk.
Don't judge a book . . .	by its cover.
Don't put all your eggs . . .	in one basket.
Don't put the cart . . .	before the horse.
Don't throw the baby . . .	out with the bathwater.

Fig. 1.18. Some English Proverbs

Every cloud has . . .	a silver lining.
Give someone an inch . . .	and they'll take a mile.
If a thing is worth doing . . .	it's worth doing well.
If at first you don't succeed . . .	try, try again.
People who live in glass houses . . .	shouldn't throw stones.

Fig. 1.18. Some English Proverbs (cont.)

How many of the proverbs did you know? If you got 16–20 correct, we will call you a "proverbial genius." If 11–15, you are "proverbially bright." If 6–10, you are struggling, and we will call you "proverbially dull." If you got only 0–5 right, you are definitely "proverbially challenged."

A number of features are common to all the proverbs listed in figure 1.18, and many of these features are also present in Hebrew proverbs, such as those found in Proverbs 10–31.

1. Proverbs are memorable.

In order to remember well, we need information that is (a) *understandable* in our language, (b) *manageable* enough to grasp, and (c) *rehearsable* enough to restate. Most proverbs are pithy, memorable, and poetic. Douglas Stuart uses the following helpful examples to draw attention to the unforgettable nature of proverbs:[65]

a. *"Look before you leap"* versus "In advance of committing yourself to a course of action, consider your circumstances and options."
b. *"A stitch in time saves nine"* versus "There are certain corrective measures for minor problems that, when taken early on in a course of action, forestall major problems from arising."

The point here is clear. Proverbs are powerful because they are memorable.

2. Many proverbs are designed for specific occasions.

Proverbs are regularly situation-specific. They often present contradictory perspectives, with each proverb being correct in certain circumstances. Note the pairs of proverbs in figure 1.19 on the next page.

65. Fee, *How to Read the Bible for All Its Worth*, 241.

1a. "Birds of a feather flock together."	1b. "Opposites attract."
2a. "Too many cooks spoil the broth."	2b. "Two heads are better than one."
3a. "He who hesitates is lost."	3b. "Look before you leap."
4a. "A bird in the hand is worth two in the bush."	4b. "A man's reach should exceed his grasp."
Prov. 26:4. Answer not a fool according to his folly, lest you be like him yourself.	Prov. 26:5. Answer a fool according to his folly, lest he be wise in his own eyes.

Fig. 1.19. Contradictory Proverbs

Proverbs supply the right word for the right time. Proverbs 25:11 declares, "A word fitly spoken is like apples of gold in a setting of silver." Yet we read in Proverbs 26:9, "Like a thorn that goes up into the hand of a drunkard is a proverb in the mouth of fools." As seen in figure 1.19, proverbs can contradict each other, but this is only because some are limited in their use and designed for particular occasions. When we neglect the intended situation for a proverb, we might use it in hurtful, unhelpful ways. But when we use a proverb rightly and wisely, we will give life to those around us. So it is that "death and life are in the power of the tongue, and those who love it will eat its fruits" (Prov. 18:21).

3. Many proverbs address ultimate and not immediate truths.

Growing out of Israel's personal relationship with the living God (Gen. 18:24–25; Job 28:28; Prov. 11:20; 15:33) and the covenantal context of blessing and curse (Lev. 26; Deut. 28), one of the principles that guides Israel's wisdom thinking is retribution theology—what some have termed the *act-consequence nexus*. Notice the examples in figure 1.20.

1.	Job 4:8	As I have seen, those who plow iniquity and sow trouble reap the same.
2.	Prov. 22:8–9	Whoever sows injustice will reap calamity, and the rod of his fury will fail. Whoever has a bountiful eye will be blessed, for he shares his bread with the poor.
3.	Prov. 26:27	Whoever digs a pit will fall into it, and a stone will come back on him who starts it rolling.

Fig. 1.20. Retribution Theology in Israel's Wisdom Tradition

4.	Prov. 28:10	Whoever misleads the upright into an evil way will fall into his own pit, but the blameless will have a goodly inheritance.
5.	Prov. 28:18	Whoever walks in integrity will be delivered, but he who is crooked in his ways will suddenly fall.

Fig. 1.20. Retribution Theology in Israel's Wisdom Tradition (cont.)

All of these texts highlight that in God's world, "you reap what you sow." Nevertheless, numerous other proverbs identify that this harvester's principle has many exceptions *in this life*. For example, the "better . . . than" proverbs clearly show that a simple act-consequence pattern does not always hold up in the present: "Better is a little with righteousness than great revenues with injustice" (Prov. 16:8). "It is better to be of a lowly spirit with the poor than to divide the spoil with the proud" (16:19). A number of other proverbs simply declare explicitly that in this cursed age, the righteous do not always prosper and the wicked sometimes do: "A gracious woman gets honor, and violent men get riches" (11:16). "The fallow ground of the poor would yield much food, but it is swept away through injustice" (13:23). The "less fitting" and "number" proverbs declare the same thing—this life does not always work out according to the act-consequence nexus: "It is not fitting for a fool to live in luxury, much less for a slave to rule over princes" (19:10). "Under three things the earth trembles; under four it cannot bear up: a slave when he becomes king, and a fool when he is filled with food; an unloved woman when she gets a husband, and a maidservant when she displaces her mistress" (30:21–23).[66]

Consider now the biblical proverbs in figure 1:21. While all offer truth claims, some of these truths (##1, 3, 6) are not apparent now but will be realized only in the future when God overcomes all evil and makes all things right.

1.	Prov. 10:27	The fear of the LORD prolongs life, but the years of the wicked will be short.
2.	Prov. 11:20	Those of crooked heart are an abomination to the LORD, but those of blameless ways are his delight.
3.	Prov. 13:21	Disaster pursues sinners, but the righteous are rewarded with good.
4.	Prov. 16:1	The plans of the heart belong to man, but the answer of the tongue is from the LORD.

Fig. 1.21. Sample Proverbs to Consider the Significance of Eschatology

66. Both the Preacher in Ecclesiastes 8:14 and the sons of Korah in Psalm 44:17–19 equally lament how retribution theology is more complex than it first appears.

5.	Prov. 16:4	The LORD has made everything for its purpose, even the wicked for the day of trouble.
6.	Prov. 16:31	Gray hair is a crown of glory; it is gained in a righteous life.
7.	Prov. 19:21	Many are the plans in the mind of a man, but it is the purpose of the LORD that will stand.
8.	Prov. 21:30	No wisdom, no understanding, no counsel can avail against the LORD.

Fig. 1.21. Sample Proverbs to Consider the Significance of Eschatology (cont.)

Proverbs that predict a certain outcome are not necessarily absolute promises *for the present age*, but they do express absolute, ultimate—even eschatological—truths that time will prove unless God intervenes for good or ill. Douglas Stuart offers the following three examples, which I have adapted for my purposes.[67]

a. Proverbs 15:25. "The LORD tears down the house of the proud but maintains the widow's boundaries."

Life and Scripture testify that there are arrogant people whose houses still stand and widows whom greedy creditors abuse or defraud. Accordingly, we read in Job 24:2–3, "Some move landmarks; they seize flocks and pasture them. They drive away the donkey of the fatherless; they take the widow's ox for a pledge." Similarly, Jesus declared in Mark 12:40, "[The religious leaders] devour widows' houses and for a pretense make long prayers. They will receive the greater condemnation." The point of Proverbs 15:25 is *not* to declare a truth that always stands in the present but rather to assert a more ultimate principle: "God opposes the proud and cares for the needy, and he will eventually make all things right." This principle is absolute, but in the present age there are many situations that counter it (see Heb. 2:8). We rest in hope, however, knowing that God's disposition is toward the broken (Deut. 10:18; James 1:27) and that God will make all things right.

b. Proverbs 22:26–27. "Be not one of those who give pledges, who put up security for debts. If you have nothing with which to pay, why should your bed be taken from under you?"

Does this passage teach that we should *never* buy a house on mortgage (a secure debt)? Will all credit-card debt automatically result in God's taking away all your possessions—including your bed? No, the proverb teaches a single principle that is always true: "Debts should be undertaken cautiously because foreclosure is very painful."

67. Fee and Stuart, *How to Read the Bible for All Its Worth*, 243–45.

c. Proverbs 29:12. "If a ruler listens to falsehood, all his officials will be wicked."

Does this proverb guarantee that a government official has no choice but to become corrupt if his superior (the king, president, prime minister, tribal chief, etc.) heeds the voices of liars? No, it simply instructs that "the ruler who insists on hearing the truth will help keep a nation's leadership honest."

In conclusion, our present lives are filled with many ironies and enigmas (see "הֶ֫בֶל ['Vanity'?] in Ecclesiastes" in chapter 7). Nevertheless, we must still heed the call to walk in wisdom, because God, who is always just and ever constant, will ultimately punish the wicked and uphold the righteous: "Be assured, an evil person will not go unpunished, but the offspring of the righteous will be delivered" (Prov. 11:21). "Fret not yourself because of evildoers, and be not envious of the wicked, for the evil man has no future; the lamp of the wicked will be put out" (24:19–20). "But these men lie in wait for their own blood; they set an ambush for their own lives. Such are the ways of everyone who is greedy for unjust gain; it takes away the life of its possessors. . . . For the simple are killed by their turning away, and the complacency of fools destroys them; but whoever listens to me will dwell secure and will be at ease, without dread of disaster" (1:18–19, 32–33).[68]

Reconsidering Proverbs 22:6

Now I want to relook at a proverb familiar to all parents—Proverbs 22:6. Regularly in my pastoral ministry and parenting I have encountered confusion regarding the meaning of this well-known verse. The whole verse has two lines, the first stating a command and the second detailing the consequence. Those who don't know Hebrew may want to jump over this section, but I encourage all to keep reading.

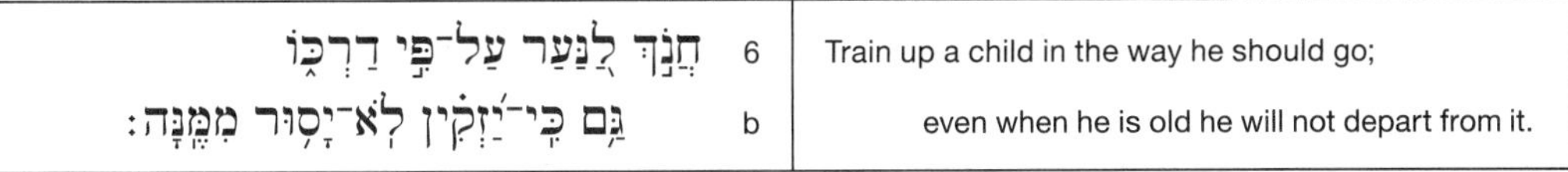

חֲנֹ֣ךְ לַ֭נַּעַר עַל־פִּ֣י דַרְכּ֑וֹ	6	Train up a child in the way he should go;
גַּ֥ם כִּֽי־יַ֝זְקִ֗ין לֹֽא־יָס֥וּר מִמֶּֽנָּה׃	b	even when he is old he will not depart from it.

Fig. 1.22. Proverbs 22:6 in the MT and ESV

68. This same eschatological hope is set forth in numerous places through the Writings (e.g., Job 19:25; 30:23; Pss. 5:11–12[H12–13]; 21:3, 6[H4, 7]; 24:5; 29:11; 67:1, 6–7[H2, 7–8]; 28:8–9; 72:17; 73:24–26; 109:26–31; 112:1–2; 115:12–15; 119:20–21; 129:8; 132:13–18; 133:3; 134:3; 147:13; Eccl. 2:11–13; 8:12–13). For a similar eschatological approach to the truths in proverbs, see Bruce K. Waltke, *The Book of Proverbs: Chapters 1–15*, NICOT (Grand Rapids: Eerdmans, 2004), 107–9.

1. Questions Arising from the Traditional Rendering

If you know Hebrew and read the text closely, two important observations become apparent as you read the traditional rendering seen in the ESV. First, in its three other occurrences, the rare verb חנך that the ESV renders "train" refers to "dedicating" houses, whether of a man (Deut. 20:5) or of God (1 Kings 8:63; 2 Chron. 7:5). This suggests that the initial imperative is calling for parents to actively devote or commit their youth to a certain, perhaps even religious, course of action—intentionally and formally pointing their child toward magnifying the greatness, worth, sufficiency, and saving power of God.[69] The point here is that "train up" may be too weak and misses the potential element of consecration to religious and moral direction.

Certainly "dedicating" a child would include the common ceremony of commitment that many parents engage in at the birth of their children. Yet most of Proverbs addresses the parenting of teenagers, suggesting that the act of dedicating in Proverbs 22:6 is focused on an intentional, sustained, God-dependent shepherding of our children's hearts as they grow into adulthood—one in which the children themselves are aware of the parents' trajectory-setting intentions. This is not a passive calling for dads and moms.

Second, the ESV's "in the way he should go" is a very idiomatic way of capturing the Hebrew "according to the dictates of [lit., the mouth of] his way" (עַל־פִּי דַרְכּוֹ).[70] We could therefore translate the command line of the proverb, "Dedicate a youth according to the dictates of his way," or, perhaps more commonly, "Dedicate your child according to what his way demands."

2. Assessing the "Way" of a Child

So what does עַל־פִּי דַרְכּוֹ ("according to the dictates of his way") most likely mean? Significantly, in wisdom literature such as Proverbs there are only two "ways"—the way of wisdom and life and the way of folly and death. The previous verse declares, "Thorns and snares are in the *way* of the crooked; whoever guards his soul will keep far from them" (Prov. 22:5). Similarly, Proverbs 11:5 says, "The righteousness of the blameless keeps his *way* straight, but the wicked falls by his own wickedness." Consider also Proverbs 14:2, which reads, "Whoever walks in uprightness fears the LORD, but he who is devious in his *ways* despises him." And again, Proverbs 16:17 says, "The highway of the upright turns aside from evil; whoever guards his *way* preserves his life."

Within Proverbs, the moral content of one's way depends on the doer—whether God (Prov. 8:22), the wise (11:5; 14:8; 16:7), humans in general (16:9; 20:24), or fools (19:3).[71] Significantly, a "youth's way" is often negative. First, when left to themselves, the "young" lack judgment and have hearts filled with foolishness: "And I have seen

69. So Bruce K. Waltke, *The Book of Proverbs: Chapters 15–31*, NICOT (Grand Rapids: Eerdmans, 2005), 204.

70. The fact that עַל־פִּי is a Hebrew idiom meaning "according to the dictates of" is clear in texts such as Genesis 41:40; 43:7; Exodus 34:7; and Deuteronomy 17:6, 10–11 (ibid., 205n62). Cf. *HALOT*, 2:826, s.v. עַל.

71. So Waltke, *The Book of Proverbs: Chapters 15–31*, 205.

among the simple, I have perceived among the youths, a young man lacking sense" (7:7). "Folly is bound up in the heart of a child, but the rod of discipline drives it far from him" (22:15). Second, without discipline, the young bring disgrace on their parents: "The rod and reproof give wisdom, but a child left to himself brings shame to his mother" (29:15). Out of this context, parents are thus exhorted to discipline their children and to instruct them in wisdom: "Discipline your son, for there is hope; do not set your heart on putting him to death" (19:18; cf. 1:1, 4; 29:15). In Proverbs the "way" of a child seems more negative than positive; it is the way without wisdom.

3. Cultivating and Shaping Potential

These texts could lead one to read Proverbs 22:6 as a sarcastic or ironic command that warns parents of the result of not establishing standards and boundaries for their children. A similar ironic command comes in Proverbs 19:27, which also begins with an imperative: "Cease to hear instruction, my son, and you will stray from the words of knowledge." If you read Proverbs 22:6 in a similar way, the principle would be, "Let a boy do what he wants, and he will become a self-willed adult incapable of change! Raise him in accordance with his wayward heart, and he will stay wayward."[72] I once read the proverb in this way.

But I now question this approach for three reasons.[73] First, the sarcastic reading requires a more passive approach to parenting that does not account for the verb חֲנֹךְ ("dedicate"), which expresses conscious intention. Certainly we as parents are always training our kids, even through our passivity. By failing to lead them to repentance before the Sovereign God, we teach them that they are fine to continue living as self-made kings and queens rather than servants. By failing to instruct them in God's commandments, we teach them that God's Word is *not* the highest authority in our lives. By failing to set boundaries, we instruct them that we really do not care whether they do good or ill. Nevertheless, this type of passive training is *not* what seems to be expressed in the imperative "Dedicate!" Rather, the sage is here calling parents to intentionally commit or orient the moral and religious trajectories of their youth.

Second, while the youth's way is naturally negative *when left to himself,* Proverbs 22:6 pictures not a self-willed individual but one who is benefiting from *the intentional discipline and instruction of his parents* ("Dedicate!"). With this, the idiomatic "according to the dictates of his way" seems most naturally to express *the way that ought to be.* That is, every youth's future is filled with possibility, and we as parents must recognize this and direct our child's path toward God. This verse is about trajectories and potential, which suggests that the ESV's "the way he should go," while missing specificity, dynamically catches the point of the text.

72. For some interpreting Proverbs 22:6 in this way, see Richard J. Clifford, *Proverbs*, OTL (Louisville: Westminster John Knox, 1999), 197; Gordon P. Hugenberger, "Train Up a Child," in *Basics of Biblical Hebrew: Grammar*, by Gary D. Pratico and Miles V. Van Pelt, 2nd ed. (Grand Rapids: Zondervan, 2007), 162–63; Douglas Stuart, *Old Testament Exegesis: A Handbook for Students and Pastors*, 4th ed. (Louisville: Westminster John Knox, 2009), 41–42.

73. I am grateful to Bruce Waltke for pushing me to reconsider my understanding of this verse; I have followed many of his exegetical decisions on this passage.

Third, the consequence of heeding the command is that "even when he grows old, he will not turn from it." In Proverbs "the wise, not fools, are crowned with the gray hair of age (20:29),"[74] so the proverb seems to anticipate a trajectory *toward wisdom*, not foolishness.

The consequence statement in Proverbs 22:6 implies that the parents' intentional moral and religious shaping early on will have a permanent effect on their child for good. This statement is not a hard-and-fast promise to parents, however, for the rest of the book makes clear that the power of the youth's future depends not only on the parents' guidance but also very much on the choices that the child himself makes. The immediately preceding verse implies that the youth must guard his soul from those who are crooked (Prov. 22:5). He could choose to follow the wicked unto death (2:12–19), or he could heed the wisdom of his parents and choose the good paths of the righteous unto life (22:1–11, 20).

4. A Proverb for Parents and Children

While Proverbs 22:6 is framed as instruction to parents, the book as a whole gives guidance to the young (1:4). This fact suggests that Proverbs 22:6 was actually intended to call straying youth back toward the right way. If you are a son or daughter who had parents who worked hard to set positive moral and religious trajectories for your life (though imperfectly), you must not counter this trajectory by making foolish decisions today.

Proverbs 22:6 sets out a principle that time will prove true unless God intervenes for good or ill. As a parent, I rejoice in the directions given me in God's Word—the Lord calls me and my wife to actively and intentionally dedicate our children to represent, reflect, and resemble the glory of God in the face of Christ.

Yet Proverbs 22:6 also reminds me how much I and my children fail, so I also rejoice in the power of the gospel to curb my own faults and the hardest of my children's hearts. God in Christ makes those dead in sin alive (Eph. 2:4–5), forgives all who confess (1 John 1:9), and overcomes the old creation with the new (2 Cor. 5:17).[75]

A Final Note on Biblical Proverbs

We have found numerous proverbs from all around the ancient world, but none of these call for the fear of YHWH. What distinguishes biblical wisdom from all the rest

74. Waltke, *The Book of Proverbs: Chapters 15–31*, 205.

75. For more on this proverb, see Ted Hilderbrandt, "Proverbs 22:6a: Train Up a Child?," *GTJ* 9, 1 (1988): 3–19; Peter J. Gentry, "Equipping the Generation: Raising Children, the Christian Way," *JDFM* 2, 2 (2012): 96–109.

is its affirmation that YHWH alone orders the universe, defines value, and clarifies right and wrong. The fear of the Lord provides the basis for wisdom because it aligns one with right order and provides the only proper disposition by which to live God's way. "The fear of the LORD is the beginning of wisdom, and the knowledge of the Holy One is insight. For by me your days will be multiplied, and years will be added to your life" (Prov. 9:10; cf. 1:7).

Throughout the Old Testament, God called people to fear him (e.g., Ex. 20:20; Deut. 10:12), but very few did, and the result was destruction. I find hope in the fact that Jeremiah predicted that in the new covenant God would supply the fear of the Lord by which we work out our salvation (Phil. 2:12). Hear the Word of the Lord in Jeremiah 32:40: "I will make with them an everlasting covenant, that I will not turn away from doing good to them. And I will put the fear of me in their hearts, that they may not turn from me." In this text God is promising to help every new covenant believer walk in the ways of wisdom.

Finally, biblical proverbs find their culmination in Christ, the one who is wisdom for us. As Paul says in 1 Corinthians 1:30, "Christ Jesus . . . became to us wisdom from God, righteousness and sanctification and redemption" (cf. 1:24). He is the ultimate one to whom Proverbs 30:4 speaks: "Who has ascended to heaven and come down? Who has gathered the wind in his fists? Who has wrapped up the waters in a garment? Who has established all the ends of the earth? What is his name, and *what is his son's name*? Surely you know!" The first name requested is most certainly *YHWH*, the one from whom wisdom comes (Job 28:23; Prov. 8:22; Eccl. 12:11). As for his "son's name," *son* in the book most commonly designates a member of the royal family (Prov. 1:1, 8; 4:1–9), who was to heed his father's teaching in order to align with the Deuteronomic ideal for kingship (Deut. 17:18–20). Thus, God's royal and wise "son" refers first to the imperfect Davidic offspring, but each of their lives served as a marker of hope for the more ultimate, perfect son of David (2 Sam. 7:14, 16; Ps. 2:7)—the one whom we now know as Jesus, the embodiment of wisdom. James tells us that for those in Christ, when we lack wisdom, all we have to do is ask, and God will give generously without reproach (James 1:5).

Key Words and Concepts

Genre and genre analysis
TaNaK
Principles of criticism, analogy, and correlation
Prophet
Oracle
Oracles of indictment, instruction, warning/punishment, and hope/salvation
Apodictic vs. casuistic laws
Criminal, civil, family, cultic/ceremonial, and compassion laws
Royal psalms
Psalms of lament, trust, thanksgiving, and praise
Proverb

Questions for Further Reflection

1. Describe the construction of Jesus' Bible in its threefold structure. How does each part contribute to the whole message of the Old Testament?
2. How should we think of the Old Testament's similarities to and differences from other ancient writings of the day?
3. How much is an account's historicity related to genre?
4. What is the problem with denying the Bible's historicity yet still claiming that the Bible bears a meaningful, authoritative message?
5. How should biblical interpreters rework the principles of criticism, analogy, and correlation for a theistic worldview?
6. What is the difference between *foretelling* and *forthtelling* in biblical prophecy?
7. How do the four types of prophetic speech relate to the Mosaic covenant? Working from figure 1.6, identify the different curse types and restoration blessing types apparent in Jeremiah 16:4, 14–15.
8. Which of the interpretive fallacies do you see yourself most prone to? Elaborate on the danger if we affirm these fallacies.
9. "The psalms that initially stood as the prayers of the Christ now become the songs of the saved." Explain what this means.
10. What are three characteristics of biblical proverbs?

Resources for Further Study

General

Eissfeldt, Otto. Part 1 in *The Old Testament: An Introduction*. New York: Harper & Row, 1965.

★ Fee, Gordon D., and Douglas Stuart. *How to Read the Bible for All Its Worth*. 4th ed. Grand Rapids: Zondervan, 2014.

House, Paul R., ed. *Beyond Form Criticism: Essays on Old Testament Literary Criticism*. SBTS 2. Winona Lake, IN: Eisenbrauns, 1992.

InterVarsity Press dictionaries on the Old Testament:

- Alexander, T. Desmond, and David W. Baker, eds. *Dictionary of the Old Testament: Pentateuch*. Downers Grove, IL: InterVarsity Press, 2003.
- Arnold, Bill T., and H. G. M. Williamson, eds. *Dictionary of the Old Testament: Historical Books*. Downers Grove, IL: InterVarsity Press, 2005.
- Boda, Mark J., and J. Gordon McConville, eds. *Dictionary of the Old Testament: Prophets*. Downers Grove, IL: InterVarsity Press, 2012.
- Longman, Tremper, III, and Peter Enns, eds. *Dictionary of the Old Testament: Wisdom, Poetry, and Writings*. Downers Grove, IL: InterVarsity Press, 2008.

Kaiser, Walter C., Jr., and Moisés Silva. *Introduction to Biblical Hermeneutics: The Search for Meaning*. 2nd ed. Grand Rapids: Zondervan, 2007.

Merrill, Eugene H., Mark F. Rooker, and Michael A. Grisanti. *The World and the Word: An Introduction to the Old Testament*. Nashville: Broadman & Holman, 2011.

★ Plummer, Robert L. *40 Questions about Interpreting the Bible*. 40 Questions. Grand Rapids: Kregel, 2010.

Ryken, Leland. *How to Read the Bible as Literature*. Grand Rapids: Zondervan, 1984.

———. *The Literature of the Bible*. Grand Rapids: Zondervan, 1974.

Ryken, Leland, and Tremper Longman III, eds. *A Complete Literary Guide to the Bible*. 2nd ed. Grand Rapids: Zondervan, 1993.

Sandy, D. Brent, and Ronald L. Giese, eds. *Cracking Old Testament Codes: A Guide to Interpreting Literary Genres of the Old Testament*. Nashville: Broadman & Holman, 1995.

Stein, Robert H. *A Basic Guide to Interpreting the Bible: Playing by the Rules*. 2nd ed. Grand Rapids: Baker Academic, 2011.

Narrative

Alter, Robert. *The Art of Biblical Narrative*. 2nd ed. New York: Basic Books, 2011.

Block, Daniel I. "Tell Me the Old, Old Story: Preaching the Message of Old Testament Narrative." In *Giving the Sense: Understanding and Using Old Testament Historical Texts: Essays in Honor of Eugene Merrill*, edited by David M. Howard and Michael A. Grisanti, 409–38. Grand Rapids: Kregel, 2003.

✪ Chisholm, Robert B., Jr. *Interpreting the Historical Books: An Exegetical Handbook*. Handbooks for Old Testament Exegesis 2. Grand Rapids: Kregel, 2006.

Fokkelmann, J. P. *Reading Biblical Narrative: An Introductory Guide*. Louisville: Westminster John Knox, 2000.

Hoffmeier, James K., and Dennis R. Magary, eds. *Do Historical Matters Matter to Faith? A Critical Appraisal of Modern and Postmodern Approaches to Scripture*. Wheaton, IL: Crossway, 2012.

Long, V. Philips. *The Art of Biblical History*. Foundations of Biblical Interpretation. Grand Rapids: Zondervan, 1994.

Millard, A. R., James K. Hoffmeier, and David W. Baker, eds. *Faith, Tradition, and History: Old Testament Historiography in Its Near Eastern Context*. Winona Lake, IN: Eisenbrauns, 1994.

Pratt, Richard L., Jr. *He Gave Us Stories: The Bible Student's Guide to Interpreting Old Testament Narratives*. Phillipsburg, NJ: P&R Publishing, 1993.

Satterthwaite, Philip E. *A Guide to the Historical Books*. Exploring the Old Testament 2. Downers Grove, IL: InterVarsity Press, 2012.

Sternberg, Meir. *The Poetics of Biblical Narrative: Ideological Literature and the Drama of Reading*. Indiana Studies in Biblical Literature. Bloomington, IN: Indiana University Press, 1985.

Prophecy and Law

Alexander, T. Desmond. *From Paradise to the Promised Land: An Introduction to the Pentateuch*. Grand Rapids: Baker Academic, 2012.

Baker, David W. "Israelite Prophets and Prophecy." In *The Face of Old Testament Studies: A Survey of Contemporary Approaches*, edited by David W. Baker and Bill T. Arnold, 266–94. Grand Rapids: Baker Academic, 2004.

Bandy, Alan S., and Bejamin L. Merkle. *Understanding Prophecy: A Biblical-Theological Approach*. Grand Rapids: Kregel, 2015.

Gentry, Peter J. *How to Read and Understand the Biblical Prophets*. Wheaton, IL: Crossway, 2017.

Gowan, Donald E. *Theology of the Prophetic Books: The Death and Resurrection of Israel*. Louisville: Westminster John Knox, 1998.

Hays, J. Daniel. *The Message of the Prophets: A Survey of the Prophetic and Apocalyptic Books of the Old Testament*. Grand Rapids: Zondervan, 2010.

McConville, J. G. *A Guide to the Prophets*. Exploring the Old Testament 4. Downers Grove, IL: InterVarsity Press, 2002.

Oswalt, John N. "Recent Studies in Old Testament Apocalyptic." In *The Face of Old Testament Studies: A Survey of Contemporary Approaches*, edited by David W. Baker and Bill T. Arnold, 369–90. Grand Rapids: Baker Academic, 2004.

Schnittjer, Gary Edward. *The Torah Story: An Apprenticeship on the Pentateuch*. Grand Rapids: Zondervan, 2006.

Schreiner, Thomas R. *40 Questions about Christians and Biblical Law*. 40 Questions. Grand Rapids: Kregel, 2010.

✪ Smith, Gary V. *Interpreting the Prophetic Books: An Exegetical Handbook*. Handbooks for Old Testament Exegesis. Grand Rapids: Kregel, 2014.

VanGemeren, Willem A. *Interpreting the Prophetic Word: An Introduction to the Prophetic Literature of the Old Testament*. Grand Rapids: Zondervan, 1996.

✪ Vogt, Peter T. *Interpreting the Pentateuch: An Exegetical Handbook*. Handbooks for Old Testament Exegesis. Grand Rapids: Kregel, 2009.

Wenham, Gordon J. *A Guide to the Pentateuch*. Exploring the Old Testament 1. Downers Grove, IL: InterVarsity Press, 2003.

Psalms and Proverbs

Alter, Robert. *The Art of Biblical Poetry*. 2nd ed. New York: Basic Books, 2011.

Anderson, Bernhard W., and Steven Bishop. *Out of the Depths: The Psalms Speak for Us Today*. 3rd ed. Louisville: Westminster John Knox, 2000.

Berlin, Adele. *The Dynamics of Biblical Parallelism*. 2nd ed. Grand Rapids: Eerdmans, 2009.

Bullock, C. Hassell. *Encountering the Book of Psalms: A Literary and Theological Introduction*. Grand Rapids: Baker Academic, 2004.

Estes, Daniel J. *Handbook on the Wisdom Books and Psalms*. Grand Rapids: Baker Academic, 2010.

Fokkelmann, J. P. *Reading Biblical Poetry: An Introductory Guide*. Louisville: Westminster John Knox, 2001.

✪ Futato, Mark D. *Interpreting the Psalms: An Exegetical Handbook*. Handbooks for Old Testament Exegesis. Grand Rapids: Kregel, 2007.

Howard, David M., Jr. "Recent Trends in Psalms Study." In *The Face of Old Testament Studies: A Survey of Contemporary Approaches*, edited by David W. Baker and Bill T. Arnold, 329–68. Grand Rapids: Baker Academic, 2004.

★ Kelby, Tom. *Psalms 1–19: A Preacher's Guide*. Webster, WI: Hands to the Plow, Inc., 2015.

Kugel, James L. *The Idea of Biblical Poetry: Parallelism and Its History*. New Haven, CT: Yale University Press, 1981; repr., Baltimore: Johns Hopkins University Press, 1998.

Longman, Tremper, III. *How to Read Proverbs*. Downers Grove, IL: InterVarsity Press, 2002.

———. *How to Read the Psalms*. Downers Grove, IL: InterVarsity Press, 1988.

Lucas, Ernest C. *A Guide to the Psalms and Wisdom Literature*. Exploring the Old Testament 3. Downers Grove, IL: InterVarsity Press, 2003.

Lunn, Nicholas P. *Word-Order Variation in Biblical Hebrew Poetry: Differentiating Pragmatics and Poetics*. Paternoster Biblical Monographs. Eugene, OR: Wipf & Stock, 2006.

O'Connor, Michael Patrick. *Hebrew Verse Structure*. 2nd ed. Winona Lake, IN: Eisenbrauns, 1997.

Waltke, Bruce K., and David Diewert. "Wisdom Literature." In *The Face of Old Testament Studies: A Survey of Contemporary Approaches*, edited by David W. Baker and Bill T. Arnold, 295–328. Grand Rapids: Baker Academic, 2004.

2

LITERARY UNITS AND TEXT HIERARCHY

Goal: Determine the limits and basic structure of the passage.

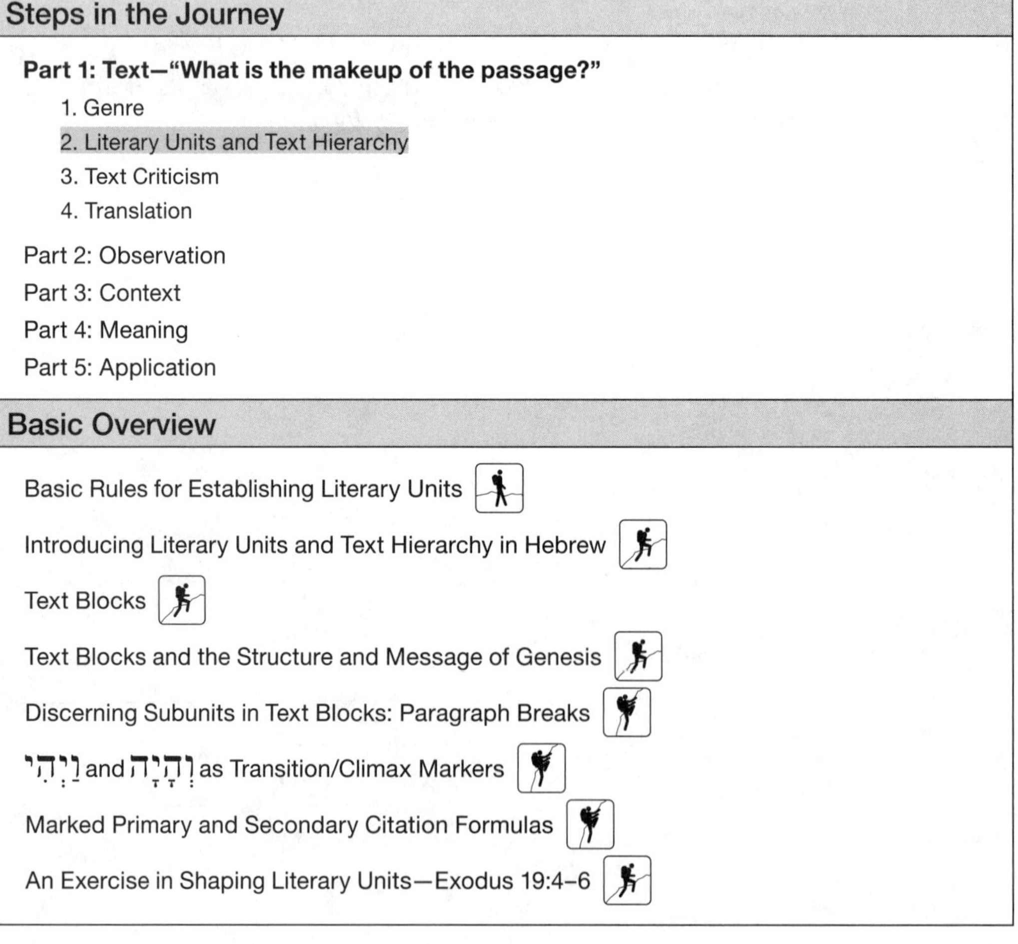

Steps in the Journey

Part 1: Text—"What is the makeup of the passage?"

1. Genre
2. Literary Units and Text Hierarchy
3. Text Criticism
4. Translation

Part 2: Observation

Part 3: Context

Part 4: Meaning

Part 5: Application

Basic Overview

Basic Rules for Establishing Literary Units

Introducing Literary Units and Text Hierarchy in Hebrew

Text Blocks

Text Blocks and the Structure and Message of Genesis

Discerning Subunits in Text Blocks: Paragraph Breaks

וַיְהִי and וְהָיָה as Transition/Climax Markers

Marked Primary and Secondary Citation Formulas

An Exercise in Shaping Literary Units—Exodus 19:4–6

Fig. 2.1. Trail Guide to Chapter 2

Basic Rules for Establishing Literary Units

After genre, the next step in your exegesis is to determine the limits of the passage that you are studying. This could be a quotation, a paragraph, a story, a song, or even an entire book. The process of establishing ***literary units*** is not random, for the biblical authors wrote with purpose, logic, and order, creating groupings and hierarchies of thought to guide understanding. As a biblical interpreter, consider whether there is a clear beginning and end to your passage. Are there clues in the content, the grammar, or both that clarify a passage's boundaries? The first section of this chapter offers some basic guidelines for establishing literary units, and then the remaining sections detail distinct ways that biblical Hebrew aids this task.

1. Don't automatically follow an English translation's verse and chapter divisions.

The chapter and verse numbers in our Bibles help us to find a given passage quickly. But they were not part of the original biblical text, and at times the divisions are misleading. For example, the narrative of the creation week stretches from Genesis 1:1 to 2:3, and then 2:4 contains the first of Genesis's ten *toledoth* formulae: "These are the generations of," each of which introduces a distinct literary unit. A proper wrestling with the preface to Genesis will cross the boundary of chapter 1 and include 2:1–3. Jewish scribes probably began to separate verses during the age of the Talmud (ca. A.D. 135–500), but the actual numbering of verses did not occur until the sixteenth century. Also, it wasn't until around the 1200s when the Roman Catholic Stephen Langton (A.D. 1150–1228) first added the chapter divisions. The point is this: Don't assume that the verse and chapter divisions in our modern translations are accurate guides to text boundaries. You need to carefully assess on your own where a passage begins and ends.

2. Remember that some multivolume works in our English Bibles were single books in Jesus' Bible.

Originally the Israelite seers, sages, and singers wrote the Old Testament with consonants only; ancient Hebrews verbalized the vowels but did not write them. This allowed them to write even big books such as 1–2 Samuel, 1–2 Kings, and 1–2 Chronicles on single scrolls. When the Jews translated the Old Testament into Greek in the third to second centuries B.C., however, they included vowels, so books doubled in size, and the longer books required more than one scroll to reproduce. Whereas 1–2 Corinthians in the New Testament are two different Pauline letters, 1–2 Chronicles in the Old Testament is a single book, and we must read it accordingly. So when wrestling with literary units in books such as Samuel, Kings, Chronicles, and even Ezra-Nehemiah (which is a single book in the Hebrew Old Testament), remember that they were all originally single volumes. Thus, literary units could cross "book" boundaries.

3. Look for recognizable beginning and ending markers.

In English, we signal sections with headings and identify paragraphs by indenting. We mark off speeches by quotation marks, and we introduce stories with phrases such as "Once upon a time . . . ." These are all literary features that mark the onset of new thought units. They're like road signs in our communication that proclaim that something new is coming.

The biblical authors used many similar features to guide their listeners' understanding of a text's structure and message. David A. Dorsey helpfully lists a number of the beginning and ending markers we find in the Old Testament. Here is a sampling of his observations:[1]

a. Beginning Markers

- *Title* (e.g., "A prayer of Habakkuk the prophet, according to Shegionoth," Hab. 3:1)
- *Introductory formulae* (e.g., "These are the generations of . . . ," Gen. 2:4; 5:1; 6:9; etc.; "And the people of Israel did what was evil in the sight of the LORD," Judg. 3:7, 12; 4:1; etc.)
- *Common beginning words or phrases* (e.g., "Thus says the LORD," Amos 1:3; "Hear!," Deut. 6:4; "Woe!," Zeph. 3:1; "And now," Deut. 4:1; "Behold," Zeph. 3:19)
- *Vocative address* (e.g., "O LORD," Ps. 8:1)
- *Rhetorical questions* (e.g., "Why do the nations rage and the peoples plot in vain?," Ps. 2:1)
- *Shifts in time* (e.g., "When Abraham was ninety-nine years old," Gen. 17:1)
- *Shifts in place* (e.g., "And the people of Israel . . . came into the wilderness of Zin," Num. 20:1)
- *Shifts in characters or speakers* (e.g., "Then Eliphaz the Temanite answered and said," Job 4:1)
- *Shifts in topic or theme* (e.g., "Comfort, comfort my people, says your God," Isa. 40:1)
- *Shifts in genre* (e.g., from narrative to genealogy in Genesis 11:10)
- *Shifts from poetry to prose or vice versa* (e.g., "In the fourteenth year of King Hezekiah" in Isaiah 36:1 after the poetry of Isaiah 35)

1. David A. Dorsey, *The Literary Structure of the Old Testament: A Commentary on Genesis-Malachi* (Grand Rapids: Baker, 1999), 22–23.

b. Ending Markers

- *Concluding formulae* (e.g., "And there was evening and there was morning," Gen. 1:5, 8, 19, etc.)
- *Poetic refrains* (e.g., "Yet you did not return to me," Amos 4:6, 8, 9, etc.)
- *Summary statements* (e.g., "This is the law of the burnt offering, of the grain offering, of the sin offering . . . , which the LORD commanded Moses," Lev. 7:37–38)
- *Conclusions* (e.g., "And the LORD gave them rest on every side," Josh. 21:43)

4. Treat literary units as wholes.

Whole *texts*, not just isolated words or clauses, supply the natural framework for verbal communication. While a text could be one clause (e.g., "YHWH is a consuming fire") or even a single word ("Run!"), usually a text contains a sequence of clauses, whether short (an answer to a question) or long (a book).

Texts themselves often divide into discrete parts or self-contained literary packages, and biblical interpreters need to work with these whole units of thought. We need to consider some of the ways in which the biblical authors signaled these literary units in their surface structure and then consider special rules associated with different genres.

a. Patterns of Similarity

A literary unit commonly distinguishes itself from others by its similar content and form. As for content, we can identify literary units by noting similar time period (e.g., the time before the fall, Gen. 2:4–25), similar location (e.g., Israel at Mount Sinai, Ex. 19:1–Num. 10:10), similar characters (e.g., the judgeship of Samson, Judg. 13:1–16:31), and similar topics or themes (e.g., the tabernacle-building instructions, Ex. 25:1–31:18). Regarding form, literary units often contain similar poetic devices (e.g., the alphabetic acrostic in Psalm 119) and similar genre (e.g., the song at the sea in Exodus 15:1–18).

b. Special Rules for Different Genres

The issue of genre demands special comment, for every genre has its own patterns for shaping literary units. For example, in *historical narrative*, we need to deal with ***scenes*** in light of ***episodes***. If we look only at a scene, we will most likely miss the point of the passage. Consider for the moment the structure of some common TV series. Shows such as *24* and *Elementary* have twenty-four episodes in a single season, and each episode may have a dozen or more different scenes. Within a single episode, each scene contributes to the overall plot of the week, and then, to a greater or lesser extent, each week's episode contributes to the plot of the season or show. Now, just as you would struggle to grasp the point of an individual scene apart from the overall episode, so, too, we will struggle to grasp the point of a biblical scene without reading it in light of its overall episode.

Genesis 39 is a good example. Casual readers of Scripture too often treat the story of "Joseph and Potiphar's Wife" as an episode, when actually it is a scene. As a scene, the narrative may simply seem to be a charge to flee sexual temptation. Certainly this is an important lesson from the story, but we cannot stop here, for this view fails to clarify why the chapter is framed with four statements that "the LORD was with Joseph." He was with Joseph when he entered Egypt as a slave (39:2); he was with Joseph as he served in Potiphar's house (39:3); he was with Joseph when Potiphar's wife unjustly accused him of sexual misconduct and had him thrown into prison (39:21); and he was with Joseph during his extended incarceration (39:23). "The LORD was with Joseph"—the repetition of this clause four times helps identify the limits of the episode and clarifies that the scene in Potiphar's house supplies an example of the type of person with whom God remains. Sexual purity is a vital expression of Godwardness worth emulating, but the episode is less about Joseph than it is about God. The Lord remains with those who consider pleasing him to be a greater prize than pleasing worldly passions.

In *prophetic sermons*, such as those found in Deuteronomy or Isaiah, paragraphs and oracles take the place of scenes and episodes. Does your paragraph contribute to the primary exhortation? Or is it part of the motivation, whether through historical reflection, promise, or prediction? The function of your text may require you to broaden the boundaries of your interpretive focus in order to properly grasp a full literary unit.

For example, very often in English Bibles Deuteronomy 5 is titled "The Ten Commandments." A careful look at the chapter, however, shows that Moses retells God's thunderous words from Mount Sinai in order to describe how the Lord appointed him as covenant mediator (Deut. 5:2–31). The whole history lesson on the giving of the Ten Commandments and the appointment of Moses then provides the reason why the new generation (postwilderness) must heed Moses' voice (5:1, 32–33). Moses is God's mouthpiece, and when the prophet speaks, God is speaking. If you don't account for the context, you may easily miss the main point.

Similarly, in *the poetry of the Psalms*, you should ideally study an entire poem and not just a single stanza (i.e., a poetic paragraph). When this is impractical (as could happen when trying to tackle a huge poem such as Psalm 119), you must deal not simply with poetic lines but with stanzas. Then you need to read those stanzas in light of the whole poem. In Psalm 1, the ESV translators distinguished three stanzas, as is evidenced by the spacing. In Psalm 2, they saw four. Your own exegesis may force you to disagree with the stanza breaks that others have proposed. Regardless, you need to be aware that verses work together less like strings of pearls and more like interwoven bracelets with a pattern, texture, and color greater than any one part. You must address verses within their immediate literary context and not in isolation.

5. Check your decision against modern translations and, if possible, the standard Hebrew text.

Bible translators use indentation to signal paragraph breaks and to distinguish literary units. The editors of the standard editions of our Hebrew Bibles make similar decisions, and it's helpful to compare our personal assessments against theirs. At times there is a level of subjectivity regarding literary units, but if you decide to start or end your passage where no editor or translator has, then it is your responsibility to argue fully for your decision.

So in summary, as you consider a text's literary units:

- Don't automatically trust English translations' verse and chapter divisions;
- Remember that some multivolume works in our English Bibles were single books in Jesus' Bible;
- Look for recognizable beginning and ending markers;
- Treat literary units as wholes; and
- Check your decision against modern translations and, if possible, the standard Hebrew text.

The next sections in this chapter are specifically intended for those who have taken at least two semesters of biblical Hebrew. If you haven't done this, you will still find some gems for biblical interpretation in what follows, or you can jump ahead to chapter 3.

Introducing Literary Units and Text Hierarchy in Hebrew

Along with surface elements such as content and literary form, biblical Hebrew uses a number of linguistic features to clarify where literary units or subunits begin and end. The rest of this chapter will highlight some of these.

1. The Hierarchy of Clauses

Every clause in Scripture fits within a relative hierarchy of prominence in relation to other clauses and its context. I represent the level of hierarchy through indentation, which helps to track the passage's thought flow (column A). Clauses that are indented support preceding higher-level clauses or units. In other words, the less indented a clause is, the more primary it is to the text's main thrust. Indented material is by no means less important; indeed, the opposite is often true. But the indented material is supporting some higher-level thought, whether by restatement or distinct statement. I call the visual display of a passage's thought flow in this manner a ***text hierarchy***.

2. The Role of וְ and Asyndeton

In biblical Hebrew, the primary factor for determining a clause's hierarchy is the presence or absence of a connector at the beginning of the clause. The most common connector is וְ (usually rendered as the coordinate conjunction "and"), and it always identifies a bound relationship between elements of equal syntactic value (e.g., phrases to phrases, clauses to clauses, larger units to larger units). The presence of וְ assumes some link to a previous thought unit, but context and broader text features alone clarify whether the relationship between clauses or text units is one of coordination, result, purpose, or some other semantic value. The semantic value of the connector וְ is regularly not "and," but its presence always creates chains of clauses that we are to read together. In other words, a וְ clause carries on the text hierarchy at the same level as the clause to which it is connected, which may or may not be the immediately preceding clause.[2]

In contrast, when a clause is not fronted by any connector, it's called an *asyndetic* clause. In Hebrew, ***asyndeton*** (i.e., lack of any fronted connector) functions to mark disjunction, for a text's movement created by the presence of וְ clauses is suddenly interrupted, thus signaling either (1) a fresh beginning (e.g., the start of a new speech act) or (2) support by restatement or distinct statement (e.g., Deut. 5:2). When functioning to mark the latter, asyndetic clauses and the units that build from them usually clarify or explain something that precedes. In the figures that follow, I identify asyndeton with the sign for a null-set (= Ø). As you will see in the examples, when shaping a text's hierarchy in Hebrew, the interpreter places farther to the right all clauses that are more primary, whereas one indents to the left those that are more dependent or supportive.[3]

3. An Example from Deuteronomy 7:2–4

These features are illustrated in the example in figure 2.2.

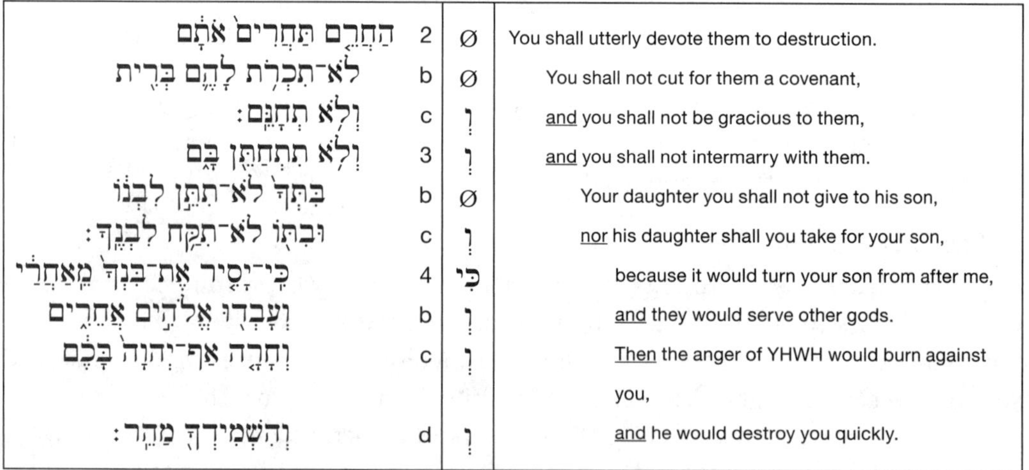

Hebrew	Verse	Connector	Translation
הַחֲרֵם תַּחֲרִים אֹתָם	2	Ø	You shall utterly devote them to destruction.
לֹא־תִכְרֹת לָהֶם בְּרִית	b	Ø	You shall not cut for them a covenant,
וְלֹא תְחָנֵּם׃	c	וְ	and you shall not be gracious to them,
וְלֹא תִתְחַתֵּן בָּם	3	וְ	and you shall not intermarry with them.
בִּתְּךָ לֹא־תִתֵּן לִבְנוֹ	b	Ø	Your daughter you shall not give to his son,
וּבִתּוֹ לֹא־תִקַּח לִבְנֶךָ׃	c	וְ	nor his daughter shall you take for your son,
כִּי־יָסִיר אֶת־בִּנְךָ מֵאַחֲרַי	4	כִּי	because it would turn your son from after me,
וְעָבְדוּ אֱלֹהִים אֲחֵרִים	b	וְ	and they would serve other gods.
וְחָרָה אַף־יְהוָה בָּכֶם	c	וְ	Then the anger of YHWH would burn against you,
וְהִשְׁמִידְךָ מַהֵר׃	d	וְ	and he would destroy you quickly.

Fig. 2.2. Text Hierarchy in Deuteronomy 7:2–4

2. For this basic approach to the connector וְ, see Richard C. Steiner, "Does the Biblical Hebrew Conjunction -וְ Have Many Meanings, One Meaning, or No Meaning at All?," *JBL* 119, 2 (2000): 249–67.

3. For more on this role of וְ and asyndeton in biblical Hebrew, see Stephen G. Dempster, *Linguistic Features of Hebrew Narrative: A Discourse Analysis of Narrative from the Classical Period* (Ph.D. diss., University of Toronto, 1985), 40–41; Jason S. DeRouchie, *A Call to Covenant Love: Text-Grammar and Literary Structure in Deuteronomy 5–11*, Gorgias Dissertations 30/Biblical Studies 2 (Piscataway, NJ: Gorgias, 2007), 107–32. From a cross-linguistic perspective, Stephen H. Levinsohn observes that in the nonnarrative texts of the New Testament, asyndeton functions in comparable ways (*Discourse Features of New Testament Greek: A Coursebook on the Information Structure of New Testament Greek*, 2nd ed. [Dallas: SIL International, 2000], § 7.2).

Notice how the hierarchy of clauses changes where there is asyndeton (2b, 3b), and notice also how a subordinate conjunction such as כִּי ("because") (4a) signals support and therefore also requires indentation. In this example, the first asyndetic clause in 2a marks a fresh beginning (it's actually the main clause following a brief temporal introduction that precedes). Then the asyndetic clauses in 2b and 3b each initiate a unit that explains its preceding clause, making each subset of clauses more dependent. Also, notice how every וְ (gloss "and") clause stands linked to the clause that precedes, building on the semantic force and function of the source clause. So for example, the logical ground initiated in verse 4a continues on through 4b–d, with each clause adding to the reason or basis. Laying out the clauses in this way allows us to determine the boundaries of the text, along with its various subunits.

Now let's reconsider the table row by row. The primary call of this text is "You shall utterly devote them to destruction" in 2a. The asyndeton and content in 2b signals that the unit that follows explains what precedes, and the two clauses fronted with וְ in 2c–3a continue the thought. By this means the initial call is unpacked negatively in three ways: utter desolation prohibits making covenants with the Canaanites, being gracious to them, or intermarrying with them (2b–3a). With the mention of intermarriage in 3a, 3bc then further details this specific prohibition, and again an asyndetic clause in 3b signals more explanation. The pair of clauses in 3bc is then followed by a כִּי ("because") clause in 4a, which is joined with three other clauses in 4b–d, all of which together ground the prohibition.

Text Blocks

What we have learned thus far has prepared us for an important concept known as a *text block*. A text block is a chain of clauses that we are to read together. This unit of discourse starts with either an asyndetic (conjunctionless) clause or a formally marked subordinate clause and continues with a succession of clauses joined by וְ (gloss "and"). An asyndetic or subordinate clause is like a train engine that can stand alone but that is often accompanied by a host of cars (i.e., clauses conjoined by וְ). Text blocks can be made up of only a single clause, but very often they extend for multiple clauses, paragraphs, or even chapters of biblical text. The main point to grasp here is this: When we see a וְ at the head of a clause, we must determine to what clause or larger text unit it is linked.

In the example from Deuteronomy 7:2–4, we find several text blocks. For now, just consider 7:4. The grounding conjunction כִּי ("because") introduces a four-clause text block that supplies the reason why interfaith marriage is prohibited—it would naturally result in apostasy from YHWH, giving rise to ruin under God's just wrath.

Consider another example in figure 2.3 from Deuteronomy 5:1, 32–33. You will recall that a וְ clause always connects to a previous thought but that the specific clause may not be the immediately preceding one. In Deuteronomy 5, verses 2–31 supply a historical-narrative digression (initially signaled by asyndeton and all of it indented) that together clarifies why Israel must heed YHWH's voice through Moses—forty years earlier, Israel requested and YHWH affirmed that Moses stand as the covenant mediator and mouthpiece of God. Verse 32 then returns to the directive speech that opened the sermon, with the וְ clause in 32a actually reaching all the way back to 1e! Once Moses completes his historical account, he returns to his exhortations begun in 5:1, continuing the original text block.

Hebrew		Connector	Translation
שְׁמַע יִשְׂרָאֵל אֶת־הַחֻקִּים וְאֶת־הַמִּשְׁפָּטִים אֲשֶׁר אָנֹכִי דֹּבֵר בְּאָזְנֵיכֶם הַיּוֹם	1c	Ø	Hear, O Israel, the statutes and the rules that I am about to speak in your hearing today.
וּלְמַדְתֶּם אֹתָם	d	וְ	<u>And</u> you shall learn them,
וּשְׁמַרְתֶּם לַעֲשֹׂתָם׃	e	וְ	<u>and</u> be careful to do them.
[Embedded narrative digression]			[---]
וּשְׁמַרְתֶּם לַעֲשׂוֹת	32	וְ	<u>And</u> you shall be careful to do
כַּאֲשֶׁר צִוָּה יְהוָה אֱלֹהֵיכֶם אֶתְכֶם	b	כַּאֲשֶׁר	just as YHWH your God commanded you.
לֹא תָסֻרוּ יָמִין וּשְׂמֹאל׃	c	Ø	You shall not turn aside to the right hand or to the left.
בְּכָל־הַדֶּרֶךְ אֲשֶׁר צִוָּה יְהוָה אֱלֹהֵיכֶם אֶתְכֶם תֵּלֵכוּ	33	Ø	In all the way that YHWH your God commanded you should walk
לְמַעַן תִּחְיוּן	b	לְמַעַן	so that you may live,
וְטוֹב לָכֶם	c	וְ	<u>and</u> it may go well with you,
וְהַאֲרַכְתֶּם יָמִים בָּאָרֶץ אֲשֶׁר תִּירָשׁוּן׃	d	וְ	<u>and</u> you may lengthen days in the land that you will possess.

Fig. 2.3. Text Hierarchy in Deuteronomy 5:1, 32–33

Verse 32c uses asyndeton to mark explication, and then 33a adds further explanation to this statement. The adverbial conjunction לְמַעַן ("so that") begins a purpose statement in 33b, which is then carried on in clauses 33cd, both of which begin with וְ. Moses gives three reasons why the Israelites should walk in YHWH's commands: *so that* they may live, *so that* it may go well with them, and *so that* they may lengthen their days.[4]

In discourse, tracking the function of וְ (gloss "and") and asyndeton is the first step in determining literary units. The connector וְ pushes the reader ahead in a text, link

4. For a developed discourse analysis of all of Deuteronomy 5–11, see DeRouchie, *A Call to Covenant Love*, 227–67.

by link by link. A lack of connection, however, forces one to pause, creating a disjunction in the text and marking something significant.

Text Blocks and the Structure and Message of Genesis

Text blocks are often short, and many are embedded within higher-level text blocks, serving to explain what precedes. As already noted, however, at the highest levels of Scripture, text blocks can stretch for chapters, and we see an example of this in the book of Genesis. The most common structural feature within Genesis is the formula אֵלֶּה תּוֹלְדוֹת, which occurs ten times and is often translated "This is the account of" or "These are the generations of" (Gen. 2:4; 5:1; 6:9; 10:1; 11:10, 27; 25:12, 19; 36:1; 37:2).[5] Its recurring placement suggests that the author used it as a shaping device for the work.

Commentators most commonly treat all ten *toledot* formulae as equal and independent, as seen in figure 2.4.

	Preface (Gen. 1:1–2:3)
1	The *toledot* of the heavens and the earth (2:4–4:26)
2	The *toledot* of Adam (5:1–6:8)
3	The *toledot* of Noah (6:9–9:29)
4	The *toledot* of Noah's sons (10:1–11:9)
5	The *toledot* of Shem (11:10–26)
6	The *toledot* of Terah (11:27–25:11)
7	The *toledot* of Ishmael (25:12–18)
8	The *toledot* of Isaac (25:19–35:29)
9	The *toledot* of Esau (36:1–37:1)
10	The *toledot* of Jacob (37:2–50:26)

Fig. 2.4. The Common View of Genesis's Structure

Yet a close look at the recurring formula shows that some of the *toledot* are preceded by the connector וְ (gloss "and"), whereas others are not. This suggests that the author

5. The אֵלֶּה תּוֹלְדוֹת pattern also occurs in Genesis 36:9, but its presence here seems secondary to the overall structure of the book, even though it appears to separate a preliminary list of Esau's descendants birthed in Canaan (36:1–8) from a more complete list of Esau's offspring, including those birthed in Edom (36:9–43). For more on the question, see footnote 1 in Jason S. DeRouchie, "The Blessing-Commission, the Promised Offspring, and the *Toledot* Structure of Genesis," *JETS* 56, 2 (2013): 219.

intended five, not ten, distinct units. Text blocks are here working at the macro-level to identify the structure of an entire biblical book.

		Preface (Gen. 1:1–2:3)
1.	Ø	These are the *toledot* of the heavens and the earth (2:4–4:26)
2.	Ø	This is the book of the *toledot* of Adam (5:1–6:8)
3.	Ø	These are the *toledot* of Noah (6:9–9:29)
	וְ	And these are the *toledot* of Noah's sons (10:1–11:9)
4.	Ø	These are the *toledot* of Shem (11:10–26)
	וְ	And these are the *toledot* of Terah (11:27–25:11)
	וְ	And these are the *toledot* of Ishmael (25:12–18)
	וְ	And these are the *toledot* of Isaac (25:19–35:29)
	וְ	And these are the *toledot* of Esau (36:1–37:1)
5.	Ø	These are the *toledot* of Jacob (37:2–50:26)

Fig. 2.5. Frontal Connection in the *Toledot* of Genesis

Whereas the connector וְ links units of equal syntactic value, asyndeton marks disjunction in the text. In the given instances, every *toledot* heading without any fronted connector identifies a fresh beginning in the narrative, whereas the headings beginning with וְ expand directly upon the previous unit. We can immediately draw three interpretive implications from these findings:

1. The length of the various *toledot* divisions gives prominence to God's covenant with the patriarchs within the book (Gen. 11:10–37:1).
2. The Shem *toledot* serves to introduce the patriarchal cycles rather than to close what has often been termed the *Primeval History*. Commonly, scholars distinguish Genesis 1–11 from 12–50, and this is not without some merit, for the narrative time slows drastically when we reach the patriarchs. Still, the וְ at the beginning of 11:27 suggests that the actual beginning of the patriarchal cycle is not chapter 12 but 11:10, with the (second) genealogy of Shem moving us from the time of Noah to the time of Abraham.
3. The five major *toledot* divisions witness a progressive narrowing that places focus on the line of promise and the centrality of Israel in God's kingdom-building plan. The shift from the heavens and earth (Gen. 2:4) to Adam (5:1) to Noah (6:9) to Shem (11:10) and to Jacob (37:2) details the movement from (a) all creation to (b) humanity in general to (c) all living humanity (after the execution of the rest) to (d) a subset of living humanity (through a shift in

genealogical focus) and finally to (e) Israel. The call of the chosen line to reflect, resemble, and represent God's excellencies is therefore placed within its global context.

While some form-driven translations such as the KJV and NASB are faithful to distinguish in English those *toledot* that begin with וְ and those that do not, very popular translations such as the NRSV, ESV, NIV, and CSB make little to no distinction. In failing to represent the connector in any way, these versions do not give the reader a structural signal that Moses intended us to see (or hear) in order to understand the outline of his book.[6] Once again, knowing Hebrew is helpful.

	2:4 Ø	5:1 Ø	6:9 Ø	10:1 וְ	11:10 Ø	11:27 וְ	25:12 וְ	25:19 וְ	36:1 וְ	37:2 Ø
KJV				Now		Now	Now	And	Now	
NASB				Now		Now	Now	Now	Now	
NRSV, ESV						Now				
NIV, CSB										

Fig. 2.6. How Some Modern Translations Render וְ and Asyndeton in the *Toledot* of Genesis

Discerning Subunits in Text Blocks: Paragraph Breaks

Any given text block can include multiple paragraphs, and the switch from one paragraph to the next is marked not only by changes in content but also by intentional changes in word order and verb pattern.[7] To discern how the Old Testament signals paragraph breaks requires first an understanding of text types and the verb patterns that signal them.

6. Whereas וְ in Hebrew is merely a default connector, the conjunction "and" in English actually marks coordination. Hebrew וְ is thus *not* equal to the English "and," which means that English translators could actually misrepresent the Hebrew by attempting to translate וְ in every instance. Ultimately, biblical interpreters will rightly identify some structural features in the Old Testament only by assessing the Hebrew text for themselves. For more on the structure and message of Genesis, see DeRouchie, "The Blessing-Commission, the Promised Offspring, and the *Toledot* Structure of Genesis," 219–47; cf. DeRouchie, review of *These Are the Generations: Identity, Covenant, and the "Toledot" Formula*, by Matthew A. Thomas, *BBR* 22, 3 (2012): 412–15.

7. Some of this material is adapted from Duane A. Garrett and Jason S. DeRouchie, *A Modern Grammar for Biblical Hebrew* (Nashville: Broadman & Holman, 2009), 291–93 (§ 37.F), 296–301 (§ 38.A), 312–14 (§ 39.A), and 330–33 (§ 40.B). Used by permission.

1. Text Types and Verb Patterns

Text types are simply the various kinds of Hebrew discourse. The three most common types are *historical* (past stories), *anticipatory* (future promises and predictions), and *directive* (commands or instructions).[8] Text blocks are usually text-type-specific, so biblical authors usually mark shifts from one type of discourse to another by starting a new text block (signaled by asyndeton or a subordinate conjunction). This feature is evident, for example, in Deuteronomy 5. Directive discourse is the primary text type (5:1, 32–33), but within it is an extended, embedded historical discourse (5:2–31). The recollection of Israel's experience at Sinai (= historical discourse) supplies a reason why the people needed to heed God's words through Moses in the present (= directive discourse).

שְׁמַע יִשְׂרָאֵל אֶת־הַחֻקִּים וְאֶת־הַמִּשְׁפָּטִים אֲשֶׁר אָנֹכִי דֹּבֵר בְּאָזְנֵיכֶם הַיּוֹם	1c	Ø	Hear, O Israel, the statutes and the rules that I am about to speak in your hearing today.	Dir Disc
וּלְמַדְתֶּם אֹתָם	d	וְ	And you shall learn them,	
וּשְׁמַרְתֶּם לַעֲשֹׂתָם׃	e	וְ	and be careful to do them.	
יְהוָה אֱלֹהֵינוּ כָּרַת עִמָּנוּ בְּרִית בְּחֹרֵב׃	2	Ø	YHWH our God cut a covenant with us at Horeb.	Hist Disc
לֹא אֶת־אֲבֹתֵינוּ כָּרַת יְהוָה אֶת־הַבְּרִית הַזֹּאת	3	Ø	Not with our fathers did he cut this covenant,	
כִּי אִתָּנוּ אֲנַחְנוּ אֵלֶּה פֹּה הַיּוֹם	b	כִּי	but with us—we, all of us here alive today.	
פָּנִים ׀ בְּפָנִים דִּבֶּר יְהוָה עִמָּכֶם בָּהָר מִתּוֹךְ הָאֵשׁ׃	4	Ø	Face to face YHWH spoke with you at the mount from the midst of the fire.	
[Continuation of embedded narrative digression through 5:31]				
וּשְׁמַרְתֶּם לַעֲשׂוֹת	32	וְ	And you shall be careful to do	Dir Disc
כַּאֲשֶׁר צִוָּה יְהוָה אֱלֹהֵיכֶם אֶתְכֶם	b	כַּאֲשֶׁר	just as YHWH your God commanded you.	
לֹא תָסֻרוּ יָמִין וּשְׂמֹאל׃	c	Ø	You shall not turn aside to the right hand or to the left.	

Fig. 2.7. Text Blocks and Text Types in Deuteronomy 5:1–4, 32

8. Some scholars simply employ different titles, such as "narrative," "promissory," and "hortatory" discourse.

Every text type is formally signaled by groupings of certain verb patterns that, by default, express temporal or logical succession within a given text type. That is, without signals that direct otherwise, the presence of these ***unmarked verb patterns*** leads us to read continuity within the text, and it is shifts away from these default verb patterns that mark literary features such as paragraph breaks. (For a developed list of the various functions of ***marked clauses***, see "More on Marked and Unmarked Clauses" in chapter 5.) In order to aid all readers in tracking the discussion of verb patterns that follows, figure 2.8 synthesizes the terminology I employ for the various verbal conjugations.

Form Title	Traditional Title	General Function
wayyiqtol	*waw*-consecutive imperfect	Context-determined tense, perfective aspect, indicative or nonindicative modality
qatal	perfect	Context-determined tense, perfective aspect, indicative or nonindicative modality
weqatal	*waw*-consecutive perfect	Context-determined tense and aspect, indicative or nonindicative modality
***(we)yiqtol* (long)**	imperfect	Context-determined tense, imperfective aspect, indicative or nonindicative modality
participle	participle	Context-determined tense, progressive aspect
***(we)yiqtol* (short)**	jussive	Context-determined tense, perfective aspect, usually volitional, nonindicative modality
imperative	imperative	Volitional, nonindicative modality

Fig. 2.8. Titles of Verbal Conjugations in This Book[9]

a. Historical Text Type

As noted, ***historical texts*** are the Old Testament's stories. Historical narrative makes up around 65 percent of the Old Testament and relays a succession of contingent events, one after another, usually in past time. In the historical text type, *wayyiqtol* clauses (= *waw*-consecutive imperfect clauses) serve as the unmarked or default verb pattern. Unless text features tell us otherwise, we by default expect that every *wayyiqtol* is simply carrying ahead the story line (= continuity). When a single clause departs from the *wayyiqtol* pattern, we often find the beginning or end of a paragraph. Take, for example, the narrative reported speech in Joshua 24:2–3.

9. Some may question the "general functions" I have assigned to the various conjugations. For more on my decisions, see "An Intermediate Look at the Hebrew Verb" in chapter 5.

Asyndeton + prepositional phrase + *qatal* (= perfect) clause initiates a new text block and marks the start of a paragraph. What follows is a chain of *wayyiqtol* clauses in Joshua 24:2b–3d. The beginning of the unit is highlighted by a non-*wayyiqtol* clause (which also happens to be asyndetic), and then *wayyiqtol* verbs carry the story along and are, by default, read as expressing temporally successive events.

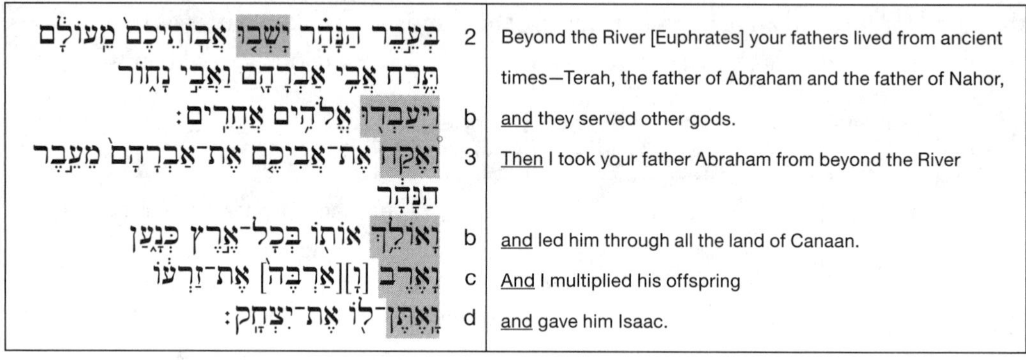

בְּעֵבֶר הַנָּהָר יָשְׁבוּ אֲבוֹתֵיכֶם מֵעוֹלָם תֶּרַח אֲבִי אַבְרָהָם וַאֲבִי נָחוֹר	2	Beyond the River [Euphrates] your fathers lived from ancient times—Terah, the father of Abraham and the father of Nahor,
וַיַּעַבְדוּ אֱלֹהִים אֲחֵרִים׃	b	and they served other gods.
וָאֶקַּח אֶת־אֲבִיכֶם אֶת־אַבְרָהָם מֵעֵבֶר הַנָּהָר	3	Then I took your father Abraham from beyond the River
וָאוֹלֵךְ אוֹתוֹ בְּכָל־אֶרֶץ כְּנָעַן	b	and led him through all the land of Canaan.
וָאֶרֶב [וָ][אַרְבֶּה] אֶת־זַרְעוֹ	c	And I multiplied his offspring
וָאֶתֶּן־לוֹ אֶת־יִצְחָק׃	d	and gave him Isaac.

Fig. 2.9. Verb Patterns in Joshua 24:2–3

b. Anticipatory Text Type

Anticipatory discourse predicts or promises forthcoming events, at times in contingent succession. Just as we have past-tense narrative, we can have future-tense narrative, describing what will happen sometime after the speech. The default verb pattern used to express anticipation is the *weqatal* (= *waw*-consecutive perfect), and single-clause departures from this pattern commonly mark the beginning and end of paragraphs. For example, after the introductory וְהָיָה ("And it will happen that") in Micah 4:1–2, we get a *yiqtol* (= imperfect) clause followed by a chain of *weqatal* clauses. The *yiqtol* verb marks the future orientation of the context, and then the further anticipations are carried on by the unmarked *weqatal* verb form.

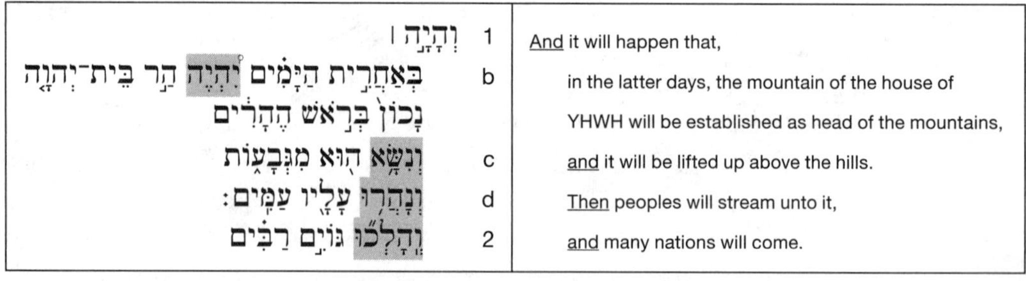

וְהָיָה ׀	1	And it will happen that,
בְּאַחֲרִית הַיָּמִים יִהְיֶה הַר בֵּית־יְהוָה נָכוֹן בְּרֹאשׁ הֶהָרִים	b	in the latter days, the mountain of the house of YHWH will be established as head of the mountains,
וְנִשָּׂא הוּא מִגְּבָעוֹת	c	and it will be lifted up above the hills.
וְנָהֲרוּ עָלָיו עַמִּים׃	d	Then peoples will stream unto it,
וְהָלְכוּ גּוֹיִם רַבִּים	2	and many nations will come.

Fig. 2.10. Verb Patterns in Micah 4:1–2

c. Directive Text Type

Directive discourse includes commands or exhortations, at times in the form of progressive instructions for a given task. Directive speech is usually marked by an initial imperative or other volitional form, which is then followed by the unmarked or default *weqatal* (as in Deut. 5:1, 32). Exodus 3:16 opens with God's giving Moses a threefold command—first by imperative ("Go") and the next two by *weqatal* clauses ("and gather . . . and say").

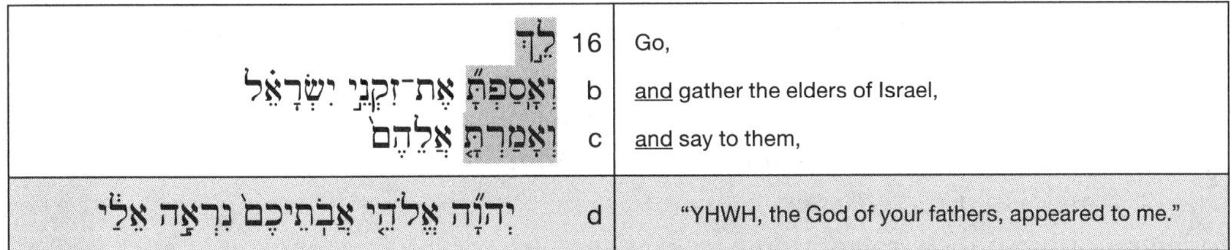

לֵךְ	16	Go,
וְאָסַפְתָּ אֶת־זִקְנֵי יִשְׂרָאֵל	b	and gather the elders of Israel,
וְאָמַרְתָּ אֲלֵהֶם	c	and say to them,
יְהוָה אֱלֹהֵי אֲבֹתֵיכֶם נִרְאָה אֵלַי	d	"YHWH, the God of your fathers, appeared to me."

Fig. 2.11. Verb Patterns in Exodus 3:16

We see a similar structure when Boaz urges Ruth to eat with him after her gleanings. He initially uses an imperative ("Approach"), and then continues his request by two *weqatal* verbs ("and eat . . . and dip"). This speech is embedded within a greater historical discourse, as signaled through the chain of *wayyiqtol* clauses in 14a, e–i.

וַיֹּאמֶר לָה בֹעַז לְעֵת הָאֹכֶל	14	And Boaz said to her at the mealtime,
גֹּשִׁי הֲלֹם	b	"Approach here,
וְאָכַלְתְּ מִן־הַלֶּחֶם	c	And eat from the bread,
וְטָבַלְתְּ פִּתֵּךְ בַּחֹמֶץ	d	and dip your morsel in the vinegar."
וַתֵּשֶׁב מִצַּד הַקּוֹצְרִים	e	So she sat beside the reapers,
וַיִּצְבָּט־לָהּ קָלִי	f	and he passed to her roasted grain.
וַתֹּאכַל	g	And she ate
וַתִּשְׂבַּע	h	and was satisfied.
וַתֹּתַר׃	i	And she left some remaining.

Fig. 2.12. Verb Patterns in Ruth 2:14

The predicate patterns in directive discourse witness a relative priority of assertive power. Imperatives (or לֹא / אַל + *yiqtol* prohibitions) bear highest directional force, followed by infinitive absolute + *yiqtol*, then *weqatal*, and then volitional *yiqtol*. This continuum of directive weight at times helps us identify an apodosis where different clauses could signal the "then" element of the two-part syntactic construction (e.g., Deuteronomy 6:10–12, where the imperative in 6:12a signals the apodosis and also identifies that the *weqatal* clauses in 6:11 continue the protasis).

2. Marked Clauses and Paragraph Breaks

In order to distinguish whether they were telling stories, making promises, or giving instructions, the Old Testament authors needed to follow the understood patterns of the language. Biblical Hebrew distinguishes unmarked and marked clauses based on text type, and the former, by default, express continuity, whereas the latter mark discontinuity. As a reader, you need to be ever mindful of the clusters of unmarked verbs—*wayyiqtol* in historical discourse and *weqatal* in anticipatory and directive discourse. This will allow you to easily identify the marked clauses and to consider their function. Later we will have an overview of the many possible functions of marked clauses (see "More on Marked and Unmarked Clauses" in chapter 5), but the one that we will focus on here is to signal the beginning or end of a paragraph within a given text block.

To help you grasp how to identify paragraphs, we are going to look at Leviticus 14:2–9, which is a directive speech that offers instructions for cleansing lepers.[10] I have included only English translation except where I mark the verb pattern in each clause. The grayed highlighting distinguishes paragraph divisions, and [x] signals any part of speech other than the main verb.[11] As you read through figure 2.13, identify the shifts in verb pattern in the translation and read the notes I make on each division.

			Verb Patterns	Notes
2a	Ø	This shall be [וְזֹאת תִּהְיֶה] the law of the leper in the day of his cleansing:	Ø [x] + *yiqtol*	Functions volitionally; an asyndetic clause introduces the text block.
2b	וְ	And he must be brought [וְהוּבָא] to the priest,	*weqatal*	Begins progression of instructions for *assessment.*
3a	וְ	and the priest must go forth [וְיָצָא הַכֹּהֵן] to the outside of the camp.	*weqatal*	
3b	וְ	And the priest must look [וְרָאָה הַכֹּהֵן]—	*weqatal*	
3c	וְ	And, behold, the affliction of the leprosy has been healed [וְהִנֵּה נִרְפָּא נֶגַע־הַצָּרַעַת] from the leper.	וְ + [x] + *qatal*	A single nondefault clause marks paragraph termination.
4a	וְ	And the priest must command [וְצִוָּה]	*weqatal*	Continues instructions, now for *preparation.*
4b	וְ	and must take [וְלָקַח] for the one cleansing himself two live clean birds and cedar wood and scarlet yarn and hyssop.	*weqatal*	
5a	וְ	And the priest must command [וְצִוָּה],	*weqatal*	

Fig. 2.13. Paragraph Breaks in Leviticus 14:2–9

10. While no imperative is present, we know that it is directive discourse because 2a calls the whole a "law" (תּוֹרָה), because the initial *yiqtol* in 2a is functioning volitionally, and because the extended chain of mostly *weqatal* clauses clearly provides step-by-step instructions.

11. Specifically, [x] stands for any subject, object, or modifier in a clause; [x] cannot stand for either a finite verb or a conjunction.

			Verb Patterns	Notes
5b	וְ	<u>and</u> he must slaughter [וְשָׁחַט] one of the birds inside an earthenware vessel over living water.	*weqatal*	
6a	Ø	As for the live bird, he must take it [אֶת־הַצִּפֹּר הַחַיָּה יִקַ אֹתָהּ] and the cedar wood and the scarlet yarn and the hyssop.	Ø [x] + *yiqtol*	6ab supply an inner-paragraph closing comment, filling final necessary information before the main instructions for cleansing ensue.
6b	וְ	<u>And</u> he must dip [וְטָבַל] them and the live bird in the blood of the slaughtered bird over the living water.	*weqatal*	The end of the inner-paragraph comment is signaled by semantic content alone.
7a	וְ	<u>And</u> he must sprinkle [וְהִזָּה] on the one cleansing himself from the leprosy seven times,	*weqatal*	Initiation of the main instructions for *cleansing, part 1*—outside the camp.
7b	וְ	<u>and</u> he will cleanse him [וְטִהֲרוֹ].	*weqatal*	Expresses result.
7c	וְ	<u>And</u> he must send out [וְשִׁלַּח] the living bird over the open field.	*weqatal*	
8a	וְ	<u>And</u> the one cleansing himself must wash [וְכִבֶּס] his clothes	*weqatal*	
8b	וְ	<u>and</u> shave [וְגִלַּח] all his hair	*weqatal*	
8c	וְ	<u>and</u> bathe [וְרָחַץ] in the water	*weqatal*	
8d	וְ	<u>and</u> become clean [וְטָהֵר].	*weqatal*	Expresses result.
8e	וְ	<u>And</u> after he enters [וְאַחַר יָבוֹא] into the camp,	וְ + [*x*] + *yiqtol*	Single nondefault clause marks paragraph initiation; continuing instructions for *cleansing, part 2*—inside the camp.
8f	וְ	<u>Then</u> he must dwell [וְיָשַׁב] outside his tent seven days.	*weqatal*	

Fig. 2.13. Paragraph Breaks in Leviticus 14:2–9 (cont.)

			Verb Patterns	Notes
9a	וְ	And it should happen [וְהָיָה] that	*weqatal* climax	Climax marker signaling the high point of the instructions—complete cleansing.
9b	Ø	in the seventh day he should shave [יְגַלַּח] all his hair—his head and his beard and his eyebrows;	[x] + *yiqtol*	
9c	וְ	even all his hair he should shave [יְגַלֵּחַ].	וְ + [x] + *yiqtol*	Identical matching with 9b [_V/_V] likely for dramatic pause.[12]
9d	וְ	And he should wash [וְכִבֶּס] his clothes,	*weqatal*	
9e	וְ	and he should bathe [וְרָחַץ] his body in water.	*weqatal*	
9f	וְ	Then he will be clean [וְטָהֵר].	*weqatal*	Final result.

Fig. 2.13. Paragraph Breaks in Leviticus 14:2–9 (cont.)

When considering the passage as a whole, we see one extended text block with title and four distinct paragraph units, each identified by both content and form and signaled by the shifts to and from gray highlighting.

- ***Title:*** the law of the leper (v. 2). It is marked by asyndeton and its title structure.
- ***Instructions for assessment*** (v. 3). The change in verb pattern in 3c marks the end of the paragraph.
- ***Instructions for preparation*** (vv. 4–6). The two-clause inner-paragraph comment in 6ab marks the paragraph's termination. The start of the inner-paragraph comment itself is signaled by an asyndetic clause (though any marked clause can signal such a comment).
- ***Instructions for cleansing, part 1***—outside the camp (vv. 7–8). This paragraph is made up completely of *weqatal* clauses.
- ***Instructions for cleansing, part 2 with climax***—inside the camp (v. 9). The paragraph's beginning is here marked by the presence of a nondefault verb pattern (וְ+ [x] + *yiqtol*). The culmination of the entire set of instructions is then signaled by the climax marker וְהָיָה—a discourse marker for which I will give an overview in the next section.

12. For a discussion of "identical matching," see "More on Marked and Unmarked Clauses" in chapter 5.

וַיְהִי and וְהָיָה as Transition/Climax Markers

Before we conclude this chapter, this section and the next will identify some more formal features that help clarify a text's shape. They are called ***discourse markers***—constructions in Hebrew whose chief purpose is to signal structural features in a text rather than to convey semantic meaning. You are already aware that at the clause level, אֶת־ as a direct-object marker is not to be translated; it operates simply as a signal.Similarly, we have seen how the connector וְ identifies some relationship between clauses or larger units while not clarifying whether those relationships are necessarily coordinate or subordinate. Its primary purpose is to couple elements of equal syntactic value, but its semantic force is clear only from the context. In Hebrew, there are many words whose primary purpose is to mark subdivisions and the relationship of various parts of a text. English, too, has discourse-structuring markers, as in the use of "well" or "now" in conversation or of "once upon a time" to begin a fairy tale.

This section addresses the discourse markers וַיְהִי and וְהָיָה, which signal transition and/or climax and introduce a new paragraph or subparagraph.[13] The verb וַיְהִי is the Qal *wayyiqtol* third masculine singular of היה, which as a full verb means "And he/it/there was." The verb וְהָיָה is the Qal *weqatal* third masculine singular of היה, which as a full verb means "And he/it/there will be."

וַיְהִי as full verb	וַֽיְהִי־הֶ֙בֶל֙ רֹ֣עֵה צֹ֔אן וְקַ֕יִן הָיָ֖ה עֹבֵ֥ד אֲדָמָֽה	And Abel was a shepherd of sheep, but Cain was a worker of ground (Gen. 4:2).
וְהָיָה as full verb	וְהָיָ֤ה זַרְעֲךָ֙ כַּעֲפַ֣ר הָאָ֔רֶץ	And your offspring will be like the dust of the earth (Gen. 28:14).

Fig. 2.14. וַיְהִי and וְהָיָה as Full Verbs

At times, however, these forms function not as normal verbs but as discourse markers that signal turning points or climaxes in texts while identifying that what follows is still linked to what precedes. When וַיְהִי and וְהָיָה function as discourse markers, they also often signal the beginning of new paragraphs. In such instances, וַיְהִי or וְהָיָה will never have a clearly defined subject or antecedent in the context and will usually front a two-part syntactic construction, otherwise known as ***protasis-apodosis*** ("if-then," "when-then," "because-therefore"). When operating

13. Much of this material is adapted from Garrett and DeRouchie, *A Modern Grammar for Biblical Hebrew*, 327–30 (§ 40.A.4). Used by permission.

as discourse markers, the "subject" of these forms is the entire paragraph or subparagraph that follows. In our look at Leviticus 14:2–9 in the previous section, we saw וְהָיָה in directive speech used to mark climax. Here, we'll consider an occurrence of וַיְהִי in historical discourse used as a climax marker, this time from from 1 Samuel 4:18.[14]

<table>
<tr><th colspan="4">1 Samuel 4:12–17 (ESV)</th></tr>
<tr><td colspan="4">A man of Benjamin ran from the battle line and came to Shiloh the same day, with his clothes torn and with dirt on his head. When he arrived, Eli was sitting on his seat by the road watching, for his heart trembled for the ark of God. And when the man came into the city and told the news, all the city cried out. When Eli heard the sound of the outcry, he said, "What is this uproar?" Then the man hurried and came and told Eli. Now Eli was ninety-eight years old and his eyes were set so that he could not see. And the man said to Eli, "I am he who has come from the battle; I fled from the battle today." And he said, "How did it go, my son?" He who brought the news answered and said, "Israel has fled before the Philistines, and there has also been a great defeat among the people. Your two sons also, Hophni and Phinehas, are dead, and the ark of God has been captured."</td></tr>
<tr><th colspan="4">1 Samuel 4:18</th></tr>
<tr><td>וַיְהִ֗י</td><td>18</td><td>וַיְהִי climax marker</td><td>And it happened that,</td></tr>
<tr><td>כְּהַזְכִּירוֹ ׀ אֶת־אֲרוֹן הָאֱלֹהִים</td><td>b</td><td>temporal protasis</td><td>as he mentioned the ark of God,</td></tr>
<tr><td>וַיִּפֹּל מֵעַל־הַכִּסֵּא אֲחֹרַנִּית בְּעַד ׀
יַד הַשַּׁעַר</td><td>c</td><td>wayyiqtol, beginning
of apodosis</td><td>then he fell from on the chair
backward by the side of the gate.</td></tr>
<tr><td>וַתִּשָּׁבֵר מַפְרַקְתּוֹ</td><td>d</td><td>wayyiqtol</td><td>And his neck was broken,</td></tr>
<tr><td>וַיָּמֹת</td><td>e</td><td>wayyiqtol</td><td>and he died</td></tr>
<tr><td>כִּי־זָקֵן הָאִישׁ וְכָבֵד</td><td>f</td><td>כִּי ground clause</td><td>because the man was old and heavy.</td></tr>
<tr><td>וְהוּא שָׁפַט אֶת־יִשְׂרָאֵל אַרְבָּעִים
שָׁנָה׃</td><td>g</td><td>וְ + [x] + qatal,
paragraph end</td><td>And he judged Israel forty years.</td></tr>
</table>

Fig. 2.15. וַיְהִי as a Climax Marker in 1 Samuel 4:18

In order to highlight the gravity of the messenger's statement that "the ark of God was taken" (1 Sam. 4:17), the narrator adds what we see in verse 18. The verse has וַיְהִי ("and it happened that") at its head, which introduces a new temporal context ("as he

14. Along with וַיְהִי and וְהָיָה, we see the same role played by the *weyiqtol* (jussive) form וִיהִי ("and it will happen that") in the directive discourse of Ruth 3:4; 2 Samuel 5:24; and 1 Chronicles 14:15. I thank my colleague John Beckman for directing me to these texts.

mentioned the ark of God," 4:18b) and initiates the dramatic response of Eli the priest to the terrible news. Notice how וַיְהִי has neither an explicit subject nor an antecedent that agrees with it in number and gender. Instead, the entire paragraph that follows is the "antecedent" referent. What was it that "happened"? The answer: Everything that follows. The fact that there is no clear subject or antecedent tells us that וַיְהִי is functioning as a transition/climax marker and not a full verb. With this, וַיְהִי introduces a protasis-apodosis construction, which is the second signal that we are looking at a discourse marker. וַיְהִי tells us that the entire narrative related to the news-bearer's message was designed to get us to this point. Verse 18 marks the climax. It also signals the start of a new paragraph.

To conclude, when וַיְהִי and וְהָיָה are operating as discourse markers, they usually introduce a new temporal context and signal that something substantial is about to be declared that grows directly out of an event, activity, or idea in the preceding context. We know that they are functioning as discourse markers when they lack any clear subject or antecedent that agrees with them in number and gender. Their "subject" is the entire paragraph or subparagraph that follows, and in most contexts, their discourse function will also include introducing a two-part syntactic construction (i.e., protasis-apodosis), though this is not necessary. If you can identify a specific subject, then וַיְהִי and וְהָיָה are operating as full verbs and *not* as transition/climax markers.

	Transition/Climax-Marking Function	Full-Verb Function
וַיְהִי	וַיְהִי לְעֵת זִקְנַת שְׁלֹמֹה נָשָׁיו הִטּוּ אֶת־לְבָבוֹ אַחֲרֵי אֱלֹהִים אֲחֵרִים	וַיְהִי הַמֶּלֶךְ שְׁלֹמֹה מֶלֶךְ עַל־כָּל־יִשְׂרָאֵל
	And it happened that, at the time of Solomon's old age, his wives turned his heart after other gods (1 Kings 11:4).	And the king Solomon was king over all Israel (1 Kings 4:1).
וְהָיָה	וְהָיָה ׀ בְּאַחֲרִית הַיָּמִים נָכוֹן יִהְיֶה הַר בֵּית־יְהוָה בְּרֹאשׁ הֶהָרִים	וְהָיָה בֵית־יַעֲקֹב אֵשׁ
	And it shall happen that, in the latter days, the mountain of YHWH's house will be established at the head of the mountains (Isa. 2:2).	And the house of Jacob will be a fire (Obad. 18).

Fig. 2.16. וַיְהִי and וְהָיָה: Climax Marker or Full Verb?

Marked Primary and Secondary Citation Formulas

This section addresses how the Old Testament identifies the onset of a speech.[15] Biblical Hebrew does not use quotation marks as we do in English. Instead, it employs introductory citation formulas, which not only signal the speech's beginning but also often clarify what type of speech it is through the use of special discourse markers.

The discussion of text types distinguished unmarked verb patterns from marked ones. Biblical Hebrew uses a comparable unmarked-marked system when introducing citations. Sometimes the type of citation is unmarked, but other times the biblical authors marked a citation as either primary or secondary.[16]

1. A ***primary citation*** has one or more of the following features:
    a. Reports a single event rather than reporting many similar speeches as one;
    b. Has its participants speak individually rather than as groups speaking chorally;
    c. Is not retold by someone else from a previous conversation;
    d. Deals with full characters in the story rather than agents or props; or
    e. Functions as the lively account of a direct conversation.
2. A ***secondary citation*** has at least one of the following features:
    a. Summarizes several similar speeches or one long speech;
    b. Presents the statements of many people as one statement;
    c. Has one character in the story quote a prior statement by another character in the story;
    d. Comes through an agent or prop rather than a full character, or is from someone who is not actually present and participating in the current conversation; or
    e. Functions as the official record of the principal points made by speakers and is a less vivid conversation.

15. Much of this material is adapted from Garrett and DeRouchie, *A Modern Grammar for Biblical Hebrew*, 323–27 (§ 40.A.3). Used by permission.

16. Linguists refer to "primary citations" as "prototypical" and "secondary citations" as "non-prototypical." For more on these issues, see Cynthia L. Miller, "Discourse Functions in Quotative Frames in Biblical Hebrew Narrative," in *Discourse Analysis of Biblical Literature: What It Is and What It Offers*, ed. Walter R. Bodine, SBLSS (Atlanta: Scholars Press, 1995), 155–82; Miller, *The Representation of Speech in Biblical Hebrew Narrative: A Linguistic Analysis*, HSM 55 (Winona Lake, IN: Eisenbrauns, 1999).

Biblical Hebrew introduces reported direct speeches in one of three ways: (1) single-verb frames; (2) double-verb frames; and (3) לֵאמֹר frames. The following chart provides an overview of the various structures and functions.

Category	Structure	Function	Example
Single-Verb Frames	Finite speech verb (usually אמר) + quotation	*Unmarked:* Either a primary or secondary citation	2 Sam. 18:29 וַיֹּאמֶר הַמֶּלֶךְ. . . "And the king said . . ."
Multiple-Verb Frames	Finite verb(s)* + finite speech verb (usually אמר) + quotation	*Marked:* A primary citation	Deut. 9:26 וָאֶתְפַּלֵּל אֶל־יְהוָה וָאֹמַר. . . "And I prayed to YHWH and said . . ."
לֵאמֹר Frames	Finite verb(s)* (at times אמר) or no verb + לֵאמֹר + quotation	*Marked:* A secondary citation	Gen. 1:22 וַיְבָרֶךְ אֹתָם אֱלֹהִים לֵאמֹר. . . "And God blessed them, saying . . ."
*At times, an infinitive construct stands in place of the initial finite verb.			

Fig. 2.17. Citation Formulas in Biblical Hebrew

Observe the following features from this chart. First, if only one finite verb (usually of the root אמר ["to say"]) introduces a citation, that citation may be primary or secondary. The citation is unmarked. Second, when לֵאמֹר is present, the citation is marked as secondary. Third, if two or more finite verbs introduce a citation, that citation is marked as primary. In biblical Hebrew, nearly every reported direct speech is introduced by a form of אמר ("to say"), so when the biblical authors wanted to specify the actual nature of the speech act, they would add another verb:

- Genesis 18:27—וַיַּעַן אַבְרָהָם וַיֹּאמַר ("And Abraham answered and said")
- Genesis 28:1—וַיְצַוֵּהוּ וַיֹּאמֶר לוֹ ("and he commanded him and said to him")
- Exodus 32:5—וַיִּקְרָא אַהֲרֹן וַיֹּאמַר ("and Aaron called out and said")

What is important to see is that the use of two or more verbs does not mean that the speaker spoke more than once. In Deuteronomy 9:26 in the chart, the quotation that follows is the content of Moses' prayer. Following the initial וָאֶתְפַּלֵּל ("And I prayed"), the second verb, וָאֹמַר ("and I said"), functions as a discourse marker, signaling the speech as primary.

1. Examples of Marked *Secondary* Citations

וַיֹּאמֶר אֲבִימֶלֶךְ וּפִיכֹל שַׂר־צְבָאוֹ אֶל־אַבְרָהָם לֵאמֹר אֱלֹהִים עִמְּךָ	And Abimelech and Phicol the commander of his army said to Abraham as follows: "God is with you."

Fig. 2.18. לֵאמֹר Frame in Genesis 21:22

In this case, the citation is secondary because it is not actually a quotation from one person. The words come from both Abimelech and Phicol but are presented as a single speech. Notice that the verb pattern is וַיֹּאמֶר . . . לֵאמֹר ("And he said . . . saying"). Clearly, לֵאמֹר was necessary only because the author wanted to mark the speech as secondary.

וּבִשְׁלֹחַ יְהוָה אֶתְכֶם מִקָּדֵשׁ בַּרְנֵעַ לֵאמֹר	And when YHWH sent you from Kadesh-barnea with the following words:

Fig. 2.19. לֵאמֹר Frame in Deuteronomy 9:23

Here Moses is secondarily recounting or retelling the essence of God's directive to Israel as he led the people from Kadesh-barnea to Canaan. It is not a direct citation of a specific speech act, so the speech is marked as secondary.

2. Examples of Marked *Primary* Citations

וָאֶשְׁאַל אֹתָהּ וָאֹמַר בַּת־מִי אַתְּ	Then I asked her and said, "Whose daughter are you?"

Fig. 2.20. Multiverb Frame in Genesis 24:47

Here Abraham's servant is giving a lively account of his conversations with Rebekah, and a multiverb frame is used to mark the citation as primary. He didn't ask one thing and say another. Rather, he asked the question, "Whose daughter are you?"

וַיִּקְרָא מֹשֶׁה אֶל־כָּל־יִשְׂרָאֵל וַיֹּאמֶר אֲלֵהֶם	And Moses called to all Israel and said to them . . .

Fig. 2.21. Multiverb Frame in Deuteronomy 5:1

In this example we find a multiverb speech frame made up of two verbs of saying: וַיִּקְרָא ("and he called") + וַיֹּאמֶר ("and he said"). This quotation frame introduces the second major prophetic address in the book of Deuteronomy. What follows appears to be a single speech, recorded in the way it was given by the prophet (Deut. 5:1–26:19). The primary speaker, Moses, is a full character in the narrative begun in 4:44, and he speaks individually throughout the discourse. We thus have a primary citation.

Citation formulas in biblical Hebrew help us identify the beginning of a speech. Even more, they often help us know whether that speech is primary or secondary. It is important to note that primary citations are not necessarily more important than secondary ones. Indeed, the reverse is often true. For example, in both Exodus 20:1 and Deuteronomy 5:5, Moses introduces the Ten Words with a secondary speech frame. Furthermore, you shouldn't think of a secondary citation as giving only the gist of a quotation. While secondary citations often do summarize, they don't need to, so both primary and secondary speech acts can give a verbatim citation of a reported speech.[17]

An Exercise in Shaping Literary Units—Exodus 19:4–6

As I noted earlier, as a pedagogical tool, each chapter of this book will analyze Exodus 19:4–6 from the perspective of the given interpretive step. We are going to look at this passage from nearly every conceivable angle, in the hope that you will get a better grasp of how to approach a single passage through the entire interpretive process, from exegesis to theology.

Sometimes establishing the beginning and end of literary units can be a complicated endeavor. Helpfully, however, this is not the case in Exodus 19:4–6. The table on the next page separates the various Hebrew clauses and includes the ESV translation of the passage. The three colors signal different levels of perspective. The narrator's voice begins and ends the unit (highlighted in white, vv. 1–3b, 7); he cites YHWH's speech to Moses (highlighted in light gray, vv. 3cd, 6b), which includes the words that Moses is to relay to the people (highlighted in darker gray, vv. 4–6a).

Exodus 19 opens with an asyndetic clause that signals a major fresh beginning within the book. Since 3:12, Moses has anticipated the day when Israel would arrive at the mountain of God to worship him, and in chapter 19 the destination is reached.

17. Sometimes the biblical authors use primary citations to report speeches by groups, with each member apparently speaking in unison. Natural contexts for this are formal occasions such as oaths in covenant ratification, where standardized wording would be expected (e.g., Ex. 19:8; 24:3; Deut. 27:14–15). Potential exceptions to this rule occur, however, when the text records with double-speech frames extended choral statements that are specific to a particular occasion (e.g., Num. 13:27–29; Deut. 1:41; Josh. 9:12, 24–25; 1 Sam. 30:22; Ezra 10:12–14). The longer and more circumstance-specific a statement and the more informal the speech and the more ad hoc the group, the less likely it is that we would expect words from multiple speakers to be spoken in unison. As noted by my colleague John Beckman, employing primary citation formulas in such contexts seems more like a stylized retelling (as when people break into song in a musical) than what we would find in a documentary film. This fact may suggest that more is at stake in such contexts. Regardless, I believe the unmarked-marked reading of speech frames works in most instances.

בַּחֹ֙דֶשׁ֙ הַשְּׁלִישִׁ֔י לְצֵ֥את בְּנֵֽי־יִשְׂרָאֵ֖ל מֵאֶ֣רֶץ מִצְרָ֑יִם בַּיּ֣וֹם הַזֶּ֔ה בָּ֖אוּ מִדְבַּ֥ר סִינָֽי׃ וַיִּסְע֣וּ מֵרְפִידִ֗ים וַיָּבֹ֙אוּ֙ מִדְבַּ֣ר סִינַ֔י וַֽיַּחֲנ֖וּ בַּמִּדְבָּ֑ר וַיִּֽחַן־שָׁ֥ם יִשְׂרָאֵ֖ל נֶ֥גֶד הָהָֽר׃ וּמֹשֶׁ֥ה עָלָ֖ה אֶל־הָאֱלֹהִ֑ים	1 2 b c d 3	1 On the third new moon after the people of Israel had gone out of the land of Egypt, on that day they came into the wilderness of Sinai. 2 They set out from Rephidim and came into the wilderness of Sinai, and they encamped in the wilderness. There Israel encamped before the mountain, 3 while Moses went up to God.
וַיִּקְרָ֨א אֵלָ֤יו יְהוָה֙ מִן־הָהָ֣ר לֵאמֹ֔ר	b	The LORD called to him out of the mountain, saying,
כֹּ֤ה תֹאמַר֙ לְבֵ֣ית יַעֲקֹ֔ב וְתַגֵּ֖יד לִבְנֵ֥י יִשְׂרָאֵֽל׃	c d	"Thus you shall say to the house of Jacob, and tell the people of Israel:
אַתֶּ֣ם רְאִיתֶ֔ם אֲשֶׁ֥ר עָשִׂ֖יתִי לְמִצְרָ֑יִם וָאֶשָּׂ֤א אֶתְכֶם֙ עַל־כַּנְפֵ֣י נְשָׁרִ֔ים וָאָבִ֥א אֶתְכֶ֖ם אֵלָֽי׃ וְעַתָּ֗ה אִם־שָׁמ֤וֹעַ תִּשְׁמְעוּ֙ בְּקֹלִ֔י וּשְׁמַרְתֶּ֖ם אֶת־בְּרִיתִ֑י וִהְיִ֨יתֶם לִ֤י סְגֻלָּה֙ מִכָּל־הָ֣עַמִּ֔ים כִּי־לִ֖י כָּל־הָאָֽרֶץ׃ וְאַתֶּ֧ם תִּהְיוּ־לִ֛י מַמְלֶ֥כֶת כֹּהֲנִ֖ים וְג֣וֹי קָד֑וֹשׁ	4 b c d 5 b c d 6	4 You yourselves have seen what I did to the Egyptians, and how I bore you on eagles' wings and brought you to myself. 5 Now therefore, if you will indeed obey my voice and keep my covenant, you shall be my treasured possession among all peoples, for all the earth is mine; 6 and you shall be to me a kingdom of priests and a holy nation.
אֵ֚לֶּה הַדְּבָרִ֔ים אֲשֶׁ֥ר תְּדַבֵּ֖ר אֶל־בְּנֵ֥י יִשְׂרָאֵֽל׃	b	These are the words that you shall speak to the people of Israel."
וַיָּבֹ֣א מֹשֶׁ֔ה וַיִּקְרָ֖א לְזִקְנֵ֣י הָעָ֑ם וַיָּ֣שֶׂם לִפְנֵיהֶ֗ם אֵ֚ת כָּל־הַדְּבָרִ֣ים הָאֵ֔לֶּה אֲשֶׁ֥ר צִוָּ֖הוּ יְהוָֽה׃	7 b c	7 So Moses came and called the elders of the people and set before them all these words that the LORD had commanded him.

Fig. 2.22. Literary Units in Exodus 19:1–7 in the MT and ESV

Following the initial asyndetic clause, we get a chain of four *wayyiqtol* clauses in verse 2, and the initial paragraph concludes with a non-*wayyiqtol* clause in 3a (i.e., וְ + subject + *qatal*). Paragraph 1 includes only the voice of the narrator.

Paragraph 2 opens in 3b with a new subject: YHWH speaks from the mountain to Moses. The speech uses a לֵאמֹר frame, which marks the quotation as secondary (see "Marked Primary and Secondary Citation Formulas" above). It could mean that we have only a synthesis of what God told Moses. But that God speaks "from the mountain" could also imply some level of mediation, which would also require a secondary speech frame. Regardless, 3c opens God's speech, and in two clauses God tells us that what follows are the words that Moses himself is to speak to the people. In verses 4–6, therefore, we have a speech within a speech (dark gray within the light gray), as highlighted in the table. Verse 6a concludes the embedded speech, and in 6b God reaffirms that these are the words that Moses is to proclaim. Verse 7 then again records the narrator's voice outside any direct reported speech.

Every chapter of this book will return to this passage. More specifically, we will consider from numerous angles the embedded words that God instructs Moses to tell the people (Ex. 19:4–6a) so that they might become "a kingdom of priests and a holy nation."

Key Words and Concepts

Literary unit
Scenes and episodes
Text hierarchy and asyndeton
Text block
Text types
Unmarked vs. marked clauses
Wayyiqtol, *qatal*, *weqatal*, *weyiqtol*, *yiqtol*, imperative
Protasis-apodosis
Discourse markers
Transition/climax markers
Primary and secondary citation formulas

Questions for Further Reflection

1. How do both content and form help to determine a passage's boundaries and to shape a literary unit?
2. What is the relationship between *scenes* and *episodes* in historical narrative? Why do we need to distinguish them? What are their counterparts in prophetic sermon and poetry?
3. What is the functional difference between a clause beginning with the connector וְ ("and") and an asyndetic (i.e., conjunctionless) clause? How do these features affect text hierarchy?
4. How are paragraphs signaled in Hebrew?
5. How does one distinguish whether וַיְהִי and וְהָיָה are functioning as discourse markers or full verbs? If operating as discourse markers, what two functions can they play?
6. What are the different functions of *primary* and *secondary citations* and how are they signaled?
7. The history of the Decalogue's interpretation has included no less than three different numbering traditions (see fig. 2.23). Using your new knowledge of literary units, how would you number the Ten Words/Commandments in

Deuteronomy 5:6–21?[18] Be sure to use the Deuteronomic version in your assessment, since it includes more signals for guiding our understanding of structure and text boundaries than are found in Exodus 20:2–17. Also, if you can't use the Hebrew text, be sure to do your analysis in the ESV, because most of the other contemporary versions fail to translate all the connectors. Which of the three major traditions do you think most faithfully represents the biblical text? As you ponder this, consider the following:

- Determine the function of each asyndetic clause, answering whether it marks the beginning of a new command (i.e., fresh beginning) or whether it signals some form of explication.
- Note how the connector וְ (gloss "and") at the head of clauses serves to identify units that are to be read together.
- Assess the person and referent of pronouns to help determine literary units.

MJ	*C-L*	*O-R*	Exodus 20:2–17 (Deuteronomy 5:6–21)
1			I am YHWH your God
2	1	1	Never other gods
		2	Never make a carved image
3	2	3	Never bear YHWH's name in vain
4	3	4	Remember (/Observe) the Sabbath
5	4	5	Honor your father and mother
6	5	6	Never murder
7	6	7	(And) Never commit adultery
8	7	8	(And) Never steal
9	8	9	(And) Never bear false witness
10	9	10	(And) Never covet your neighbor's house (/wife)
	10		(And) Never covet (/desire) your neighbor's wife, etc. (/house, his field, etc.)
MJ = Majority Jewish; *C-L* = Catholic-Lutheran; *O-R* = Orthodox-Reformed			

Fig. 2.23. The Numbering of the Decalogue in the History of Interpretation

18. For a full assessment of the question, see Jason S. DeRouchie, "Counting the Ten: An Investigation into the Numbering of the Decalogue," in *For Our Good Always: Studies on the Message and Influence of Deuteronomy in Honor of Daniel I. Block*, ed. Jason S. DeRouchie, Jason Gile, and Kenneth J. Turner (Winona Lake, IN: Eisenbrauns, 2013), 93–125.

Resources for Further Study

Dawson, D. A. *Text-Linguistics and Biblical Hebrew.* JSOTSup 177. Sheffield, UK: Sheffield Academic, 1994.

Dempster, Stephen G. *Linguistic Features of Hebrew Narrative: A Discourse Analysis of Narrative from the Classical Period.* Ph.D. diss., University of Toronto, 1985.

de Regt, L. J., J. de Waard, and J. P. Fokkelman, eds. *Literary Structure and Rhetorical Strategies in the Hebrew Bible.* Winona Lake, IN: Eisenbrauns, 1996.

DeRouchie, Jason S. "The Blessing-Commission, the Promised Offspring, and the *Toledot* Structure of Genesis." *JETS* 56, 2 (2013): 219–47.

———. *A Call to Covenant Love: Text-Grammar and Literary Structure in Deuteronomy 5–11.* Gorgias Dissertations 30/Biblical Studies 2. Piscataway, NJ: Gorgias, 2007.

———. "Counting the Ten: An Investigation into the Numbering of the Decalogue." In *For Our Good Always: Studies on the Message and Influence of Deuteronomy in Honor of Daniel I. Block*, edited by Jason S. DeRouchie, Jason Gile, and Kenneth J. Turner, 93–125. Winona Lake, IN: Eisenbrauns, 2013.

★ Dorsey, David A. Pages 21–35 in *The Literary Structure of the Old Testament: A Commentary on Genesis-Malachi.* Grand Rapids: Baker, 1999.

Garrett, Duane A., and Jason S. DeRouchie. Pages 283–348 (chs. 37–41) in *A Modern Grammar for Biblical Hebrew.* Nashville: Broadman & Holman, 2009.

Heller, Roy L. *Narrative Structure and Discourse Constellations: An Analysis of Clause Function in Biblical Hebrew Prose.* Harvard Semitic Studies 55. Winona Lake, IN: Eisenbrauns, 2004.

★ Kaiser, Walter C., Jr. Pages 87–104, 165–81 in *Toward an Exegetical Theology: Biblical Exegesis for Preaching and Teaching.* Grand Rapids: Baker Academic, 1981.

Longacre, Robert E. *Joseph: A Story of Divine Providence—A Text Theoretical and Textlinguistic Analysis of Genesis 37 and 39–48.* 2nd ed. Winona Lake, IN: Eisenbrauns, 2003.

Robar, Elizabeth. *The Verb and the Paragraph in Biblical Hebrew: A Cognitive-Linguistic Approach.* Studies in Semitic Languages and Linguistics 78. Leiden: Brill, 2014.

van Wolde, Ellen, ed. *Narrative Syntax and the Hebrew Bible: Papers of the Tilburg Conference 1996.* Biblical Interpretation 29. Leiden: Brill, 1997.

3

TEXT CRITICISM

Goal: Establish the passage's original wording.[1]

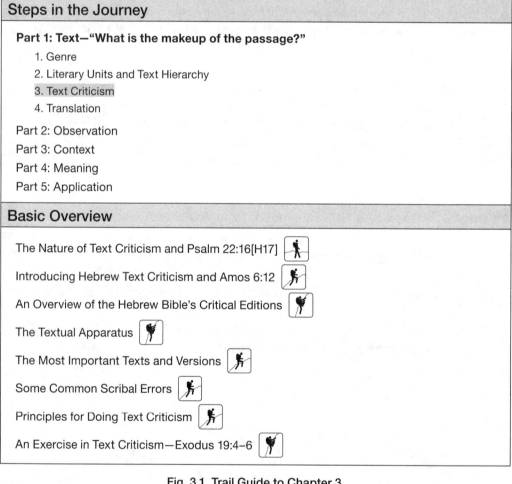

Steps in the Journey

Part 1: Text—"What is the makeup of the passage?"

1. Genre
2. Literary Units and Text Hierarchy
3. Text Criticism
4. Translation

Part 2: Observation

Part 3: Context

Part 4: Meaning

Part 5: Application

Basic Overview

The Nature of Text Criticism and Psalm 22:16[H17]

Introducing Hebrew Text Criticism and Amos 6:12

An Overview of the Hebrew Bible's Critical Editions

The Textual Apparatus

The Most Important Texts and Versions

Some Common Scribal Errors

Principles for Doing Text Criticism

An Exercise in Text Criticism—Exodus 19:4–6

Fig. 3.1. Trail Guide to Chapter 3

1. Some of what follows is adapted from Duane A. Garrett and Jason S. DeRouchie, *A Modern Grammar for Biblical Hebrew* (Nashville: Broadman & Holman, 2009), 349–65 (§ App. 1). Used by permission. See also Jason S. DeRouchie, "Textual Criticism," "Texts of the Old Testament," and "The Ancient Translations," in *Archaeological Study Bible*, ed. Walter C. Kaiser Jr. and Duane A. Garrett (Grand Rapids: Zondervan, 2005), 1151, 1491–92.

The Nature of Text Criticism and Psalm 22:16[H17]

For all their care and attention to detail, the scribes who copied and recopied the Hebrew Bible were not perfect. Errors in copying did occur. Poor memory, impaired judgment, mishearing, and errors of sight or misunderstanding often caused the best-intentioned scribes to omit, substitute, or repeat letters or entire words. At times, scribes made matters worse when they deliberately altered the text in an attempt to correct what they perceived to be a problem. The ultimate result was a series of accidental corruptions or intended improvements that departed from the original text.

For this reason, interpreters must sometimes engage in text criticism, identifying a scribal error and arguing for a more accurate, original reading. ***Text criticism*** is the discipline of restoring the biblical authors' original words by comparing and contrasting the various copies and translations of the Bible. Here, *criticism* means not "finding fault with" but "evaluating" the existing copies.

Significantly, while textual errors do exist among the biblical witnesses, they do not destroy the Bible's credibility or message. Just as an alert reader can understand a book or article that has typographical errors in it, so, too, God's Word is able to speak for itself in spite of the minor corruptions that have arisen through scribal transmission. Most of the biblical text is certain, and where variations do occur among existing copies, we can usually determine the original wording with a good degree of certainty. Most modern translations use footnotes to let readers know where the text is difficult or where scribal errors may exist.

A well-known example of a text problem is found in Psalm 22, the "My God, my God, why have you forsaken me?" psalm. The New Testament refers to this psalm numerous times in relation to Christ's suffering, death, and resurrection.[2] In verse 16[H17] the ESV reads, "They have pierced my hands and feet," which is also the preferred reading in all the other major English versions except the NET Bible, which reads, "Like a lion *they pin* my hands and feet."[3] These two renderings reflect different opinions on which manuscripts preserve the most original reading. An ESV footnote alerts the reader that its translation follows some Hebrew manuscripts, the Greek Septuagint, Latin Vulgate, and Syriac Peshitta, whereas most Hebrew manuscripts read "like a lion, my

2. See Ps. 22:7[H8] in Matt. 27:39; Ps. 22:8[H9] in Matt. 27:43; Ps. 22:15[H16] in John 19:28; Ps. 22:16[H17] in Luke 24:40 with John 20:25; Ps. 22:18[H19] in John 19:24 and Matt. 27:35; Ps. 22:22[H23] in Heb. 2:12 and Matt. 28:10; John 20:17; Rom. 8:29; Ps. 22:24[H25] in Heb. 5:7.

3. The italicized words are not in the Hebrew texts, but the translators added them in an attempt to make sense of the verse.

hands and feet."[4] The NET Bible notes affirm the "grammatically awkward" Hebrew phrasing, which led the translators to supply the clause's subject and verb, "they pin." Nevertheless, they suggest that the difficult syntax may be by "rhetorical design" in order "to convey the panic and terror felt by the psalmist."[5]

There is a difference between a construction that is "grammatically awkward" but still makes sense and one that is completely unintelligible. As it stands, the grouping of words in the majority of Hebrew manuscripts of Psalm 22:16[H17] is nonsensical, which raises the possibility that this is one of a number of examples in the Old Testament in which the bias of later Jewish scribes against Christianity moved them (consciously or unconsciously) to vocalize the Hebrew text in a less messianic way.[6] Not only this, including "lion" in verse 16[H17] would break what appears to be an intentional inversion within the text. In verses 12–18 the psalmist lists his enemies as "bulls," a "lion," "dogs," and armed "evildoers" (vv. 12, 13, 16[H13, 14, 17]), and then in verses 20–21 he restates these antagonists in reverse order: "the sword," "the dog," "the lion," and the

4. The Leningrad Codex found in the *BHS* reads כָּאֲרִי יָדַי וְרַגְלָי ("like a lion my hands and my feet"). In contrast, a DSS fragment (4QPs^{f} [4Q88 f1 2.25]) containing Psalm 22:13–16[H14–17] reads כר[ו]ידי ורגלי, and a Nahal Hever scroll fragment (5/6HevPs [5/6Heb1b f8 9:12]) containing most of Psalm 22 reads כארו ידיה ורגלי. The form כרו in 4QPs^{f} is clearly a Qal *qatal* 3mp from the verb I-כרה, which consistently means "to borrow, hollow, dig," whether of a well (Gen. 26:25), a cistern (Ps. 7:15[H16]), a pit (Ps. 57:6[H7]), a pond (Ps. 94:13), or a grave (2 Chron. 16:14). While the only biblical reference of I-כרה to the human body is used metaphorically of an ear opened to hear from God (Ps. 40:6[H7]), it is a fine verb choice for expressing the "gouging" or "piercing" of the Christ's hands and feet. The other natural option would have been דקר ("to pierce"), which occurs in Zechariah 12:10 with the same predictive effect (see John 19:37; cf. 20:25; Luke 24:40). As for כארו in 5/6HevPs, the root occurs elsewhere only in the nonbiblical pesher on Nahum 3:6–7a (4QpNah [4Qp169 f3 4iii:2 and 4iii:4]), and there it means "to repulse" (II-כאר). *DCH*, however, proposes the meaning "to mutilate" in 5/6HebPs on Psalm 22:16[H17] (*DCH* 4:349). While possible, in light of the reading in 4QPs^{f}, it seems more likely that כארו in 5/6HevPs is a bi-form of I-כרה and should thus be translated "they bore/gouged/pierced." This appears to be the perspective of DSS scholars James C. VanderKam and Peter Flint, who write of the Nahal Hever fragment, "For the crucial word (כארו) the Hebrew form is grammatically difficult, but it is clearly a verb, not a noun, and means *they have bored* or *they have dug* or *they have pierced*" (*The Meaning of the Dead Sea Scrolls: Their Significance for Understanding the Bible, Judaism, Jesus, and Christianity* [San Francisco: HarperSanFrancisco, 2004], 125).

5. W. Hall Harris III and Michael Burer, eds., *The NET Bible* (Richardson, TX: Biblical Studies Press, 1996–2006), s.v. Ps. 22:16 n36.

6. Various types of Jewish postbiblical interpretation are evident through the MT. For example, in Judges 18:30 the Masoretes changed the name *Moses* (מֹשֶׁה) to *Manasseh* (מְנַשֶּׁה) through the addition of a raised letter נ, likely in order to safeguard the honor of the prophet. Similarly, the foreign deity title המלך (= "the king" הַמֶּ֫לֶךְ) is consistently spelled הַמֹּלֶךְ ("the Molek-*god*"), using the vowels for בֹּשֶׁת ("shame") (see Lev. 18:21; 20:2–5; 2 Kings 16:3; 21:6; 23:10; Jer. 32:35). Other proposed examples that directly relate to messianic interpretations are reading "Gog" instead of "Agag" in Numbers 24:7; understanding David's last words to concern "the Christ" instead of himself in 2 Samuel 23:1; viewing Psalm 72:5 as a prayer for the unending reign of the hoped-for king and not for the people to fear him; treating "Mighty God" and "Everlasting Father" as titles for the promised child and not God the Father in Isaiah 9:6[H5]; and reading the time frame of "the anointed" one's coming in Daniel 9:25 to be aligned with the appearing of Jesus (after 7 weeks + 62 weeks) and not some other much earlier figure (e.g., Nehemiah). For an overview of these latter texts, see especially Michael Rydelnik, *The Messianic Hope: Is the Hebrew Bible Really Messianic?*, NAC Studies in Bible and Theology 9 (Nashville: Broadman & Holman, 2010), 34–46, along with the discussions in Roger T. Beckwith, "Daniel 9 and the Date of the Messiah's Coming in Essene, Hellenistic, Pharisaic, Zealot, and Early Christian Computation," *RevQ* 40 (1981): 521–42; John H. Sailhamer, *Introduction to Old Testament Theology: A Canonical Approach* (Grand Rapids: Zondervan, 1995), 204–5, 220–21.

horned "wild oxen."[7] In all likelihood, Psalm 22:16[H17] stands alongside Zechariah 12:10 (which uses a different verb for "pierced" [דקר]) in supplying a direct prediction of the Messiah's death (Matt. 27:35; Mark 15:24; Luke 23:33), which included the piercing of his hands and feet (John 19:37; cf. 20:25; Luke 24:40).

No major doctrines are at stake in this text-critical issue. Jesus' feet and hands were pierced for our transgressions regardless of whether Psalm 22:16[H17] predicted it or not (cf. Isa. 53:5). As here, most other scribal questions in Scripture involve only minor points in the text. We have good reason to be confident that the translations now available faithfully, yet never perfectly, reflect what the seers, sages, and songwriters originally wrote. The presence of scribal errors should not cause fear or move us to think the Bible untrustworthy. Instead, we should rejoice that God has preserved his Word through the ages and has raised up faithful scholars in our day to help establish the best readings when textual variants are present.

The remaining sections in this chapter help clarify the nature and practice of text criticism, especially for those who have at least two semesters of biblical Hebrew. If you know only English but want to learn more about text criticism, read the next section and then jump ahead to "The Most Important Texts and Versions." In that section and the two that follow it, I will introduce the most important texts and versions, set out an overview of common scribal errors, and then offer guidelines for Hebrew text criticism. If you are already feeling that you are in over your head, jump ahead to the discussion of "Translation" in chapter 4.

Introducing Hebrew Text Criticism and Amos 6:12

Hebrew text criticism can be challenging on a number of levels. One of the difficulties comes in shaping legitimate justification for proposed emendations. In text criticism, ***emendation*** is the process of altering a known text in an attempt to return it to its more original reading. A famous but debatable example of an emended text is in Amos 6:12, where the prophet is speaking of things that are obviously absurd or impossible. He says, "Do horses run in a rocky place, or does one plow with oxen [אִם־יַחֲרוֹשׁ בַּבְּקָרִים]? Yet you have turned justice into poison . . . ." The problem, of course, is that although horses do not gallop on stones (or at least should not), people do plow with oxen, and therefore the whole comparison looks irrational. By emending the text to אִם־יַחֲרוֹשׁ בַּבָּקָר יָם, however, we can obtain the rendering "Or does one plow the sea with an ox?" The answer would certainly be "No!" Many argue that this makes more sense.

7. For a full text-critical argument in favor of the LXX reading, see Conrad R. Gren, "Piercing the Ambiguities of Psalm 22:16 and the Messiah's Mission," *JETS* 48, 2 (2005): 283–99.

Because we no longer have the biblical authors' original documents (the ***autographs***), ancient manuscripts and fragments of the Hebrew Scriptures (called ***texts***) and ancient translations of the Old Testament (called ***versions***) are the basic tools of text criticism. These witnesses indicate different readings that have existed through the centuries.

Of course, there are problem passages for which the texts and versions give no real help, and in these cases a scholar must use context and analogy in order to proceed. The alteration of wording in Amos 6:12 has no manuscript or versional support; it is only a scholar's guess that the words בַּבָּקָר יָם ("with an ox the sea") were accidentally joined as one word בַּבְּקָרִים ("with oxen").

Few readers of this book will have access to all the texts and versions that might have a bearing on the text criticism of the Old Testament. For the most part, however, the textual apparatus of the standard Hebrew editions (i.e., *Biblia Hebraica Stuttgartensia* [*BHS*] and *Biblia Hebraica Quinta* [*BHQ*]) and the text-critical notes found in most major Old Testament commentaries will suffice. In addition, there are three other important resources to aid the beginner. First is the United Bible Societies' five-volume *Preliminary and Interim Report of the Hebrew Old Testament Text Project*,[8] which is set up much like Bruce Metzger's well-known *A Textual Commentary on the Greek New Testament*.[9] Second are the notes in the NET Bible, which are especially focused on textual and grammatical challenges in the biblical text. Third, while not yet complete, the new critical edition titled *Biblia Hebraica Quinta* is accompanied by a text-critical commentary that addresses every major issue that translators must tackle.

The NET Bible on Amos 6:12 follows the proposed emendation, rendering the question "Can one plow the sea with oxen?" In contrast, the *Preliminary and Interim Report* favors the traditional Hebrew text with a "B" reading.[10] Similarly, the editor of the *BHQ* volume on *The Twelve Minor Prophets* cautions against the emendation.[11] We should always be hesitant to follow any emendation that has no textual support, and in this instance an easy solution for interpretation is available without any changes to the text. Look again at the Hebrew of Amos 6:12:

12 הֲיְרֻצוּן בַּסֶּלַע סוּסִים
b אִם־יַחֲרוֹשׁ בַּבְּקָרִים (or בַּבָּקָר יָם)
c כִּי־הֲפַכְתֶּם לְרֹאשׁ מִשְׁפָּט

Fig. 3.2. Amos 6:12 in the MT

8. Dominique Barthélemy et al., *Preliminary and Interim Report of the Hebrew Old Testament Text Project*, 5 vols. (New York: United Bible Societies, 1974–80).

9. Bruce M. Metzger, *A Textual Commentary on the Greek New Testament*, 2nd ed. (Peabody, MA: Hendrickson, 2005).

10. Dominique Barthélemy et al., *Preliminary and Interim Report on the Hebrew Old Testament Text Project*, vol. 5, *Prophetical Books II—Ezekiel, Daniel, Twelve Minor Prophets* (New York: United Bible Societies, 1980), 289.

11. Anthony Gelston, "Introduction and Commentaries on the Twelve Minor Prophets," in *The Twelve Minor Prophets*, *BHQ* 13 (Stuttgart: Deutsche Bibelgesellschaft, 2010), 85*.

Although we have warrant for proposing a reading that does not occur in any text, we should be very careful in doing so. If there is a good way to render a text without changing it, we should, and this is the case with Amos 6:12. Rather than emend the text, we should probably assume that בַּסֶּ֫לַע ("in a rocky place") in the first half does "double duty" in both clauses, a practice that occurs in poetry and that is known as *gapping* or *ellipsis*. Taken this way, the whole means, "Do horses run in a rocky place, or does one plow (in a rocky place) with oxen?" The image of someone trying to plow the sea with an ox just seems so far-fetched and implausible that it does not make for a good analogy. But this image works well: a foolish farmer trying to plow through a field when he has not taken the time to remove the stones. This rendering is preferred in the ESV, which translates, "Do horses run on rocks? Does one plow *there* with oxen? But you have turned justice into poison."

An Overview of the Hebrew Bible's Critical Editions

In order to engage in text criticism, we need to know our way around the Hebrew Bible. Until the sixth century A.D., the Hebrew text contained only consonants; the Jews passed the vowels on orally but did not write them. Between A.D. 500 and 1000, however, a group of Jewish scholars known as the *Masoretes* (from מסר, "hand on, transmit") developed a system of vowel pointing, cantillation marks, notes, and various other conventions designed to guarantee a more accurate reading and transmission of the sacred text. Their work, known as the Masoretic Text (MT), was and still remains authoritative, and what we have termed *biblical Hebrew* grows out of the Masoretic tradition.

Today the standard Hebrew text, known in successive editions as the *Biblia Hebraica Stuttgartensia* (*BHS*) and the *Biblia Hebraica Quinta* (*BHQ*), is a copy of the Leningrad Codex (A.D. 1008), the earliest complete Masoretic manuscript.[12] Since the completion of the *BHS* in 1977, new discoveries and advances in text criticism have justified the creation of the updated *BHQ*, which numerous scholars are producing one fascicle (usually a single biblical book) at a time and which will one day replace the *BHS*. While the beginning student will likely use the *BHS* until a single volume of the whole *BHQ* is complete, it is good to become acquainted with the structure and component parts of both editions.

12. Intriguingly, though both the *BHS* and *BHQ* use the *text* of the Leningrad Codex, neither follows its arrangement, which places 1–2 Chronicles before Psalms at the head of the Writings.

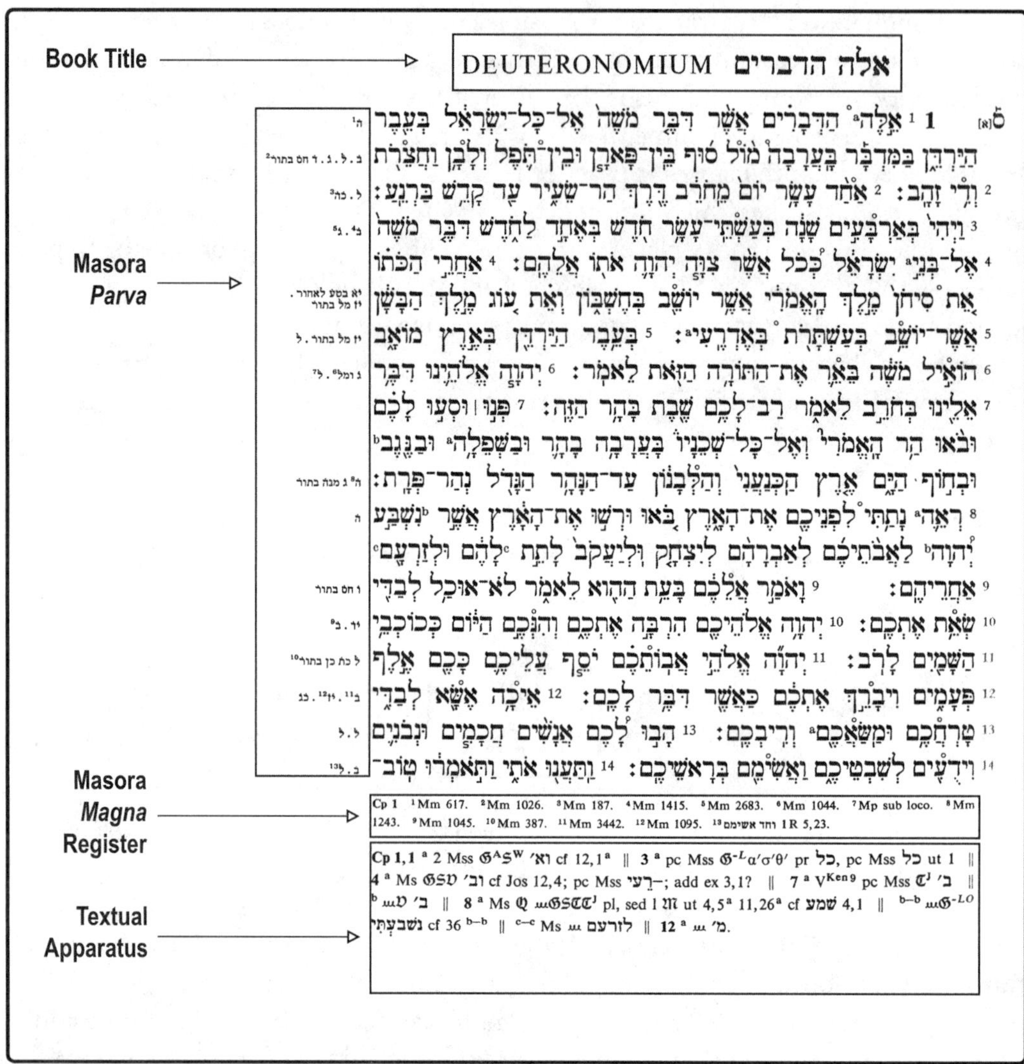

Fig. 3.3. Sample *BHS* Page[14]

14. *BHS*, 283. Used by permission.

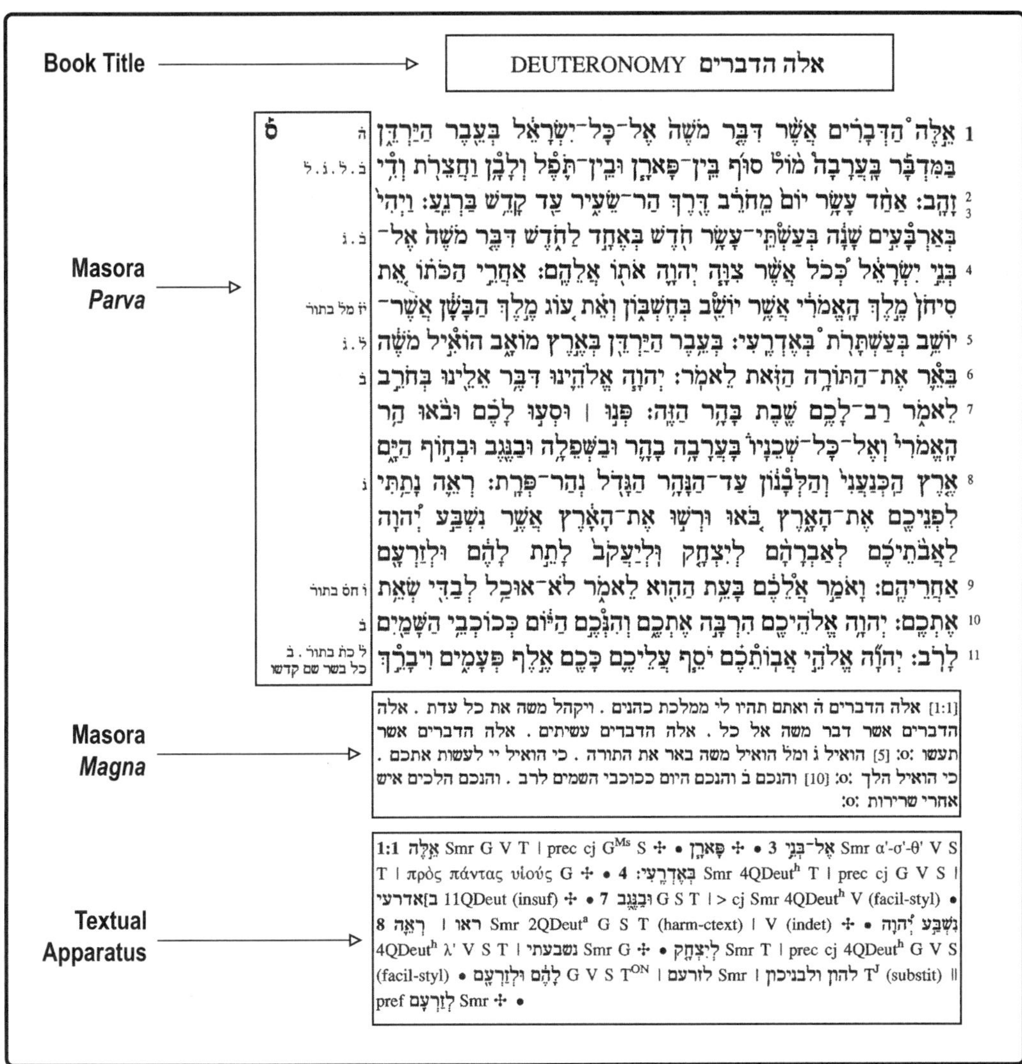

Fig. 3.4. Sample *BHQ* Page[15]

15. Carmel McCarthy, ed., *Biblia Hebraica Quinta, Fascicle 5: Deuteronomy* (Stuttgart: Deutsche Bibelgesellschaft, 2007), 3. Used by permission.

Book Titles and Arrangement

If you own a copy of the *BHS*, open it up to the first page of Deuteronomy (283). If you do not, you can look at the reproductions on the preceding pages (figs. 3.3–3.4).[13] As you turn there, notice that in the *BHS* the biblical book titles are located at the top center of each page: the Hebrew title on even pages and the Latin title on odd pages. The same pattern is followed in the *BHQ*, except that English has replaced the Latin. The first page of each book includes both the Hebrew title and the Latin (*BHS*) or English (*BHQ*) title together.

As I already noted, while all the biblical books are the same in the English and Hebrew Old Testaments, they are ordered differently, and some are grouped as single books where our English Bibles distinguish them. The result is that the Hebrew Old Testament has twenty-four books instead of thirty-nine. Figure 3.5 highlights the arrangement of biblical books in the *BHS* and *BHQ*, which is a little different from the ordering found in *Baba Bathra* 14b noted earlier in chapter 1.

Law	Former & Latter Prophets		Former & Latter Writings	
Genesis Exodus Leviticus Numbers Deuteronomy	Joshua Judges 1–2 Samuel 1–2 Kings	Isaiah Jeremiah Ezekiel The Twelve	Psalms Job Proverbs Ruth Song of Songs Ecclesiastes Lamentations Esther	Daniel Ezra-Nehemiah 1–2 Chronicles

Fig. 3.5. The Arrangement of Books in the *BHS* and *BHQ*

13. I thank the German Bible Society for allowing me to reproduce pages from both the *BHS* and *BHQ* in this book.

Paragraph, Lesson, Verse, and Chapter Divisions

The Hebrew Bible marks a number of divisions; all but the chapter divisions have been present in some form among the Jews for a long time. You should be aware of the following dividers.

1. Paragraphs

The entire Hebrew Old Testament (except the Psalter) is divided into extended paragraphs. In a properly laid-out liturgical text, an "open" paragraph, prefixed by a small פ and known as *Pethuchah* (פְּתוּחָא = "opened"), is one that starts a new line after an empty or incomplete line. In contrast, a "closed" paragraph, marked by a small ס and known as *Sethumah* (סְתוּמָא = "closed"), is separated from its preceding paragraph by a short space within the line. The excerpts from Deuteronomy 1 do not contain any paragraph marks, but a Pethuchah can be seen at Deuteronomy 5:1 (*BHS*, 294) and a host of Sethumah occur between each of the Ten Words in 5:6–22 (*BHS*, 295). While the *BHS* starts every Pethuchah on a new line, the *BHQ* patterns the spacing as if it were a Sethumah. The tendency to place spaces between paragraphs is evident as early as the DSS, and while no one today is certain why some paragraphs were Sethumah and others were Pethuchah, their presence can still at times aid in clarifying literary structure.

2. Lessons

Throughout history, Jews have grouped certain texts to guide the reading of the Hebrew Bible. Jews in Palestine created a three-year lectionary cycle of 452 readings known as *Sedarim* (from סֵדֶר, "order, sequence"). The beginning of each Seder is marked in the Hebrew Scriptures by what looks like a sideways Qamets over the top of a large ס (not to be confused with Sethumah). An example of this mark is found in the margin (inner for *BHS* and outer for *BHQ*) next to the first line of Deuteronomy 1. Similarly, Jews in Babylon, who read through the Torah each year, divided the first five books into fifty-four (or fifty-three) weekly lessons known as *Parashoth*, the beginning of which are marked by the characters פרש in the margin (inner for *BHS* and outer for *BHQ*). For an example of this marking, see Deuteronomy 3:23 in the *BHS* (290).

3. Verses

In biblical Hebrew, the Sof Pasuq (lit., "end of verse"), which looks similar to an English colon (׃), signals the conclusion of a verse (though perhaps not the end of a sentence). The Jewish scribes probably began to separate verses during the age of the Talmud (ca. A.D. 135–500), but the actual numbering of verses did not occur until the sixteenth century. In the *BHS* and *BHQ*, the verse numbers are marked as superscripts at the inside margin. The *BHS* also includes the superscript numbers after each Sof Pasuq. Occasionally, especially in the Psalter, the Hebrew and English verse numbers do not align.

4. Chapters

The Hebrew Bible did not include chapters until the early fourteenth century A.D. Intriguingly, the presence of these divisions derived from the Christian tradition of the Latin Vulgate. The Roman Church had adopted a system developed by Stephen Langton (1150–1228), and this scheme has been used in nearly all biblical texts and versions to the present day. In both the *BHS* and *BHQ*, large numbers at the inside margin signal the beginning of new chapters.

With the possible exception of the paragraph divisions, the principal purpose of the lessons, verses, and chapters has always been to make reading of and reference to the Hebrew Bible more manageable and easy. The purpose was never to guide interpretation. Interpreters should therefore use care in allowing the marked divisions to influence their understanding of the text's component boundaries and message.

The Masorah

One of the contributions the Masoretes made was a series of notes designed to assist a copyist in preserving an unaltered biblical text. Known as the *Masorah*, these notes are located in the manuscript margins and at the end of each book or canonical section (e.g., at the end of the Law). The marginal notes are distinguished between the *Masorah parva* ("small Masorah") and the *Masorah magna* ("large Masorah"), and the concluding notes are called the *Masorah finalis* ("final Masorah"). While the Masorah is written only in consonants (usually Aramaic), the *BHS* and *BHQ* assist the reader by including in the introduction a glossary of common terms. The glossary translations of the Aramaic/Hebrew are in Latin in the *BHS* but in English in the *BHQ*. Furthermore, in a separate section of each fascicle, the *BHQ* provides an English translation of and commentary on the Masorah parva and magna. (When the *BHQ* is complete, these latter elements will be included in a separate volume.)

For our purposes, the ***Masorah parva*** (or "small Masorah") needs some additional comment. It is located in the outer page margins of the *BHS* and *BHQ*. It offers an array of statistical details regarding word counts, word placement (e.g., in the exact middle of the book), and spelling peculiarities, all designed to protect the text from scribal error. A small circle in the body of the text above a word or phrase (°) signals the reader to the marginal comment. For example, in Deuteronomy 1:1, a circle over the phrase אֵלֶּה הַדְּבָרִים ("these are the words") sends the reader to the margin, where the letter ה with a dot over it (הׄ) informs the reader that the phrase shows up five total times in the Hebrew Old Testament (here in Deuteronomy 1:1 and then in Exodus 19:6; 35:1; Isaiah 42:16; Zechariah 8:16). (The Medieval Jews editing the biblical text applied numerical values to all the alphabet, with א–ט representing the units [1–9]—e.g., א stands for 1 and ה for 5). With this information in hand, the copyist was charged to make sure that the phrase occurred only this many times in his text.

While most notes in the Masorah parva are of little value to the interpreter, two should be given more care: Kethiv-Qere and unique forms known as *hapax legomena*.

1. Kethiv-Qere

There were times when the scribes believed that a word written one way (the Kethiv[16]) should be read another way (the Qere[17]). In such instances, they would leave the consonants of the Kethiv but point it with the vowels of the Qere; the consonants of the Qere would then be written in the Masorah parva and usually be marked by a ק with a dot over it (קׄ, short for the Aramaic קְרֵי). While there are no Kethiv-Qere issues in the Deuteronomy 1 samples, one is recorded in Deuteronomy 2:33 (*BHS*, 288). There we are told that the word written בנו ("his son," בְּנוֹ) should be read בָּנָיו ("his sons").

2. Unique Forms

The Masorah parva uses the sigla לׄ (short for the Aramaic לֵיתָא ["There is no (other)"]) to mark when certain forms occur only once in the Hebrew Bible. This feature of ***hapax legomenon*** could mean that the word is unique or that the spelling alone is unique. An example is found in Deuteronomy 1:1. After the Masorah parva notes that מוֹל ("opposite") occurs only twice (בׄ), we are informed that the form תֹּפֶל ("Tophel"), a place name related to Israel's location during Moses' Deuteronomic sermons, shows up only here in the biblical text.

The Textual Apparatus

When a critical edition uses a single manuscript as its base, it is called a ***diplomatic text***. This contrasts with an ***eclectic text***, for which the body text is not tied to a single manuscript but already displays the fruits of text-critical investigation and presents the editor's decisions on what the editor believes to be the most original text. Whereas the

16. Aramaic כְּתִיב, related to the Hebrew root כתב ("to write").
17. Aramaic קְרֵי, related to the Hebrew root קרא ("to call, recite, read").

critical editions of the New Testament follow the latter pattern, all Biblia Hebraica editions to date are diplomatic texts, using the text of the Leningrad Codex (A.D. 1008) as their base.[18] They include a textual apparatus at the bottom of each page that interacts with the most important textual variants for translation and exegesis. As already noted, one of the nice features of the *BHQ* is that it also adds a text-critical commentary that helps the interpreter wade through the data of the apparatus.

The contemporary scholar who edited the particular biblical book in either the *BHS* or *BHQ* is the one who prepared the apparatus. The textual notes included are of three sorts:

- Those that cite minor irregularities in the Leningrad Codex in distinction from other Masoretic manuscripts (e.g., accent or vocalization distinctions).
- Those that give the editor's suggestion for a textual emendation.
- Those that show alternative readings in other Hebrew texts or ancient translations. These notes are by far the most important.

For native English speakers, the *BHQ* apparatus is relatively easy to understand, for it employs English abbreviations for both the textual witnesses and the notes. This is not the case, though, in the *BHS*, whose apparatus uses a mixture of symbols and Latin abbreviations. You can find a full list of the sigla and definitions for the Latin in the introduction to the *BHS* and *BHQ*, but both features still make working through the *BHS* apparatus difficult. The *BHS* and *BHQ* are distinct in the way they present the apparatus notations. Keep your eye on figures 3.3–3.4 as I give an overview of the two apparatuses, and take comfort in knowing that you don't have to memorize all the sigla.

1. *BHS* Apparatus

The body of the *BHS* uses raised English letters to signal when words or phrases are addressed in the apparatus. When a single word is discussed, it is followed by a superscript lowercase English letter, as with [a]אֵלֶּה ("these"), the first word of Deuteronomy 1:1. Two or more words that are addressed as a group are bracketed by the same raised lowercase letter, as in 1:8, where we read [b]נִשְׁבַּע יְהוָה[b] ("YHWH swore"). In the first of these instances, the note tells us that two Hebrew manuscripts (Mss), one Greek manuscript ($\mathfrak{G}^{A}$), and one Syriac manuscript ($\mathfrak{S}^{W}$) add the connector before the word (= וְאֵלֶּה). In the example from 1:8, we see that the Samaritan Pentateuch ($\mathfrak{m}$) and two Greek versions ($\mathfrak{G}^{-LO}$) have the verb in first person

18. Currently, three other groups are creating critical editions of the Hebrew Old Testament. The first two are diplomatic texts, utilizing the Aleppo Codex, which dates to A.D. 900–925 but which is incomplete, lacking almost all of the Pentateuch as well as some or all of Song of Songs, Ecclesiastes, Lamentations, Esther, Daniel, and Ezra: (1) The Hebrew University Bible Project, http://www.hum.huji.ac.il/english/units.php?cat=4980; (2) Miqraot Gedolot HaKeter, http://www1.biu.ac.il/indexE.php?id=6261&pt=1&pid=43&level=3&cPath=6261. In contrast to these, the third project is a critical eclectic text: (3) Ronald Hendel, ed., The Hebrew Bible: A Critical Edition (HBCE) (formerly The Oxford Hebrew Bible Project), http://hbceonline.org/.

in accordance with the fact that YHWH is speaking in the context. As should be clear, the apparatus distinguishes chapter divisions by the abbreviation Cp, verses through the inclusion of verse numbers separated on each side by a space, and notes by two parallel vertical lines (||).

2. *BHQ* Apparatus

In contrast to the pattern in the *BHS*, the *BHQ* offers no markings in the body of the text to signal comment in the apparatus. Each new entry in the *BHQ* apparatus, however, begins with a listing of the word or phrase in the Leningrad Codex that is being addressed. So, for example, אֵ֣לֶּה is listed first after 1:1 in the apparatus, followed directly by those witnesses that agree with the Leningrad Codex: the Samaritan Pentateuch (Smr), the old Greek (G), the Vulgate (V), and the Targum (T). After a single vertical separator line, which marks that what follows disagrees with the reading of the Leningrad Codex, we read that a single Greek manuscript (G^{Ms}) and the Syriac (S) precede (prec) אֵ֣לֶּה with the conjunction (cj). The cross symbol (⁜) indicates that the apparatus commentary has a discussion of this case, and the black dot (●) concludes the note. Occasionally, before the note is concluded, two parallel vertical lines (||) will signal the case conclusion, followed by a comment detailing the editor's preferred reading. For example, the last note in Deuteronomy 1:8 reveals that the editor believes the Samaritan Pentateuch retains the most original reading, one that does not include לָהֶ֥ם וּ ("to them and") before לְזַרְעָ֑ם ("to their offspring").

The Most Important Texts and Versions

From the earliest period of the Bible's origin, God's people had a tendency to preserve the text and to update things such as the Hebrew script, spelling developments, and geographical data for later generations. The Jews saw the Scriptures as God's lasting and authoritative Word, so they sought not only to copy the text with great care but also to explain (through the Masorah), update (in the ways noted above), and translate the text so that the meaning was preserved.

Not one of the original biblical manuscripts still exists. But through the years, faithful scribes, translators, and expositors have preserved the Scriptures. For the Old Testament, we have ancient manuscripts in Hebrew, Greek, Aramaic, Syriac, and Latin. There are also thousands of leather and papyrus scroll fragments, some more than two thousand years old. These sources bear witness to the "original" Old Testament. The Hebrew witnesses are called *texts*, whereas the translations are called *versions*. I want to supply an overview of the most important of these now.

Hebrew Texts

The primary witnesses to the original Old Testament are the copies written in Hebrew. The most significant of these texts are the ***Masoretic Text***(s), the ***Dead Sea Scrolls***, and the ***Samaritan Pentateuch***.

1. The Masoretic Text(s) (𝔐 [*BHS*], M [*BHQ*])

The MT is the received standard text of the Hebrew Scriptures. It is called *Masoretic* because it is the text tradition of the Jewish scholars known as the *Masoretes*, who worked between A.D. 500 and 1000 to add to the consonantal Hebrew text a system of vowels, accents, and notes that guaranteed a more accurate transmission of the biblical text. No other text from the ancient world was as carefully safeguarded as the MT. Its tradition came to be regarded as authoritative, and we can still consider it highly trustworthy. Today the earliest complete Masoretic manuscript, the Leningrad Codex (A.D. 1008), is used for the standard edition of the Hebrew Old Testament. Another ancient copy, the Aleppo Codex, is even earlier (A.D. 925), but part of the Pentateuch is missing.

2. The Dead Sea Scrolls (𝔔, Q for Qumran)

Up until the discovery of the Dead Sea Scrolls (DSS) in 1947, the earliest known copies of the Hebrew Bible were those produced by the Masoretes in the Middle Ages. But with the eight hundred scrolls found in the Judaean Desert, dating from approximately 250 B.C. to A.D. 135 and including every Old Testament book except Esther, our knowledge of the Old Testament text was pushed back a thousand years! The DSS contained Hebrew, Greek, and Aramaic manuscripts and fragments, many of which are biblical in nature. A great number of the Old Testament manuscripts found reflect essentially the same text inherited by the Masoretes, confirming the antiquity and authority of the MT. The most famous DSS text is the great Isaiah scroll (1QIsa[a]), which contains the entire book of Isaiah.

3. The Samaritan Pentateuch (𝔐𝔰, Smr)

This is the Pentateuch of the Samaritan community, the semi-Jewish breakaway group that grew up in the region of Samaria after Assyria's occupation (2 Kings 17:29) and that Jesus encountered several times in his ministry (e.g., John 4). The Samaritans recognized only the Pentateuch as canonical. In some places the Samaritan Pentateuch seems to have been deliberately altered to support the theology of the Samaritans, but many differences between it and the MT are merely spelling-related (orthographic), so we can still use it for text-critical purposes.

Versions/Translations

Since the discovery of the DSS, the ancient versions (or translations) of the Bible have become less important for establishing the original Old Testament text. Nevertheless, readings that differ from the MT are still evaluated in at least four early versions: the Greek ***Septuagint***, the Aramaic ***Targums***, the Syriac ***Peshitta***, and the Latin ***Vulgate***.

1. The Septuagint (𝔊, G)

The most important of all versions, the Septuagint is the translation of the Old Testament into Greek that became the Bible of the early church. Although its origins are debated, the process of translation probably began around the mid-third century B.C. in Alexandria, Egypt. It does not appear to be the work of a single translator or even of a single group of translators; it has been called a collection of translations. Some books in the LXX are translated skillfully and accurately, but others, such as Job, are very free renditions. It is the most useful version for helping us establish the original Old Testament text because (a) it is the earliest translation of the entire Old Testament, (b) it is well attested in numerous manuscripts, and (c) it contains more significant variant readings than any other version. Still, very few scholars would regard it as superior to the MT, even though some of its readings are supported in Qumran material.

2. The Targums (𝔗, T)

A *Targum*, Aramaic for "translation" or "interpretation," is an Aramaic translation of the Hebrew Scriptures made for postexilic Jews whose mother tongue was Aramaic. Targums tend to paraphrase freely—at times exceedingly so. Targum Onkelos is the official Targum for the Law, and Targum Jonathan is the official Targum for the Prophets, but there are also a number of unofficial Targums. While they appear to have been translated from a text very similar to the MT, they are so interpretive, loosely translated, and filled with comments that it is hard to use them to establish the original Hebrew text.

3. The Peshitta (𝔖, S for Syriac)

The *Peshitta*, Syriac for "simple" or "straightforward," is the authorized Bible of the Syrian church. Syriac is a later dialect of Aramaic. Although the history of the Syriac text is complex and debated, it appears that it has Jewish rather than Christian origin, dating no later than the fourth century A.D. It was originally translated relatively literally from the Hebrew, so it can still be of help in text criticism.

4. The Vulgate (𝔙, V)

Vulgate is Latin for "common" or "popular," and since the late fourth century the Vulgate has served as the standard Bible of the Western church. The Old Testament portion is made up of the church father Jerome's translation of the Hebrew text into Latin. Because Jerome was largely dependent on the Septuagint and because his own translation varies in literalness, we need to use the Old Testament Vulgate cautiously as a witness to the Hebrew original.

Some Common Scribal Errors

Having reviewed the most important texts and versions, we are in a position to consider some common scribal errors and the practice of text criticism itself. In order to do text criticism, you need to have some idea about the kinds of errors that a scribe was likely to make. Scholars have catalogued these errors by carefully analyzing the various texts and versions in relation to one another, by identifying scribal tendencies, and by drawing reasoned conclusions from the data. Errors of sight, understanding, sound, judgment, or memory often caused the best-intentioned scribes to omit, substitute, or repeat letters or entire words. While very few errors were likely ever brought about on purpose, scribes made both unintentional and intentional alterations to the text, which ultimately resulted in a departure from the original.

We find three main types of textual changes: ***accidental***, ***unintentional***, and ***intentional***.[19]

1. Accidental Changes

These are errors that are due to the physical deterioration of a manuscript.

2. Unintentional Changes

These are (a) errors related to the manuscript's being copied, (b) errors of the scribe's fallibility, (c) errors related to dictation/faulty hearing, and (d) errors of the scribe's judgment.

a. Errors Related to the Manuscript's Being Copied

- *Confusion of similar letters*. Hebrew students can understand this problem very well. Both in the archaic script and in the later square script that you likely

19. I have taken the structure and some of the content of this discussion from Ellis R. Brotzman and Eric J. Tully, *Old Testament Textual Criticism: A Practical Introduction*, 2nd ed. (Grand Rapids: Baker Academic, 2016), 117–29. The beginning student will find this introductory guide a great first step into the science and art of Old Testament text criticism.

learned in Hebrew class, certain letters are easily confused. In the square script, consider ב and כ (in 1 Chron. 17:20), י and ו (in Isa. 30:4), ה and ת (in Ex. 34:19), and ח and ת (in Ps. 49:15).

- *Wrong word division*. Very often in ancient manuscripts, letters are closely placed, challenging one's reading. A common example in English is the unseparated phrase GODISNOWHERE, which could be separated GOD IS NOW HERE or GOD IS NOWHERE. The proposed emendation of Amos 6:12 from בבקרים (i.e., בַּבְּקָרִים ["with oxen"]) to בבקר ים (i.e., בַּבָּקָר יָם ["with an ox the sea"]) is an example of this; scholars suggest that the words have been incorrectly joined.
- *Wrong assignment of vowels*. The incorrect placement of a vowel letter or a misreading of an ambiguous vowel letter could cause a scribe to misidentify or mistranslate a word.
- *Abbreviations*. An earlier scribe may have used an abbreviation that a later scribe misunderstood.
- *Homoioteleuton*. *Homoioteleuton* means "similar ending," and it refers to an error of omission brought about by the similarity of the ending of neighboring words. For example, if two phrases end with the same word, the scribe's eye might jump from the end of the first phrase to the end of the second phrase without copying the words of the second phrase. Anyone who has copied something by hand knows how easily this error can happen when you are moving your eye from the text being copied to the copy itself.
- *Homoioarcton*. *Homoioarcton* means "similar beginning," and it refers to an error of omission brought about by the similarity of the beginning of neighboring words.

b. Errors of the Scribe's Fallibility

- *Haplography*. This is writing a word or letter once where it should have been written twice.
- *Dittography*. This is writing a word or letter twice where it should have been written once.
- *Transposition (Metathesis)*. A scribe inadvertently switched the places of two letters, as when we type the definite article *the* as "teh."

c. Errors Related to Dictation/Faulty Hearing

- *Misunderstanding a spoken text*. It appears that sometimes the scribes wrote as another scribe read the text aloud. Some may have made mistakes based on words that sound alike. For example, at times we see לוֹ in the text where we should see לֹא, or the reverse.

d. Errors of the Scribe's Judgment

- *Faulty memory*. Sometimes scribes lapsed into copying from mistaken memory rather than from the manuscript(s) before them.

- *Improper conformity to parallels.* At other times scribes appear to have unintentionally made a text conform to a parallel reading.
- *Insertion of marginal note.* Some scholars suggest that occasionally a note in the margin of a text was accidentally inserted into the text itself.

3. Intentional Changes

These include (a) deliberate alterations, (b) deliberate omission of words or phrases, (c) explanatory glosses, and (d) euphemisms.

a. Deliberate alterations. In comparing manuscripts of the Hebrew Old Testament, we occasionally see evidence that an early scribe engaged in a kind of textual emendation. For example, scribes may correct spelling or even grammatical peculiarities, update or clarify archaic or unclear words or phrases, adapt readings that were believed theologically questionable or disrespectful to God, conform divergent readings with parallel passages, or fix what were believed to be historical or geographical problems. While these kinds of changes are quite rare and could in certain circumstances be justified, they could also create further distance between the copied text and the original.

b. Deliberate omission of words or phrases. From Jewish sources, we learn of seventeen instances in the whole Old Testament where scribes felt certain words were out of place or improper in context.

c. Explanatory glosses. Some scholars suggest that occasionally a scribe added a clarifying note into the text.

d. Euphemisms. In some instances, scribes apparently viewed what was written to be indelicate or offensive and so altered the text to something less offensive.

While textual changes resulting in error do exist among the biblical witnesses, and while some Old Testament books such as Samuel and Jeremiah witness major differences between the MT and other texts and versions, most textual variations are quite small and have little impact on either the text's credibility or its message.[20] Most of the biblical text is undisputed, and for the questions that exist among the biblical witnesses, scholars can usually establish the original wording with a high degree of certainty because of their thorough acquaintance with the available manuscripts and the context.

As an interpreter, you do well to remember that you are not alone in this process. Not only do we have many exceptional English translations based on solid text-critical work, we also have great tools such as technical commentaries and the NET Bible notes that help us work through the various problems.

20. For a discussion of these and many other matters, see the "Resources for Further Study" at the end of this chapter.

Principles for Doing Text Criticism

The reader of the Hebrew Old Testament frequently encounters variant readings and must evaluate them to decide whether a given emendation should be followed. This issue cannot be avoided. For the beginning reader, this is a bewildering enterprise, but the following guidelines should prove helpful.

THE GUIDING PRINCIPLE:
The more original reading is the one that best explains the rise of all the others.

The interpreter must assess which reading most likely came first and how other readings could have come about. In doing so, text critics must evaluate both external and internal evidence. ***External evidence*** deals with the age and quality of the manuscripts. Older manuscripts may be closer to the original, but they could also contain old errors, so we must be cautious. Wrestling with ***internal evidence*** involves deciding what the author most likely wrote and which variant readings are best explained as unintentional or intentional changes made by copyists.

With these aspects in mind, at least one of the following should be true in order to justify emending a text:

- The Hebrew of the received text is unintelligible or at least very strange. Sometimes the interpretation of a problematic line is so speculative in nature that it is difficult to have confidence in the text or in any translation allegedly based on that text.
- Support exists in Hebrew manuscripts for the proposed emendation.
- There is support in the versions or the history of interpretation (e.g., the New Testament) for the proposed emendation, and we can offer a clear explanation of how the correct reading reflected in the version became corrupted to what we see in the MT.
- There is strong contextual support for emendation.

These principles noted, you would do well to heed another fundamental rule of Old Testament text criticism: Emend with caution! Why? I have seven reasons:

1. We are dealing with the very Word of God. This is no ordinary human book.
2. The Masoretes were very careful. They were not flawless, and at times their bias against Christianity may have caused them (whether consciously or unconsciously)

to favor nonmessianic readings. Nevertheless, the last hundred years of textual research has shown that they preserved the text remarkably well.

3. Every argument for emending a text can be countered. For example, we may assert that the Hebrew is unclear. But Hebrew that appears to us to be unintelligible may simply be using an idiom that we do not know. We should bear in mind how little we know of ancient Israelite culture and dialect.
4. The versions (LXX, etc.) have numerous problems of their own (inept or biased translators, corrupt manuscripts, use of paraphrase, etc.).
5. Emendations are sometimes driven by theological considerations or some other agenda. A scholar may want to emend the text because the text contradicts a thesis that he or she is trying to push. Such emendations have little to commend them.
6. Emendations tend to make a dynamic text flat or dull. A heavily emended version of a Hebrew text often reads as generic Hebrew and lacks literary power. Moreover, a willingness to work with a text as it stands often yields a profound, or at least clear, sense of what the passage means.
7. An excessively emended text is a new edition of the Scriptures! Someone who emends the text liberally has taken the position of being a redactor—one might say a coauthor—of a biblical text. There is an inverse relationship between how much emending a scholar does and how much confidence people have in that scholar's results.

With these guidelines, you should be ready to begin your hand at text criticism. Before concluding this chapter, let us consider the text-critical issues that arise in Exodus 19:4–6.

An Exercise in Text Criticism—Exodus 19:4–6

The *BHS* apparatus lists three text problems associated with Exodus 19:4–6. None of them are substantial.

4 אַתֶּם רְאִיתֶם אֲשֶׁר עָשִׂיתִי לְמִצְרָיִם [a]וָאֶשָּׂא אֶתְכֶם עַל־[b]כַּנְפֵי נְשָׁרִים וָאָבִא אֶתְכֶם אֵלָי׃ 5 וְעַתָּה אִם־שָׁמוֹעַ תִּשְׁמְעוּ בְּקֹלִי וּשְׁמַרְתֶּם אֶת־בְּרִיתִי וִהְיִיתֶם לִי [a]סְגֻלָּה מִכָּל־הָעַמִּים כִּי־לִי כָּל־הָאָרֶץ׃ 6 וְאַתֶּם תִּהְיוּ־לִי מַמְלֶכֶת כֹּהֲנִים וְגוֹי קָדוֹשׁ אֵלֶּה הַדְּבָרִים אֲשֶׁר תְּדַבֵּר אֶל־בְּנֵי יִשְׂרָאֵל׃	4 You yourselves have seen what I did to the Egyptians, and how I bore you on eagles' wings and brought you to myself. 5 Now therefore, if you will indeed obey my voice and keep my covenant, you shall be my treasured possession among all peoples, for all the earth is mine; 6 and you shall be to me a kingdom of priests and a holy nation.

4 [a] mlt Mss 𝔗[Ms] בְּמִ׳ || [b] 𝔊(𝔖𝔗[JP]) ὡσεὶ ἐπί
5 [a] 𝔊(𝔗[P]) + λαός

Fig. 3.6. Text-Critical Issues in the *BHS* of Exodus 19:4–6 (with ESV)

In Exodus 19:4 problem "a," we read that multiple medieval Hebrew manuscripts (mlt Mss) and a single Targum manuscript (𝔗[Ms]) read בְּמִצְרָיִם ("in Egypt") rather than לְמִצְרָיִם ("to Egypt"). The ESV translates מִצְרָיִם as "Egyptians," but the plural gentilic "Egyptians" is actually מִצְרִים (e.g., Gen. 12:12, 14; 43:32; Deut. 26:6).[21] מִצְרָיִם is the proper name "Egypt," which can refer to a place (thus "in Egypt," בְּמִצְרָיִם, see Ex. 12:40) or can collectively stand for the nation (cf. 18:8–10). Because ב (*beth*) and ל (*lamed*) are not easily confused letters in either the square script or the archaic script (𐤁 and 𐤋), it seems most likely that the translators of the multiple Hebrew manuscripts and the single Targum read "Egypt" as the place instead of as the people and therefore felt compelled to switch the preposition from לְ ("to") to בְּ ("in").

In problem "b" of Exodus 19:4, we read that the Greek Septuagint (𝔊), the Syriac Peshitta (𝔖), and the entire Targum tradition (𝔗), including Targum Pseudo-Jonathan to the Pentateuch (𝔗[J]) and the Palestinian Targum (𝔗[P]), read the compound preposition כְּעַל ("as on") rather than the single preposition עַל ("on"). This variant likely grew not out of an actual Hebrew text but more simply from a translator's making explicit the implied simile in order to ensure that readers recognized the metaphorical language and didn't imagine something like Tolkien's great eagles from *Lord of the Rings* rescuing the Israelites from the clutches of the Egyptians!

Problem "a" in Exodus 19:5 simply notes that the Septuagint (𝔊) and Palestinian Targum (𝔗[P]) add עַם ("people") into the text before סְגֻלָּה ("treasured possession"). Because the Greek term consistently used to translate סְגֻלָּה is the adjective περιούσιος ("special") and not a noun, the inclusion of λαός was imperative to make sense of the clause. Hebrew and Greek are not equivalent languages, so two words were required to unpack what in Hebrew was represented by a single word. As with the previous text problems, there is no evidence here that a different Hebrew text including עַם stands behind what is found in the LXX. The Greek is just making a dynamic equivalent of the Hebrew.

21. The term *gentilic* (or *demonym*) is a substantival adjective that in grammar relates to words that refer to residents or natives of a particular place, whose title is derived from the name of that particular place (e.g., *Egyptians* is the gentilic from *Egypt*).

Text criticism can be tedious work, but the process gives us confidence that we are faithfully exegeting the original biblical text that God gave us. And that is what we want—God's Word, not man's words. As noted, in New Testament studies the UBS and Nestle Aland critical editions are eclectic texts, not being based on any single Greek manuscript but already showing the labors of text-critical reconstruction. This is not the case for our study of the Hebrew Old Testament. The *BHS* and *BHQ* reproduce a single medieval Hebrew manuscript, the Leningrad Codex. A translation such as the NASB simply renders this text, whereas the translation teams of versions such as the ESV and NIV actually did some of their own textual assessment. An example of this comes when we read in an ESV footnote that the English translation follows the Septuagint or Vulgate instead of the Hebrew (e.g., 1 Sam. 10:5; 14:41).

As with each of the text problems in Exodus 19:4–6, most of those we face in Scripture have little bearing on the message of the text itself. But this is not always the case, so you need to keep your eye out for more substantial problems and then do your own text-critical work.

Key Words and Concepts

Text criticism
Emendation
Autograph
Texts and versions
Masorah parva
Kethiv-Qere
Hapax legomenon
Diplomatic and eclectic texts
Masoretic Text (MT), Dead Sea Scrolls (DSS), and Samaritan Pentateuch
Septuagint (LXX), Targums, Peshitta, and Vulgate
Accidental, unintentional, and intentional changes
External and internal evidence

Questions for Further Reflection

1. How should we respond when we learn that the biblical manuscripts that stand behind our modern versions can have scribal errors in them?
2. If you were teaching from Amos 6:12 this week, what would your conclusion be regarding the best reading of the text? In your answer, explain both sides of the argument.
3. What is significant about the Leningrad Codex?
4. What are the most important texts and versions? Assess how they are helpful or unhelpful in text criticism.
5. Explain some of the ways that scribes made errors in their copying.

6. Explain this axiom: "The more original reading is the one that best explains the rise of all the others."
7. Why must we be cautious when proposing an emendation?

Resources for Further Study

Ready-Reference Tools

Barthélemy, Dominique, et al. *Preliminary and Interim Report of the Hebrew Old Testament Text Project*. 5 vols. New York: United Bible Societies, 1974–80.

"Commentary on the Critical Apparatus." In *BHQ*.

Comprehensive Aramaic Lexicon. http://cal1.cn.huc.edu/.

Computer resources: *Accordance* (http://www.accordancebible.com/), *BibleWorks* (http://www.bibleworks.com/), *Logos Bible Software* (https://www.logos.com/).

Evangelical Textual Criticism (blog). http://www.evangelicaltextualcriticism.blogspot.com/.

Harris, W. Hall, III, and Michael H. Burer, eds. *The NET Bible*. Richardson, TX: Biblical Studies Press, 1996–2006. https://bible.org/netbible/.

Judaica Electronic Texts. http://www.library.upenn.edu/cajs/etexts.html.

Latin Vulgate. http://www.latinvulgate.com/.

Septuagint Online. http://www.kalvesmaki.com/LXX/.

Text-critical notes in series such as Anchor Bible Commentary, Hermeneia, and Word Biblical Commentary.

Tov, Emanuel, ed. *Electronic Resources Relevant to the Textual Criticism of Hebrew Scripture*. http://rosetta.reltech.org/TC/vol08/Tov2003.html.

Overviews of the Discipline

Barthélemy, Dominique. *Studies in the Text of the Old Testament: An Introduction to the Hebrew Old Testament Text Project*. Textual Criticism and the Translator 3. Winona Lake, IN: Eisenbrauns, 2012.

Gentry, Peter J. "The Text of the Old Testament." *JETS* 52, 1 (2009): 19–45.

Soderland, S. K. "Text and MSS of the OT." *ISBE* 4:798–814.

✪ Tov, Emanuel. "Textual Criticism (OT)." *ABD* 4:393–412.

Waltke, Bruce K. "Old Testament Textual Criticism." In *Foundations for Biblical Interpretation*, edited by David S. Dockery, Kenneth A. Mathews, and Robert B. Sloan, 156–86. Nashville: Broadman & Holman, 1994.

———. "Textual Criticism of the Old Testament." In *Introductory Articles*, vol. 1 of Expositor's Bible Commentary, edited by Frank E. Gaebelein, 211–28. Grand Rapids: Zondervan, 1979.

Wolters, Al. "The Text of the Old Testament." In *The Face of Old Testament Studies: A Survey of Contemporary Approaches*, edited by David W. Baker and Bill T. Arnold, 19–37. Grand Rapids: Baker Academic, 2004.

Introductions to Methodology

Barthélemy, Dominique. *Studies in the Text of the Old Testament: An Introduction to the Hebrew Old Testament Text Project*. Textual Criticism and the Translator 3. Winona Lake, IN: Eisenbrauns, 2012.

⭘ Brotzman, Ellis R., and Eric J. Tully. *Old Testament Textual Criticism: A Practical Introduction*. 2nd ed. Grand Rapids: Baker Academic, 2016.

McCarter, P. Kyle, Jr. *Textual Criticism: Recovering the Text of the Hebrew Bible*. Guides to Biblical Scholarship, Old Testament. Minneapolis: Augsburg Fortress, 2001.

⭘ Tov, Emanuel. *Textual Criticism of the Hebrew Bible*. 3rd ed. Minneapolis: Fortress, 2011.

Wegner, Paul D. *A Student's Guide to Textual Criticism of the Bible: Its Methods and Results*. Downers Grove, IL: InterVarsity Press, 2006.

Introductions to Major Texts, Versions, and Critical Editions

General

Birdsall, J. Neville. "Versions, Ancient (Introduction)." *ABD* 6:787–93.

Danker, Frederick W. *Multipurpose Tools for Bible Study*. 2nd ed. Minneapolis: Fortress, 2003.

Eissfeldt, Otto. Part 5 in *The Old Testament: An Introduction*. New York: Harper & Row, 1965.

Harrison, R. K. Part 4 in *Introduction to the Old Testament*. Grand Rapids: Eerdmans, 1969; repr., Peabody, MA: Hendrickson, 2016.

⭘ Würthwein, Ernst, and Alexander Achilles Fisher. *The Text of the Old Testament: An Introduction to the Biblia Hebraica*. Translated by Errol F. Rhodes. 3rd ed. Grand Rapids: Eerdmans, 2014.

Masoretic Text and Masorah

Biblia Hebraica Quinta: General Introduction and Megilloth. Stuttgart: Deutsche Bibelgesellschaft, 2004.

Garrett, Duane A., and Jason S. DeRouchie. Pages 349–65 in *A Modern Grammar for Biblical Hebrew*. Nashville: Broadman & Holman, 2009.

Ginsburg, Christian D. *Massorah*. 4 vols. 1865–1905; repr., New York: Ktav, 1975.

Kelley, Page H., Daniel S. Mynatt, and Timothy G. Crawford. *The Masorah of Biblia Hebraica Stuttgartensia: Introduction and Annotated Glossary*. Grand Rapids: Eerdmans, 1998.

Scott, William R., Harold Scanlin, and Hans Peter Rüger. *A Simplified Guide to BHS: Critical Apparatus, Masora, Accents, Unusual Letters and Other Markings*. 4th ed. N. Richland Hills, TX: D&F Scott Publishing, 2007.

Wonneberger, Reinhard. *Understanding BHS: A Manual for the Users of Biblia Hebraica Stuttgartensia*. 2nd ed. Rome: Pontifical Biblical Institute, 1990.

Dead Sea Scrolls

Flint, Peter W., ed. *The Bible at Qumran: Text, Shape, and Interpretation*. Studies in the Dead Sea Scrolls and Related Literature. Grand Rapids: Eerdmans, 2001.

Henze, Matthias, ed.. *Biblical Interpretation at Qumran*. Studies in the Dead Sea Scrolls and Related Literature. Grand Rapids: Eerdmans, 2004.

Orion Center for the Study of the Dead Sea Scrolls and Associated Literature at Hebrew University of Jerusalem. http://orion.mscc.huji.ac.il/.

Schiffman, Lawrence H., and James C. VanderKam, eds. *Encyclopedia of the Dead Sea Scrolls*. 2 vols. New York: Oxford University Press, 2000.

Tov, Emanuel. *Scribal Practices and Approaches Reflected in the Texts Found in the Judean Desert*. Studies on the Texts of the Desert of Judah 54. Atlanta: SBL, 2009.

———, ed. *The Texts from the Judaean Desert: Indices and an Introduction to the Discoveries in the Judaean Desert Series*. DJD 39. Oxford: Clarendon, 2002.

Ulrich, Eugene. *The Dead Sea Scrolls and the Origins of the Bible*. Studies in the Dead Sea Scrolls and Related Literature. Grand Rapids: Eerdmans, 1999.

VanderKam, James C. *The Dead Sea Scrolls and the Bible*. Grand Rapids: Eerdmans, 2012.

Septuagint

Computer Assisted Tools for Septuagint/Scriptural Study. http://ccat.sas.upenn.edu/rs/rak/catss.html.

Dines, Jennifer M. *The Septuagint*. Understanding the Bible and Its World. London: Bloomsbury, 2004.

Greenspoon, Leonard J. "Versions, Ancient (Greek)." *ABD* 6:793–94.

Jellicoe, Sidney. *The Septuagint and Modern Study*. Winona Lake, IN: Eisenbrauns, 1978; repr., 2014.

Jobes, Karen H., and Moisés Silva. *Invitation to the Septuagint*. 2nd ed. Grand Rapids: Baker Academic, 2015.

Marcos, Natalio Fernández. *The Septuagint in Context: Introduction to the Greek Version of the Bible*. Atlanta: SBL, 2009.

Septuagint Online. http://www.kalvesmaki.com/LXX/.

Swete, Henry Barclay. *An Introduction to the Old Testament in Greek*. 2nd ed. Cambridge: Cambridge University Press, 1914; repr., Eugene, OR: Wipf & Stock, 2003.

Theological and Academic Resources for the Septuagint. http://www.kalvesmaki.com/.

Tov, Emanuel. *The Text-Critical Use of the Septuagint in Biblical Research*. 3rd ed. Winona Lake, IN: Eisenbrauns, 2015.

United Bible Societies. *Septuagint Bibliography*. http://www.ubs-translations.org/cgi-bin/dbman/db.cgi?db=lxxbib&uid=default.

Samaritan Pentateuch

Crown, Alan D., and Terry Giles. "Samaritan Pentateuch." *NIDB* 6:73–74.

Waltke, Bruce K. "Samaritan Pentateuch." *ABD* 5:932–40.

Peshitta and Targums

Alexander, Philip S. "Targum, Targumim." *ABD* 6:320–31.

Brock, S. P. "Versions, Ancient (Syriac)." *ABD* 6:794–99.

Reviews of Peshitta and Targum scholarship. http://www.targum.info/biblio/reviews.htm.

Vulgate and Old Latin

Bogaert, P.-M. "Bulletin de la Bible latine. VII. Première série." *RBén* 105 (1995): 200–38.

———. "Bulletin de la Bible latine. VII. Deuxième série." *RBén* 106 (1996): 386–412.

———. "Bulletin de la Bible latine. VII. Troisième série." *RBén* 108 (1998): 359–86.

———. "Versions, Ancient (Latin)." *ABD* 6:799–803.

Hartman, L. F., B. M. Peebles, and M. Stevenson. "Vulgate." *NCE* 14:591–600.

Critical Text Editions and Translations

Computer Aids

Comprehensive Aramaic Lexicon. http://cal1.cn.huc.edu/.

Computer resources: *Accordance* (http://www.accordancebible.com/), *BibleWorks* (http://www.bibleworks.com/), *Logos Bible Software* (https://www.logos.com/).

Evangelical Textual Criticism (blog). http://www.evangelicaltextualcriticism.blogspot.com/.

Judaica Electronic Texts. http://www.library.upenn.edu/cajs/etexts.html.

Septuagint Online. http://www.kalvesmaki.com/LXX/.

Tov, Emanuel, ed. *Electronic Resources Relevant to the Textual Criticism of Hebrew Scripture.* http://rosetta.reltech.org/TC/vol08/Tov2003.html.

Masoretic Text

Elliger, Karl, et al., eds. *Biblia Hebraica Stuttgartensia.* 5th rev. ed. Stuttgart: Deutsche Bibelgesellschaft, 1983.

Hebrew University Bible Project. http://www.hum.huji.ac.il/english/units.php?cat=4980.

Hendel, Ronald, ed. The Hebrew Bible: A Critical Edition (HBCE). Formerly The Oxford Hebrew Bible Project. http://hbceonline.org/.

Miqraot Gedolot HaKeter. http://www1.biu.ac.il/indexE.php?id=6261&pt=1&pid=43&level=3&cPath=6261.

Schenker, Adrian, et al., eds. *Biblia Hebraica Quinta.* Stuttgart: Deutsche Bibelgesellschaft, 2004–.

Dead Sea Scrolls

Abegg, Martin G., Jr., James E. Bowley, and Edward M. Cook, eds. *The Dead Sea Scrolls Concordance.* Vol. 3, *The Biblical Texts from Qumran and Other Sites.* Leiden: Brill, 2009.

Abegg, Martin G., Jr., Peter Flint, and Eugene Ulrich. *The Dead Sea Scrolls Bible.* San Francisco: HarperSanFrancisco, 1999.

Discoveries in the Judaean Desert. 32 vols. Oxford: Oxford University Press, 1951–2011.

Martínez, Florentino García, and Eibert J. C. Tigchelaar. *The Dead Sea Scrolls Study Edition.* 2 vols. Grand Rapids: Eerdmans, 1997–98.

Vermes, Geza. *The Complete Dead Sea Scrolls in English*. 7th ed. London: Penguin Books, 2012.

Wise, Michael, Martin Abegg Jr., and Edward Cook. *The Dead Sea Scrolls: A New Translation*. San Francisco: HarperSanFrancisco, 2005.

Samaritan Pentateuch

Tal, Abraham, ed. *The Samaritan Pentateuch: Edited according to MS 6 of the Shekem Synagogue*. Tel-Aviv: Tel-Aviv University Press, 1994.

Von Gall, August, ed. *Der hebräische Pentateuch der Samaritaner: Genesis-Deuteronomy*. 5 vols in 1. Giessen: Töpelmann, 1918; repr., Berlin: de Gruyter, 1965.

Septuagint

Brenton, Lancelot C. *The Septuagint with Apocrypha: Greek and English*. 1844; repr., Peabody, MA: Hendrickson, 1986.

Brooke, Alan E., Norman McLean, and Henry St. J. Thackeray, eds. *The Old Testament in Greek*. 3 vols. Cambridge: Cambridge University Press, 1906–40.

Pietersma, Albert, and Benjamin G. Wright. *A New English Translation of the Septuagint*. Oxford: Oxford University Press, 2007.

Rahlfs, Alfred, and Robert Hanhart, eds. *Septuaginta*. Stuttgart: Deutsche Bibelgesellschaft, 2007.

Septuaginta: Vetus Testamentum Graecum Auctoritate Societatis Litterarum Gottingensis Editum. 24 vols. Göttingen: Vandenhoeck & Ruprecht, 1931–2006.

Septuagint Online. http://www.kalvesmaki.com/LXX/.

Peshitta and Targums

The Aramaic Bible. 19 vols. Collegeville, MN: Liturgical Press, 1987–2007.

Comprehensive Aramaic Lexicon. http://cal1.cn.huc.edu/.

Etheridge, J. W. *The Targums of Onkelos and Jonathan ben Uzziel on the Pentateuch*. 2 vols. 1862–65; repr., Piscataway, NJ: Gorgias, 2005.

Grossfeld, Bernard, ed. *The Targum to the Five Megilloth*. New York: Hermon, 1973.

Judaica Electronic Texts. http://www.library.upenn.edu/cajs/etexts.html.

Kiraz, George A., ed. *The Antioch Bible: The Syriac Peshitta Bible with English Translation*. 35 vols. Piscataway, NJ: Gorgias, 2012–.

Lamsa, George M. *The Holy Bible from Ancient Eastern Manuscripts*. Philadelphia: Holman, 1957.

Peshitta Institute of Leiden, ed. *The Old Testament in Syriac*. Leiden: Brill, 1972–.

Sperber, Alexander, ed. *The Bible in Aramaic*. 4 vols. Leiden: Brill, 1959–73.

Vetus Testamentum Syriace et Neosyriace. 1852; repr., London: Trinitarian Bible Society, 1954.

Vulgate and Old Latin

Colunga, Alberto, and Laurentio Turrado, eds. *Biblia Vulgata*. Madrid: Biblioteca de Autores Cristianos, 1953; repr., 1977.

Knox, Ronald Arbuthnott. *The Old Testament: Newly Translated from the Vulgate Latin*. 2 vols. New York: Sheed & Ward, 1950.

Latin Vulgate. http://www.latinvulgate.com/.

Vetus latina: Die Reste der altlateinischen Bibel nach Petrus Sabatier neu gesammelt und in Verbindung mit der Heidelberger Akademie der Wissenschaften herausgegeben von der Erzabtei Beuron. Freiburg: Herder, 1949–.

Weber, Robert, and Roger Gryson, eds. *Biblia sacra: Iuxta Vulgatam versionem*. 4th ed. Stuttgart: Deutsche Bibelgesellschaft, 1994.

4

TRANSLATION

Goal: Translate the text and compare other translations.

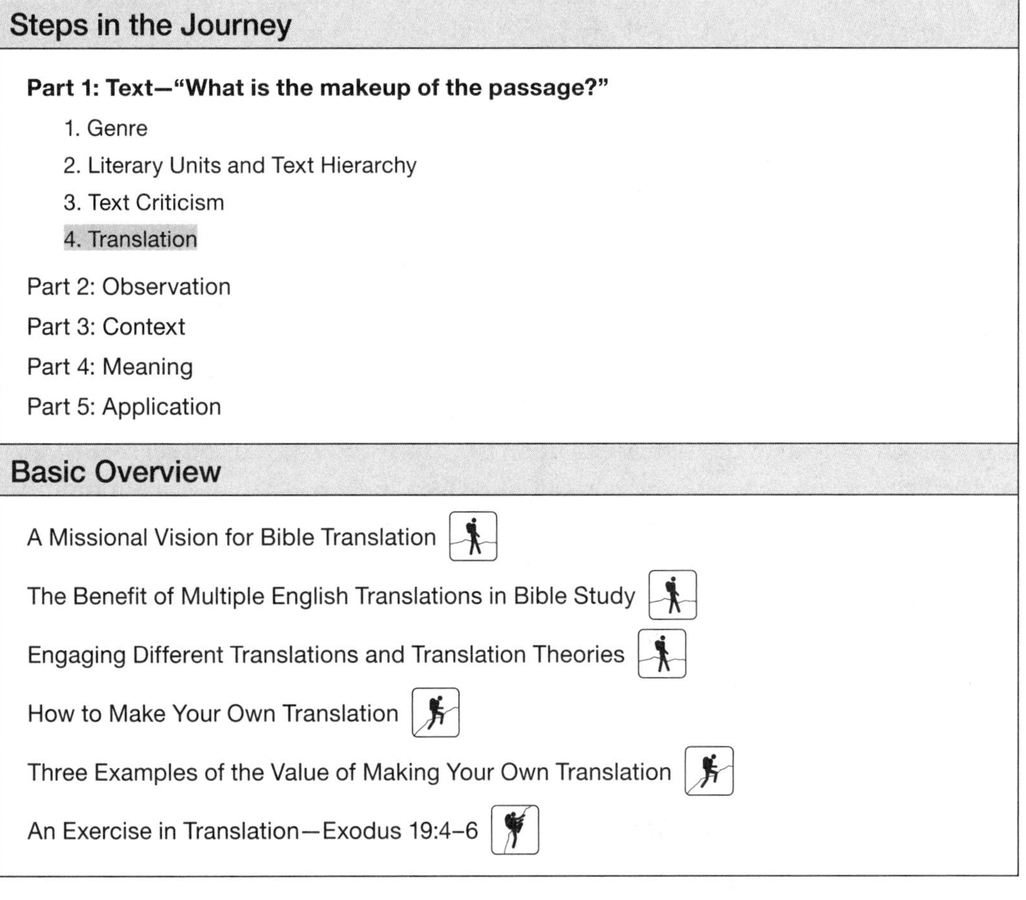

Steps in the Journey

Part 1: Text—"What is the makeup of the passage?"

1. Genre
2. Literary Units and Text Hierarchy
3. Text Criticism
4. Translation

Part 2: Observation

Part 3: Context

Part 4: Meaning

Part 5: Application

Basic Overview

A Missional Vision for Bible Translation

The Benefit of Multiple English Translations in Bible Study

Engaging Different Translations and Translation Theories

How to Make Your Own Translation

Three Examples of the Value of Making Your Own Translation

An Exercise in Translation—Exodus 19:4–6

Fig. 4.1. Trail Guide to Chapter 4

A Missional Vision for Bible Translation

Wycliffe Global Alliance estimates that right now only 2,932 of the approximately 7,000 languages in the world have at least some of the Bible, leaving 3,955 languages without any access to Scripture.[1] Because "faith comes from hearing, and hearing from the word of Christ" (Rom. 10:17), the translated Word of God is essential.

Christianity is distinctive in the way its sacred Scripture maintains all its power even when rendered in different tongues. While the Old Testament was originally drafted (mostly) in Hebrew, the heart language of the Old Testament prophets and the nation of Israel,[2] the New Testament apostles do not hesitate to preach from the Septuagint for their Greek-speaking audience, being convinced that "whatever was written in former days was written for our instruction" (Rom. 15:4; cf. the LXX quotation of Ps. 69:9[H10] in Rom. 15:3). Similarly, Ezra and the Levites helped their non-Hebrew-speaking audience "understand the Law," likely by translating it (Neh. 8:7–8; cf. 13:24), and at Pentecost God allowed Jews "from every nation under heaven" to hear "the mighty works of God" in their "own language" (Acts 2:5–6, 11).

In response to the Tower of Babel debacle, YHWH both "dispersed" the seventy "families" deriving from Noah across the globe and "confused the language of all the earth" (Gen. 10:32; 11:9). It is to these "families" that God promised his "blessing" to come through Abram and his seed (12:3; 22:18), and it is to the "daughter" community of these "dispersed" ones that God promised to one day change their "speech . . . to a pure speech, that all of them may call upon the name of the LORD and serve him with one accord" (Zeph. 3:9–10). The portrait of heaven in Revelation displays a multilingual community from every nation on earth—a community that declares in unified voice, "Salvation belongs to our God who sits on the throne, and to the Lamb!" (Rev. 7:9–10; cf. 5:9–10; Zech. 14:9). Thus Babel has been reversed! Both Revelation 5:9 and 7:9 suggest that God will receive praise in multiple languages forever, so as to supply a lasting testimony of his curse-overcoming power.

With this hope set before us, may the church of Christ Jesus gain increasing passion to see the ministry of Bible translation flourish in the twenty-first century. We should also encourage the updating of present translations in light of changes in language and culture. But until Christ returns, we must utilize the access to Scripture that so

1. Wycliffe Global Alliance, "2015 Bible Translation Statistics FAQ: Going Deeper," downloaded from http://resources.wycliffe.net/statistics/WycliffeGA_stats_2015_FAQs_EN.pdf. The statistics were as of October 1, 2015.

2. Along with classical Hebrew, the Old Testament includes a small amount of Aramaic, most notably in Daniel and Ezra-Nehemiah, which were written when Aramaic was the common tongue of diplomacy (Dan. 2:4b–7:28; Ezra 4:8–6:18; 7:12–26; cf. Gen. 31:47; Jer. 10:11).

many around the globe already have in order to proclaim Jesus as the divine, crucified, and resurrected Messiah, the world's only Savior. We must also pray for God to raise up new laborers—perhaps you—to target the unreached and unengaged, a task that often requires Bible translation.[3] "How beautiful are the feet of those who preach the good news!" (Rom. 10:15).

The Benefit of Multiple English Translations in Bible Study

With so many peoples globally having no Scripture in their heart language, English speakers should stand in awe of the plethora of solid Bible translations that we have. Whether you know the biblical languages or not, several good English translations will serve you well in Bible study and teaching preparation. As for study, those who don't know the original languages and who rely fully on translations are at the mercy of the translator(s), who themselves have made interpretive decisions about the meaning of the Hebrew or Greek text (see "The Benefits of Hebrew Exegesis" in the introduction). And if you use only one translation, you are all the more limited in your ability to identify and evaluate interpretive options when they are present. With respect to teaching, your audience could be using over a dozen different contemporary English translations, many of which will differ to greater or lesser degrees. So the more you can familiarize yourself with the various translations, the more confident you'll be that you have made the best exegetical choices and the more prepared you'll be to answer questions as they arise.

Consider, for example, some various renderings of the Shema in Deuteronomy 6:4 displayed in figure 4.2.

4 3 2 1 שְׁמַע יִשְׂרָאֵל יְהוָה אֱלֹהֵינוּ יְהוָה ׀ אֶחָד		1 2 3 4 "Hear, Israel: YHWH our-God YHWH one"		
	A	**B**	**Version**	**Distinct Significance**
1.	God our God,	God the one and only!	MSG	Slogan: Stresses sole allegiance to YHWH
2.	The LORD our God	is one LORD.	ASV, KJV, BBE	Confronts poly-YHWHism

Fig. 4.2. The Shema: Different Translations of Deuteronomy 6:4

3. For more on this important missional necessity, see the website of the Wycliffe Global Alliance: http://www.wycliffe.net/en/.

A	B	Version	Distinct Significance
3. The LORD our God,	the LORD is one.	NKJV, ESV, NIV, CSB	Stresses YHWH's supremacy and uniqueness
4a. The LORD is our God,	the LORD alone.	NRSV	Identifies YHWH as our only God
4b. Our God is the LORD,	only the LORD!	CEB	Asserts that our only God is YHWH
5. The LORD is our God;	the LORD is one.	NASB, WEB, NET Bible	Combines 3 and 4

Fig. 4.2. The Shema: Different Translations of Deuteronomy 6:4 (cont.)

Even if you are not using Hebrew, a quick glimpse at these translations identifies some key questions that you would probably have missed had you looked at only a single translation. For example, how should we understand the structure of the Shema? Is it a verbless slogan (#1), a single sentence (##2, 3, 4), or two sentences (#5)? This decision will impact our understanding of the whole. Also, what is the meaning of YHWH's oneness? Is this oneness bound up in God's nature (##2, 3, 5), or does it point to the direction of our allegiance (#4)? If you are slated to teach this passage, simply comparing the translations lets you know that you have some important exegetical work to do in order to rightly understand the text's message. For a number of reasons, some of which I'll discuss under "Verbless Clauses" in chapter 5, the ESV and NIV represent the most exegetically sound interpretation of these words. But had you used only the NRSV or NASB, you would have never seen it as an option.

For the purposes of Bible memorization and consistency in teaching, using a single high-quality translation is best. In my sphere of ministry, the most common are the NASB, ESV, NIV, and CSB, but there are other solid options. For the purpose of Bible *study*, however, multiple well-chosen translations will supply the interpreter with the greatest awareness of exegetical options and the greatest preparedness for ministry in the English-speaking world.

Engaging Different Translations and Translation Theories

Bible translations differ on whether they are form-, sense-, or idea-driven and to what degree they are gender-inclusive. Different translation theories actually stand behind the various versions, creating a continuum of equivalence (displayed in fig. 4.3)

based on how they handle lexical, grammatical, and historical correspondences. ***Lexical correspondence*** relates to how closely translators attempt to render single words in the source text into individual words in the target language. ***Grammatical correspondence*** addresses how closely word order and syntax in the original language is aligned with word order and syntax in translation. Finally, ***historical correspondence*** concerns how closely the translators retain the factual and cultural elements connected with the biblical times. You may think that the more rigorously tied a translation is to lexical, grammatical, and historical correspondence, the more "biblical" or faithful the translation will be. But liberal-versus-conservative theology does not appear to play a role in which translation theory scholars prefer. Each of the various approaches to translation has its own strengths and weaknesses, and often the choice of one approach over another is driven by distinct purposes.

Form-Equivalence			Sense-Equivalence			Idea-Equivalence	
YLT	KJV/NKJV	RSV/NRSV	CSB	NAB	JB	NEB	TLB
	NASB/NASU	ESV	NET Bible	NJB	GNB	CEB	MSG
			NIV		REB		
					NLT		

Fig. 4.3. A Continuum of Bible Translations

1. Form-Equivalence

Versions that strive for ***form-equivalence*** try to retain correspondence of words, grammar, and history as much as possible between the original and receptor language. Some people refer to these as "literal" translations, but such terminology is a misnomer because no two languages enjoy one-to-one correspondence in everything, and often the English equivalent requires a more dynamic rendering to actually capture the sense of the original in the receptor language. The older Young's Literal Translation (YLT, 1862) actually failed to recognize this point, assuming that complete grammatical and lexical equivalence was always possible. The result was that the translation regularly disregarded the normal structures of the English language, making the text almost nonsensical.

Two of the best form-driven translations are the New American Standard Bible (NASB, 1995) and the English Standard Version (ESV, 2016). The former is especially helpful when trying to track an author's flow of thought because it renders almost all the connecting words, which serve as signals for text structure (see "Introducing Literary Units and Text Hierarchy in Hebrew" in chapter 2 and "Step 1b: Create an Argument Diagram" in chapter 6). This type of translation is the least interpretive, and because of this I choose a formally equivalent translation as my primary English version for Bible study. While form-driven translations can be understandable, however, they often use cumbersome English rather than contemporary English, and they also require the teacher to clarify meaning more often. The ESV strikes a helpful balance between form and meaning, but in the Old Testament it fails to translate many of the connectors, making it more difficult to use for tracing an argument.

2. Sense-Equivalence

Sense-equivalent translations such as the New International Version (NIV, 2011) and the New Living Translation (NLT, 2004) provide beautiful and meaningful contemporary English. They seek functional/dynamic correspondence, retaining the historical-factual features of the text and capturing the meaning of the Hebrew and Greek, while not hesitating to translate the words, grammar, and style into common English words, structures, and idioms. More interpretation takes place here, but if the translators do their job well, the result is a clear and faithful rendering of God's Word that can serve everyone, but especially those who need more help in grasping the meaning of the Bible's propositions.

When there is greater interpretation in translation, however, there is also more opportunity for the preacher or teacher to disagree with the translator's choices. Furthermore, translations that seek sense-equivalence often fail to represent important text features such as connectors and discourse markers (some of which have no English equivalent, e.g., "Marked Primary and Secondary Citation Formulas" in chapter 2). Without these structural signals, the interpreter cannot track the author's argument as easily, so he or she is further distanced from the ancient book.

3. Idea-Equivalence

Versions that seek ***idea-equivalence*** such as The Living Bible (TLB, 1971) and The Message (MSG, 2002) are better called *paraphrases*, since they strive only to convey the concepts of Scripture with little attempt to retain lexical, grammatical, or historical correspondence. These have their place in contemporizing God's Word, but they are less helpful for study or teaching because they have distanced themselves so far from the original.

As an example of the equivalence continuum at work, compare the following renderings of Psalm 119:105 in the YLT, NASB, ESV, NIV, NLT, TLB, and MSG (see fig. 4.4). The right-hand columns identify how closely the translation corresponds to the Hebrew with respect to lexical (L), grammatical (G), and historical (H) features. The number 5 represents the highest level of correspondence, and 1 represents the least.

			L	G	H
	MT	נֵר־לְרַגְלִי דְבָרֶךָ וְאוֹר לִנְתִיבָתִי			
Form-Equivalence	YLT	[Nun] A lamp to my foot [is] Thy Word, And a light to my path.	5	5	5
	NASB	Your word is a lamp to my feet and a light to my path.	4	4	5
	ESV	Your word is a lamp to my feet and a light to my path.	4	4	5

Fig. 4.4. Psalm 119:105 in Various Translations

			L	G	H
Sense-Equivalence	NIV	Your word is a lamp for my feet, a light on my path.	3	3	5
	NLT	Your word is a lamp to guide my feet and a light for my path.	2	3	5
Idea-Equivalence	TLB	Your words are a flashlight to light the path ahead of me and keep me from stumbling.	1	1	2
	MSG	By your words I can see where I am going; they throw a beam of light on my dark path.	1	1	3

Fig. 4.4. Psalm 119:105 in Various Translations (cont.)

An overview of the translations shows that some vary drastically, but others not so much. With respect to the form-equivalent translations, the YLT notes up front with the word *Nun* that Psalm 119:105 is part of an alphabetical acrostic and falls in the section where the poetic lines begin with the Hebrew letter נ (*Nun*). It identifies the verse as a verbless clause, placing "is" in brackets, and it retains the singular Hebrew "foot." It maintains Hebrew word order and offers an equivalent for every Hebrew morph (i.e., linguistic form), but it does so at the cost of making the English unsmooth. The NASB and ESV, while having smoother English, still preserve the conjunction "and" (וְ) and the repeated preposition "to" (לְ). But they also reverse the word order at the front of the first clause, allowing for more natural English, and they read the singular "foot" collectively as "feet." While they fully maintain historical correspondence, they somewhat minimize lexical and grammatical correspondence in order to communicate more effectively in English.

The NIV and NLT, as sense-driven translations, attempt to make the English even more flowing. The NIV also renders "foot" as "feet," but it drops the conjunction and changes the second preposition, probably for stylistic variation. The NLT retains the conjunction, alters the second preposition, and then adds the dynamic infinitive "to guide" for clearer comprehension. Both the NIV and NLT retain full historical correspondence, but both are even more willing than the ESV to drop lexical and grammatical correspondence for the sake of readability. Whether they sacrifice literalness is debatable.

The mere fact that both TLB and the MSG have more words identifies that they are rendering concepts, not words or phrases. TLB is a complete paraphrase that bears little if any lexical, grammatical, or historical equivalence. Was there a "flashlight" in the Old Testament period? God's "word" is changed to "words," and both clause structure and word order are transformed. As for the MSG, it, too, is a complete paraphrase that creates two independent clauses and loses nearly all lexical and grammatical correspondence, while retaining historical equivalence.

There are strengths and challenges to every theory of Bible translation. We must judge the quality of a translation not simply on its faithfulness to the Hebrew or Greek original but also in light of its target audience and communicative purpose. Public reading of Scripture may benefit from a more sense-driven translation such as the NLT, which will often capture the meaning of the original in fresh, evocative ways. Idea-equivalent versions can be helpful for those who have little to no exposure to the Bible or have limited understanding of English, such as children and students for whom English is a second language.

For personal study and lesson preparation, I encourage you to interact with at least three versions that stand at different points along the equivalence continuum. My preferences are the NASB, ESV, and NIV. If you don't know Hebrew, the more form-based translations will ensure that you spot more of the connectors and discourse markers so as to better track the author's intended thought flow. But engaging more dynamically equivalent translations can also help you better grasp the sense of given clauses and phrases. In teaching situations, be sure to know the main translation that your audience is using.

How to Make Your Own Translation

Having established a passage's genre, literary units, and original wording, one who knows Hebrew is now ready to prepare a tentative translation of the text. If you don't know Hebrew and don't wish to engage with it, feel free to move ahead to chapter 5.

While God has graciously granted English speakers a wealth of faithful translations that can serve various purposes in different contexts, there is no substitute for you becoming familiar enough with your own passage in Hebrew so as to render it faithfully in your own words in English. Only then will you best be in a position to fairly evaluate other translations and the reflections of commentators. Here is the process that I suggest:

1. **Create a working draft, grasping the meaning and relationship of all the words.** As you begin, try to translate afresh on your own without the help of English versions. Using a standard Hebrew lexicon such as Koehler and Baumgartner's *HALOT*,[4] look up all the words whose range of meaning you are not fully certain of. Ensure that you understand the function of every word and its relationship to all others.
2. **Write down all your questions.** The very process of shaping a translation will raise all types of interpretive questions. Jot these down for future reference. Highlight the most significant words or concepts that will demand further

4. Ludwig Koehler, Walter Baumgartner, and Johann Jakob Stamm, eds., *The Hebrew and Aramaic Lexicon of the Old Testament: Study Edition*, trans. M. E. J. Richardson, 2 vols. (Leiden: Brill, 2001). See "An Overview of Concordances, Lexicons, and Theological Wordbooks" in chapter 7 for discussion of the most common lexicons.

study. Note any questions of syntax, historical context, or theology to which you will need to return.

3. **Compare your translation with others.** Once you've got a working draft, then compare your translation to at least three contemporary versions at different points on the equivalence continuum, evaluating your decisions at every point. Revise your translation now, and then continue to revise it until the end of your exegesis, sharpening and honing it at every stage.

There is a tricky balance when it comes to providing your own rendering of a passage that differs from the mainstream. On the one hand, most readers of this book are not scholars—at least not yet! So you might ask, "What right do I have to propose a different reading from the translators of the ESV or NIV?" This is a fair question, but you shouldn't downplay either the value of doing your own work first or the possibility that you will see something that others haven't. A number of factors when it comes to Bible translation should free you to really consider a fresh take on your passage.

First, all modern translations were shaped either by committees working under time deadlines or by individuals who cannot possibly know the whole Bible well enough in the original to produce a flawless translation at every point. The amount of time you get to spend on any given text may be more than the Bible translator(s) had.[5]

Second, in the modern business of Bible publishing, the more "different" a translation is, the greater the risk of lowered sales. Thus, pressures are placed on those doing the translation work to keep renderings as familiar as possible, while still being as faithful as possible to the original. So many people have memorized the KJV's "Yea, though I walk through the valley of the shadow of death" in Psalm 23:4 that some translation teams still struggle to speak of walking "through a valley of deep darkness," even if the translation more accurately conveys the meaning of the Hebrew.[6]

Third, a translation written for the entire English-speaking world is not the place to offer new renderings, so translators almost always fall back on the side of caution and historical tradition. This leaves it to ministers such as you and me to clarify for our congregations the details of the biblical text.

As you work on your translation, just remember that your people are looking to you to clarify for them the meaning of God's Word. Wrestle on your own, and be very aware of the translations from which your listeners will most likely be working. *If you can faithfully exposit the original text using the translation of choice, then do that*, for it will

5. For a fascinating look at how the "ESV Bible Translators Debate the Word 'Slave' at Tyndale House, Cambridge," see https://www.youtube.com/watch?v=Mx06mtApu8k. My colleague Andy Naselli directed me to this four-minute video, and now I use it in class in order to illustrate the complexities of translating the Bible into English. The BBC filmed this segment during a meeting of the ESV Translation Oversight Committee in summer 2010. The question was, "What is the best way to translate the Hebrew word עֶבֶד (*'ebed*) and the Greek word δοῦλος (*doulos*)?" This video condenses hours of discussion. Members of the committee who speak in this video include Jack Collins, Peter Williams, Gordon Wenham, Paul House, Wayne Grudem, and Lane Dennis.

6. The NRSV, NET Bible, 2011 NIV, and CSB actually depart from the traditional reading, whereas the NASB, 1984 NIV, and ESV retain the traditional reading and place the alternative in a footnote.

bolster your hearers' faith in their Bibles, teaching them that they don't have to be scholars to rightly read God's Word. If you need to diverge from the common translation, however, see if you can find another one that supports your rendering. Regardless, clarify your reasoning and then proclaim what you believe to be God's Word boldly and articulately, speaking "as one who speaks oracles of God" (1 Peter 4:11).

Three Examples of the Value of Making Your Own Translation

The Importance of Day 6 in Genesis 1

I now want to supply some examples of how a fresh translation of the Hebrew text and how comparison with other translations reveal some helpful insights. Our first illustration comes from the repeated day-end formula in Genesis 1. The text is so familiar that a small addition in day 6 could easily be missed, as appears to have happened in most English translations. Here is what we read:

וַֽיְהִי־עֶ֥רֶב וַֽיְהִי־בֹ֖קֶר . . .	And there was evening, and there was morning....
יֹ֥ום אֶחָֽד	Day one / A first day (1:5).
יֹ֥ום שֵׁנִֽי	A second day (1:8).
יֹ֥ום שְׁלִישִֽׁי	A third day (1:13).
יֹ֥ום רְבִיעִֽי	A fourth day (1:19).
יֹ֥ום חֲמִישִֽׁי	A fifth day (1:23).
יֹ֥ום הַשִּׁשִּֽׁי	***The*** sixth day (1:31).

Fig. 4.5. The Day-End Formula in Genesis 1

Most English translations, including the NKJV, NRSV, ESV, NIV, and CSB, render all six days as if they each had the definite article ("*the* first day . . . *the* second day," etc.). Both the NASB and NET Bible, however, recognize that only day 6 provides such specification—"the sixth day." The use of the definite article is one of a number of features that the author of Genesis 1 used to direct the reader's attention to day 6 of the creation week.

1. Day 6 climaxes God's creative work, for in it he creates humanity and defines his relationship with them.
2. Day 6 gets the most literary space and includes the longest speeches.
3. Only at the end of day 6 does God declare creation "*very* good" (Gen. 1:31).
4. Only on this day is the definite article "the" added to the day-ending formula.

Day 6 portrays humanity as the culmination of God's creative works. Yet as soon as human readers find ourselves in the creation week, our focus is pushed off ourselves back to God! Humans are to image *God* (Gen. 1:26–27), and it is toward this end of reflecting, resembling, and representing *him* that we are called to "be fruitful and multiply and fill the earth and subdue it" (1:28). The ultimate end is that the earth may be "filled with the knowledge of the glory of the LORD as the waters cover the sea" (Hab. 2:14; cf. Num. 14:21; Ps. 72:19; Isa. 11:9). Humanity exists *for God*, and the use of the definite article at day 6 pushes us to recognize this.

Kept in Perfect Peace in Isaiah 26:3

Since Jesus inaugurated the new creation, one of the great promises that is "Yes" in Christ (2 Cor. 1:20) appears in Isaiah 26:3 (for more on claiming Old Testament promises today, see "Old Testament Promises and the Christian" in chapter 12). I want to translate this promise afresh and see what we find. This section may be too technical for those without Hebrew, but I believe that you will be edified if you keep reading.

בָּטוּחַ׃	בְּךָ	כִּי	שָׁלוֹם ׀ שָׁלוֹם	תִּצֹּר	סָמוּךְ	יֵצֶר	You keep him in perfect peace whose mind
Adj	PrepPh	Conj	Nouns-accus	V(S)	PassPtc	DO	is stayed on you, because he trusts in you.

Fig. 4.6. Isaiah 26:3 in the MT and ESV

Passing over the direct object that starts the sentence, the main clause and subordinate clause together read, "You keep/preserve [Qal *yiqtol* second masculine singular of נצר] in peace-peace [= perfect peace] because in you [he] is trusting." For whom does God preserve peace? The ESV says that it is to the one "whose mind is stayed on you." Where does the ESV get this translation? יֵצֶר is the direct object; סָמוּךְ is a passive participle of סמך, meaning "what is supported." סָמוּךְ serves as an appositive, restating the direct object. So what does the direct object יֵצֶר mean?

The noun יֵצֶר comes from the verb יצר ("to form, fashion"), as a potter does with clay. In Isaiah 29:16, the ESV translates יֵצֶר as "the thing formed," and here we also see the substantival participle of the verb rendered both as "potter" and as "one who forms": "Shall the potter [הַיֹּצֵר] be regarded as the clay, that the thing made should say of its maker, 'He did not make me'; or the thing formed [וְיֵ֫צֶר] say of him who formed it [לְיוֹצְרוֹ], 'He has no understanding'?" (Cf. 45:9 for the same verb form.)

When יֵ֫צֶר is linked with the passive participle סָמוּךְ, we get the rendering "a thing formed that is being supported." The image is of a potter's upholding in his hands the clay that he is shaping. The clay is what is formed, what is being supported. In the hands of the potter, the clay is kept, upheld, sustained. The whole sentence would then be translated, *"A thing formed that is being supported you keep in perfect peace, because in you (he) is trusting."* Trusting God is the means by which the hands of God hold us. As we put our faith in his promises, he builds a wall of protection around us so that we are secure, and in turn we gain peace—perfect peace. This makes me think of Philippians 4:6–7, where Paul asserts: "Do not be anxious about anything, but in everything by prayer and supplication with thanksgiving let your requests be made known to God. And the peace of God, which surpasses all understanding, will guard your hearts and your minds in Christ Jesus." The ESV renders יֵצֶר סָמוּךְ as "whose mind is stayed" on God. This may be an adequate dynamic equivalent, but I suggest that a rendering closer to Isaiah's theology and to the semantic range of these words is "a thing formed that is being supported."

As we close, note how well the new translation fits into the context. Isaiah 26:1–4 reads:

> In that day [when death is defeated and the LORD stands in victory] this song will be sung in the land of Judah: "We have a strong city; he sets up salvation as walls and bulwarks. Open the gates, that the righteous nation that keeps faith may enter in. A thing formed that is being supported you preserve in perfect peace, because he is trusting in you. Trust in the LORD forever, for the LORD GOD is an everlasting rock."

In Jesus, the powers of hell have already been conquered, so this song can, in many respects, already be sung. May we be among those who find our gracious, victorious Maker helping us trust in him, that we may know his peace.

Made for Praise in Zephaniah 3:20[7]

As with the previous example, this discussion is quite technical and may require a knowledge of Hebrew to track. If you haven't had any Hebrew, feel free to press ahead, but you can also jump to chapter 5.

בָּעֵ֤ת הַהִיא֙ אָבִ֣יא אֶתְכֶ֔ם וּבָעֵ֖ת קַבְּצִ֣י אֶתְכֶ֑ם כִּֽי־אֶתֵּ֨ן אֶתְכֶ֜ם לְשֵׁ֣ם וְלִתְהִלָּ֗ה בְּכֹל֙ עַמֵּ֣י הָאָ֔רֶץ בְּשׁוּבִ֧י אֶת־שְׁבוּתֵיכֶ֛ם לְעֵינֵיכֶ֖ם אָמַ֥ר יְהוָֽה׃	"At that time I will bring you in, at the time when I gather you together; for I will make you renowned and praised among all the peoples of the earth, when I restore your fortunes before your eyes," says the LORD.

Fig. 4.7. Zephaniah 3:20 in the MT and ESV

With Judah's punishment for covenant rebellion on the horizon, YHWH used the prophet Zephaniah to muster tireless trust in God's faithfulness to preserve and ultimately satisfy his believing remnant. One of the greatest motivations that Zephaniah provides for "seeking" and "waiting upon" God together (2:1, 3; 3:8) comes in the glorious portrayal of future hope that is held out for all who persevere in faith.

Part of this promise is found in the book's last verse (Zeph. 3:20), which begins בָּעֵת הַהִיא ("at that time")—specifically, the day of the Lord when YHWH removes the proud and preserves the God-dependent (3:11–13), when the saving king's irreversible victory gives rise to shouts of joy from those rescued (3:14–15), and when YHWH both delivers and takes delight in his remnant (3:16–19). "At that time" YHWH will rally his redeemed together for a key reason (3:20): כִּי־אֶתֵּן אֶתְכֶם לְשֵׁם וְלִתְהִלָּה בְּכֹל עַמֵּי הָאָרֶץ. The NASB, ESV, and NIV all treat the admiration and acclaim (שֵׁם "name" and תְּהִלָּה "praise") as something that the onlooking world gives to the preserved remnant: "I will give you renown/honor and praise among all the peoples of the earth" (NASB/NIV); "I will make you renowned and praised among all the peoples of the earth" (ESV).

Elsewhere, God clearly promises to exalt his people before the world's eyes. But this text does not simply say that YHWH will give his redeemed fame and acclaim. Instead, using the לְ preposition ("to/for"), the verse declares that YHWH will set his people in the center of the world "*for* a name and *for* praise" (לְשֵׁם וְלִתְהִלָּה). As rendered in the YLT, "For I give you for a name, and for a praise, among all peoples of the land." About whose name and whose praise is Zephaniah talking? The closest

7. This theological reflection is adapted from the author's previously published work. Taken from *Devotions on the Hebrew Bible: 54 Reflections to Inspire and Instruct*, edited by Milton Eng and Lee M. Fields. Copyright © 2015 by Milton Eng and Lee M. Fields. Used by permission of Zondervan. www.zondervan.com.

parallel texts suggest that *YHWH*'s worth and honor is the ultimate goal of the new creation. It is God's name, God's glory, that is to be exalted in the lives of his saints.

Specifically, YHWH declared through Jeremiah, Zephaniah's contemporary, that he originally set his people apart in order "that they might be *for me* [לִי] a people, a name, a praise, and a glory, but they would not listen" (Jer. 13:11; cf. Deut. 26:19). Nevertheless, in the new covenant, when sins are forgiven and loyalty is enabled, YHWH asserted that his people "shall be *to me* [לִי] a name of joy, a praise and a glory before all the nations of the earth" (Jer. 33:9). As Ezekiel later testified, by YHWH's delivering his people before the eyes of the nations, he will act "for the sake of my holy name" (Ezek. 36:22–23). The prophet Zechariah captured the meaning well when he claimed that the delivered flock of God would be "like the jewels of a crown" that would magnify God's "goodness" and God's "beauty" (Zech. 9:16–17).

The ultimate end of new covenant transformation is worship. All things are from God, through God, and to God (Rom. 11:36). The new creation, now inaugurated through Christ and his church (2 Cor. 5:17; Gal. 6:15), is about God. It's about his glory, his Son, his greatness, his exaltation among the peoples of the planet. May your life be marked by the matchless worth of God in Christ, that all "may see your good works and give glory to your Father who is in heaven" (Matt. 5:16).

An Exercise in Translation—Exodus 19:4–6

It's now time to take our first pass at translating Exodus 19:4–6 and to compare a number of English translations. Those without Hebrew will likely not benefit here, so you can move directly to chapter 5.

It's important to note that very often a first draft of a translation will be very different from the final draft after all exegesis is complete. As we make fresh observations and new discoveries, they will challenge our initial decisions. Take a moment right now to translate these verses on your own. As you do, jot down all major observations and questions. Then compare and contrast your translation with my initial work below and with a number of other contemporary versions. Note further observations and questions, and tweak your translation as necessary. Everything done at this stage is provisional. In figure 4.8 I note my own observations and questions.

MT	DeRouchie's Initial Translation
4 אַתֶּם רְאִיתֶם אֲשֶׁר עָשִׂיתִי לְמִצְרָיִם וָאֶשָּׂא אֶתְכֶם עַל־כַּנְפֵי נְשָׁרִים וָאָבִא אֶתְכֶם אֵלָי׃ 5 וְעַתָּה אִם־שָׁמוֹעַ תִּשְׁמְעוּ בְּקֹלִי וּשְׁמַרְתֶּם אֶת־בְּרִיתִי וִהְיִיתֶם לִי סְגֻלָּה מִכָּל־הָעַמִּים כִּי־לִי כָּל־הָאָרֶץ׃ 6 וְאַתֶּם תִּהְיוּ־לִי מַמְלֶכֶת כֹּהֲנִים וְגוֹי קָדוֹשׁ	4 You have seen what I did to Egypt, and [how] I lifted you on wings of eagles, and [how] I brought you to myself. 5 And now, if you will indeed listen unto my voice and [then(?)] keep my covenant and [then(?)] be my [for me a (?)] treasured possession from [more than (?)] all the peoples, for [though(?)] all the earth is mine [for me (?)], 6 and [then(?)] you will be for me a [my(?)] kingdom of priests and a holy nation.
YLT	**NASB**
4 Ye—ye have seen that which I have done to the Egyptians, and I bear you on eagles' wings, and bring you in unto Myself. 5 'And now, if ye really hearken to My voice, then ye have kept My covenant, and been to Me a peculiar treasure more than all the peoples, for all the earth [is] Mine; 6 and ye—ye are to Me a kingdom of priests and a holy nation.	4 You yourselves have seen what I did to the Egyptians, and how I bore you on eagles' wings, and brought you to Myself. 5 Now then, if you will indeed obey My voice and keep My covenant, then you shall be My own possession among all the peoples, for all the earth is Mine; 6 and you shall be to Me a kingdom of priests and a holy nation.
ESV	**NIV**
4 You yourselves have seen what I did to the Egyptians, and how I bore you on eagles' wings and brought you to myself. 5 Now therefore, if you will indeed obey my voice and keep my covenant, you shall be my treasured possession among all peoples, for all the earth is mine; 6 and you shall be to me a kingdom of priests and a holy nation.	4 You yourselves have seen what I did to Egypt, and how I carried you on eagles' wings and brought you to myself. 5 Now if you obey me fully and keep my covenant, then out of all nations you will be my treasured possession. Although the whole earth is mine, 6 you will be for me a kingdom of priests and a holy nation.

Fig. 4.8. Translations of Exodus 19:4–6a

1. Key Observations on Exodus 19:4–6

a. The explicit second masculine plural pronoun אַתֶּם ("you") at the head of verse 4 is unnecessary syntactically but is likely present in order to mark the paragraph's initiation, using a marked, nondefault verb pattern ([x] + *qatal*).[8] It may also give added stress that it was the *Israelites* ("you!") who saw God's works.

b. In verse 4, the first common singular *wayyiqtol* (*waw*-consecutive imperfect) verbs וָאֶשָּׂא ("and I lifted") and וָאָבִא ("and I brought") appear to be building on the *qatal* (perfect) first common singular relative clause אֲשֶׁר עָשִׂיתִי ("what

8. For marked versus default clause patterns, see "Discerning Subunits in Text Blocks: Paragraph Breaks" in chapter 2 and "More on Marked and Unmarked Clauses" in chapter 5. [x] stands for any subject, object, or modifier in a clause. [x] cannot stand for either a finite verb or a conjunction.

I did"). That is, Israel saw not only *what* God did but *how* he lifted the people and *how* he brought them to himself.

c. וְעַתָּה ("And now") in verse 5 is an inference marker (see "The Inference Markers לָכֵן and וְעַתָּה" in chapter 5), and the inference itself has both a marked protasis (אִם־ "if") and an unmarked apodosis ("then").

2. Key Questions on Exodus 19:4–6

a. As noted, אִם־ ("if") at the beginning of verse 5 signals a conditional protasis. Where does the apodosis begin? The YLT begins it with the first *weqatal* (*waw*-consecutive perfect) (וּשְׁמַרְתֶּם "and you shall keep"), but most other English translations place it at the second *weqatal* (וִהְיִיתֶם "and you shall be") (cf. KJV, NKJV, NRSV, NASB, NET Bible, ESV, NIV, CSB). It's noteworthy that the majority view stretches way back to the sixteenth century, which could suggest a firmly fixed tradition rather than careful exegetical assessment.

b. What is a סְגֻלָּה, rendered in the ESV of verse 5 as "treasured possession"?

c. Does the fronted preposition מִן ("from") in the phrase מִכָּל־הָעַמִּים in verse 5 express separation (i.e., "from all the peoples") or comparison (i.e., "more than all the peoples")?

d. Does the כִּי clause in verse 5 function as a ground for what precedes (= "for/because," so ESV) or as a concessive for what precedes or follows (= "though/although," so NIV)?

e. As at the front of verse 4, the וְאַתֶּם ("and you") in verse 6 is intrusive and unnecessary grammatically. Why is it part of the speech at this point?

f. What is the significance of "a kingdom of priests and a holy nation"?

g. Do the various לִי prepositional phrases in verses 5–6 express divine possession (i.e., "mine") or divine advantage (i.e., "to/for me")? Most English translations treat the two occurrences in verse 5 as expressing possession and the single occurrence in verse 6 as expressing advantage.

As we proceed through our exegesis to theology, we will want to keep these observations and questions in mind. We have an initial translation and a good list of observations and questions from which to build. We are now ready to move from the "Text" stage into "Observation."

Key Words and Concepts

Lexical, grammatical, and historical correspondence
Form-, sense-, and idea-equivalence

Questions for Further Reflection

1. The chapter began by talking about the importance of translating the Bible for peoples who do not yet have access to God's Word in their heart language. Prayerfully consider and reflect on how God is calling you to be a part of this mission. Will you become equipped and then go to give your life to this task? Will you stay and work hard, that you may send others to give their lives to this? What is God impressing on you?
2. When studying Scripture, what is the benefit of using multiple translations?
3. What accounts for the differences between Bible translations?
4. Describe the strengths and weaknesses of the different types of Bible translations.
5. Even though there are already several good English translations of the Bible, why is it a good idea to translate a passage for yourself when studying it?
6. What are the steps of making your own translation?
7. Why is it at times justifiable to vary from mainstream translations?

Resources for Further Study

Translation Theory and Practice

Beekman, John, and John Callow. *Translating the Word of God*. Dallas: Summer Institute of Linguistics, 1974.

★ Brunn, Dave. *One Bible, Many Versions: Are All Translations Created Equal?* Downers Grove, IL: InterVarsity Press, 2013.

Dewey, David. *A User's Guide to Bible Translations: Making the Most of Different Versions*. Downers Grove, IL: InterVarsity Press, 2005.

"ESV Bible Translators Debate the Word 'Slave' at Tyndale House, Cambridge," https://www.youtube.com/watch?v=Mx06mtApu8k.

★ Fee, Gordon D., and Mark L. Strauss. *How to Choose a Translation for All Its Worth: A Guide to Understanding and Using Bible Versions*. Grand Rapids: Zondervan, 2007.

Fee, Gordon D., and Douglas Stuart. Pages 36–56 in *How to Read the Bible for All Its Worth*. 4th ed. Grand Rapids: Zondervan, 2014.

Köstenberger, Andreas J., and David A. Croteau, eds. *Which Bible Translation Should I Use? A Comparison of 4 Major Recent Versions*. Nashville: Broadman & Holman, 2012.

Kubo, Sakae, and Walter Specht. *So Many Versions?* Grand Rapids: Zondervan, 1975.

Metzger, Bruce M. *The Bible in Translation: Ancient and English Versions*. Grand Rapids: Baker Academic, 2001.

Nida, Eugene A. "Theories of Translation." *ABD* 6:512–15.

Nida, Eugene A., and Charles R. Taber. *The Theory and Practice of Translation*. Leiden: Brill, 1969; repr., 2003.

Porter, Stanley E., and Richard S. Hess, eds. *Translating the Bible: Problems and Prospects*. Sheffield, UK: Sheffield Academic, 1999.

Wegner, Paul D. *The Journey from Texts to Translations: The Origin and Development of the Bible*. Grand Rapids: Baker, 2004.

Challenging Questions in Translation

Carson, D. A. *The Inclusive-Language Debate: A Plea for Realism*. Grand Rapids: Baker, 1998.

———. *The King James Version Debate: A Plea for Realism*. Grand Rapids: Baker, 1978.

———. "The Limits of Functional Equivalence in Bible Translation—and Other Limits, Too." In *The Challenge of Bible Translation: Communicating God's Word to the World; Understanding the Theory, History, and Practice: Essays in Honor of Ronald F. Youngblood*, edited by Glen G. Scorgie, Mark L. Strauss, and Steven M. Voth, 65–113. Grand Rapids: Zondervan, 2003.

Combs, William W. "The History of the NIV Translation Controversy." *DBSJ* 17 (2012): 3–34.

Decker, Rodney J. "An Evaluation of the 2011 Edition of the New International Version." *Themelios* 36, 3 (2011): 415–56.

"The Development and Use of Gender Language in Contemporary English: A Corpus Linguistic Analysis; Prepared for the Committee on Bible Translation by Collins Dictionaries." September 2010. http://www.thenivbible.com/wp-content/uploads/2015/02/Collins-Report-Final.pdf.

Moo, Douglas J., ed. "Updating the New International Version of the Bible: Notes from the Committee on Bible Translation." August 2010. Available at http://www.thenivbible.com/wp-content/uploads/2014/11/2011-Translation-Notes.pdf.

———. *We Still Don't Get It: Evangelicals and Bible Translation Fifty Years after James Barr*. Grand Rapids: Zondervan, 2014. Available at http://www.thenivbible.com/wp-content/uploads/2014/11/We-Still-Dont-Get-It.pdf.

Nida, Eugene A. "The Sociolinguistics of Translating Canonical Religious Texts." *Traduction, Terminologie, Rédaction* 7, 1 (1994): 191–217.

Nida, Eugene A., and Jan de Waard. *From One Language to Another: Functional Equivalence in Bible Translation*. Nashville: Thomas Nelson, 1986.

Poythress, Vern S., and Wayne A. Grudem. *The TNIV and the Gender-Neutral Bible Controversy*. Nashville: Broadman & Holman, 2004.

Ryken, Leland. *The ESV and the English Bible Legacy*. Wheaton, IL: Crossway, 2011.

Scorgie, Glen G., Mark L. Stauss, and Steven M. Voth, eds. *The Challenge of Bible Translation: Communicating God's Word to the World*. Grand Rapids: Zondervan, 2003.

Strauss, Mark L. "Why the English Standard Version (ESV) Should Not Become the Standard English Version: How to Make a Good Translation Much Better." Paper presented at the National Meeting of the Evangelical Theological Society, Providence, RI, November 21, 2008. Available at http://zondervan.typepad.com/files/improvingesv2.pdf.

White, James R. *The King James Only Controversy: Can You Trust Modern Translations?* 2nd ed. Minneapolis: Bethany House, 2009.

Translation Aids

Hebrew-English Interlinears

Blair, Thom, ed. *The Hebrew-English Interlinear ESV Old Testament: Biblia Hebraica Stuttgartensia (BHS) and English Standard Version (ESV)*. Wheaton, IL: Crossway, 2014.

Green, Jay Patrick, ed. *The Interlinear Bible: Hebrew, Greek, English*. Peabody, MA: Hendrickson, 2005.

Kohlenberger, John R., III, ed. *The Interlinear NIV Hebrew-English Old Testament*. Grand Rapids: Zondervan, 1993.

Reader's Edition. Logos Bible Software.

Scripture 4 All: Hebrew Interlinear Bible (OT). http://www.scripture4all.org/OnlineInterlinear/Hebrew_Index.htm.

Hebrew Analytical Lexicons and Reader's Bibles

Brown, A. Philip, II, and Bryan W. Smith. *A Reader's Hebrew Bible*. Grand Rapids: Zondervan, 2008.

Busby, Douglas L., Terry A. Armstrong, and Cyril F. Carr. *A Reader's Hebrew-English Lexicon of the Old Testament*. Grand Rapids: Zondervan, 1989.

Davidson, Benjamin. *The Analytical Hebrew and Chaldee Lexicon*. 2nd ed. 1848; repr., Grand Rapids: Zondervan, 1993.

Owens, John Joseph. *Analytical Key to the Old Testament*. 4 vols. Grand Rapids: Baker Academic, 1989.

Vance, Donald A., George Athas, and Yael Avrahami, eds. *Biblia Hebraica Stuttgartensia: A Reader's Edition*. Peabody, MA: Hendrickson, 2015.

Hebrew and Aramaic Lexicons

Brown, Francis, S. R. Driver, and Charles A. Briggs. *The New Brown-Driver-Briggs Hebrew and English Lexicon*. Peabody, MA: Hendrickson, 1979.

Clines, David J. A., ed. *The Concise Dictionary of Classical Hebrew*. Sheffield, UK: Sheffield Phoenix, 2009.

———, ed. *The Dictionary of Classical Hebrew*. 9 vols. Sheffield, UK: Sheffield Phoenix, 1993–2014.

Comprehensive Aramaic Lexicon. http://cal1.cn.huc.edu/.

Einspahr, Bruce. *Index to Brown, Driver & Briggs Hebrew Lexicon*. 2nd ed. Chicago: Moody, 1976.

Holladay, William L. *A Concise Hebrew and Aramaic Lexicon of the Old Testament*. Grand Rapids: Eerdmans, 1988.

Jastrow, Marcus. *A Dictionary of the Targumim, the Talmud Babli and Yerushalmi, and the Midrashic Literature*. 2nd ed. 2 vols. in 1. 1926; repr., New York: Judaica, 1996. Available at http://www.tyndalearchive.com/tabs/jastrow/.

✪ Koehler, Ludwig, Walter Baumgartner, and Johann Jakob Stamm, eds. *The Hebrew and Aramaic Lexicon of the Old Testament: Study Edition*. Translated by M. E. J. Richardson. 2 vols. Leiden: Brill, 2001.

★ Mounce, William D., ed. *Mounce's Complete Expository Dictionary of Old and New Testament Words*. Grand Rapids: Zondervan, 2006.

Sokoloff, Michael. *A Dictionary of Jewish Babylonian Aramaic*. Baltimore: Johns Hopkins University Press, 2003.

———. *A Dictionary of Jewish Palestinian Aramaic of the Byzantine Period*. 2nd ed. Baltimore: Johns Hopkins University Press, 2002.

Vine, W. E., Merrill F. Unger, and William White Jr. *Vine's Complete Expository Dictionary of Old and New Testament Words*. London: Oliphants, 1939; repr., Nashville: Thomas Nelson, 1996.

Vogt, Ernesto. *Lexicon Linguae Aramaicae Veteris Testamenti Documentis Antiquis Illustratum*. Rome: Pontifical Biblical Institute, 1991.

Dead Sea Scrolls

Abegg, Martin G., Jr., James E. Bowley, and Edward M. Cook, eds. *The Dead Sea Scrolls Concordance*. Vol. 3, *The Biblical Texts from Qumran and Other Sites*. Leiden: Brill, 2009.

Abegg, Martin G., Jr., Peter Flint, and Eugene Ulrich. *The Dead Sea Scrolls Bible*. San Francisco: HarperSanFrancisco, 1999.

Martínez, Florentino García, and Eibert J. C. Tigchelaar. *The Dead Sea Scrolls Study Edition*. 2 vols. Grand Rapids: Eerdmans, 1997–98.

Vermes, Geza. *The Complete Dead Sea Scrolls in English*. 7th ed. London: Penguin Books, 2012.

Wise, Michael, Martin Abegg Jr., and Edward Cook. *The Dead Sea Scrolls: A New Translation*. San Francisco: HarperSanFrancisco, 2005.

Septuagint

Brenton, Lancelot C. *The Septuagint with Apocrypha: Greek and English*. 1844; repr., Peabody, MA: Hendrickson, 1986.

Danker, Frederick W., et al. *Greek-English Lexicon of the New Testament and Other Early Christian Literature*. 3rd ed. Chicago: University of Chicago Press, 2000.

Liddell, H. G., and R. Scott. *Greek-English Lexicon with a Revised Supplement*. 9th ed. Oxford: Clarendon, 1996.

Louw, Johannes P., and Eugene A. Nida, eds. *Greek-English Lexicon of the New Testament: Based on Semantic Domains*. 2nd ed. 2 vols. New York: United Bible Societies, 1989.

Moulton, Harold K., ed. *The Analytical Greek Lexicon Revised*. 1852; repr., Grand Rapids: Zondervan, 1979.

Muraoka, T. *A Greek-English Lexicon of the Septuagint*. Leuven: Peeters, 2010.

Pietersma, Albert, and Benjamin G. Wright. *A New English Translation of the Septuagint*. Oxford: Oxford University Press, 2007.

Septuagint Online. http://www.kalvesmaki.com/LXX/.

Thesaurus Linguae Graecae. http://stephanus.tlg.uci.edu/.

Peshitta and Targums

See Hebrew and Aramaic Lexicons above.

The Aramaic Bible. 19 vols. Collegeville, MN: Liturgical Press, 1987–2007.

Comprehensive Aramaic Lexicon. http://cal1.cn.huc.edu/.

Etheridge, J. W. *The Targums of Onkelos and Jonathan ben Uzziel on the Pentateuch*. 2 vols. 1862–65; repr., Piscataway, NJ: Gorgias, 2005.

Grossfeld, Bernard, ed. *The Targum to the Five Megilloth*. New York: Hermon, 1973.

Judaica Electronic Texts. http://www.library.upenn.edu/cajs/etexts.html.

Kiraz, George A., ed. *The Antioch Bible: The Syriac Peshitta Bible with English Translation*. 35 vols. Piscataway, NJ: Gorgias, 2012–.

Lamsa, George M. *The Holy Bible from Ancient Eastern Manuscripts*. Philadelphia: Holman, 1957.

Smith, R. Payne, ed. *A Compendious Syriac Dictionary*. Oxford: Clarendon, 1903; repr., Eugene, OR: Wipf & Stock, 1999.

Latin Vulgate and Old Latin

Glare, P. G. W., ed. *Oxford Latin Dictionary*. 2nd ed. 2 vols. Oxford: Oxford University Press, 2012.

Knox, Ronald Arbuthnott. *The Old Testament: Newly Translated from the Vulgate Latin*. 2 vols. New York: Sheed & Ward, 1950.

Latin Vulgate. http://www.latinvulgate.com/.

Morwood, James, ed. *The Oxford Latin Desk Dictionary*. Oxford: Oxford University Press, 2005.

Simpson, D. P., ed. *Cassell's Latin Dictionary*. New York: Macmillan, 1968.

PART 2

OBSERVATION—"HOW IS THE PASSAGE COMMUNICATED?"

5

CLAUSE AND TEXT GRAMMAR

Goal: Assess the makeup and relationship of words, phrases, clauses, and larger text units.

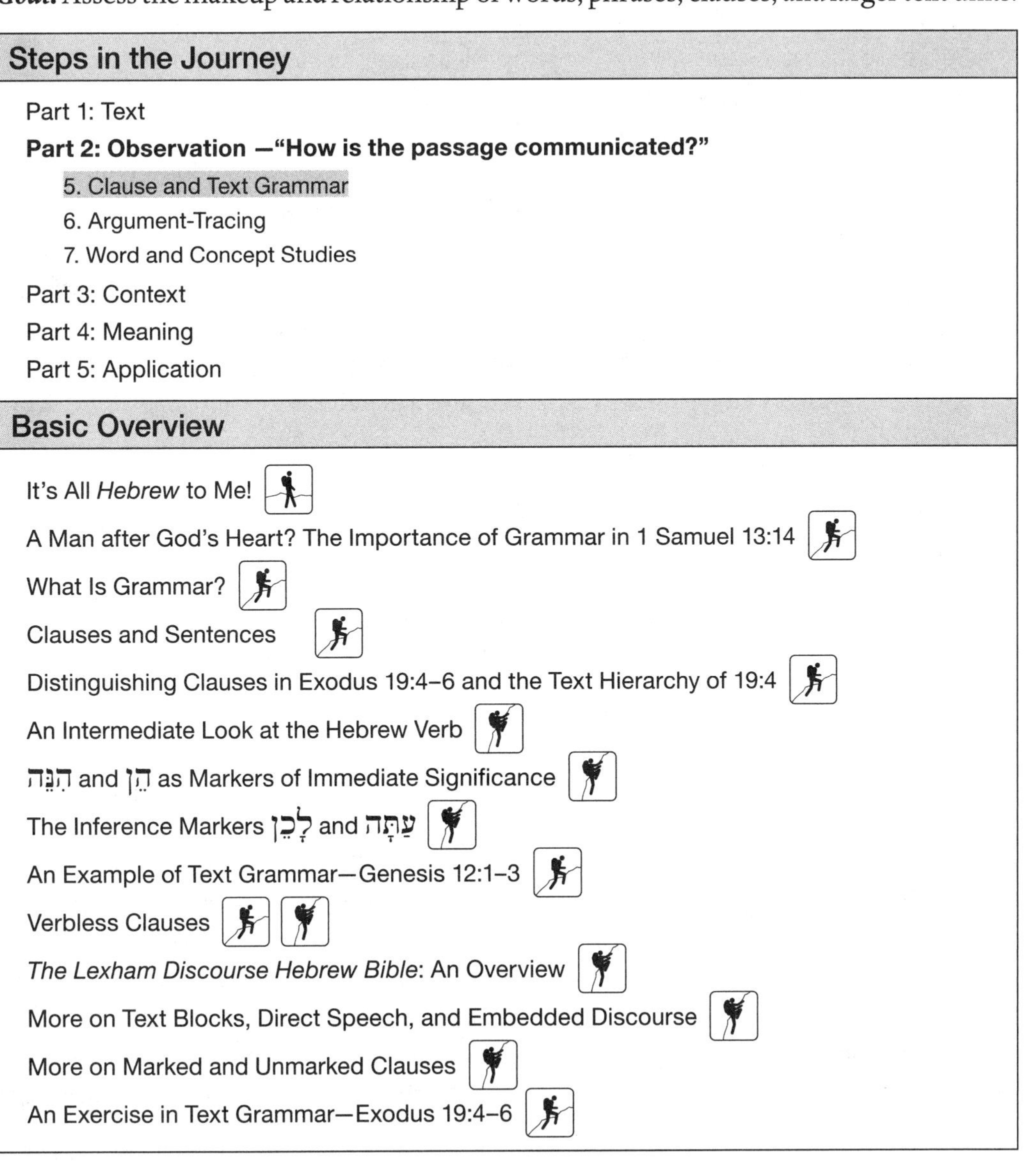

Steps in the Journey

Part 1: Text

Part 2: Observation —"How is the passage communicated?"

5. Clause and Text Grammar
6. Argument-Tracing
7. Word and Concept Studies

Part 3: Context

Part 4: Meaning

Part 5: Application

Basic Overview

It's All *Hebrew* to Me!

A Man after God's Heart? The Importance of Grammar in 1 Samuel 13:14

What Is Grammar?

Clauses and Sentences

Distinguishing Clauses in Exodus 19:4–6 and the Text Hierarchy of 19:4

An Intermediate Look at the Hebrew Verb

הִנֵּה and הֵן as Markers of Immediate Significance

The Inference Markers לָכֵן and עַתָּה

An Example of Text Grammar—Genesis 12:1–3

Verbless Clauses

The Lexham Discourse Hebrew Bible: An Overview

More on Text Blocks, Direct Speech, and Embedded Discourse

More on Marked and Unmarked Clauses

An Exercise in Text Grammar—Exodus 19:4–6

Fig. 5.1. Trail Guide to Chapter 5

It's All *Hebrew* to Me!

Grammar is not always a student's favorite subject. Nevertheless, things such as prepositions and participles, paradigms and the logical relationship of propositions are all a pleasing pain if you recognize that through them you can get closer to rightly understanding God's Book.

For those who don't know Hebrew, simply learning the Hebrew alphabet and grasping some basics about how Hebrew nouns, verbs, and other words relate and operate will open a whole world of advanced Bible study tools and help you better track the discussions in commentaries. A useful guide to this end is Lee Fields's *Hebrew for the Rest of Us*, which provides an overview of some of the basics of Hebrew word construction and function and supplies a brief guide to word studies, translation choice, and tools.[1]

This chapter seeks to show how grammar is important for exegesis and how it helps us track an author's flow of thought. Much of the treatment is targeted toward those with at least two semesters of Hebrew, but most of the discussion should be clear to all. If you are one who says, "It's all Hebrew to me," and if you are already beginning to break out in hives because I mentioned the word *grammar*, feel free to jump ahead to chapter 6.

A Man after God's Heart? The Importance of Grammar in 1 Samuel 13:14

In 1993 I spent a semester studying in Israel. As I went, I prayed that God would increasingly make me "a man after his heart." I was echoing 1 Samuel 13:14, where, speaking of Saul's replacement, the prophet declared, "The Lord has sought for himself a man after his own heart" (NASB). What does this mean? If you were to pray this, for what would you be asking God? I think for me it was something like this: "God, let my desires, thoughts, delights, and hates be like yours; let my heart be like your heart." Or it could have been: "Help me be a man who pursues after your heart."

The essence of both of these prayers is good. But what is clear is that I was interpreting the passage in a certain way. In fact, even though I never consciously thought

1. Lee M. Fields, *Hebrew for the Rest of Us: Using Hebrew Tools without Mastering Biblical Hebrew* (Grand Rapids: Zondervan, 2008).

about it, I was assuming something about the grammar of 1 Samuel 13:14—that the prepositional phrase "after/like/according to his heart" (כִּלְבָבוֹ) was describing something about the "man." This, however, is not the only possibility for understanding the phrase. Let's consider the text in interlinear fashion, identifying the verb (V), subject (S), direct object (DO), and modifiers (M).[2] Remember that Hebrew reads right to left.

MT		ESV
וְעַתָּה מַמְלַכְתְּךָ לֹא־תָקוּם	14	But now your kingdom shall not continue.
בִּקֵּשׁ יְהוָה לוֹ אִישׁ כִּלְבָבוֹ	b	The LORD has sought out a man after his own heart,
וַיְצַוֵּהוּ יְהוָה לְנָגִיד עַל־עַמּוֹ	c	and the LORD has commanded him to be prince over his people,
כִּי לֹא שָׁמַרְתָּ אֵת אֲשֶׁר־צִוְּךָ יְהוָה׃	d	because you have not kept what the LORD commanded you.

כִּלְבָבוֹ	אִישׁ	לוֹ	יְהוָה	בִּקֵּשׁ
M	DO	M	S	V
after/like/according-to-his-heart	a-man	for-himself	YHWH	sought

Fig. 5.2. 1 Samuel 13:14 in MT, ESV, and Hebrew-English Interlinear

In English, the preposition *after* can mean "in pursuit of," as in "the cop went *after* the robber." Yet the Hebrew preposition כְּ ("like/according to") never functions this way, so the construction אִישׁ כִּלְבָבוֹ can't mean "a man who pursues God's heart." That cancels out one of the possible ways in which I may have interpreted this statement decades ago. Instead, כְּ most often expresses either (1) a relationship of correspondence or identity ("like, just as") or (2) agreement in kind, manner, or norm ("according to").[3]

The next thing to recognize is that prepositional phrases are modifiers, characterizing either nouns (functioning adjectivally) or verbs (functioning adverbially). Most prepositional phrases in Hebrew are adverbial, but the traditional interpretation of 1 Samuel 13:14 treats the prepositional phrase כִּלְבָבוֹ adjectivally. Let's look at three possibilities for interpreting 1 Samuel 13:14.

First, if כִּלְבָבוֹ ("after/like/according to his heart") is functioning adjectivally, modifying the direct object "man" (אִישׁ), and if "heart" (לֵבָב) refers to God's character or loyalty, then the clause would mean that "YHWH has sought a man whose character or loyalty in some way corresponded to God's character or loyalty." This is the traditional reading, and a number of English translations make this view explicit: "The Lord, searching for a man who is pleasing to him in every way" (BBE); "The

2. For those without Hebrew, a Hebrew-English interlinear can be a useful tool for tracking grammatical discussions. The very best interlinear of which I am aware is Logos Bible Software's *Reader's Edition*, which allows you to set the parameters for word inclusion based on a set word list or the number of occurrences you have already learned. There are also a number of good options available in print: John R. Kohlenberger III, ed., *The Interlinear NIV Hebrew-English Old Testament* (Grand Rapids: Zondervan, 1993); Jay Patrick Green, ed., *The Interlinear Bible: Hebrew, Greek, English* (Peabody, MA: Hendrickson, 2005); Thom Blair, ed., *The Hebrew-English Interlinear ESV Old Testament: Biblia Hebraica Stuttgartensia (BHS) and English Standard Version (ESV)* (Wheaton, IL: Crossway, 2014).

3. *IBHS* 202–5, § 11.2.9.

Lord has sought out for himself a man who is loyal to him" (NET Bible); "The Lord has found a man loyal to him" (HCSB);[4] "The Lord will search for a man following the Lord's own heart" (CEB).

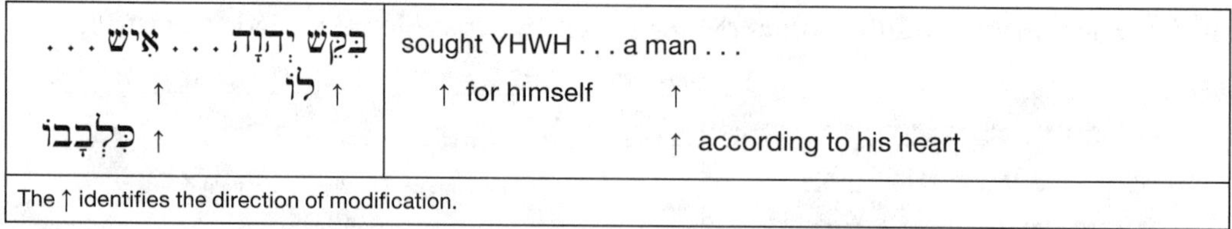

Fig. 5.3. Adjectival View of כִּלְבָבוֹ in 1 Samuel 13:14

Second, when reading כִּלְבָבוֹ adjectivally, another possibility arises if "heart" refers not to God's character but to his "desire" or "choice." Here God's elective purpose corresponds with or finds fulfillment in the "man." McCarter made this view popular in his Anchor Bible commentary on 1 Samuel, and many scholars today are following this reading.[5] Here the basic idea would be that "YHWH sought for himself a man who was in accord with his own choosing." Some contemporary versions employ this reading: "God is out looking for your replacement right now. This time he'll do the choosing" (MSG). "The Lord will search for a man of his own choosing" (CEBA).

There is still a third way of reading the passage, and I think it is to be preferred—that the prepositional phrase כִּלְבָבוֹ functions not adjectivally, modifying "man," but adverbially, modifying the main verb בִּקֵּשׁ ("he sought"). In this instance, YHWH's "heart/will" serves as the standard or norm by which he sought a new king: "YHWH sought for himself according to his own will a man." In this reading, the verse says nothing explicit about the man's character or loyalty. Instead, it focuses on how YHWH's act of discretion in selecting David grew out of a previous act of willing—he sought in accordance with a mental image he had in mind.

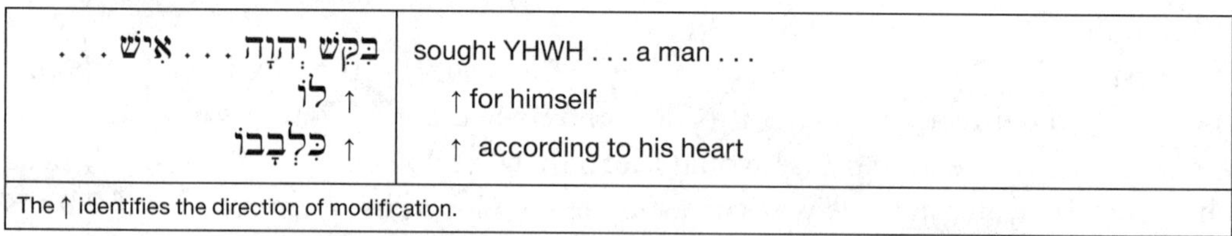

Fig. 5.4. Adverbial View of כִּלְבָבוֹ in 1 Samuel 13:14

Support for the adverbial reading comes from grammatical parallels, ancient Near Eastern comparisons (see "The Historical Context of 1 Samuel 13:14" in chapter 8), and biblical theology, all of which I have addressed elsewhere.[6] Now, if the adverbial reading

4. The newer CSB returns to a more traditional rendering: "The Lord has found a man after his own heart."

5. P. Kyle McCarter Jr., *1 Samuel: A New Translation with Introduction and Commentary*, AB 8 (New York: Doubleday, 1980), 229.

6. Jason S. DeRouchie, "The Heart of YHWH and His Chosen One in 1 Samuel 13:14," *BBR* 24, 4 (2013): 467–89.

is correct, even though the verse tells us nothing explicit about Saul's replacement, it may still tell us something implicitly. If YHWH, in part, selected David because his life aligned more closely to God's mental ideal for kingship than Saul's life did (i.e., Deut. 17:14–20), then even with the adverbial reading, we may learn something about David's character or loyalty.

In 1 Samuel 15:28 Samuel tells Saul that YHWH has given the kingdom "to a neighbor of yours, who is better than you." Then in 16:7, God rejects all of David's brothers from kingship but declares David to be the heir to the throne, asserting that "the LORD sees not as man sees; man looks on the outward appearance, but the LORD looks on the heart." YHWH sought the one whose life aligned most closely with his ideal for kingship as described in Deuteronomy 17:14–20. David was not perfect—indeed, he was far from it. But his inner disposition truly did align more with God's desires than Saul's did. Even more, his life pointed to his greater Son, Jesus, who perfectly matches God's ideal image of kingship.[7]

My point in this illustration is to stress the value of knowing Hebrew grammar. In our look at 1 Samuel 13:14, our awareness that prepositional phrases can function both adjectivally and adverbially has opened up new avenues for questions and interpretation.

What Is Grammar?

Grammar is important because it is the whole system and structure that a language uses for communicating effectively, and it is the means that God used to give us his Word. For those who have worked through a year of biblical Hebrew, your study has included four areas: orthography, phonology, morphology, and syntax. ***Orthography*** is the study of an alphabet and of how its letters combine to represent sounds and to form words. ***Phonology*** is the study of a language's system of sounds (phonemes). ***Morphology*** is the study of the formation of words. All the paradigms from first-year Hebrew are part of morphology, as are the rules for accent shift and vowel change. ***Syntax*** deals with how words combine to form phrases, clauses, sentences, and even larger discourse structures. Micro-syntax focuses on the shaping of clauses and sentences, whereas macro-syntax addresses the shaping of whole texts.

7. The apostle Paul alluded to 1 Samuel 13:14 in a sermon to the Jews in the synagogue at Pisidian Antioch during his first missionary journey (Acts 13:22). The fact that Paul's speech came over a thousand years after David's rise explains both the inclusion of David's identity and the shift in verbs from "sought" to "found." Thus, the prepositional phrase "according to my heart" could be either adjectival or adverbial, with the apostle merely quoting the text as it stands. I do not believe there is enough evidence to assert that Paul followed the traditional adjectival reading of כִּלְבָבוֹ in 1 Samuel 13:14. For more on this, see ibid., 488–89.

In the exegetical process, you need to identify every major grammatical issue in your text, whether orthographic, morphologic, or syntactic. Questions related to these issues include:

- Could any clauses or groups of clauses be understood differently if the grammar were construed differently?
- Have I accounted for all spelling irregularities?
- Why were certain stems chosen instead of others—for example, a Hithpael over a Niphal?
- Have I identified the antecedent referent of every pronoun and the subject of every verb?
- Do I understand the function of every subordinate conjunction and asyndetic clause, and have I determined the start of every chain of coordinated וְ ("and") clauses?
- Have I grasped the role of every discourse marker and the function of every marked clause?
- Do I know what the cantillation marks say about the Jewish interpretation?

Most likely, your study of Hebrew has focused almost solely on morphology and micro-syntax—the formation of words and the shaping of those words into clauses and sentences. This is where study of any language must begin, but it cannot end there. Interpreters of Scripture need to exegete more than clauses; we exegete texts such as paragraphs and pericopes, and this is what this chapter is about. It is built on what was already addressed in chapter 2, "Literary Units and Text Hierarchy."

Clauses and Sentences[8]

In assessing grammar we must begin with the clause, for it is the basic building block of text analysis. A ***clause*** is a grammatical construction that is made up of a subject and its predicate. For example, "he prayed" is a clause, with "he" being the subject and "prayed" being the predicate. By contrast, "in the house" is only a phrase, for the collection of words has no subject and predicate and is therefore not a clause.

The ***predicate*** is the part of a clause that refers to the state, process, or action associated with the subject. In Hebrew, the predicate either may be a finite verb with all its complements (resulting in what we call a *verbal clause*) or may be another noun

8. This material is adapted from Duane A. Garrett and Jason S. DeRouchie, *A Modern Grammar for Biblical Hebrew* (Nashville: Broadman & Holman, 2009), 283–84 (§ 37.B). Used by permission.

or an adjective without any explicit verb (resulting in what we call a *verbless clause*). The subject and its predicate make up the essential nucleus (Nuc) of a clause (Cl). Along with the clause nucleus can be various modifiers (Mod) and connectors (Con), such as conjunctions, exclamations, adverbs, and prepositional phrases

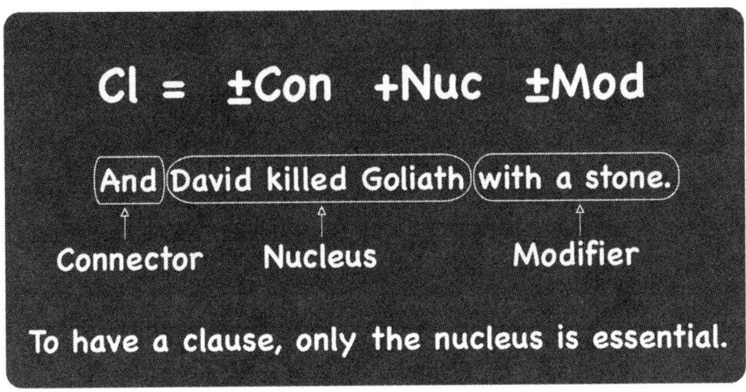

You can think of a clause as having grammatical slots: one slot for an optional connector, one slot for a mandatory nucleus (subject and predicate), and any number of slots for optional modifiers. The modifier slots may be filled by a word (such as an adverb), a phrase (such as a prepositional phrase), or even a whole clause (such as a relative clause). Figure 5.5 supplies some examples of the different kinds of modifiers.

1. Word	"**Yesterday** David slew Goliath."
	Here, "yesterday" is an adverbial modifier.
2. Phrase	"David slew Goliath **in the afternoon**."
	"In the afternoon" is an adverbial prepositional phrase that functions collectively as a single modifier.
3. Clause	"David, **who is but a boy**, slew Goliath."
	The words "who is but a boy" include a subject and predicate, but they form a relative clause and serve as a modifier of "David." They are in a subordinate position.

Fig. 5.5. Modifiers as Words, Phrases, and Clauses

Our study of grammar begins with the following definitions:

1. A ***phrase*** is a group of words that fills a single slot in a clause.
2. A ***subordinate clause*** is a clause that serves as a modifier and is embedded in a higher-level clause, as in "who is but a boy" in my earlier example.

3. A ***main clause*** (*matrix* "mother" clause) is not grammatically subordinate to any other higher-level clause.[9] In the construction "David, who is but a boy, slew Goliath," the words "David . . . slew Goliath" form the main clause.
4. A ***sentence*** is a main clause with all its subordinate clauses.

In the process of Old Testament exegesis, a good initial step for assessing grammar and structure is to divide the text into its discrete clauses. Once this is accomplished, you can begin to evaluate how those clauses come together to form texts. In the next section, we will divide Exodus 19:4–6 into clauses and then consider some of the grammatical questions that we raised during translation.

Distinguishing Clauses in Exodus 19:4–6 and the Text Hierarchy of 19:4

We will continue our assessment of Exodus 19:4–6 by first distinguishing all the clauses. Before reading ahead, try to delimit the various clauses in this passage on your own. You can do this even if you don't know Hebrew. Remember that the necessary elements to make a clause are a subject and its predicate. To test whether you have identified a clause, simply drop off all connectors and modifiers and see whether it makes sense on its own. Every clause nucleus should supply a complete thought. When you've finished, compare your work to figure 5.6.

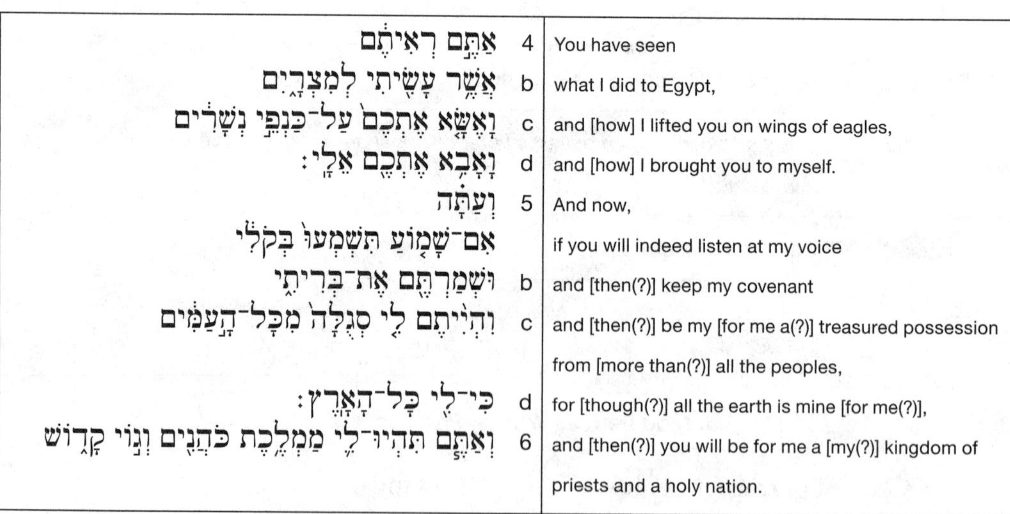

אַתֶּ֣ם רְאִיתֶ֔ם	4	You have seen
אֲשֶׁ֥ר עָשִׂ֖יתִי לְמִצְרָ֑יִם	b	what I did to Egypt,
וָאֶשָּׂ֤א אֶתְכֶם֙ עַל־כַּנְפֵ֣י נְשָׁרִ֔ים	c	and [how] I lifted you on wings of eagles,
וָאָבִ֥א אֶתְכֶ֖ם אֵלָֽי׃	d	and [how] I brought you to myself.
וְעַתָּ֗ה	5	And now,
אִם־שָׁמ֤וֹעַ תִּשְׁמְעוּ֙ בְּקֹלִ֔י		if you will indeed listen at my voice
וּשְׁמַרְתֶּ֖ם אֶת־בְּרִיתִ֑י	b	and [then(?)] keep my covenant
וִהְיִ֨יתֶם לִ֤י סְגֻלָּה֙ מִכָּל־הָ֣עַמִּ֔ים	c	and [then(?)] be my [for me a(?)] treasured possession
		from [more than(?)] all the peoples,
כִּי־לִ֖י כָּל־הָאָֽרֶץ׃	d	for [though(?)] all the earth is mine [for me(?)],
וְאַתֶּ֧ם תִּהְיוּ־לִ֛י מַמְלֶ֥כֶת כֹּהֲנִ֖ים וְג֣וֹי קָד֑וֹשׁ	6	and [then(?)] you will be for me a [my(?)] kingdom of
		priests and a holy nation.

Fig. 5.6. Delimiting Clauses in Exodus 19:4–6

9. Some main clauses can still bear levels of dependence, as when subject or object pronouns have their antecedents stated elsewhere.

I have marked the start of each verse with the verse number and then every clause that follows within the verse with a letter. In 5a, I separated the "And now" (וְעַתָּה) from the "if" (אִם־) clause because וְעַתָּה modifies the entire sentence that runs from verses 5–6. Even though 5a is broken over two lines, there is only one clause.

Next, let's consider how the clauses relate to each other, specifically by shaping a text hierarchy (see "Introducing Literary Units and Text Hierarchy in Hebrew" in chapter 2 and "Text Blocks" in chapter 2). Remember that indents indicate which clauses are more dominant (less indented) or more dependent (more indented). Starting the text hierarchy is relatively easy in verse 4. We have a main clause in 4a followed by the relative object clause in 4b (beginning with אֲשֶׁר "what"). Because the object clause complements the main clause, we indent 4b one tier to the left (or right in English).

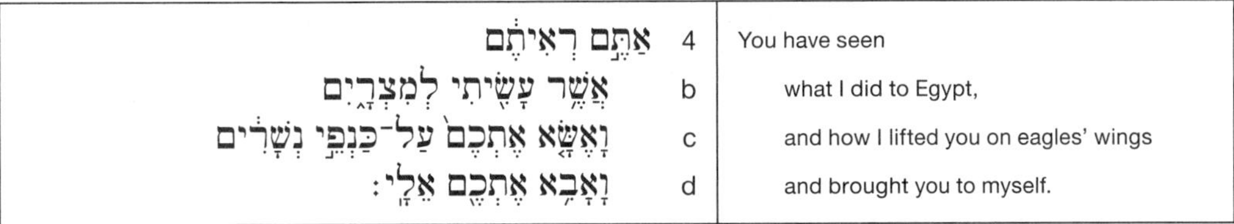

אַתֶּם רְאִיתֶם	4	You have seen
אֲשֶׁר עָשִׂיתִי לְמִצְרָיִם	b	what I did to Egypt,
וָאֶשָּׂא אֶתְכֶם עַל־כַּנְפֵי נְשָׁרִים	c	and how I lifted you on eagles' wings
וָאָבִא אֶתְכֶם אֵלָי׃	d	and brought you to myself.

Fig. 5.7. Text Hierarchy of Exodus 19:4

Next, we see that the two verbal clauses 4cd further describe what Israel "saw" or experienced in Egypt. That is, the וְ connectors at the front of the *wayyiqtol* verbs in 4cd (וָאֶשָּׂא "*and* I lifted"; וָאָבִא "*and* I brought") are building on the relative אֲשֶׁר ("which, that, what") clause and therefore must be joined to it and thus indented once as well. The relative particle אֲשֶׁר, initially translated "what," controls not only 4b but also 4cd because the וְ conectors at the front of 4cd are joined to it. The shift in verbal meaning requires translating the first clause with "what" and the next two with "how," but all three clauses operate together as the object of the main verb רְאִיתֶם ("you have seen") in 4a. God's people had seen *what* God did, *and how* he lifted them, *and how* he brought them to himself.

At verse 5 we begin to face the grammatical questions raised in our translation. The two main questions that need to be answered are (1) where do we start the apodosis (i.e., "then") in verses 5–6, and (2) is the subordinate conjunction כִּי in 5d providing a ground/reason ("because/for" = ESV) for what precedes, or is it concessive ("although" = NIV), introducing what precedes or follows? We'll tackle these questions later in the chapter.

An Intermediate Look at the Hebrew Verb[10]

Figure 5.8 is an overview of the various verbal conjugations used in biblical Hebrew.[11] In this section I want to develop these concepts.

Sphere	Form Title	Traditional Title	General Function
Past/ Perfective	*wayyiqtol*	waw-consecutive imperfect	Context-determined tense, perfective aspect, indicative or nonindicative modality
	qatal	perfect	Context-determined tense, perfective aspect, indicative or nonindicative modality
	weqatal	waw-consecutive perfect	Context-determined tense and aspect, indicative or nonindicative modality
Imperfective/ Progressive	*(we)yiqtol* (long)	imperfect	Context-determined tense, imperfective aspect, indicative or nonindicative modality
	participle	participle	Context-determined tense, progressive aspect
Volitional Modality[12]	*(we)yiqtol* (short)	jussive	Context-determined tense, perfective aspect, usually volitional, nonindicative modality
	imperative	imperative	Volitional, nonindicative modality

Fig. 5.8. The Hebrew Verb

10. Some of this material is adapted from Garrett and DeRouchie, *A Modern Grammar for Biblical Hebrew*, 33–40, 64–66, 220–23 (§§ 6, 10.D, 30). Used by permission.

11. See Peter J. Gentry, "The System of the Finite Verb in Classical Biblical Hebrew," *HS* 39 (1998): 7–39; John A. Cook, "The Hebrew Verb: A Grammaticalization Approach," *ZAH* 14, 4 (2001): 117–43.

12. Volitional modality relates to the moral realm and refers to the logic of obligation and permission; scholars usually refer to it as deontic modality (David A. Crystal, *A Dictionary of Linguistics and Phonetics*, 5th ed., Language Library [Malden, MA: Blackwell, 2003], 130).

Defining Terms

English speakers have been taught to think of verbs first in terms of *tense* and then in terms of *voice* and *mood*. For biblical Hebrew, we also need to be aware of *aspect* and *Aktionsart*.

Tense tells us whether the situation expressed by the verb is past, present, or future. English uses, for example, simple past ("Barney ate it") and future ("Moses will eat it").

Voice tells us whether the subject of a verb acts or is acted on. English has the *active* voice ("Joey hit the ball") and the *passive* voice ("The ball was hit by Joey").

Mood (or *modality*) tells us whether the action or state expressed in a verb is actual (*was, is, will*) or merely possible (*may, should, would, could*). The *indicative mood* conveys real situations and facts ("Ruthie *eats* cookies"), whereas various *nonindicative moods* indicate situations that are potential but not realized (e.g., "Ruthie *could eat* vegetables"). Some nonindicative modals are tagged as *volitives*, because they express the volition or will of the speaker. Among these are the imperatives, which form commands ("*Run*, Ezra!") or prohibitions ("Please *don't run*, Ezra!"). Also among these are the subjunctives, which express doubts, wishes, requests, or desires (e.g., "*May* Joy *sing*?" or "Joy *should sing*"). Some nonindicatives express conditions or contingency, in which the validity or realization of one proposition is dependent on a condition's being met ("If . . . then"). Other nonindicatives express purpose ("Jason stood by the road so that he *would see* Teresa go by").

Aspect relates to how a speaker portrays an action, whether it is presented as a whole event ("it happened") or as a process ("it was happening"). We are concerned with two aspects: perfective and imperfective. ***Perfective aspect*** portrays an action as a whole. Its focus is on the fact that an action took place, as opposed to viewing an activity in process as it happens or happened. English examples of perfectives are as follows:

- *"Isaac ate the apples."* This is a past action viewed as a whole, stated as a simple act that took place in the past.
- *"Isaac has eaten the apples."* This is a completed action.
- *"Isaac eats apples."* Here, although the tense is present, the action is portrayed as a whole rather than as ongoing. It could answer the question, "Should I give him an apple to eat?" and imply, "Yes, give him one; he likes them." This is not the same as "He is eating apples," which indicates ongoing activity in the present. Notice also that "He eats apples" is perfective but does not imply a completed action; it merely states that such an action takes place.

Imperfective aspect portrays an action *in process* rather than as a whole. It is sometimes open-ended as to the outcome, and it may be habitual or repeated.

- *"Janie was driving home after work."* Here, focus is on the process of driving home. It is open-ended because we don't know whether she made it home or not. Contrast "She drove home after work," which is perfective in that it portrays the action as a whole and implies the outcome: She arrived at her home.
- *"Janie used to drive home."* This describes an action that habitually took place in the past.

Aktionsart (German for "kind of action") is principally a lexical feature of language (i.e., bound up in the inherent meaning of each verb) and relates to the actual (and not just portrayed) procedural characteristics attributed to a verb phrase. *Dynamicity* (dynamic vs. stative), *durativity* (durative vs. punctiliar), and *telicity* (telic vs. atelic) are all features of *Aktionsart*.[13] These terms express qualities of action or state that are usually lexically determined and thus have little to do with the communicator's viewpoint or portrayal of events (i.e., aspect). In English, for example, the *Aktionsart* of the verb *strike* is punctiliar regardless of context or morphology, but grammar and context alone reveal the author's perspective on this event. "He struck" is perfective in aspect and portrayed as a complete entity, whereas "he is striking" is imperfective and portrayed as a process.

Tense, *Aktionsart*, Mood, and Aspect: *Yiqtol*, *Qatal*, *Wayyiqtol*

1. Introduction

Many Western languages, such as French, Latin, and Greek, have elaborate inflection systems that explicitly mark their verbs with such things as past and present tense or indicative and subjunctive mood. In contrast, biblical Hebrew finite verbs do not inflect verbs specifically for tense or mood. No Hebrew verb form is solely used for the "future tense" or the "indicative mood." But for the *yiqtol*, *qatal*, and *wayyiqtol*, these general rules apply:

a. *Tense*: The *yiqtol* is more likely to be future, and the *wayyiqtol* and *qatal* are more likely to be past. All three can be present tense in certain contexts.

b. *Voice*: Hebrew marks passive voice independently of whether the verb is *yiqtol*, *qatal*, or *wayyiqtol*. Along with the Qal passive participle, the Niphal, Pual, Hophal, and Hithpael all can express passivity.

13. John A. Cook, *The Biblical Hebrew Verbal System: A Grammaticalization Approach* (Ph.D. diss., University of Wisconsin—Madison, 2002), 26; cf. Cook, *Time and the Biblical Hebrew Verb: The Expression of Tense, Aspect, and Modality in Biblical Hebrew*, LSAWS 7 (Winona Lake, IN: Eisenbrauns, 2012).

c. *Mood*: The *qatal* and *wayyiqtol* are much more likely to be indicative (a real situation), though both can be nonindicative in contingent contexts (e.g., Num. 5:27; 1 Sam. 25:34; Job 9:16). The *yiqtol* may be either indicative or nonindicative (a possible or desirable situation), and as we will see, the latter is usually marked by the verb's placement in first position.

d. *Aspect*: Speakers who wish to portray perfective aspect usually use *qatal* and *wayyiqtol*. They normally indicate imperfective action through the *yiqtol*. This does not mean, however, that every *yiqtol* implies continuous or repeated action. The *yiqtol* is likely to be imperfective if it is in the past or present tense (not future) and is indicative.

e. *Aktionsart*: As a lexical feature of individual verbs, *Aktionsart* influences the possible nuances of various conjugations in given contexts. For more on this, see below.

2. Tense and *Aktionsart* in the Hebrew Verb

a. Overview

The various Hebrew conjugations are not tense-specific. Nevertheless, certain verbal conjugations more naturally align with past or nonpast contexts.

Yiqtol verbs are often future tense. This is why the gloss for a form such as יִפֹּל (Qal *yiqtol* third masculine singular of נפל "to fall") is "he *will fall*." But the *yiqtol* can mark ongoing present activity (e.g., "he *falls*") or recurrent or habitual past action (e.g., "he *used to fall*"). A *yiqtol* is rarely if ever translated as a simple past, such as "he fell." Here are three places where one might use יִפֹּל as the verb: (1) Future tense: "Within a year, that evil man *will fall*." The *yiqtol* here marks a simple act (not repeated action or action in process) in the future. (2) Present tense: "The old man regularly *falls* when he tries to walk." Action verbs in present-time contexts can take the *yiqtol*. (3) Past imperfect: "The old man *would fall* when he tried to walk." Notice that the translation is imperfective and not a simple past tense as in: "He *fell* when he tried to walk."

Qatal verbs most commonly represent the past tense, and thus the gloss for קָם is "he arose." Yet *qatal* does not equal past tense, because it can also express present states or past events that bear present results or significance (i.e., a persistent present perfect). Also, the *qatal* may or may not describe completed action. Note the following examples: (1) Simple past tense: "He *rose* to power at a young age." The simple past is the default translation (the gloss). (2) A past tense indicating completed action: "He *has arisen*." (3) A persistent present perfect, in which a completed action bears sustained significance in the present, often when identifying a common practice: "The people *have risen* [i.e., often rise] when the king enters the room."

Wayyiqtol verbs most often express simple past action (and also have the connector *and*), and thus the gloss for וַיָּסָב is "*and* he *encircled*." This is the default, but in present-time contexts, it can also serve as a persistent present perfect, expressing completed action that bears continuing results (e.g., "*and* he *has encircled*").

b. The Role of Context and Aktionsart in Determining Tense[14]

We have seen that יִפֹּל might mean "he *will fall*" or "he *used to fall*." Both meanings are indicative, but how do we tell whether יִפֹּל is future or past in meaning? One answer is *context*. Context describes the situation in which a statement is made. If יִפֹּל is in a narrative about the past, it is a past imperfective ("he *used to fall*"). If יִפֹּל is in a future context, it has a future meaning. The future meaning of the *yiqtol* is far more common than the past imperfect. Context will also determine the tense of a *qatal* verb. The *qatal* in verbs describing what one thinks or feels is often present perfect tense. For example, "They have known [this is a *qatal* verb] the way of YHWH" (Jer. 5:5); "I have loved [this is a *qatal* verb] the habitation of your house" (Ps. 26:8). Usually, however, *qatal* is past tense.

Along with context, another feature that can guide our assessment of tense is *Aktionsart*. As noted, *Aktionsart* is a lexical designation that relates to the "kind of action" expressed by a Hebrew verb. Most important for our purposes is whether a verb is dynamic or stative. ***Dynamic verbs*** (also known as *fientive*) are action verbs, showing continued or progressive action on the part of a subject. In contrast, ***stative verbs*** describe the condition of their subject rather than an action and often relate to thoughts, emotions, relationships, senses, or states of being. Figure 5.9 shows how *Aktionsart* works with the *qatal* and *yiqtol* conjugations to express tense.

Aktionsart	Tense-Aspect		
	Past	***Present***	***Future***
Dynamic	*qatal* *yiqtol* (recurring actions)	*yiqtol* *qatal* (persistent perfect)	*yiqtol*
Stative	*qatal*	*qatal*	*yiqtol*

Fig. 5.9. Tense and *Aktionsart* in *Qatal* and *Yiqtol* Verbs

The tense of Hebrew verbs is context-determined, but there are still limits to usage that are controlled by a verb's *Aktionsart* in relation to its conjugation's aspect. With both dynamic and stative verbs, for example, biblical authors use normal *qatal* to express simple past time, whereas they commonly use *qatal* only with stative verbs in present time. In our examples above from Jeremiah 5:5 and Psalm 26:8, however, we already saw how dynamic *qatal* verbs can participate in the present time frame when operating as persistent perfects—when a past action has continuing results or significance in the present (e.g., "The enemies have torn down the walls"). The same can happen with

14. I have built much of this discussion from two studies: Brian L. Webster, *The Cambridge Introduction to Biblical Hebrew* (Cambridge: Cambridge University Press, 2009), 295–305; Webster, "The Perfect Verb and the Perfect Woman in Proverbs," in *Windows to the Ancient World of the Hebrew Bible: Essays in Honor of Samuel Greengus*, ed. Bill T. Arnold, Nancy L. Erickson, and John H. Walton (Winona Lake, IN: Eisenbrauns, 2014), 261–71.

wayyiqtol (e.g., Ps. 41:13; Nah. 3:16).[15] More commonly, however, dynamic verbs use *yiqtol* in the present. *Yiqtol* is also the conjugation of choice for all future expressions with both dynamic and stative verbs, and *yiqtol* can also be used in past-tense contexts when the action is recurring or in progress.

These distinctions greatly help us understand what is going on in Hebrew poetic parallelism. Translators of the Psalms and Proverbs have long struggled to discern how apparent parallel statements in present time could include both *yiqtol* and *qatal* forms.[16] In my assessment, the answer is found in recognizing how a verb's *Aktionsart* works with conjugation type to inform tense. I believe that Hebrew verbs function the same way in poetry as they do in prose. Dynamic *yiqtol*, stative *qatal*, and dynamic *qatal* can all stand in relation to one another (along with verbless clauses) in a stanza concerned with the present time, so long as we rightly recognize the way in which each conjugation type expresses itself.

15. Waltke and O'Connor follow the common view that *qatal* and *wayyiqtol*, along with functioning as present statives and persistent present perfects, can function as persistent or habitual gnomic perfectives, which occur in present time in proverbs or similar short, pithy maxims or aphorisms (*IBHS* §§ 30.4b, 30.5.1c, 33.3.1.b [485, 488, 555–56]). For the *qatal*, their examples include Jeremiah 8:7 ("The dove . . . and the bulbul *observe* the time of their migration") and Isaiah 40:7 ("Grass *withers*, flowers *fade*"). For the *wayyiqtol*, they point to Isaiah 40:24 ("He blows upon them *and* they *wither*"); Job 7:9 ("The cloud wastes away *and vanishes*"); and Proverbs 11:2 ("When pride comes, *so does* disgrace"), all of which also include their proposed gnomic *qatal*. In each of these examples, however, I see no reason not to retain the persistent present *perfect* reading of both the *qatal* and *wayyiqtol* forms: Jeremiah 8:7 ("And the dove . . . and the bulbul *have observed* the time of their migration"); Isaiah 40:7 ("The grass *has withered*, the flower *has faded*"); Isaiah 40:24 ("And also he *has blown* upon them, *and* they *have withered*"); Job 7:9 ("The cloud *has wasted away and has vanished*"); Proverbs 11:2 ("Pride *has come, and* disgrace *has come*"). For more on the approach I follow, see the resources in the previous footnote.

16. Many scholars assume that in Hebrew poetry the *qatal* forms of dynamic verbs often bear present and future meanings, much in contrast to their use in prose, where they by default express past tense or present perfect tense (see the citations from Waltke and O'Connor in the previous footnote). Alviero Niccacci summarizes this approach when he observes that scholars commonly think that "the verbal forms in poetry, more so than in prose, can be taken to mean everything the interpreter thinks appropriate according to his understanding of the context" ("The Biblical Hebrew Verbal System in Poetry," in *Biblical Hebrew in Its Northwest Semitic Setting: Typological and Historical Perspectives*, ed. Steven Ellis Fassberg and Avi Hurvitz [Winona Lake, IN: Eisenbrauns, 2006], 247). In contrast, I think that the Hebrew verb functions in biblical poetry the same way it does in prose and that the *qatal* never expresses a "gnomic" present but always signals past or persistent present perfect tense in all its contexts, so long as the root is not stative. See Webster's studies noted above.

	MT	DeRouchie	ESV
1.	Proverbs 12:21		
	לֹא־יְאֻנֶּה לַצַּדִּיק כָּל־אָוֶן וּרְשָׁעִים מָלְאוּ רָע׃	No disaster befalls the righteous; but the wicked are full of trouble.	No ill befalls the righteous, but the wicked are filled with trouble.
	Dynamic *yiqtol* as present; stative *qatal* as present.		
2.	Proverbs 14:1		
	חַכְמוֹת נָשִׁים בָּנְתָה בֵיתָהּ וְאִוֶּלֶת בְּיָדֶיהָ תֶהֶרְסֶנּוּ׃	She has built her house with the wisdom of wives; but folly with her own hands tears it down.	The wisest of women builds her house, but folly with her own hands tears it down.
	Dynamic *qatal* as persistent present perfect; dynamic *yiqtol* as present.		
3.	Psalm 50:19		
	פִּיךָ שָׁלַחְתָּ בְרָעָה וּלְשׁוֹנְךָ תַּצְמִיד מִרְמָה׃	You have loosed your mouth with evil; and your tongue frames deceit.	You give your mouth free rein for evil, and your tongue frames deceit.
	Dynamic *qatal* as persistent present perfect; dynamic *yiqtol* as present		

Fig. 5.10. Examples of Present-Tense *Qatal* and *Yiqtol* in Parallelism

c. Proverbs 31:10–31 as a Case Study in Tense

The epilogue in Proverbs is well known for its portrayal of embodied wisdom in the wife of noble character (Prov. 31:10–31). Yet how reachable is this picture? In my own ministry, I find that women generally struggle with this text, feeling unable to match up with its ideal. Furthermore, reading this text has made a number of my single male students believe they may never find such a woman.

The poem is an alphabetic acrostic, structured with twenty-two lines, each beginning with a consecutive letter of the Hebrew alphabet. Every possible word-shaper is utilized in order to highlight the excellent wife and the need for men to surround themselves with this kind of woman.

Duane A. Garrett has noted that the poem's content is shaped in a chiastic pattern, with each step having a corresponding note (see fig. 5.11). Within this structure, the young noblemen and prospective husbands who stand as the primary audience of Proverbs find themselves at the center in verse 23, the only statement in the poem that does not focus on the remarkable woman.

A: High value of a good wife (v. 10)
B: Husband benefited from the wife (vv. 11–12)
C: Wife worked hard (vv. 13–19)
D: Wife gave to the poor (v. 20)
E: Wife had no fear of snow (v. 21a)
F: Children were clothed in scarlet (v. 21b)
G: Coverings for bed, wife wore linen (v. 22)
H: Public respect for husband (v. 23)
G': Sold garments and sashes (v. 24)
F': Wife was clothed in dignity (v. 25a)
E': Wife had no fear of future (v. 25b)
D': Wife spoke wisdom (v. 26)
C': Wife worked hard (v. 27)
B': Husband and children praised wife (vv. 28–29)
A': High value of a good wife (vv. 30–31)

Adapted from Duane A. Garrett, *Proverbs, Ecclesiastes, Song of Songs*, NAC 14 (Nashville: Broadman & Holman, 1993), 248.

Fig. 5.11. The Chiastic Structure of Proverbs 31:10–31

Translators have usually rendered all of Proverbs 31:10–31 in present tense. But it is dominated by *qatal* and *wayyiqtol* forms, which elsewhere would normally be translated as past. When one removes the introductory comment (v. 10) and concluding statement (vv. 30–31), there are nineteen *qatal* and nine *wayyiqtol* forms. In contrast, excluding the frame, there are five *yiqtol* forms, all of which can legitimately be rendered as habitual or recurring past actions when showing up in past-time contexts. Rather than overthrow the normal past-time reference of twenty-eight *qatal* and *wayyiqtol* verbs on the basis of five *yiqtol* forms, it is better to understand the *yiqtol* verbs in light of the *qatal* and *wayyiqtol* verbs and to render all the verbs in the body in past tense.

ESV	DeRouchie's Modified Translation
10 An excellent wife who can find? She is far more precious than jewels.	10 An excellent wife who can find? She is far more precious than jewels.
11 The heart of her husband **trusts** in her, and he **<u>will have no lack of</u>** gain. 12 She **does** him good, and not harm, all the days of her life. 13 She **seeks** wool and flax, ***and works*** with willing hands.	11 The heart of her husband **trusted** in her, and he **<u>had no lack of</u>** gain. 12 She **did** him good, and not harm, all the days of her life. 13 She **sought** wool and flax, ***and worked*** with willing hands.

Fig. 5.12. Proverbs 31:10–31 in the ESV and DeRouchie's Modified Translation

ESV	DeRouchie's Modified Translation
14 She **is** like the ships of the merchant; she **brings** her food from afar. 15 She ***rises*** while it is yet night ***and provides*** food for her household and portions for her maidens. 16 She **considers** a field **and buys** it; with the fruit of her hands she **plants** a vineyard. 17 She **dresses** herself with strength **and makes** her arms **strong**. 18 She **perceives** that her merchandise is profitable. Her lamp **does not go** out at night. 19 She **puts** her hands to the distaff, and her hands **hold** the spindle. 20 She **opens** her hand to the poor and **reaches** out her hands to the needy. 21 She **is not afraid** of snow for her household, for all her household are clothed in scarlet. 22 She **makes** bed coverings for herself; her clothing is fine linen and purple.	14 She **was** like the ships of the merchant; she **would bring** her food from afar. 15 ***And*** she ***rose*** while it was yet night ***and provided*** food for her household and portions for her maidens. 16 She **considered** a field ***and bought*** it; with the fruit of her hands she **planted** a vineyard. 17 She **dressed** herself with strength ***and made*** her arms ***strong***. 18 She **perceived** that her merchandise was profitable. Her lamp **did not go out** at night. 19 She **put** her hands to the distaff, and her hands **held** the spindle. 20 She **opened** her hand to the poor and **reached** out her hands to the needy. 21 She **was not afraid** of snow for her household, for all her household were clothed in scarlet. 22 She **made** bed coverings for herself; her clothing was fine linen and purple.
23 Her husband is known in the gates when he sits among the elders of the land.	23 Her husband is known in the gates when he sits among the elders of the land.
24 She **makes** linen garments **and sells** them; she **delivers** sashes to the merchant. 25 Strength and dignity are her clothing, **and** she **laughs** at the time to come. 26 She **opens** her mouth with wisdom, and the teaching of kindness is on her tongue. 27 She looks well to the ways of her household and **does not eat** the bread of idleness. 28 Her children **rise** up ***and call*** her blessed; her husband also, ***and*** he ***praises*** her: 29 "Many women **have done** excellently, but you **surpass** them all."	24 She **made** linen garments ***and sold*** them; she **delivered** sashes to the merchant. 25 Strength and dignity were her clothing, ***and*** she ***laughed*** at the time to come. 26 She **opened** her mouth with wisdom, and the teaching of kindness was on her tongue. 27 She looked well to the ways of her household and **did not eat** the bread of idleness. 28 Her children **have arisen *and called*** her blessed; her husband also, ***and*** he ***has praised*** her: 29 "Many women **have done** excellently, but you ***have surpassed*** them all."
30 Charm is deceitful, and beauty is vain, but a woman who fears the Lord is to be praised. 31 Give her of the fruit of her hands, and let her works praise her in the gates.	30 Charm is deceitful, and beauty is vain, but a woman who fears the Lord—she is to be praised. 31 Give her of the fruit of her hands, so that her works may praise her in the gates.

Note: The nineteen *qatal* verbs are **bold**; the nine *wayyiqtol* verbs are ***bold italics***; the five *yiqtol* verbs are **bold underline**.

Fig. 5.12. Proverbs 31:10–31 in the ESV and DeRouchie's Modified Translation (cont.)

Brian L. Webster helpfully summarizes the significance of this change of perspective as follows:[17]

> But what does this mean for our understanding of the woman? Instead of what she does, the description says what she did and what she used to do. Likewise, her children have risen and blessed her. If her grown children have risen and blessed her, then we have not been talking about a prospective spouse that a young bachelor is trying to find and marry. She is not even a young wife, who would still be in the process of becoming such a woman. The passage describes the mature woman who has done it. It describes a woman whose husband and household have benefited from her character and labor. She did not necessarily stay up late every night and get up early every morning. But she did whichever may have been needed when it was necessary. She did not necessarily have ongoing concurrent businesses in real estate, farming, tanning, and textiles. But over the years she has done such things. The behaviors are typical, not constant and simultaneous. We are reading about a lifetime achievement recognition, not her daily planner.
>
> The shift away from present-tense translation removes possible overtones of workaholism and adds the quality of persevering faithfulness. She is still an ideal. She has demonstrated that beauty is vain by having lived out what is important. She fears God, speaks with wisdom, is industrious, valuable, valiant. But she is perhaps a bit more human, a bit more possible to imitate. If the perfect [*qatal*] verbs are translated as past and perfective, then the perfect woman is more possible to find in the present.

3. Mood in the Hebrew Verb: *Yiqtol*

As explained, a speaker can describe a situation as actual (indicative mood) or as merely desirable or possible (nonindicative mood). For nonindicative statements, Hebrew is far more likely to use a *yiqtol* (or *weqatal*) than a *qatal* or *wayyiqtol*. There are patterns in which Hebrew uses a *qatal* for a nonindicative, such as in contrary-to-fact statements (a *qatal* is used in "we would have been like Sodom" [Isa. 1:9]), but these are not common. We will focus here on nonindicative statements that employ the *yiqtol*.

The basic question is this: "How do you tell whether a *yiqtol* such as יִפֹּל is a future indicative, 'He will fall,' or a nonindicative, 'He should fall'?" Once again, you need to be aware of *context*, but you also need to look at *syntax*. Context is the situation in which a statement is made, and syntax is how a sentence is put together (i.e., its word order and its use of certain modifiers such as "perhaps" or "in order that").

You should not be surprised that context is important for understanding *yiqtol* verbs. Context is important in many languages. For example, in English we say that "will (do)" is future tense, but it is actually more complex than that. Consider the following:

- An investment counselor tells a client, "Don't worry, you will make money this year." The counselor is making a prediction (future tense).

17. Webster, "The Perfect Verb and the Perfect Woman in Proverbs," 271.

- A sergeant tells his troops, "You will stay together and you will not talk!" He is not making a prediction; he is giving a command.
- An employee tells a coworker, "I will ask the boss for a raise!" He is not really making a prediction; he is expressing determination to do something.

Nothing distinguishes these three sentences grammatically, but in each case the meaning of "will (do)" is different. The important point is this: *Context often plays a key role in determining the mood of a verb.*

With respect to syntax, one general rule can help you refine your translations: pay attention to where the *yiqtol* verb is placed in the sentence. This will help you determine whether the verb is indicative or nonindicative.

- If the *yiqtol* is the first word in the sentence, it is probably nonindicative. Thus, when it is the first word in a sentence, a *yiqtol* verb usually means "he should do" or "may he do," or it expresses possibility or determination to do something.
- If the *yiqtol* is not the first word in the sentence, it is probably indicative. Remember: Depending on context, it could be a future ("he will do") or a past imperfect ("he used to do"). Most often, it will be future, and this should be your default translation.

There are exceptions to the rules above. For example, a *yiqtol* in a question may be nonindicative regardless of its position in a sentence. As a question, אִשָּׁה תִּפֹּל בְּצָבָא could mean "Should a woman fall in battle?" Also, occasionally a *yiqtol* is nonindicative even when it is not first—something that happens often when God is the subject. Therefore, while a sentence such as אֱלֹהִים יִתֵּן אוֹת might mean "God will give a sign," it could mean "May God give a sign!" Finally, if the *yiqtol* is in a conditional statement, the question of indicative or nonindicative is determined by context. A conditional statement is an "If . . . then" sentence. The "if" clause is called a *protasis*, and the "then" clause is called an *apodosis*, as in the following:

- *Protasis*: "If you worship other gods,"
- *Apodosis*: "then you will die."

Similar patterns are found when the conditional sentence is temporal ("When . . . then") or causal ("Because . . . therefore"). In such cases, word position does not indicate whether a *yiqtol* is indicative or nonindicative; it is simply conditional, and the translation you apply will depend on context.

4. Aspect in the Hebrew Verb: *Yiqtol*

For the imperfective aspect, the *yiqtol* is much more likely to be used than the *qatal* and *wayyiqtol*. In many cases, however, even the *yiqtol* does not describe repeated or habitual action, and there is no reason to think of it as describing a process. This is especially so if the *yiqtol* is either future tense or nonindicative, as in these two examples:

- *Future*: "He who is near will fall [יִפֹּל] by the sword" (Ezek. 6:12).
- *Nonindicative*: "A thousand may fall [יִפֹּל] at your side" (Ps. 91:7).

An imperfective aspect for a *yiqtol* is more likely if the clause is either past or present tense and in the indicative mood, as in these two examples:

- *Present imperfective*: "Why do you keep looking [this is a *yiqtol* verb] at each other?" (Gen. 42:1).
- *Past imperfective*: "Whenever the cloud was taken up . . . , the Israelites would move out [this is a *yiqtol* verb] on each stage of their journey" (Ex. 40:36).

In summary, figure 5.13 provides an overview of some basic guidelines for determining the tense, mood, and aspect of *yiqtol* verbs.

Guideline	Hebrew	Example
1. The default for the *yiqtol* is future indicative.	מֶ֫לֶךְ יִפֹּל	A king *will fall.*
2. In the first position, the *yiqtol* is usually nonindicative.	יִתֵּן אֱלֹהִים אוֹת	*May* God *give* a sign!
3. Not in the first position, the *yiqtol* is usually indicative.	כֹּהֵן יִתֵּן בְּרָכָה	A priest *will give* a blessing!
4. In a question, a *yiqtol* not in the first position may be nonindicative.	אִשָּׁה תִּפֹּל בְּצָבָא	*Should* a woman *fall* in battle?
5. If God is the subject, a *yiqtol* not in the first position may be nonindicative.	אֱלֹהִים יִתֵּן אוֹת	*May* God *give* a sign!
6. If the *yiqtol* is indicative, the context determines its tense.	. . . יִפֹּל . . .	Tomorrow *he will fall.* In his childhood, *he used to fall.*
7. If the *yiqtol* is indicative and past or present, it is probably imperfective.	. . . יִפֹּל . . .	He *used to fall* a lot when he skied, but he does better now.
8. A conditional sentence: Protasis Apodosis	אִם יֶחֱטָא אִישׁ יִפֹּל	If a man *should sin,* *he will fall.*

Fig. 5.13. Tense, Mood, and Aspect of the *Yiqtol*

The *Weqatal*

In form, the *weqatal* is nothing more than a *qatal* with a simple וְ connector in front of it (וְקָטַל). Because of this, scholars have at times called it the *conjoined perfect*.

While not always the case, the accent on the *weqatal* generally shifts to the ultima in the second masculine singular and first common singular (וְקָטַלְתָּ֫ and וְקָטַלְתִּ֫י; contrast the simple *qatals* קָטַ֫לְתָּ and קָטַ֫לְתִּי). Accent shift does not affect the vowels of the *weqatal*; the vowels are the same as in the regular *qatal*.

The *weqatal* works in a way that most students of Hebrew find surprising. Consider the following sentence: הַמֶּ֫לֶךְ יֵשֵׁב בֶּחָצֵר וְשָׁפַט אֶת־הָעָם ("The king would sit in the courtyard and judge the people"). Depending on context, you can translate the sentence either as a past imperfect (as above) or as a future ("The king will sit in the courtyard and judge the people"). Notice that וְשָׁפַט is a *weqatal* and that it appears to have similar if not the same significance as the *yiqtol* verb יֵשֵׁב. Depending on the translation, both verbs refer to actions done repeatedly in the past or both verbs refer to future actions.

Now look at another example: יִשְׁמַע הַמֶּ֫לֶךְ אֶת־הַתּוֹרָה וְשָׁפַט אֶת־הָעָם ("The king should hear the Law and judge the people"). In this case, יִשְׁמַע is clearly nonindicative (note that it is in first position) and describes what ought to be done. But notice that וְשָׁפַט in this sentence appears to have a similar if not the same function. It, too, is nonindicative modality, expressing either a further desire of the speaker or the ultimate purpose for which he should "hear."

Now consider the following: אִם יָשׁוּב הַמֶּ֫לֶךְ וְשָׁפַט אֶת־הָעָם ("If the king returns, then he will judge the people"). Here, we have a conditional statement with the *yiqtol* יָשׁוּב as the protasis and the *weqatal* וְשָׁפַט marking the apodosis. That is why וְשָׁפַט is translated "then he will judge."

Finally, examine this example: לֵךְ וְשָׁפַטְתָּ אֶת־הָעָם ("Go and judge the people!" *or* "Go, so that you may judge the people!"). לֵךְ is an imperative, a word used to make a command, and it means "go!" The *weqatal* is second person (וְשָׁפַטְתָּ) because a command is by nature a second-person statement. וְשָׁפַטְתָּ might simply have the force of another command (first translation), or it might express purpose (second translation). Either way, its meaning is closely tied to the imperative לֵךְ ("Go!").

How can the *weqatal* have all these meanings, and why is it so different from the normal *qatal* without conjunction, which frequently just expresses simple past tense, indicative mood, and perfective aspect? Why is וְשָׁפַט not translated "and he judged" in any of the sentences above? Scholars have long debated this, and there is no certain answer. Here are some possibilities:

1. **A converting וְ.** The traditional view is that the connector וְ "converts" the *qatal* so that it simply has the same significance as the verb in front of it. Thus, if a future-tense *yiqtol* is followed by a *weqatal*, the *weqatal* is also future. If an imperative is followed by a *weqatal*, the *weqatal* is also a command. As a rule of thumb, this regularly works, but often the force of the *weqatal* is not precisely the same as that of the preceding verb. Furthermore, scholars today no longer believe that וְ carries "converting" power.
2. **Contingent modality.** Some scholars believe that the *weqatal* is a type of nonindicative modal, marked by virtue of always being the first word in its clause. In

this instance, the modality is not subjunctive but *contingent*, wherein the *weqatal* always stands as an outgrowth of an initial verb and expresses potential, telic, resultative, or imperatival force.

3. **An unmarked form.** Somewhat similar to the above, other scholars think that the *qatal* should be considered basically an "unmarked" form in terms of tense, mood, and aspect. When a *qatal* is by itself (with no connector וְ), it usually has a default meaning of past tense, indicative mood, and perfective aspect. When the *qatal* has the connector, however, its meaning corresponds to its context. Thus, *weqatal* can be a future, a past imperfect, an apodosis, a purpose clause, or a command, depending on its placement in a text.

It is important to realize that you don't have to determine the correct theory about the *weqatal* in order to understand how to read it. Also, in English we have a similar pattern that we use all the time. Look at the examples in figure 5.14.

1. As an Apodosis	Keep this law, *and live*; don't keep it, *and die*.
2. As a Subjunctive	He should learn this law, *and keep* it *and teach* it to his children.
3. In a Series of Commands	Go, *and stay* in your homes, *and watch over* your families.
4. As a Prediction	The king of Nineveh will come here *and destroy* this city *and take away* the people.

Fig. 5.14. English Examples Comparative to the *Weqatal*

Example 1 is really two conditional sentences; the phrases "and live . . . and die" form the apodosis parts of each conditional statement. In effect, what is being said is "If you keep this law, then you will live; if you don't keep it, then you will die." In example 2, "he should learn" is subjunctive, implying moral obligation, and the phrases "and keep . . . and teach" have a similar force. The latter verbs could be understood to express the ultimate purpose of the first action. In example 3, "and stay . . . and watch" follow the command "go" and are also in effect commands growing out of the initial order. In example 4, "and destroy . . . and take away" are in essence future tense and continue the prediction begun with "The king of Nineveh will come."

By itself, the significance of a phrase such as "and live" or "and teach" is unclear. It is, in effect, unmarked. Within a context, however, the meaning of each verb with "and" is fairly obvious. The Hebrew *weqatal* is similar to English in this way. Keep this in mind, and you should have no problem with the *weqatal*.

The Nonindicative *Yiqtol* and *Weyiqtol*

1. The Volitive *Yiqtol*

Scholars often call imperatives *volitives* because they always convey a speaker's will (i.e., volition). At times, *yiqtol* verbs can also function as volitives, especially when in first position within a clause. Commonly, scholars tag first-person volitive *yiqtol* forms as *cohortatives* ("Let's do this!") and third-person volitive *yiqtol* forms as *jussives* ("May he do this!").

You may recall that in the Qal, most first-person volitives include a paragogic *hey* (ָה) suffix. This ending is a likely signal that you are looking at a volitional *yiqtol*. What you must recognize, however, is that some "cohortatives," especially those with a III-ה root, do not take paragogic *hey* (ָה) and are formally identical to the nonindicative first-person *yiqtol*. Similarly, whereas beginning students are usually told that "jussives" are third-person volitional *yiqtol* forms that "apocopate," this shortening of the form occurs only in verbs that are hollow (bi-consonantal), III-ה, or original I-ו. Most third-person volitives are formed in exactly the same way as the simple *yiqtol*, and context and syntax alone signal the volitional meaning. יִקְטֹל can mean "he will kill" or "may he kill."

In parsing, therefore, it is best simply to identify a form as a *yiqtol* and then note whether it includes a paragogic ה or is apocopated. Your translation then identifies whether the *yiqtol* is functioning as an indicative (e.g., "he will kill") or nonindicative (e.g., "he should kill").

2. Negative Commands

A negative command (prohibition) in Hebrew is created by adjoining a negative particle (either לֹא or אַל) before a second-person *yiqtol* form. לֹא is usually used with simple ("long") *yiqtol* verbs and generally expresses permanent prohibitions (e.g., לֹא תִּנְאָף "Never commit adultery!"). אַל commonly occurs with "short" *yiqtol* verbs and expresses immediate commands that apply to specific situations (e.g., אַל־תַּבִּיט אַחֲרֶיךָ "Don't look behind you!"). This distinction suggests that long *yiqtols* are likely imperfective in aspect, whereas short *yiqtols* (like the *wayyiqtol* form to which they may be related) are perfective in aspect.

3. The *Weyiqtol*

Adding the connector וְ to a *yiqtol* generally does more than simply add the word *and*. Often it has distinctive usage and meaning. We may call this form the *weyiqtol*.

The *weyiqtol*'s form and placement (always in first position) suggest that it is a nonindicative rather than an indicative *yiqtol*. *Weyiqtols* often appear in volitional contexts to express purpose or intent, regardless of whether the forms are apocopated (i.e., shortened). For example, 1 Kings 22:20 has: "Who will entice Ahab, so that he will go up . . ." (using the apocopated form וְיַ֫עַל). But 1 Kings 15:19 has: "Break your covenant with King Baasha of Israel, so that he will go up . . ." (using the simple וְיַעֲלֶה). The *weyiqtol* is used in at least four ways.

1. The *weyiqtol* frequently appears in the context of a volitive. When following an imperative or volitional *yiqtol*, it often indicates purpose or result, as in "so that he may do." Genesis 1:6 can be translated "And God said, 'Let there be an expanse in the middle of the waters, so that there may be [וִיהִי] a divider between the [two] waters.'"
2. *Weyiqtols* that continue a series of volitional *yiqtol* forms have high thematic prominence (they are important). This contrasts with *weqatals* that continue a volitional *yiqtol* series; they typically do not have high thematic prominence.
3. The *weyiqtol* is rarely just a simple future. It usually connotes purpose or, if referring to the future, makes a more dramatic, prominent proclamation than a simple *yiqtol* or *weqatal* would. Genesis 12:2 has three *weyiqtol* forms, which may express prominent future but more likely express purpose: "so that I may make of you a great nation, and so that I may bless you, and so that I may make great your name."
4. Occasionally, *weyiqtol* conveys "and" + volitional meaning to the verb, as in "and let him do." Genesis 9:27 is an example: וְיִשְׁכֹּן בְּאָהֳלֵי־שֵׁם וִיהִי כְנַ֫עַן עֶ֫בֶד לָמוֹ ("And may he dwell in the tents of Shem, and may Canaan be his servant").

הִנֵּה and הֵן as Markers of Immediate Significance[18]

In chapter 2, I noted that Hebrew employs words whose chief purpose is to signal structural features in a text. We identified two such discourse markers: (1) the transition/climax markers and (2) citation formulas. A third type is the presentative particles, הִנֵּה and הֵן (with or without וְ [gloss "and"]), which I call ***markers of immediate significance***. The words הִנֵּה and הֵן are clause modifiers that point forward in a discourse, focusing attention on the following content. These particles always introduce an event or situation that has special relevance with respect to the actual moment of communication. They can provide a basis for a forthcoming statement or command or set a temporal connection, occasion, or condition for an ensuing clause. While they are traditionally translated with the archaic "Behold," I usually try to translate them with a more modern idiom, such as "Look here" or "Well, now."

18. This material is adapted from Garrett and DeRouchie, *A Modern Grammar for Biblical Hebrew*, 321–22 (§ 40.A.1). Used by permission.

23 וַתִּקְרְבוּן אֵלַי כָּל־רָאשֵׁי שִׁבְטֵיכֶם וְזִקְנֵיכֶם 24 וַתֹּאמְרוּ הֵן הֶרְאָנוּ יְהוָה אֱלֹהֵינוּ אֶת־כְּבֹדוֹ וְאֶת־גָּדְלוֹ וְאֶת־קֹלוֹ שָׁמַעְנוּ מִתּוֹךְ הָאֵשׁ . . . 25 וְעַתָּה לָמָּה נָמוּת כִּי תֹאכְלֵנוּ הָאֵשׁ הַגְּדֹלָה הַזֹּאת	23 And all the heads of your tribes and your elders approached me [Moses] 24 and said, "Now look, YHWH our God has shown us his glory and his unstyled greatness, and his voice we have heard out of the midst of the fire. . . . 25 And now, why should we die, for this great fire will consume us?"

Fig. 5.15. הֵן Focusing Attention in Deuteronomy 5:23–25

In this example, הֵן directs the audience's attention to the leaders' testimony of their recent encounter with YHWH and ties this past event with their present conversation with Moses. Specifically, their encounter with God is the basis for their question, "And now, why should we die?"

The form הִנֵּה can also mark the immediate significance of an event or situation by indicating how something looked through a character's eyes.

וַיִּשָּׂא עֵינָיו וַיַּרְא וְהִנֵּה שְׁלֹשָׁה אֲנָשִׁים נִצָּבִים עָלָיו	And he lifted his eyes and looked, and—get this—three men were standing before him!

Fig. 5.16. הִנֵּה Introducing a Point of View in Genesis 18:2

Here the narrator uses וְהִנֵּה to draw attention to what Abraham saw: שְׁלֹשָׁה אֲנָשִׁים נִצָּבִים עָלָיו ("three men were standing before him"). It's as though, for a brief moment, the reader were looking through Abraham's eyes, seeing what he is seeing.

The Inference Markers לָכֵן and עַתָּה

This section introduces a fourth set of discourse markers—the ***inference markers*** לָכֵן ("therefore") and וְעַתָּה ("and now"). These forms can function at a micro-level as general adverbials between two sentences, in which לָכֵן identifies an immediate conclusion from a defined ground statement and וְעַתָּה indicates a contrast between "then" *"and now."* Yet both can function at a more macro-level, marking a logical inference that is drawn from a greater literary context. We are addressing the latter function here.

לָכֵן as an Inference Marker

As a discourse marker, לָכֵן ("therefore") usually introduces a declaration or command after an extended discussion that serves as its basis or reason. We see an example of this in Zephaniah 3:8–10, where YHWH uses a plural imperative to call the righteous remnant to "wait" for him to act, first as punisher of his enemies and then as Savior of his faithful. The command for patience is an inference from the previous extended section in 2:5–3:7, where he unpacks the lamentable state and fate of the rebels from the foreign nations (2:5–15) and Jerusalem (3:1–7). So the logic is this: Because God still intends to destroy his enemies, how should the righteous remnant respond?

לָכֵן חַכּוּ־לִי נְאֻם־יְהוָה לְיוֹם קוּמִי לְעַד[19]	Therefore, wait for me—the announcement of YHWH— for the day of my rising as witness.

Fig. 5.17. לָכֵן as Inference Marker in Zephaniah 3:8

וְעַתָּה as an Inference Marker and Its Use in Exodus 19:5[20]

Although וְעַתָּה can simply indicate the present time of an action (= "and now") in contrast to what was "then," more often it indicates that a present event or situation is the natural consequence or logical conclusion of an event or topic that directly precedes. We see an example of this in Exodus 10:16–17. Having recognized his guilt, Pharaoh now calls Moses and Aaron, as representatives of YHWH, to pardon him.

19. The MT actually reads לָעַד "for prey" (= 2-עַד). The LXX, however, renders the phrase εἰς μαρτύριον ("as a witness"), reading עֵד ("witness"), which is the more likely reading in light of the use of עֵד in similar contexts throughout the Prophets (Jer. 29:23; 42:5; Mic. 1:2; Mal. 3:5). The verse is speaking about God's arising as a covenant witness to the world's covenant (in)fidelity (so too NIV).

20. This material is adapted from Garrett and DeRouchie, *A Modern Grammar for Biblical Hebrew*, 322–23 (§ 40.A.2). Used by permission.

וַיְמַהֵר פַּרְעֹה לִקְרֹא לְמֹשֶׁה וּלְאַהֲרֹן וַיֹּאמֶר חָטָאתִי לַיהוָה אֱלֹהֵיכֶם וְלָכֶם	16	16 And Pharaoh hastened to call Moses and Aaron, and he said, "I have sinned against YHWH your God and against you.
וְעַתָּה שָׂא נָא חַטָּאתִי	17	17 And now [since I have realized and expressed my error], please forgive my sin!"

Fig. 5.18. וְעַתָּה as Inference from Immediate Context in Exodus 10:16–17

As shown in this example, usually the reason and its inference occur in the same paragraph. At times, however, the causal ground can span several chapters before the inference is made. Such is the case in Deuteronomy 10:12, which builds an inference from material begun in 9:1 (cf. also how 4:1 draws an inference from 1:5–3:29). In Deuteronomy 9:1–10:11 Moses calls Israel to know YHWH as a consuming fire (9:3) and to know that, because of the people's stubbornness of heart, all benefits that God gives them come by mercy alone (9:6). All the rest of the unit from 9:7 to 10:11 clarifies through numerous examples the truths of these points. Then in 10:12 the inference is drawn.

וְעַתָּה יִשְׂרָאֵל מָה יְהוָה אֱלֹהֶיךָ שֹׁאֵל מֵעִמָּךְ כִּי אִם־לְיִרְאָה אֶת־יְהוָה אֱלֹהֶיךָ לָלֶכֶת בְּכָל־דְּרָכָיו	And now, Israel, what is YHWH your God asking from you, but to fear YHWH your God by walking in all his ways?

Fig. 5.19. וְעַתָּה as Inference from Extended Context in Deuteronomy 10:12

אַתֶּם רְאִיתֶם אֲשֶׁר עָשִׂיתִי לְמִצְרָיִם וָאֶשָּׂא אֶתְכֶם עַל־כַּנְפֵי נְשָׁרִים וָאָבִא אֶתְכֶם אֵלָי׃	4 b c d	You have seen what I did to Egypt, and [how] I lifted you on wings of eagles, and [how] I brought you to myself.
וְעַתָּה אִם־שָׁמוֹעַ תִּשְׁמְעוּ בְּקֹלִי וּשְׁמַרְתֶּם אֶת־בְּרִיתִי וִהְיִיתֶם לִי סְגֻלָּה מִכָּל־הָעַמִּים כִּי־לִי כָּל־הָאָרֶץ׃ וְאַתֶּם תִּהְיוּ־לִי מַמְלֶכֶת כֹּהֲנִים וְגוֹי קָדוֹשׁ	5 a b c d 6	And now, if you will indeed listen at my voice and [then?] keep my covenant and [then?] be to me a treasured possession from all the peoples, for [although?] all the earth is to me, and [then?] you will be to me a kingdom of priests and a holy nation.

Fig. 5.20. The Inference Marker וְעַתָּה in Exodus 19:4–6

וְעַתָּה stands as an inference marker at the front of Exodus 19:5 (fig. 5.20). In 19:4 we learn of God's great deliverance of Israel through the exodus, and then verses 5–6 assert that because God has saved the Israelites, they must *therefore* live for the honor of his name among the nations—serving as a kingdom of priests and a holy nation. Because וְעַתָּה carries the primary weight of the discourse and identifies what precedes as the basis for the call to give witness to God's worth, I have shifted all of verse 4 one indent more than the inference marker. We'll establish the text hierarchy of the rest of the passage in a later section.

An Example of Text Grammar—Genesis 12:1–3

We are now in a position to consider the text hierarchy of one of Scripture's most important passages. Genesis 12:1–3 details the commissioning of Abram (i.e., Abraham), and figure 5.21 includes my clause breakdown and translation of these three verses.

וַיֹּ֤אמֶר יְהוָה֙ אֶל־אַבְרָ֔ם	1	And YHWH said to Abram,
לֶךְ־לְךָ֛ מֵאַרְצְךָ֥ וּמִמּֽוֹלַדְתְּךָ֖ וּמִבֵּ֣ית אָבִ֑יךָ אֶל־הָאָ֖רֶץ אֲשֶׁ֥ר אַרְאֶֽךָּ׃	b	Go from your land and from your kindred and from your father's house to the land that I will show you,
וְאֶֽעֶשְׂךָ֙ לְג֣וֹי גָּד֔וֹל	2	so that I may make you into a great nation,
וַאֲבָ֣רֶכְךָ֔	b	and may bless you,
וַאֲגַדְּלָ֖ה שְׁמֶ֑ךָ	c	and may make your name great.
וֶהְיֵ֖ה בְּרָכָֽה׃	d	Then be a blessing,
וַאֲבָֽרְכָה֙ מְבָ֣רְכֶ֔יךָ	3	so that I may bless those who bless you,
וּמְקַלֶּלְךָ֖ אָאֹ֑ר	b	but the one who curses you I will bind with a curse,
וְנִבְרְכ֣וּ בְךָ֔ כֹּ֖ל מִשְׁפְּחֹ֥ת הָאֲדָמָֽה׃	c	with the result that in you all the families of the ground may be blessed.

Fig. 5.21. Text Hierarchy of Genesis 12:1–3

The speech frame (in light gray) that opens verse 1 is unmarked, so it does not tell us whether the reported speech that follows is primary or secondary (see "Marked Primary and Secondary Citation Formulas" in chapter 2). The speech itself is a single text block (see "Introducing Literary Units and Text Hierarchy in Hebrew" and "Text Blocks" in chapter 2), as is clear from the chain of וְ ("and")-fronted clauses after the asyndetic imperative לֶךְ־ ("Go!") in 1b.

While every clause is part of the same text block, there are two clear sections to God's commissioning of Abram, both distinguished by imperatives. The first imperative לֶךְ ("Go!") is followed by three *weyiqtol* (*waw* + cohortative) verb forms, which is a common pattern in Hebrew for expressing purpose or consequence.[21] Thus I have translated the *weyiqtol* forms in 2a–c "*so that I may* make you into a great nation, and may bless you, and may make your name great." Often English translations fail to account for the second imperative וֶהְיֵה ("And be!"). The common thought is that when two imperatives are conjoined by וְ, then the second stands as a consequence of the first.[22] But while the second command form is contingent on the initial imperative, the second does not lose its imperatival force.[23]

The command to "be a blessing" in 2d is itself followed in verse 3 by one *weyiqtol* (cohortative) form that expresses purpose and one *weqatal* form that provides the ultimate result of Abram's commission. The initial verb-first clause starts with a verb (V_) in 3a and is immediately followed by a non-verb-first clause (_V) in 3b. Thus a V_ + _V pattern emerges, which can signal *contrastive matching* (see "More on Marked and Unmarked Clauses" below), which occurs when two adjacent clauses provide contrasting parts of a single event or idea: "so that I may bless those who bless you, but the one who curses you I will bind with a curse." That the final verb-first clause is the only one that uses a *weqatal* and not a volitional *weyiqtol* suggests that 3c stands as the ultimate consequence and thus the ultimate goal of all the obedience that is demanded: "*Go* to the land, . . . then *be* a blessing, . . . *with the [ultimate] result that* in you all the families of the ground may be blessed."

By analyzing the grammar, we see that Genesis 12:1–3 has two distinct units, with the second being conditioned on the fulfillment of the first. Abram must "go" to the land in order to become a nation, and there he must "be a blessing" in order that the curse from Genesis 3 may be overcome and all the world may be blessed. The Old Testament makes clear that the patriarch's descendants known as the nation of Israel experienced the fulfillment of stage 1 during the era of the Mosaic covenant. The patriarchal promises (e.g., Gen. 15:13–14; 17:8) grounded the inauguration of this covenant (e.g., Ex. 2:24; 6:4–8; Deut. 1:8; 9:5), and the ministries of Joshua and David/Solomon identified their fulfillment (cf. Gen. 15:18; 17:8; 22:17 with Josh. 21:43; 1 Kings

21. *GKC* 320 (§ 108d); Paul Joüon and T. Muraoka, *A Grammar of Biblical Hebrew*, Subsidia Biblica 27 (Rome: Pontifical Biblical Institute, 2006), 352–54 (§ 116a–b); Thomas O. Lambdin, *Introduction to Biblical Hebrew* (New York: Scribner's Sons, 1971), 119 (§ 107c).

22. *GKC* 325 (§ 110f, i); Joüon and Muraoka, *A Grammar of Biblical Hebrew*, 355–56 (§ 116f).

23. So too Peter J. Gentry and Stephen J. Wellum, *Kingdom through Covenant: A Biblical-Theological Understanding of the Covenants* (Wheaton, IL: Crossway, 2012), 230–34; cf. Paul R. Williamson, *Sealed with an Oath: Covenant in God's Unfolding Purpose*, NSBT 23 (Downers Grove, IL: InterVarsity Press, 2007), 78–79. Some would counter that when purpose semantics are already established through volitional *yiqtol* forms (i.e., cohortatives), וְ + imperative can be command (e.g., Gen. 34:12; 47:19; Ex. 33:13) or purpose (e.g., Gen. 18:5; 19:8, 34; 45:18). I propose that the imperatival force is still evident in all these contexts, even if purpose is also present.

4:20–21; see also Neh. 9:8). But although some levels of representative obedience and international blessing were evident in this period (e.g., in the lives of Joseph [Gen. 39:5; 41:56–57] and David [1 Sam. 17:43–54]), Moses, Israel's histories, and the Latter Prophets make clear that we must wait until the coming of Christ to see the ultimate realization of stage 2—blessing to the world (Ps. 72:17; Isa. 49:6; Amos 9:11–12; cf. Gen. 22:17b–18 with Acts 3:25–26; Gal. 3:8, 14, 16, 29). Stated succinctly, the first half of Abram's commission focuses on what is accomplished in the Mosaic covenant (stage 1 fulfillment), whereas the second addresses a divine work of restoration that is accomplished only through Jesus Christ in the new covenant (stage 2 fulfillment).

The rest of Genesis supports this conclusion, for it distinguishes Abraham's serving as a father of a single nation from his future role as "the father of a multitude of nations" (Gen. 17:4–5). It also distinguishes the initial age of blessing and life in the Promised *Land* [singular]—made up of Canaan (Gen. 17:8, tribal allotments) and the extended region of suzerain oversight (15:18; cf. 1 Kings 4:20–21)—from the broader *lands* [plural] that Abraham's offspring would inherit when they multiply as "the stars of heaven" and when "all the nations of the earth shall be blessed" (Gen. 26:3–4; cf. 15:5). The kingdom would expand in this way only with the rising of a single male deliverer who would both possess enemy gates and serve as the agent of God's blessing to the world (22:17b–18; cf. 3:15; 24:60).[24]

Furthermore, Paul stresses how stage 2 fulfillment of the Abrahamic covenant is already being realized in Jesus through his church. Christ Jesus' redeeming work has made Abraham the father of both Jews and Gentiles in Christ (Rom. 4:16–18; cf. Gal. 3:29), and "in Christ Jesus the blessing of Abraham [has] come to the Gentiles, so that we might receive the promised Spirit through faith" (Gal. 3:14; cf. Acts 3:25–26). God's Spirit is "the guarantee of our inheritance" (Eph. 1:14), which will completely fulfill "the promise to Abraham and his offspring that he would be heir of the world" (Rom. 4:13). The macro-structure of Genesis 12:1–3 points to a major covenantal progression in salvation history.

24. For more on this two-stage fulfillment of the Abrahamic covenant, see Jason S. DeRouchie, "Counting Stars with Abraham and the Prophets: New Covenant Ecclesiology in OT Perspective," *JETS* 58, 3 (2015): 445–85; DeRouchie, "Father of a Multitude of Nations: New Covenant Ecclesiology in OT Perspective," in *Progressive Covenantalism: Charting a Course between Dispensational and Covenant Theologies*, ed. Stephen J. Wellum and Brent E. Parker (Nashville: Broadman & Holman, 2016), 7–38.

Verbless Clauses

Subject vs. Predicate in Verbless Clauses[25]

1. Grasping the Basics of Verbless Clauses

One feature of biblical Hebrew is that you can have a complete clause with no finite verb. We call this a ***verbless clause*** (or *nominal clause*). For example, an adjective can be used as a predicate in expressions such as הָאִשָּׁה טוֹבָה ("the woman *is* good"). A participle can function similarly, as in מֹשֶׁה רֹעֶה אֶת־צֹאן אָבִיו ("Moses *was* shepherding the flock of his father"). In such clauses, the predicate is made up of an understood *to be* verb, which we supply in translation, plus a complement, which could be a noun, an adjective, a prepositional phrase, a participle, an infinitive construct, or some other nominal form or phrase. We call this complement the *predicate*.

Clauses with the verb *to be*—whether visually present or not (i.e., lexicalized or unlexicalized)—express "being, existence, or occurrence," which distinguishes them from most other clauses. In Hebrew, verbs rendered with the *to be* verb link a subject to its location, possession, identity, class, or status, among other things. In the example "the woman is good," "the woman" is classified or described as "good." In the example "Moses was shepherding the flock of his father," "Moses" is identified or characterized as "shepherding" Jethro's sheep.

2. Distinguishing Subject and Predicate in Verbless Clauses

A verbless clause may have no more than two nominals (e.g., noun, pronoun, adjective, etc.) standing side by side. Because the predicate in verbless clauses is not identified by an explicit verb, it is sometimes difficult to distinguish the subject (S) and the predicate (P). While the default word order in nominal clauses appears to be S–P,[26] the pattern is often reversed, whether to help orient the audience to the greater context (= ***contextualizing constituent***) or to highlight prominent information (= ***focus***).[27] In that case, how does the reader know which noun is the subject and which is the predicate?

25. This material is adapted from Garrett and DeRouchie, *A Modern Grammar for Biblical Hebrew*, 314–15, 371–72 (§§ 39.B.1–2, App. 3). Used by permission.

26. So Randall Buth, "Word Order in the Verbless Clause: A Generative-Functional Approach," in *The Verbless Clause in Biblical Hebrew: Linguistic Approaches*, ed. Cynthia L. Miller, LSAWS 1 (Winona Lake, IN: Eisenbrauns, 1999), 79–108.

27. Randall Buth, "Topic and Focus in Hebrew Poetry—Psalm 51," in *Language in Context: Essays for Robert E. Longacre*, ed. S. J. J. Hwang and W. R. Merrifield, SIL and University of Texas at Arlington Publications in Linguistics 107 (Dallas: SIL, 1992), 83–96; Buth, "Functional Grammar, Hebrew, and Aramaic: An Integrated, Textlinguistic Approach to Syntax," in *Discourse Analysis of Biblical Literature: What It Is and What It Offers*, ed. Walter

THE GUIDING PRINCIPLE:
The subject is usually more defined or known in the communication situation than the predicate.

Although certain kinds of definiteness are associated with specific forms such as the definite article, all nominals have a relative level of definiteness in relation to one another. So, for example, a proper noun such as *Ruth* is more defined or known than an indefinite common noun such as *house*. But *house* is more defined than an adjective such as *red*.

Generally, the more definite noun or noun phrase will be the subject. Let's consider some examples.

- In the clause וְעַבְדִּי דָוִד מֶ֫לֶךְ (Ezek. 37:24), the subject is the definite noun phrase וְעַבְדִּי דָוִד ("and my servant David") and the predicate is the indefinite noun מֶ֫לֶךְ ("king"). It means "and my servant David [will be] king."
- In a clause such as כִּי אֵל רַחוּם יְהוָה אֱלֹהֶ֫יךָ (Deut. 4:31), where we see an indefinite noun phrase (אֵל רַחוּם "compassionate God") and a proper name (יְהוָה אֱלֹהֶ֫יךָ "YHWH your God") standing side by side, the proper name is more defined or specific and is therefore likely the subject: "for YHWH your God is a compassionate God" (rather than "for a compassionate God is YHWH your God").

Sometimes it may be unclear or debatable which of two nominals is more defined and thus the subject instead of the predicate. In Exodus 9:27 we have יְהוָה הַצַּדִּיק, which could be translated either as "YHWH *is* in the right" or as "The one in the right *is* YHWH."

The list in figure 5.22 shows one proposal for the relative levels of definiteness expressed by the various phrase types found in nominal clauses.[28] The higher the number, the higher the level of relative definiteness. You can use this continuum to distinguish subjects and predicates.

R. Bodine, SBLSS (Atlanta: Scholars Press, 1995), 84–85. What Christo H. J. van der Merwe, Jackie A. Naudé, and Jan H. Kroeze refer to as the "focus of topicalization" (*A Biblical Hebrew Reference Grammar*, Biblical Languages: Hebrew 3 [Sheffield, UK: Sheffield Academic, 2002], 347–48 [§ 47.2(ii)]), Buth refers to as a "contextualizing constituent," distinct from "focus."

28. Adapted from Janet W. Dyk and Eep Talstra, "Paradigmatic and Syntagmatic Features in Nominal Clauses," in *The Verbless Clause in Biblical Hebrew: Linguistic Approaches*, ed. Cynthia L. Miller, LSAWS 1 (Winona Lake, IN: Eisenbrauns, 1999), 152.

Always the subject
10. Pronominal suffix on יֵשׁ, on אַ֫יִן, on הִנֵּה, on עוֹד, or on a locative
Either the subject or predicate
9. Demonstrative pronoun 8. Personal pronoun 7. Definite noun phrase or definite participle 6. Proper noun or name 5. Indefinite noun phrase or indefinite participle 4. Interrogative pronoun or interrogative noun phrase 3. Infinitive construct 2. Adjective
Always the predicate
1. Prepositional phrase or locative (e.g., שָׁם)

Fig. 5.22. Relative Definiteness in Clauses

To use figure 5.22 with a verbless clause, find the two elements of your clause in the list. Whichever element has the highest number is probably the subject, for that element bears a higher level of definiteness or specification. For example, we see in Exodus 16:15 the following verbless clause (with a modifying relative clause):

הוּא הַלֶּ֫חֶם אֲשֶׁר נָתַן יְהוָה לָכֶם לְאָכְלָה	That is the bread that YHWH gave to you for food.

Fig. 5.23. Subject vs. Predicate in Exodus 16:15

In this case, הוּא ("That") is the subject and הַלֶּ֫חֶם ("the bread") is the predicate because הוּא is a demonstrative pronoun (level 9 on the list) and הַלֶּ֫חֶם is a definite noun (level 7).

What I have offered here are general guidelines for interpreting verbless clauses, and understanding these issues will help you to analyze a text more intelligently. You should know, however, that scholars are still investigating these matters, and there is room for exceptions or disagreement. Above all, you should be careful about interpreting a clause in an unusual way, because such interpretations are often forced or unnatural.

The Grammar and Meaning of the Shema in Deuteronomy 6:4

Having considered verbless clauses in the previous section, we can now consider what is perhaps the most important verbless construction in the Old Testament. In chapter 4 on translation, I already highlighted a number of different renderings of the Shema in Deuteronomy 6:4.

4 3 2 1 — שְׁמַע יִשְׂרָאֵל יְהוָה אֱלֹהֵינוּ יְהוָה I אֶחָד	1 2 3 4 — "Hear, Israel: YHWH our-God YHWH one"		
A	**B**	**Version**	**Distinct Significance**
1. God our God,	God the one and only!	MSG	Slogan: Stresses sole allegiance to YHWH
2. The LORD our God	is one LORD.	ASV, KJV, BBE	Confronts poly-YHWHism
3. The LORD our God,	the LORD is one.	NKJV, ESV, NIV, CSB	Stresses YHWH's supremacy and uniqueness
4a. The LORD is our God,	the LORD alone.	NRSV	Identifies YHWH as our only God
4b. Our God is the LORD,	only the LORD!	CEB	Asserts that our only God is YHWH
5. The LORD is our God;	the LORD is one.	NASB, WEB, NET Bible	Combines 3 and 4

Fig. 5.24. The Shema: Different Translations of Deuteronomy 6:4

With the four nominal constituents placed side by side, how do we distinguish which reading is correct? Let me first make a couple of observations and then overview what I did to determine the most likely reading.

Figure 5.22 in the previous section identifies the relative definiteness of various nominals and by this helps us distinguish subjects and predicates in verbless clauses. When two constituents stand adjacent to each other in a verbless construction, the one aligning with the higher number is most defined and therefore more likely the subject. If the first two nominals in the Shema, יְהוָה אֱלֹהֵינוּ ("YHWH our-God"), are indeed a clause, then the chart would suggest that "our God" is the subject and "YHWH" is the predicate, because definite noun phrases (#7) bear a higher level of definiteness on the chart than proper names (#6). This is the rendering of the CEB's "Our God is the LORD" in contrast to the NRSV's and NASB's "The LORD is our God."

The second pair of words in the Shema offers no ambiguity, because the proper name "YHWH" (#6) is clearly more defined than the adjective "one" (#2). If it is a clause, we would translate the second half as something like "the LORD is one," as seen in the ESV, NIV, and NASB, though we would need to also consider the meaning of אֶחָד ("one").

Now to which translation we should follow. We begin by focusing on the initial pair of words: יְהוָה אֱלֹהֵינוּ. To determine whether they together form a clause ("Our God is YHWH") or not ("YHWH our God"), I catalogued all the occurrences of אֱלֹהִים

("God") + suffix in Deuteronomy. Phrases such as "his God," "your God," "my God," "their God," and "our God" show up a total of 321 times in the book, which provides a lot of data from which to look for patterns. I can't go into all the details here, but I can summarize my findings and note their implications for our understanding of Deuteronomy 6:4.

Deuteronomy has 321 total occurrences of אֱלֹהִים ("God") + suffix: 10 refer to other "gods"[29] and 311 refer to יְהוָה ("YHWH"). Of the latter group, only 3 are not immediately preceded by יְהוָה (see 10:21; 31:17; 32:3). The other 308 instances have the divine name directly in front of אֱלֹהִים + suffix, and all but 4 clearly have "God" in apposition to "YHWH."[30] For example, in 6:15 we read, "For the LORD your God in your midst is a jealous God" (כִּי אֵל קַנָּא יְהוָה אֱלֹהֶיךָ בְּקִרְבֶּךָ). Here, אֱלֹהֶיךָ ("your God") stands adjacent to "YHWH," filling the same grammatical slot. The two terms refer to the same person and do not allow any predication. This is the common pattern throughout the book, which moves me to draw the following conclusions:

- Because 304 of the total 308 occurrences of יְהוָה אֱלֹהִים + suffix in Deuteronomy are unambiguously appositional (= 98.7%), the most likely rendering of the Shema's first pair is "YHWH our God," not "Our God *is* YHWH," or the like.
- While there are four instances in Deuteronomy in which אֱלֹהִים ("God") + suffix may stand as the predicate complement to a pronoun referring to YHWH (e.g., "I am your God," Deut. 5:6, 9; 10:21; 29:5[6]), there are no instances in which אֱלֹהִים + suffix stands in a predicate relationship with the proper name יְהוָה ("YHWH") itself. That is, not one of the 307 parallel constructions within the book of Deuteronomy include the rendering "Our God *is* YHWH" or "YHWH *is* our God" (= 0.0%). Therefore, there is little support for reading the Shema this way.

The best translation for the first half of the Shema is "The LORD our God," as found in the ESV and NIV. The renderings "Our God is the LORD" in the CEB and "The LORD is our God" in the NRSV, NASB, and NET Bible have no parallel within Deuteronomy.

With this understanding in mind, we are now ready to assess the second half of the Shema. How should we render יְהוָה אֶחָד ("YHWH one")? To answer this, we must move beyond grammar into deeper exegetical and theological wrestling, as taught in the rest of this book. Six observations strongly support that the ESV and NIV provide the best reading (#3): "The LORD our God, *the* LORD *is one*."

29. Third masculine singular suffix: Deut. 32:37; third masculine plural suffix: 7:16, 25; 12:2, 3, 30[2×], 31[2×]; 20:18.

30. Along with Deuteronomy 6:5, the other three questionable instances have אָנֹכִי יְהוָה אֱלֹהֶיךָ/אֱלֹהֵיכֶם, which can read either "I am YHWH your God" (= אֱלֹהִים + suffix in apposition to יְהוָה) or "I, YHWH, am your God" (אֱלֹהִים + suffix standing as the predicate complement to an explicit pronoun, which itself has יְהוָה in apposition) (see 5:6, 9; 29:6[H5]).

First, when the KJV renders אֶחָד ("one") as an attributive adjective (= "one LORD"), it either treats יְהוָה ("YHWH") as a title instead of the divine name (e.g., "one Lord" in Ephesians 4:5) or assumes a problem of poly-YHWHism for which we have no biblical support. While certain Israelites may have viewed localized idols as distinct and perhaps even contrasting manifestations of YHWH, nothing in the texts identifies YHWH with specific locations in a way that suggests that the inspired biblical authors were thinking this way.[31]

Second, because verbless slogans are so rare and because communication is driven by clauses, the rendering in the MSG (#1) is unlikely. Similarly, if we are expecting the Shema to express a full clause and if the first half is best rendered "YHWH our God," the second half must include predication. This fact cancels out the translations "the LORD alone" in the NRSV (#4a) and "only the LORD" in the CEB (#4b).

Third, while the adjective אֶחָד ("one") can refer to "oneness" in both quantity (i.e., one in number, single; e.g., Gen. 11:1; Deut. 32:30) and quality (i.e., unique, distinct, singular; e.g., 2 Sam. 7:23; Song 6:9),[32] the renderings "the LORD alone" (NRSV) and "only the LORD" (CEB) are quite unnatural grammatically and would more likely be expressed through the composite adverb לְבַד + suffix, as in לְבַדּוֹ ("only him," Isa. 2:11, 17; cf. 2 Kings 19:19).

Fourth, the NRSV and CEB treat Deuteronomy 6:4 as a cry of allegiance and not as a monotheistic confession.[33] In contrast, I believe Deuteronomy 6:4 declares loudly YHWH's sole supremacy and exclusive sovereignty, and only after calling people to hear this assertion (6:4) does Moses then charge God's people to love the Lord with all, serving him exclusively (6:5). In support of this claim, the Shema parallels numerous texts in Deuteronomy that emphasize the foundational truth of the biblical worldview. That is, within the pantheon of heaven, YHWH stands alone. He operates as the sole causer, chief authority, and supreme Sovereign of the universe. He may work through a heavenly assembly (e.g., 1 Kings 22:19–22; Job 1:6–12; 2:1–7; Pss. 82:1; 89:5–7[H6–8]), but none of these "angels" or "gods" are equal to YHWH; they are all subordinate and subservient, serving him (1 Kings 22:19), bowing to him (Ps. 29:2), obeying him (103:20–21), and praising him (148:2–5). YHWH is "God of gods and Lord of lords, the great, the mighty, and the awesome God" (Deut. 10:17). Therefore, we must affirm YHWH's assertion that "there is no God besides me" (Deut. 4:35, 39; 5:7; 32:39). "You shall have no other gods before me" (5:7) speaks not of priority but of space, so that

31. For example, YHWH is God at Bethel (Gen. 31:13; 35:7), Sinai (Deut. 33:2; Judg. 5:5), Seir (Deut. 33:2), Mount Paran (Deut. 33:2; Hab. 3:3), Shiloh (1 Sam. 1:3; 4:4), Teman (Hab. 3:3), Mount Zion (Isa. 8:18; 18:7; 24:23), and Jerusalem (Zech. 8:22). But nothing in these texts suggests that each site contained different manifestations of the same deity or different deities by the same name. The singular God YHWH was simply worshiped at or in some way associated with these various sites.

32. *DCH* 1:179–81, s.v. אֶחָד; cf. Frederick W. Danker, et al., *Greek-English Lexicon of the New Testament and Other Early Christian Literature*, 3rd ed. (Chicago: University of Chicago Press, 2000), 291, s.v. εἷς.

33. So too Daniel I. Block, "How Many Is God? An Investigation into the Meaning of Deuteronomy 6:4–5," *JETS* 47, 2 (2004): 193–212.

God is calling us to envision the pantheon of heaven as including only him.[34] In this sense, "YHWH is *one*."

Fifth, the quotations and allusions to the Shema throughout the rest of Scripture appear united in interpreting Deuteronomy 6:4 as a declaration of monotheism (in oneness of both quantity and quality) and not allegiance.[35] For example, Paul notes that all sorts of peoples can be saved in this new covenant day because "there is one God [εἷς θεός], and there is one mediator [εἷς μεσίτης] between God and men, the man Christ Jesus" (1 Tim. 2:5; cf. Rom. 3:29–30; Gal. 3:20). Similarly, after affirming that, from a certain perspective, "there are many 'gods' and many 'lords,'" the apostle highlights: "Yet for us there is one God [εἷς θεὸς], the Father, from whom are all things and for whom we exist, and one Lord [εἷς κύριος], Jesus Christ, through whom are all things and through whom we exist" (1 Cor. 8:5–6). Paul's point is not to stress the Christian's unidirected allegiance but instead to highlight that, as the true God, the Father is the one and only uncaused one and that Jesus is intimately related to him.[36]

Finally, in Mark 12 a scribe asks Jesus what the most important commandment is. He replies by quoting Deuteronomy 6:5 verbatim from the LXX: ἄκουε, Ἰσραήλ, κύριος ὁ θεὸς ἡμῶν κύριος εἷς ἐστιν ("Hear, O Israel: the Lord our God, the Lord is one," Mark 12:29). At this, the scribe then responds by affirming Jesus' statement and interpreting his words: "You are right, Teacher. You have truly said that he is one, and there is no other besides him" (12:32). We then read, "And when Jesus saw that he answered wisely, he said to him, 'You are not far from the kingdom of God'" (12:34). From Jesus' perspective, a "wise" reading of the Shema results in treating it as a statement that "there is no other besides" God. This is the meaning of the Shema in Deuteronomy 6:4. And in this light, the Lord then calls his people to "love the LORD your God with all your heart and with all your soul and with all your might" (Deut. 6:5).

Deuteronomy 6:4 supplies a good example of how rigorous grammatical wrestling gives clarity to meaning and opens the door for more advanced exegetical and theological interpretation. Nothing is more fundamental to the biblical worldview than that YHWH is one. The Lord is the only uncaused one—the ultimate Judge and the sole Source, Sustainer, and Goal of all things (Rom. 11:36; Col. 1:16). And because of this, he deserves our highest respect and surrender. The God who is over all cares for the small, so may we praise him, love him, and live for him.

34. For this interpretation of the first of the Ten Words, which the Shema echoes, see John H. Walton, "Interpreting the Bible as an Ancient Near Eastern Document," in *Israel: Ancient Kingdom or Late Invention?*, ed. Daniel I. Block (Nashville: Broadman & Holman, 2008), 305–9; Jason S. DeRouchie, "Making the Ten Count: Reflections on the Lasting Message of the Decalogue," in *For Our Good Always: Studies on the Message and Influence of Deuteronomy in Honor of Daniel I. Block*, ed. Jason S. DeRouchie, Jason Gile, and Kenneth J. Turner (Winona Lake, IN: Eisenbrauns, 2013), 422–23.

35. See, e.g., Job 31:15; Eccl. 12:11; Ezek. 34:23; 37:22, 24; Zech. 14:9; Mal. 2:10; Matt. 19:17; 23:9; Mark 2:7; 12:29, 32, 34; John 10:16; Rom. 3:29–30; 1 Cor. 8:4–6; Gal. 3:20; Eph. 4:4–6; 1 Tim. 2:5; Heb. 2:11; James 2:19; 4:12.

36. On this issue, N. T. Wright is correct: "Paul has placed Jesus *within* an explicit statement of doctrine that Israel's God is the one and only God, the creator of the world. . . . Paul has redefined [the Shema] christologically, producing what we can only call a sort of christological monotheism" (*The Climax of the Covenant: Christ and the Law in Pauline Theology* [Minneapolis: Fortress, 1993], 129).

The Lexham Discourse Hebrew Bible: An Overview

At this point, I want to highlight an important resource that is offered only in Logos Bible Software (https://www.logos.com/). It's *The Lexham Discourse Hebrew Bible* and the accompanying *High Definition Old Testament: ESV Edition.*[37] This tool, produced by Drs. Steven E. Runge and Joshua R. Westbury, supplies a visual portrait of some of the discourse grammar of every passage in Jesus' Bible. It distinguishes simple sentences from complex sentences and subpoints, supporting information, or elaboration. And then it uses a number of custom-made symbols (with easy-to-access pop-up definitions) to draw attention to key discourse features that are often missed by commentators but that can help you hear rightly the message of God's Word.

Whether you're engaged in sermon preparation, Bible translation, rigorous first-hand research, or classroom instruction, *The Lexham Discourse Hebrew Bible* will aid the task. Let's take a look at what it clarifies in Deuteronomy 6:4.

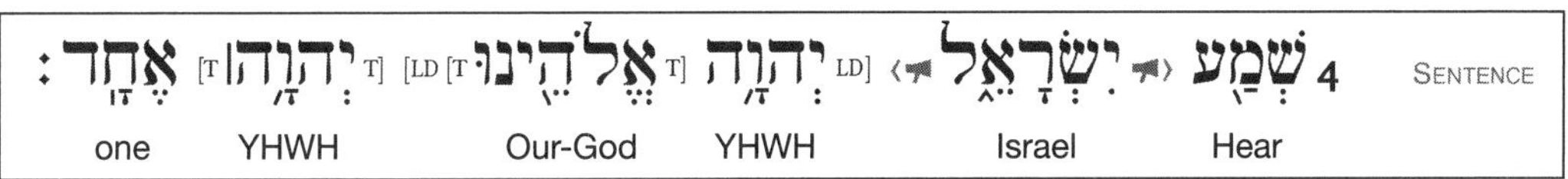

Fig. 5.25. Deuteronomy 6:4 in *The Lexham Discourse Hebrew Bible*

Right up front Runge and Westbury tag Deuteronomy 6:4 as a "sentence," as opposed to a slogan, as found in the MSG paraphrase. Next, the megaphone symbols around יִשְׂרָאֵל ("Israel") indicate "*Thematic Address:* The use of vocatives or nominatives of address containing extra descriptive information that is not required to identify the addressee(s). The information characterizes the addressee(s), based on how the speaker perceives them." In this instance, יִשְׂרָאֵל is a vocative.

Next, the "LD" in brackets around יְהוָה אֱלֹהֵינוּ ("YHWH our God") stands for "*Left-Dislocation:* Introducing information that is syntactically outside the main clause (i.e., it is dislocated) but that is reiterated somewhere within the main clause using a pronoun or other generic reference. Left-dislocations typically introduce something that is too complex to include in the main clause, where it might otherwise cause confusion. The element of the left-dislocation that resumes the information essentially summarizes new content, allowing the writer to easily comment about the new entity." It is important to note that in Hebrew what is called *left-dislocation* actually requires

37. Steven E. Runge and Joshua R. Westbury, *Lexham Discourse Hebrew Bible* and *High Definition Old Testament: ESV Edition* (Bellingham, WA: Lexham, 2012).

moving the dislocated material to the *right*. *Left-dislocation* is common linguistic terminology in languages such as English that are left-to-right, in which placing material outside the clause would require moving it to the left. In Hebrew, though, this means moving it to the right, because Hebrew starts from the right.

The "T" in brackets around אֱלֹהֵינוּ ("our God") introduces the last note on this verse. The notes state: "*Topic:* A label to identify the topic or subject of a clause where no finite verb form is present." Significantly, because Runge and Westbury read יְהוָה אֱלֹהֵינוּ as outside the main clause (= left-dislocation), it's clear that they are reading the text as a single independent clause in the pattern of the ESV or NIV (contra NRSV or CEB), not as a slogan (MSG) or two independent clauses (NASB; NET Bible). אֱלֹהֵינוּ then provides the topic, and the second יְהוָה supplies the subject of the main clause: "YHWH is one."

I highly recommend to you *The Lexham Discourse Hebrew Bible*. It's not an infallible guide to grammar, but it is a good one. If you want to read the Old Testament for depth and not just distance, this is a resource that will serve you long-term.

More on Text Blocks, Direct Speech, and Embedded Discourse[38]

In the next several sections we are going to look further at macro-syntax—the way in which various clauses work together to form texts. Already in our discussion of literary units ("Introducing Literary Units and Text Hierarchy in Hebrew" and "Text Blocks" in chapter 2) I have noted how Hebrew uses the connector וְ (gloss "and") and asyndeton (Ø) to create text blocks, discrete chains of clauses that we are to read together. The connector וְ links grammatical units of equal value, highlighting that all clauses within a given group are related in some way. וְ is a coordinator, and its presence assumes a preceding structure; therefore, we do not expect וְ to occur at the beginning of a new unit. In contrast, within contexts of coordination, asyndeton—the absence of a connector—often signals disjunction, either to identify the start of a new unit of discourse (= fresh beginning) or to restate, clarify, or support a previous text unit (= explication). In most instances, context alone clarifies which function asyndeton is performing.

What I want to note now is how text blocks are often interrupted by other ***embedded discourse units***. This is especially common with quotations—what we call ***direct speech***, when an actual utterance is placed within a text without any modification. Consider the following in English:

38. This material is adapted from Garrett and DeRouchie, *A Modern Grammar for Biblical Hebrew*, 285–87 (§ 37.D). Used by permission.

> The night wore on, and Nehemiah thought that he was ready for bed. So he said to his mother, "I am going to leave now." And he got up, and he left the courtyard.

In this illustration, the reported speech, "I am going to leave now," is set within a larger discourse. The direct speech itself, however, is an independent text unit. We have the narrator's larger discourse and, within that, Nehemiah's reported speech. We already saw this pattern at work in Deuteronomy 5 ("Introducing Literary Units and Text Hierarchy in Hebrew" in chapter 2), where the quotation containing the Ten Words (Deut. 5:6–21) or any number of the other speeches that Moses recalls (5:24b–27, 28c–31) are embedded in and set apart from the higher levels of the discourse.

As we also noted in the example from Deuteronomy 5, sometimes speakers insert one discourse type within another discourse even when there is no reported speech. We saw this in the way that the historical discourse in 5:2–31 served to support and give reason for heeding the directive discourse in 5:1, 32–33. Similarly, a storyteller may narrate a brief aside that gives background information but is actually not part of the main narrative.

The two examples that follow show how larger text blocks can include embedded discourse. Note especially the way in which asyndeton (Ø) and וְ work together to signal the beginning and end of the embedded units.

אֱמֹר לָהֶם	–	Ø	30b
שׁוּבוּ לָכֶם לְאָהֳלֵיכֶם׃	–	Ø	30c
וְאַתָּה פֹּה עֲמֹד עִמָּדִי	↑	וְ	31a
וַאֲדַבְּרָה אֵלֶיךָ אֵת כָּל־הַמִּצְוָה וְהַחֻקִּים וְהַמִּשְׁפָּטִים	↑	וְ	31b

30b	Say to them,
30c	"Return to your tents."
31a	But you, stand here with me,
31b	and I will tell you the whole commandment and the statutes and the rules . . .

Fig. 5.26. Reported Direct Speech in Deuteronomy 5:30–31

In this example from Deuteronomy 5:30–31, clauses 31ab are part of a single text block initiated at 30b. This is marked by the fact that both 31ab continue the second masculine singular address and link to 30b by the connector וְ. The clause in 30c, however, is direct speech, standing as an independent discourse. It is not directly linked to anything that precedes because it is the beginning of a speech, and therefore 30c is asyndetic. After the reported speech, clause 31a resumes the prior discourse (30b) and thus begins with the connector וְ.

Now, in cases in which one text block is embedded within another without reported speech, the embedded material often explains or emphasizes something in the larger text unit.

וַיִּשְׁכַּב דָּוִד עִם־אֲבֹתָיו	↑	וַ	10a
וַיִּקָּבֵר בְּעִיר דָּוִד׃	↑	וַ	10b
וְהַיָּמִים אֲשֶׁר מָלַךְ דָּוִד עַל־יִשְׂרָאֵל אַרְבָּעִים שָׁנָה	↑	וְ	11a
בְּחֶבְרוֹן מָלַךְ שֶׁבַע שָׁנִים	–	Ø	11b
וּבִירוּשָׁלַםִ מָלַךְ שְׁלֹשִׁים וְשָׁלֹשׁ שָׁנִים׃	↑	וּ	11c

10a	And David lay down with his fathers,
10b	and he was buried in the city of David.
11a	And the days that David reigned over Israel were forty years.
11b	In Hebron he reigned seven years,
11c	and in Jerusalem he reigned thirty-three years.

Fig. 5.27. Inner-Paragraph Comment in 1 Kings 2:10–11

Notice how this example from historical discourse begins with two *wayyiqtol* clauses that are carrying along the narrative. *Wayyiqtol* is the default or unmarked verb pattern in the historical text type. Then in 11a we get a non-*wayyiqtol* clause, which is probably marking the close of this particular paragraph. But before the paragraph is fully complete we get the embedded discourse in 11bc, which explains the "forty years" mentioned in 11a. Note that the embedded text block begins with asyndeton, marking the explication (Ø).

You must recognize that the most important material thematically in a text is not necessarily to be found in the primary line of textual development. In fact, you will usually find a passage's main point within the text's embedded material. For example, although the primary story line in historical narrative is never embedded, the core message that gives us understanding in how to read the story is usually found not in the characters' actions but in their speech acts, which are always embedded. When God speaks, we need to listen, and his speeches are usually embedded within other material.

More on Marked and Unmarked Clauses[39]

In our discussion of literary units in chapter 2, we noted how in the various text types (whether historical, anticipatory, or directive) any switch away from the unmarked, default verb pattern signals something significant in the discourse ("Discerning Subunits in Text Blocks: Paragraph Breaks"). Paragraph division is only one reason why the

39. This material is adapted from ibid., 287–90 (§ 37.E). Used by permission.

biblical authors departed from the default pattern. There are a host of other possibilities, for which I will now give an overview. Whenever you find a marked (nondefault) predication pattern or clause structure in the Old Testament, it is usually functioning in one of four ways.

1. To Give Background Information

A clause that alters from the default pattern can describe the setting or situation at the time of a main action.

וַיָּקָם ׀	10	And he [Elijah] arose,
וַיֵּלֶךְ צָרְפַתָה	b	and he went to Zarephath.
וַיָּבֹא אֶל־פֶּתַח הָעִיר	c	And he came to the opening of the city,
וְהִנֵּה־שָׁם אִשָּׁה אַלְמָנָה מְקֹשֶׁשֶׁת עֵצִים	d	and behold, a widow woman was there gathering wood.
וַיִּקְרָא אֵלֶיהָ	e	And he called to her
וַיֹּאמַר . . .	f	and said . . .

Fig. 5.28. Background Information in 1 Kings 17:10

In this example, the continuous chain of וְ-fronted clauses identifies the entire verse as part of the same text block. All the clauses have *wayyiqtol* verbs except 10d. The narrative runs without a break through 10a–c, but then the reader's attention is grabbed through the marked nominal participial clause that begins with וְהִנֵּה־שָׁם ("and behold, there"), using the marker of immediate significance. Verse 10d tells us what Elijah saw when he arrived at the city gate—a widow woman gathering sticks. Because 10e ("And he called to her") does not appear to start a new paragraph, 10d seems to be offering necessary background information so that we can know whom he called. Verse 10d introduces the widow into the story. Each unmarked *wayyiqtol* clause carries the historical account forward; the marked non-*wayyiqtol* clause provides essential background material that we need for understanding the narrative.

2. To Match Multiple Aspects of the Same Event

A single event may have two or more components or aspects, which may be contrasted or aligned.

Contrastive matching occurs when an unmarked clause and an adjacent marked clause are together treated as two contrasting parts of a single event or idea. This type of matching is often expressed when a default verb-first clause (i.e., *wayyiqtol* or *weqatal* = V_) is directly followed by a marked, non-verb-first clause (_V), resulting in the following pattern: V_ + _V. ***Identical matching*** happens when there is a series of marked clauses that describe two or more aligned elements of a single event. Here two or more marked, non-verb-first clauses stand adjacent, resulting in the following pattern: _V + _V.

Let's first look at an example of contrastive matching from Genesis 1:4–5.

וַיַּרְא אֱלֹהִים אֶת־הָאוֹר כִּי־טוֹב	4	And God saw that the light was good.
וַיַּבְדֵּל אֱלֹהִים בֵּין הָאוֹר וּבֵין הַחֹשֶׁךְ	b	And God separated between the light and the darkness.
וַיִּקְרָא אֱלֹהִים לָאוֹר יוֹם	5	And God called the light Day,
וְלַחֹשֶׁךְ קָרָא לָיְלָה	b	but the darkness he called Night.

Fig. 5.29. Contrastive Matching in Genesis 1:4–5

Here all the clauses begin with וְ, but in 5b the *wayyiqtol* pattern is halted with a וְ + prepositional phrase + *qatal* clause. The repetition of the verb קרא ("to call") in both 5a and 5b suggests that we actually have a match here, and the fact that 5a is verb-first (V_) and 5b non-verb-first (_V) suggests that the match is contrastive. The action of calling the darkness "night" is conceptually simultaneous with and contrasted with the calling of the light "day." There are therefore three (not four) events in these verses: (a) God saw that it was good, (b) then God separated light from darkness, and (c) then God called the light "day" and the darkness "night." Light and darkness are not equals but opposites, so the author used contrastive matching.

We see identical matching in 2 Kings 17:29–30.

וַיִּהְיוּ עֹשִׂים גּוֹי גּוֹי אֱלֹהָיו	29	And nation after nation was making its gods.
וַיַּנִּיחוּ בְּבֵית הַבָּמוֹת אֲשֶׁר עָשׂוּ הַשֹּׁמְרֹנִים גּוֹי גּוֹי בְּעָרֵיהֶם אֲשֶׁר הֵם יֹשְׁבִים שָׁם	b	And they placed them in the shrine of the high places that the Samaritans had made—nation after nation in the cities in which they lived.
וְאַנְשֵׁי בָבֶל עָשׂוּ אֶת־סֻכּוֹת בְּנוֹת	30	And the men of Babylon made Succoth-benoth,
וְאַנְשֵׁי־כוּת עָשׂוּ אֶת־נֵרְגַל	b	and the men of Cuth made Nergal,
וְאַנְשֵׁי חֲמָת עָשׂוּ אֶת־אֲשִׁימָא׃	c	and the men of Hamath made Ashima.

Fig. 5.30. Identical Matching in 2 Kings 17:29–30

Notice once again the chain of וְ-fronted clauses. After two *wayyiqtol* clauses in 29ab, we switch to three marked non-verb-first clauses in 30a–c. All three of these intrusive, nondefault clauses build on the earlier statements regarding the nations that crafted gods and placed them in the city shrines. Each nation's idolatrous actions are identical to those of all the others, and together they are here portrayed as a single event, each part clarifying the whole. The threefold non-verb-first pattern (_V + _V + _V) signals identical matching.

3. To Signal an Interruption or Transition

This action breaks the main flow of thought, whether to mark dramatic pause, thematic division, or flashback. We have already seen this use in the way in which a marked clause can signal a turning point, whether by identifying the beginning or end of a paragraph or by introducing an entirely new text section. At other times, such clauses mark thematically prominent material, meaning that their content sticks out as a high point from the rest of the text. Such clauses can be very important. We see an example of this type in Jonah 1:3–4.

וַיָּקָם יוֹנָה לִבְרֹחַ תַּרְשִׁישָׁה מִלִּפְנֵי יְהוָה	3	And he arose to flee to Tarshish from the presence of YHWH.
וַיֵּרֶד יָפוֹ	b	And he went down to Joppa
וַיִּמְצָא אָנִיָּה בָּאָה תַרְשִׁישׁ	c	and he found a ship going to Tarshish.
וַיִּתֵּן שְׂכָרָהּ	d	And he paid its fare
וַיֵּרֶד בָּהּ לָבוֹא עִמָּהֶם תַּרְשִׁישָׁה מִלִּפְנֵי יְהוָה	e	and he went down in it to go with them to Tarshish away from the presence of YHWH.
וַיהוָה הֵטִיל רוּחַ־גְּדוֹלָה אֶל־הַיָּם. . . .	4	But YHWH hurled a great wind upon the sea . . . .

Fig. 5.31. Thematic Prominence in Jonah 1:3–4

In this example we have five *wayyiqtol* clauses in verse 3, each event naturally building on the previous and allowing us to move quickly through Jonah's journey of flight: "he arose . . . and he went down . . . and he found . . . and he paid . . . and he went down." Verse 4, however, diverges from this development with the marked וְ + subject + *qatal* clause: "But YHWH hurled a great wind upon the sea." The clause draws attention to YHWH's action and provides a surprising interruption in the story flow. The marked clause in 4a makes God's action more thematically prominent than Jonah's actions, which are represented through the unmarked *wayyiqtol* clauses in 3a–e. The intrusion of the marked clause into the text suggests that the action is sudden, unexpected, and important.

4. To Signal Negated Actions

Here an action does not move the story along but clarifies what did not happen. As a general rule, a negative does not carry the action forward in a text. Nevertheless, very often negated clauses provide the most thematically prominent and critical material in a discourse. We see a good example in 2 Samuel 11:8–10.

וַיֵּצֵא אוּרִיָּה מִבֵּית הַמֶּלֶךְ	8	And Uriah went out of the king's house,
וַתֵּצֵא אַחֲרָיו מַשְׂאַת הַמֶּלֶךְ	b	and a present from the king went out after him.
וַיִּשְׁכַּב אוּרִיָּה פֶּתַח בֵּית הַמֶּלֶךְ אֵת כָּל־עַבְדֵי אֲדֹנָיו	9	And Uriah slept at the door of the king's house with all the servants of his lord,
וְלֹא יָרַד אֶל־בֵּיתוֹ	b	but he did not go down to his house.
וַיַּגִּדוּ לְדָוִד	c	And they told David . . . .

Fig. 5.32. Negation in 2 Samuel 11:8–10

Here we have a chain of *wayyiqtol* clauses that is interrupted with the וְ + negative (לֹא) + *qatal* clause in 9b. The negative clause pattern highlights what did not happen and marks this information as important. Naturally, the narrator stresses that "he did not go down to his house" in order to emphasize that Bathsheba's pregnancy was due to David's sexual sin and not to Uriah.

In summary, default, unmarked material carries ahead the flow of thought, whereas marked material creates disjunction, drawing attention to itself for some reason. Whereas at times the marked clauses signal paragraph divisions, at other times their purpose is to supply background information or to highlight thematically prominent material.

An Exercise in Text Grammar—Exodus 19:4–6

Determining the Protasis and Apodosis in Exodus 19:5–6

In this section we want to consider where the apodosis begins in Exodus 19:5–6. The protasis or "if" section of this two-part syntactic construction clearly starts with the אִם־ ("if") in 5a ("If you will indeed listen unto my voice . . ."). But where do we start the "then"? Our translation revealed three possibilities: 5b, 5c, and 6a.

At times there is difficulty discerning the beginning of an apodosis because Hebrew usually doesn't use an explicit conjunction such as *then* or *therefore* to mark it. Instead, Hebrew relies on a mixture of content and grammatical signals. What we are looking for is a clear formal (i.e., grammatical) cue to identify the shift from protasis to apodosis—perhaps a new verb pattern, a change in subject, or the use of an unnecessary

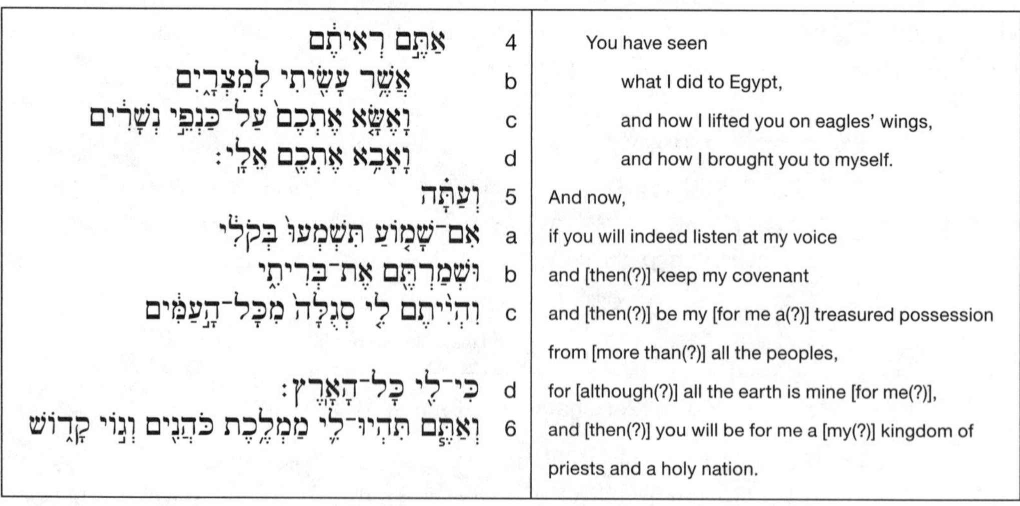

אַתֶּם רְאִיתֶם	4	You have seen
אֲשֶׁר עָשִׂיתִי לְמִצְרָיִם	b	what I did to Egypt,
וָאֶשָּׂא אֶתְכֶם עַל־כַּנְפֵי נְשָׁרִים	c	and how I lifted you on eagles' wings,
וָאָבִא אֶתְכֶם אֵלָי׃	d	and how I brought you to myself.
וְעַתָּה	5	And now,
אִם־שָׁמוֹעַ תִּשְׁמְעוּ בְּקֹלִי	a	if you will indeed listen at my voice
וּשְׁמַרְתֶּם אֶת־בְּרִיתִי	b	and [then(?)] keep my covenant
וִהְיִיתֶם לִי סְגֻלָּה מִכָּל־הָעַמִּים	c	and [then(?)] be my [for me a(?)] treasured possession from [more than(?)] all the peoples,
כִּי־לִי כָּל־הָאָרֶץ׃	d	for [although(?)] all the earth is mine [for me(?)],
וְאַתֶּם תִּהְיוּ־לִי מַמְלֶכֶת כֹּהֲנִים וְגוֹי קָדוֹשׁ	6	and [then(?)] you will be for me a [my(?)] kingdom of priests and a holy nation.

Fig. 5.33. Preliminary Text Hierarchy of Exodus 19:4–6

explicit pronoun. So let's consider our three possibilities for the apodosis in Exodus 19:5–6. Figure 5.33 identifies where we left off our text hierarchy, having finalized the thought flow only through verse 4.

1. Option 1: Placing the Apodosis at 5b

The 1862 YLT placed the apodosis in 5b, directly following the אִם־ ("if") protasis of 5a: "And now, if ye really hearken to My voice, then ye have kept My covenant, and been to me a peculiar treasure." Positively, this view includes a marked shift from the *yiqtol* תִּשְׁמְעוּ ("you will listen") in the protasis of 5a to the *weqatal* וּשְׁמַרְתֶּם ("and you will keep") in 5b. But the challenge is that if 5b were a continuation of the protasis, it would have looked exactly the same way. *Weqatal* usually follows *yiqtol* when a protasis extends over multiple clauses, so we ought to expect a greater marked shift than a simple change from *yiqtol* to *weqatal* in order to signal the start of the apodosis.

2. Option 2: Placing the Apodosis at 5c

Since the 1611 KJV, most English translations have placed the apodosis at 5c. For example, the NASB reads, "Now then, if you will indeed obey My voice and keep My covenant, then you shall be My own possession among all the peoples, for all the earth is Mine." Note, however, that 5c simply begins with the *weqatal* verb וִהְיִיתֶם ("and you will be"), which is the same conjugation represented in וּשְׁמַרְתֶּם ("and you will keep") in 5b. There is no grammatical shift at all between 5b and 5c, and no other markers would tell us that the apodosis should begin in 5c. This lack of signal calls into question the majority view. Indeed, this may be an instance in which tradition rather than careful reading has guided most of the translations.

3. Option 3: Placing the Apodosis at 6a

What is noteworthy in 6a is the explicit presence of the unnecessary pronoun וְאַתֶּם ("and you [masculine plural]") before the verb תִּהְיוּ ("you [masculine plural] will be"): "And *you* will be to me a kingdom of priests and a holy nation." The inclusion of a lexicalized, unnecessary pronoun is exactly what we would expect to mark an apodosis when the main subject does not change.

Deuteronomy 26:17–19 is a parallel text that supports viewing the start of the apodosis in Exodus 19:6a. Deuteronomy 26:17–19 stands as the climax to the Moab covenant, in which God renews his relationship with the post-Sinai generation. Figure 5.34 shows my translation and basic outline of the passage. You'll notice a number of allusions to Exodus 19:4–6.

Today you have caused YHWH to declare to be your God and [for you] to walk in his ways, to keep his statutes, his commandments, and his judgments, and to heed his voice. 18 And today YHWH has caused you to declare to be a people of treasured possession, just as he declared to you, and to keep all his commandments, 19 and [for him] to place you high over all nations for praise and for fame and for beauty and to make you a people holy to YHWH your God, just as he declared.
1. You have today caused YHWH to declare (v. 17): a. YHWH's *commitment*: to be God to you b. YHWH's expectations: i. To walk in his ways ii. To keep his statutes, commands, and judgments iii. To heed his voice **2. YHWH has today caused you to declare (vv. 18–19):** a. Israel's *commitment* (v. 18): i. To be a treasured possession for YHWH ii. To keep all his commands b. Israel's *expectations* (v. 19) i. To set Israel high above the nations ii. To be a holy people to YHWH

Fig. 5.34. DeRouchie's Translation and Outline of Deuteronomy 26:17–19[40]

There are two parties in the covenant (YHWH and Israel), and here each party's readiness to enter into covenant moves the other to formalize both his covenantal commitments (obligations) and expectations (stipulations). The commitments of one party are equivalent to the expectations of the other. Focusing on the terms that are parallel with Exodus 19:5–6, in Deuteronomy 26 we see God *expecting* Israel to "keep" covenantal statutes, commands, and judgments and to "heed [ESV = obey] his voice" (26:17). We also see Israel *committing* to be a "treasured possession" and "to keep" the covenantal commands (26:18). YHWH calls Israel *to do* these things; they are not what Israel is hoping to become. These divine expectations and human commitments suggest that all three main clauses in Exodus 19:5 serve as the protasis and that only in 19:6a do we arrive at the apodosis: "If Israel will surely heed his voice and keep his covenant and be a treasured possession—living as if they are

40. Deuteronomy 26:17–18 contains the only instances of the Hiphil of אמר ("to say") in the Hebrew Old Testament. The default meaning behind the Hiphil is causative, but most translators render the form as a simple declarative (see Walter T. Claassen, "The Declarative-Estimative Hiph'il," *JNSL* 2 [1972]: 5–16). In contrast, my rendering retains the causative force, reading it within the covenantal ratification context. Thus, Israel first causes YHWH to declare both obligation and stipulation, and then YHWH causes Israel to declare both obligation and stipulation. A more periphrastic rendering would be: "Today you have ratified YHWH's declaration . . . . Today YHWH has ratified your declaration . . . ." My proposal is adapted from Steven Ward Guest, *Deuteronomy 26:16–19 as the Central Focus of the Covenantal Framework of Deuteronomy* (Ph.D. diss., The Southern Baptist Theological Seminary, 2009), 72–129, esp. 77–88. I disagree, however, with Guest's treatment of "treasured possession" in verse 18 (118–19). My rendering is somewhat comparable to the NRSV: "Today you have obtained the LORD's agreement . . . . Today the LORD has obtained your agreement" (Deut. 26:17–18). It is also similar to Patrick D. Miller, *Deuteronomy, Interpretation* (Louisville: John Knox, 1990), 185–86; and Daniel I. Block, "The Privilege of Calling: The Mosaic Paradigm for Missions (Deu 26:16–19)," *BSac* 162, 648 (2005): 387–405.

valued by God, *then* they will fulfill their calling as a kingdom of priests and holy nation" (author's paraphrase). Notice how Deuteronomy 26:19 includes Israel's becoming "a holy" people in their expectation. This, too, indicates that Exodus 19:6 is indeed the apodosis. We can thus display a basic outline of Exodus 19:5–6 like this:

1. **Protasis:** "If you will . . ." (v. 5)
   a. Heed God's voice
   b. Keep his covenant
   c. Be his treasured possession
2. **Apodosis:** "Then you shall be . . ." (v. 6)
   a. Kingdom of priests
   b. Holy nation

The Text Hierarchy of Exodus 19:4–6

If we are on track with the placement of the protasis and apodosis in Exodus 19:5–6, we can expand our text hierarchy of the passage. Laying out the hierarchy of clauses helps us visualize the relationship of all the parts. It helps us differentiate subordination, embedding, and the various text blocks.

What you must remember as you visually represent your structural analysis through a text hierarchy is that you mark subordination by indenting and that in given text blocks you should always be able to follow the chain of וְ ("and")-fronted clauses to their source, whether it is an asyndetic clause or a subordinate clause marked by a subordinate conjunction. Our exegetical decisions to date lead us to the breakdown shown in figure 5.35.

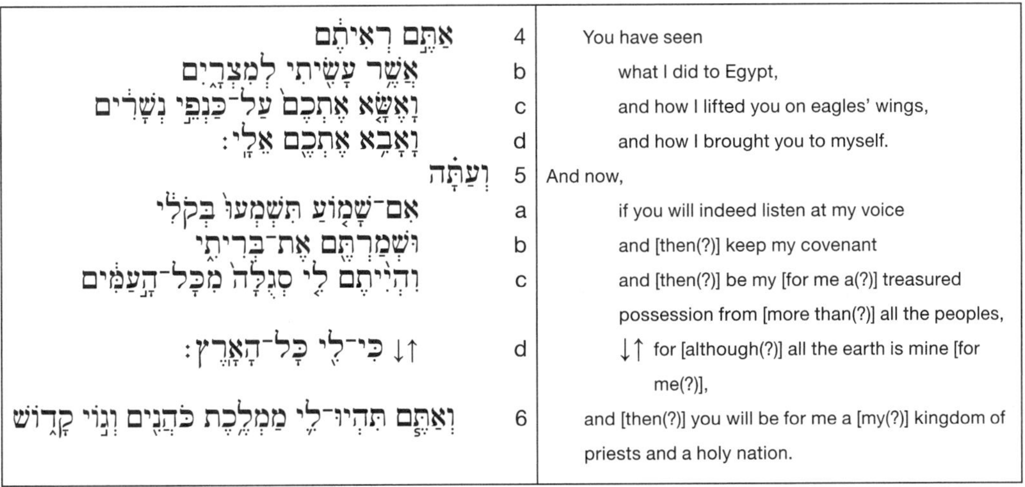

אַתֶּ֣ם רְאִיתֶ֔ם	4	You have seen
אֲשֶׁ֥ר עָשִׂ֖יתִי לְמִצְרָ֑יִם	b	what I did to Egypt,
וָאֶשָּׂ֤א אֶתְכֶם֙ עַל־כַּנְפֵ֣י נְשָׁרִ֔ים	c	and how I lifted you on eagles' wings,
וָאָבִ֥א אֶתְכֶ֖ם אֵלָֽי׃	d	and how I brought you to myself.
וְעַתָּ֗ה	5	And now,
אִם־שָׁמ֤וֹעַ תִּשְׁמְעוּ֙ בְּקֹלִ֔י	a	if you will indeed listen at my voice
וּשְׁמַרְתֶּ֖ם אֶת־בְּרִיתִ֑י	b	and [then(?)] keep my covenant
וִהְיִ֨יתֶם לִ֤י סְגֻלָּה֙ מִכָּל־הָ֣עַמִּ֔ים	c	and [then(?)] be my [for me a(?)] treasured possession from [more than(?)] all the peoples,
↓↑ כִּי־לִ֖י כָּל־הָאָֽרֶץ׃	d	↓↑ for [although(?)] all the earth is mine [for me(?)],
וְאַתֶּ֧ם תִּהְיוּ־לִ֛י מַמְלֶ֥כֶת כֹּהֲנִ֖ים וְג֣וֹי קָד֑וֹשׁ	6	and [then(?)] you will be for me a [my(?)] kingdom of priests and a holy nation.

Fig. 5.35. Text Hierarchy of Exodus 19:4–6

One feature of my text hierarchy worth mentioning is that with both וְעַתָּה ("and now") in 5a and וְאַתֶּם ("and you [masculine plural]") in 6a, the connector וְ ("and") is not linked to anything before it. Scholars call this the "*waw* of apodosis," which usually stands as an optional marker of the main consequence clause following the subordinate protasis: "if-*then*, when-*then*, because-*therefore*." When וְ signals an apodosis, this coordinator does not join elements of equal syntactic value. The protasis is always subordinate to the apodosis, and I have identified this subordination by indenting both the unmarked protasis of verse 4 and the embedded אִם-protasis in verse 5.[41]

The Function of מִן and לְ in Exodus 19:5–6

We are now ready to clarify the function of the single מִן preposition and three לְ prepositions in Exodus 19:5–6. Was Israel to be a treasured possession to God in distinction "from" all the peoples of the earth (separative מִן) or "more than" all the peoples of the earth (comparative מִן)? Two arguments stand against the comparative reading and therefore support the view that the preposition expresses a relationship of separation between Israel and the rest of the peoples. First, elsewhere Scripture designates old covenant Israel and the church as a "treasured possession" only in relation to God (Deut. 7:6; 14:2; 26:18; Ps. 135:4; Mal. 3:17; Titus 2:14; 1 Peter 1:14). Indeed, as we will see in chapter 7, the very meaning of סְגֻלָּה ("treasured possession") implies a unique and distinctive status. The translation "more than" requires that the peoples of the earth were still, in some lower sense, God's special treasure, but this is *not* what the rest of the Bible teaches. Second, rendering מִן as comparative sets us up to read the כִּי as a concessive statement (i.e., "though, although"). The result would be something like this: "You shall be to me a treasured possession *more than* all the peoples, *though* all the earth is mine"). As the next section highlights, however, a concessive translation of כִּי as "though, although" is highly unlikely, and without the contrary-to-fact statement, a translation of מִן as "more than" makes little sense. We

41. Richard C. Steiner has proposed that even in conditional sentences, the "*waw* of apodosis" may actually still be a coordinator through an abbreviated form of logic. He proposes that the pattern "If A, then B" is equivalent to "If A, then A *and* B," which both English and Hebrew can express as "If A, then *also* B" (cf. Lev. 6:21 with Jer. 31:37; 33:20–21; Zech. 3:7; "Does the Biblical Hebrew Conjunction -ו Have Many Meanings, One Meaning, or No Meaning at All?," *JBL* 119, 2 [2000]: 264). While Steiner's proposal provides a likely explanation for the origin of the *waw* of apodosis, one struggles to see explicit patterns in biblical Hebrew for the use or nonuse of the *waw* of apodosis. Its presence or absence seems optional in most two-part syntactic constructions. For a synthesis of Steiner's article, see Jason S. DeRouchie, *A Call to Covenant Love: Text-Grammar and Literary Structure in Deuteronomy 5–11*, Gorgias Dissertations 30/Biblical Studies 2 (Piscataway, NJ: Gorgias, 2007), 108–10.

should translate מִן as "from," highlighting YHWH's call for Israel to stand distinct *from* the nations.

The prepositional phrase לִי occurs in 5cd and 6a, and each instance most likely expresses either divine possession ("mine") or divine advantage ("to/for me"). Is Israel to be *YHWH's* treasured possession or a treasured possession *to YHWH*? Is all the earth *God's*, or is all the earth *for God*? Will the Israelites' obedience result in their being *YHWH's* kingdom of priests and holy nation, or are God's people to become a kingdom of priests and a holy nation *for God's sake*? The exegetical decisions here are not easy, but thankfully we can say that all these options are true teachings in Scripture. Nevertheless, the question is "What exactly is the Lord calling for or declaring *in this passage*?"

As suggested in the major translations, the two instances of לִי in verse 5 are probably possessive, stressing that Israel was to exist as *God's* special treasure and that the whole earth was the *Lord's*. Only this interpretation counters the unnecessary redundancy of "You shall be a treasured possession *to YHWH* because all the earth exists *for me*." The use of לִי in 6a, however, is different. Israel's priesthood was always *for YHWH's* sake (Ex. 28:1; 1 Chron. 23:13), designed to promote his holiness and display his beauty. Most translations render 6a as "And you shall be *to me* a kingdom of priests and a holy nation," and this pattern seems sound.

The Function of כִּי in Exodus 19:5

The final major grammatical question in Exodus 19:5 relates to whether the particle כִּי marks 5d as supplying a logical ground for what precedes (i.e., "for, because") or signals a concessive relationship with what precedes or follows (i.e., "though, although"). Compare the ESV and NIV translations.

MT		ESV	NIV
וְעַתָּ֗ה אִם־שָׁמ֤וֹעַ תִּשְׁמְעוּ֙ בְּקֹלִ֔י	5	5 Now therefore, if you will	5 Now if you obey me fully and
וּשְׁמַרְתֶּ֖ם אֶת־בְּרִיתִ֑י	b	indeed obey my voice and keep	keep my covenant, then out of all
וִהְיִ֨יתֶם לִ֤י סְגֻלָּה֙ מִכָּל־הָ֣עַמִּ֔ים	c	my covenant, you shall be my	nations you will be my treasured
כִּי־לִ֖י כָּל־הָאָֽרֶץ׃	d	treasured possession among all	possession. *Although the whole*
וְאַתֶּ֧ם תִּהְיוּ־לִ֛י מַמְלֶ֥כֶת כֹּהֲנִ֖ים	6	peoples, *for all the earth is mine*; 6	*earth is mine*, 6 you will be for me
וְג֣וֹי קָד֑וֹשׁ		and you shall be to me a kingdom	a kingdom of priests and a holy
		of priests and a holy nation.	nation.

Fig. 5.36. The Function of כִּי in Exodus 19:4–6

The NIV renders the clause in 5d (כִּי־לִי כָּל־הָאָֽרֶץ) concessively with what follows: *"Although the whole earth is mine*, you will be for me a kingdom of priests and a holy nation." While גַּם כִּי ("even though") is the more natural way in Hebrew to express concession (e.g., Ps. 23:4; Isa. 1:15), scholars recognize that a כִּי clause can bear concessive force when it precedes the main clause (e.g., Jer. 51:53; Ezek. 11:16).[42] A strength of the NIV's rendering is that it explains the explicit subject וְאַתֶּם ("and you") in 6a by seeing it as emphasizing contrast with what precedes—as if God were saying, "Although I own all the world, *you alone* are my kingdom of priests." Furthermore, the NIV translation of 5d–6a reads smoothly, treating the last sentence of the speech as an inner-paragraph restatement of 5c. In this interpretation, being God's "treasured possession" (5c) is parallel to Israel's being a "kingdom of priests and a holy nation" (6a), whereas "out of all nations" (5c) is parallel to "the whole earth is mine" (5d).

In spite of these strengths, the NIV reading fully depends on viewing the statement about the "treasured possession" in 5c as the start of the apodosis. And I already showed the unlikelihood of this reading, since no grammatical signals suggest that any major change happens in 5c ("Determining the Protasis and Apodosis in Exodus 19:5–6" above). The explicit subject וְאַתֶּם ("and you") in 6a marks the start of the apodosis, and we should therefore read the כִּי as supplying support to what precedes. Scholars believe that the concessive force is unlikely whenever כִּי follows its main clause,[43] so we are on most stable ground to treat the כִּי as causal (i.e., "because, for"), supplying a reason why Israel needed to live as a treasured possession.

The offspring of Abraham were to exist with a conscious sense that they were God's special treasure from all peoples *because* all the earth is the Lord's. How does God's ownership of all the earth supply a reason for Israel's being a treasured possession? It must mean that the Israelites' living with a recognition of their special status before God would have served as a means for God's global sovereignty to be re-realized. We could paraphrase the whole in this way: "Because I deserve allegiance from all the earth, I am giving you a sacred task, part of which is for you to exist as a treasured possession among all peoples. As you revel in my closeness and take pleasure in your sonship, you will in turn point the rest of the world back to the only Savior, Sovereign, and Satisfier. And they will see your good works and glorify your Father in heaven." This interpretation best fits the grammar in these verses.

We have concluded that כִּי in Exodus 19:5 is best read causally ("because, for"). When the conclusions from the last three sections are joined, the result is the following text hierarchy and translation for Exodus 19:5–6:

42. Joüon and Muraoka, *A Grammar of Biblical Hebrew*, 602 (§ 171b).

43. Ibid., 602n1; Anneli Aejmelaeus, "Function and Interpretation of כי in Biblical Hebrew," *JBL* 105, 2 (1986): 198–9, 205–7.

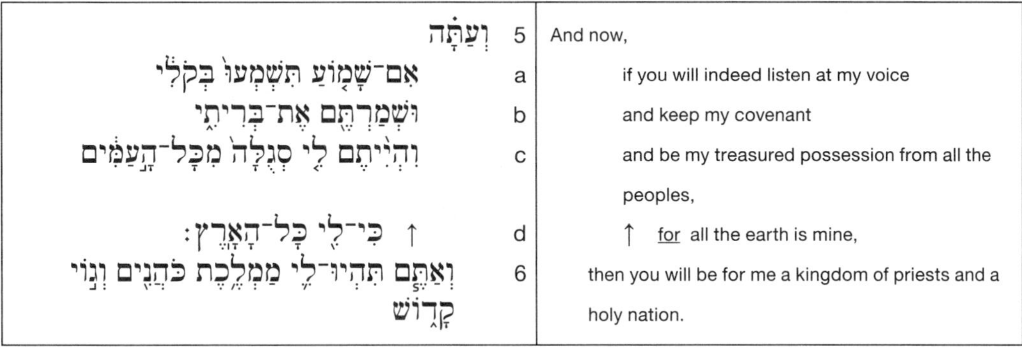

וְעַתָּה	5	And now,
אִם־שָׁמוֹעַ תִּשְׁמְעוּ בְּקֹלִי	a	if you will indeed listen at my voice
וּשְׁמַרְתֶּם אֶת־בְּרִיתִי	b	and keep my covenant
וִהְיִיתֶם לִי סְגֻלָּה מִכָּל־הָעַמִּים	c	and be my treasured possession from all the peoples,
↑ כִּי־לִי כָּל־הָאָרֶץ׃	d	↑ for all the earth is mine,
וְאַתֶּם תִּהְיוּ־לִי מַמְלֶכֶת כֹּהֲנִים וְגוֹי קָדוֹשׁ	6	then you will be for me a kingdom of priests and a holy nation.

Fig. 5.37. Text Hierarchy of Exodus 19:5–6

Key Words and Concepts

Grammar
Orthography, phonology, morphology, and syntax
Clause
Predicate
Phrase, subordinate clause, main clause, and sentence
Tense, voice, mood, aspect, and *Aktionsart*
Perfective and imperfective aspect
Dynamic and stative verbs
Markers of immediate significance
Inference markers
Verbless clause
Contextualizing constituent and focus
Embedded discourse units and direct speech
Contrastive and identical matching

Questions for Further Reflection

1. The goal of this chapter was "to show how grammar is important for exegesis and how it helps us track an author's flow of thought." Upon reading it, how would you say that grammar is important for exegesis?
2. Explain the concept of a clause having grammatical slots.
3. What role do context and *Aktionsart* play in clarifying the use of *qatal* and *yiqtol* verbs in past, present, and future tense?
4. What syntactical clues help distinguish whether a *yiqtol* is functioning indicatively or nonindicatively (e.g., volitionally)?
5. What is the difference between לֹא and אַל negatives?
6. How do the relative levels of definiteness in a clause (see fig. 5.22) help to identify the subject from the predicate in verbless clauses?
7. Explain the concept of *embedding*. How is this helpful for exegesis?
8. What are the varying purposes of a marked clause?

Resources for Further Study

Guides to Hebrew Tools (for those who don't know Hebrew)

★ Fields, Lee M. *Hebrew for the Rest of Us: Using Hebrew Tools without Mastering Biblical Hebrew.* Grand Rapids: Zondervan, 2008.

Goodrick, Edward W. *Do It Yourself Hebrew and Greek: A Guide to Biblical Language Tools.* Grand Rapids: Zondervan, 1980.

Ready-Reference Tools by Passage

Baylor *Handbooks on the Hebrew Bible.* Waco, TX: Baylor University Press, 2006–.

Runge, Steven E., and Joshua R. Westbury. *Lexham Discourse Hebrew Bible* and *High Definition Old Testament: ESV Edition.* Bellingham, WA: Lexham, 2012. Available from Logos Bible Software.

Beginning Hebrew Grammars

Cook, John A., and Robert D. Holmstedt. *Beginning Biblical Hebrew: A Grammar and Illustrated Reader.* Grand Rapids: Baker Academic, 2013.

Fuller, Russell T., and Kyoungwon Choi. *An Invitation to Biblical Hebrew: A Beginning Grammar.* Grand Rapids: Kregel, 2006.

Futato, Mark D. *Beginning Biblical Hebrew.* Winona Lake, IN: Eisenbrauns, 2003.

Garrett, Duane A., and Jason S. DeRouchie. *A Modern Grammar for Biblical Hebrew* and *Workbook.* Nashville: Broadman & Holman, 2009.

Hackett, Jo Ann. *A Basic Introduction to Biblical Hebrew.* Peabody, MA: Hendrickson, 2010.

Pratico, Gary D., and Miles V. Van Pelt. *Basics of Biblical Hebrew: Grammar* and *Workbook.* 2nd ed. Grand Rapids: Zondervan, 2007.

Ross, Allen P. *Introducing Biblical Hebrew.* Grand Rapids: Baker Academic, 2001.

Webster, Brian L. *The Cambridge Introduction to Biblical Hebrew.* Cambridge: Cambridge University Press, 2009.

Intermediate Hebrew Grammars

Arnold, Bill T., and John H. Choi. *A Guide to Biblical Hebrew Syntax.* Cambridge: Cambridge University Press, 2003.

Fuller, Russell T., and Kyoungwon Choi. *An Invitation to Biblical Hebrew Syntax: An Intermediate Grammar.* Grand Rapids: Kregel, 2016.

Garrett, Duane A., and Jason S. DeRouchie. Pages 33–40, 64–66, 273–374 (chs. 6, 10.D, 36–41 + Appendixes 1–4) in *A Modern Grammar for Biblical Hebrew.* Nashville: Broadman & Holman, 2009.

✪ Merwe, Christo H. J. van der, Jackie A. Naudé, and Jan H. Kroeze. *A Biblical Hebrew Reference Grammar.* Biblical Languages: Hebrew 3. Sheffield, UK: Sheffield Academic, 2002.

Waltke, Bruce K., and M. O'Connor. *An Introduction to Biblical Hebrew Syntax.* Winona Lake, IN: Eisenbrauns, 1990.

✪ Williams, Ronald J., and John C. Beckman. *Williams' Hebrew Syntax*. 3rd ed. Toronto: University of Toronto Press, 2007.

Advanced Hebrew Grammars

Joüon, Paul, and T. Muraoka. *A Grammar of Biblical Hebrew*. 2nd ed. Subsidia Biblica 27. Rome: Gregorian & Biblical, 2011.

Kautzsch, E., ed. *Gesenius' Hebrew Grammar*. Translated by A. E. Cowley. 2nd ed. Oxford: Clarendon, 1910.

Aramaic Grammars

Greenspahn, Frederick E. *An Introduction to Aramaic*. 2nd ed. Atlanta: SBL, 2003.

Johns, Alger F. *A Short Grammar of Biblical Aramaic*. 2nd ed. Berrien Springs, MI: Andrews University Press, 1982.

Jumper, James N. *A Short Grammar of Biblical Aramaic: An Annotated Answer Key*. Berrien Springs, MI: Andrews University Press, 2003.

Rosenthal, Franz. *A Grammar of Biblical Aramaic*. Index of Biblical Citations compiled by Daniel M. Gurtner. 7th ed. Leipzig: Harrassowitz, 2006.

Stevenson, William B. *Grammar of Palestinian Jewish Aramaic*. Oxford: Clarendon, 1962; repr., Eugene, OR: Wipf & Stock, 2000.

Van Pelt, Miles V. *Basics of Biblical Aramaic: Complete Grammar, Lexicon, and Annotated Text*. Grand Rapids: Zondervan, 2011.

Historical Hebrew and Comparative Semitic Grammars

Bauer, Hans, and Pontus Leander. *Historische Grammatik der hebräischen Sprache des Alten Testamentes*. 2 vols. Halle: Niemeyer, 1918–22.

Bennett, Patrick R. *Comparative Semitic Linguistics: A Manual*. Winona Lake, IN: Eisenbrauns, 1998.

Bergsträsser, Gotthelf. *Hebräische Grammatik*. 2 vols. in 1. Leipzig: Hinrichs, 1929; repr., Hildesheim: Olms, 1962.

Goldenberg, Gideon. *Studies in Semitic Linguistics: Selected Writings*. Jerusalem: Magnes, 1998.

Lipiński, Edward. *Semitic Languages Outline of a Comparative Grammar*. 2nd ed. Orientalia Lovaniensia Analecta 80. Leuven: Peeters, 2000.

———. *Semitic Linguistics in Historical Perspective*. Orientalia Lovaniensia Analecta 230. Leuven: Peeters, 2014.

O'Leary, De Lacy. *Comparative Grammar of the Semitic Languages*. London: Routledge, 2001.

Sperber, Alexander. *A Historical Grammar of Biblical Hebrew*. Leiden: Brill, 1966.

Select Special Studies

Andersen, Francis I. *The Hebrew Verbless Clause in the Pentateuch*. JBLMS 14. Nashville: Abingdon, 1970.

———. *The Sentence in Biblical Hebrew*. Janua Linguarum, Series Practica 231. The Hague: Mouton, 1974.

Bergen, R. D., ed. *Biblical Hebrew and Discourse Linguistics*. Summer Institute of Linguistics. Winona Lake, IN: SIL, 1994.

Bodine, Walter, R., ed. *Discourse Analysis of Biblical Literature: What It Is and What It Offers*. SBLSS. Atlanta: Scholars Press, 1995.

Carson, D. A. "Grammatical Fallacies." In *Exegetical Fallacies*, 65–86. 2nd ed. Grand Rapids: Baker Academic, 1996.

Cook, John A. *Time and the Biblical Hebrew Verb: The Expression of Tense, Aspect, and Modality in Biblical Hebrew*. LSAWS 7. Winona Lake, IN: Eisenbrauns, 2012.

Dawson, D. A. *Text-Linguistics and Biblical Hebrew*. JSOTSup 177. Sheffield, UK: Sheffield Academic, 1994.

Dempster, Stephen G. *Linguistic Features of Hebrew Narrative: A Discourse Analysis of Narrative from the Classical Period*. Ph.D. diss., University of Toronto, 1985.

de Regt, L. J., J. de Waard, and J. P. Fokkelman, eds. *Literary Structure and Rhetorical Strategies in the Hebrew Bible*. Winona Lake, IN: Eisenbrauns, 1996.

DeRouchie, Jason S. *A Call to Covenant Love: Text-Grammar and Literary Structure in Deuteronomy 5–11*. Gorgias Dissertations 30/Biblical Studies 2. Piscataway, NJ: Gorgias, 2007.

Exter Blockland, A. F. den. *In Search of Syntax: Towards a Syntactic Text-Segmentation Model for Biblical Hebrew*. Amsterdam: VU University Press, 1995.

Gentry, Peter J. "The System of the Finite Verb in Classical Biblical Hebrew." *HS* 39 (1998): 7–39.

Heimerdinger, Jean-Marc. *Topic, Focus and Foreground in Ancient Hebrew Narratives*. JSOTSup 295. Sheffield, UK: Sheffield Academic, 1999.

Heller, Roy L. *Narrative Structure and Discourse Constellations: An Analysis of Clause Function in Biblical Hebrew Prose*. Harvard Semitic Studies 55. Winona Lake, IN: Eisenbrauns, 2004.

Longacre, Robert E. *Joseph: A Story of Divine Providence—A Text Theoretical and Textlinguistic Analysis of Genesis 37 and 39–48*. 2nd ed. Winona Lake, IN: Eisenbrauns, 2003.

Lunn, Nicholas P. *Word-Order Variation in Biblical Hebrew Poetry: Differentiating Pragmatics and Poetics*. Paternoster Biblical Monographs. Eugene, OR: Wipf & Stock, 2006.

Miller, Cynthia L. *The Representation of Speech in Biblical Hebrew Narrative: A Linguistic Analysis*. HSM 55. Winona Lake, IN: Eisenbrauns, 1999.

———, ed. *The Verbless Clause in Biblical Hebrew: Linguistic Approaches*. LSAWS 1. Winona Lake, IN: Eisenbrauns, 1999.

O'Connor, Michael Patrick. *Hebrew Verse Structure*. 2nd ed. Winona Lake, IN: Eisenbrauns, 1997.

Robar, Elizabeth. *The Verb and the Paragraph in Biblical Hebrew: A Cognitive-Linguistic Approach*. Studies in Semitic Languages and Linguistics 78. Leiden: Brill, 2014.

van Wolde, Ellen, ed. *Narrative Syntax and the Hebrew Bible: Papers of the Tilburg Conference 1996*. Biblical Interpretation 29. Leiden: Brill, 1997.

6

ARGUMENT-TRACING

Goal: Finish tracing the literary argument and create a message-driven outline that is tied to the passage's main point.

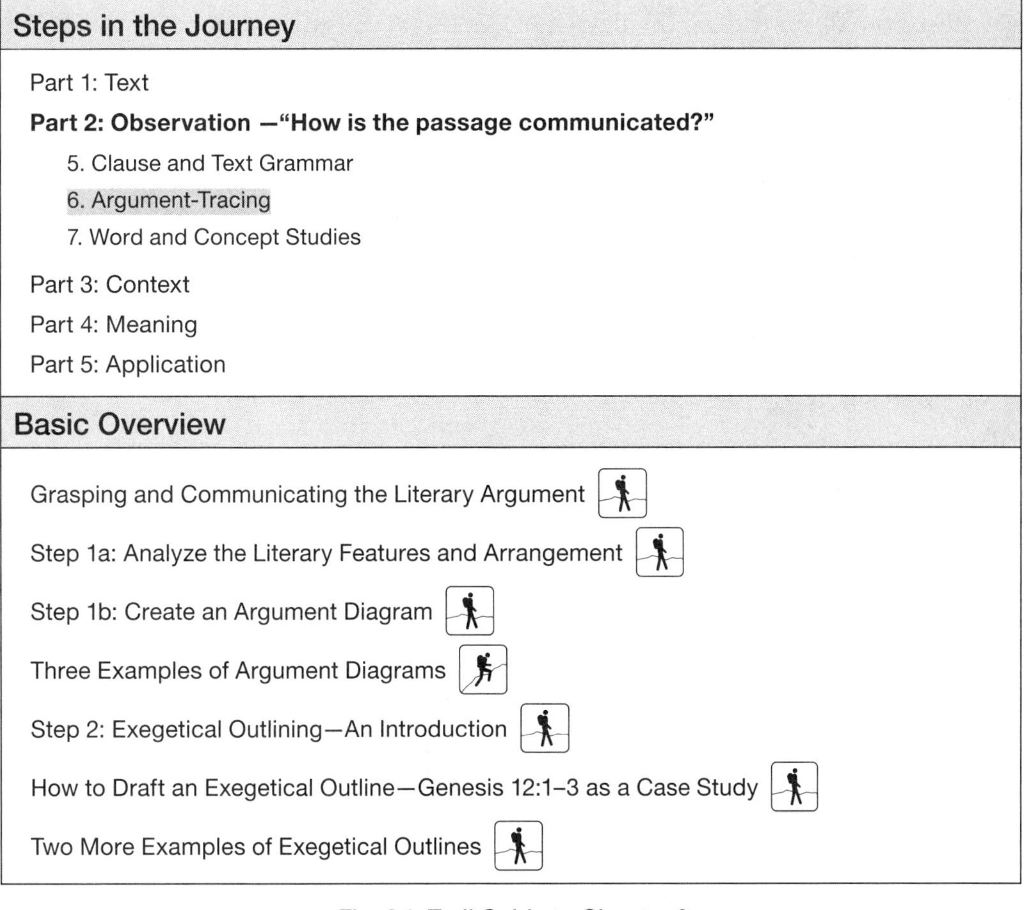

Steps in the Journey

Part 1: Text

Part 2: Observation —"How is the passage communicated?"

5. Clause and Text Grammar
6. Argument-Tracing
7. Word and Concept Studies

Part 3: Context

Part 4: Meaning

Part 5: Application

Basic Overview

Grasping and Communicating the Literary Argument

Step 1a: Analyze the Literary Features and Arrangement

Step 1b: Create an Argument Diagram

Three Examples of Argument Diagrams

Step 2: Exegetical Outlining—An Introduction

How to Draft an Exegetical Outline—Genesis 12:1–3 as a Case Study

Two More Examples of Exegetical Outlines

Fig. 6.1. Trail Guide to Chapter 6

Grasping and Communicating the Literary Argument

Once we establish the text's genre, literary units, and text hierarchy (chaps. 1–2), determine its original wording (chap. 3), and translate and assess the grammar (chaps. 4–5), we are ready to study more closely the compositional features and arrangement of the parts. Perhaps more than any other step in the exegetical process, this one helps us grasp a passage's message. This level of structural analysis has two parts:

1. Analyze Literary Features and Arrangement and Create an Argument Diagram

Drawing on what we already started in our assessment of genre and literary units, we must now finish tracing the details of the literary argument in order to finalize our understanding of the thought flow. Here we seek to grasp how the author communicates his message and to establish the interrelationship and development of all the parts. By ***literary argument*** I mean the way in which an author structures his thoughts in order to communicate reality as he intends his audience to view it. Seeing this reality rightly *will* change us. Arguments seek to compel beliefs or actions, and they come in all genres, whether narrative plots, hortatory sermons, poetic prayers, or the like.

Argument-tracing is often aided by creating a graphic diagram of a passage. *Arcing* and *bracketing* are two helpful ways to do this, as I will illustrate below. This argument diagram visually captures the relationships of the various ***propositions*** (i.e., the distinct thoughts in a passage).

2. Draft an Exegetical Outline

Once we grasp the entire thought flow, we should articulate the passage's structure by means of an exegetically grounded, message-driven outline. The best outlines focus on message and not just content and clarify how the passage fills out its main idea.

Step 1a: Analyze the Literary Features and Arrangement

It is important for us to recognize that the biblical authors wrote their words for the *ears* and not just the eyes. Moses set this pattern when he commissioned the priests to "*read* this law before all Israel in their *hearing*" every seven years (Deut. 31:9–11). The textual law would become an oral law, and with this, Moses' call to "today" heed God's voice (e.g., 4:39–40; 6:6; 8:1) would stand as a fresh commission from generation to generation.

Within this context, audiences would have certainly heard the repetition of the connector וְ (gloss "and") + verb at the head of most Hebrew clauses, and so departures from this pattern would have caused them to pause, guiding their understanding of literary structure and of the author's emphases, agenda, main point, and so on.[1] Furthermore, a text's grammatical features (conjunctions, discourse markers, verb patterns, etc.) are almost always accompanied by shifts in content and style. The biblical authors used both the formal and literary elements to help listening audiences discern a passage's thought flow and message. Among these artistic surface features are repetition, inclusio (or book-ending), terseness, ellipsis (gapping), rhyme or other sound patterns, and parallelism as a structuring feature ("Guidelines for Interpreting the Psalms" in chapter 1).

As an example of assessing literary features and arrangement, let's consider the book of Jonah, whose biographical nature sets it apart among the Prophets. The entire story is framed by the prophet's flight from God (Jonah 1:3) and the reason for his flight (4:2). Immediately after the Ninevites repent, Jonah declares, "O Lord, is not this what I said when I was yet in my country? That is why I made haste to flee to Tarshish; for I knew that you are a gracious God and merciful, slow to anger and abounding in steadfast love, and relenting from disaster" (4:2). The prophet of YHWH does not like the character of YHWH, and this irony is matched by a number of other literary features in the book. For example, the pagan sailors honor God by sacrifice (1:16), whereas YHWH's own prophet is defiant. Jonah declares at the end of his song of deliverance, "Salvation belongs to the Lord!" (2:9[H10]), and this truth is then evidenced both in Nineveh's repentance and in YHWH's withholding punishment (3:6–10). Nevertheless, while God rescues the prophet from death, in the end Jonah wishes to die rather than live (4:8) because God allowed the Ninevites to live instead of die (3:10). Even as YHWH's prophet, Jonah cannot accept God's "steadfast love" (4:2)—unless he is the recipient (2:8–9[H9–10]).

The story of Jonah witnesses both a linear and parallel pattern that we could lay out as A-B-C-D-A′-B′-C′-D′-E. It's the unexpected nature of the last unit that calls us to find in it the main point of the story—YHWH's lesson on steadfast love.

1. In his commentary on Genesis, Robert Alter retained "every 'and' and every element of parataxis" in translation, being convinced that the authors intended their listeners to hear the repeated connector וְ. He writes, "The general practice of modern English translators of suppressing the 'and' when it is attached to a verb has the effect of changing the tempo, rhythm, and construction of events in biblical narrative. . . . The *waw*, whatever is claimed about its linguistic function, is by no means an inaudible element in the phonetics of the Hebrew text: we must keep constantly in mind that these narratives were composed to be *heard*, not merely to be decoded by a reader's eye. The reiterated 'and,' then, plays an important role in creating the rhythm of the story, in phonetically punctuating the forward-driving movement of the prose" (*Genesis: Translation and Commentary* [New York: Norton, 1996], xix–xx).

I. Jonah's first experience of YHWH's steadfast love (1:1–2:10[H11])
- A. YHWH's initial call for a message of steadfast love (1:1–2)
- B. Jonah's personal need for steadfast love (1:3–16)
- C. YHWH's demonstration of steadfast love (1:17[H2:1])
- D. Jonah's positive response to YHWH's steadfast love (2:1–10[H2:2–11])

II. Jonah's second experience of YHWH's steadfast love (3:1–4:11)
- A. YHWH's second call for a message of steadfast love (3:1–2)
- B. Nineveh's corporate need for steadfast love (3:3–9)
- C. YHWH's demonstration of steadfast love (3:10)
- D. Jonah's negative response to YHWH's steadfast love (4:1–3)
- E. Conclusion: YHWH's lesson on his steadfast love (4:4–11)

Fig. 6.2. Exegetical Outline of Jonah

From the beginning of the drama to its end, the author pushes the reader to stand in awe of YHWH and to not want to be like Jonah. *YHWH* calls Jonah to Nineveh (1:2). *He* sends the storm when Jonah disobeys (1:4). *He* intensifies the storm to force the sailors to toss Jonah overboard (1:13). *He* is the object of the sailors' praise (1:16). *He* provides the great fish to rescue Jonah (1:17[H2:1]). *He* stands as the object of Jonah's praise from the fish's belly (2:2–9[H3–10]). *He* moves the fish to vomit up Jonah on the beach (2:10[H11]). *He* graciously resends Jonah to call Nineveh to repent (3:1–2). *He* responds to the Ninevites' repentance by relenting from punishing them (3:10). *His* steadfast love toward those who call on him makes Jonah angry (4:1–2). *YHWH* provides the plant, the worm, and the scorching east wind to instruct Jonah in his ways (4:6–8). *He* calls his prophet to value human life and to celebrate his bestowal of steadfast love. YHWH is the main character in the drama. Jonah is but a foil for exalting YHWH and his steadfast love.

To determine a text's message, we must carefully assess the passage's compositional features and arrangement. Doing so helps us better grasp the author's agenda and main point.

Step 1b: Create an Argument Diagram

To understand a passage's structure, we must evaluate the relationship of every proposition, clause, and larger text unit. This type of appraisal is most natural when the argument is chronologically or logically linear (A-B-C-D-E) as opposed to parallel

(A-B-C-A′-B′-C′) or symmetric (A-B-C-B′-A′). Regardless, in each structure every proposition contributes in its own way to developing the passage's main idea. The relationships between propositions can be either coordinate or subordinate.

1. ***Coordinate relationships*** are those that stand side by side. These elements could operate independently in *series*, in *progression* pointing to a climax, as *alternative* possibilities of a given situation, or as *both* true or *both* false.
2. ***Subordinate relationships*** always have a main clause or text unit and then another that restates, stands distinct from, or stands contrary to the main clause or text.
   a. *Restatement* exists:
      i. When a stated action is followed by the manner for fulfilling that action,
      ii. When a comparison between two or more entities exists,
      iii. When the same thing is stated both negatively and positively,
      iv. When there is a question and an answer,
      v. When an idea is then explained,
      vi. When a general statement is then specified, or
      vii. When a fact is then interpreted.
   b. *Distinct statements* are evident:
      i. When one statement provides a ground or reason for another statement,
      ii. When one statement draws an inference from another,
      iii. When a single statement bilaterally grounds two different statements that frame it,
      iv. When there is an action and its result or an action and its purpose,
      v. When there is a condition for meeting a greater end,
      vi. When there is a specific temporal or locative marker, or
      vii. When anticipation through promise is accompanied by its fulfillment.
   c. *Contrary statements* exist:
      i. When a concessive relationship is marked through a term such as *although*, or
      ii. When a stated situation is followed by a response.

I use these categories to assess every clause and text unit of every passage that I exegete, whether in biblical prose, prophecy, or poetry. Figure 6.3 lists the most common types of coordinate and subordinate relationships present in texts. I have included abbreviations or symbols that you may find helpful in marking up your own passage.[2]

2. My approach to analyzing discourse and tracing arguments in both the Old and New Testaments is highly indebted to the teaching and unpublished hermeneutics notes of Daniel P. Fuller (1925–), professor emeritus of hermeneutics at Fuller Theological Seminary and only child of Charles E. Fuller, cofounder of the school. My first encounters with the methodology related directly to the study of the English Bible and Greek New Testament and came in the classrooms and writings of his former students—Ted Dorman (Taylor University, 1993), Scott J. Hafemann (Gordon-Conwell Theological Seminary, 1995), John Piper (*Biblical Exegesis: Discovering the Meaning of*

Coordinate
• ***Series (S)*:** Each proposition makes its own independent contribution to a whole (English signal: *and, moreover, likewise, neither, nor*).
• ***Progression (P)*:** Like series, but each proposition is a further step toward a climax (English signal: *then, and, moreover, furthermore*).
• ***Alternate (A)*:** Each proposition expresses a different possibility arising from a situation (English signal: *or, but, while, on the other hand*).
• ***Both-And (B&)*:** Two propositions that are surprisingly both true or both false (English signal: *both . . . and, neither . . . nor*).
Subordinate
Restatement
• ***Action-Manner (Ac/Mn)*:** An action and a more precise statement indicating the way or manner in which the action is carried out (also called Way-End) (English signal: *in that, by + participles*).
• ***Comparison (Cf)*:** An action and a statement that clarifies that action by showing what it is like (English signal: *even as, as . . . so, like, just as*).
• ***Negative-Positive (–/+)*:** Two statements, one of which is denied so that the other is enforced. This is also the relationship implicit in contrasting statements (English signal: *not . . . but*).
• ***Question-Answer (Q/A)*:** The statement of a question and the answer to that question (English signal: *?*).
• ***Idea-Explanation (Id/Exp)*:** The relationship between a statement and another clarifying its meaning by expounding on a single word or the entire idea (English signal: *that is, in other words*).
• ***General-Specific (Gn/Sp)*:** A proposition stating a whole and a second stating one or more parts of that whole (English signal: *such as, for example*).
• ***Fact-Interpretation (Ft/In)*:** A statement and its interpretation (English signal: *that is, which is, meaning*).

Fig. 6.3. Definitions for the Various Propositional Relationships

---

Biblical Texts [Minneapolis: Desiring God, 1999], http://cdn.desiringgod.org/pdf/booklets/BTBX.pdf), and Thomas R. Schreiner (*Interpreting the Pauline Epistles*, 2nd ed. [Grand Rapids: Baker Academic, 2011], 97–124). Both Piper (11) and Schreiner (98n2) openly acknowledge their indebtedness to Fuller's teaching. Then, in my doctoral thesis, I sought to discover how to track thought flow and to trace arguments in reported speech of Old Testament prose—a context in which almost every clause begins with the connector וְ (gloss "and"). During this time I noted that Robert E. Longacre, the father of Old Testament discourse analysis, also attributes his earliest motivation into the field to Fuller's 1959 hermeneutics notes (*Joseph: A Story of Divine Providence—A Text Theoretical and Textlinguistic Analysis of Genesis 37 and 39–48*, 2nd ed. [Winona Lake, IN: Eisenbrauns, 2003], 60). While a number of Old and New Testament scholars have proposed similar categories, I use Fuller's categories and approach because of their simplicity and clarity (cf. Francis I. Andersen, *The Sentence in Biblical Hebrew*, Janua Linguarum, Series Practica 231 [The Hague: Mouton, 1974], 24–28, 36; L. J. de Regt, *A Parametric Model for Syntactic Studies of a Textual Corpus, Demonstrated on the Hebrew of Deuteronomy 1–30* and *Supplement*, 2 vols. [Assen: Van Gorcum, 1988], 1:10, 34–43; Longacre, *Joseph*, 83, 107; George H. Guthrie and J. Scott Duvall, *Biblical Greek Exegesis: A Graded Approach to Learning Intermediate and Advanced Greek* [Grand Rapids: Zondervan, 1998], 43–52). For my application of the model in Deuteronomy 5–11, see Jason S. DeRouchie, *A Call to Covenant Love: Text-Grammar and Literary Structure in Deuteronomy 5–11*, Gorgias Dissertations 30/Biblical Studies 2 (Piscataway, NJ: Gorgias, 2007), esp. 87–92, 217–67. For both training and practice in this approach to establishing a text's structure, visit www.Biblearc.com.

Distinct Statement
• **Ground (G):** A statement and the argument or reason for that statement (supporting proposition follows) (English signal: *for, because, since*). • ***Inference (∴):*** A statement and the argument or reason for that statement (supporting proposition precedes) (English signal: *therefore, accordingly, so*). • ***Bilateral (BL):*** A proposition that supports two other propositions, one preceding and one following (English signal: *for, because, therefore, so*). • ***Action-Result (Ac/Res):*** An action and a consequence or result that accompanies that action (also called *Cause-Effect*) (English signal: *so that, that, with the result that*). • ***Action-Purpose (Ac/Pur):*** An action and its intended result (also called *End-Means*) (English signal: *in order that, so that, that, lest*). • ***Conditional (If/Th):*** Like action-result except that the existence of the action is only potential and the result is contingent on that action (English signal: *if . . . then, provided that, except, unless*). • ***Temporal (T):*** A statement and the occasion when it is true or can occur (English signal: *when, whenever, after, before*). • ***Locative (L):*** A statement and the place where it is true or can occur (English signal: *where, wherever*). • ***Anticipation-Fulfillment (Ant/F):*** A promise with its accompanying fulfillment (English signal: *and so*).
Contrary Statement
• ***Concessive (Csv):*** A main clause that stands despite a contrary statement (also called *Adversative*) (English signal: *although, though, yet, nevertheless, but, however*). • ***Situation-Response (Sit R):*** A situation and a surprising or counterintuitive response (English signal: *and*).
All these definitions are taken from https://Biblearc.com.

Fig. 6.3. Definitions for the Various Propositional Relationships (cont.)

All these relationships are helpfully defined and reviewed at https://Biblearc.com. This is one of the best online resources for personal Bible study, and it's my favorite tool for doing the actual brain work of analyzing a passage's thought flow and propositional relationships. Here you can create a text hierarchy through the *phrasing* module. Then, in the *discourse* module, you can identify the logical relationships of the various parts of your passage through arcing or bracketing. The process of arcing or bracketing a passage assists our interpretation in at least five ways:

- Arcing or bracketing pushes us to recognize that the Bible presents profound and often complex arguments and not bullet points of unrelated truths;
- Arcing or bracketing forces us to take every connecting word seriously;

- Arcing or bracketing helps us to ensure that we do not leave any clause or proposition unexamined;
- Arcing or bracketing causes us to ask many questions that we may have otherwise not considered;
- Arcing or bracketing moves us to the main point of the passage.

Naturally, the best way to be certain that you are tracing an argument correctly is to use the Hebrew, but a form-equivalent translation such as the New American Standard Bible (NASB) works very well. As an example of the approach in English, let's consider Deuteronomy 7:2–4, a text that we already looked at back in chapter 2.

		Connectors	Relationship
2	Then you shall utterly destroy them.	"Then"	Temporal marker
b	You shall make no covenant with them	Ø	Explanation of 2a
c	and show no favor to them.	"and"	Cont. explanation of 2a
3	Furthermore, you shall not intermarry with them;	"Furthermore"	Cont. explanation of 2a
b	you shall not give your daughters to their sons,	Ø	Explanation of 3a
c	nor shall you take their daughters for your sons.	"nor"	Cont. explanation of 3a
4	For they will turn your sons away from following Me to serve other gods;	"For"	Reason for 3bc
b	then the anger of the LORD will be kindled against you	"then"	Further reason for 3bc
c	and He will quickly destroy you.	"and"	Further reason for 3bc

Fig. 6.4. Text Hierarchy of Deuteronomy 7:2–4 in NASB

The text hierarchy in figure 6.4 represents the general thought flow and units of the discourse. The middle column identifies the various conjunctions (the null-set sign [Ø] represents the absence of any conjunction), and the far right column lists the types of relationships that the conjunctions signal.

Moses opens the passage in 2a by commanding Israel to destroy the Canaanites. The lack of conjunction in 2b signals that the unit initiated by 2b supplies an explanation of the command. I indented 2b and the clauses coordinated to it one tier to the right to signal the subordination to 2a. 2a supplies the *Idea* (Id), and what follows gives the *Explanation* (Exp) in 2b–4c. Specifically, destroying the Canaanites (2a) means at least three things: Israel should make no covenants with them, show them no favor, and not intermarry with them (2b–3a). The three prohibitions stand in *Series* (S) with

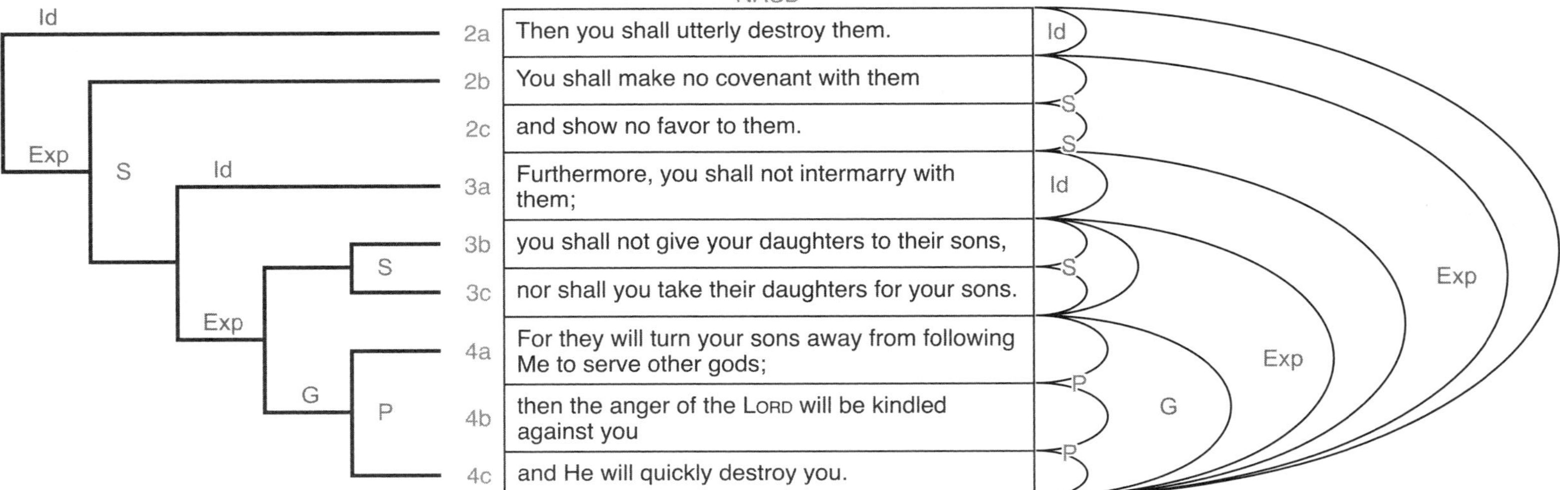
NASB
2a Then you shall utterly destroy them.
2b You shall make no covenant with them
2c and show no favor to them.
3a Furthermore, you shall not intermarry with them;
3b you shall not give your daughters to their sons,
3c nor shall you take their daughters for your sons.
4a For they will turn your sons away from following Me to serve other gods;
4b then the anger of the LORD will be kindled against you
4c and He will quickly destroy you.
Id
Exp
S
Id
Exp
S
G
P
Id
S
S
Id
S
P
P
G
Exp
Exp

Fig. 6.5. Bracket and Arc of Deuteronomy 7:2–4

each other, the initial two joined by *and* and the latter two joined by *Furthermore*. The lack of initial conjunction in 3b and the content in 3bc then signal that 3bc supplies an *Explanation* (Exp) of the *Idea* (Id) presented in 3a. I have indented the material accordingly. Not intermarrying means not giving one's daughters to their sons and not taking their daughters for one's sons. The "For" conjunction in 4a then begins an extended three-clause reason or *Ground* (G) why the Israelites must not intermarry with the Canaanites (4a–c)—because the pagans would move the Israelites to turn from YHWH, which would in turn kindle his anger, which would then result in his destroying them.

We can aid our visualization of the various relationships by bracketing (left) or arcing (right) the passage (fig. 6.5). Note how both the bracket and the arc identify two main sections—the initial command in 2a supplies the *Idea* (Id), whereas the rest of the unit in 2b–4c supplies the *Explanation* (Exp). Within the latter, 2b and 2c provide stand-alone comments in *Series* (S), whereas 3a includes its ow n *Explanation* (Exp), which has parallel prohibitions in *Series* (S) (3bc) followed by a *Ground* (G), which itself includes a *Progression* (P) of thought (4a–c).

You can go to https://Biblearc.com for further definitions, examples, and a host of training videos to show you how to trace the biblical authors' arguments. Biblearc has training both for English-only interpreters and for those using the original languages. In the rest of this chapter, I'll provide some examples that will help clarify why it is so crucial to discern the coordinate and subordinate relationships of the various parts of a passage. While I will include the Hebrew, I will also translate everything, so I encourage everyone to press ahead. The exegetical payoff will be beautiful.

Coordinate	Subordinate	
	Restatement	***Distinct Statement***
Series (S)	Action-Manner (Ac/Mn)	Ground (G)
Progression (P)	Comparison (Cf)	Inference (∴)
Alternate (A)	Negative-Positive (–/+)	Bilateral (BL)
Both-And (B&)	Question-Answer (Q/A)	Action-Result (Ac/Res)
	Idea-Explanation (Id/Exp)	Action-Purpose (Ac/Pur)
	General-Specific (Gn/Sp)	Conditional (If/Th)
	Fact-Interpretation (Ft/In)	Temporal (T)
	Contrary Statement	Locative (L)
	Concessive (Csv)	Anticipation-Fulfillment Ant/F)
	Situation-Response (Sit/R)	

Fig. 6.6. Types of Propositional Relationships

Three Examples of Argument Diagrams

Argument Diagram of Genesis 12:1–3

Picking up from the previous chapter (see "An Example of Text Grammar—Genesis 12:1–3" in chapter 5), this section will finish tracking the thought flow of Genesis 12:1–3. Because our study of logical relationships is built on our understanding of a passage's macro-structure, let me first recall my text hierarchy and translation of the passage. You will remember that the two imperatives "Go" (לֶךְ) and "Then be a blessing" (וֶהְיֵה) in 1a and 2d identify two distinct units, and each is followed by a chain of verbs (the initial grouping has three *weyiqtol* forms in 2a–c, and the next grouping has a *weyiqtol* and *weqatal* in 3a, c). These express the consequences that will result when Abram or those whom his covenant headship represents obey the commands.

The promises that motivate "going" all relate to Abram's offspring becoming a renowned nation. This is stage 1 of the Abrahamic covenant and is realized under the *Mosaic covenant* during Israel's initial tenure in the Promised Land. Next, the call is to "be a blessing," which is motivated by promises that culminate in stage 2 of the Abrahamic covenant—what we know as the *new covenant*. "Being a blessing" will result in God's bestowing favor and protection on his own (3ab) and ultimately in all the families of the earth being blessed (3c), the reversal of the Adamic curse.

וַיֹּ֤אמֶר יְהוָה֙ אֶל־אַבְרָ֔ם	1	And YHWH said to Abram,
לֶךְ־לְךָ֛ מֵאַרְצְךָ֥ וּמִמּֽוֹלַדְתְּךָ֖ וּמִבֵּ֣ית אָבִ֑יךָ אֶל־הָאָ֖רֶץ אֲשֶׁ֥ר אַרְאֶֽךָּ׃	b	Go from your land and from your kindred and from your father's house to the land that I will show you,
וְאֶֽעֶשְׂךָ֙ לְג֣וֹי גָּד֔וֹל	2	*so that* I may make you into a great nation,
וַאֲבָ֣רֶכְךָ֔	b	and may bless you,
וַאֲגַדְּלָ֖ה שְׁמֶ֑ךָ	c	and may make your name great.
וֶהְיֵ֖ה בְּרָכָֽה׃	d	Then be a blessing,
וַאֲבָֽרְכָה֙ מְבָ֣רְכֶ֔יךָ	3	*so that* I may bless those who bless you,
וּמְקַלֶּלְךָ֖ אָאֹ֑ר	b	but the one who curses you I will bind with a curse,
וְנִבְרְכ֣וּ בְךָ֔ כֹּ֖ל מִשְׁפְּחֹ֥ת הָאֲדָמָֽה׃	c	*with the result that* in you all the families of the ground may be blessed.

Fig. 6.7. Text Hierarchy of Genesis 12:1–3

At this point, our goal is to identify how all the parts correlate with one another. To do this, we will draw on the categories of coordinate and subordinate relationships highlighted in figures 6.5–6.6, and I will also create both an arc (see fig. 6.8) and a bracket (fig. 6.9) of the passage, which will help display the various relationships in an easy-to-track schematic. Whether you choose to arc or bracket your passage is simply a matter of preference, since both accomplish the same purpose. I have included both here simply to help visualize the different ways that each tool represents the propositional relationships. As noted, www.Biblearc.com provides a great one-stop shop for this type of exegetical analysis.

The goal in arcing and bracketing is to help visualize the relationships of all the parts in a given passage. We begin by identifying the most major units and assessing their logical relationships. In Genesis 12:1–3 we have the speech frame in 1a and the speech itself in 1b–3c. The *Idea* is presented in 1a, and the speech provides the *Explanation* for that idea. I have thus marked the respective units with "Id/Exp."

1a	וַיֹּ֤אמֶר יְהוָה֙ אֶל־אַבְרָ֔ם	And YHWH said to Abram,	Id
1b	לֶךְ־לְךָ֛ מֵאַרְצְךָ֥ וּמִמּֽוֹלַדְתְּךָ֖ וּמִבֵּ֣ית אָבִ֑יךָ אֶל־הָאָ֖רֶץ אֲשֶׁ֥ר אַרְאֶֽךָּ׃	"Go from your land and from your kindred and from your father's house to the land that I will show you,	Ac
2a	וְאֶֽעֶשְׂךָ֙ לְג֣וֹי גָּד֔וֹל	so that I may make you into a great nation,	P
2b	וַאֲבָרֶכְךָ֔	and may bless you,	P Pur
2c	וַאֲגַדְּלָ֖ה שְׁמֶ֑ךָ	and may make your name great.	
2d	וֶהְיֵ֖ה בְּרָכָֽה׃	Then be a blessing,	Ac P
3a	וַאֲבָֽרְכָה֙ מְבָ֣רְכֶ֔יךָ	so that I may bless those who bless you,	S Ac
3b	וּמְקַלֶּלְךָ֖ אָאֹ֑ר	but the one who curses you I will bind with a curse,	Pur
3c	וְנִבְרְכ֣וּ בְךָ֔ כֹּ֖ל מִשְׁפְּחֹ֥ת הָאֲדָמָֽה׃	with the result that in you all the families of the ground may be blessed."	Res

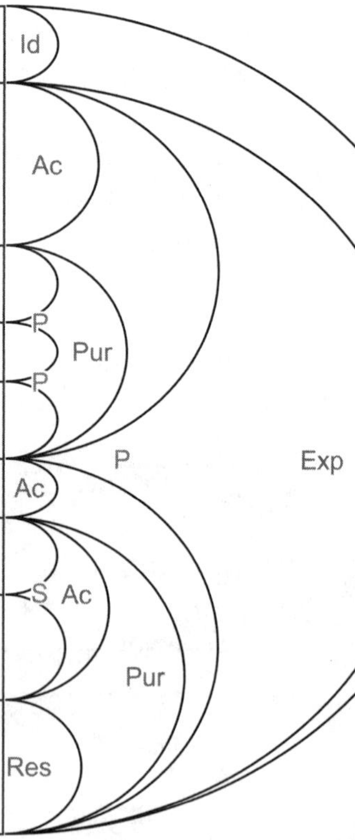

Exp

Fig. 6.8. Arc of Genesis 12:1–3

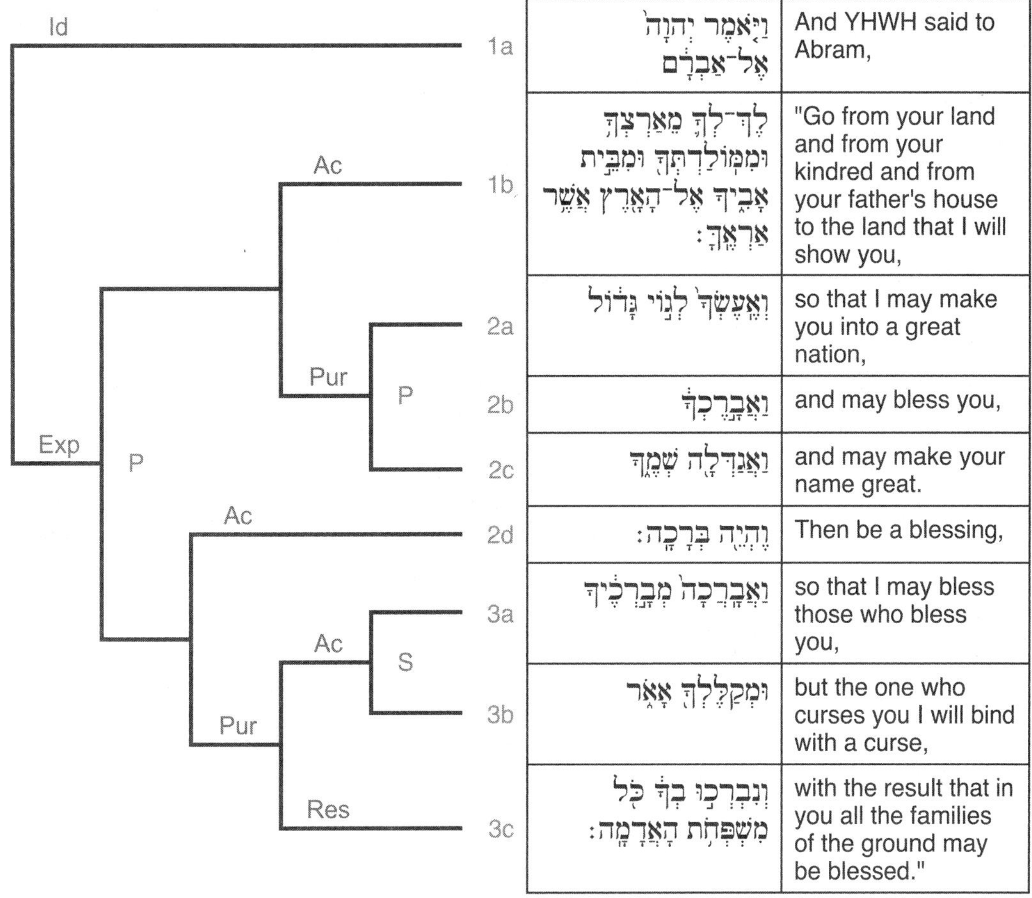

1a	וַיֹּאמֶר יְהוָה אֶל־אַבְרָם	And YHWH said to Abram,
1b	לֶךְ־לְךָ מֵאַרְצְךָ וּמִמּוֹלַדְתְּךָ וּמִבֵּית אָבִיךָ אֶל־הָאָרֶץ אֲשֶׁר אַרְאֶךָּ׃	"Go from your land and from your kindred and from your father's house to the land that I will show you,
2a	וְאֶעֶשְׂךָ לְגוֹי גָּדוֹל	so that I may make you into a great nation,
2b	וַאֲבָרֶכְךָ	and may bless you,
2c	וַאֲגַדְּלָה שְׁמֶךָ	and may make your name great.
2d	וֶהְיֵה בְּרָכָה׃	Then be a blessing,
3a	וַאֲבָרְכָה מְבָרְכֶיךָ	so that I may bless those who bless you,
3b	וּמְקַלֶּלְךָ אָאֹר	but the one who curses you I will bind with a curse,
3c	וְנִבְרְכוּ בְךָ כֹּל מִשְׁפְּחֹת הָאֲדָמָה׃	with the result that in you all the families of the ground may be blessed."

Fig. 6.9. Bracket of Genesis 12:1–3

Within the "explanation" section, the two imperatives in 1b and 2d mark the beginning of two discrete units. You will recall that when two imperatives are joined by the connector וְ (gloss "and"), the second imperative stands as a consequence or progression from the first. I have thus grouped each imperative unit together under a single arc (1b–2c and 2d–3c) and placed between them a *P*, which stands for *Progression*. Progression is a coordinate relationship like a series, but in a progression each proposition is a further step toward a climax. We often signal it in English with *then*, *and*, *moreover*, or *furthermore*. I have used *then* in my translation.

Next let us consider the initial imperatival unit in 1b–2c. There we have the imperative action followed by three consequences, which could express purpose or result. I have called 1b the *Action* (Ac) and 2a–c the *Purpose* (Pur). Within the purpose, I also placed under three arcs the three coordinated statements, which themselves appear to stand in *Progression*. I have thus added a *P* between the arcs. God's making Abram into a great nation will lead to blessing, which will lead to a great name.

As in the initial imperatival unit in 1b–2c, the second also has *Action* (Ac) in 2d and *Purpose* (Pur) in 3a–c. Here, rather than three promises, there is only one main one in 3a, with 3c providing an ultimate result. Verses 3ab shapes a unit by contrastive matching (V_ + _V) (see "More on Marked and Unmarked Clauses" in chapter 5). I have placed 3a and 3b in *Series*, marked by the *S*, because the order has no bearing on the logic. Furthermore, because I believe that the shift from *weyiqtol* to *weqatal* in 3c signals that the anticipation of blessing the world is the ultimate result and goal of all the obedience, I have marked the relationship between 3ab and 3c as *Result* (Res) in order to highlight climax.

With just a glimpse at either the arc or the bracket, I see that of the two units in the *Explanation* (Exp), the second bears more rhetorical weight. The *Progression* (P) at 2d marks this. Then the *Result* (Res) at 3c immediately shows me that the culminating goal of the entire passage is that all the families of the ground would be blessed in Abram. I am now in a position to attempt to capture the message and flow of the passage in an outline, which we will do after a couple more examples of the arcing and bracketing process.

Argument Diagram of Habakkuk 3:17–19

One of the great Old Testament expressions of persevering faith comes in Habakkuk 3:17–19. I want to walk through my text hierarchy (fig. 6.10), and then we will track the logical relationships through an arc and a bracket.

כִּֽי־תְאֵנָ֣ה לֹֽא־תִפְרָ֗ח	17	When the fig tree has not budded
וְאֵ֤ין יְבוּל֙ בַּגְּפָנִ֔ים	b	and there is no fruit at the vines,
כִּחֵשׁ֙ מַעֲשֵׂה־זַ֔יִת	c	the produce of the olive has failed
וּשְׁדֵמ֖וֹת לֹא־עָ֣שָׂה אֹ֑כֶל	d	and the fields do not yield food,
גָּזַ֤ר מִמִּכְלָה֙ צֹ֔אן	e	when the fold has not divided sheep,
וְאֵ֥ין בָּקָ֖ר בָּרְפָתִֽים׃	f	and there is no cattle in the stalls,
וַאֲנִ֖י בַּיהוָ֣ה אֶעְל֑וֹזָה	18	then I will exult in YHWH.
אָגִ֖ילָה בֵּאלֹהֵ֥י יִשְׁעִֽי׃	b	I will rejoice in the God of my salvation.
יְהוִ֤ה אֲדֹנָי֙ חֵילִ֔י	19	YHWH my Lord is my strength;
וַיָּ֤שֶׂם רַגְלַי֙ כָּֽאַיָּל֔וֹת	b	and he has made my feet like the does',
וְעַ֥ל בָּמוֹתַ֖י יַדְרִכֵֽנִי	c	and on the heights he makes me walk.

Fig. 6.10. Text Hierarchy of Habakkuk 3:17–19

Reading the translation, you can see that the passage has two parts—the temporal protasis beginning with כִּי ("when") in verse 17, and the declarative apodosis starting in verse 18 with the explicit first common singular pronoun וַאֲנִי ("then I"). The protasis itself has two parts: agricultural devastation in 17a–d and the ruin of the livestock in 17ef. The apodosis opens in 18a with a statement, "then I will exult in YHWH" (וַאֲנִי בַּיהוָה אֶעְלוֹזָה), which is then explained in 18b, "I will rejoice in the God of my salvation" (אָגִילָה בֵּאלֹהֵי יִשְׁעִי). Asyndeton marks the explanation. Then what follows in verse 19 is a further inner-paragraph comment, signaled also by asyndeton, which appears to express the reason why Habakkuk commits to celebrate his God—he will do so because "YHWH my Lord is my strength" (יְהוִה אֲדֹנָי חֵילִי, in 19a), and because he has empowered him to rise above his adversities through faith (19bc).

With this basic thought flow in hand, let us now create an argument diagram, considering the logical relationships evident in the text. I will again both arc (fig. 6.11) and bracket (fig. 6.12) the passage, but you need engage in only one of these options.

17a כִּי־תְאֵנָה לֹא־תִפְרָח When the fig tree has not budded
17b וְאֵין יְבוּל בַּגְּפָנִים and there is no fruit at the vines,
17c כִּחֵשׁ מַעֲשֵׂה־זַיִת the produce of the olive has failed,
17d וּשְׁדֵמוֹת לֹא־עָשָׂה אֹכֶל and the fields do not yield food,
17e גָּזַר מִמִּכְלָה צֹאן when the fold has not divided sheep,
17f וְאֵין בָּקָר בָּרְפָתִים׃ and there is no cattle in the stalls,
18a וַאֲנִי בַּיהוָה אֶעְלוֹזָה then I will exult in YHWH.
18b אָגִילָה בֵּאלֹהֵי יִשְׁעִי׃ I will rejoice in the God of my salvation.
19a יְהוִה אֲדֹנָי חֵילִי YHWH my Lord is my strength;
19b וַיָּשֶׂם רַגְלַי כָּאַיָּלוֹת and he has made my feet like the does',
19c וְעַל בָּמוֹתַי יַדְרִכֵנִי and on the heights he makes me walk.
S
Id
S
Exp
T
S
S
Id
Exp
S
G
P

Fig. 6.11. Arc of Habakkuk 3:17–19

First we must distinguish the temporal protasis in 17a–f from the declarative apodosis in 18a–19c. I use the symbol *T* to mark the *Temporal* nature of the protasis. The temporal unit distinguishes between God's curse on crops in 17a–d and his curse on domesticated animals in 17e–f, so I put arcs or brackets over the various sections.

Note that each unit bears a parallel structure: a finite verb clause in 17a and 17e is followed by a verbless clause beginning with the negative particle אֵין ("there is not") in 17b and 17f. These two groupings are coordinate and interchangeable, so I mark the relationship as *Series* with the symbol *S*. Within the first of these units, I have also treated 17cd as an *Explication* (Exp) of the *Idea* (Id) presented in 17ab. The second pair of clauses build on the content of the initial two clauses, developing the concept of agricultural devastation. We could translate it: "When the fig tree has not budded, and there is no fruit at the vines—I mean when the produce of the olive has failed, and the fields do not yield food."

Coming to the declarative apodosis in verses 18–19, we begin with an *Idea-Explanation* (Id/Exp) in 18ab. After declaring, "Then I will exult in YHWH" (וַאֲנִי בַּיהוָה אֶעְלוֹזָה), Habakkuk clarifies that what he means is "I will rejoice in the God of my salvation" (אָגִילָה בֵּאלֹהֵי יִשְׁעִי). The explanation is signaled by asyndeton.

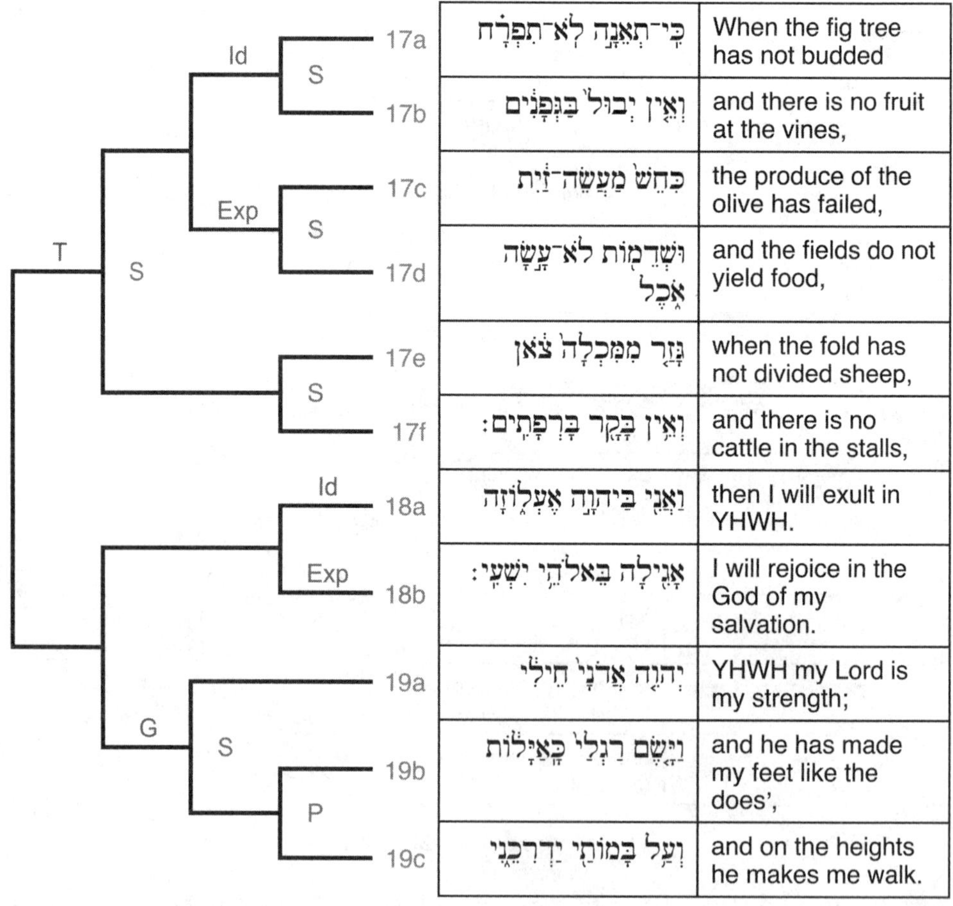
T
S
G
Id
Exp
S
P
17a כִּי־תְאֵנָה לֹא־תִפְרָח When the fig tree has not budded
17b וְאֵין יְבוּל בַּגְּפָנִים and there is no fruit at the vines,
17c כִּחֵשׁ מַעֲשֵׂה־זַיִת the produce of the olive has failed,
17d וּשְׁדֵמוֹת לֹא־עָשָׂה אֹכֶל and the fields do not yield food,
17e גָּזַר מִמִּכְלָה צֹאן when the fold has not divided sheep,
17f וְאֵין בָּקָר בָּרְפָתִים׃ and there is no cattle in the stalls,
18a וַאֲנִי בַּיהוָה אֶעְלוֹזָה then I will exult in YHWH.
18b אָגִילָה בֵּאלֹהֵי יִשְׁעִי׃ I will rejoice in the God of my salvation.
19a יְהוִה אֲדֹנָי חֵילִי YHWH my Lord is my strength;
19b וַיָּשֶׂם רַגְלַי כָּאַיָּלוֹת and he has made my feet like the does',
19c וְעַל בָּמוֹתַי יַדְרִכֵנִי and on the heights he makes me walk.

Fig. 6.12. Bracket of Habakkuk 3:17–19

What follows in verse 19 unpacks further why the prophet will rejoice in God, and even though there is not a formal causal conjunction such as כִּי ("because, for"), the relationship between verses 18 and 19 appears to be a *Ground* (G): "*Because* YHWH my Lord is my strength and empowers me to rise above my challenges, *therefore* I will rejoice in the God of my salvation." Oh, that we would continue to savor our Savior amid times of testing (Matt. 5:11–12; Rom. 5:3; James 1:2)! The last two clauses are tied together thematically and appear to express a *Progression* (P): God first makes Habakkuk's feet like the does' and then moves him to walk in the heights.

Some of the logical relationships that I identified when doing my text hierarchy I have now been able to concretize and display through arcing or bracketing the passage. I hope that you can begin to see the benefit of identifying the coordinate and subordinate relationships. Engaging in arcing or bracketing forces us to ask all the right questions and allows us to visualize in an instant the way in which all the parts of a text relate to one another.

Argument Diagram of Exodus 19:4–6

We are now ready to finish tracing the argument in Exodus 19:4–6 (fig. 6.13). Before taking this step, it is always helpful to look over our text hierarchy in order to recall the passage's main sections.

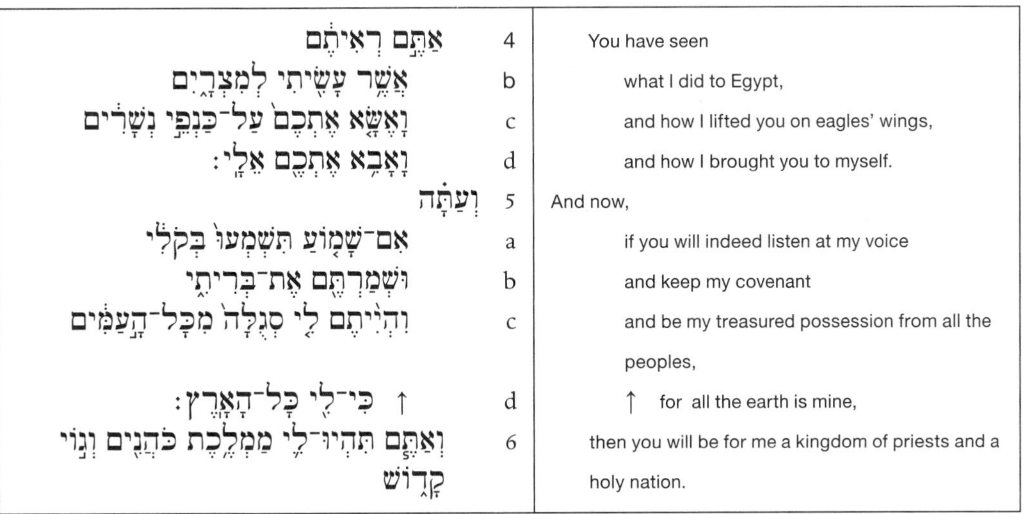

אַתֶּם רְאִיתֶם	4	You have seen
אֲשֶׁר עָשִׂיתִי לְמִצְרָיִם	b	what I did to Egypt,
וָאֶשָּׂא אֶתְכֶם עַל־כַּנְפֵי נְשָׁרִים	c	and how I lifted you on eagles' wings,
וָאָבִא אֶתְכֶם אֵלָי׃	d	and how I brought you to myself.
וְעַתָּה	5	And now,
אִם־שָׁמוֹעַ תִּשְׁמְעוּ בְּקֹלִי	a	if you will indeed listen at my voice
וּשְׁמַרְתֶּם אֶת־בְּרִיתִי	b	and keep my covenant
וִהְיִיתֶם לִי סְגֻלָּה מִכָּל־הָעַמִּים	c	and be my treasured possession from all the peoples,
↑ כִּי־לִי כָּל־הָאָרֶץ׃	d	↑ for all the earth is mine,
וְאַתֶּם תִּהְיוּ־לִי מַמְלֶכֶת כֹּהֲנִים וְגוֹי קָדוֹשׁ	6	then you will be for me a kingdom of priests and a holy nation.

Fig. 6.13. Text Hierarchy of Exodus 19:4–6

Note that verse 4 recalls YHWH's great deliverance of Israel from Egypt. And then, with the inference marker וְעַתָּה ("and now") in 5a, verses 5–6 draw a conclusion from the great salvation related to Israel's sacred task. The inference section itself has two units: the conditional protasis in verse 5 ("if") and the apodosis in verse 6 ("then") (see "Determining the Protasis and Apodosis in Exodus 19:5–6" in chapter 5). Because God saved Israel, if the people will heed his voice, keep his covenant, and be his treasured possession from all the earth, then they will serve for him as a kingdom of priests and holy nation. We can now display these various relationships through an arc (fig. 6.14) or bracket (fig. 6.15).

Our first step is to distinguish the understood *Ground* (G) in verse 4 from the *Inference* (∴) in verses 5–6. There is no כִּי ("because, for") in verse 4, but we do find וְעַתָּה ("and now") in verse 5, which identifies the inference.

Within 4a we have the initial statement that Moses' audience had seen something. This is the *Idea* (Id), which is then unpacked through the *Explanation* (Exp) given in the compound relative clauses in 4b–d. A *Progression* (P) is evident: They saw or experienced (1) what God did to Egypt, and (2) how he carried them, and then (3) how he brought them to himself. Now they were with God at his mountain, and he identifies the implications of this reality in verses 5–6.

The inference section has a conditional protasis in verse 5 and an apodosis in verse 6, which I identify with *If-Then* (If-Th). The "if" section contains a progression

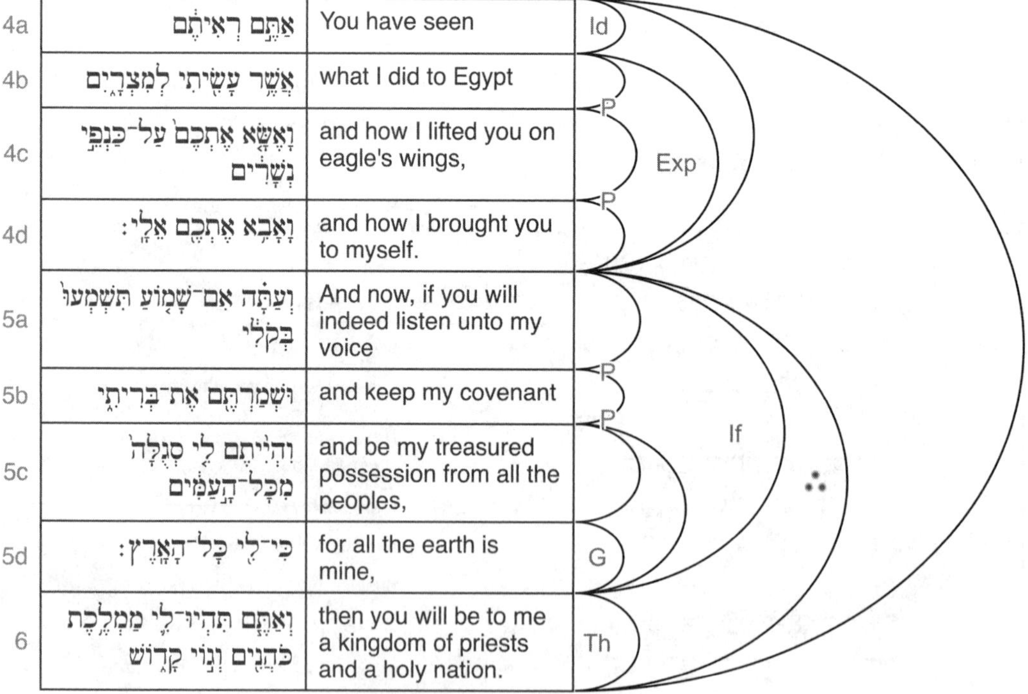

Fig. 6.14. Arc of Exodus 19:4–6

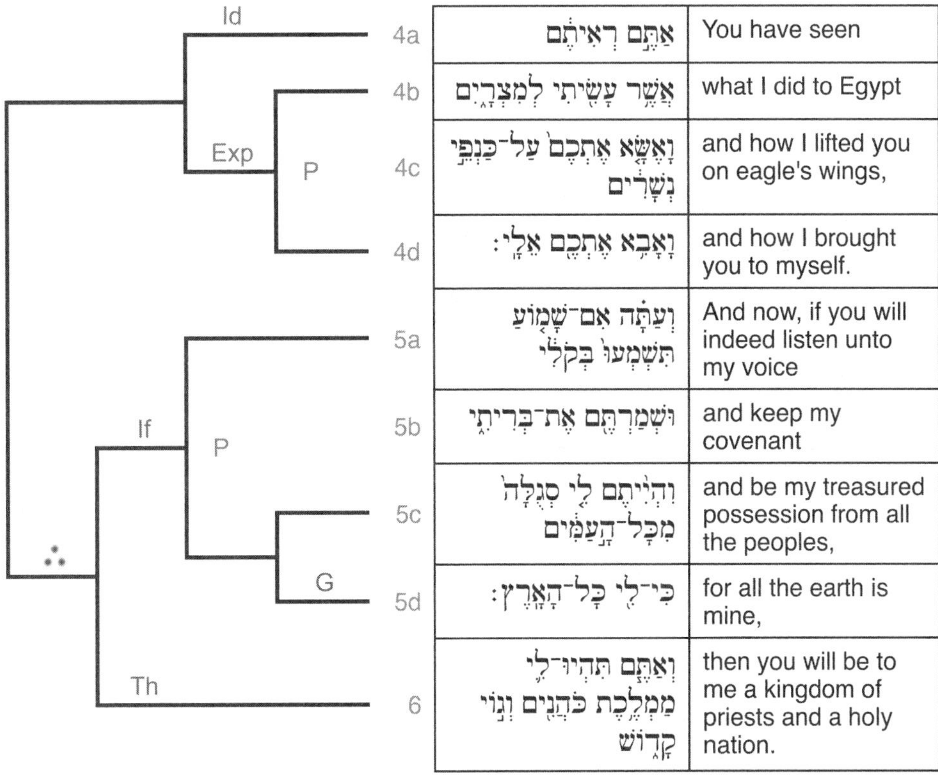

4a	אַתֶּם רְאִיתֶם	You have seen
4b	אֲשֶׁר עָשִׂיתִי לְמִצְרָיִם	what I did to Egypt
4c	וָאֶשָּׂא אֶתְכֶם עַל־כַּנְפֵי נְשָׁרִים	and how I lifted you on eagle's wings,
4d	וָאָבִא אֶתְכֶם אֵלָי׃	and how I brought you to myself.
5a	וְעַתָּה אִם־שָׁמוֹעַ תִּשְׁמְעוּ בְּקֹלִי	And now, if you will indeed listen unto my voice
5b	וּשְׁמַרְתֶּם אֶת־בְּרִיתִי	and keep my covenant
5c	וִהְיִיתֶם לִי סְגֻלָּה מִכָּל־הָעַמִּים	and be my treasured possession from all the peoples,
5d	כִּי־לִי כָּל־הָאָרֶץ׃	for all the earth is mine,
6	וְאַתֶּם תִּהְיוּ־לִי מַמְלֶכֶת כֹּהֲנִים וְגוֹי קָדוֹשׁ	then you will be to me a kingdom of priests and a holy nation.

Fig. 6.15. Bracket of Exodus 19:4–6

of three actions that appear to serve as the means by which the Israelites will reach God's goal of their serving as a kingdom of priests and a holy nation. Later we will consider more fully what this task actually means, but here I want to note the type of condition that is evident. I could say, "If I fly on the airplane, I will arrive in Chicago." Here the arrival in Chicago is an ultimate goal not enjoyed until *after* the flight is complete. In contrast, I could also say, "If I fly on the airplane, I will get some extended time to read." Here the apodosis is fulfilled while the condition is being met, not after. While I am flying, I am getting to read. This latter example clarifies the type of conditional relationship evident in Exodus 19:5–6. At the very time while Israel is pursuing God by heeding his voice, keeping his covenant, and existing as his treasured possession, the people will be serving as a kingdom of priests and a holy nation on behalf of God for the sake of the world. The apodosis identifies the God-honoring calling, and the protasis the means for fulfilling that calling.

The final arc is between 5cd, with 5d providing the *Ground* (G) or reason for 5c. Israel must serve as God's treasured possession amid the earth, *because* all the earth is the Lord's. As I already noted, the logic here appears to be that the Israelites bear a God-exalting calling and that their role of serving as God's treasured people is part of YHWH's means for reclaiming his rightful place as the recognized and praised Lord of the earth. Because all the world is indeed his, Israel must complete its purpose of reflecting and representing YHWH's supremacy over the world.

These are the logical relationships in Exodus 19:4–6. We now move to step 2 in finalizing our understanding of thought flow—drafting the exegetical outline.

Step 2: Exegetical Outlining—An Introduction

Once you have created an argument diagram of your passage, the next natural step is to craft your message-driven exegetical outline. If you look in a commentary or study Bible, most outlines of biblical books or passages address only content. They restate what is there but do not show why it's there, what it means, and how all the parts relate to shape a single main idea or thesis statement for the whole.

Compare the *ESV Study Bible*'s outline of Ruth[3] with Daniel I. Block's outline[4] in his New American Commentary (NAC):

Content Outline: *ESV Study Bible*	Exegetical Outline: D. I. Block
1. Introduction: Naomi Bereft of Family (1:1–5) 2. Scene 1: Naomi Returns to Bethlehem with Ruth (1:6–22) 3. Scene 2: Ruth Gleans in Boaz's Field (2:1–23) 4. Scene 3: Ruth, at the Threshing Floor, Asks Boaz to Marry Her (3:1–18) 5. Scene 4: Boaz Arranges Redemption at the Gate (4:1–12) 6. Conclusion: Naomi Blessed with a New Family (4:13–17) 7. Genealogy: Extended Blessing (4:18–22)	1. Act 1: The Crisis for the Royal Line (1:1–21) 2. Act 2: The Ray of Hope for the Royal Line (1:22–2:23) 3. Act 3: The Complication for the Royal Line (3:1–18) 4. Act 4: The Rescue of the Royal Line (4:1–17) 5. Epilogue: The Genealogy of the Royal Line (4:18–22)

Fig. 6.16. A Content Outline vs. an Exegetical Outline of Ruth

Whereas the content-driven outline gives you a sense for Ruth's story line, it does not help you assess the narrative's "argument"—the sermon behind the story. In contrast, upon a single read of Block's outline you already know that this is a book about

3. Ronald Bergey, "Ruth" notes in *ESV Study Bible*, ed. Lane T. Dennis and Wayne Grudem (Wheaton, IL: Crossway, 2008), 477.

4. Daniel I. Block, *Judges, Ruth: An Exegetical and Theological Exposition of Holy Scripture*, NAC 6 (Nashville: Broadman & Holman, 1999), 621.

the royal line of promise that includes crisis, hope, complication, and rescue. Block summarizes *Ruth's main point* this way: "the providential hand of God in the preservation of Israel's royal line during the dark days of the judges."[5] A message-driven outline captures more fully the Old Testament's nature as Scripture.

Figure 6.17 is another example from my recent work in Zephaniah. Compare the outline of Zephaniah in Zondervan's original *NIV Study Bible*[6] with my outline[7] for the Zondervan Exegetical Commentary on the Old Testament (ZECOT):

Content Outline: ***NIV Study Bible***	**Exegetical Outline:** J. S. DeRouchie
1. Introduction (1:1–3) 2. The Day of the Lord Coming on Judah and the Nations (1:4–18) 3. God's Judgment on the Nations (2:1–3:8) 4. Redemption of the Remnant (3:9–20)	1. The Superscription of the Savior's Summons to Satisfaction (1:1) 2. The Setting of the Savior's Summons to Satisfaction: A Call to Revere God in Light of the Coming Day of the Lord (1:2–18) 3. The Substance of the Savior's Summons to Satisfaction: Charges to Patiently Pursue the Lord Together in Order to Avoid Punishment and to Enjoy Satisfying Salvation (2:1–3:20)

Fig. 6.17. A Content Outline vs. an Exegetical Outline of Zephaniah

One outline pattern simply focuses on content. The other tries to capture the argument and message of the whole. My synthesis of *Zephaniah's main point* is: "In light of the impending day of his wrath, the Lord summons his faithful remnant to patiently pursue him together in order to avoid punishment and to enjoy satisfying salvation, all for God's joy and glory." Thus in my outline I have connected each step in the book to the Savior's summons to satisfaction.[8]

What Block and I are doing in these examples at the book level actually begins with careful evaluation of each part. For every passage I exegete, for every passage I preach, I try to capture the main idea in a single statement and try to draft a message-driven outline that aligns with it.

A number of years ago I was teaching through the historical narrative of Samuel. I grew to see that the initial two stories in chapters 1–2 introduce the message of the book by contrasting two episodes in the life of Israel. The first unpacks the principle

5. Ibid., 620.

6. R. K. Harrison, "Zephaniah" notes in *NIV Study Bible*, ed. Kenneth L. Barker (Grand Rapids: Zondervan, 2002), 1418–19.

7. Jason S. DeRouchie, *Zephaniah*, ZECOT (Grand Rapids: Zondervan, forthcoming).

8. For a complete walk through the book of Zephaniah, see "Zephaniah: The Savior's Summons to Satisfaction" in chapter 9.

that "holy YHWH helps those who honor him" by recounting Hannah's God-honoring plea for a child and the Lord's gracious gift of Samuel (1 Sam. 1:1–2:11). In contrast, the narrative of Eli's rebellious sons stresses that "holy YHWH destroys those who dishonor him" (2:12–36). Both narrative episodes include an extended drama (1:1–28 // 2:12–26) followed by a long speech (2:1–11 // 2:27–36) that climaxes with statements about the coming messianic king-priest (2:10 // 2:35). These long speeches capture the book's thesis. Hannah declares, "[YHWH] will guard the feet of his faithful ones, but the wicked shall be cut off in darkness" (2:9). Similarly, the man of God asserts to Eli, "Those who honor me I will honor, and those who despise me shall be lightly esteemed" (1 Sam. 2:30). The two stories of Hannah's exaltation and Hophni and Phinehas's downfall provide introductory examples to these truths. In light of this, I attempted to craft an exegetical, message-driven outline that was faithful to the main point of the narrative. Here was the result, though I will give only the main headings:

1. **Holy YHWH Helps One Who Honors Him (1:1–2:11)**
    a. The prelude to YHWH's helping of one who honors him: Days past (1:1–3)
    b. The setting for YHWH's helping of one who honors him: One day in Shiloh (1:4–19)
    c. The nature of YHWH's helping of one who honors him: A new day in Shiloh (1:20–2:11)

2. **Holy YHWH Destroys Those Who Dishonor Him (2:12–36)**
    a. The setting for YHWH's promise to destroy those who dishonor him: Dark days in Shiloh (2:12–26)
    b. The nature of YHWH's promise to destroy those who dishonor him: Deadly storms foretold in Shiloh (2:27–36)

How, then, do we move from tracing the argument to a message-driven outline? We'll consider that next with Genesis 12:1–3; Habakkuk 3:17–19; and then Exodus 19:4–6.

How to Draft an Exegetical Outline—Genesis 12:1–3 as a Case Study

This section will give an overview of the four steps for shaping an exegetical outline and main-idea statement for a passage. We will use Genesis 12:1–3 as an example, but before we begin, let's recall the arc of the passage displayed in figure 6.18.

Fig. 6.18. Arc of Genesis 12:1–3

You'll remember that there were two primary divisions in the text, each introduced by a command form (i.e., imperative) followed by a progression of finite verbs that identify the purpose (or consequence) of the patriarch's obedience. Abram needed to "go" to the Promised Land (1b) in order to become a nation of renown, blessed by God (2a–c). And once there, he needed to "then be a blessing" (2d) in order for God to bless others, ultimately resulting in all the families of the ground being blessed in him (3a–c). With this in mind, let's now walk through the steps for drafting an exegetical outline:

1. Draft a basic logical outline.

Building on the traced argument visualized in your arc or bracket, the initial step is to sketch a rough outline of the passage that distinguishes the major and minor clause groupings, based on whether the propositional relationships are coordinate or subordinate. The delimitation of primary headings and subheadings in the outline should align with the primary and embedded arcs in the diagram. In Genesis 12:1b–3, we begin by distinguishing the two main units of command and promise (1b–2c, 2d–3c), the first of which addresses Abram's becoming a God-blessed kingdom of renown and the second of which focuses on his serving as an agent of blessing. Each of these units has two parts.

I. YHWH's Initial Command to Go to the Land (12:1b–2c)
- A. YHWH's Command to Go to the Land (12:1b)
- B. YHWH's Promise of a Consequent Kingdom (12:2a–c)
  1. YHWH's gift of nationhood (12:2a)
  2. YHWH's favor/blessing (12:2b)
  3. YHWH's gift of renown (12:2c)

II. YHWH's Consequent Command to Be an Agent of Blessing to the World (12:2d–3)
- A. YHWH's Command to Be a Blessing (12:2d)
- B. YHWH's Promise of a Consequent Role as Agent of Blessing (12:3)
  1. YHWH's blessing all who bless Abram but cursing the one who curses (12:3ab)
  2. The ultimate result: YHWH's blessing all the families of the ground in Abram (12:3c)

Fig. 6.19. Basic Logical Outline of Genesis 12:1–3

2. Clarify the main purpose.

Once a rough outline is set, define the main purpose of the passage. What did the author seek to accomplish by his words? This is different from the main point. Did he intend to inform, instruct, motivate, challenge, warn, plea, encourage, or something else?

What is clear in Genesis 12:1–3 is that while YHWH is commanding Abram to act, YHWH himself remains the primary mover. *He* gives the commands, *his* promises motivate the obedience, and *he* is the one who would ultimately fulfill the promises. What could cause a person such as Abram, born into a family of idolaters (Josh. 24:2), to leave the comforts of family, friends, and the familiar to pursue promises that are humanly impossible to fulfill? How could he ever truly expect to enjoy a land that was not his to inherit, to grow into a nation when he had a barren wife, and to see the global curse and the animosity between God and man overcome by blessing and reconciliation? Stephen's response in Acts 7:2 is that "the God of glory appeared" to Abraham. In Mesopotamia the patriarch encountered something so beautiful and so compelling that he could not help but follow. He stepped out in hope because the promise-maker showed himself believable and because his promises were so desirable. Faith in God's promises would motivate every step of Abram's obedience. Faith would be the root, obedience the fruit. "By faith Abraham obeyed when he was called to go out to a place that he was to receive as an inheritance. And he went out, not knowing where he was going" (Heb. 11:8).

How, then, should we understand God's purpose in his words? We must see more than just commands. It is a commission that includes both commands and a goal. This goal is clarified through remarkable promises that would inspire and stimulate Abram's wholehearted obedience. God compelled the patriarch to action with this commission. Only by grace did God give Abram commands and promises. The commands would guide his steps, and the promises of future grace would fuel both his radical going and his radical witness.

To compel Abram to kingdom growth and impact.

Fig. 6.20. Main Purpose of Genesis 12:1–3

3. State the main idea.

Step 3 is to capture the main idea of the passage in a single sentence. Whereas the statement of purposes captures the author's goal, the main-idea statement captures his point. This statement should (a) give emphasis to the primary subject of the passage while relating it to the supporting complement; (b) focus on the passage's message, not just its content; (c) align with the passage's main purpose; and (d) use signal words to clarify the nature of the relationships.

Propositional Relationship	Question Raised	Signal Words
Action-Manner (Ac/Mn)	How?	"The method/manner/means of"
Ground (G) / Bilateral (BL)	Why? (on what basis?)	"The reason/cause/foundation of"
Inference (∴)	So what?	"The conclusion/significance of"
Action-Purpose (Ac/Pur)	Why? (for what end?)	"The goal/aim/motivation of"
Action-Result (Ac/Res)	What was the result?	"The consequence/effect of/outcome of"
Conditional (If/Th)	If this, then what?	"The condition for/context of"
Temporal (T)	When?	"The time/context of"
Locative (L)	Where?	"The place/location of"

Fig. 6.21. Some Signal Words That Express Propositional Relationships

When it comes to Genesis 12:1–3, the commands to "go" and "be a blessing" shape the subject, whereas the promises to make Abram into a renowned nationhood and to use him as an instrument of blessing complement the subject by motivating Abram's loyalty and witness. Together the commands and promises work to commission the patriarch to a life of radical obedience. So I propose the following main-idea statement:

God commissions Abram to kingdom growth (by commanding him to follow for the purpose of becoming an exalted kingdom) and, consequentially, to kingdom impact (by calling him to be a blessing for the purpose of serving as the agent of worldwide blessing).

Fig. 6.22. Main Idea of Genesis 12:1–3

4. Reword the basic outline into a message-driven outline.

The last step is to rework the rough logical outline into an exegetically grounded, message-driven outline. The outline should align with the passage's purpose and identify how the passage communicates its main idea. There are three steps: (a) If possible, transform your statements of fact into statements of principle. (b) Relate each statement to the passage's main idea. (c) Put your statements/conclusions into the form of headings, not using finite verbs and making frequent use of signal words (see fig. 6.21) to clarify the various propositional relationships. As you work through these steps, try to establish coherence between headings by repeating a word from the main heading in the subheadings.

Go from your land and from your kindred and from your father's house to the land that I will show you, 2 so that I may make you into a great nation and may bless you and may make your name great. Then be a blessing, 3 so that I may bless those who bless you, but the one who curses you I will bind with a curse, with the result that in you all the families of the ground may be blessed.	**I. YHWH's Initial Commission to Kingdom Growth (12:1b–2c)** A. YHWH's Command to Go to the Land of Kingdom Growth (12:1b) B. YHWH's Motivating Promise of Kingdom Growth (12:2a–c) 1. YHWH's gift of nationhood (12:2a) 2. YHWH's favor/blessing (12:2b) 3. YHWH's gift of renown (12:2c) **II. YHWH's Consequent Commission to Kingdom Impact (12:2d–3)** A. YHWH's Command to Make a Kingdom Impact (12:2d) B. YHWH's Motivating Promise of Kingdom Impact (12:3) 1. YHWH's blessing all who bless Abram but cursing the one who curses (12:3ab) 2. YHWH's ultimate commitment to bless all the families of the ground in Abram (12:3c)

Fig. 6.23. Exegetical Outline of Genesis 12:1–3

The goal of an exegetical outline is to capture the message of your passage in a clear and logical way. There is *not* only one "right way" of doing this. Your own outline of this passage would likely look different from mine, but there should also be elements that identify common threads and a similar understanding of the passage's overall structure and message.

Most commentaries supply only content outlines and walk through passages verse by verse or phrase by phrase while giving little thought to the overall flow of the argument. An exception to this pattern is ZECOT. This entire series works hard to trace arguments in the various books. The discussion of each passage includes a main-idea statement and a carefully crafted message-driven outline that clarifies how every clause and text unit contributes to the main idea. I strongly encourage you to check out the series.

Two More Examples of Exegetical Outlines

Exegetical Outline of Habakkuk 3:17–19

In this section I want to establish an exegetical outline for Habakkuk 3:17–19. You'll recall when we made the arc of the passage that there were two distinct sections: a temporal *when* section addressing the potential reality of coming curse and then the prophet's assertion that, come what may, he would ever rejoice in the God of his salvation.

17a
כִּי־תְאֵנָה לֹא־תִפְרָח
When the fig tree has not budded
17b
וְאֵין יְבוּל בַּגְּפָנִים
and there is no fruit at the vines,
17c
כִּחֵשׁ מַעֲשֵׂה־זַיִת
the produce of the olive has failed,
17d
וּשְׁדֵמוֹת לֹא־עָשָׂה אֹכֶל
and the fields do not yield food,
17e
גָּזַר מִמִּכְלָה צֹאן
when the fold has not divided sheep,
17f
וְאֵין בָּקָר בָּרְפָתִים׃
and there is no cattle in the stalls,
18a
וַאֲנִי בַּיהוָה אֶעְלוֹזָה
then I will exult in YHWH.
18b
אָגִילָה בֵּאלֹהֵי יִשְׁעִי׃
I will rejoice in the God of my salvation.
19a
יְהוִה אֲדֹנָי חֵילִי
YHWH my Lord is my strength;
19b
וַיָּשֶׂם רַגְלַי כָּאַיָּלוֹת
and he has made my feet like the does',
19c
וְעַל בָּמוֹתַי יַדְרִכֵנִי
and on the heights he makes me walk.
S
Id
S
Exp
S
S
T
Id
Exp
S
G
P

Fig. 6.24. Arc of Habakkuk 3:17–19

In order to create an exegetical outline, we'll follow the same four-step process that I offered in the previous section.

1. Draft a basic logical outline of the passage.

I. The Temporal Context for Habakkuk's Joy in God (v. 17)
- A. Crop devastation (v. 17a–d)
- B. Livestock devastation (v. 17e–f)

II. The Declaration of Habakkuk's Joy in God (vv. 18–19)
- A. The assertion of joy in God (v. 18)
- B. The basis of joy in God (v. 19)

Fig. 6.25. Basic Logical Outline of Habakkuk 3:17–19

2. Clarify the main purpose of the passage.

To motivate fellow believers to follow Habakkuk in rejoicing in his saving God, even when tasting the impact of covenant curse, because they can be confident in YHWH's ability and faithfulness to strengthen and ultimately sustain them through the trial.

Fig. 6.26. Main Purpose of Habakkuk 3:17–19

3. State the main idea of the passage in a single sentence.

Every believer should rejoice in the saving God amid trial because the Lord is both able and committed to strengthen and sustain.

Fig. 6.27. Main Idea of Habakkuk 3:17–19

4. Reword the basic outline into an exegetically grounded, message-driven outline.

When the fig tree has not budded and there is no fruit at the vines, the produce of the olive has failed, and the fields do not yield food, when the fold has not divided sheep, and there is no cattle in the stalls, 18 **then I will exult in YHWH**. I will rejoice in the God of my salvation. 19 YHWH my Lord is my strength; and he has made my feet like the does', and on the heights he makes me walk.	**I. The Temporal Cursed Context for a Believer's Joy in the Saving God (v. 17)** A. Lack of earthly provision: Crop devastation (v. 17a–d) B. Lack of earthly provision: Livestock devastation (v. 17e–f) **II. The Believer's Declaration of Sustained Joy in the Saving God (vv. 18–19)** A. The assertion of joy in the saving God (v. 18) B. The basis of joy in the saving God: His ability and commitment to strengthen and sustain (v. 19)

Fig. 6.28. Exegetical Outline of Habakkuk 3:17–19

Exegetical Outline of Exodus 19:4–6

In this final section of the chapter, we will establish an exegetical outline for Exodus 19:4–6. Before working through the four steps, let's recall my arc of the passage.

Fig. 6.29. Arc of Exodus 19:4–6

1. Draft a basic logical outline of the passage.

I. God Redeems Israel from Egypt (v. 4)
II. Implication ("And now"): Israel bears a calling to make much of God (vv. 5–6)
- A. The condition ("if") (v. 5)
  1. Heed God's voice
  2. Keep God's covenant
  3. Be God's treasured possession in the context of the world
- B. The result ("then") (v. 6)
  1. Be a kingdom of priests
  2. Be a holy nation

Fig. 6.30. Basic Logical Outline of Exodus 19:4–6

2. Clarify the main purpose of the passage.

To motivate Israel to mediate and display God's greatness and worth in response to God's gracious redemption and by means of a lifestyle of radical God-centeredness.

Fig. 6.31. Main Purpose of Exodus 19:4–6

3. State the main idea of the passage in a single sentence.

In response to God's gracious redemption, the Lord calls his people to a God-exalting task of mediating and displaying his greatness and worth to the world through radical God-centered living.

Fig. 6.32. Main Idea of Exodus 19:4–6

4. Reword the basic outline into an exegetically grounded, message-driven outline.

You have seen what I did to Egypt and how I lifted you on eagles' wings, and how I brought you to myself. 5 And now, if you will indeed listen unto my voice and keep my covenant and be my treasured possession from all the peoples, for all the earth is mine, 6 **then you will be to me a kingdom of priests and a holy nation.**	**I. The Basis of God's Calling for His People: God's Deliverance (v. 4)** **II. The Nature of God's Calling for His People: To Exalt God in the World (vv. 5–6)** A. The means for fulfilling the calling to exalt God in the world: radical God-centered living (v. 5) 1. Heed God's voice 2. Keep God's covenant 3. Exist as God's treasured possession in the context of the world B. The essence of the calling to exalt God in the world (v. 6) 1. Serving as a kingdom of priests: mediate God's greatness and worth 2. Serving as a holy nation: display God's greatness and worth

Fig. 6.33. Exegetical Outline of Exodus 19:4–6

While I will comment more about this later, it is important at this point to note that there is an analogy between the structure of grace in the old covenant and the structure of grace in the new. In the old covenant, God graciously redeemed Israel from Egypt and only in light of this called the people to a life of radical obedience and witness in the world. Following God in obedience was not the means for getting saved from slavery but the proper response to being saved. This is the structure of grace we see in the new covenant as well. God graciously redeems us in Christ and only then calls us to radical Christ-centered living. We bring nothing to our initial salvation. Only after a disciple is reborn does he or she become an obedient follower of all that Jesus commanded.

You now have a solid introduction to tracking thought flow in Old Testament texts. You have learned how to create a text hierarchy and how to trace biblical arguments by carefully assessing coordinate and subordinate relationships through the tool of arcing or bracketing. You have also become acquainted with exegetical, message-driven outlines. We are now ready to move on to the seventh stage of the interpretive process—word/concept studies.

Key Words and Concepts

Literary argument
Proposition
Coordinate and subordinate relationships

Questions for Further Reflection

1. What are the two steps for grasping and communicating a passage's thought flow?
2. In what way can we consider a biblical narrative to contain an "argument"?
3. What types of linguistic and literary features help us grasp an author's flow of thought?
4. What are the benefits to assessing the various propositional relationships listed in figure 6.3 by developing an arc or bracket of a passage?
5. How can this process of tracing an argument be used on an entire book? In your response, clarify the difference between a content-driven and message-driven outline of Ruth or Zephaniah.
6. What is the difference between clarifying the main purpose and stating the main idea?

Resources for Further Study

Literary Analysis

Alter, Robert. *The Art of Biblical Narrative.* 2nd ed. New York: Basic Books, 2011.
———. *The Art of Biblical Poetry.* 2nd ed. New York: Basic Books, 2011.
Block, Daniel I. "Tell Me the Old, Old Story: Preaching the Message of Old Testament Narrative." In *Giving the Sense: Understanding and Using Old Testament Historical Texts: Essays in Honor of Eugene Merrill*, edited by David M. Howard and Michael A. Grisanti, 409–38. Grand Rapids: Kregel, 2003.
de Regt, L. J., J. de Waard, and J. P. Fokkelman, eds. *Literary Structure and Rhetorical Strategies in the Hebrew Bible.* Winona Lake, IN: Eisenbrauns, 1996.
Dorsey, David A. *The Literary Structure of the Old Testament: A Commentary on Genesis-Malachi.* Grand Rapids: Baker, 1999.
Fokkelmann, J. P. *Reading Biblical Narrative: An Introductory Guide.* Louisville: Westminster John Knox, 2000.
———. *Reading Biblical Poetry: An Introductory Guide.* Louisville: Westminster John Knox, 2001.

Hayes, John H., and Carl R. Holladay. "Literary Criticism: The Composition and Rhetorical Style of the Text." In *Biblical Exegesis: A Beginner's Handbook*, 90–103. 3rd ed. Louisville: Westminster John Knox, 2007.

House, Paul R., ed. *Beyond Form Criticism: Essays on Old Testament Literary Criticism*. SBTS 2. Winona Lake, IN: Eisenbrauns, 1992.

Kaiser, Walter C., Jr. Pages 87–104, 149–81 in *Toward an Exegetical Theology: Biblical Exegesis for Preaching and Teaching*. Grand Rapids: Baker Academic, 1981.

Longman, Tremper, III. "Literary Approaches to the Old Testament." In *The Face of Old Testament Studies: A Survey of Contemporary Approaches*, edited by David W. Baker and Bill T. Arnold, 97–115. Grand Rapids: Baker Academic, 2004.

Ryken, Leland. *How to Read the Bible as Literature*. Grand Rapids: Zondervan, 1984.

———. *The Literature of the Bible*. Grand Rapids: Zondervan, 1974.

Ryken, Leland, and Tremper Longman III, eds. *A Complete Literary Guide to the Bible*. 2nd ed. Grand Rapids: Zondervan, 1993.

Argument-Diagramming

★ *Biblearc*. http://www.Biblearc.com/.

DeRouchie, Jason S. Pages 87–92, 217–67 in *A Call to Covenant Love: Text-Grammar and Literary Structure in Deuteronomy 5–11*. Gorgias Dissertations 30/Biblical Studies 2. Piscataway, NJ: Gorgias, 2007.

Piper, John. Appendix in *Reading the Bible Supernaturally: Seeing and Savoring the Glory of God in Scripture*. Wheaton, IL: Crossway, 2017.

Schreiner, Thomas R. "Tracing the Argument." In *Interpreting the Pauline Epistles*, 69–124. 2nd ed. Grand Rapids: Baker Academic, 2011.

Exegetical Outlining

Block, Daniel I. "Tell Me the Old, Old Story: Preaching the Message of Old Testament Narrative." In *Giving the Sense: Understanding and Using Old Testament Historical Texts: Essays in Honor of Eugene Merrill*, edited by David M. Howard and Michael A. Grisanti, 409–38. Grand Rapids: Kregel, 2003.

DeRouchie, Jason S. Pages 87–92, 217–67 in *A Call to Covenant Love: Text-Grammar and Literary Structure in Deuteronomy 5–11*. Gorgias Dissertations 30/Biblical Studies 2. Piscataway, NJ: Gorgias, 2007.

Kaiser, Walter C., Jr. Pages 87–104, 149–81 in *Toward an Exegetical Theology: Biblical Exegesis for Preaching and Teaching*. Grand Rapids: Baker Academic, 1981.

Zondervan Exegetical Commentary on the Old Testament. Grand Rapids: Zondervan, 2015–.

7

WORD AND CONCEPT STUDIES

Goal: Clarify the meaning of key words, phrases, and concepts.

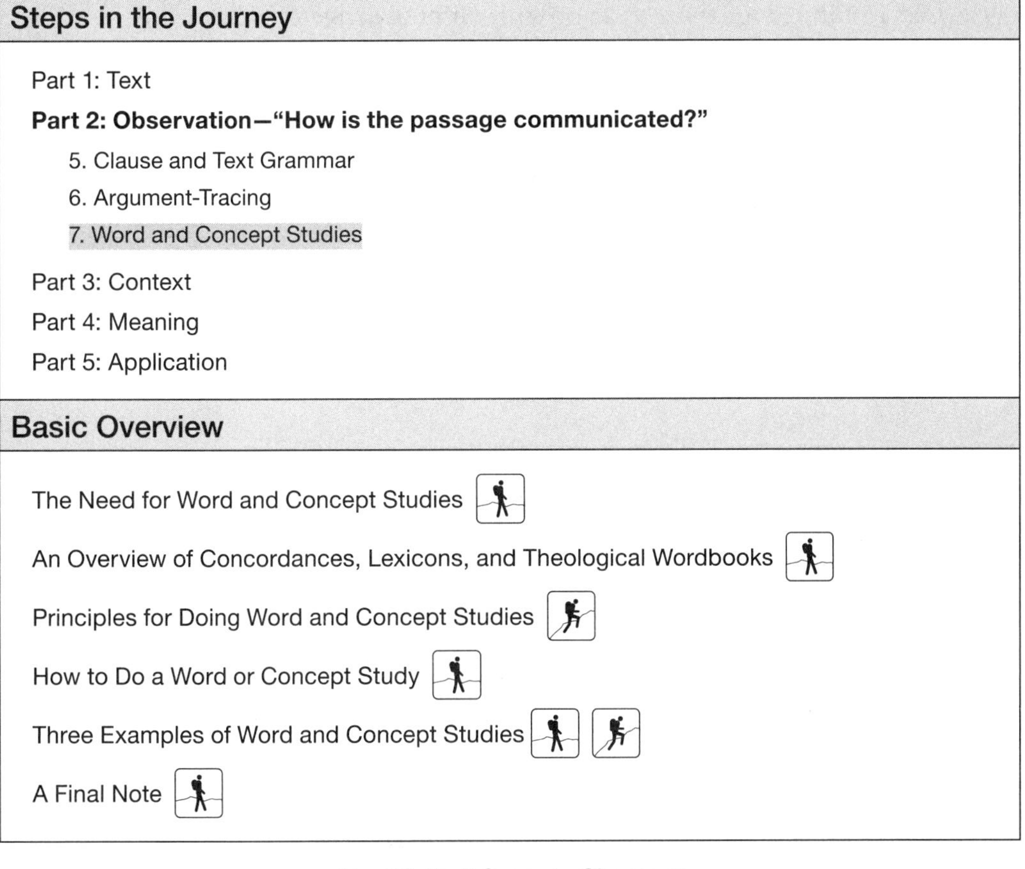

Steps in the Journey
Part 1: Text
Part 2: Observation—"How is the passage communicated?"
5. Clause and Text Grammar
6. Argument-Tracing
7. Word and Concept Studies
Part 3: Context
Part 4: Meaning
Part 5: Application
Basic Overview
The Need for Word and Concept Studies
An Overview of Concordances, Lexicons, and Theological Wordbooks
Principles for Doing Word and Concept Studies
How to Do a Word or Concept Study
Three Examples of Word and Concept Studies
A Final Note

Fig. 7.1. Trail Guide to Chapter 7

The Need for Word and Concept Studies

Words often have a range of meanings. If I say "trunk," many different images may come to mind: (1) the main woody stem of a tree, (2) the torso of a person's or animal's body, (3) the extended nose of an elephant, (4) a large box with hinged lid, and (5) the storage compartment located at the rear of a vehicle.

Because word meanings can overlap, in any given context an author could choose different words to communicate the same reality. Even when a certain word is not present, the concept may still be. Because the message of every passage of Scripture is dependent on the meaning of words, phrases, and concepts, knowing how to grasp such meaning is vitally important for interpretation. This chapter will provide an overview of the key tools, principles, and process for doing word and concept studies in the Old Testament for those with or without knowledge of Hebrew.

An Overview of Concordances, Lexicons, and Theological Wordbooks

We begin with the tools of the trade for word and concept studies. There are three main ones: concordances, lexicons, and theological wordbooks.

1. Concordances

A Hebrew concordance is the most important tool in a word/concept-study toolbox. A ***concordance*** lists all instances of a word or phrase within a given Testament, usually followed by a sampling of its use in specific contexts. By far, concordance searches are most efficient and detailed when done electronically through one of the following programs: *Accordance*[1] (http://www.accordancebible.com/), *BibleWorks*[2] (http://www.bibleworks.com/), or *Logos Bible Software*[3] (https://www.logos.com/). For those who still prefer print editions, the two best options are Evan-Shoshan's *A New Concordance*

1. *Accordance* (Mac, Windows, mobile devices), from Oak Tree Software, http://www.accordancebible.com/. For my positive review of *Accordance 11 Ultimate Collection*, see *BBR* 25, 2 (2015): 225–26.

2. *BibleWorks* (Mac, Windows), from BibleWorks, http://bibleworks.com/. For David Instone Brewer's positive review of *BibleWorks 10*, see http://tyndaletech.blogspot.com/2015/07/bw10.html.

3. *Logos Bible Software* (Mac, Windows, mobile devices), from Faithlife Corporation, https://www.logos.com/. For Jeffrey Kranz's positive review of *Logos 6*, see http://overviewbible.com/batmobile-bible-study-logos-bible-software-6/.

of the Old Testament Using the Hebrew and Aramaic Text[4] and Kohlenberger and Swanson's *The Hebrew-English Concordance to the Old Testament*.[5] The latter of these resources is especially useful for those without any knowledge of Hebrew, for all the Scripture translations are from the NIV.

Even if you have never learned Hebrew, you should learn to use a *Hebrew* word-based concordance. Why? Concordances that are based on English word searches show only the uses of a given *English* word within a single English-based translation. And because Hebrew words have their own range of meanings, a passage list from an English-only concordance will miss all occurrences of the Hebrew word that are translated differently in other passages. With this, lists of verses in an English-only concordance will usually contain instances of multiple Hebrew words that the English translators happened to render with the same English term found in your passage. It is vital, therefore, that everyone learn to do word and concept studies in the original languages. Thankfully, for those who don't know Hebrew, there are helpful tools to guide your way, and I'll focus more closely on these when I detail the process for doing word and concept studies ("How to Do a Word or Concept Study" below).

2. Lexicons

A ***lexicon*** is similar to a dictionary. It lists the words of a language, usually in alphabetical order, and gives their range of meaning through equivalent words in a different language. In a Hebrew lexicon, specific biblical references usually accompany the various word glosses, allowing the lexicon to serve both as a dictionary and as a sort of concordance. Lexicons can be valuable time-savers in the interpretive process, and having a solid Hebrew lexicon is essential for exegesis. Nevertheless, you should know that lexicons are not infallible resources and that their purpose is principally to list a word's possible range of meanings. Therefore, we as interpreters must evaluate every word use in context in order to decide which meaning best fits.

The standard Hebrew-English lexicon is Koehler and Baumgartner's *The Hebrew and Aramaic Lexicon of the Old Testament* (*HALOT*).[6] Brill published the two-volume study edition in 2001, and this is one resource worth budgeting for in an electronic format, because it will be massively valuable to your ministry over the long term. With *HALOT* is Holladay's *A Concise Hebrew and Aramaic Lexicon of the Old Testament*, which is based on an earlier edition of *HALOT*.[7] It offers nothing that the bigger edition does not already offer, but it is cheaper if you need a lexicon to get by with until you can acquire *HALOT*. Next would be Clines's *The Concise Dictionary of Classical Hebrew* (*CDCH*),[8] which is an abridged version of the masterful nine-volume *The Dictionary*

4. Abraham Evan-Shoshan, ed., *A New Concordance of the Old Testament Using the Hebrew and Aramaic Text* (Grand Rapids: Baker Academic, 1989).

5. John R. Kohlenberger III and James A. Swanson, *The Hebrew-English Concordance to the Old Testament* (Grand Rapids: Zondervan, 1998).

6. Ludwig Koehler, Walter Baumgartner, and Johann Jakob Stamm, eds., *The Hebrew and Aramaic Lexicon of the Old Testament: Study Edition*, trans. M. E. J. Richardson, 2 vols. (Leiden: Brill, 2001).

7. William L. Holladay, *A Concise Hebrew and Aramaic Lexicon of the Old Testament* (Grand Rapids: Eerdmans, 1988).

8. David J. A. Clines, ed., *The Concise Dictionary of Classical Hebrew* (Sheffield, UK: Sheffield Phoenix, 2009).

of Classical Hebrew (*DCH*).[9] This is the first Hebrew dictionary to cover all the literature of classical Hebrew, including the Old Testament, DSS, Ben Sira, and the ancient Hebrew inscriptions.

HALOT, Holladay, *CDCH*, and *DCH* all structure their entries alphabetically by first letter, making it easy to look up any given word, as long as you can remember the alphabet. Some exegetes, however, still prefer the older standard, which is now commonly called *The Brown-Driver-Briggs Hebrew and English Lexicon* (normally abbreviated as *BDB*).[10] In contrast to the other lexicons, BDB is not alphabetical, at least with respect to how it handles nouns. Instead, it arranges everything in the lexicon alphabetically by root. For example, the Hebrew noun מִזְבֵּחַ ("altar") is not found with words beginning with מ but with the entry for the Hebrew verb זבח, which in the Piel stem means "to sacrifice" (זִבַּח). To use BDB effectively, you need to know the root behind every noun, you need to have it on your computer so that you can still search it alphabetically, or you need to acquire Einspahr's *Index to Brown, Driver & Briggs Hebrew Lexicon*, which lists in alphabetical order the consonantal form of every Hebrew word in BDB, gives its general meaning, and identifies its location in the lexicon.[11]

Naturally, without a knowledge of the Hebrew alphabet, you will not be able to access these top lexicons. For those without the biblical languages, a secondary tool that should be useful is *Mounce's Complete Expository Dictionary of Old and New Testament Words* (*MCED*).[12] Unlike the older layperson's standard *Vine's Complete Expository Dictionary of Old and New Testament Words*,[13] *MCED* builds on the best of contemporary evangelical scholarship and employs both the Strong's and Goodrick/Kohlenberger (G/K) numbering systems, the latter of which is often supplanting the former as the standard instrument for identifying Hebrew and Greek words.[14] So if you know the number associated with a Hebrew or Greek word, you can find a definition that includes the word's range of meaning throughout the given Testament.

3. Theological Wordbooks

Along with lexicons, you should be aware of some extremely helpful word-study dictionaries, also known as ***theological wordbooks***. These multivolume tools, most of which are available for your electronic Bible software, include articles that survey all major uses of a given term throughout Scripture and also often comment on its use outside the Bible. Here I will review the most substantial tools for Old Testament studies.

The initial two resources were written from a broadly evangelical perspective. Pride of place goes to VanGemeren's five-volume *New International Dictionary of Old Testament*

9. David J. A. Clines, ed. *The Dictionary of Classical Hebrew*, 9 vols. (Sheffield, UK: Sheffield Phoenix, 1993–2014).

10. Francis Brown, S. R. Driver, and Charles A. Briggs, *The New Brown-Driver-Briggs Hebrew and English Lexicon* (Peabody, MA: Hendrickson, 1979).

11. Bruce Einspahr, *Index to Brown, Driver & Briggs Hebrew Lexicon*, 2nd ed. (Chicago: Moody, 1976).

12. William D. Mounce, ed., *Mounce's Complete Expository Dictionary of Old and New Testament Words* (Grand Rapids: Zondervan, 2006).

13. W. E. Vine, Merrill F. Unger, and William White Jr., *Vine's Complete Expository Dictionary of Old and New Testament Words* (London: Oliphants, 1939; repr., Nashville: Thomas Nelson, 1996).

14. While Strong's numbers are the long-held standard, the G/K numbers are more in touch with the existence of homonyms, as is common in up-to-date Hebrew lexicons.

Theology and Exegesis (*NIDOTTE*).[15] *NIDOTTE* is my top pick for Old Testament theological wordbooks. The essays are usually of manageable size for sermon preparation, and all are accessible through G/K numbers (a Strong's-to-G/K number index is in the back of volume 5). Each study helpfully synthesizes how a given Hebrew term is used throughout the entire Old Testament, and most entries set theological trajectories into the New Testament. This is a resource well worth having in your library. A similar volume, though older and smaller, is Harris, Archer, and Waltke's *Theological Wordbook of the Old Testament* (*TWOT*).[16] As above, this tool is tied to Strong's numbers, making it accessible to those who don't know the biblical languages.

My next two wordbooks are of comparable structure, but both were written by German liberal scholars who have very unorthodox views of the Bible's composition, dating, and authority. The first is Jenni and Westermann's three-volume *Theological Lexicon of the Old Testament* (*TLOT*).[17] Except for its higher-critical bias, this has all the benefits of *NIDOTTE*. Last is Botterweck, Ringgren, and Fabry's fifteen-volume *Theological Dictionary of the Old Testament* (*TDOT*).[18] This is a massive, very thorough work, and if you can keep the different presuppositions in mind, it can greatly serve detailed exegetical study.

All of us need these kinds of tools. But they are best used to offer initial perspective or to provide a comparison for word and concept studies that we have already done on our own.

Principles for Doing Word and Concept Studies

A lexicon is a great tool for giving us a quick snapshot of a word's range of meanings and for associating the use of a term in one passage with its use in others. Sadly, interpreters often make errors in establishing a word's meaning because they fail to heed a few guiding principles:[19] (1) The history and makeup of a word are not reliable guides to meaning. (2) Usage in context determines meaning. (3) Authorial, historical,

15. Willem A. VanGemeren, ed., *New International Dictionary of Old Testament Theology and Exegesis*, 5 vols. (Grand Rapids: Zondervan, 1997).

16. R. Laird Harris, Gleason L. Archer Jr., and Bruce K. Waltke, *Theological Wordbook of the Old Testament*, rev. 1-vol. ed. (Chicago: Moody, 2003).

17. Ernst Jenni and Claus Westermann, eds., *Theological Lexicon of the Old Testament*, trans. Mark E. Biddle, 3 vols. (Peabody, MA: Hendrickson, 1994).

18. G. Johannes Botterweck, Helmer Ringgren, and Heinz-Josef Fabry, eds., *Theological Dictionary of the Old Testament*, 15 vols. (Grand Rapids: Eerdmans, 1974–2006).

19. The initial two principles and some of the examples are adapted from John H. Walton, *Chronological and Background Charts of the Old Testament*, 2nd ed. (Grand Rapids: Zondervan, 1994), 94–95. He expanded this information in his essay titled "Principles for Productive Word Study" in *NIDOTTE* 1:158–68.

geographical, and formal correspondences matter when determining meaning. If you don't know Hebrew and prefer not to see a number of Hebrew words with their translations, jump ahead to "How to Do a Word or Concept Study."

1. The history and makeup of a word are not reliable guides to meaning.

a. Past usage is not necessarily equivalent to current usage.

Just because people in the past used a word in a certain way does not mean that people are still using it that way. The original meaning (etymology) of a word is an unreliable guide to its contemporary use. For example, *awful* in English used to express reverence (i.e., "full of awe"), but today it most commonly describes something that is very bad or unpleasant. Similarly, while זָקָן ("beard") in Hebrew was originally related to the idea of being old (cf. verb זָקֵן [Qal], "grow old"; adjective זָקֵן, "old"), this connection is not necessarily apparent in Scripture.

b. Similar roots do not necessarily have similar meanings.

Verbs and nouns that share the same root do not always share the same semantic meaning. An example in English is the verb *undertake* versus the noun *undertaker*, the latter of which has a much more limited range of usage. In Hebrew, the noun מִדְבָּר ("wilderness") bears no connection in meaning to the Piel verb דִּבֵּר ("speak"). Furthermore, the various stems of a particular verbal root are not necessarily related in meaning. While English has no parallel in its use of verbs, the noun *adult* has no direct link with the noun *adultery*. Similarly, in Hebrew, the Qal verb כָּפַר ("cover") may have no direct connection to the Piel כִּפֵּר ("atone").

c. Comparative languages are unreliable guides.

Similar vocabulary from a related language (i.e., a ***cognate***) is an unreliable guide to meaning. Just as we cannot determine the meaning of the English *dynamite* from the Greek cognate δύναμις ("power"), so, too, we cannot reliably determine from Arabic usage the specific meaning of the Hebrew תְּשׁוּקָה ("desire") in Genesis 3:16 and 4:7.[20] There are times when we are forced to look at cognates to assess the possible meaning of a term, but we must recognize any conclusions as tentative.

2. Usage in context determines meaning.

a. Context is king.

The historical and literary context is always determinative for meaning, most significantly when several different meanings exist for a given word. For example, in English, *minutes* can be parts of an hour or notes from a meeting, and context alone clarifies which meaning is in use. In Hebrew, רוּחַ can mean either "wind" or "spirit,"

20. BDB relates תשׁוקה to the Arabic root *šāqa* ("to desire, excite desire"), but the phonemic equivalent of the Hebrew שׁ (*š*) is *s* in Arabic, making the proper etymology in Arabic *sāqa* ("to urge, drive on, impel") (so Susan T. Foh, "What Is the Woman's Desire?," *WTJ* 37, 3 [1975]: 376–83). Regardless, biblical context and not Arabic should serve as the primary guide for our word-study decisions.

depending on the context. Interpreters are not at liberty to choose whichever meanings they want for a given word but must determine what the author intended.

To understand the importance of a particular word in context, we need to know what choices (synonyms) were available to the author, and what is signified by the choice he made. In English usage, the choice of *stallion* leads to certain conclusions, because the author did not use *steed* or *charger*. Similarly, in Hebrew, the nouns עַלְמָה ("a girl able to be married, usually a virgin"), בְּתוּלָה ("a woman old enough to bear children"), and נַעֲרָה ("young [un]married girl") overlap in meaning, but each term has its own semantic range. The interpreter must not only determine this range, but also clarify whether there is significance to why a certain word was chosen over another (see עַלְמָה in Isaiah 7:14).[21]

When a word has both a general and a technical sense, context alone must determine which the author intended. For example, in English *reformed* can be a general adjective ("a reformed man"), but it can also be a technical term for a specific system of Christian doctrine ("Reformed theology"). In Hebrew, שָׂטָן may refer generally to an "adversary, accuser," whether human (1 Kings 11:23) or angelic (Num. 22:22), or it may refer to the prince of demons himself—"Satan." In order to render שָׂטָן as "Satan," however, the interpreter must defend his translation from context; it is not necessarily the default meaning.

b. Look out for idioms.

One must consider whether combinations of verb + preposition take on special meanings. In English, the idiomatic expression "just a minute" refers to an undefined period and could not be applied to, for example, the statement "Class will be fifty minutes long." So, too, in the Hebrew phrase "the day of YHWH," יוֹם ("day") does not refer to a twenty-four-hour period, even though this is clearly the meaning in other contexts.

c. Assigned meanings must not be too limited.

While context is paramount for determining meaning, the interpreter must construe a term's meaning broadly enough to fit all appropriate contexts (except in cases of idiomatic or technical usage). For example, in English we should not define the verb *swim* by a particular arm stroke, for numerous arm strokes would qualify for "swimming." Accordingly, the Qal verb בָּרָא ("create") cannot mean "create out of

21. Scholars usually render בְּתוּלָה as the Old Testament term for "virgin" (*HALOT*, 1:166–67), citing texts such as Genesis 24:16; Leviticus 21:14; Deuteronomy 22:15–19; and Isaiah 62:5. In Joel 1:8, however, the one referred to as בְּתוּלָה is a widow longing for the husband of her youth, so she is probably *not* a virgin, though her man's death has again rendered her unmarried. Furthermore, the fact that Genesis 24:16 adds the explanatory statement "a man had not known her" suggests that the term does not by itself mean "virgin"; otherwise, the addition would be unnecessary. I suggest instead that בְּתוּלָה means something like "a woman old enough to bear children." In contrast, scholars have typically translated עַלְמָה as "a girl able to be married" (*HALOT*, 2:835–36), but in all seven occurrences "virgin" could work (the only potential exception being Proverbs 30:19, though even here the mystery of verses 18–19 is heightened if the "maiden" of verse 19 points to one who has no sexual experience). While there is not enough data to say that עַלְמָה means "virgin," this meaning is likely within its semantic range.

nothing," for this meaning cannot apply to Genesis 5:1, where we are told that God "created" man (cf. Gen. 2:7).

3. Authorial, historical, geographical, and formal correspondences matter when determining meaning.

a. Authorial Correspondence

A given author's use of a term elsewhere should bear greater influence in your assessment than the uses of other authors. So, for example, if you're considering the meaning of the feminine noun צְדָקָה ("righteousness") in Genesis 15:6, the eight other occurrences in the law of Moses should bear a priority in your analysis.[22] Also, the comparative significance increases all the more when an author uses the term in the same book.

b. Historical Correspondence

Because languages evolve over time, comparing word usage of authors living at the same time is normally more helpful than comparing authors from different historical eras. For example, if you are working through Micah 5:2 and want to better grasp the meaning of the substantive Qal participle מוֹשֵׁל ("ruler" in ESV), the eleven occurrences of the same verb in his contemporary prophet Isaiah would be helpful. But there is an important qualification here. When an author is drawing his language from previous Scripture, the earlier biblical usage often controls the later meaning.[23]

c. Geographical Correspondence

Linguists recognize that geography influences speech patterns.[24] In Judges 12:5–6 we read this somewhat humorous story: "And the Gileadites captured the fords of the Jordan against the Ephraimites. And when any of the fugitives of Ephraim said, 'Let me go over,' the men of Gilead said to him, 'Are you an Ephraimite?' When he said, 'No,' they said to him, 'Then say Shibboleth [שִׁבֹּלֶת],' and he said, 'Sibboleth [סִבֹּלֶת],' for he could not pronounce it right." Anyone who hears my voice would know that I come from the Midwest and not the South or the United Kingdom. As in English, classical Hebrew had its own dialects, and these geographical distinctions could influence not only intonation but also word usage and meanings. Thus, considering whether you are reading a northern or southern prophet could influence your word study.

22. With these, you would be aided by comparing and contrasting the various uses of צְדָקָה with the Pentateuch's twelve instances of the masculine noun צֶדֶק ("righteousness"), seventeen instances of the adjective צַדִּיק ("righteous, upright"), and four instances of the verb צדק ("to be just, righteous").

23. An additional element to keep in mind is that the entire Old Testament witnesses to some, though minimal, textual updating, probably limited to switching from the paleo-Hebrew script to Aramaic square script and *plene* spelling and to some updating related to geography, grammar, and lexicon. The result is that historical distinctions in the language are minimized. For more on this, see Bruce K. Waltke, "Old Testament Textual Criticism," in *Foundations for Biblical Interpretation*, ed. David S. Dockery, Kenneth A. Mathews, and Robert B. Sloan (Nashville: Broadman & Holman, 1994), 156–86; Peter J. Gentry, "The Text of the Old Testament," *JETS* 52, 1 (2009): 19–45.

24. E.g., W. Randall Garr, *Dialect Geography of Syria-Palestine, 1000–586 B.C.E.* (Winona Lake, IN: Eisenbrauns, 2004).

d. Generic or Formal Correspondence

Here we simply recognize that certain genres may prefer certain word meanings over others. For example, if you are working through Psalm 33, a psalm of praise, the term תְּרוּעָה is less likely a "war cry" (Jer. 4:19) and more likely a "shout of joy": "Sing to him a new song; play skillfully on the strings, *with loud shouts* [בִּתְרוּעָה]" (Ps. 33:3).

How to Do a Word or Concept Study

Because effective communication depends on the meanings of words, word and concept studies are a vital part of the interpretive enterprise. Before turning immediately to a secondary source, such as a lexicon or theological wordbook that gives you the results of word and concept studies that other people have done, you should always consider doing a word study yourself. The process of personal discovery can be both edifying and rewarding. It will also help you better recognize careful research when you find it. There are three steps to the process: (1) Choose a Hebrew word to study. (2) Discover the range of meaning for your Hebrew word (*external data*). (3) Determine the meaning of your Hebrew word in the target text (*internal assessment*). We will examine each step in turn.

1. Choose a Hebrew word to study.

Which word(s) you target for study will vary from passage to passage. Here are some factors to keep in mind when choosing:

a. *Study words or phrases that are theologically significant or crucial to a passage's understanding.* Examples are the meaning of the noun סְגֻלָּה (Strong's [S] 5459; G/K 6035; "treasured possession," ESV) in Exodus 19:5 or the verb אהב (S 157; G/K 170; "to love," ESV) in Deuteronomy 6:5.

b. *Study words or phrases that are puzzling or unclear,* such as הֶבֶל (S 1892; G/K 2039; "vanity," ESV) in Ecclesiastes 1:2.

c. *Study words or phrases that have figurative meanings,* as in the verb phrase וּמָל אֶת־לְבָבְךָ ("and [the LORD your God] will circumcise your heart," ESV) in Deuteronomy 30:6.

d. *Study words or phrases that are apparent synonyms or antonyms,* such as the verbs כבד (S 3513; G/K 3877; Piel "to honor," ESV) and קלל (S 7043; G/K 7837; "to curse," ESV) in 1 Samuel 2:30.

e. *Study words or phrases that are repeated and/or clearly central to the meaning of a passage.* An example is the repeated טוֹב (S 2896; G/K 3202; "good," ESV) in Genesis 1:4, 10, 12, 18, 21, 25, 31.

f. *Study words or phrases that are infrequent*, such as the construction אָסֹף אָסֵף ("I will utterly sweep away," ESV) in Zephaniah 1:2 (cf. Jer. 8:13).

If you don't already know Hebrew, you will need to find the G/K and Strong's numbers associated with your word, for these numbers will give you access to many of the best word-study tools. To acquire these numbers, simply look up your English word in something like *The Strongest NIV Exhaustive Concordance*, and then find your passage. The G/K number is listed to the right of the verse, and you can find the Strong's number by looking at the G/K-to-Strong's index in the back of the *Concordance* or in another tool such as *NIDOTTE*.

2. Discover the range of meaning for your Hebrew word (external data).

Before determining the meaning of your chosen word within a given passage, you must have a clear grasp of the range of the word's meanings throughout the entire Old Testament. As highlighted in "Principles for Doing Word and Concept Studies" above, there are different levels of correspondences or contexts that we need to keep in mind when doing word and concept studies. At the center of focus is (a) our target verse (e.g., Gen. 15:6) within which our chosen word occurs (e.g., צְדָקָה "righteousness"; S 6666; G/K 7407). Next is (b) the context of the whole book (Genesis) and then (c) other books by the same author (Exodus–Deuteronomy). Then we consider (d) other books of the same historical period, genre (prophetic sermons), or canonical division. Beyond this is (e) all the rest of the Old Testament. Thorough word and concept studies will then also need to account for (f) how Hebrew literature outside the Bible used the word, (g) how ancient versions such as the Septuagint translated the word, and finally (h) how similar languages render cognates of the same word. You can usually find comments on the latter three elements in a good lexicon.

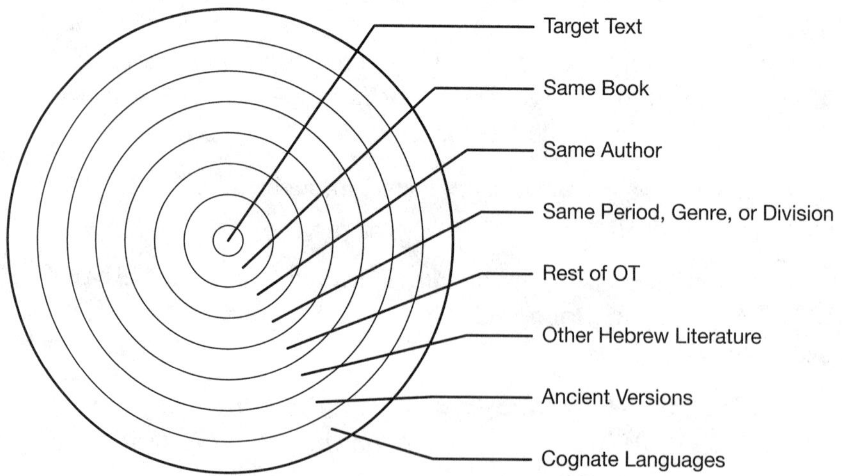

Fig. 7.2. Contexts for a Word/Concept Study[25]

25. A similar image is found in Lee M. Fields, *Hebrew for the Rest of Us: Using Hebrew Tools without Mastering Biblical Hebrew* (Grand Rapids: Zondervan, 2008), 222.

As you move out from the center, you increase the number of possible contexts for your word. Because immediate context is always most determinative for meaning, a high number of examples toward the center may lessen the busy teacher's need to extend the search outward. Nevertheless, thorough study requires this, and the investment can be massively rewarding.

a. Generate a list of texts.

For word studies I first generate a list of all the texts, which is easy to do in any of the major Bible software programs. For those who don't know Hebrew, the best tool at this point is Kohlenberger and Swanson's *The Hebrew-English Concordance to the Old Testament* (see "An Overview of Concordances, Lexicons, and Theological Wordbooks" above). With your G/K number in hand, you simply locate your Hebrew word, which is followed by a complete list of texts in the Old Testament containing it, and all are followed by NIV translations that give context.

b. Categorize meanings.

With the complete list of texts in hand, I then systematically work through every passage, categorizing various meanings and nuances in each context. I did this, for example, with all 229 occurrences of the noun זֶ֫רַע ("seed, offspring"; S 2233; G/K 2446) in the Old Testament. My inspiration for the study arose when I considered how Paul in Romans 4:17–18 and Galatians 3:28–29 portrays Gentile participation in the new covenant as fulfilling Old Testament "seed" promises when those promises themselves, at least initially, appear to *distinguish* the "seed" from the nations. For example, God promises to bless the "nations/Gentiles" in or through the "seed": "in your offspring shall all the nations of the earth be blessed" (Gen. 22:18; cf. 26:4; 28:14).

c. Catalogue and assess your data.

A written word study is not just your lexical homework but the fruits of your labors. After I categorize all texts, I then catalogue and assess my findings. For my study of זֶ֫רַע ("seed, offspring"), I produced the following chart:[26]

	Totals
1. Plant seed or seed time	43 (18.78%)
2. Animal natural seed	3 (1.31%)
3. Human seed	
a. Male semen	7 (3.06%)
b. Natural seed, all-inclusive	87 (37.99%)

Fig. 7.3. Categories of זֶ֫רַע in the Old Testament

26. For my full study, including the chart with all Scripture passages attached, see Jason S. DeRouchie, "Counting Stars with Abraham and the Prophets: New Covenant Ecclesiology in OT Perspective," *JETS* 58, 3 (2015), 445–85, chart on 448–49.

c. Special natural seed: Preexilic old covenant community	49 (21.40%)
d. Special natural seed: Postexilic old covenant community	5 (2.18%)
e. Special natural seed: Singular, male descendant with key role in redemptive history (type and antitype)	9 (3.93%)
f. Special regenerated, adopted seed: Redeemed new covenant community (includes ethnic Israelites and Gentiles)	26 (11.35%)
TOTAL	229

Fig. 7.3. Categories of זֶ֫רַע in the Old Testament (cont.)

I noted a number of features from these data. First, when referring to humans, some instances of זֶ֫רַע ("seed, offspring") are not all-inclusive but restrictive, pertaining to a certain group of "offspring" or even an individual descendant within the greater unit. So, for example, while Ishmael was called Abraham's "seed" (Gen. 21:13), he was not among the "seed" that would inherit the Promised Land (12:7; 17:20). We also note that the use of the third masculine *singular* pronoun identifies three texts in Genesis that explicitly anticipate a unique male deliverer who would overcome Adam's curse and enemy hostility and serve as the agent of blessing to the world (3:15; 22:17b–18; 24:60).[27]

Second, when "seed" refers to humans in the Old Testament, it almost always denotes natural children. In Genesis, for example, Eliezer of Damascus was Abram's heir and a member of his household but not his "seed" (15:2–3), whereas Moab and Ben-ammi were the biological "offspring" of Lot's daughters (19:32, 34, 37–38). The only exception to human "seed" referring to physical descent comes in Old Testament promise texts that address the makeup of the new covenant community (category 3f in fig. 7.3). What my study revealed was that the combination of the old covenant's restriction of "seed" to natural descent and of the new covenant's lack of such restriction highlights a substantial progression in the makeup of the old and new covenant communities and brings focus to the centrality of Christ in redemptive history.

Third, Genesis and several Old Testament prophetic texts anticipate the expansion of "the seed of Abraham" to include those redeemed from both ethnic Israel and the nations during the age of the Messiah. Christ is the "seed" of Abraham (Gal. 3:16), and

27. God declares to the serpent in Genesis 3:15, "I will put enmity between you and the woman, and between your offspring and her offspring; *he* [הוּא] shall bruise your head, and you shall bruise his heel." Similarly, in Genesis 22:17b the Lord declares to Abraham, "And your offspring shall possess the gate *of his enemies* [אֹיְבָיו]." These singular references for זֶ֫רַע stand in contrast to the author's third masculine *plural* suffix in Genesis 17:9: "As for you, you shall keep my covenant, you and your offspring after you *through their generations* [לְדֹרֹתָם]." Moses was able to distinguish singular "seed" (Gen. 3:15; 22:17b; 24:60) from plural "seed" (17:9) when he wanted to do so. For more on this, see Jack Collins, "A Syntactical Note (Genesis 3:15): Is the Woman's Seed Singular or Plural?," *TynBul* 48, 1 (1997): 139–48; T. Desmond Alexander, "Further Observations on the Term 'Seed' in Genesis," *TynBul* 48, 2 (1997): 363–67; Jason S. DeRouchie and Jason C. Meyer, "Christ or Family as the 'Seed' of Promise? An Evaluation of N. T. Wright on Galatians 3:16," *SBJT* 14, 3 (2010): 36–48.

all those who identify with him by faith in turn become the "seed" of Abraham (3:29). Paul's including "nations/Gentiles" among the "seed" (Rom. 4:16–18) fulfills an Old Testament eschatological hope that is linked with the new covenant and associated directly with the representative saving work of the promised royal deliverer, Messiah Jesus (Gal. 3:8, 14, 16, 29).

Assessing the external data at this stage of a word study can exhaust us. Yet it can also help us exult in the Lord for his magnificent revelation.

d. Expand your assessment.

As you work through the various texts containing your word, be mindful of other words that occur in relation to it. Are there regular synonyms or closely related terms that can inform your understanding of the word's meaning in your passage? Does your study help clarify what a term *cannot* mean in your text? For example, in spite of the long history of reading Proverbs 29:18 as a verse related to planning based on forethought ("Where there is no *vision*, the people perish," KJV), חָזוֹן never means "plan" in any of its other thirty-four occurrences but instead consistently points to true or false divine revelations or messages (S 2377; G/K 2606; e.g., 1 Sam. 3:1; Isa. 1:1; Jer. 14:14; Dan. 1:17; Nah. 1:1). Similarly, if your word is a verb, are there common subjects or objects associated with it? For example, in the entire Old Testament, the Lord alone is the subject of the verb ברא ("to create"; S 1254; G/K 1343). Certainly this is significant! If your word is an adjective, are there specific nouns that it commonly modifies? For example, if you are assessing the adjective גָּבֹהַּ ("high"; S 1364; G/K 1469) or noun גֹּבַהּ ("height"; S 1363; G/K 1470), a careful look at all occurrences would reveal that the entire Old Testament highlights only the heights of Saul (1 Sam. 9:2), Eliab (16:7), and Goliath (17:4), all of whom stand as literary foils to David. Thus Hannah's words at the front of the book become significant: "Talk no more so very proudly [אַל־תַּרְבּוּ תְדַבְּרוּ גְּבֹהָה גְבֹהָה],[28] let not arrogance come from your mouth, for the LORD is a God of knowledge and by him actions are weighed. The bows of the mighty are broken, but the feeble bind on strength" (1 Sam. 2:3–4).

3. Determine the meaning of your Hebrew word in the target text (internal assessment).

Having worked diligently to discover the range of meanings for your word in the Old Testament, you are now ready to determine its specific meaning in your passage. Carefully assess the closest contexts, considering the implications for your word's meaning. Does your author use the same term elsewhere in the book? Do other Old Testament authors appropriate the term in similar settings or when addressing similar issues? Does the New Testament ever quote or allude to your text, and if so, does the interpretation offer any clarity? Does your author appear to use the word in a different manner from the way others do?

28. Word for word: "Do not multiply [or] say, 'high! high!'"

Decide what you believe to be your word's meaning within your passage, and then argue your case in writing, because it will help you refine your thought. In the process, consider the lasting theological significance of your decision. How does it impact your passage's overall message?

Once you come to a conclusion, verify your decision against the most important lexicons and theological wordbooks (see "An Overview of Concordances, Lexicons, and Theological Wordbooks" above). Remember: There is no substitute for performing your *own* word study before seeing what others have said. Only with your own research in hand will you be able to evaluate others' claims and to evaluate your own decisions against theirs. Finalize your decision in writing, clarifying for others the meaning of your word within your specific passage and in light of its full range of meaning within the Old Testament.

Nearly every passage with which you wrestle will have important words or concepts that you need to understand in order to fully grasp the meaning of the passage. Careful firsthand wrestling through the data of your concordance matched with interaction with lexicons and theological wordbooks will give you great help in discerning the meaning of the words in your passage.

In the remaining portion of this chapter, I will supply three examples of word and concept studies. Because even those who don't know Hebrew need to learn to do Hebrew-based word studies following the process I detailed above, I encourage all readers to push ahead. If, however, you don't want to engage any more Hebrew at this time, jump ahead to "'YHWH' in Zephaniah" to read an example of a "concept study" in which Hebrew is restricted only to tracking the name of God.

Three Examples of Word and Concept Studies

סְגֻלָּה ("Treasured Possession") in Exodus 19:5

One of the words on which the meaning of Exodus 19:5 hangs is סְגֻלָּה (S 5459; G/K 6035), which the ESV renders "treasured possession." In previous chapters, we finalized our translation of verse 5 as follows: "If you will indeed listen unto my voice and keep my covenant and be my treasured possession from all the peoples . . . ." The term סְגֻלָּה shows up eight times in the Old Testament (Ex. 19:5; Deut. 7:6; 14:2; 26:18; 1 Chron. 29:3; Ps. 135:4; Eccl. 2:8; Mal. 3:17). Its first use in Scripture is in our text, which, as we will see, appears to have impacted the majority of other occurrences, thus showing the foundational role that Exodus 19:4–6 played in shaping Israel's self-understanding.

1. External Data

I have classified the eight passages containing סְגֻלָּה into two groups: (a) nontheological uses and (b) theological uses. This distinction is important, for God's theological use of the term in our text is most probably applying in a spiritual or religious context how the greater society was using the term in everyday life—its more common or secular use.

a. Nontheological uses (2×)

Our first example comes from Ecclesiastes 2:8, where the Preacher, reflecting on his kingship in Jerusalem, declares, "I also gathered for myself silver and gold *and the treasure of kings* [וּסְגֻלַּת מְלָכִים] and provinces. I got singers, both men and women, and many concubines, the delight of the sons of man." Similarly, in 1 Chronicles 29:3, King David asserts of the temple, "Moreover, in addition to all that I have provided for the holy house, I have *a treasure* [סְגֻלָּה] of my own of gold and silver, and because of my devotion to the house of my God I give it to the house of my God."

In both these texts, the סְגֻלָּה appears to be costly, valued, private property of the king that is normally reserved for his sole use and special purposes. Not only this, both instances show that the property is movable—not palaces but treasures associated with silver and gold that could be gathered from others or given for the building of the temple on the king's own prerogative. Ecclesiastes 2:8 may also add that the treasury is something personally gained.

In contrast to the narrow focus of סְגֻלָּה, we find in 1 Chronicles 27:25–31 a list of all the stewards who were over King David's "property" (רְכוּשׁ), which is the broadest term for one's possessions or goods. For David this meant his entire royal estate reaching over the entire kingdom, including all treasuries, workers of the fields for tilling the soil, vineyards, produce from the vineyards for the wine cellars, olive and sycamore trees in the Shephelah, stores of oil, herds that pastured in Sharon and in the valleys, camels, donkeys, and flocks. Because the text distinguishes "the king's treasuries" (אֹצְרוֹת הַמֶּלֶךְ) from those "treasuries" in the country, the cities, the villages, and towers, it seems likely that the סְגֻלָּה was restricted to the private physical but nonliving wealth that David retained in his personal "treasury of the king."

Synthesis: Based on these texts, the common, everyday use of סְגֻלָּה appears to have been "a king's costly, valued, private, movable, nonliving, personally gained property normally reserved for his sole use and special purposes."

b. Theological uses (5× + Exodus 19:5)

We first assess the *Law*, which is the canonical section in which our passage falls, the bulk of which Moses authored. Outside Exodus 19:5, the initial few references are all from Deuteronomy. The first two are worded almost identically, and both are tied to a reaffirmation of Israel's identity as a holy people, which, with סְגֻלָּה, alludes to Exodus 19:5–6. Deuteronomy 7:6 gives the reason why Israel must utterly destroy all Canaanite worship implements: "For you are a people holy to the Lord your God. The Lord your God has chosen you to be a people for his *treasured possession* [סְגֻלָּה],

out of all the peoples who are on the face of the earth." Similarly, Deuteronomy 14:2 stresses why God's people must not engage in pagan worship practices: "For you are a people holy to the Lord your God, and the Lord has chosen you to be a people for his *treasured possession* [סְגֻלָּה], out of all the peoples who are on the face of the earth." As in Exodus 19:5, YHWH's intent for Israel to be his סְגֻלָּה is something not true of all other peoples on the planet. God is calling Israel to live out a distinct status. The text stresses that YHWH *chose* Israel to be a סְגֻלָּה, which highlights the value he places on his people.

We already encountered the next text in our earlier grammatical discussion of the protasis and apodosis in Exodus 19:5–6 (see "Determining the Protasis and Apodosis in Exodus 19:5–6" in chapter 5). Deuteronomy 26:18 reads, "And the Lord has today confirmed your declaration to be a people of treasured possession [סְגֻלָּה], just as he declared to you, and to keep all his commandments" (author's translation). Here, once again, living as YHWH's סְגֻלָּה is God's expectation for Israel.

We next assess the Prophets and Writings. While YHWH called Israel to holiness and to serve as his kingdom of priests by pursuing him wholly, the history of Israel showed that the people's hearts were far from God. Thus, because they would not know him intimately, God declared through his prophet Hosea, "My people are destroyed for lack of knowledge; because you have rejected knowledge, I reject you from being a priest to me" (Hos. 4:6). What we see in the final two texts, however, is that this was not the final verdict and that YHWH would one day empower a remnant from Israel to be who the nation could not be on its own.

First, we read in Malachi 3:17, "They shall be mine, says the Lord of hosts, in the day when I make up my *treasured possession* [סְגֻלָּה], and I will spare them as a man spares his son who serves him." No harm will come to those who are God's. God will protect them, but he will punish the wicked. Malachi goes on to distinguish the righteous from the wicked as "one who serves God and one who does not serve him" (3:18). To be God's סְגֻלָּה—his "treasured possession"—means that you will be his servant. When, therefore, YHWH charges Israel in Exodus 19:5 to "be my treasured possession" (וִהְיִיתֶם לִי סְגֻלָּה), it seems likely that he is calling Israel to live in his service.

The last Old Testament text is in Psalm 135:3–4: "Praise the Lord, for the Lord is good; sing to his name, for it is pleasant! For the Lord has chosen Jacob for himself, Israel *as his own possession* [לִסְגֻלָּתוֹ]." The final book of the Psalter celebrates the God who restores and renews in anticipation of his full Davidic kingdom fulfillment.[29] Psalm 132 has just reaffirmed the Davidic covenant, and Psalms 133 and 134 celebrate the unity of the righteous and the hope for God's blessing. Into this context Psalm 135 reaffirms YHWH's claim on his own: "The Lord has chosen Jacob for himself, Israel *as his own possession*." The wording is more specific and personal than in earlier texts, using the third masculine singular suffix to emphasize that Israel is *his*.

29. For this reading, see Michael K. Snearly, "The Return of the King: Book V as a Witness to Messianic Hope in the Psalter," in *The Psalms: Language for All Seasons of the Soul*, ed. Andrew J. Schmutzer and David M. Howard (Chicago: Moody Press, 2014), 209–17.

2. Internal Assessment: The Meaning of סְגֻלָּה in Exodus 19:5

The nontheological uses of סְגֻלָּה in Ecclesiastes 2:8 and 1 Chronicles 29:3 pointed to the word meaning "a king's costly, valued, private, movable, nonliving, personally gained property normally reserved for his sole use and special purposes." סְגֻלָּה was indeed the king's "treasured possession."

The theological uses of סְגֻלָּה suggest that this is exactly how the Israelites were to think of themselves in their relationship with God. They were his costly, valued, private, personally gained property reserved for his special purpose. They stood distinct from the world as his special treasure (Ex. 19:5; Deut. 7:6; 14:2). Their responsibility was to live like it, which meant fleeing wickedness and serving YHWH (Mal. 3:17). In time, Israel's rebellion caused the people to lose their priestly status (Hos. 4:6). Nevertheless, in the context of celebrating God's greatness and the hope of complete Davidic kingdom restoration, the psalmist affirms YHWH's claim on Israel, his treasure (Ps. 135:4). The Lord also promises that one day he would bring about by his power what the people could not accomplish on their own (Mal. 3:17). They would live as his servants and in so doing mediate and magnify his greatness to the world.

The LXX translates סְגֻלָּה in Exodus 19:5 as λαὸς περιούσιος, which is the same phrase Paul employs in Titus 2:14, where he highlights that Jesus Christ "gave himself for us to redeem us from all lawlessness and to purify for himself a people for his own possession [λαὸν περιούσιον] who are zealous for good works." Thus the church is now fulfilling the God-honoring calling of Israel by the power supplied through Christ. Jesus mediated and magnified the majesty of God perfectly in his life, death, and exaltation, and now in him we are enabled to do the same.

Similarly, in a context of calling the church to holiness (1 Peter 1:14–16) and stressing that those who come to Christ "are being built up . . . to be a holy priesthood, to offer spiritual sacrifices acceptable to God through Jesus Christ" (2:5), Peter alludes to Exodus 19:5, using περιποίησις, which means the same thing—a "treasured possession" of God: "But you are a chosen race, a royal priesthood, a holy nation, *a people for his own possession* [λαός εἰς περιποίησις], that you may proclaim the excellencies of him who called you out of darkness into his marvelous light" (1 Peter 2:9). In Exodus 19 Israel's call to be a "treasured possession" was only potential, but in the church of Christ it is already being realized. In Jesus we are enabled to live as God's "treasured possession," serving him in the strength he supplies (1 Peter 4:11), and by this we are functioning as a kingdom of priests and a holy nation under our king, to the praise of his glorious grace.

הֶבֶל ("Vanity"?) in Ecclesiastes

The thematic motto of the entire book of Ecclesiastes is captured in 1:2: הֲבֵל הֲבָלִים אָמַר קֹהֶלֶת הֲבֵל הֲבָלִים הַכֹּל הָבֶל (ESV = "Vanity of vanities, says the Preacher, vanity of vanities! All is vanity."). The key term הֶבֶל (S 1892; G/K 2039) is repeated five times in this one verse and thirty-eight times in the whole book, including in the final refrain of 12:8, just before the book's conclusion. Following the path set by the Latin Vulgate's *vanitas*, most recent translators render the term negatively as "vanity" (NASB, NRSV, ESV), "meaninglessness" (NIV), "futility" (NET Bible, CSB), or "absurdity" (various commentators[30]). Because *everything* is הֶבֶל, according to the Preacher, assigning a negative meaning to the term colors the book's message with dark hues. Indeed, some view the Preacher Qoheleth's teaching to be unorthodox, pessimistic, and fatalistic, and they compare it with the statements of Job's three friends that God condemns (Job 42:7). These same scholars often contrast this misguided "voice" with that of the final narrator, whose own orthodoxy is highlighted in the book's final verses: "The end of the matter; all has been heard. Fear God and keep his commandments" (Eccl. 12:13).[31]

Not all scholars agree. Indeed, many see theological unity in the entire book and prefer tagging Qoheleth as a "preacher of joy,"[32] a "godly sage,"[33] or an orthodox "realist."[34] Often this alternative approach is colored by a more positive definition of הֶבֶל, whether as "transient, temporary, or fleeting" on the one hand or what is "mysterious, incomprehensible, or enigmatic" on the other.

30. E.g., Michael V. Fox, "The Meaning of *Hebel* for Qohelet," *JBL* 105, 3 (1986): 409–27; Fox, *Qoheleth and His Contradictions*, JSOTSup 71 (Sheffield, UK: Almond Press, 1989), 29–46; Duane A. Garrett, *Proverbs, Ecclesiastes, Song of Songs*, NAC 14 (Nashville: Broadman & Holman, 1993), 283.

31. So Tremper Longman III, *Ecclesiastes*, NICOT (Grand Rapids: Eerdmans, 1998), 32–36; Gordon D. Fee and Douglas Stuart, *How to Read the Bible for All Its Worth*, 2nd ed. (Grand Rapids: Zondervan, 1993), 214.

32. R. N. Whybray, "Qoheleth, Preacher of Joy," *JSOT* 7, 23 (1982): 87–98; cf. Douglas Wilson, *Joy at the End of the Tether: The Inscrutable Wisdom of Ecclesiastes* (Moscow, ID: Canon, 1999).

33. Ardel B. Caneday, "Qoheleth: Enigmatic Pessimist or Godly Sage?," *GTJ* 7, 1 (1986): 21–56; Robert V. McCabe, "The Message of Ecclesiastes," *DBSJ* 1, 1 (1996): 85–112 (see 87 for the title "godly sage").

34. Daniel C. Fredericks, "Ecclesiastes," in *Ecclesiastes and The Song of Songs*, by Daniel C. Fredericks and Daniel J. Estes, ApOTC 16 (Downers Grove, IL: InterVarsity Press, 2010), 40–41.

	Less Abstract	*More Abstract*
Negative view of הֶבֶל	(1) Vanity, meaninglessness (of things); futility (of actions) —— *"All things in this world are worthless, valueless, or profitless."*	(2) Irrationality, senselessness, absurdity —— *"All things in this world are counter-rational or a violation of reason."*
Positive view of הֶבֶל	(3) Transience, temporariness, fleetingness, ephemerality —— *"All things in this world are brief."*	(4) Mystery, incomprehensibility, ungraspability, enigma —— *"All things in this world are not fully in humanity's power to comprehend."*

Fig. 7.4. Categories of Meaning Assigned to הֶבֶל in Ecclesiastes

1. External Data: Overview of הֶבֶל outside Ecclesiastes

At base, הֶבֶל means "wisp of air, breath, vapor." The initial aspirated "h" followed by the spirant "v" sound suggests that the word is probably onomatopoeic, which means that it is spoken by the exhalation of "breath" that the word itself denotes: "*hébel*." Only three instances of actual physical "breath" are found in the Old Testament, and even with these the point is to stress the breathlike futility of wickedness (Ps. 62:9[H10]; Prov. 21:6; Isa. 57:13). In all the rest of the occurrences, including all thirty-eight in Ecclesiastes, the nominal and verbal instances are metaphorical.

Many of the occurrences outside Ecclesiastes retain the sense of the "ephemeral" or "fleeting" (e.g., Job 7:16; Pss. 39:6[H7], 11[H12]; 144:4). In other instances, the noun denotes "valuelessness" or "inefficacy" (and so "vanity"), in that something does not or cannot fulfill what it implicitly promises (e.g., Job 9:29; Isa. 30:7; 49:4; Jer. 10:2). Accordingly, הֶבֶל appears to denote "worthlessness" in a number of contexts where it parallels nouns such as תֹּהוּ ("nothingness"); רִיק ("emptiness"); לֹא יוֹעִיל ("it is not profitable"); and the like (Isa. 30:6–7; 49:4; 57:12–13; Jer. 16:19). Furthermore, in contexts where הֶבֶל parallels nouns such as אָוֶן ("misdeed"); כָּזָב ("delusion"); מַעַל ("unfaithfulness"); שָׁוְא ("worthless, without result"); and שֶׁקֶר ("falsehood"), it carries the sense of "deceit" (e.g., Job 21:34; Ps. 62:10; Prov. 31:30; Zech. 10:2). Out of this framework, הֶבֶל also serves as a designation for false gods (e.g., Deut. 32:21; 2 Kings 17:15; Jer. 8:19; 14:22; 16:19; Jonah 2:8[H9]). Finally, in some texts הֶבֶל appears to express that which is "senseless, foolish, or without thought," as when Elihu states that "Job opens his mouth in empty talk [הֶבֶל]; he multiplies words without knowledge" (Job 35:16; cf. Ps. 39:6[H7]; Jer. 10:3, 8).

2. Internal Assessment: הֶבֶל in Ecclesiastes

In its refrain, Ecclesiastes equates הֶבֶל with "everything" (Eccl. 1:2; 12:8). This fact, along with the formulaic character of the הֶבֶל-judgments throughout the rest of the book, suggests that there is a common definition to the book's various occurrences and that 1:2 and 12:8 summarize Qoheleth's thought on reality.

What types of things does the Preacher judge to be הֶבֶל? First would be human activity, such as toil and its products (Eccl. 2:11, 18–26; 4:4, 7–8, 15–16; 5:10; 6:1–2), pleasure (2:1; 6:9), wisdom and growing wise (2:15; 7:15–16), and words (5:6–7; 6:10–11): "Then I considered all that my hands had done and the toil I had expended in doing it, and behold, all was *hébel* and a striving after wind, and there was nothing to be gained under the sun" (2:11). Next, he considers as הֶבֶל living beings and times in their lives (3:18–19; 6:12; 7:15–16; 9:9; 11:10): "For who knows what is good for man while he lives the few days of his *hébel* life, which he passes like a shadow? For who can tell man what will be after him under the sun?" (6:12). Finally, divine behavior is הֶבֶל, whether portrayed broadly as "everything" that happens (1:2, 14; 2:17; 6:3–4; 11:8–9; 12:8) or as divine justice in particular (2:15, 26; 6:1–2; 8:10, 14): "There is a *hébel* that takes place on earth, that there are righteous people to whom it happens according to the deeds of the wicked, and there are wicked people to whom it happens according to the deeds of the righteous. I said that this also is *hébel*" (8:14).

While certain contexts may support "vanity, emptiness" (Eccl. 2:1, 11, 19, 21) or "transience" (2:15; 3:19; 6:12), neither of these options fits all instances. Furthermore, in light of the Preacher's calls to joy and affirmation of the need to fear and remember God, it is difficult to believe that he views life as "worse than pointless" and "absurd." I think "enigma" (i.e., not fully comprehensible but still meaningful) best captures the overall thrust of הֶבֶל in every instance throughout the book.

a. הֶבֶל *as "meaninglessness, pointlessness, or absurdity"*

There are at least four reasons not to render הֶבֶל as that which is "meaningless, pointless, or absurd." First, common synonyms for הֶבֶל when it means "meaninglessness" or "valuelessness" are completely absent in Ecclesiastes—e.g., רֵיק ("empty, idle, worthless"); רִיק ("emptiness"); שָׁוְא "worthless, without result"; תֹּהוּ ("nothingness"). Second, the Preacher often says that one thing is "better than" another (e.g., "Two are better than one, because they have a good reward for their toil," 4:9; cf. 3:22; 5:1; 7:1–3, 5, 8, 10; 9:4, 16–18). These "better than" statements all suggest that there is meaning in life. If all things are completely without meaning (i.e., meaningless), how, then, can something be more meaningless or more absurd than something else? Third, if all is "meaningless" or "absurd," why should we listen to Qoheleth's own conclusions, which would themselves be pointless? Nevertheless, he expects us to learn from his teaching and to heed his wisdom. Fourth, the Preacher affirmed deep meaning in life, for he tagged much in this life as "evil, trouble" (9:3), "grievous evil" (5:13, 16; 6:2), "great evil" (2:21), and "unhappy business" (1:13; 4:8)—all declarations that uphold a standard of truth and rightness and a conviction that the universe needs "straightening" (1:14–15;

7:13). Pain or offense testifies to one's innate sense of meaning and purposefulness, whether accurate or misguided.

b. הֶבֶל *as "transience, temporariness, or fleetingness"*

There are also a number of reasons not to translate הֶבֶל as that which is "transient, temporary, or fleeting." First, while the Preacher addresses the unchanging cycles of "every matter under heaven" (Eccl. 3:1; cf. 1:4–11; 3:2–8; 12:2–7), the point of affirming life's repetitions and even brevity is not to highlight life's temporariness but to identify the enigma of history's recursive nature and of each generation's relative insignificance in the scope of God's story. For example, after observing the Lord's call on mankind to live wisely in all seasons of life (3:1–10), Qoheleth clarified the point of his temporal observations—no one is able to fully grasp God's purposes from start to finish: "He has made everything beautiful in its time. Also, he has put eternity into man's heart, yet so that he cannot find out what God has done from the beginning to the end" (3:11). Second, as the Preacher describes life's unhappy business, he portrays an existence that is anything but temporary, at least from the perspective of the human experiencing it. For example, the workaholic has "no end to all his toil"; his greed is "never satisfied"; and he "never asks, 'For whom am I toiling and depriving myself of pleasure?'" (4:8). Furthermore, the leaving of one's wealth to another who never worked for it (2:19, 21, 23) is not simply הֶבֶל but a "great evil" (2:21) that leads to a lifetime of "sorrow" and "vexation," "despair over all the toil of my labors under the sun" (2:20, 23).

c. הֶבֶל *as "enigma or frustrating mystery"*

The Preacher says in Ecclesiastes 11:7–8, "Light is sweet [not meaningless or absurd], and it is pleasant [not pointless or senseless] for the eyes to see the sun. So if a person lives many years [far from brief], let him rejoice in them all [far from meaningless or absurd]; but let him remember that the days of darkness will be many [not few and fleeting]. All that comes is *enigma* [הֶבֶל]" (modified ESV). Along with the challenges to the other views, rendering הֶבֶל as "enigma" finds much support in Ecclesiastes.

First, when Qoheleth asserted that "all" in creation was הֶבֶל, numerous verses suggest that he meant that nothing in the universe this side of eternity was fully understandable, whether bad or good. "I saw all the work of God, that man cannot find out the work that is done under the sun. However much man may toil in seeking, he will not find it out. Even though a wise man claims to know, he cannot find it out" (Eccl. 8:17). The point is not that truth is "unknowable" or "unintelligible" but that reality is ultimately "unfathomable." While we are able to know and understand some truths, realities such as the repetitive character of life and nature (1:4–7, 9–10), the soul's inability to be satisfied (1:8), and the failure of every new generation to learn from the past (1:11) make existence in this present age "wearisome" at best (1:8; cf. 8:17; Ps. 73:16). All things bear a level of mystery and frustration, and this is the meaning of הֶבֶל. From this framework, the Preacher writes: "[God] has put eternity into man's hearts, yet so that he cannot find out what God has done from the beginning to the end" (Eccl. 3:11). "Consider the work of God: who can make straight what he has made crooked? In the day of prosperity be joyful, and in the day of adversity consider: God has made the one as well as the other, so that man may not find out anything that will be after him" (7:13–14). "As you do not know the way the spirit comes to the bones in the womb of a woman with child, so you do not know the work of God who makes everything" (11:5; cf. 1:17–18; 6:11–12; 8:5–7).

Second, while the world as we know it is far from meaningless, absurd, or fleeting, for Qoheleth it is impossible to fully understand. Both the "evil" and the "good" raise mental dilemmas. On the one hand, the Preacher calls aspects of life עִנְיַן רָע ("a bad business, an evil occupation," Eccl. 1:13; 4:8; 5:13), חֳלִי רָע ("a sickness of evil," 6:2), and the like, as when life seems "unfair": "Sometimes a person who has toiled with wisdom and knowledge and skill must leave everything to be enjoyed by someone who did not toil for it. This also is an *enigma* [הֶבֶל] and a *great evil* [2:21) "[רָעָה רַבָּה], author's translation). On the other hand, affirming the complete depravity of mankind (7:20; cf. 4:4; 7:29; 9:3) and recognizing the global impact of the curse (7:13; 11:5), the Preacher struggles to understand how justice could ever happen, as when "to one who pleases him God has given wisdom and knowledge and joy, but to the sinner he has given the business of gathering and collecting, only to give to one who pleases God. This is an *enigma* [הֶבֶל] and a shepherding of wind" (2:26, author's translation). Similarly, the sweetness of fresh mercies at dawn and of pleasures during cloud-cast skies (11:7–8) was as much הֶבֶל as the unjust gain of the wicked (8:14). For Qoheleth, life clearly has meaning, for there is "evil" and there is "good." Nevertheless, the presence of both challenges the mind, and the reality of this internal wrestling suggests that הֶבֶל means "enigma."

Third, support for reading הֶבֶל as "enigma" also comes from two recurring phrases that are regularly appended to Qoheleth's הֶבֶל-judgments, bearing the same contexts and referents: רְעוּת רוּחַ ("a shepherding of wind") (Eccl. 1:14; 2:11, 17, 26; 4:4, 6; 6:9) and רַעְיוֹן רוּחַ ("a thought of wind") (1:17; 4:16). The ESV translates both phrases "a striving after wind," but their distinction in the Hebrew text suggests that we should render them differently. Nevertheless, the point of these phrases is the same—that grasping why the world works the way it does is like trying to grab wind by its tail. It can't be done.

Besides the nine combined instances of "a shepherding of wind" and "a thought of wind" in Ecclesiastes, the only other occurrence of the root רעה ("to shepherd") is in Ecclesiastes 12:11, where the words of the wise are said to be "given by *one Shepherd* [רֹעֶה אֶחָד]." While many scholars have thought that a reference to God as "one Shepherd" is intrusive and does not fit the context of Ecclesiastes, I believe that no better title could have been chosen. Indeed, when people find themselves in a world that makes little sense—a world where trying to understand reality is like shepherding the wind—what is needed is confidence in one Shepherd who has been guiding all things well for all time (3:11). God creates everything (12:1), yet he does so in a way that makes it so that we cannot grasp all his purposes (11:5; cf. 7:13–14). He works his providence this way "so that people fear before him" (3:14), for "it will be well with those who fear God, . . . but it will not be well with the wicked" (8:12–13). The one Shepherd is the great provider and protector of his own, and fearing him amid life's enigmas enables one to find joy in this painful existence as we await the day when he, through his "one shepherd," will triumph over all wrongs and establish peace for his people (Ezek. 34:23; 37:24; John 10:16).[35]

"YHWH" in Zephaniah

I have given some examples of general word studies. In this section I want to show how a word study often requires branching out to the concept associated with a term. By *concept* I mean that often we cannot simply look up a single word but must also consider the other words or concepts most related to it. In Zephaniah 2:3 the prophet urges, "Seek the Lord, all you humble of the land, who do his just commands; seek righteousness; seek humility; perhaps you may be hidden on the day of the anger of the Lord." You know that whenever our English translations use "Lord" in large and small caps, the term represents God's proper name, YHWH. If I were preaching this text, I might want to pause to consider what the book of Zephaniah itself tells me about this God who is to be sought and whose anger will pour forth at the day of the Lord. To consider such things, I need to do more than a simple word study. I must do a concept study, for all I need to know about YHWH will be gained only if I look beyond the name itself. I need to know what titles are associated with him and in what contexts. I need to know what the book tells me God does and who the book says he is. So I start with the titles. As we will see, a key purpose of the book is clearly to exalt YHWH God as the sovereign Judge and supreme Savior who deserves everyone's reverence.

The proper name "YHWH" (יהוה, used 34×; S 3068; G/K 3378) is God's most common designation, with ten of these coming from the Lord himself. The name firmly fits the book within the Mosaic covenant (cf. Ex. 3:14–16; 6:6–8; 34:6–7, 14), a fact also highlighted by the frequent allusions to the Law in the various indictments, instructions, curses, and blessings. The name likely comes from the causative Hiphil stem of the *to be* verb היה (S 1961; G/K 2118). If so, the name "YHWH" also stresses God as the only uncaused one, who creates and controls all things visible and invisible, material and immaterial (see Rom. 11:36; Col. 1:16; Heb. 1:3). The book confirms and builds on this point by summarizing its contents (Zeph. 1:1) and God's purposed

35. For an expanded version of this word study with more theological reflection and direct interaction with scholars holding other views, see Jason S. DeRouchie, "Shepherding Wind and One Wise Shepherd: Grasping for Breath in Ecclesiastes," *SBJT* 15, 3 (2011): 4–25.

activity (2:5) as "the word of YHWH" and by emphasizing both the Lord's "utterance" (1:2–3, 10; 2:9; 3:8) and the outworkings of his "decree" (2:2), of all he has "appointed" (3:7), and of his "decision" (3:8).

When referring to the coming restoration, Zephaniah joins the name "YHWH" with the title "their/your God" (Zeph. 2:7; 3:17) to offer comfort to the remnant. In contrast, the prophet calls him "the Sovereign YHWH" (1:7) when demanding reverence in view of the impending day of the Lord. Accordingly, when castigating Moab and the sons of Ammon for their pride and aggression against his people, God tags himself as "YHWH of hosts/armies" (2:9–10) and then underlines his favor toward his own with the title "the God of Israel" (2:9). Elsewhere Zephaniah designates the Lord as "her [Jerusalem's] God" (3:2), and then he calls him "the King of Israel" (3:15; cf. 2:5) and "a Warrior" (3:17; cf. 3:14) when stressing the certainty of the remnant's deliverance. Along with these titles, the prophet designates YHWH's character as "righteous" (3:5a) and notes his homage-demanding presence as both "awesome" (2:11a) and "in your [Jerusalem's] midst" (3:15c, 17a).

Of the no less than thirty-seven different verbal roots used in relation to the Lord, all are fientive, focusing on God's actions. In what follows, I synthesize all roots used two or more times, along with some others. While the complacent in Jerusalem declared that God would neither "do good" nor "do ill" (Zeph. 1:11), Zephaniah's message of retribution stresses otherwise. YHWH is the one who "gathers" and "assembles" for the purpose of punishment (1:2–3; 3:8) and restoration (3:18–20). When he "attends to" someone, there is either chastisement (1:8–9, 12; 3:7) or redemption (2:7). When he "stretches out" his hand (1:4; 2:13), he "cuts off" (1:3–4, 11; 3:6–7) and "destroys" (2:5, 13). He "pours out" both indignation (3:8) and blood (1:17), so that all opponents are "consumed" (1:18; 3:8). Why? It is because "against YHWH they have sinned" (1:17; cf. 2:9). YHWH always "does" what is just (3:5) and will "deal" with all the wicked (1:18), including oppressors (3:19). He will "remove" the proud enemies (3:11, 15) but will "save" his humble followers (3:17, 19) and "restore" their fortunes (2:7; 3:20). He will "make" Nineveh for a desolation (2:13) but his redeemed for praise and renown (3:19). Indeed, he will "give" his elect for name and acclaim (3:20), as he carries on his daily purpose to "give" his justice for light (3:5). In 3:20 the prophet couches all his words as that which YHWH "has said," but God also has two embedded reported speech acts that declare his past longing for his people's repentance (3:7) and his future commitment to fully save and savor his redeemed (3:16).

As the supreme Sovereign, Savior, and Satisfier, YHWH deserves highest allegiance, and it is his just "jealousy" for the fame of his own name that kindles his sacrificial fires of punishment against the ungodly (Zeph. 1:18; 3:8; cf. Ex. 34:14). Because he has diminished "all the gods of the earth," every knee "shall bow" to him (Zeph. 2:11; cf. Isa. 45:23; Rom. 14:11; Phil. 2:10), some as condemned prisoners of war (Zeph. 3:15, 19; cf. Isa. 45:14; Ezek. 39:6; Mic. 7:16–17) and others as redeemed worshipers (Zeph. 3:9–10; cf. Isa. 2:3; 66:20; Zech. 8:22–23). In the end, YHWH will celebrate over his purified remnant of faithful (Zeph. 3:17) whom he is transforming as a people of joy (3:14) for his "praise" and his "renown" throughout the earth (3:19–20; cf. Jer. 13:11; 33:9).

When Zephaniah calls his audience to "seek YHWH" (Zeph. 2:3), the object of his focus is quite defined. I gained all this information by walking verse by verse through the book and writing down all that I learned about YHWH. I catalogued all the verbs and titles, noted where similar titles and verbs were used and in what contexts, and then restated what I learned in this flowing overview. This study shows that we often need to look beyond a single word to uncover what we need to know about a single concept in a passage. Any given word may carry a lot of theological freight, and we will gain much by thinking through synonyms and related concepts when assessing our texts.

A Final Note

We are now ready to move to our next step in the interpretive process and from the "Observation" stage into "Context." Text → Observation → *Context* → Meaning → Application. From this point forward in the book, nearly every section should be accessible to all readers, regardless of whether you know Hebrew.

Key Words and Concepts

Concordance, lexicon, and theological wordbook
Cognate

Questions for Further Reflection

1. Why are word and concept studies important?
2. List some of the fallacies commonly committed when doing a word study.
3. What is the importance of context in determining a word's meaning?
4. What are the most important factors to consider when determining how much the meaning of a word in a different passage should bear on our understanding of its meaning in our passage? How do you know which occurrences should influence your study the most?
5. What are some of the factors in selecting which word to study in a passage?
6. Which of the three examples of word and concept studies did you find the most helpful? Why?

Resources for Further Study

Word-Study Theory and Methodology

Barr, James. *The Semantics of Biblical Language*. London: Oxford University Press, 1961; repr., Eugene, OR: Wipf & Stock, 2004.

Carson, D. A. "Word-Study Fallacies." In *Exegetical Fallacies*, 27–64. 2nd ed. Grand Rapids: Baker Academic, 1996.

★ Fields, Lee M. "What Do You Mean?—Hebrew Word Studies." In *Hebrew for the Rest of Us: Using Hebrew Tools without Mastering Biblical Hebrew*, 221–33. Grand Rapids: Zondervan, 2008.

Gibson, Arthur. *Biblical Semantic Logic: A Preliminary Analysis*. Sheffield, UK: Sheffield Academic, 2002.

Oxford English Dictionary. http://www.oed.com/.

Silva, Moisés. *Biblical Words and Their Meaning: An Introduction to Lexical Semantics*. 2nd ed. Grand Rapids: Zondervan, 1994.

———. "God, Language, and Scripture: Reading the Bible in the Light of General Linguistics." In *Foundations of Contemporary Interpretation*, edited by Moisés Silva, 193–280. Grand Rapids: Zondervan, 1996.

Walton, John H. "Principles for Productive Word Study." *NIDOTTE* 1:161–70.

Hebrew and Aramaic Lexicons

Brown, Francis, S. R. Driver, and Charles A. Briggs. *The New Brown-Driver-Briggs Hebrew and English Lexicon*. Peabody, MA: Hendrickson, 1979.

Clines, David J. A., ed. *The Concise Dictionary of Classical Hebrew*. Sheffield, UK: Sheffield Phoenix, 2009.

———, ed. *The Dictionary of Classical Hebrew*. 9 vols. Sheffield, UK: Sheffield Phoenix, 1993–2014.

Comprehensive Aramaic Lexicon. http://cal1.cn.huc.edu/.

Einspahr, Bruce. *Index to Brown, Driver & Briggs Hebrew Lexicon*. 2nd ed. Chicago: Moody, 1976.

Holladay, William L. *A Concise Hebrew and Aramaic Lexicon of the Old Testament*. Grand Rapids: Eerdmans, 1988.

Jastrow, Marcus. *A Dictionary of the Targumim, the Talmud Babli and Yerushalmi, and the Midrashic Literature*. 2nd ed. 2 vols. in 1. 1926; repr., New York: Judaica, 1996. Available at http://www.tyndalearchive.com/tabs/jastrow/.

✪ Koehler, Ludwig, Walter Baumgartner, and Johann Jakob Stamm, eds. *The Hebrew and Aramaic Lexicon of the Old Testament: Study Edition*. Translated by M. E. J. Richardson. 2 vols. Leiden: Brill, 2001.

★ Mounce, William D., ed. *Mounce's Complete Expository Dictionary of Old and New Testament Words*. Grand Rapids: Zondervan, 2006.

Sokoloff, Michael. *A Dictionary of Jewish Babylonian Aramaic*. Baltimore: Johns Hopkins University Press, 2003.

———. *A Dictionary of Jewish Palestinian Aramaic of the Byzantine Period*. 2nd ed. Baltimore: Johns Hopkins University Press, 2002.

Vine, W. E., Merrill F. Unger, and William White Jr. *Vine's Complete Expository Dictionary of Old and New Testament Words*. London: Oliphants, 1939; repr., Nashville: Thomas Nelson, 1996.

Vogt, Ernesto. *Lexicon Linguae Aramaicae Veteris Testamenti Documentis Antiquis Illustratum*. Rome: Pontifical Biblical Institute, 1991.

Hebrew and Hebrew-English Concordances

Computer resources: *Accordance* (http://www.accordancebible.com/), *BibleWorks* (http://www.bibleworks.com/), *Logos Bible Software* (https://www.logos.com/).

Evan-Shoshan, Abraham, ed. *A New Concordance of the Old Testament Using the Hebrew and Aramaic Text*. Grand Rapids: Baker Academic, 1989.

★ Kohlenberger, John R., III, and James A. Swanson. *The Hebrew-English Concordance to the Old Testament*. Grand Rapids: Zondervan, 1998.

Greek Septuagint Lexicons

Chamberlain, Gary Alan. *The Greek of the Septuagint: A Supplemental Lexicon*. Peabody, MA: Hendrickson, 2011.

Danker, Frederick W., et al. *Greek-English Lexicon of the New Testament and Other Early Christian Literature*. 3rd ed. Chicago: University of Chicago Press, 2000.

Liddell, H. G., and R. Scott. *Greek-English Lexicon with a Revised Supplement*. 9th ed. Oxford: Clarendon, 1996.

Louw, Johannes P., and Eugene A. Nida, eds. *Greek-English Lexicon of the New Testament: Based on Semantic Domains*. 2nd ed. 2 vols. New York: United Bible Societies, 1989.

Muraoka, T. *A Greek-English Lexicon of the Septuagint*. Leuven: Peeters, 2010.

Taylor, Bernard A. *Analytical Lexicon to the Septuagint*. 2nd ed. Peabody, MA: Hendrickson, 2009.

Thesaurus Linguae Graecae. http://stephanus.tlg.uci.edu/.

Greek Septuagint Concordances

Computer resources: *Accordance* (http://www.accordancebible.com/), *BibleWorks* (http://www.bibleworks.com/), *Logos Bible Software* (https://www.logos.com/).

Hatch, Edwin, and Henry A. Redpath. *A Concordance to the Septuagint and the Other Greek Versions of the Old Testament*. 2nd ed. Grand Rapids: Baker Academic, 1998.

Morrish, George. *A Handy Concordance of the Septuagint: Giving Various Readings from Codices Vaticanus, Alexandrinus, Sinaiticus, and Ephraemi*. London: Bagster, 1887; repr., Eugene, OR: Wipf & Stock, 2008.

Muraoka, T. *Greek-Hebrew/Aramaic Two-Way Index to the Septuagint*. Leuven: Peeters, 2010.

———. *Hebrew/Aramaic Index to the Septuagint Keyed to the Hatch-Redpath Concordance*. Grand Rapids: Baker Academic, 1998.

Dead Sea Scrolls Concordance

Abegg, Martin G., Jr., James E. Bowley, and Edward M. Cook, eds. *The Dead Sea Scrolls Concordance.* 3 vols. Leiden: Brill, 2003–9.

Computer resources: *Accordance* (http://www.accordancebible.com/), *BibleWorks* (http://www.bibleworks.com/), *Logos Bible Software* (https://www.logos.com/).

Theological Wordbooks

Old Testament

Botterweck, G. Johannes, Helmer Ringgren, and Heinz-Josef Fabry, eds. *Theological Dictionary of the Old Testament.* 15 vols. Grand Rapids: Eerdmans, 1974–2006.

★ Harris, R. Laird, Gleason L. Archer Jr., and Bruce K. Waltke. *Theological Wordbook of the Old Testament.* Rev. 1-vol. ed. Chicago: Moody, 2003.

Jenni, Ernst, and Claus Westermann, eds. *Theological Lexicon of the Old Testament.* Translated by Mark E. Biddle. 3 vols. Peabody, MA: Hendrickson, 1994.

✪ VanGemeren, Willem A., ed. *New International Dictionary of Old Testament Theology and Exegesis.* 5 vols. Grand Rapids: Zondervan, 1997.

Other

Alexander, T. Desmond, and Brian S. Rosner, eds. *New Dictionary of Biblical Theology: Exploring the Unity and Diversity of Scripture.* Downers Grove, IL: InterVarsity Press, 2000.

Bauer, Johannes B., ed. *Encyclopedia of Biblical Theology.* 3 vols. London: Sheed & Ward, 1970; repr., New York: Crossroad, 1981.

Kittel, Gerhard, and Gerhard Friedrich, eds. *Theological Dictionary of the New Testament.* Translated by Geoffrey W. Bromiley. 10 vols. Grand Rapids: Eerdmans, 1964–76.

Silva, Moisés, ed. *New International Dictionary of New Testament Theology and Exegesis.* 2nd ed. 5 vols. Grand Rapids: Zondervan, 2014.

Spicq, Ceslas, ed. *Theological Lexicon of the New Testament.* Translated by James D. Ernest. 3 vols. Peabody, MA: Hendrickson, 1993.

PART 3

CONTEXT—"WHERE DOES THE PASSAGE FIT?"

8

HISTORICAL CONTEXT

Goal: Understand the historical situation from which the author composed the text and identify any historical details that the author mentions or assumes.

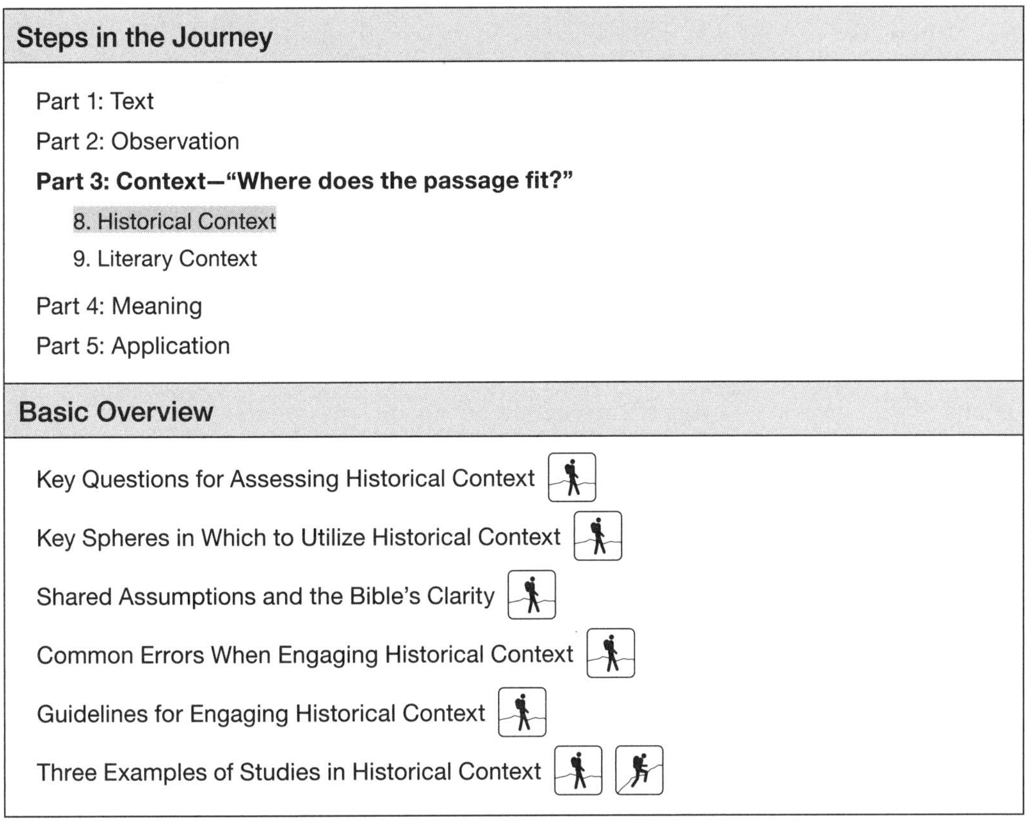

Steps in the Journey

Part 1: Text
Part 2: Observation
Part 3: Context—"Where does the passage fit?"
8. Historical Context
9. Literary Context
Part 4: Meaning
Part 5: Application

Basic Overview

Key Questions for Assessing Historical Context
Key Spheres in Which to Utilize Historical Context
Shared Assumptions and the Bible's Clarity
Common Errors When Engaging Historical Context
Guidelines for Engaging Historical Context
Three Examples of Studies in Historical Context

Fig. 8.1. Trail Guide to Chapter 8

Key Questions for Assessing Historical Context

Earlier in chapter 1 we wrestled with the question of the biblical text's historicity (see "History, Myth, and the Biblical Narratives"). Now we will consider a text's ***historical context*** by asking, "Where does this passage fit in space and time, and how do these data points inform the reading of our passage?" Here we seek to understand the nature and implications of the temporal, social, and physical situation in which the author wrote the text and to identify any historical-cultural-geographical details that the author mentions or assumes. Some of the questions that we need to ask are:

1. **Who?** The *authorship, audience, and major figures and powers* of the passage.
2. **When?** The *original date* of the message in relation to major periods and powers, including assessment of what events precede and follow (with consideration of potential influence either way).
3. **Where?** The *physical location and geography* pointed to in the text.
4. **Why?** The *cause and purpose* of the message.
5. **How?** The *genre and thought flow* of the passage. At stake here is answering, "Why did he say it that way?"

We gain answers to these questions mostly from a close reading of the biblical text itself. The more we understand the Bible as a whole, the better we can understand the details of its parts. The better we are aware of the ancient context, the easier it is for us to cross the bridge from the modern world into the ancient world.

For help on historical matters, you can always consult good Bible dictionaries, commentaries, or tools such as the *ESV Study Bible* and *NIV Zondervan Study Bible*. Just remember that for the most part, the scholars who wrote the various essays or notes were restricted to the same data you are—the biblical passage, the section, the book, and the broader canon. Because our knowledge of the ancient world is relatively small, most of our wrestling with historical context must come from within Scripture itself and must be tested by the data found in the text. We must read, read, and reread the Bible.

Now, all this information is important to historical context, but at the heart of this exegetical stage is identifying the *shared assumptions* between author and audience—elements that were clear to them but may not be as clear to us. Thus, I want to add one more question that is related to the questions above but whose answer assumes a little more from the reader. As God's Word spoken through human words in history, every biblical book was conditioned by the language, culture, and situations of the time—some of which are like those of our age but a lot of which are not. If you, as a twenty-first-century interpreter, don't have some grasp of the "clean and unclean" laws from Leviticus, Ezekiel's comparison of Israel to a woman in her menstrual impurity will likely not make much sense to you (Ezek. 36:17; cf. Lev. 15:19–33). Similarly, unless you are already aware of the Pentateuch's discussion of levirate marriage (e.g., Deut. 25:5–10), the process by which Boaz redeemed Ruth will seem quite strange (Ruth 4:1–14). How does removing one's sandal and giving it to another party actually "confirm a transaction" (4:7)? These kinds of historical details are addressed when we ask:

6. **What?** Here our focus is less on *what* is said and more on *what* is assumed with respect to detailed knowledge of at least seven areas:[1]

   a. *Linguistic familiarity.* Every biblical author assumed that his words would be understood, which requires either a shared knowledge of Hebrew, Aramaic, or Greek or the certainty of a translation into a known tongue.

   b. *Worldview.* Here I refer to the shared values, perspectives, mind-set, and outlook of the writer, recipients, key figures mentioned in the text, or society.

   c. *Societal and economic systems.* These are the relationships and social structures that determine everyday life: common history of families or groups, marriage and family patterns, gender roles, social status, ethnicity, trades and vocations, slavery, and wealth and poverty. All of these are features that the author often assumes his reader will understand, and because we are so far removed from the original setting, grasping the various societal and economic structures can be difficult.

   d. *Behavioral patterns*, such as dress and community or family customs.

   e. *Political climate.* Here we mean the governmental power centers, structures, loyalties, and personnel. Biblical authors, for example, don't always explain the distinction between an officer and a judge but instead assume that we already know the difference.

   f. *Religious practices.* These are the convictions, rituals, affiliations, personnel, and sacred structures associated with Israel's worship or that of its neighbors.

   g. *Physical features*, such as climate and weather, topography, architecture, transportation, and plants and animals.

We can gain clarity on much of these data within the confines of the biblical text itself. At times, however, understanding these things requires reaching beyond the text to our knowledge of life in this created world or to extrabiblical sources. I'll look into these various spheres in the next section, but right now remember this: As you work

1. Adapted from Gordon D. Fee, *New Testament Exegesis: A Handbook for Students and Pastors*, 3rd ed. (Louisville: Westminster John Knox, 2002), 96; Craig L. Blomberg, *A Handbook of New Testament Exegesis* (Grand Rapids: Baker Academic, 2010), 84.

through historical-context issues, the goal is not simply to identify the author, date, or cause of writing or to grasp a historical detail but also to clarify how these data affect the interpretation of your passage. The aim is to gain greater specific understanding of God's Word and not just general understanding of the book or a historical event to which the passage points.

Key Spheres in Which to Utilize Historical Context

Historical context often relates to shared assumptions between the author and reader—elements that are understood but not necessarily explicitly stated. At least four broad spheres intersect with the question of historical context. Few question the validity of looking for historical context amid the initial three, but the fourth raises more questions.

1. A Proper Grasp of Linguistic Signs

At base, reading Scripture rightly demands that the interpreter, or at least a translator, rightly understand the linguistic signs in which God gave us his Word. The original languages are part of the historical context. So a primary-level reading of the Bible demands a knowledge of Hebrew, Aramaic, and/or Greek, depending on which part of Scripture you are interpreting.

2. A Detailed Grasp of the Persons, Institutions, and Events of Scripture

Biblical interpreters must also have a mastery of the persons, institutions, and events of Scripture. We can understand the Bible, but this often takes a lot of work. In Paul's words to Timothy, we must "think over" Scripture, confident that "the Lord will give . . . understanding in everything" (2 Tim. 2:7). This God-dependent thinking often demands rigorous study. The more we recognize the key persons, institutions, and events of Scripture, the better interpreters we will be. And the more we know, the less we will need to rely on secondary sources for help. For example, knowing Israel's covenantal history and its relations with the neighboring nations helps us grasp the prophets' numerous public condemnations. Similarly, I love Deuteronomy because the worldview it presents, the various instructions it gives, and the portrait of the future it depicts all help me understand the rest of the Bible better. The Pentateuch was the foundational Scripture for the Old Testament prophets, priests, and poets and for all the New Testament authors, so the more familiar we are with the foundation, the more we'll appreciate the structure that builds on it.

3. A General Awareness of Life in This Created World

Exegetes also need to be conscious of the world around them in order to properly understand the Bible. "Go to the ant, O sluggard; consider her ways, and be wise" (Prov. 6:6). This kind of command demands that we know what an ant is and that we have an ability to "consider [its] ways." "The heavens declare the glory of God, and the sky above proclaims his handiwork" (Ps. 19:1). "Lift up your eyes on high and see: who created these?" (Isa. 40:26). Jesus said, "Look at the birds of the air. . . . Consider the lilies of the field" (Matt. 6:26, 28). All these statements necessitate that we be generally aware of life in this created world. That is historical context.

4. A Proper Approach to Extrabiblical Data

Finally, we must address how to handle extrabiblical materials. With every new textual and material find from the ancient world (e.g., an inscription on a tablet or a painting on a temple tomb wall), the shared assumptions between the biblical author and his original audience have the potential of becoming more clear to us. Without any added texts or artifacts from outside the Bible, Scripture itself is sufficiently clear, supplying us with "all things that pertain to life and godliness" (2 Peter 1:3). Nevertheless, extrabiblical data of this sort can inform and add to our understanding of a passage, not only by filling in factual data (such as the common price for slaves in Egypt during the days of Joseph or the topography of the Sinai Peninsula) but also by helping to clarify a text's rhetorical impact. Let me unpack what I mean.

While I can understand the general sense and message of the Bible's creation account as it stands, it is the comparative creation accounts that raise fresh possibilities for the Old Testament as polemical theology—its critique of the false worldviews of the day. Ancient Near Eastern extrabiblical data rarely if ever provide *necessary* details for grasping the message of the biblical text itself, but they do inform our reading and raise new rhetorical possibilities in our understanding that we would otherwise have likely not considered.

For example, in Ezekiel 1 the prophet unfolds a remarkable vision of God's glory, which he saw on the banks of the Chebar canal in Babylon. Included in his depiction are heavenly beings with four wings, human hands, and four faces with the likeness of a human, a lion, an ox, and an eagle. Every reading of this text witnesses these remarkable creatures as servants to the exalted God who is seated on his throne in brightness and rainbows. The point that is clear for every culture and time is that YHWH's glory is great and that he is exalted over every other heavenly being and over every created earthly thing, whether human, wild beast, domesticated animal, or flying creature. But in the last century we have unearthed numerous reliefs and statues that depict the gods of Babylon in the days of Ezekiel, and they are often pictured as multiwinged creatures with multiple faces including human, lion, ox, and eagle. We didn't need these findings to grasp the sense of Ezekiel 1, but their presence raises the possibility that God disclosed himself to Ezekiel in Babylon in a way that would have directly confronted the Babylonian exiles and called them to flee idolatry. The Babylonian pagans worshiped gods with multiple wings and faces, but Ezekiel's vision shows that all such realities are themselves submitted to the supreme God, YHWH, who is seated on the throne and whose likeness we cannot compare!

In my view, the biblical authors assume an awareness of the biblical languages, a robust knowledge of the biblical text itself, and a general awareness of real life in this created world. This much is needed to properly grasp the message of Scripture. Beyond this, while the essence or general sense of the biblical message would rarely, if ever, be contingent on details gained only from extrabiblical sources, such information can serve to elucidate Scripture's meaning in fuller ways.

Shared Assumptions and the Bible's Clarity

As previously noted, historical context is about the *shared assumptions* between author and audience—knowledge that they took for granted but to which we may not be privy. For example, when did Amos preach? Was he a prophet of the northern or southern kingdom? Who was "Assyria"? What is a "siege mound"? How big is a "cubit"? What was the value of a "shekel"? Such are the questions of historical context.

All effective communication is guided by an unstated but assumed understanding between the speaker and the recipient. Determining what the biblical authors expect of their readers is not always easy. Recently, one scholar asserted: "Determining the genre of Gen. 1–11 and its proper interpretation is an extremely difficult task. To do it competently, one must be able to read Genesis in Hebrew and Greek, have a knowledge of the history of its interpretation, be acquainted with critical methods and conclusions, understand the various theories of historiography and the ways in which ancient authors composed narratives of the past, be able to compare Gen. 1–11 with cognate texts, and so on."[2]

My question is, "Did the author really assume that we would have to do that much just to grasp that Genesis 1–11 is historical narrative?" This would mean that no interpreter until the last hundred years could really know the genre of Genesis 1–11. I question this approach to historical context.

But how much and which historical information *is* necessary as we approach the biblical text? We can determine this only by considering whether and in what ways

2. Charles Halton, "Conclusion: We Disagree. What Now?," in *Genesis: History, Fiction, or Neither? Three Views on the Bible's Earliest Chapters*, ed. Charles Halton, Counterpoints (Grand Rapids: Zondervan, 2015), 160. For my review of this volume, see Jason S. DeRouchie, Review of *Genesis: History, Fiction, or Neither?*, in *Themelios* 40, 3 (2015): 485–90. An abridged version of this review is available at http://www.thegospelcoalition.org/article/book-reviews-genesis-history-fiction-or-neither-three-views.

any given historical fact of which we are aware impacts the meaning that the writer was trying to convey. We must ask, "Are there clues in the literary context that certain historical data are important?"

For example, when we read that Ezra journeyed from Babylon to Jerusalem (Ezra 7:9), do we need to have in mind that the journey was about 900 miles (1,448 km) through a desert? Did the author expect us to know this? While the specific distance may not be necessary, the rest of Ezra-Nehemiah highlights that the distance between Babylon and Jerusalem was great and that this created a number of obstacles that the reader is expected to feel. Indeed, it was only "*because* [כִּי] the good hand of his God was on him" that Ezra and his company made it safely to Jerusalem (7:9). Furthermore, Ezra himself underlines the difficulties when he writes in 8:21–22:

> Then I proclaimed a fast . . . , that we might humble ourselves before our God, to seek from him a safe journey for ourselves, our children, and all our goods. For I was ashamed to ask the king for a band of soldiers and horsemen to protect us against the enemy on our way, since we had told the king, "The hand of our God is for good on all who seek him, and the power of his wrath is against all who forsake him."

Ezra's move from Babylon to Jerusalem was less like a journey across town and more akin to moving to a different state but doing so with camels, carts, and at least a couple thousand people (8:1–20).[3] The text wants us to feel the weight of this journey, so whether we go outside the text to identify its nine-hundred-mile distance, there is enough within the text to say that knowledge of the distance was indeed assumed and expected to be appreciated.

While it is not always easy to know how much the authors assume of their readers, the very nature of God's Word demands that its message can be understood in any culture and in any age. Historically, the church has called this the doctrine of ***Scripture's perspicuity***, or clarity. The Bible is sufficiently clear, but not everything in it is equally clear. It is sufficiently clear to allow us to grasp the portrait of God's supremacy and his overarching kingdom purposes climaxing in the saving work of Jesus, but some other elements in Scripture are less lucid. In his article titled "The Perspicuity of Scripture," Wayne Grudem helpfully notes that the Bible itself testifies that we can understand it, but:[4]

- Not all at once;
- Not without effort;
- Not without ordinary means;
- Not without the reader's willingness to obey it;

3. Ezra highlights 1,496 men, 38 Levites, and 220 temple servants (Ezra 8:1–20); to this we must add the women and children.

4. Wayne A. Grudem, "The Perspicuity of Scripture," *Themelios* 34, 3 (2009): 288–309. Andy Naselli directed me to this reference.

- Not without the help of the Holy Spirit;
- Not without human misunderstanding;
- Never completely.

Even where the Bible is less clear, we can always discern truth and preach life-giving sermons. For example, the book of Zephaniah stands as a summons for believers to find their ultimate satisfaction in the Lord. One way in which the prophet motivates his listeners to patiently pursue God in the present is by identifying their sins and declaring the nearness of YHWH's day of wrath. In 1:9 we are told, "On that day I will punish everyone who leaps over the threshold." The temple threshold was the base area at the entrance to the Holy or Most Holy Place. Why were people leaping over it, and what was wrong with this? We don't know. This is a piece of historical data that has been lost to us. The only other Scripture that talks about leaping a threshold is 1 Samuel 5:5, which says that the Philistine priests of Dagon in Ashdod would "not tread on the [temple] threshold." But this story from 1 Samuel does not appear to have any direct link with Zephaniah's oracle, and we can't have certainty that this pagan superstition stands behind Zephaniah's denunciations. Perhaps future extrabiblical findings will cast more light on this text. But until that happens, I can still preach the passage with an awareness that God condemned what the people were doing and that it was most likely connected to pagan religious rituals. More information would inform my reading, but it would not change my basic understanding.

Common Errors When Engaging Historical Context

We can derail our biblical interpretation by approaching a text in the wrong way. We need to avoid three common errors when addressing historical context.

1. Missing the Text's Point

Many scholars and pastors get so enthralled with supposed historical backgrounds that they fail to highlight what the text actually says in the foreground. I see this regularly in Old Testament surveys or commentaries, which too often major on background and content rather than on message. Don't miss the text's main point; hear the message of Scripture.

2. Eliminating Rather than Illuminating the Text

There are other scholars who shape complex theories about the meaning of a text on the basis of little or debatable evidence. For example, in much of the twentieth century, the study of the Psalms was dominated by a form-critical approach that posited elaborate life settings in Israel's worship for each of the different genres. The challenge, of course, is that we actually find very little historical data in the titles or psalms themselves. Theories are necessary and can be helpful, but a historical reconstruction is likely valid only (a) when it grows out of the text itself, (b) when it reinforces rather than disturbs the apparent meaning of the text, and (c) when it helps make sense of difficult statements in the text.[5] Summarizing my friend and colleague Andy Naselli, legitimate theories about historical context will *illuminate* rather than *eliminate* the biblical text.

3. Emphasizing Similarities but Not Differences

Some scholars appear quick to identify genuine parallels between the Bible and extrabiblical texts, but they then fail to draw attention to the differences that often set Scripture apart. It is these dissimilarities that regularly suggest that the biblical authors wrote not only to present true doctrine but also to confront the twisted views of Israel's pagan neighbors. The best comparative work will identify both similarities *and* differences and consider the significance of each.

Historical backgrounds can be fascinating. Nevertheless, I urge you: Guard yourself against these three errors. Confess your weaknesses often, and ask God for wisdom in your exegesis.

Guidelines for Engaging Historical Context

I have five guidelines to help at this step in the exegetical process: Be clear, be careful, be certain, be restrained, and be relentless.

1. *Be clear* on the type of historical-context information you are assessing.

Does it answer Who? When? Where? Why? How? or What?

2. *Be careful* in your assessment of comparative literature.

Examine both similarities and differences with the biblical material, and seek to discern the rhetorical purpose of the biblical message. While growing up in an ancient context filled with pagan perspectives, powers, and practices, Scripture has a tendency not to appropriate but to dispute and repudiate pagan myths, ideas, identities, and customs. As I noted earlier in my discussion of genre in chapter 1 ("History, Myth,

5. See Walter C. Kaiser Jr. and Moisés Silva, *Introduction to Biblical Hermeneutics: The Search for Meaning*, 2nd ed. (Grand Rapids: Zondervan, 2007), 179.

and the Biblical Narratives"), the Bible often does this (a) by establishing the authentic original historical event that was vulgarized and distorted through polytheism, magic, violence, and paganism; or (b) by showing that what was myth in the ancient world has real substance and is factual in Israel's story. Be careful in your assessment of comparative literature.

3. *Be certain* that you can clarify the background information's relevance.

You must be able to explain how the historical details help us grasp the author's intended point. If you can't do this, the historical datum is likely not one of the shared assumptions necessary for grasping the passage's message. Include only relevant, needed information in your presentation of historical context.

4. *Be restrained* in your use of historical-context material.

Before going outside the Bible for answers, wrestle within the Scripture itself, considering the Bible in its entirety in order to grasp the author's message. As preachers and teachers of God's Word, we have as our goal to unpack the message of Scripture, not to major on the periphery that is interesting but ultimately unhelpful in understanding the author's main point. We must ask, "Is the Scripture sufficient, and do we have all we need for life and godliness?" May you not be like Paul's opponents, who desired to be teachers of the Old Testament and yet taught different doctrines and devoted themselves to myths and endless genealogies that promoted speculation rather than advancing God's work (1 Tim. 1:3–7). Thus, when you draw on background information from outside the biblical text, use only that material that aligns with and upholds the flow and message of the text itself.

5. *Be relentless* in your commitment to draw your message from the text.

A proper use of historical context will support, not subvert, the text's apparent meaning. One way to ensure that you are drawing your assertions of historical relevance from the text is to look for authorial clues regarding the purpose of historical data. This can serve to guide your assessment about why certain historical details may be present in the text.

For example, the book of Kings emphasizes in nearly every chapter the covenant rebellion of the northern and southern kingdoms, which climaxes in the exile of both from the land. If the small remnant in exile did not yet grasp why the twelve tribes were decimated and why Jerusalem fell, 2 Kings 17 uses explicit language to clarify the cause. The narrator writes: "And this occurred because the people of Israel had sinned against the Lord their God . . . . They despised his statutes and his covenant that he made with their fathers and the warnings that he gave them" (2 Kings 17:7, 15). The narrator recorded every expression of faithlessness and every act of rebellion within the book in order to clarify that the Israelites were in exile because they sinned. God turned from them *because* they had first turned from him. The historical details in the book are heading somewhere, and the narrator himself tells us where. We need to follow his lead in our interpretation of the historical data.

Consider also the nine chapters of tribal allotments that the narrator painstakingly details in Joshua 13–21. At one point in my life I actually worked my way through these chapters, drawing maps of the various tribal boundaries. This is a fine exercise, but doing so could easily cause us to miss the narrator's own cue for why he so carefully laid out each detail. We read this in the concluding comment in Joshua 21:43–45: "Thus the LORD gave to Israel all the land that he swore to give to their fathers. And they took possession of it, and they settled there. And the LORD gave them rest on every side just as he had sworn to their fathers. Not one of all their enemies had withstood them, for the LORD had given all their enemies into their hands. Not one word of all the good promises that the LORD had made to the house of Israel had failed; all came to pass."

These verses tell us that the point of giving so many details in the discussion of tribal allotments was not simply to clarify for future generations which tribe got what turf. Rather, all this information was given to magnify the greatness of YHWH's faithfulness: "Not one word" of all of God's good promises failed. He is always faithful to his Word, and the penetrating question in Joshua is this: "Will you be? Will you be as faithful to God's Word as he is?"

Three Examples of Studies in Historical Context

The Historical Context of 1 Samuel 13:14

In one of the opening sections on clause and text grammar ("A Man after God's Heart? The Importance of Grammar in 1 Samuel 13:14" in chapter 5), I addressed the proper translation of 1 Samuel 13:14. The clause itself comes to us in the form of Verb (V)-Subject (S)-Modifier (M)-Direct Object (DO)-Modifier (M).

כִּלְבָבוֹ	אִישׁ	לוֹ	יְהוָה	בִּקֵּשׁ
M	DO	M	S	V
after/like/according-to-his-heart	a-man	for-himself	YHWH	sought

Fig. 8.2. 1 Samuel 13:14 Hebrew-English Interlinear

I argued that the translation "a man after God's heart" is inappropriate and that the prepositional phrase כִּלְבָבוֹ ("like/according to his heart") modifies not the direct object אִישׁ ("man") but the main verb בִּקֵּשׁ ("he sought"). It functions adverbially, clarifying the standard by which YHWH sought Saul's replacement. I translated the clause: "YHWH sought for himself according to his own will a man."

In this section I want to supply ancient Near Eastern comparative support for this reading. All the texts I address deal with a superior's selection of a king. In each of the contexts, the *heart* idiom refers to the suzerain or god's mental conception or choice of a new king rather than to the like-mindedness of the vassal or to the loyalty of the new king as the standard for his selection. For the sake of ease, I will include only English translations of the various texts, which means that the cognate for *heart* will not always be apparent.

1. Texts in Which a Suzerain's Heart Gives Rise to the Selection of a King

a. *Hittite New Kingdom treaty (ca. 1250–1225* B.C.*)*: "Whatever son Kurunta prefers, whether the son of his wife or the son of some other woman, whatever the son is the choice of Kurunta, whatever son Kurunta prefers, [let him place him in kingship in the land of Tarhuntassa]."

b. *Babylonian Chronicles (ca. 550–400* B.C.*)*: "The seventh year: In the month of Kislev the king of Akkad [Nebuchadnezzar II] mustered his army and marched to Hattu. He encamped against the city of Judah and on the second day of the month Adar he captured the city [and] seized [its] king. A king of his own choice he appointed in the city [Jerusalem] [and] taking the vassal tribute he brought it into Babylon."

2. Texts in Which a God's "Heart" Gives Rise to the Selection of a King

a. *King Eannatum, Dynasty of Lagash (ca. 2500–2335* B.C.*)*: "[My] name was called to mind by Enlil; endowed with strength by Ningirsu; envisaged by Nansh in [her] heart; truly and rightly suckled by Ninhursaga; named by Inanna."

b. *King Gudea, Dynasty of Akkad (ca. 2335–2112* B.C.*)*: "Shepherd envisaged by Ningirsu in [his] heart, steadfastly regarded by Nanshe; endowed with strength by Nindar; the man described[?] by Baba."

c. *King Gudea, Dynasty of Akkad*: "Being the one at whom Nanshe looked with favor, being the man of the heart of Enlil, being the ruler . . . [?] of Ningirsu, Gudea, being born in a lofty sanctuary of Gatumdug."

d. *King Shu-Sin, Ur III Period (ca. 2112–2004* B.C.*)*: "Shu-Sin, called by name by the god An, beloved of the god Enlil, king whom the god Enlil chose in his [own] heart as shepherd of the land and of the four quarters, mighty king, king of Ur, king of the four quarters."

e. *Neo-Assyrian liver omen (ca. 668–627* B.C.*)*: "If the Presence is turned upside down: Enlil will install a king of his own choice."

f. *Cyrus Cylinder (ca. 539* B.C.*)*: "[Marduk] surveyed and looked throughout all the lands, searching for a righteous king according to the desire of his heart, so as to grasp his hand. He called his name Cyrus, king of Anshan; he pronounced his name to be king over all [the world]."

All these extrabiblical texts address a superior's selection of a king. Whether human suzerain or a god, each of these passages has the *heart* idiom referring to the sovereign's conception or choice of a new king rather than to the like-mindedness of the vassal to his superior or to the loyalty of the new king as the standard for his selection. This comparative ancient Near Eastern material, therefore, counters the traditional adjectival rendering of כִּלְבָבוֹ ("like, according to his heart") and supports the view that the Hebrew idiom focuses more on YHWH's choice of Saul's replacement. The historical-context material is in no way conclusive in determining the meaning of 1 Samuel 13:14. Yet it does supply supportive information for one interpretation over another.

Geographical Details in Deuteronomy 1:1

Most of us in the West give little thought to the geographical notations in Scripture. There are times, however, when the author's assumption that the reader knows the location of place names may actually have a substantial impact on our understanding of a passage or book.

We know that Deuteronomy is made up of three sermons, a warning song, and a deathbed blessing that Moses spoke to the postexodus generation of Israel across from Jericho after the forty years in the wilderness. Before the first sermon, Deuteronomy 1:5 clarifies the location of Moses' address: "Beyond the Jordan, in the land of Moab, Moses undertook to explain this law, saying . . . ." Before the second sermon, we read something similar: "These are the testimonies, the statutes, and the rules, which Moses spoke to the people of Israel when they came out of Egypt, beyond the Jordan in the valley opposite Beth-peor, in the land of Sihon the king of the Amorites" (Deut. 4:45–46). Finally, after the warning song, the narrator states, "That very day the LORD spoke to Moses, 'Go up this mountain of the Abarim, Mount Nebo, which is in the land of Moab, opposite Jericho, and view the land of Canaan, which I am giving to the people of Israel for a possession'" (32:48–49). It's clear that Moses gave the various messages of Deuteronomy east of the Jordan River in the land of Moab. But now let's go back and read Deuteronomy 1:1.

אֵ֣לֶּה הַדְּבָרִ֗ים אֲשֶׁ֨ר דִּבֶּ֤ר מֹשֶׁה֙ אֶל־כָּל־יִשְׂרָאֵ֔ל בְּעֵ֖בֶר הַיַּרְדֵּ֑ן בַּמִּדְבָּ֡ר בָּעֲרָבָה֩ מ֨וֹל ס֜וּף בֵּֽין־ פָּארָ֧ן וּבֵֽין־תֹּ֛פֶל וְלָבָ֥ן וַחֲצֵרֹ֖ת וְדִ֥י זָהָֽב׃	These are the words that Moses spoke to all Israel beyond the Jordan in the wilderness, in the Arabah opposite Suph, between Paran and Tophel, Laban, Hazeroth, and Dizahab.

Fig. 8.3. Deuteronomy 1:1 in MT and ESV

This is the introductory statement for the entire book. In it we read a number of place names that clarify the location where Moses initially gave Deuteronomy's message. What is striking is that the locations listed suggest that Moses proclaimed God's Deuteronomic word *not* on the north side of the Dead Sea across from Jericho in Moab but rather somewhere southwest in the area associated with the first generation's initial journey to the Promised Land.

1. "Beyond the Jordan"

This is a general designation most often associated with entrance to the Promised Land. Like all other sacred space in the ancient world, the main entrance of the Promised Land (at least from a theological perspective) was on the east side, so the final narrator, writing from within the Promised Land, tells us that Moses spoke from outside, "beyond the Jordan."

2. "In the Wilderness"

This, too, is general language associated with all of Israel's experience from leaving Egypt to the borders of the Promised Land. It can refer to the area in which Israel journeyed from Egypt to Mount Sinai (Ex. 14:11), to the region of Mount Sinai itself (Num. 1:1), and to the entire location of Israel's wanderings after Sinai up to the point of Moses' death (14:32–33). In Moses' words from Deuteronomy 8:2: "And you shall remember the whole way that the LORD your God has led you these forty years *in the wilderness* [בַּמִּדְבָּר], that he might humble you, testing you to know what was in your heart, whether you would keep his commandments or not."

3. "In the Arabah"

In Deuteronomy 1:7 we learn that this was the region through which Israel journeyed in order to get to Canaan the first time: "Turn and take your journey, and go to the hill country of the Amorites and to all their neighbors *in the Arabah* [בָּעֲרָבָה], in the hill country and in the lowland and in the Negeb and by the seacoast, the land of the Canaanites, and Lebanon, as far as the great river, the river Euphrates." The Arabah is the dry depression that runs north from the Dead Sea up to Galilee (Deut. 3:17) and south down from the Dead Sea through Edom to the Red Sea and beyond (2:8).

4. "Opposite Suph"

We are not certain as to the location of "Suph" (סוּף), but we do know that what we tag as the "Red Sea" Scripture titles יַם סוּף ("Reed Sea"). This could suggest that

Suph is the region directly associated with the Reed (or Red) Sea, which would be far in the south, away from Moab.

5. "Between Paran and Tophel, Laban, Hazeroth, and Dizahab"

We know of only two of these places from elsewhere in Scripture. "Paran" (פָּארָן) was an early stopping place after Sinai (Num. 10:12; 12:16; 13:3, 26), and with this, Hazeroth was a later stopping place (11:35; 12:16; 33:17–18).

So what does all this mean? I think we gain clarity when we read all of Deuteronomy 1:1–3 together.

> These are the words that Moses spoke to all Israel beyond the Jordan in the wilderness, in the Arabah opposite Suph, between Paran and Tophel, Laban, Hazeroth, and Dizahab. 2 It is eleven days' journey from Horeb by the way of Mount Seir to Kadesh-barnea. 3 In the fortieth year, on the first day of the eleventh month, Moses spoke to the people of Israel according to all that the Lord had given him in commandment to them.

Fig. 8.4. Deuteronomy 1:1–3 in ESV

I see three important implications of the geographical notations for our reading of Deuteronomy. First, the geographical description in 1:1 is complemented by the contrast of "eleven days" in verse 2 and "in the fortieth year" in verse 3. This suggests that the first generation heard the heart of Deuteronomy forty years before—after the departure from Sinai but prior to the faithlessness of the ten spies and the rest of the unbelieving nation.

Second, it is now forty years later. The first generation is dead due to sin, and God has graciously raised up a new generation to carry on his vision for global redemption. God's approach to the new generation is no different from his approach to the previous one. They have the same responsibility to respond to the same revelation. The question is, "Will they?"

Third, frequently in Deuteronomy, the present Moab generation is treated as though the Horeb covenant were theirs—as though they had been the ones at the mountain of God. For example, in 5:3–4, Moses writes, "Not with our fathers did the Lord make this covenant, but with us, who are all of us here alive today. The Lord spoke with you face to face at the mountain, out of the midst of the fire" (cf. 6:20–25). This transgenerational nature of the book is something that the very initial verses highlight. What was true in the past is equally true in Moses' present. The earlier generation heard the essence of Deuteronomy, but they rejected it. How will the new generation respond?

This brief study highlights how historical-geographical data can at times serve our understanding of God's Word. I found information about the various locations within the Bible itself. The narrator of Deuteronomy expected me to know Israel's story, and after I went back to read what God had already given, the geography lesson paid off on clarifying part of the rhetorical purpose of Deuteronomy's beginning.

The Historical Context of Exodus 19:4–6

Let us consider the historical context of Exodus 19:4–6. Something I mentioned at the beginning of this book is the natural challenge we face in separating all the exegetical steps. In historical-narrative texts, for example, it is often difficult to discern the difference between historical and literary context, since the history is bound up in the narrative itself. Such is the case as we approach Exodus 19:4–6.

In light of this challenge, I have decided to deal with only the most general historical data here, and I will leave a more thorough analysis of the Exodus narrative for the "Literary Context" discussion in the next chapter. As we approach the historical context, I have chosen two areas on which to focus: (1) the event of the exodus, which 19:4 tells us grounds Israel's God-honoring calling; and (2) the nature and significance of the "covenant" mentioned in 19:5.

1. The Exodus

After the Israelites dwelt in Egypt's east Delta for several centuries (Ex. 12:40–41),[6] God commissioned Moses to lead a deliverance before the eyes of both Israel and

6. Exodus 12:40–41 tells us that Israel sojourned in Egypt 430 years, and then "at the end of the 430 years, on that very day, all the hosts of the LORD went out from the land of Egypt." While many scholars believe this means 430 years from the time Jacob entered Egypt to the time of the exodus, Jewish tradition, John Calvin, and some contemporary scholars such as John Bimson and David Rohl propose that the time was only 210 years, based on genealogical data and other specific statements from the biblical texts. In my own assessment, at least five observations support this shorter period: (1) Kohath was born before the entry into Egypt (Gen. 46:12, 26), and his son Amram (Ex. 6:18) was the father of Moses and Aaron (6:20). Kohath lived 133 years (6:18), Amram lived 137 years (6:20), and Moses was 80 years old at the exodus (7:7). This means that *at the very most* Israel was in Egypt for 350 years (133 + 137 + 80), and that assumes the unlikely possibility that each man had his son in the year of his death. More likely is the fact that the nation's time in Egypt was much shorter. (2) The 400 years promised in Genesis 15:13 most likely refers *not* to the length of Egyptian oppression but to the time until the oppression will cease—about 400 years from the Abrahamic covenant. Indeed, we know the oppression was not 430 years, for Israel lived in solace under Joseph for many years. (3) Paul's statement that the law came 430 years after "the promises were made to Abraham" (Gal. 3:16–17) implies a shorter Egyptian sojourn, for his point of departure is the promises to *Abraham* and not the patriarchs in general or the entrance of Jacob and his sons into Egypt. (4) In Acts 13:17–20 Paul states that "all this" from the choosing of the patriarchs through the period of the judges took "about 450" years. If the time reference indeed refers to everything mentioned in verses 17–20, the actual period from Jacob's entrance into Egypt to the exodus was *not* 430 years but much, much shorter. (5) While less specific, Acts 7:17–19 states that already after Joseph's death but before Egypt actually enslaved the Israelites "the time of the [Gen. 15:13] promise [fulfillment] drew near." This would be strange to say if many centuries of enslavement were still ahead, but if the enslavement happened only toward the end of the Egyptian sojourn, Stephen's stress on the "nearness" of the fulfillment makes more sense. How, then, do we reconcile the 430-year period in Exodus 12:40–41? I propose that Moses' "430 years" could be counting from the time when the father of their nation (Abraham) first sojourned in Egypt, which happens as early as Genesis 12:10–20 around Abram's seventy-fifth

the world. This stood in fulfillment of his earlier promise to Abraham in Genesis 15:13–14: "Then the LORD said to him, 'Know for certain that for four hundred years your descendants will be strangers in a country not their own and that they will be enslaved and mistreated there. But I will punish the nation they serve as slaves, and afterward they will come out with great possessions'" (NIV).

Scholars are not united on the dating of the exodus, partly because the pharaoh of the exodus is not named. A straightforward reading of the biblical text, especially 1 Kings 6:1, would put the exodus in 1446 B.C., probably during Egypt's Eighteenth Dynasty during the reign of Amenhotep II (ca. 1450–1425 B.C.). While there is much corroborative evidence for the Israelite exodus in 1446 B.C.,[7] there is no explicit evidence in the materials of the Egyptians that they, as the greatest empire on earth, were drastically humbled by the God of a massive band of foreign slaves. But this should not even be expected, for we know of no kings in the ancient world who were quick to retain for posterity stories of their own humiliation. What we do know is that the biblical details associated with Egyptian culture line up perfectly and that nothing in Egyptian history counteracts the Bible's claims.[8] Finally, as for Amenhotep II, we know that he began his kingship during Egypt's zenith of global power and influence. He was a successful military warrior and made several campaigns into Canaan. But then, for whatever reason, he abruptly stopped his military activity. While not conclusive, the Dream Stele of Thutmose IV, son and successor of Amenhotep II, notes that Thutmose IV was not the firstborn son of Amenhotep II, which could be an allusion to the tenth plague on the firstborn of Egypt.

What is most significant with respect to this piece of historical context is that Exodus 19:4–6 assumes with much of the rest of Scripture that the exodus actually occurred in space and time—that Israel's God, YHWH, miraculously and with great power delivered the Israelites personally and visibly, making certain that all future deliverance was sure to come.

2. The Covenant

In his excellent coauthored work *Kingdom through Covenant*, Peter Gentry has noted that Scripture applies the term בְּרִית ("covenant") to numerous oath-bound commitments: international treaties (Josh. 9:6; 1 Kings 15:19), clan alliances (Gen. 14:13), personal agreements (Gen. 31:44), national agreements (Jer. 34:8–10), and loyalty agreements

---

year, soon after his initial entrance into Canaan. The promise of 400 years in Genesis 15:13 is not associated with a specific age of Abram but came somewhere between his seventy-fifth and eighty-sixth years (Gen. 12:4; 16:16).

7. See Charles F. Aling, *Egypt and Bible History: From Earliest Times to 1000 B.C.*, Baker Studies in Biblical Archaeology (Grand Rapids: Baker, 1981); John Bimson, *Redating the Exodus and Conquest*, 2nd ed., JSOTSup 5 (Sheffield, UK: Almond Press, 1981); David Rohl, *Exodus: Myth or History?* (St. Louis Park, MN: Thinking Man Media, 2015); Timothy P. Mahoney with Steven Law, *Patterns of Evidence: Exodus* (St. Louis Park, MN: Thinking Man Media, 2015).

8. See especially Aling, *Egypt and Bible History*; James K. Hoffmeier, *Israel in Egypt: The Evidence for the Authenticity of the Exodus Tradition* (Oxford: Oxford University Press, 1996); K. A. Kitchen, *On the Reliability of the Old Testament* (Grand Rapids: Eerdmans, 2003), 241–312.

(1 Sam. 20:14–17), including marriage.[9] In another exceptional study titled *Marriage as a Covenant*, Gordon Hugenberger helpfully defines *covenant* as "an elected, as opposed to natural, relationship of obligation under oath."[10] This definition fits well the nature of covenantal relationships that we see throughout both the Bible and the ancient world. At the heart of a covenant is a relationship—one established by choice and not by birth, though it is modeled on family relationships. Thus suzerains tagged themselves as "fathers," vassals "sons," and fellow vassals "brothers." This covenant relationship bore obligations for both parties, who established this relationship in the context of promise, or oath, usually with the gods as witnesses for curse or blessing.

In Exodus 19:5, YHWH calls Israel to "keep my covenant." Since God's dealing with Noah, YHWH has called his various relationships with humans "covenants" (Gen. 6:8; 9:9–17; 15:18; 17:2–22; Ex. 2:24; 6:4–5). This implies both his fatherly and sovereign authority and his intention to relate with the people of his creation. When we arrive at Exodus 19:5, the only two divine-human relationships tagged as "covenants" are the Noahic and Abrahamic covenants. Now in Exodus 19–20, God is establishing what he later calls a "covenant" (Ex. 24:8; 34:10, 27–28) specifically associated with Horeb, or Mount Sinai (Deut. 5:2; 29:1[H28:69]). The question becomes this: "What historical covenant is God pointing to in Exodus 19:5?" "If you . . . keep *my covenant* . . . ."

In Exodus, the narrator opens the story of deliverance by saying, "God remembered his covenant with Abraham, with Isaac, and with Jacob" (Ex. 2:24). Then in Exodus 6:4–5, YHWH himself asserts, "I also established my covenant with them to give them the land of Canaan, the land in which they lived as sojourners. Moreover, I have heard the groaning of the people of Israel whom the Egyptians hold as slaves, and I have remembered my covenant." YHWH had promised Abraham in Genesis 12:2 that he would make Abraham into a renowned nation, and then in 17:7–8 he promised, "And I will establish *my covenant* between me and you and your offspring after you throughout their generations for an everlasting covenant, to be God to you and to your offspring after you. And I will give to you and to your offspring after you the land of your sojournings, all the land of Canaan, for an everlasting possession, and I will be their God." These promises find their fulfillment in the Mosaic covenant established at Sinai.

William Dumbrell has argued that because Exodus has mentioned only the Abrahamic covenant to this point, God is calling Israel in 19:5 to keep the Abrahamic covenant.[11] Other scholars struggle with this because Exodus 19–20 is the very context in which God makes the Sinai covenant. Indeed, the call to "listen unto [his] voice" in 19:5 appears to anticipate the introduction to the Ten Words in 20:1, where we read, "And God spoke all these words, saying . . . ."

9. Peter J. Gentry and Stephen J. Wellum, *Kingdom through Covenant: A Biblical-Theological Understanding of the Covenants* (Wheaton, IL: Crossway, 2012), 130–31.

10. Gordon P. Hugenberger, *Marriage as a Covenant: Biblical Law and Ethics as Developed from Malachi* (Grand Rapids: Baker, 1998), 11.

11. William J. Dumbrell, *Covenant and Creation: An Old Testament Covenant Theology*, 2nd ed. (Milton Keynes, UK: Paternoster, 2013), 110–11.

I suggest that we do not have to choose between the two, for Genesis anticipates that God's relationship with Israel established at Sinai is actually the fulfillment of stage 1 of his promises to Abraham—those promises directly related to Israel's nationhood and tenure in the land. Stage 2 of the Abrahamic covenant, which includes blessing reaching the nations through a male deliverer (Gen. 12:3; 22:17b–18) and Abraham's standing as the father of a multitude of nations (17:4–6), is developed in the Mosaic covenant but explicitly fulfilled only in the new covenant in Christ (Acts 3:25–26; Rom. 4:13–18; Gal. 3:7–29) (see "An Example of Text Grammar—Genesis 12:1–3" in chapter 5). In Exodus 19:5 God is calling Israel to work out stage 1 of the Abrahamic covenant, which will mean the need to abide by the Ten Words and all other regulations, all in order to mediate and display the holiness of God to the world.

Key Words and Concepts

Historical context
Perspicuity of Scripture

Questions for Further Reflection

1. Where do Scripture scholars find most of their historical-context information?
2. What is at the heart of studying historical context, and in what areas were there often shared assumptions between the author and his audience?
3. What is the place of extrabiblical writings when studying historical context?
4. What are three common errors in engaging historical context? Elaborate on the one you feel most prone toward.
5. What are the five guidelines to engage in historical context?
6. Using either 1 Samuel 13:14 or Ezekiel 1, clarify how extrabiblical sources are helpful but unnecessary to understand a text's main point.

Resources for Further Study

Historical Context: Biblical Book- and Passage-Specific

Hill, Andrew E., and John H. Walton. *A Survey of the Old Testament*. 2nd ed. Grand Rapids: Zondervan, 2000.

House, Paul R., and Eric Mitchell. *Old Testament Survey*. 2nd ed. Nashville: Broadman & Holman, 2007.

★ Kaiser, Walter C., Jr., and Duane A. Garrett, eds. *NIV Archaeological Study Bible*. Grand Rapids: Zondervan, 2005.

LaSor, William Sanford, David Allan Hubbard, and Frederic William Bush. *Old Testament Survey: The Message, Form, and Background of the Old Testament*. 2nd ed. Grand Rapids: Eerdmans, 1996.

Longman, Tremper, III, and Raymond B. Dillard. *An Introduction to the Old Testament*. 2nd ed. Grand Rapids: Zondervan, 2006.

Merrill, Eugene H., Mark F. Rooker, and Michael A. Grisanti. *The World and the Word: An Introduction to the Old Testament.* Nashville: Broadman & Holman, 2011.

✪ Walton, John H., ed. Zondervan Illustrated Bible Backgrounds Commentary: Old Testament. 5 vols. Grand Rapids: Zondervan, 2009.

★ Walton, John H., and Craig S. Keener, eds. *NIV Cultural Backgrounds Study Bible.* Grand Rapids: Zondervan, 2016.

★ Walton, John H., Victor H. Matthews, and Mark W. Chavalas, eds. The IVP Bible Background Commentary: Old Testament. Downers Grove, IL: InterVarsity Press, 2000.

Historical Context: General

Beale, G. K. "The Relevance of Jewish Backgrounds for the Study of the Old Testament in the New." In *Handbook on the New Testament Use of the Old Testament: Exegesis and Interpretation*, 103–32. Grand Rapids: Baker Academic, 2012.

Chavalas, Mark W., and Murray R. Adamthwaite. "Archaeological Light on the Old Testament." In *The Face of Old Testament Studies: A Survey of Contemporary Approaches*, edited by David W. Baker and Bill T. Arnold, 59–96. Grand Rapids: Baker Academic, 2004.

Chavalas, Mark W., and Edwin C. Hostetter. "Epigraphic Light on the Old Testament." In *The Face of Old Testament Studies: A Survey of Contemporary Approaches*, edited by David W. Baker and Bill T. Arnold, 38–58. Grand Rapids: Baker Academic, 2004.

Chavalas, Mark W., and K. Lawson Younger Jr., eds. *Mesopotamia and the Bible: Comparative Explorations.* Grand Rapids: Baker Academic, 2002.

Coogan, Michael D., ed. *The Oxford History of the Biblical World.* Oxford: Oxford University Press, 1999.

Currid, John D. *Against the Gods: The Polemical Theology of the Old Testament.* Wheaton, IL: Crossway, 2013.

Frankfort, Henri. *Kingship and the Gods: A Study of Ancient Near Eastern Religion as the Integration of Society and Nature.* Chicago: University of Chicago Press, 1978.

Freedman, David Noel, ed. *The Anchor Bible Dictionary.* 6 vols. New York: Doubleday, 1992.

Hoerth, Alfred J., Gerald L. Mattingly, and Edwin M. Yamauchi, eds. *Peoples of the Old Testament World.* Grand Rapids: Baker, 1994.

Hoffmeier, James K., and Dennis R. Magary, eds. *Do Historical Matters Matter to Faith? A Critical Appraisal of Modern and Postmodern Approaches to Scripture.* Wheaton, IL: Crossway, 2012.

InterVarsity Press dictionaries on the Old Testament:

- Alexander, T. Desmond, and David W. Baker, eds. *Dictionary of the Old Testament: Pentateuch.* Downers Grove, IL: InterVarsity Press, 2003.
- Arnold, Bill T., and H. G. M. Williamson, eds. *Dictionary of the Old Testament: Historical Books.* Downers Grove, IL: InterVarsity Press, 2005.
- Boda, Mark J., and J. Gordon McConville, eds. *Dictionary of the Old Testament: Prophets.* Downers Grove, IL: InterVarsity Press, 2012.

• Longman, Tremper, III, and Peter Enns, eds. *Dictionary of the Old Testament: Wisdom, Poetry, and Writings*. Downers Grove, IL: InterVarsity Press, 2008.

Livingston, G. Herbert. *The Pentateuch in Its Cultural Environment*. 2nd ed. Grand Rapids: Baker, 1987.

Long, V. Philips. *The Art of Biblical History*. Foundations of Biblical Interpretation. Grand Rapids: Zondervan, 1994.

———. "Historiography of the Old Testament." In *The Face of Old Testament Studies: A Survey of Contemporary Approaches*, edited by David W. Baker and Bill T. Arnold, 145–75. Grand Rapids: Baker Academic, 2004.

Matthews, Victor H. *Manners and Customs in the Bible: An Illustrated Guide to Daily Life in Bible Times*. 3rd ed. Peabody, MA: Hendrickson, 2006.

Matthews, Victor H., and James C. Moyer. *The Old Testament: Text and Context*. 3rd ed. Grand Rapids: Baker Academic, 2012.

Millard, A. R., James K. Hoffmeier, and David W. Baker, eds. *Faith, Tradition, and History: Old Testament Historiography in Its Near Eastern Context*. Winona Lake, IN: Eisenbrauns, 1994.

Niehaus, Jeffrey J. *Ancient Near Eastern Themes in Biblical Theology*. Grand Rapids: Kregel, 2008.

Sakenfeld, Katharine Doob, ed. *The New Interpreter's Dictionary of the Bible*. 5 vols. Nashville: Abingdon, 2009.

Sasson, Jack M., ed. *Civilizations of the Ancient Near East*. 2 vols. Peabody, MA: Hendrickson, 2001.

Snell, Daniel C. *Life in the Ancient Near East, 3100–332 B.C.E.* New Haven, CT: Yale University Press, 1998.

Soden, Wolfram von. *The Ancient Orient: An Introduction to the Study of the Ancient Near East*. Translated by Donald G. Schley. Grand Rapids: Eerdmans, 1994.

Tenney, Merrill C., and Moisés Silva, eds. *The Zondervan Encyclopedia of the Bible*. 2nd ed. 5 vols. Grand Rapids: Zondervan, 2009.

Vaux, Roland de. *Ancient Israel: Its Life and Institutions*. Grand Rapids: Eerdmans, 1997.

Walton, John H. *Ancient Near Eastern Thought and the Old Testament: Introducing the Conceptual World of the Hebrew Bible*. Grand Rapids: Baker Academic, 2006.

———. *Chronological and Background Charts of the Old Testament*. 2nd ed. Grand Rapids: Zondervan, 1994.

Yamauchi, Edwin M. *Persia and the Bible*. Grand Rapids: Baker, 1990.

Yamauchi, Edwin M., and Marvin R. Wilson. *Dictionary of Daily Life in Biblical and Post-Biblical Antiquity*. 4 vols. Peabody, MA: Hendrickson, 2014–16.

Ancient Near Eastern Texts (in English) and Pictures Related to the Old Testament

⋆ Arnold, Bill T., and Bryan Beyer, eds. *Readings from the Ancient Near East: Primary Sources for Old Testament Study*. Encountering Biblical Studies. Grand Rapids: Baker Academic, 2002.

Beyerlin, Walter. *Near Eastern Religious Texts Relating to the Old Testament*. Philadelphia: Westminster, 1978.

✪ Hallo, William W., and K. Lawson Younger Jr., eds. *The Context of Scripture*. Vol. 1, *Canonical Compositions from the Biblical World*. Leiden: Brill, 1997.

✪ ———, eds. *The Context of Scripture*. Vol. 2, *Monumental Inscriptions from the Biblical World*. Leiden: Brill, 2000.

✪ ———, eds. *The Context of Scripture*. Vol. 3, *Archival Documents from the Biblical World*. Leiden: Brill, 2002.

Hays, Christopher B. *Hidden Riches: A Sourcebook for the Comparative Study of the Hebrew Bible and Ancient Near East*. Louisville: Westminster John Knox, 2014.

Matthews, Victor H., and Don C. Benjamin. *Old Testament Parallels: Laws and Stories from the Ancient Near East*. 3rd ed. New York: Paulist, 2006.

★ Pritchard, James B., ed. *The Ancient Near East: An Anthology of Texts and Pictures*. Foreword by Daniel E. Flemming. Princeton, NJ: Princeton University Press, 2011. Reprinted from 2 vols. in 1958, 1975.

✪ ———, ed. *Ancient Near Eastern Texts Relating to the Old Testament*. 3rd ed. Princeton, NJ: Princeton University Press, 1969.

———, ed. *The Ancient Near East in Pictures Relating to the Old Testament*. 2nd ed. Princeton, NJ: Princeton University Press, 1994.

SBL Writings from the Ancient World. Atlanta: SBL, 1990–.

Sparks, Kenton L. *Ancient Texts for the Study of the Hebrew Bible: A Guide to the Background Literature*. Peabody, MA: Hendrickson, 2005.

Walton, John H. *Ancient Israelite Literature in Its Cultural Context*. Grand Rapids: Zondervan, 1994.

✪ Younger, K. Lawson, Jr., ed. *The Context of Scripture*. Vol. 4, *Supplements*. Leiden: Brill, 2016.

History of Israel and of the Ancient Near East

Bright, John. *A History of Israel*. 4th ed. Louisville: Westminster John Knox, 2000.

Hallo, William W., and William Kelly Simpson. *The Ancient Near East: A History*. 2nd ed. New York: Harcourt, Brace, 1998.

★ Kaiser, Walter C., Jr., and Paul D. Wegner. *A History of Israel: From the Bronze Age through the Jewish Wars*. 2nd ed. Broadman & Holman, 2016.

★ Merrill, Eugene H. *Kingdom of Priests: A History of Old Testament Israel*. 2nd ed. Grand Rapids: Baker, 2008.

✪ Provan, Iain W., V. Philips Long, and Tremper Longman III. *A Biblical History of Israel*. 2nd ed. Louisville: Westminster John Knox, 2015.

Issues of Dating

Freedman, David Noel, A. Dean Forbes, and Francis I. Andersen, eds. *Studies in Hebrew and Aramaic Orthography*. Winona Lake, IN: Eisenbrauns, 1992.

Robertson, David A. *Linguistic Evidence in Dating Early Hebrew Poetry*. Missoula, MT: Scholars Press, 1973.

Steinmann, Andrew E. *From Abraham to Paul: A Biblical Chronology*. St. Louis: Concordia, 2011.

Thiele, Edwin R. *The Mysterious Numbers of the Hebrew Kings*. 2nd ed. Grand Rapids: Zondervan, 1983.

Walton, John H. *Chronological and Background Charts of the Old Testament*. 2nd ed. Grand Rapids: Zondervan, 1994.

Young, Ian, Robert Rezetko, and Martin Ehrensvärd. *Linguistic Dating of Biblical Texts: An Introduction to Approaches and Problems*. 2 vols. London: Routledge, 2014.

Young, Rodger C. All his published essays found at http://www.rcyoung.org/papers.html.

Historical Geography

Aharoni, Yohanan. *The Land of the Bible: A Historical Geography*. 2nd ed. Philadelphia: Westminster, 1979.

✪ Aharoni, Yohanan, Michael Avi-Yonah, Anson F. Rainey, Ze'ev Safrai, and R. Steven Notley. *The Carta Bible Atlas*. 5th ed. Jerusalem: Carta, 2011.

Beitzel, Barry J. *The New Moody Atlas of the Bible*. Chicago: Moody, 2009.

Currid, John D., and David P. Barrett. *Crossway ESV Bible Atlas*. Wheaton, IL: Crossway, 2010.

Curtis, Adrian. *Oxford Bible Atlas*. 4th ed. Oxford: Oxford University Press, 2009.

Hoppe, Leslie J. *A Guide to the Lands of the Bible*. Collegeville, MN: Glazier, 1999.

Monson, James M. *The Land Between: A Regional Study Guide to the Land of the Bible*. Highland Park, IL: Institute of Holy Land Studies, 1983.

✪ Rainey, Anson F., and R. Steven Notley. *The Sacred Bridge: Carta's Atlas of the Biblical World*. 2nd ed. Jerusalem: Carta, 2015.

Rasmussen, Carl. *Zondervan Atlas of the Bible*. 2nd ed. Grand Rapids: Zondervan, 2010.

★ Schlegel, William. *The Land and the Bible: A Historical Geographical Companion to the Satellite Bible Atlas*. Available at http://www.bibleplaces.com/wp-content/uploads/2015/08/The-Land-and-the-Bible.pdf.

★ ———. *Satellite Bible Atlas*. Israel: William Schlegel, 2013.

Smith, George Adam. *The Historical Geography of the Holy Land*. London: Hodder and Stoughton, 1894; repr., New York: Harper & Row, 1966.

Historiography

Arnold, Bill T., and Richard S. Hess, eds. *Ancient Israel's History: An Introduction to Issues and Sources*. Grand Rapids: Baker Academic, 2014.

Block, Daniel I., ed. *Israel: Ancient Kingdom or Late Invention?* Nashville: Broadman & Holman, 2008.

Fischer, David Hackett. *Historians' Fallacies: Toward a Logic of Historical Thought*. New York: Harper & Row, 1970.

★ Hoffmeier, James K., and Dennis R. Magary, eds. *Do Historical Matters Matter to Faith? A Critical Appraisal of Modern and Postmodern Approaches to Scripture*. Wheaton, IL: Crossway, 2012.

Kitchen, K. A. *On the Reliability of the Old Testament*. Grand Rapids: Eerdmans, 2003.

Kofoed, Jens Bruun. *Text and History: Historiography and the Study of the Biblical Text.* Winona Lake, IN: Eisenbrauns, 2005.

★ Long, V. Philips. *The Art of Biblical History.* Foundations of Biblical Interpretation. Grand Rapids: Zondervan, 1994.

Long, V. Philips, ed. *Israel's Past in Present Research: Essays on Ancient Israelite Historiography.* SBTS 7. Winona Lake, IN: Eisenbrauns, 1999.

Millard, A. R., James K. Hoffmeier, and David W. Baker, eds. *Faith, Tradition, and History: Old Testament Historiography in Its Near Eastern Context.* Winona Lake, IN: Eisenbrauns, 1994.

Miller, J. Maxwell, and John H. Hayes. *A History of Ancient Israel and Judah.* Philadelphia: Westminster, 1986.

Archaeology

Ben-Tor, Amnon, ed. *The Archaeology of Ancient Israel.* Translated by R. Greenberg. New Haven, CT: Yale University Press, 1994.

Currid, John D. *Doing Archaeology in the Land of the Bible: A Basic Guide.* Grand Rapids: Baker, 1999.

Harrison, R. K., and E. M. Blaiklock, eds. *The New International Dictionary of Biblical Archaeology.* Grand Rapids: Zondervan, 1983.

Hoerth, Alfred J. *Archaeology and the Old Testament.* Grand Rapids: Baker Academic, 2009.

Hoffmeier, James K. *The Archaeology of the Bible.* Oxford: Lion, 2008.

Kitchen, K. A. *The Bible in Its World: The Bible and Archaeology Today.* Downers Grove, IL: InterVarsity Press, 1977.

Mazar, Amihay, Ephraim Stern, Eric M. Meyers, and Mark A. Chancey. *Archaeology of the Land of the Bible.* 3 vols. New York: Doubleday, 1990.

McRay, John, and Alfred Hoerth. *Bible Archaeology: An Exploration of the History and Culture of Early Civilizations.* Grand Rapids: Baker, 2006.

Meyers, Eric M., ed. *The Oxford Encyclopedia of Archaeology in the Near East.* 5 vols. New York: Oxford University Press, 1997.

Stern, Ephraim, Ayelet Leyinzon-Gilboʿa, and Joseph Aviram, eds. *The New Encyclopedia of Archaeological Excavations in the Holy Land.* 4 vols. New York: Simon & Schuster, 1993–2008.

9

LITERARY CONTEXT

Goal: Comprehend the role that the passage plays in the whole book.

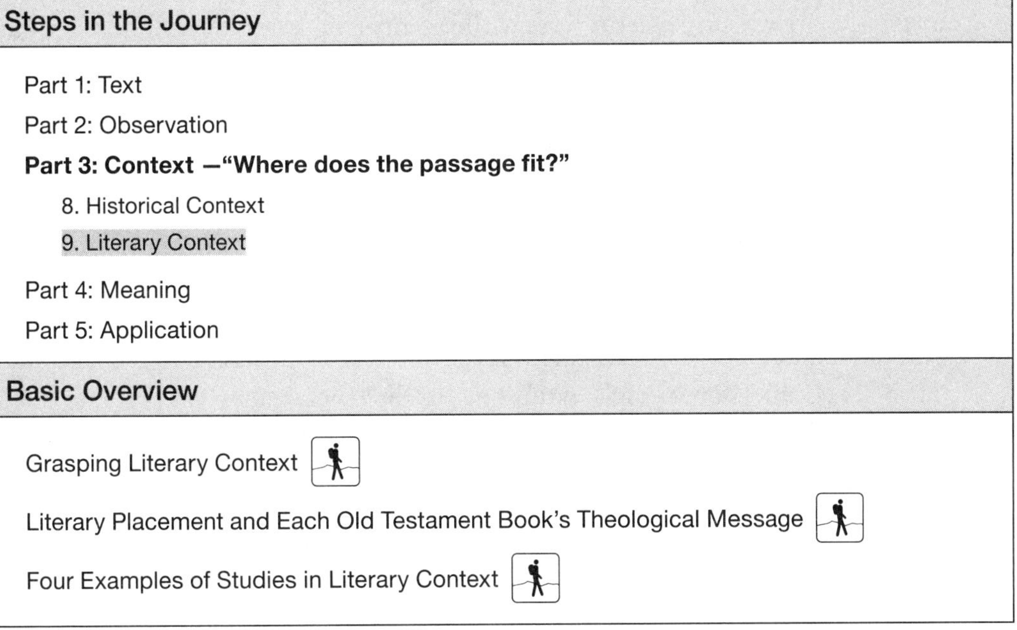
Steps in the Journey

Part 1: Text
Part 2: Observation
Part 3: Context —"Where does the passage fit?"
8. Historical Context
9. Literary Context
Part 4: Meaning
Part 5: Application

Basic Overview

Grasping Literary Context
Literary Placement and Each Old Testament Book's Theological Message
Four Examples of Studies in Literary Context

Fig. 9.1. Trail Guide to Chapter 9

Grasping Literary Context

God gave us his Word in a Book that is made up of multiple books. We will see that biblical theology looks more at Scripture as a whole, but literary context focuses on the individual parts as they come to us within their overall canonical context. It's the difference between looking at a whole quilt and looking at one of its single squares, which itself has its own color, texture, and story.

The question in ***literary context*** is, "How does the passage contribute to the overall story or argument of the book?" To answer this, we need to have a solid grasp of the book's thought flow, which is best initiated by reading the whole book several times on your own, each in a single sitting and while comparing a number of book outlines drafted by those who have spent far more time in the book than you have.

As you examine your passage in light of the whole book, you want to keep in mind at least three areas: literary placement, literary function, and literary details.

1. Literary Placement

Literary placement refers to your passage's location. Is the passage part of a larger literary grouping that has a discernible beginning, middle, or end? What leads up to the passage? What flows from it? How is the book organized, and how does the passage fit within the section, book, canonical division, Testament, and Bible—in that order?

The book of Daniel, for example, is most naturally structured in two parts: (a) God's sovereign control in the present (chs. 1–6) and (b) God's sovereign control in the future (chs. 7–12). Part 1 includes a progression of court stories about the exaltation of Daniel and his three friends. Together they stress that, while not always clear in the present, Israel's God is sovereign over all things and is working for his own against the world's rebellion. Part 2 then supplies a series of apocalyptic visions about the rise and fall of succeeding empires. Together these emphasize that, while it may not always be evident in the future, Israel's God is controlling all things according to his purposes and will ultimately establish his kingdom through his Messiah, destroying all evil.

If you were studying the episode of the fiery furnace in Daniel 3, it would be good to know its placement in part 1 between the stories of Nebuchadnezzar's statue-dream in chapter 2 and the king's punishment and restoration in chapter 4. It would also be good to know that in Jesus' Bible, Daniel's hope of God's kingdom opens the final narrative portion of the Writings, which sought to remind the believers who were in exile and slavery (Ezra 9:9; Neh. 9:36) that YHWH's power and kingdom purposes still stand. In this context, Daniel follows Lamentations and affirms the concluding statement, "But you, O Lord, reign forever; your throne endures to all generations"

(Lam. 5:19). Furthermore, in response to the lamenter's final cry, "Renew our days as of old—unless you have utterly rejected us, and you remain exceedingly angry with us" (5:21–22), Daniel declares that God had not completely rejected and would both restore and renew. Standing in the concluding portion of the Hebrew Scriptures, Daniel plays a vital role in thrusting the reader's eyes toward the New Testament, in which God's kingdom purposes begin to be realized.

2. Literary Function

Literary function addresses your text's purpose and contribution. What is the main thrust of the book as a whole, and what role does this particular passage play in the book's story line or reasoning? Does the passage fill in, add on to, introduce, bring to completion, or counterbalance the portion or book of which it is a part? What does it add to the overall picture? What does the overall picture add to it? If this passage were missing from the book, what would be lost?

If the book of Daniel as a whole supplies a glorious, hopeful vision of God's kingship over all, how does the story of Daniel 3 contribute to this message? In Daniel 2, King Nebuchadnezzar dreamed of a statue with four parts, each of which represented an earthly kingdom that would ultimately be overthrown by God's kingdom that would never perish (Dan. 2:44). Babylon, led by Nebuchadnezzar, was the first of these kingdoms (2:37–38). In Daniel 3, Nebuchadnezzar appears to have gotten caught up in his dream from chapter 2, but he is determined to be not just the head of gold but the whole. He erected a massive image of himself that all peoples, nations, and languages were to worship, lest they be immediately cast into a blazing furnace (3:1–7). Daniel's three friends, Shadrach, Meshach, and Abednego, were unrelentingly committed to YHWH and refused to bow down (3:16–18), resulting in their punishment. But they were not burned, for one "like a son of the gods" protected them (3:25). Therefore, Nebuchadnezzar declared them to be "servants of the Most High God" (3:26), praised their God for his mighty act (3:28), and then decreed that none should speak against their God (3:29).

This episode plays a key role in showing how Nebuchadnezzar was growing in his awareness of YHWH's sovereign control of the present. This recognition would only grow until in Daniel 4:37 we read, "Now I, Nebuchadnezzar, praise and extol and honor the King of heaven, for all his works are right and his ways are just; and those who walk in pride he is able to humble."

3. Literary Details

Literary details are the particular features or aspects of the text that set it apart and that help identify its overall contribution. How comprehensive or selective is the passage? Do any details help you decide whether or not the author wrote it in connection with a specific cultural or historical situation? Does the passage relay material from a distinctive perspective? What does this tell you about the author's intentions?

The biblical author clearly wrote Daniel 3 to remind the audience of YHWH's greatness and worth and of his ability to save either out of suffering or through suffering. Nebuchadnezzar's initial pride in questioning the three, "Who is the god who will deliver out of my hands?" (3:15), is contrasted with his later declaration, "There is no other god who is able to rescue in this way" (3:29). The king's initial challenge is also countered by Shadrach, Meshach, and Abednego's relentless commitment to the true God and their confidence that he was able to rescue: "Our God whom we serve is able to deliver us from the burning fiery furnace, and he will deliver us out of your hand, O king. But if not, be it known to you, O king, that we will not serve your gods or worship the golden image that you have set up" (Dan. 3:17–18). The three did not presume that they fully knew the Lord's will, but regardless of his pleasure they would trust and obey. Such details force readers to decide whether we will equally surrender to the supreme Sovereign and Savior in this story. Furthermore, when read in light of the whole book, the emphasis that one "like a son of the gods" protected the three in the furnace (3:25) likely anticipates the "one like a son of man" in 7:13–14—the one who will reign over God's kingdom. Later this figure is probably tagged as the "Messiah," during whose ministry God intends "to finish the transgression, to put an end to sin, and to atone for iniquity, to bring in everlasting righteousness, to seal both vision and prophet, and to anoint a most holy place" (9:24, 26). So Daniel 3 does not merely add general hope in a delivering God; it also fuels anticipation for the Messiah's reign.

Literary context is an essential step in exegeting a text, for it identifies the unique role that a passage plays in the overall flow of a book. This in turn helps us make explicit the author's intention in giving us these words in this way.

Literary Placement and Each Old Testament Book's Theological Message[1]

The Bible describes how God reigns, saves, and satisfies through covenant for his glory in Christ.[2] The Old Testament provides the foundation for this kingdom message, and the New Testament details its fulfillment. Jesus' Bible was the Old Testament, which highlights through narrative and commentary how the Mosaic old covenant was established in the Law, enforced in the Prophets, and enjoyed in the Writings (see "Putting Genre within Its Biblical Context" in chapter 1). In this section I want to share an overview of the theological message of each Old Testament book and to show how each book contributes to the message of the whole.

1. See http://www.desiringgod.org/messages/the-old-testament-in-ten-minutes.

2. Andy Naselli and I partnered in the shaping of this statement, building on some earlier conversations I had with my colleague Jason Meyer.

The Bible opens with the five narrative books of Moses, which together are called the *Law*. Here God *establishes* the old covenant. **Genesis** introduces God's universal kingdom program by highlighting the need for and provision of universal blessing. It also supplies the context for Israel's global mission. Sin has resulted in worldwide curse, and Abraham and his offspring's climaxing in a single, male, royal descendant in the line of Judah would be the means for the curse to be overcome by blessing. The remaining four books of the Law then clarify how the promise of offspring and the hope of the Promised Land find initial fruition in the Mosaic old covenant, all in the anticipation of the royal Redeemer. **Exodus** highlights King YHWH's global purposes through Israel, stressing the centrality and necessity of his presence and detailing both Israel's salvation and calling—Israel is to serve as a kingdom of priests and a holy nation in the context of the world (remember Exodus 19:4–6). In **Leviticus**, holy YHWH calls his people to be holy and clarifies how their pursuit of God will be empowered by his sanctifying presence and promises of blessing and curse. **Numbers** contrasts faithful YHWH with unfaithful Israel and describes an extended season of discipline in the wilderness during which Israel was supposed to learn to wait on and follow God. **Deuteronomy** is the "Constitution of the United Tribes of Israel" and calls for obedience leading to lasting covenant relationship. It also clarifies, however, that God would not overcome Israel's stubborn rebellion and enable love until the latter days after Israel would enter, lose, and be restored to the land. Then he would circumcise the people's hearts, empowering them to love God with all.

Next is the *Prophets*, which are to be read in light of the law of Moses and the hope of the coming royal deliverer. Here God *enforces* the old covenant, and the material is divided into two parts. The Former Prophets provide a narrative history of what happened to Israel from the conquest of the Promised Land, through the rise of the united and divided monarchies, to the exile from the land. The grouping begins with **Joshua**, which highlights YHWH's covenant faithfulness in giving the land and calls for Israel's covenant faithfulness. Will the people meditate on the law day and night, or will they go their own way? **Judges** answers Joshua's question by detailing Israel's covenant faithlessness and highlights that its chaotic, sinful existence was partly due to the fact that there was no king in Israel. Then **1–2 Samuel** outlines the rise of kingship, stresses the Davidic kingdom hope, and clarifies the importance of honoring YHWH above all else—something especially important for Israel's king. The narrative portion of the Former Prophets ends with **1–2 Kings**, which outlines Israel's covenant failure, especially the kings' failures, which in turn resulted in the kingdom's division and destruction. Nevertheless, it also retains hope in a Davidic king whose throne would last forever.

At this point the Old Testament narrative pauses, and the Latter Prophets offer prophetic commentary on why Israel's history resulted in exile. **Jeremiah** stresses Israel's lack of covenant loyalty and the eschatological promise of covenant loyalty in the age of the new covenant, when God would write his law on the heart. **Ezekiel** focuses on Israel's loss of God's presence from Jerusalem and the eschatological promise of his Spirit's presence in the age of resurrection. **Isaiah** unpacks Israel's rejection of God's kingship and the eschatological promise of his universal kingdom through the peace-establishing, justice-working servant-king, who would reign over transformed ethnic Israelites and Gentiles in the new creation. **The Twelve** Minor Prophets—Hosea, Joel, Amos, Obadiah, Jonah, Micah, Nahum, Habakkuk, Zephaniah, Haggai, Zechariah, Malachi—are united into a single volume in Jesus' Bible. Through the themes of sin, punishment, and restoration, they detail Israel's spiritual unfaithfulness and the eschatological promise of divine faithfulness. At this, the Prophets come to a close, and the focus on Israel's sin now shifts to a focus on kingdom hope.

In the *Writings*, the faithful remnant are found *enjoying* the old covenant relationship with YHWH. The Former Writings are principally poetic commentary on how the loyal remnant of YHWH was to live in a context of darkness, maintaining the belief that YHWH was still on the throne and would one day right all wrongs through his royal Redeemer. This commentary portion opens with **Ruth**, a narrative prelude that affirms the kingdom hope of YHWH's redeeming grace through the line of David. Just as God used Boaz of Bethlehem to redeem King David's ancestors, so also God would raise up another Kinsman-Redeemer of Bethlehem to restore David's descendants. Exile was not the final word, and this messianic hope provides the lens for reading Psalms and beyond. The rest of the Former Writings detail specifically the type of lifestyle by which one gains real kingdom hope. **Psalms** stresses that there is hope for those delighting in and submitting to God's kingship by walking, waiting, and worshiping in light of the Messiah. Through the five books of the Psalter, the prayers of the Christ become the songs of the saved as the messianic music moves from lament to praise and from kingdom crisis to kingdom consummation. **Job** gives hope for those fearing God for who he is and not for what he gives or takes away. **Proverbs** then provides kingdom hope for those acting wisely, who fear God, turn from evil, and live in light of the future; in the process it details how the future royal deliverer would live. **Ecclesiastes** details hope for those fearing and following God in pleasure and pain despite life's enigmas. And **Song of Songs** gives hope for those celebrating human sexuality in the context of marriage; only those who fan the flame of YHWH in the proper context will enjoy the ultimate union of the groom of heaven with his bride. **Lamentations** supplies hope for those remaining confident in God's reign and faithfulness to his own. With the promise of fresh mercies at dawn, the laments of Lamentations end the commentary portion of the Old Testament and provide a bridge for the reader back into the context of exile, which is picked up in the four final narrative books.

In the Latter Writings, we gain tangible signs of kingdom hope. **Daniel** reiterates the promise of God's universal kingdom: God reigns over every kingdom of the earth and will establish his kingdom over all through an Anointed One like a son of man. **Esther** details the preservation of God's kingdom people through whom the Messiah would come; God would not let his kingdom promises die. **Ezra-Nehemiah** stands as one book in Jesus' Bible and together foreshadows the restoration of God's kingdom people and land that was still to come. Then, with a focus on the Davidic covenant, **1–2 Chronicles** recaps in positive terms the purposes of God from Adam to Cyrus's call for the Jews to return to Jerusalem, thus affirming YHWH's universal kingship and kingdom promises.

The Old Testament closes without all the promises' having reached fulfillment, and therefore the end demands a sequel—a sequel that ultimately comes in the New Testament. God will reign over God's people in God's land. God will see his kingdom purposes accomplished. He establishes the old covenant in the Law, enforces it in the Prophets, and allows it to be enjoyed in the Writings. While the old covenant bore a ministry of condemnation, the Old Testament itself ends in hope and provides a foundation for the fulfillment found in Christ and the New Testament wherein the new covenant brings a ministry of righteousness. In the whole, God stands as the ultimate Lord, Savior, and Treasure, who reigns, saves, and satisfies through covenant for his glory in Christ.

Four Examples of Studies in Literary Context

Exodus 19:4–6 in Its Literary Context

We begin our examples of literary context by returning to Exodus 19:4–6. Perhaps more than any other book in Scripture, Exodus is an extended narrative treatise on the nature of YHWH as God. The whole book is designed to highlight his rightful, necessary, and loving passion for his own glory above all things. It does this by focusing on two main areas: (1) his redemption of his people (chs. 1–18) and (2) his relationship with his people (chs. 19–40).

Figure 9.2 on the next page contains my exegetical outline for Exodus. Note where 19:4–6 falls:

I. YHWH's Self-Exalting, Gracious Redemption of His People (1:1–18:27)

- A. Historical Background to Redemption (1:1–4:31)
  1. Setting the stage for redemption (1:1–2:25)
  2. Calling of God's messenger of redemption (3:1–4:31)
- B. The Call for and Experience of Redemption (5:1–15:21)
  1. Moses' challenge to Pharaoh and Israel (5:1–6:27)
  2. Ten plagues: proclaiming the power and presence of YHWH (6:28–11:10)
  3. The memorialization of redemption: the Passover (12:1–36)
  4. The experience of redemption (12:37–14:31)
  5. The celebration of redemption (15:1–21)
- C. The Ramifications of Redemption (15:22–18:27)
  1. For Israel: the life of faith as trust for provision (15:22–17:16)
  2. For Moses: the life of faith as trust for guidance (18:1–27)

II. YHWH's Self-Exalting, Gracious Relationship with His People (19:1–40:38)

- A. The Covenant Embodying YHWH's Relationship with Israel (19:1–24:11)
  1. The manifestation of and response to YHWH's presence and word (19:1–20:21)
  2. The nature of the relationship expounded (20:22–23:33)
  3. The ratification of the covenant (24:1–11)
- B. Sacred Space as the Emanating Center of YHWH's Relationship with Israel (24:12–40:38)
  1. The manifestation of God's glory and the description of sacred space (24:12–31:18)
  2. YHWH's response to Israel's failure to reckon with his presence (32:1–34:35)
  3. YHWH's gracious manifestation of his presence among his people (35:1–40:38)

Fig. 9.2. Exegetical Outline of Exodus

1. Literary Placement and Function

Redemption and relationship through covenant and divine presence are the hallmarks of the way in which YHWH discloses himself in Exodus. Since each of these elements is present in Exodus 19:4–6, this passage has a foundational place in the book. Redemption and divine presence are manifest in verse 4, whereas the covenant and its purpose of mediating and magnifying God's presence are the focus of verses 5–6.

Chapters 19–40 address two things: (a) how the Mosaic covenant (19:1–24:11) set the boundaries and purpose of Israel's relationship with YHWH and (b) how the tabernacle (25:1–40:38) provided the context for this relationship. Within this framework, Exodus 19:4–6 introduces the section on covenant, describing its core. Exodus 19:4–6 is YHWH's first speech in the main part of the book, which itself gives the text priority.

Chapters 19–40 stand as the heart of the book for at least three reasons. First, these chapters carry the most literary weight, standing twice as long as what comes before. Second, Exodus 19:4–6 is explicit that the redemption detailed in chapters 1–18 grounds and gives rise to the relationship and the calling that flows from it. Third, the narrative itself has been anticipating Israel's arrival at Mount Sinai since 3:12, where God declared to Moses at the burning bush, "I will be with you, and this will be the sign for you, that I have sent you: when you have brought the people out of Egypt, you shall serve [worship] God on this mountain." Exodus 19:2 then tells us, "They . . . came into the wilderness of Sinai. . . . There Israel encamped before *the* mountain."

2. Literary Details

a. Background: Destruction and Deliverance

Using the translation I gave in chapter 4, Exodus 19:4 reads, "You have seen what I did to Egypt, and how I lifted you on wings of eagles, and how I brought you to myself." The task to which YHWH calls Israel in these verses is grounded in what he had just accomplished on the nation's behalf. With their own eyes, the people had witnessed the ten devastating plagues that YHWH brought on Egypt, and they had experienced a remarkable salvation.

Pharaoh had asked in Exodus 5:2, "Who is the Lord, that I should obey his voice and let Israel go?" The plagues provided YHWH's systematic response to this query. It is intriguing that the text never names the pharaoh of the exodus. Oh, how historians wish that he were identified! But a theological point is being made. Pharaoh was god on earth for the Egyptians, yet he remains nameless. In contrast, the God over both heaven and earth from whom everything derives bears the name *YHWH* (Ex. 3:14–15). He is jealous to be known (34:14), and the whole book of Exodus works to unpack the significance of his name.

The battle in Egypt took place first in the heavenlies—it was a battle of the gods, during which YHWH as the only uncaused one defeated Egypt's powers. Nearly every one of the ten plagues is known to have confronted an Egyptian deity.[3] Furthermore, we have such texts as this: "For I will pass through the land of Egypt that night, and I will strike all the firstborn in the land of Egypt, both man and beast; and on all the gods of Egypt I will execute judgments: I am the Lord" (Ex. 12:12). "On the day after the Passover, the people of Israel went out triumphantly in the sight of all the Egyptians, while the Egyptians were burying all their firstborn, whom the Lord had struck down among them. On their gods also the Lord executed judgments" (Num. 33:3–4). "And who is like your people Israel, the one nation on earth whom God went to redeem to be his people, making himself a name and doing for them great and awesome things by driving out before your people . . . for yourself from Egypt, a nation and *its gods*?" (2 Sam. 7:23).

YHWH declares in Exodus 19:4, "You yourselves have seen!" The destruction of Egypt and the people's own deliverance happened before their very eyes. Faced with the amazing majesty and mercy of God, they sang, "Who is like you, O Lord, among the gods? Who is like you, majestic in holiness, awesome in glorious deeds, doing wonders?" (Ex. 15:11). The answer: No one! Thus they declared, "The Lord will reign

3. See John H. Walton, *Chronological and Background Charts of the Old Testament*, 2nd ed. (Grand Rapids: Zondervan, 1994), 85.

forever and ever" (15:18). Others outside Israel also expressed similar awe. Jethro, Moses' father-in-law, declared, "Blessed be the LORD, who has delivered you out of the hand of the Egyptians and out of the hand of Pharaoh and has delivered the people from under the hand of the Egyptians. Now I know that the LORD is greater than all gods" (18:10).

This amazing display of majesty and mercy sets the literary backdrop to our passage. Just before the seventh plague, YHWH told Pharaoh through Moses, "For by now I could have put out my hand and struck you and your people with pestilence, and you would have been cut off from the earth. But for this purpose I have raised you up, to show you my power, so that my name may be proclaimed *in all the earth*" (Ex. 9:15–16). God is intent to exalt his power in the sight of all—with every people, every power knowing that he alone is God. He had raised up Pharaoh for this ultimate end. He destroyed Egypt and delivered Israel for the fame of his name, and this God-exalting motivation is what grounds the God-honoring calling detailed in Exodus 19:5–6.

b. Foreground: Covenant and Calling

Exodus 19:5–6 reads, "And now, if you will indeed listen unto my voice and keep my covenant and be to me a treasured possession from all the peoples, for all the earth is mine, then you will be to me a kingdom of priests and holy nation" (author's translation). When YHWH asserted that Israel should indeed "listen unto [his] voice," this implied his authority over his people. YHWH speaks as a sovereign, and therefore, his words are by nature authoritative and, when written, canonical. The call to "listen unto [his] voice" in 19:5 appears to anticipate the introduction to the Ten Words in 20:1, which reads, "And God spoke all these words, saying . . . ." The voice that the people are to obey is, at the very least, disclosed in the words that YHWH is about to proclaim.

God calls Israel specifically to keep his "covenant," which, as I noted in my discussion of "Historical Context," refers to the Sinai covenant as the fulfillment of the first stage of the Abrahamic covenant ("The Historical Context of Exodus 19:4–6" in chapter 8). YHWH had promised Abraham that he would become a nation in the land, and the Mosaic covenant revealed initially in Exodus 19–20 is the working out of this promise.

Exodus 20 highlights the way in which the encounter with God's presence mentioned in Exodus 19:4 grounds and gives rise to the calling of verses 5–6. At the mountain YHWH had disclosed both his person and word in power through the giving of the Ten Words. The crashing and piercing sounds and the visible display of fire and smoke had caused the people to tremble and to back away from the mountain (Ex. 20:18). YHWH is not safe, but he is good. At this Moses came to them and declared in Exodus 20:20: "Do not fear, for God has come in order to test you and in order that the fear of him may be before you, that you may not sin" (author's translation). The logic of this text is important. God came to test the Israelites and to generate holy fear in them in order that they might not sin. Sin implies a lack of Godward fear, and a lack of Godward fear implies that we are not encountering God.

In Exodus 19:5–6, the means for fulfilling the calling to mediate God's greatness as a kingdom of priests and to magnify this greatness as a holy people was through their heeding his voice, keeping his covenant, and being a treasured possession. The Israelites needed to obey God's law to show the world the value of God, but they would not do so apart from his merciful disclosure of himself. This is Moses' point at the end of the book when, after the golden-calf episode, he pleads for God's presence to remain in their midst. Exodus 33:16 says, "For how shall it be known that I have found favor in your sight, I and your people? Is it not in your going with us, so that we are distinct, I and your people, from every other people on the face of the earth?" In Exodus 19:5–6, what will make Israel a light in the world will be its radical surrender to God and his ways. In Exodus 33:16, what will make Israel a light to the world will be the presence of God. Exodus 20:20 clarifies that God's presence generates fear that in turn leads to obedience.

As I conclude this section, I offer a challenge. Examine your life. Where are your biggest struggles with sin? We rebel against God only when we don't fear him enough, and fear is generated with a personal encounter with his presence. Plead to God to make his presence known to you. I love the promise in Jeremiah 32:40 regarding the new covenant: "I will make with them an everlasting covenant, that I will not turn away from doing good to them. And I will put the fear of me in their hearts, that they may not turn from me." Pray that God will work within you the fear that leads to holiness, for the glory of his name.

Psalm 121 in Its Literary Context

Here is another example of a literary-context analysis of a single psalm. Psalm 121 is one of my favorites.

Main Idea: The psalmist calls others to join him in celebrating YHWH's guardianship in their lives.	
1 A SONG OF ASCENTS	
I lift up my eyes to the hills. From where does my help come? 2 My help comes from the LORD, who made heaven and earth.	**I. The Personal Celebration of YHWH's Guardianship (vv. 1–2)** A. The posture of the guarded (v. 1) B. The confidence of the guarded (v. 2)

Fig. 9.3. Main Idea and Exegetical Outline of Psalm 121

3 He will not let your foot be moved; he who keeps you will not slumber. 4 Behold, he who keeps Israel will neither slumber nor sleep.	**II. The Assurance to Others of YHWH's Guardianship (vv. 3–8)** A. The nature of YHWH's guardianship declared (vv. 3–4) 1. The ensurer of our perseverance (v. 3a) 2. The constant watcher over his own (vv. 3b–4)
5 The LORD is your keeper; the LORD is your shade on your right hand. 6 The sun shall not strike you by day, nor the moon by night. 7 The LORD will keep you from all evil; he will keep your life. 8 The LORD will keep your going out and your coming in from this time forth and forevermore.	B. The nature of YHWH's guardianship expounded (vv. 5–8) 1. His identity: the ever-present defender (vv. 5–6) 2. His actions (vv. 7–8) a. The life-preserver (v. 7) b. The lasting protector (v. 8)

Fig. 9.3. Main Idea and Exegetical Outline of Psalm 121 (cont.)

In Psalm 121 the psalmist expresses his confidence in YHWH as his helper, and he builds his belief in God's protection by rehearsing to himself and to others the qualities of God's faithfulness that he has grown to know are true. As we begin to consider this psalm's literary context, you will recall that the book of Psalms is found in the Writings, the third major section of the Old Testament. The Writings are devoted to showing God's people how the remnant made it through Israel's rough history by trusting the promises of YHWH's eternal kingdom. Psalm 121 contributes to this message.

Within the Hebrew Old Testament, Psalms is the first major book in the Writings, according to the canonical arrangement that I believe is most original (see "Putting Genre within Its Biblical Context" in chapter 1), coming after Ruth, which serves as a narrative preface focusing on the Davidic kingdom hope of the coming Messiah. Psalms first supplies the prayers by and about the Christ, which in turn become the songs of those he saves (see "Psalms" in chapter 1). The Psalms give voice to the Godward laments, thanksgivings, and praises that rise from those finding refuge in the royal Son in this beautiful but often chaotic and broken world. Psalms predictively provided Christ with words to capture his own heart cries, and now, for those in Christ, Psalms models how to remain Godward and hopeful at points of desperation and exhilaration, both individually throughout the week and corporately when believers gather together.

Psalms is messianic music that God's people sang before and after exile. In days of imperfect Davidic kings or of no king at all, the Psalms promised that the future

Davidic king would indeed triumph through tribulation, that light would overcome darkness, and that praise would supplant lament. From beginning to end, the Psalter portrays the sufferings of the Christ and the hope of his kingdom. For generations the Psalms have helped readers see how completely the Christ identified with us in sin and suffering and how only in him is there possibility for life.

Psalm 121 occurs in the fifth book of the Psalms (Pss. 107–150). This section offers reflections on the return to the land after exile and presents YHWH as the one who restores and renews his people, all with an eye to the consummate fulfillment of his Davidic kingdom promises. Much like David's own prayer in Psalm 14:7 (cf. 1 Chron. 16:35), Book IV ended with the psalmist praying for return from exile. He cries in Psalm 106:47: "Save us, O Lord our God, and gather us from among the nations, that we may give thanks to your holy name and glory in your praise." The psalmist is most likely hoping not simply for a physical return but for the climactic second exodus of which the prophets spoke that would align with the coming messianic kingdom (e.g., Isa. 11:1–12:5; 49:1–6; Jer. 23:5–8; Ezek. 34:16, 22–24; 37:20–28; Hos. 3:5). Now Book V opens in Psalm 107 with praise to God for answering this prayer. We read in Psalm 107:1–3: "Oh give thanks to the Lord, for he is good, for his steadfast love endures forever! Let the redeemed of the Lord say so, whom he has redeemed from trouble and gathered in from the lands, from the east and from the west, from the north and from the south."

After this, the remaining parts of Psalm 107, along with Psalms 108–109, emphasize YHWH's unrelenting affection for all who trust him (cf. Pss. 107:33–43; 108:11). With glorious messianic hope, Psalm 110 then stresses that the Davidic covenant has not been set aside. Quoting Psalm 110, Hebrews 1:13 tells us that Jesus is David's "Lord" of whom YHWH declared, "Sit at my right hand until I make your enemies a footstool for your feet" (cf. Matt. 22:41–45). Psalms 111–118 stress that the God who works on behalf of his people deserves wholehearted worship and loyalty at all times and in all circumstances. Such a call stresses the importance of God's Word, which is celebrated in Psalm 119. It also requires the centrality of YHWH's presence in the lives of God's people, which is the focus of the Songs of Ascent in Psalms 120–134. In these Songs of Ascent we find Psalm 121, which supplies hope-filled assurance in YHWH's guardianship and gives cause for enjoying his presence. Building on Psalm 121:6, Revelation 7:16 declares that for all who die in the great tribulation, having identified themselves with the slain Lamb, "They shall hunger no more, neither thirst anymore; *the sun shall not strike them*, nor any scorching heat." The favor that God shows his Christ becomes the favor that he shows all who are identified with him. The longest of the Songs of Ascent is Psalm 132, which emphasizes the fulfillment of YHWH's promise to David that he would indeed have a king on the throne of Jerusalem forever.

Psalms 135–138 summarize God's work through creation and providence on behalf of his people, with Psalm 138 returning to psalms of David, which continue through Psalm 145. These psalms depict the anointed royal figure as requesting God's help in both spiritual and temporal matters (Pss. 139–144) and then celebrating YHWH's character and work (Ps. 145). The five books conclude with a string of five praise psalms that exalt the excellencies of God over all (Pss. 146–150).

Standing as the second of the Songs of Ascent, Psalm 121 sets the readers' gaze upward toward God and his holy mountain: "I lift my eyes to the hills. From where does my help come?" Looking up means one thing: the psalmist was down. Nevertheless, in his pain, in his anxiety he looked Godward to the one who had made heaven and earth. He says, "He will not let your foot be moved" (Ps. 121:3). Your guardian never sleeps, and because of that you can. He was a refuge for Christ, and he will continue to guard all who find refuge in him. You can rest today because the all-satisfying Savior reigns in the person of Jesus. The Davidic hope has reached its fulfillment, and now the very psalms that Jesus drew from to clarify his own mission of triumph through tribulation can become the very cries of our hearts. "The Lord is your keeper . . . . The Lord will keep your going out and your coming in from this time forth and forevermore" (Ps. 121:5, 8).

Flow of Thought in the Book of the Twelve

To many people, one of the surprising features of Jesus' Bible is that the Minor Prophets stand together as a twelve-part book—the Book of the Twelve. Stephen, the first known Christian martyr, referred to this book when quoting Amos, saying, "As it is written in *the book* of the prophets . . ." (Acts 7:42). In my mind, each individual prophetic book stands on its own without clear signs of outside editorial updating. Nevertheless, the nonchronological arrangement of the Twelve suggests the work of a theologically minded editor, who grouped certain works together by theme and catchphrases. Affirming the independent role of each book, what I want to do in this section is simply draw attention to the fact that together the twelve individual books proclaim a message greater than they do when each is read alone.

Scholars have noted three main themes in the Twelve: sin, punishment, and restoration. While all these elements are clearly apparent at some level in each of the twelve books, Paul House has helpfully noted how the initial six books, Hosea–Micah, bear a deeper affinity toward addressing *sin*, that the next three, Nahum–Zephaniah, focus more closely on *punishment*, and that the final three, Haggai–Malachi, call higher attention to *restoration*.[4]

4. Paul R. House, *The Unity of the Twelve*, JSOTSup 97 (Sheffield, UK: Almond Press, 1990).

Sin	Hosea, Joel, Amos, Obadiah, Jonah, Micah
Punishment	Nahum, Habakkuk, Zephaniah
Restoration	Haggai, Zechariah, Malachi

Fig. 9.4. The Unity of the Twelve

Along with these features, I think that we can get a deeper sense of the unity of the Twelve by reading the books in light of one another and in light of the overall flow of the collection. Simply synthesizing the message of each book in succession reveals a coherent flow of thought that pronounces a message greater than the parts.

1. **Hosea.** "Israel, YHWH has a case against you: You have played the harlot and been like an unfaithful wife, departing from faithfulness, steadfast love, and knowledge. Please return to YHWH, your husband!"
2. **Joel.** "For the day of YHWH is at hand, and repentance is your only hope! I will be a refuge to my people, but a roaring, devouring lion against all who fail to heed my voice!"
3. **Amos.** "How secure you feel, yet how insecure you actually are! I have disciplined you, yet you have not learned from the discipline. You anticipate my coming, but for you this day will be darkness, not light. Prepare to meet your God, for the fulfillment of my kingdom promises is only for those who truly repent!"
4. **Obadiah.** "Know this: Pride and hatred have no place in my coming kingdom; this is why your brother Edom will be destroyed."
5. **Jonah.** "Yet be warned, for your own pride and hatred of others resembles that of Edom and stands in direct contrast to the steadfast love YHWH gives to whomever he wills. Don't be like Jonah; be like YHWH and extend compassion rather than gloating in others' destruction, lest God's punishment fall on you!"
6. **Micah.** "YHWH, from his courtroom, has found you and the nations guilty! Yet your final judgment day has not come, and in his mercy, he will still forgive your sins, if you but return. Soon God, through his Word and Messiah, will be exalted over all things. Will you be a part of the punishment or the redemption?"
7. **Nahum.** "Know this for certain: YHWH is a stronghold only for those who accept his terms of peace, but he will justly judge all his unrepentant enemies."
8. **Habakkuk.** "YHWH is just, and in his time he will indeed punish all wrongdoers and preserve all who walk by faith, looking to him for help, guidance, and satisfaction."

9. **Zephaniah.** "Please be part of the remnant that draws near to YHWH, so that the coming day may be one of rejoicing! Yet for all who fail to heed God's voice, the day of YHWH the warrior will be sure destruction!"
10. **Haggai.** "Drawing near to God necessitates that you take seriously the need for his presence in your midst, that he might bring forth the fulfillment of all he has promised, blessing for you and for the nations who surrender to him."
11. **Zechariah.** "You need YHWH's presence among you, for his kingdom restoration will be brought not by human effort but by the power of his Spirit working through his slain and yet victorious Priest-King."
12. **Malachi.** "This restoration is for you, if you will but fear and honor YHWH in all areas of your life, awaiting the day when curse will give rise to full restoration blessing!"

When assessing literary context in the Minor Prophets, keep in mind that together they shape a single twelve-part book. Whichever prophet you assess, consider how his message contributes to the overall message of the Twelve.

Zephaniah: The Savior's Summons to Satisfaction

Martin Luther once declared, "Among the minor prophets, [Zephaniah] makes the clearest prophecies about the kingdom of Christ."[5] I want to conclude this chapter on literary context by reviewing the thought flow and message of the entire book of Zephaniah. Because it is only fifty-three verses long, I encourage you to take ten minutes to read through the three chapters and then to refer back to the biblical book as I walk through the whole. Figure 9.5 reviews the overall structure and argument levels of the book, and figure 9.6 supplies my main-idea statement and exegetical outline.

5. Martin Luther, *Lectures on the Minor Prophets I: Hosea–Malachi*, ed. Hilton C. Oswald, Luther's Works 18 (St. Louis: Concordia, 1975), 320.

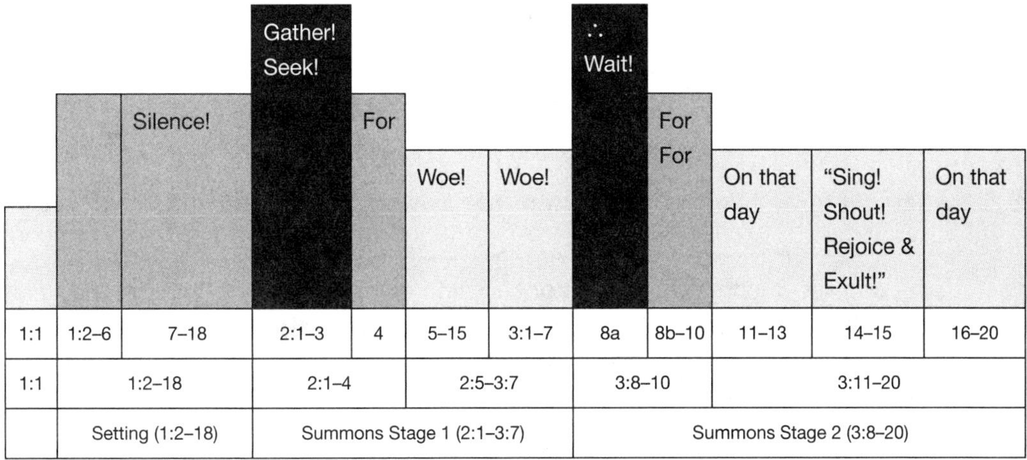

Fig. 9.5. Structural Overview of Zephaniah

Main Idea: In light of the impending day of his wrath, the Lord summons his faithful remnant to patiently pursue him together in order to avoid punishment and to enjoy satisfying salvation, all for God's joy and glory.

I. The Superscription to the Savior's Summons to Satisfaction (1:1)

II. The Setting for the Savior's Summons to Satisfaction: A Call to Revere God (1:2–18)

- A. The Context for the Call to Revere God: Coming Punishment (1:2–6)
- B. The Makeup of the Call to Revere God (1:7–18)

III. The Substance of the Savior's Summons to Satisfaction: Charges to Patiently Pursue the Lord Together (2:1–3:20)

- A. Stage 1: Seek the Lord Together to Avoid Punishment (2:1–3:7)
  - 1. The Charge to Gather Together before the Lord (2:1–2)
  - 2. The Charge to Seek the Lord in Righteousness and Humility (2:3–3:7)
    - a. The charge to seek the Lord (2:3)
    - b. An initial reason to seek the Lord (2:4)
    - c. Some expounded reasons to seek the Lord (2:5–3:7)
      - i. Reason 1 ("Woe"): The lamentable state and fate of the rebels from the foreign nations (2:5–15)
      - ii. Reason 2 ("Woe"): The lamentable state and fate of the rebels from Jerusalem (3:1–7)
- B. Stage 2: Wait on the Lord to Enjoy Satisfying Salvation (3:8–20)
  - 1. The Charge to Wait for the Lord (3:8a)
  - 2. Two Reasons to Wait for the Lord (3:8b–10)
  - 3. Promises to Motivate Waiting for the Lord: The Remnant's Satisfying Salvation (3:11–20)
    - a. The promise that the Lord will not put Jerusalem to shame (3:11–13)
    - b. A parenthetical call to rejoice as if the great salvation had already occurred (3:14–15)
    - c. The promise that the Lord will save completely (3:16–20)

Fig. 9.6. Main Idea and Exegetical Outline of Zephaniah

1. The Superscription to the Savior's Summons to Satisfaction (1:1)

In introducing this prophetic call to satisfying salvation, the book's superscription highlights its nature and source (the Word of God), its messenger (Zephaniah, a Judaean in the Davidic royal line), and its historical backdrop (the days of Josiah's reformation).

2. The Setting for the Savior's Summons to Satisfaction: A Call to Revere God (1:2–18)

This section sets a context for the book's main exhortations in chapters 2–3. The prophet cries, "Be silent before the Lord God!" (Zeph. 1:7), which is a call to revere the Lord in light of the nearness and nature of YHWH's impending judgment on Judah and the world. Verses 2–6 highlight the context for the call (i.e., global judgment), and verses 7–18 define the makeup of the call.

a. The Context for the Call to Revere God: Coming Punishment (1:2–6)

YHWH promises to bring devastating judgment on the broad world (Zeph. 1:2–3) and on Judah and Jerusalem in particular (vv. 4–6). Destruction will come because of rampant wickedness and idolatrous rebellion.

b. The Makeup of the Call to Revere God (1:7–18)

Like a herald readying an audience for an angry king's arrival, Zephaniah charges his audience to become quiet before the Lord (Zeph. 1:7a). He then further describes the basis for the call, detailing the imminent timing and sacrificial makeup of YHWH's impending judgment day with respect to both Judah (vv. 7b–13) and the whole world (vv. 14–18). Fascinatingly, the prophet portrays the day of the Lord as both war (1:15–16) and sacrifice (1:7, 18), which gives clarity to what is taking place in Old Testament atonement and in the work of Christ at the cross. Because God poured out on Christ the just wrath he had toward us—making "him to be sin who knew no sin" (2 Cor. 5:21; cf. Gal. 3:13)—we will now "be saved by him from the wrath of God" (Rom. 5:9). Jesus bore the day of the Lord's wrath on behalf of all who are in him.

3. The Substance of the Savior's Summons to Satisfaction: Charges to Patiently Pursue the Lord Together (2:1–3:20)

In light of the call to revere God sparked by the encroaching day of YHWH (Zeph. 1:2–18), the book's main section calls the righteous remnant to seek the Lord together and to wait for him (2:1, 3; 3:8). The dual charges frame 2:5–3:7, which highlight the lamentable state and fate of the rebels from the foreign nations (2:5–15) and from Jerusalem (3:1–7) in order to clarify some reasons why the remnant should patiently pursue YHWH.

a. Stage 1: Seek the Lord Together to Avoid Punishment (2:1–3:7)

Stage 1 in the summons to satisfaction is communal Godward pursuit, defined here in two parts as gathering together (Zeph. 2:1–2) and seeking YHWH (v. 3abc). The remnant must join arms before the day of divine wrath comes, and they must seek God in righteousness and humility. Only by this means may they "perhaps . . . be sheltered" from God's destruction of the wicked (v. 3d), like those from Philistia (v. 4).

The main reasons to seek God together are then expounded (Zeph. 2:5–3:7). This unit develops the punishment mentioned in 2:4 and by this unpacks the rational basis for the charges to "seek" and "wait" found in 2:3 and 3:8. The rebellious listeners should patiently pursue YHWH because he has promised to punish not only the rebels of the foreign nations (2:5–15) but also those from Jerusalem (3:1–7). Each reason for patiently pursuing God begins with the term "woe" (2:5; 3:1) and laments the state and fate of the respective groups.

The first reason relates to the lamentable state and fate of the rebels from the foreign nations (Zeph. 2:5–15). With the call to Judah to repent in focus (2:1–4), this unit builds a compass of punishment around Israel, announcing God's wrath against the Philistines to the west (vv. 5–7), the Moabites and Ammonites to the east (vv. 8–11), and the Cushites/Ethiopians and Assyrians to the south and north (vv. 12–15). Implied is that the punishment that spans the populated world will reach Judah (cf. Hab. 2:16–17) unless the people return to YHWH and become part of the preserved remnant (see Zeph. 3:7, 9).

The second reason for seeking the Lord concerns the lamentable state and fate of the rebels from Jerusalem (Zeph. 3:1–7). As implied in the preceding lament ("woe") against the rebels from the foreign nations (2:5–15), this brief unit further unpacks the sinful makeup and certain punishment of those in Jerusalem by highlighting their stubborn resistance to learn from God's correction of them or from his destruction of the foreign nations. In turn, it provides a further reason why the remnant should indeed pursue YHWH ("gather" and "seek," 2:1–3) with patient trust ("wait," 3:8).

b. Stage 2: Wait on the Lord to Enjoy Satisfying Salvation (3:8–20)

Added to the order to pursue the Lord together (Zeph. 2:1–3) is here a call to enduring patience (3:8): "'Therefore, wait for me,' declares the LORD." The charges to seek the Lord together and to wait for him make up Zephaniah's two-stage summons that explains the means to lasting joy—a joy that culminates in God's delight in those he has saved (3:17).

Following the initial call to patient trust in 3:8a, Zephaniah supplies two reasons to wait for the Lord (3:8b–10). The ESV marks each with the conjunction "for": "*For* my decision is to gather nations . . . . *For* at that time I will change the speech of the peoples." The remnant should continue to wait upon YHWH because he still intends both to judge the rebel nations (3:8b; cf. Hab. 1:2; 3:17–19) and to save a group from the nations of the world, reversing the effects of the Tower of Babel (Zeph. 3:9–10; cf. Gen. 11:9). Specifically, on the very day that YHWH stands in judgment as covenant witness ("then"), he will do a work of new creation, transforming peoples from all over the world into true worshipers. Peoples from beyond ancient Ethiopia (Cush) will call on God's name and serve him with one accord—all predictions initially fulfilled in the days of Pentecost (Acts 2:4–6, 21, 38, 42–47; 8:26–40) and now realized eternally in the church (Matt. 28:18–20; Rom. 11; Eph. 2:11–22; Rev. 5:9–10; 7:9–10).

This initial promise of new creation centered in a new Jerusalem is then followed by further promises to motivate waiting for the Lord (Zeph. 3:11–20). The lack of a connector at the head of 3:11 and the content that focuses on the remnant's satisfying salvation suggest that the whole unit from 3:11–20 clarifies the implications of the global transformation highlighted in 3:8b–10.

For those whom God preserves in Jerusalem (which includes both ethnic Israelites and others from the nations, Zeph. 3:9–10; cf. 2:9), the restoration will include the removal of the proud and the preservation of the God-dependent (3:11–13), the verbal expression of joy in the wake of the King's irreversible victory (3:14–15), and YHWH's deliverance of and delight in his remnant, which secures provision and protection (3:16–20). The call to joy in 3:14–15 is especially important, for it treats the deliverance as though it had already happened: "Rejoice and exult with all your heart, O daughter of Jerusalem! The Lord has taken away the judgments against you; he has cleared away your enemies. The King of Israel, the Lord, is in your midst; you shall never again fear evil." Strikingly, in recording Jesus' triumphal entry into Jerusalem, John appears to blend both Zechariah 9:9 and Zephaniah 3:14–15, the latter of which is the only place in the Old Testament that includes the phrases "daughter of Zion," "King of Israel," and "fear not": "So they took branches of palm trees and went out to meet [Jesus], crying out, 'Hosanna! Blessed is he who comes in the name of the Lord, even the *King of Israel*!' And Jesus found a young donkey and sat on it, just as it is written, '*Fear not, daughter of Zion*; behold, your king is coming, sitting on a donkey's colt!'" (John 12:13–15). John sees Jesus as initiating the end-times salvation for which Zephaniah longed.

The three-part call to rejoice in Zephaniah 3:14–15 ("Sing aloud . . . ; shout . . . ! Rejoice and exult!") is matched by the three declarations of YHWH's joy in his redeemed in 3:17 ("He will rejoice over you . . . ; he will quiet you . . . ; he will exult over you . . . ."). Together these highlight that the book is indeed a summons to satisfying salvation. The highest motivation for answering the call to patiently pursue YHWH (2:1–3; 3:8) is the joy set before us. Hearers should hunt and hope, entreat and trust, look and long—all for the day when God will completely remove every oppressor, heal the broken, and sing over those he has saved (3:17, 19–20). Significantly, these are all elements that Christ inaugurated in his first coming and that he will consummate when he returns. This is the word of the Lord to Zephaniah.

Key Words and Concepts

Literary context
Literary placement, function, and details

Questions for Further Reflection

1. In order to engage in literary context, you must first have a good grasp of the whole book's thought flow. What is the best way to grasp this?
2. What are the kinds of questions to ask when considering literary placement, function, and details?
3. According to DeRouchie, what is the main point of the Bible? How do the Old and New Testaments develop this point?

4. Which example of engaging in literary context did you find the most insightful? In your own words, explain the process of engaging in literary context.

Resources for Further Study

✪ Alexander, T. Desmond, and Brian S. Rosner, eds. *New Dictionary of Biblical Theology: Exploring the Unity and Diversity of Scripture.* Downers Grove, IL: InterVarsity Press, 2000.

Carson, D. A., ed. *NIV Zondervan Study Bible.* Grand Rapids: Zondervan, 2015.

Dempster, Stephen G. *Dominion and Dynasty: A Biblical Theology of the Hebrew Bible.* NSBT 15. Downers Grove, IL: InterVarsity Press, 2003.

★ DeRouchie, Jason S., ed. *What the Old Testament Authors Really Cared About: A Survey of Jesus' Bible.* Grand Rapids: Kregel, 2013.

Dever, Mark. *The Message of the Old Testament: Promises Made.* Wheaton, IL: Crossway, 2006.

Dyer, John. *Best Commentaries: Reviews and Ratings of Biblical, Theological, and Practical Christian Works.* http://www.bestcommentaries.com/.

Fee, Gordon D., and Douglas Stuart. *How to Read the Bible Book by Book: A Guided Tour.* Grand Rapids: Zondervan, 2002.

Grudem, Wayne H., ed. *The ESV Study Bible.* Wheaton, IL: Crossway, 2008.

Hill, Andrew E., and John H. Walton. *A Survey of the Old Testament.* 2nd ed. Grand Rapids: Zondervan, 2000.

✪ House, Paul R. *Old Testament Theology.* Downers Grove, IL: InterVarsity Press, 1998.

★ House, Paul R., and Eric Mitchell. *Old Testament Survey.* 2nd ed. Nashville: Broadman & Holman, 2007.

InterVarsity Press dictionaries on the Old Testament:

- Alexander, T. Desmond, and David W. Baker, eds. *Dictionary of the Old Testament: Pentateuch.* Downers Grove, IL: InterVarsity Press, 2003.
- Arnold, Bill T., and H. G. M. Williamson, eds. *Dictionary of the Old Testament: Historical Books.* Downers Grove, IL: InterVarsity Press, 2005.
- Boda, Mark J., and J. Gordon McConville, eds. *Dictionary of the Old Testament: Prophets.* Downers Grove, IL: InterVarsity Press, 2012.
- Longman, Tremper, III, and Peter Enns, eds. *Dictionary of the Old Testament: Wisdom, Poetry, and Writings.* Downers Grove, IL: InterVarsity Press, 2008.

LaSor, William Sanford, David Allan Hubbard, and Frederic William Bush. *Old Testament Survey: The Message, Form, and Background of the Old Testament.* 2nd ed. Grand Rapids: Eerdmans, 1996.

Leithart, Peter J. *A House for My Name: A Survey of the Old Testament.* Moscow, ID: Canon, 2000.

Schreiner, Thomas R. *The King in His Beauty: A Biblical Theology of the Old and New Testaments.* Grand Rapids: Baker Academic, 2013.

★ Van Pelt, Miles V., ed. *A Biblical-Theological Introduction to the Old Testament: The Gospel Promised.* Wheaton, IL: Crossway, 2016.

PART 4

MEANING—"WHAT DOES THE PASSAGE MEAN?"

10

BIBLICAL THEOLOGY

Goal: Consider how your passage connects to the Bible's overall story line or message and points to Christ.

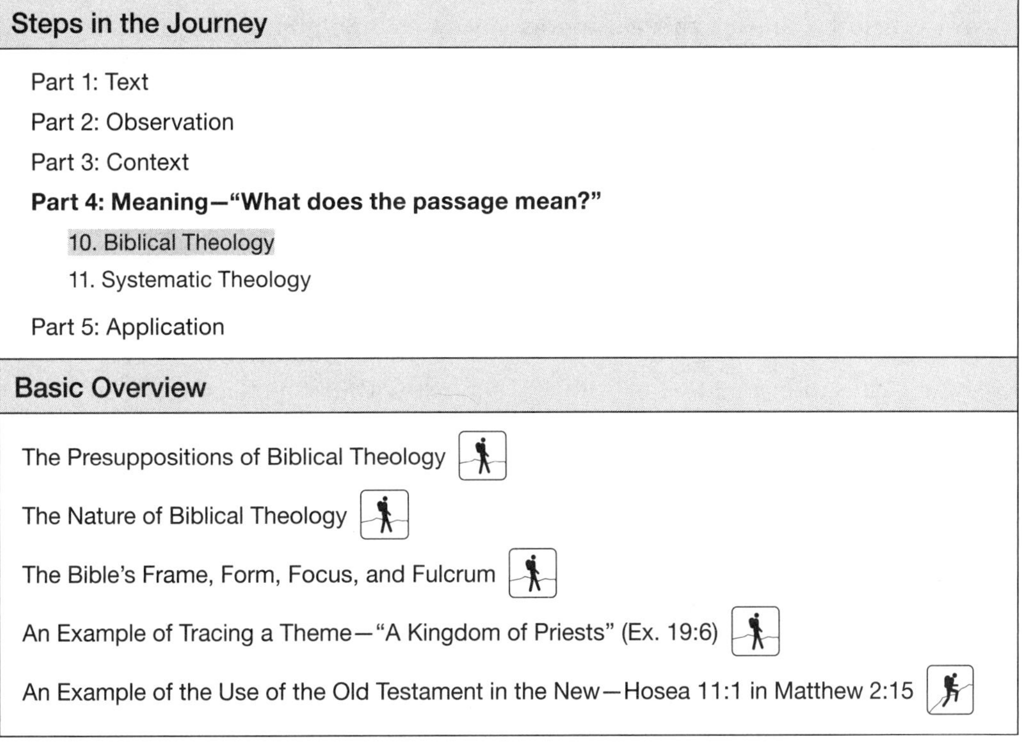

Steps in the Journey

Part 1: Text
Part 2: Observation
Part 3: Context
Part 4: Meaning—"What does the passage mean?"
  10. Biblical Theology
  11. Systematic Theology
Part 5: Application

Basic Overview

The Presuppositions of Biblical Theology
The Nature of Biblical Theology
The Bible's Frame, Form, Focus, and Fulcrum
An Example of Tracing a Theme—"A Kingdom of Priests" (Ex. 19:6)
An Example of the Use of the Old Testament in the New—Hosea 11:1 in Matthew 2:15

Fig. 10.1. Trail Guide to Chapter 10

The Presuppositions of Biblical Theology

As we move into biblical theology, we shift from the formal category of exegesis into the area of theology. It is in our wrestling with biblical, systematic, and practical theology that we truly begin to synthesize the lasting message of a passage.

The question before us now is "What is biblical theology?" In this discipline, we consider how all the Bible fits together and points to Christ. More specifically, as I approach the task, **biblical theology** is a way of analyzing and synthesizing what the Bible reveals about God and his relations with the world that makes organic salvation-historical and literary-canonical connections with the whole of Scripture on its own terms, especially with respect to how the Old and New Testaments progress, integrate, and climax in Christ.

Now, before I unpack this definition, I want to highlight four contrasting poles of focus related to the task. I note them because since the rise of the biblical-theology movement in the 1960s, many scholars have approached this discipline in ways different from my approach. So I want to be clear up front regarding my methodological presuppositions.[1]

1. **Event vs. Text:** Is the locus of special revelation a historical event in space and time or a written account?

God certainly reveals himself in history, but this revelation becomes clearly understandable to us only through his written Word. Therefore, biblical theology is a *textual discipline* that is informed by the historical context within which it developed.

2. **Criticism vs. Canon:** What is the nature and object of biblical-theological inquiry?

With respect to *the nature of the discipline*, there are two primary approaches: (a) the critical and deconstructive approach, in which man is the decisive authority, and (b) the submissive and constructive approach, in which God's Word remains the decisive authority. For some, the *critical and deconstructive approach* is evidenced through a type of source criticism that breaks the biblical text into hypothetical sources and only then attempts to establish the message of each independent source—a theology of "J" (the Jahwist) or "P" (the Priestly source), for example. For others, the deconstruction comes in accepting or rejecting the text's claims of faith, ethics, or fact based on one's personal biases. The result is a personal canon within the canon, with certain parts bearing more authority than others.

1. I adapted some of these methodological presuppositions from John H. Sailhamer, *Introduction to Old Testament Theology: A Canonical Approach* (Grand Rapids: Zondervan, 1995), 27–194.

In contrast, the *submissive and constructive approach* is my desired method because it is the only one that remains faithful to the nature of the Bible as God's Word. It states that we can rightly perform biblical theology only when we submit our lives to Scripture as canonical, authoritative revelation and when we affirm the values and claims that the text itself makes. In this view, the various forms of critical inquiry have their place only insofar as the scholars using them observe accurately what is in the text, understand rightly in alignment with the intentions of the biblical authors, and evaluate fairly the claims of the text in accordance with its nature. That covers the nature of the discipline.

But the issue of criticism versus canon also relates to the inquiry regarding *the object of biblical theology*. With respect to *scope*, biblical theology must restrict itself to the final form of the canon as God has revealed it to us—not a hypothetical reconstruction driven by the varied presuppositions of scholars, and not additional material that neither the Bible nor historical tradition has recognized as canonical. The object of biblical-theological inquiry must ever remain and be limited to the Christian Bible, made up of the sixty-six books that embody God's Word written and that therefore alone bear a unique nature and authority (2 Tim. 3:16–17; 1 Peter 1:20–21).

With respect to the *makeup* of the biblical text, we must first consider the text's unity and diversity. How do we find unity when the Bible comes to us over a 1,500-year period through numerous genres and multiple hands? The answer comes in the fact that God himself is the decisive author of the whole; he guided the biblical authors, who wrote his words. Second, we must consider canonical arrangement. How important is the received ordering of the Old and New Testaments? Should the fact that Jesus employs a three-part canon (Luke 24:44; cf. 11:51) inform our exegesis of at least the Old Testament? What about the structure of the New? The evangelical church has not yet come to terms with this question, but I anticipate that the next decade will provide a context for further discussions. I am one who is becoming increasingly convinced that Jesus' statement in Luke 24:44 regarding the Law, the Prophets, and the Psalms not only suggests a three-part Old Testament canon but calls us to do biblical theology within this framework.

3. **Descriptive vs. Prescriptive:** Do we approach the Bible like all other literature, or does the nature of Scripture as God's Word demand a special interpretive approach for a unique purpose?

The Bible is a book, having many features like other books, but in many respects, it is unlike any other book. Through use of sources and under divine guidance, the Old Testament was formed over approximately a thousand-year period. As God's Word spoken through human words in history, every individual book was conditioned by the language, culture, and situations of the time. Thus, biblical theology has a descriptive element, for the message of Scripture at one level is historically bound. We put in fresh words what is already in the text; we describe it.

Nevertheless, the biblical text is also God's Word, and what is spiritually given must be spiritually appraised.[2] The discipline of biblical theology necessitates understanding

2. See John Piper, *Reading the Bible Supernaturally: Seeing and Savoring the Glory of God in Scripture* (Wheaton, IL: Crossway, 2017).

not only the biblical author's intended meaning but also his intended effect. While the former is possible at some level for nonbelievers, seeing God's Word change our lives happens only through his Spirit's work. Paul said, "The natural person does not accept the things of the Spirit of God, for they are folly to him, and he is not able to understand them because they are spiritually discerned" (1 Cor. 2:14; cf. Matt. 16:17; John 14:26; 16:13; Acts 8:31; Rom. 8:7–8).

There is no true biblical theology without a conviction that the Bible is God's Word and therefore manifests an overarching unity. While biblical theology is a descriptive discipline, it also grows out of a confessional (Christian-theistic and submissive) framework and bears a normative goal, prescribing a certain lifestyle and worldview for all its readers and seeking to enliven within them worship and deeper surrender to the living God through Christ.

4. **Theologies vs. Theology:** Is it enough to interpret the biblical books historically as distinct theologies (parts), or must we also consider them in light of one another as a unity (whole)?

God and not any human person is the ultimate author of Scripture: "Men spoke from God as they were carried along by the Holy Spirit" (2 Peter 1:21). This means that biblical theology's task cannot end by shaping theologies of corpora (the Law, the Latter Prophets, etc.) or theologies of various human authors (Moses, Isaiah, etc.). We must push to grasp the unified theology of the whole Bible, which comes from the only uncaused one and discloses his character and purposes in space and time.

Some would compare the Bible to a wall of fabric, with each bolt bearing its own makeup. In contrast, I propose that Scripture is much more like a massive, intentionally crafted quilt, with each square (or biblical book) bearing its own color, texture, and story, but with the whole displaying a message far greater than the parts.

The Nature of Biblical Theology

I have defined biblical theology as a way of analyzing and synthesizing what the Bible reveals about God and his relations with the world that makes organic salvation-historical and literary-canonical connections with the whole of Scripture on its own terms, especially with respect to how the Old and New Testaments progress, integrate, and climax in Christ. In this section, I want to unpack this definition under six headings.

The Task, Part 1:

Biblical theology analyzes and synthesizes what the Bible (Old and New Testaments) reveals about God and his relations with the world.

Biblical theology seeks to interpret the final form of the Christian Bible—to analyze and synthesize God's special revelation embodied in the Old and New Testaments. While the task is in part descriptive, it also requires a preceding conviction that the object of study is God's Word and therefore bears authority in our lives. Because Scripture is the revelation of God, we need to engage biblical theology humbly and with a desire to encounter the living God and to be changed more completely into his likeness.

That the early church tagged the Bible's two parts as *Testaments* rightly highlights that Scripture is grounded in history and bears a covenantal (i.e., testamental) and thus canonical makeup. Covenants come from kings, and the written witness to a covenant is by nature authoritative for the recipients.[3] Everything in Scripture addresses God and his relationship with his world at various covenantal stages.

That God's special revelation comes through *Old* and *New Testaments* highlights both Scripture's unity and its diversity. The one Bible has two necessary parts, each of which we must read in light of the other—a foundation in the Old Testament upon which is built the fulfillment or climax in the New Testament, ultimately in Messiah Jesus.

The Task, Part 2:

Biblical theology makes organic connections with the whole of Scripture on its own terms.

Biblical theology is about making natural, unforced connections within Scripture in a way that recognizes growth or progress in a thought or concept and lets the Bible speak in accordance with its own contours, structures, language, and flow. This is what I mean when I say "*organic* connections" and approaching the Bible "on its own terms."

Although Scripture was developed by dozens of prophets in various places over thousands of years using multiple genres, all the Bible came from a unified God. It is his Word, and it is all guided by a common message, which I summarize as "God

3. Meredith G. Kline, *The Structure of Biblical Authority*, 2nd ed. (Eugene, OR: Wipf & Stock, 1997), 37.

reigns, saves, and satisfies through covenant for his glory in Christ." All the Bible grows out of the unchanging nature of God and must be understood to align with his unified purpose of exalting himself over all things, ultimately through Jesus (Eph. 1:10; Col. 1:20). This unity is what makes biblical theology possible and necessary. Because God is the ultimate author of Scripture, we must believe that themes will develop in "organic" or natural ways and that true fulfillment of past predictions will always stand in alignment with their prophetic intent. Just as we can witness how an acorn grows into a mighty oak, so, too, biblical theology analyzes and synthesizes the progression of biblical revelation, identifying the remarkable unity amid all the diversity.

Salvation-Historical Connections:

Biblical theology makes organic salvation-historical connections with the whole of Scripture on its own terms.

When it comes to tracking the progressive growth of themes and fulfillment on the Bible's own terms, Scripture itself encourages us to make organic connections on two planes, the first of which is salvation history. ***Salvation history*** is the progressive narrative unfolding of God's kingdom plan through the various covenants, events, people, and institutions, all climaxing in the person and work of Jesus. Redemptive history moves from creation to the fall to redemption to consummation. It's what frames all of Scripture from Genesis to Revelation. Some have termed it "the story of God's glory."[4]

Old Testament Narrative Foundation	K	1. Kickoff and rebellion	Creation, fall, and flood
	I	2. Instrument of blessing	Patriarchs
	N	3. Nation redeemed and commissioned	Exodus, Sinai, and wilderness
	G	4. Government in the land	Conquest and kingdoms
	D	5. Dispersion and return	Exile and initial restoration
New Testament Narrative Fulfillment	O	6. Overlap of the ages	Christ's work and the church age
	M	7. Mission accomplished	Christ's return and kingdom consummation

Fig. 10.2. God's KINGDOM Plan

4. John Piper, "The Goal of God in Redemptive History," in *Desiring God: Meditations of a Christian Hedonist*, 3rd ed. (Sisters, OR: Multnomah, 2003), 308–21; this appendix is also found in the 2011 hardback edition.

All of history is indeed *His-story*, and we read about it as we track the Bible's story line. I have tried to capture this plot in seven developing stages. I use the acronym ***KINGDOM*** to help trace the redemptive flow of God's kingdom-building plan. Figure 10.2 gives an overview of the plan itself, and then figure 10.3 synthesizes the whole through images.

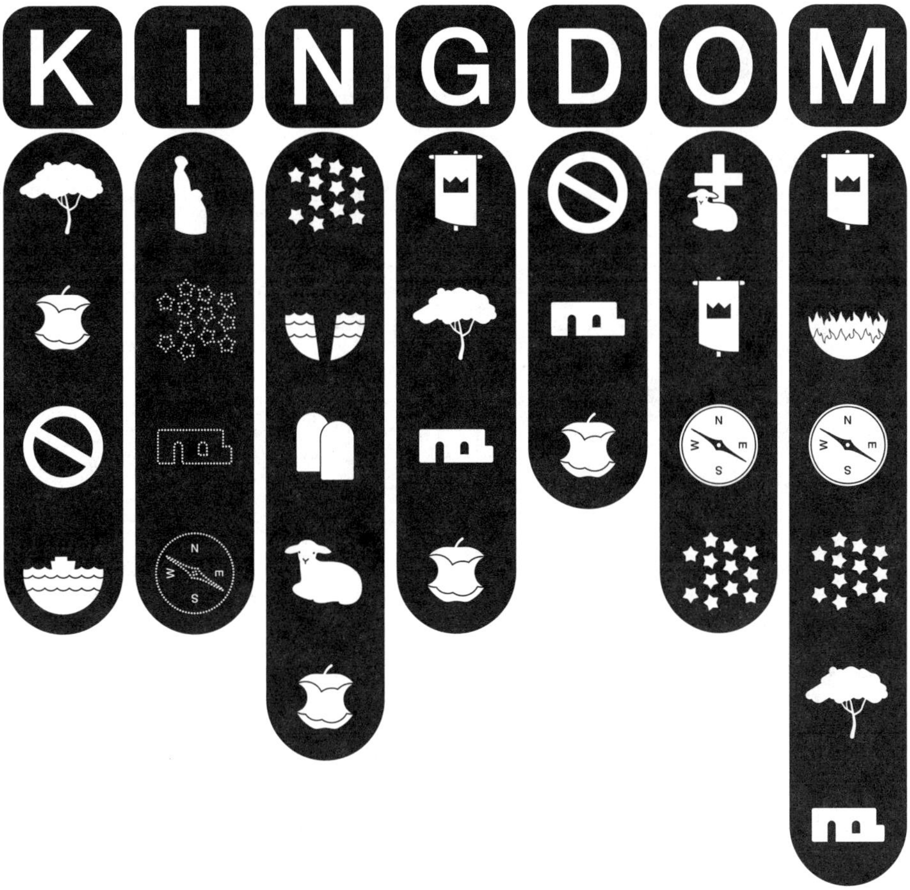

K I N G D O M

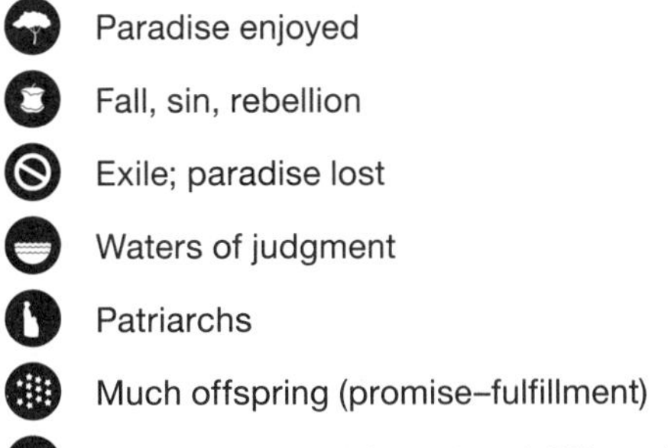

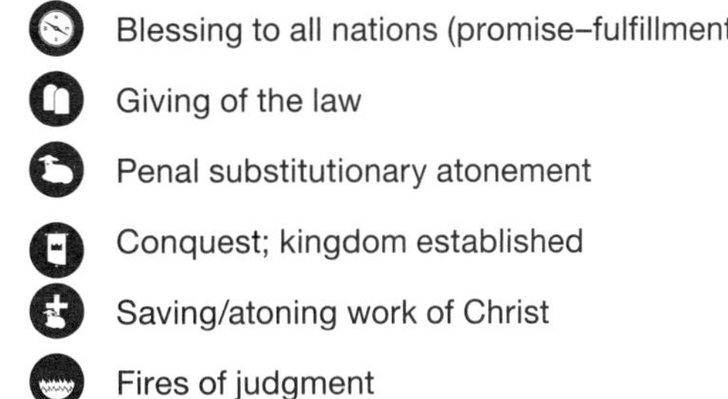

Fig. 10.3. God's KINGDOM Plan through Images[5]

5. This diagram originally appeared in Jason S. DeRouchie, ed., *What the Old Testament Authors Really Cared About: A Survey of Jesus' Bible* (Grand Rapids: Kregel, 2013), 31. Used by permission.

	Covenants	Stages of Redemptive History	Major Literary Divisions: Narrative	Major Literary Divisions: Commentary
Old Testament	Adamic / Noahic	1. Creation, fall & flood	Law	
	Abrahamic	2. Patriarchs		
	Mosaic (Old)	3. Exodus, Sinai & wilderness		
	Davidic	4. Conquest & kingdoms (united & divided)	Former Prophets	
				Latter Prophets
				Former Writings
		5. Exile & initial restoration	Latter Writings	
New Testament	Christ Jesus	6. Christ's work	Gospels	
		& the church age	Acts	
	New			Pauline Epistles & Hebrews
				General Epistles
		7. Christ's return & kingdom consummation	Revelation	

Fig. 10.4. Salvation History in the Context of Scripture[6]

This is Scripture's story of God's glory in Christ. And within this framework, we can make salvation-historical connections in at least five different ways:

1. Thematic Development

We can trace a theme through the story of redemption from Genesis to Revelation. In chapter 7's discussion of three steps for doing word studies ("How to Do a Word or Concept Study"), I highlighted how I did this in a number of articles with the theme of *seed*, showing the progressive growth from Genesis to Paul's statements in Galatians 3 that the "seed/offspring" of Abraham "is Christ" (3:16) and that on this side of the cross you become "Abraham's offspring, heirs according to promise," only "if you are Christ's" (3:29). Other themes could include *the glory of God*, *creation*, *sin*, *covenant*, *kingdom*, *law*, *temple*, *atonement*, *holiness*, and many more. Two resources that have done a great job with biblical-theological thematic studies are *NDBT* and the *NIV Zondervan Study Bible*.[7]

2. Covenantal Continuity and Discontinuity

Here we compare and contrast how the progress of the covenants maintains, transforms, alters, or escalates various elements in God's relations with his people and the world. Interwoven into salvation history is the progression of five overlapping covenants, which portray the development of God's global purposes with humanity. The interrelationship of the covenants can be portrayed like an hourglass, with the most universal scope occurring at the two ends and the work of Christ as the center (see fig. 10.4). The Adamic-Noahic, Abrahamic, Mosaic, and Davidic covenants are all named in light of the covenant head or mediator through whom God entered into a relationship with his elect. The new covenant is titled in light of its contrast to the "old" Mosaic administration and provides climax to all of God's purposes in history (see Jer. 31:31–34; Heb. 8:6–13). Some books that helpfully wrestle with the relationship and progression of the biblical covenants are O. Palmer Robertson's *The Christ of the Covenants*, David Baker's *Two Testaments, One Bible*, and Peter Gentry and Stephen Wellum's *Kingdom through Covenant*.[8]

6. This image originally appeared in DeRouchie, *What the Old Testament Authors Really Cared About*, 32. Used by permission.

7. D. A. Carson, ed., *NIV Zondervan Study Bible* (Grand Rapids: Zondervan, 2015), 2629–96. See also the lexical and topical articles in *NIDOTTE*.

8. O. Palmer Robertson, *The Christ of the Covenants* (Phillipsburg, NJ: Presbyterian and Reformed, 1987); David L. Baker, *Two Testaments, One Bible: The Theological Relationship between the Old and New Testaments*, 3rd ed. (Downers Grove, IL: InterVarsity Press, 2010); Peter J. Gentry and Stephen J. Wellum, *Kingdom through Covenant: A Biblical-Theological Understanding of the Covenants* (Wheaton, IL: Crossway, 2012). For a recent survey of the discussion, see G. K. Beale, *Handbook on the New Testament Use of the Old Testament: Exegesis and Interpretation* (Grand Rapids: Baker Academic, 2012), 1–13. For a very helpful essay wrestling with the question, see D. A. Carson, "Mystery and Fulfillment: Toward a More Comprehensive Paradigm of Paul's Understanding of the Old and New," in *The Paradoxes of Paul*, vol. 2 of *Justification and Variegated Nomism*, ed. D. A. Carson, Peter T. O'Brien, and Mark A. Seifrid, 2 vols., WUNT 181 (Grand Rapids: Baker Academic, 2004), 393–436. I wrestle with covenantal continuity and discontinuity with respect to the theme of ecclesiology in my essay "Counting Stars with Abraham and the Prophets: New Covenant Ecclesiology in OT Perspective," *JETS* 58, 3 (2015)," 445–85; abridged as "Father of

3. Type and Antitype

G. K. Beale defines ***typology*** as follows: "The study of analogical correspondences among revealed truths about persons, events, institutions, and other things within the historical framework of God's special revelation, which, from a retrospective view, are of a prophetic nature and are escalated in their meaning."[9] While there is some question as to how much the Old Testament authors knew they were predicting the future (see "The Relationship of the Testaments" below), both Old and New Testament authors regularly identify predictive thematic anticipations or types rooted in the progressive development of Scripture's historical record (e.g., Rom. 5:14; 1 Cor. 10:6, 11; Col. 2:16–17; Heb. 8:5; 9:24; 1 Peter 3:21). By God's design, types are prophetic and prospective by nature, even when interpreters discover them only retrospectively.[10] Ultimately, all types culminate in the life and work of Christ Jesus. For example, Jesus is the ultimate "prophet like Moses" to whom peoples were to listen (Deut. 18:15) and who, through his death and resurrection, performs a second, greater exodus (Luke 9:30–31, 35; Acts 3:20–22). He is also the substance of all old covenant shadows, whether temple, festival, new moon, Sabbath, or the like (John 2:19–21; Col. 2:16–17).[11]

4. Promise and Fulfillment

Fulfillment grows out of different types of predictions. Here our attempt is to track specific promises and then to identify their partial, progressive, and/or ultimate fulfillment at various stages in salvation history, ever remembering Paul's declaration that "all the promises of God find their Yes in [Christ]" (2 Cor. 1:20). An example here

a Multitude of Nations: New Covenant Ecclesiology in OT Perspective," in *Progressive Covenantalism: Charting a Course between Dispensational and Covenant Theologies*, ed. Stephen J. Wellum and Brent E. Parker (Nashville: Broadman & Holman, 2016), 7–38. I consider how the makeup of the new covenant community differs from that of the old—how the coming of Jesus marks a shift from a community made up of both remnant and rebel to a community made up solely of remnant incorporated into Christ.

9. G. K. Beale, *Handbook on the New Testament Use of the Old Testament*, 14; cf. Beale, "Did Jesus and His Followers Preach the Right Doctrine from the Wrong Texts? An Examination of the Presuppositions of the Apostles' Exegetical Method," in *The Right Doctrine from the Wrong Texts? Essays on the Use of the Old Testament in the New*, ed. G. K. Beale (Grand Rapids: Baker Academic, 1994), 387–404, esp. 394; repr. from *Themelios* 14, 3 (1989): 89–96. See also Richard Davidson, *Typology in Scripture: A Study of Hermeneutical TUPOS Structures*, Andrews University Seminary Doctoral Dissertation Series 2 (Berrien Springs, MI: Andrews University, 1981); Douglas J. Moo, "The Problem of *Sensus Plenior*," in *Hermeneutics, Authority, and Canon*, ed. D. A. Carson and John D. Woodbridge (Grand Rapids: Zondervan, 1986), 175–211, 397–405; Richard Lints, *The Fabric of Theology: A Prolegomenon to Evangelical Theology* (Grand Rapids: Eerdmans, 1993), 304–10; Gordon P. Hugenberger, "Introductory Notes on Typology," in *The Right Doctrine from the Wrong Texts? Essays on the Use of the Old Testament in the New*, ed. G. K. Beale (Grand Rapids: Baker Academic, 1994), 331–41; Carson, "Mystery and Fulfillment," 393–436, esp. 404; Gentry and Wellum, *Kingdom through Covenant*, 94–95, 101–8, 606–8; Douglas J. Moo and Andrew David Naselli, "The Problem of the New Testament's Use of the Old Testament," in *The Enduring Authority of the Christian Scriptures*, ed. D. A. Carson (Grand Rapids: Eerdmans, 2016), 725–28.

10. So too Brent E. Parker, "The Israel-Christ-Church Relationship," in *Progressive Covenantalism: Charting a Course between Dispensational and Covenant Theologies*, ed. Stephen J. Wellum and Brent E. Parker (Nashville: Broadman & Holman, 2016), 48n20.

11. For more on typology, see the same works listed under the discussion in "2. Covenantal Continuity and Discontinuity." For a survey of the discussion, see Beale, *Handbook on the New Testament Use of the Old Testament*, 13–25.

is Micah 5:2's declaration that the royal deliverer will rise out of Bethlehem and Matthew's declaration that this is fulfilled (Matt. 2:5–6). For a helpful book that unpacks many of the direct predictions of the Messiah in the Old Testament, see Walter Kaiser's *The Messiah in the Old Testament*.[12]

5. Use of the Old Testament in the Old and New Testaments

Here we assess the way in which later biblical writers interpret and/or apply earlier canonical revelation. Two very helpful books that wrestle with these issues are G. K. Beale and D. A. Carson's *Commentary on the New Testament Use of the Old Testament* and Beale's *Handbook on the New Testament Use of the Old Testament*.[13] I will address the biblical authors' own interpretive method below.

Literary-Canonical Connections:

Biblical theology makes organic literary-canonical connections with the whole of Scripture on its own terms.

Most definitions of biblical theology do not stress ***literary-canonical connections***. The focus here is on the Bible's final-form composition and structure and its historical details, all of which I believe should influence the shaping of biblical theology.

1. The Bible's Composition and Structure

Earlier I noted how Scripture includes groupings of narrative books that frame commentary books. When we read the Old Testament in the three-part arrangement of Jesus' Bible, we see a comparable structure between the Old and New Testaments.

	Covenant Established	*Covenant Enforced*		*Covenant Enjoyed*	
OT	Law	Former Prophets	Latter Prophets	Former Writings	Latter Writings
NT	Gospels	Acts	Pauline Epistles & Hebrews	General Epistles	Revelation
	Narrative	**Narrative**	***Commentary***	***Commentary***	**Narrative**

Fig. 10.5. Narrative and Commentary in the Bible's Covenantal Structure

12. Walter C. Kaiser Jr., *The Messiah in the Old Testament*, SOTBT (Grand Rapids: Zondervan, 1995).

13. G. K. Beale and D. A. Carson, eds., *Commentary on the New Testament Use of the Old Testament* (Grand Rapids: Baker Academic, 2007); Beale, *Handbook on the New Testament Use of the Old Testament*.

Biblical theology arises out of the narrative framework of salvation history, but we cannot restrict the discipline to redemptive-historical connections because the Bible includes more than the story of God's glory in Christ. We must consider every passage in light of its placement and role within the canon as a whole, which contains two Testaments, each with corresponding narrative and commentary sections and each with a potentially corresponding three-part structure.

The narrative history of redemption frames both the Old and New Testaments and therefore calls us to relate everything to the story of salvation that moves from Genesis to Revelation.[14] But the Bible also includes prophetic commentary—sermons and songs, preaching and poetry, letters and laments, wisdom and worship—that informs our reading of the story and contributes in its own way to the portrait of God's glory in Christ. The Latter Prophets and Former Writings in the Old Testament and the Pauline Epistles-Hebrews and General Epistles in the New Testament supply color and shape to the Bible's message, clarifying through propositions, predictions, prayers, and praises the character of God in Christ and the nature of faith, hope, and love.[15]

Furthermore, the Bible that Jesus used bore a three-part structure—Law, Prophets, Writings (see Luke 24:44)—and this structure may also have influenced the structuring of the New Testament. Of all five major biblical covenants, the most dominant from a literary perspective are the old (Mosaic) covenant and the new covenant in Christ. On the whole, the Mosaic covenant represented an age of death, and it is this covenant that controls the Old Testament's three divisions. God *establishes* the old (Mosaic) covenant in the Law, with Genesis providing the kingdom prologue that sets the stage for Israel's calling, which is detailed in Exodus–Deuteronomy. God then *enforces* the old covenant in the Prophets, with the Former Prophets (Joshua–Kings) narrating what happened in Israel's downward spiral from conquest through monarchy to exile, and the Latter Prophets (Jeremiah–the Twelve [Minor Prophets]) developing through prophetic commentary why the drama went the way it did. The Writings are dominated by a positive thrust, giving voice to the faithful who were *enjoying* the old covenant, while

14. Although Revelation is not strictly "narrative," it does complete the story line that is begun in the Old Testament and carried on in the Gospels and Acts. Furthermore, like Chronicles at the end of the Old Testament, which reviews all history from Adam to the initial restoration, Revelation at the end of the New Testament reviews redemptive history from the first coming of Christ to eternity.

15. David Trobisch has argued that the New Testament canon was fixed as early as A.D. 125 and originally bore a different arrangement in the commentary section, the General Epistles being placed before Paul's letters and Hebrews: Matthew, Mark, Luke, John, Acts, James, 1 Peter, 2 Peter, 1 John, 2 John, 3 John, Jude, Romans, 1 Corinthians, 2 Corinthians, Galatians, Ephesians, Philippians, Colossians, 1 Thessalonians, 2 Thessalonians, Hebrews, 1 Timothy, 2 Timothy, Titus, Philemon, Revelation (David Trobisch, *Paul's Letter Collection: Tracing the Origins* [Minneapolis: Fortress, 1994]; cf. Trobisch, *The First Edition of the New Testament* [Oxford: Oxford University Press, 2000]; C. E. Hill, "The New Testament Canon: Deconstructio ad Absurdum?," *JETS* 52, 1 [2009]: 101–19; Hill, *Who Chose the Gospels? Probing the Great Gospel Conspiracy* [Oxford: Oxford University Press, 2010]). In contrast, Brevard S. Childs gives priority to the Muratorian fragment and various comments from Irenaeus, Tertullian, and Origen, which place Paul's epistles directly after the Gospels and Acts (*The Church's Guide for Reading Paul: The Canonical Shaping of the Pauline Corpus* [Grand Rapids: Eerdmans, 2008], 225–26). Significantly, regardless of how the New Testament commentary books are ordered, the general pattern Narrative → Narrative → Commentary → Commentary → Narrative remains parallel to the structure of Jesus' Bible.

hoping in the complete fulfillment of God's kingdom promises. The Former Writings (Ruth/Psalms–Lamentations) supply poetic commentary on how those looking ahead to kingdom fulfillment were to live, and the Latter Writings (Daniel–Chronicles) narrate the continuing drama of the exilic and initial-restoration generations as they long for complete kingdom realization.[16]

While a comparable pattern is not as clear in the New Testament, some may find it helpful to identify such a pattern. The new covenant is established in the Gospels, enforced in Acts and the Pauline Epistles-Hebrews, and enjoyed in the General Epistles and Revelation. As in the Old Testament Writings, the "joy" is one of hope in the midst of trial, of God-oriented satisfaction experienced through suffering, in the battle against false teaching, and in light of the glory that is to be revealed at the consummation of the kingdom.

2. The Bible's Historical Details

Along with final-form composition and structure, literary-canonical connections include the historical details that tie the canon together. Here I refer to information regarding authorship, date, or provenance of a given passage. Where God reveals such information, it is fair and appropriate to use it to consider how books or passages that are historically united address various themes or contribute to our knowledge of a given topic. In contrast to the books in the New Testament, not one Old Testament book explicitly mentions its human author, though many individual psalm titles identify their composer and prophetic books such as Isaiah and Jeremiah identify the various oracles as deriving from the prophet associated with the book's title. Accordingly, we know, for example, that Moses spoke and wrote the sermons within Deuteronomy and the poetry of Psalm 90 and perhaps 91. The editor of Genesis–Numbers also identifies many speeches with Moses, and the rest of the biblical tradition treats Moses himself as the substantial author of all five books.

What this means is that the text itself gives us freedom to ask not only "What does the Law say about X?" but also "What did *Moses* teach about Y?" We could also query, "How did the eighth-century prophets approach Z?" or "What do we learn from the postexilic books about X?" In the New Testament, along with treating Luke as part of the Synoptics and reading Acts in the light of all the Gospels and as the historical prelude to Paul's Epistles, the historical data in Acts 1:1 calls us to read the book of Acts itself as the second part of Luke's account of Jesus. The Gospel of Luke tells us all that "Jesus began to do and teach" (Acts 1:1), whereas Acts clarifies what he continues to do and teach by his Spirit working through his apostles and his church (1:8; cf. 16:7).

In summary, we engage in biblical theology by keeping our eyes on the redemptive-historical trajectories found in our text. We ask, "How does our passage fit within the progressive story of God's kingdom purposes?" But biblical theology also considers how the various canonical groupings treat a given theme, be it atonement, sonship,

16. For a more detailed overview of the Law, Prophets, and Writings as the old covenant established, enforced, and enjoyed, see DeRouchie, *What the Old Testament Authors Really Cared About*, 41–49, 55–57, 163–66, 319–23.

temple, or the like. Here we ask, "How does the Law set a foundation for our knowledge of X?" or "How do the Latter Prophets approach Y?" Finally, biblical theology must account for the historical details given in Scripture, building connections between the God-given temporal, political, and social markers. It's within this overall framework that I say that biblical theology makes organic literary-canonical connections with the whole of Scripture on its own terms.

The Relationship of the Testaments:
Biblical theology wrestles with how the
Old and New Testaments progress and integrate.

The relationship of the Testaments is perhaps the biggest question faced in biblical theology. Scripture was not shaped in a day. God produced it over time, progressively disclosing his kingdom purposes climaxing in Christ and pointing ultimately to the consummation. Biblical theology gives significant effort to tracking this progression and to considering how the two Testaments integrate in God's overarching kingdom plan.

1. Prophetic Fulfillment: Prospect and Retrospect

Central in this process is grappling with how the Old and New Testament authors interpret earlier Scripture. Perhaps more than any other contemporary scholar, G. K. Beale has worked hard to understand the New Testament authors' approach to their Scriptures. Years ago he identified five principles that guided their interpretive conclusions,[17] and he has recently showed how all of these are rooted in the Old Testament's own story of salvation history.[18]

- There is an ever-present assumption of *corporate solidarity*, in which one can represent the many.
- The Messiah is viewed as *representing the true (remnant) Israel* of the old covenant *and the true (consummate) Israel, the church*, of the new covenant.
- *History is unified* by a wise and sovereign plan so that God designs the earlier parts to correspond and point to the latter parts.
- The age of *eschatological fulfillment* has come in Christ.
- *Christ as the center of history* is the key to interpreting the earlier portions of the Old Testament and its promises.

17. Beale, "Did Jesus and His Followers Preach the Right Doctrine from the Wrong Texts?," 392; cf. Beale, *Handbook on the New Testament Use of the Old Testament*, 52–53, 95–102.

18. Beale, *Handbook on the New Testament Use of the Old Testament*, 96–102.

Scholars have differing views on how much the Old Testament authors actually understood of what God was predicting through them.[19] I'll address broader questions of the "mystery" of the kingdom in chapter 12 under "God Gave the Old Testament to Instruct Christians." Here, however, I want to note that Jesus does say that "Abraham rejoiced that he would see my day. He saw it and was glad" (John 8:56). Similarly, reflecting on Psalm 16, Peter claims that David was "a prophet" and that, "knowing that God had sworn with an oath to him that he would set one of his descendants on his throne, he foresaw and spoke about the resurrection of the Christ" (Acts 2:30–31). From Peter's perspective, David grasped that he was speaking about the Messiah. Elsewhere the apostle further states that the Old Testament prophets "searched and inquired carefully, inquiring what person or time the Spirit of Christ in them was indicating when he predicted the sufferings of Christ and the subsequent glories" (1 Peter 1:10–11). The New Testament is clear that the Old Testament authors were often well aware that they were predicting the Messiah's work and the mission that would follow (see Luke 24:45–47; Acts 26:22–23). They may not have known Jesus' name, but they knew what type of person he would be and generally when he would come. This is further confirmed by Jesus' own claim that the Scriptures "bear witness about me" (John 5:39)—a statement that John frequently uses to speak of a verbal testimony after a visible encounter (e.g., 1:34; 3:11, 32; 19:35). Philip declared to Nathanael, "We have found him of whom Moses in the Law and also the prophets wrote, Jesus of Nazareth" (1:45; cf. 5:46). Through these Old Testament authors the Father bears witness to his Son (5:37, 39).

Building on these New Testament statements, the longer I study the Old Testament itself, the more I find support for the view that, in at least a high percentage of instances, the Old Testament authors themselves (though not most of their contemporaries) already visualized the nature of the fulfillment that the New Testament identifies (or at least understood that their texts were typological and pointed to something greater).[20] This is not to deny the progress of revelation, but it is to stress that the progress is often simply between conscious, prospective prediction (whether direct or typological) and fulfillment (as opposed to a prediction of which only God was originally aware but that we now identify retrospectively). This possibility is strengthened when we allow our grammatical-historical exegesis to assess not only what is explicitly stated but also all implications—those subsidiary or implicit meanings that we can show fall within the author's cognitive peripheral vision, though he may not have been conscious of them.[21] Often, we are able to better grasp these implications by considering how previous

19. For a helpful assessment of the data associated with this question, see Carson, "Mystery and Fulfillment," 393–436; G. K. Beale, "The Cognitive Peripheral Vision of the Biblical Authors," *WTJ* 76, 2 (2014): 263–93.

20. For a similar conclusion, see Robert L. Plummer, "Righteousness and Peace Kiss: The Reconciliation of Authorial Intent and Biblical Typology," *SBJT* 14, 2 (2010): 54–61; Beale, "The Cognitive Peripheral Vision of Biblical Authors," 263–93. Beale writes, "There is always a related range of meaning that appropriately is an expansion of the explicit meaning that is expressed. . . . OT authors may have had some inkling of how the meaning of their texts would be later interpreted in what would appear to us surprising interpretations" (ibid., 265, 283); cf. Beale and Gladd, *Hidden but Now Revealed*, 343, 359.

21. See especially Robert H. Stein, *A Basic Guide to Interpreting the Bible: Playing by the Rules*, 2nd ed. (Grand Rapids: Baker Academic, 2011), 30–38; Stein, "The Benefits of an Author-Oriented Approach to Hermeneutics,"

Scripture[22] and the patterns in Israel's redemptive story[23] inform our reading—by appreciating, for example, how Genesis 3:15 or 22:17b–18 shape and inform messianic hope in all the rest of the Bible, how associations between YHWH and his Messiah (e.g., Hos. 3:5) may influence later readings that mention only YHWH (e.g., Hos. 11:10–11), or how past types such as sacrifice may guide a messianic reading within later texts (e.g., of the day of the Lord as sacrifice in Zephaniah 2:7). The Old Testament prophets and New Testament authors seem to have read their Scriptures in this way.

These things stated, the ultimate divine intent of Old Testament texts (with respect to both sense and referent) may legitimately transcend any given human author's immediate written speech, while still organically growing out of it and never contradicting it (see John 11:51).[24] This is so because God's purposes often far exceed human

JETS 44, 3 (2001): 451–66; Beale, "The Cognitive Peripheral Vision of Biblical Authors," 263–93, esp. 266–70; Beale and Gladd, *Hidden but Now Revealed*, 344–47.

22. On this point, I agree with Walter C. Kaiser Jr., who stresses that before considering how subsequent revelation handles our passage, we must first use "all the divine revelation found in the books that *preceded* [historically] the selected text we are reading or studying as the context and 'informing theology' that could have the first input to 'thicken' the meaning" ("Single Meaning, Unified Referents: Accurate and Authoritative Citations of the Old Testament by the New Testament," in *Three Views on the New Testament Use of the Old*, ed. Kenneth Berdin and Jonathan Lunde, Counterpoints [Grand Rapids: Zondervan, 2008], 53; cf. 72, 75). Similarly, though rightfully allowing for interaction with historically later works as well, Beale writes, "When a NT writer refers to an OT passage, both the explicit and subsidiary understanding of the OT author's meaning compose what we would call the NT writer's respect for the OT contextual meaning. In addition to the explicit meaning from the specific text quoted and explicitly attended to by the NT author, this contextual meaning may include ideas from the immediate or nearby OT context that are in mind, as well as ideas from other OT books that are related to the meaning of the focus text" ("The Cognitive Peripheral Vision of Biblical Authors," 273; cf. Beale and Gladd, *Hidden but Now Revealed*, 349).

23. See Beale, *Handbook on the New Testament Use of the Old Testament*, 96–102.

24. Since E. D. Hirsch's landmark volume *Validity in Interpretation* (New Haven, CT: Yale University Press, 1967), scholars have often limited meaning to human authorial intent, and I am highly sympathetic to this view. Numerous scholars, however, have offered fair critique of this perspective, since one of Scripture's authors is God, whose purpose was not simply to write books but a Book (see Philip B. Payne, "The Fallacy of Equating Meaning with the Human Author's Intention," *JETS* 20, 3 [1977]: 243–52; Raju D. Kunjummen, "The Single Intent of Scripture—Critical Examination of a Theological Construct," *GTJ* 7, 1 [1986]: 81–110; Peter Enns, "Apostolic Hermeneutics and an Evangelical Doctrine of Scripture: Moving beyond a Modernist Impasse," *WTJ* 65, 2 [2003]: 263–87; Vern S. Poythress, "The Presence of God Qualifying Our Notions of Grammatical-Historical Interpretation: Genesis 3:15 as a Test Case," *JETS* 50, 1 [2007]: 87–103; Jared M. Compton, "Shared Intentions? Reflections on Inspiration and Interpretation in Light of Scripture's Dual Authorship," *Themelios* 33, 3 [2008]: 23–33; Poythress, "Dispensing with Merely Human Meaning: Gains and Losses from Focusing on the Human Author, Illustrated by Zephaniah 1:2–3," *JETS* 57, 3 [2014]: 481–99; Moo and Naselli, "The Problem of the New Testament's Use of the Old Testament," 702–46). Significantly, Hirsch himself has refined his statements, affirming that his original line between *meaning* (which is textually bound) and *significance* (which is fluid) is not as fixed as he once thought (E. D. Hirsch, "Meaning and Significance Reinterpreted," *Critical Inquiry* 11, 2 [1984]: 202–24; Hirsch, "Transhistorical Intentions and the Persistence of Allegory," *New Literary History* 25, 3 [1994]: 549–67; cited in Darrell L. Bock, "Single Meaning, Multiple Contexts and Referents: The New Testament's Legitimate, Accurate, and Multifaceted Use of the Old," in *Three Views on the New Testament Use of the Old*, ed. Kenneth Berdin and Jonathan Lunde, Counterpoints [Grand Rapids: Zondervan, 2008], 123n15). On the question of the New Testament's use of the Old, Walter C. Kaiser Jr. is perhaps the strongest voice arguing that human authorial intent exhausts the full meaning of every Old Testament text, so that the New Testament authors are in *every instance* simply identifying what the Old Testament authors already meant in full (*The Uses of the Old Testament in the New* [Chicago: Moody, 1985]; Kaiser, "Single Meaning, Unified Referents," 45–89). Another following this basic

understanding (Deut. 29:29; Eccl. 8:16–17; Isa. 55:8–9) and because God was authoring not simply books but a Book (2 Tim. 3:16; 2 Peter 1:21) whose parts were "incomplete" until Jesus "fulfilled" them by his coming (Matt. 5:17; 11:13; Rom. 10:4).[25]

Christian interpretation of Scripture requires considering questions not simply related to grammar and historical occasion but also related to redemptive history and canonical placement. With some instances of typology, for example, the God-established historical predictive analogy between the Old Testament person, event, or institution and its escalated antitype may not be completely apparent until the fulfillment is realized.[26] While the types' predictive nature was innately present from the beginning (see 1 Cor. 10:6, 11), we may at times recognize the anticipatory elements only in retrospect.

In regard to these matters, Darrell Bock writes, "Later revelation can complete and fill meaning that was initially, but not comprehensively, revealed in the original setting, so that once the progress of revelation emerges, the earlier passage is better and more comprehensively understood."[27] He continues, "The force of earlier passages in God's plan becomes clearer and more developed as more of the plan is revealed in later events and texts. This increase in clarity often involves the identification of new referents, to which the initial referents typologically point forward."[28] Similarly, G. K. Beale notes:[29]

> It is quite possible that the OT authors did not exhaustively understand the meaning, implications, and possible applications of all that they wrote. Subsequently, the NT Scripture interprets the OT Scripture by expanding its meaning, seeing new implications in it and giving it new applications. . . . This expansion does not contravene the integrity of the earlier texts but rather develops them in a way which is consistent with the OT author's understanding of the way in which God interacts with his people—which is the unifying factor between the Testaments.

What these authors are stressing is that even if the Old Testament authors were not always *fully* aware of all that God was speaking through them, they at least retrospectively would have affirmed the trajectories defined by the later biblical authors.[30] As Beale states:

---

approach to biblical interpretation is Stein, "The Benefits of an Author-Oriented Approach to Hermeneutics," 451–66; Stein, *A Basic Guide to Interpreting the Bible*.

25. So too Moo and Naselli, "The Problem of the New Testament's Use of the Old Testament," 735.

26. For an example of typology that is viewed to be primarily retrospective and not prospective, see Andrew David Naselli, *From Typology to Doxology: Paul's Use of Isaiah and Job in Romans 11:34–35* (Eugene, OR: Pickwick, 2012).

27. Darrell L. Bock, "Response to Kaiser," in *Three Views on the New Testament Use of the Old*, ed. Kenneth Berdin and Jonathan Lunde, Counterpoints (Grand Rapids: Zondervan, 2008), 92.

28. Bock, "Single Meaning, Multiple Contexts and Referents," 114.

29. Beale, "Did Jesus and His Followers Preach the Right Doctrine from the Wrong Texts?," 394.

30. LaSor once stated, "An ordinary seed contains in itself everything that will develop in the plant or tree to which it is organically related: every branch, every leaf, every flower. Yet no amount of examination by available scientific methods will disclose to us what is in that seed. However, once the seed has developed to its fullness, we can see how the seed has been fulfilled" (William Sanford LaSor, "Prophecy, Inspiration, and *Sensus Plenior*," *TynBul* 29 [1978]: 55–56). I appreciate here the stress on the organic connection between acorn and oak, or apple seed and apple tree. But while not true in every instance, the Old Testament authors do often appear to have known a lot about both the organic trajectory and its ultimate fulfillment.

> When there is a divine understanding that transcends the conscious intention of the human author, the divine understanding is still organically related to the human author's understanding or "willed type." What God knew more fully than the prophet consciously knew would be an interpretive implication that would fit within the human author's "willed type," and, if asked later, the prophet would say, "Yes, I see how that is the wider, thicker meaning of what I intended originally to say." We must say that in every case God had a more exhaustive understanding than biblical authors had of what they wrote.[31]

The New Testament Scripture in many ways operates like an answer key that unlocks the Old Testament as Christian Scripture.[32] Grasping how Jesus and the New Testament authors approached their Bible enables us to see better the divine author's intent in Scripture. It also gives us protective guides for keeping our interpretations grounded and not overly subjective.

2. A Process for Assessing the New Testament's Use of the Old Testament

Assessing how the Old Testament and New Testament progress and integrate is an essential part of biblical theology. Beale and Carson propose a six-step process when it comes to evaluating the New Testament use of the Old Testament, and this process is a great starting place for also assessing the use of the Old Testament in the Old Testament.[33]

a. *New Testament context.* Exegete the New Testament text, identify the Old Testament reference, and discern whether it is a quotation or allusion.
b. *Old Testament context.* Exegete the Old Testament text, giving attention to whether the text itself may build on an earlier Old Testament text.
c. *Relevant uses of the Old Testament passage in extrabiblical Jewish literature.*
d. *Textual issues.* Here we seek to establish the potential source text for the New Testament quotation or allusion, performing text-critical analysis of the New Testament, MT, LXX, Targums, and any Jewish citations and then comparing them.
e. *The New Testament author's textual and hermeneutical warrant for using the Old Testament text.* Beale highlights twelve possible ways in his *Handbook on the New Testament Use of the Old Testament:*[34]

31. Beale, "The Cognitive Peripheral Vision of Biblical Authors," 283; cf. Beale and Gladd, *Hidden but Now Revealed*, 358.

32. Moo and Naselli assert, "The most basic of all NT 'hermeneutical axioms' . . . is the authors' conviction that the God who had spoken in the OT continued to speak to them and that it was this final divine context for all of Scripture that determines the meaning of any particular text" ("The Problem of the New Testament's Use of the Old Testament," 737).

33. Beale and Carson, "Introduction," in *Commentary on the New Testament Use of the Old Testament*, xxiv–xxvi. On the use of the Old Testament in the Old Testament, see, e.g., Richard L. Schultz, *The Search for Quotation: Verbal Parallels in the Prophets*, JSOTSup 180 (Sheffield, UK: Sheffield Academic, 1999); Derek Drummond Bass, *Hosea's Use of Scripture: An Analysis of His Hermeneutics* (Ph.D. diss., The Southern Baptist Theological Seminary, 2008).

34. Beale, *Handbook on the New Testament Use of the Old Testament*, 55–93.

- To indicate direct fulfillment of Old Testament prophecy.
- To indicate indirect fulfillment of Old Testament typological prophecy.
- To indicate affirmation that a not-yet-fulfilled Old Testament prophecy will assuredly be fulfilled in the future.
- To indicate an analogical or illustrative use of the Old Testament.
- To indicate the symbolic use of the Old Testament.
- To indicate an abiding authority carried over from the Old Testament.
- To indicate a proverbial use of the Old Testament.
- To indicate a rhetorical use of the Old Testament.
- To indicate the use of an Old Testament segment as a blueprint or prototype for a New Testament segment.
- To indicate an alternative textual use of the Old Testament.
- To indicate an assimilated use of the Old Testament.
- To indicate an ironic or inverted use of the Old Testament.

f. The New Testament author's theological and rhetorical uses of the Old Testament text. This is the synthesis statement of all conclusions. What theological or rhetorical point is the New Testament author making by using the Old Testament text in the way that he is?

The Centrality of Christ:
Biblical theology wrestles with how the Old and New Testaments climax in Christ.

The ultimate end of biblical theology is Jesus. The salvation history that frames Scripture all points and progresses to Christ, and all fulfillment flows from and through him.

The Old Testament is ***Christotelic*** (from the Greek τέλος, meaning "goal, end"), with all its history (Matt. 2:15), laws (5:17–18), and prophecy (Acts 3:18) pointing to Jesus. I believe the Old Testament was a messianic document written to instill messianic hope. Jesus told the religious leaders: "You search the Scriptures because you think that in them you have eternal life; and it is they that bear witness about me" (John 5:39). "Many prophets and righteous people longed to see what you see, and did not see it, and to hear what you hear, and did not hear it" (Matt. 13:17; cf. John 8:56; Heb. 11:13, 39–40). "Your father Abraham rejoiced that he would see my day. He saw it and was glad" (John 8:56). Jesus fulfills all that the Old Testament hoped for (Matt. 5:17; Luke 24:44). In Christ, anticipation gives rise to realization (Matt. 11:13; Luke 16:16; Heb. 1:1–2).

Paul said, "I stand here testifying both to small and great, saying nothing but what the prophets and Moses said would come to pass: that the Christ must suffer and that, by being the first to rise from the dead, he would proclaim light both to our people and to the Gentiles" (Acts 26:22–23). In the apostle's mind, every part of the Old Testament anticipates the Messiah and the mission that his victorious death and resurrection would spark (cf. Luke 24:47). Paul declared, "We preach Christ crucified" (1 Cor. 1:23), and he even asserted, "I decided to know nothing among you except Jesus Christ and him crucified" (2:2).

The good news that the reigning God saves and satisfies believing sinners through Christ Jesus' life, death, and resurrection is of "first importance" (1 Cor. 15:3), yet so many biblical interpreters and Christian preachers treat these truths as tangential, at least in practice. Paul's gospel-centrality should *not* appear radical from a Christian expositor, but sadly many "Christian" sermons from the Old and New Testaments do not magnify the majesty of our Messiah. Indeed, many Old Testament teachers suggest that we should approach Jesus' Bible as though Jesus hadn't come. Yet this was never God's intent. Like any good mystery novel, reading the last chapter forces us to rethink the entire plotline. When reading in light of the revelation of Christ, the New Testament authors saw that the gospel concerning God's Son that they preached arose out of the promises of the Old Testament itself (Rom. 1:1–3). Indeed, the apostles recognized that the Lord foretold by the mouth of *all* the prophets from Moses forward the tribulation and triumph of the Christ and the subsequent glories (Acts 3:18, 24; 10:43; 1 Peter 1:10–12; cf. Rom. 3:21).

We must interpret the Old Testament in light of Christ's coming and through the lens of the apostles' teaching. Jesus is the Bible's fulcrum, marking the central turning point in history and inaugurating the climactic new covenant. The entire Old Testament points to him, and all fulfillment comes from and through him. The Old Testament is foundation; the New Testament is fulfillment. All true biblical theology will make much of Jesus.

We must read the Old Testament as Christians and not as though Christ had not come, for this is how the divine author intended us to read his Book. Once Luke and John, Paul and Peter encountered the resurrected Christ, they could not help but read their Old Testament in the knowledge of Christ's person and work. Indeed, as I'll note in chapter 12, numerous Old and New Testament passages suggest that Christians are in a better place to understand the Old Testament's actual meaning than most in the old covenant community were. We now have eyes to see and to savor the one to whom the Old Testament pointed all along. His name is *JESUS*!

We can legitimately tag whole-Bible preaching today as Christian only if it is "built on the foundation of the apostles and prophets, Christ Jesus himself being the cornerstone" (Eph. 2:20). We must, like the believers after Pentecost, devote ourselves to "the apostles' teaching" (Acts 2:42), which means studying the New Testament and following the apostles' pattern of interpreting the Old in the light of Christ's coming. If we fail to do this, we are not approaching the Old Testament as Jesus and his apostles were, and therefore we have no ground to actually call our interpretation "Christian."

Now, to say that all the Old Testament points to Christ does not mean that all of it does so in the same way. In chapter 12, we'll consider various ways by which we can faithfully see and ultimately proclaim Christ and the gospel in the Old Testament.

Summary of the Nature of Biblical Theology

In his book *The Fabric of Theology*, Richard Lints encourages evangelicals to shape theology within three distinct but overlapping spheres:[35]

- ***The Textual Horizon.*** Our focus here is on what the passage meant to its original author. The textual horizon addresses the immediate literary context, accounting for both the words and the informing theology that may have influenced those words.
- ***The Epochal Horizon.*** This perspective relates to the place of the passage within salvation history. Where does it fit within the unfolding of God's kingdom purposes, ultimately culminating in Christ?
- ***The Canonical Horizon.*** This view of the text considers how the placement and use of the text within the broader canon informs our understanding of God's intent for the passage. Here we keep in mind: (1) the progressive nature of revelation; (2) that all history is influenced by the defining work of Christ; and (3) that the divine authorship of Scripture allows for later texts to clarify, enhance, or deepen the meaning of earlier texts.

These three spheres of biblical interpretation necessitate a methodology for biblical theology that includes both grammatical-historical exegesis and salvation-historical and literary-canonical assessment. In this regard, Stephen Wellum writes: "Texts must be read not only in terms of their immediate context but also in terms of the 'whole.' Scripture is both unified and progressive. Thus biblical theology is concerned to read 'parts' in terms of the 'whole' and to trace out how God's plan develops *throughout* redemptive-history, leading us to its fulfillment in Christ and ultimately to the consummation."[36]

35. Lints, *The Fabric of Theology*, 293–310.

36. Gentry and Wellum, *Kingdom through Covenant*, 34n30.

To me, this approach seems most faithful to the biblical text itself and best aligns with how the New Testament authors are approaching their Bible. In summary, biblical theology is *a way of analyzing and synthesizing what the Bible reveals about God and his relations with the world that makes organic salvation-historical and literary-canonical connections with the whole of Scripture on its own terms, especially with respect to how the Old and New Testaments progress, integrate, and climax in Christ.*

The Bible's Frame, Form, Focus, and Fulcrum[37]

In this section I seek simply to synthesize where we have come in our discussion of biblical theology. I want to clarify what we have learned regarding what the Bible is about (its ***frame***), how it is transmitted (its ***form***), why it was given (its ***focus***), and around whom it is centered (its ***fulcrum***).

1. The Frame (Content: What?)

The Bible is the revelation of God, who reigns over all and who saves and satisfies all who look to him. In short, it's about his kingdom. He is the only uncaused one—the Source, Sustainer, and Goal of all things (Rom. 11:36). Through creation, fall, redemption, and consummation, this supreme Sovereign, Savior, and Satisfier has been shaping a people for himself in the context of the world. The Bible is about his kingdom-building process—God's reign over God's people in God's land for God's glory (Luke 4:43; Acts 1:3; 20:25; 28:23, 31).

2. The Form (Means: How?)

Throughout salvation history, God has maintained his relationship with the world through a series of covenants. The most dominant of these are the old (Mosaic) covenant and the new covenant in Christ. The old covenant brought forth an age of death, bearing a ministry of condemnation; the new covenant brought with it life, bearing a ministry of righteousness (2 Cor. 3:9). Moses recognized Israel's stubbornness and predicted the old covenant's failure (Deut. 9:6–7; 31:27–29). But he also envisioned that God would mercifully overcome curse with restoration blessing (4:30–31) in what we now know as the *new covenant* (Jer. 31:31). A prophetic, new covenant Mediator would facilitate this era of blessing (Deut. 18:15), which would include God's transforming the hearts of covenant members in a way that would generate love and obedience

37. I am certain that some of the synthesis that follows is indebted to conversations I enjoyed with my friend Miles Van Pelt during our doctoral studies at Southern Baptist Theological Seminary. You can find his synthesis of the Bible's message in the "Introduction" to Van Pelt, ed., *A Biblical-Theological Introduction to the Old Testament: The Gospel Promised* (Wheaton, IL: Crossway, 2016), 23–42.

(30:6, 8). God would curse all his enemies (30:7) and broaden the makeup of his people to include some from the nations (32:21, 43; cf. Gen. 17:4–5). Christ is the Mediator of the new covenant (1 Tim. 2:5; Heb. 9:15; 12:24), which has superseded the old (Rom. 10:4; Gal. 3:24–25), made every promise "Yes" (2 Cor. 1:20), and secured for us every spiritual blessing (Eph. 1:3) and "an inheritance that is imperishable, undefiled, and unfading" (1 Peter 1:4).

3. The Focus (Purpose: Why?)

The ultimate goal behind all of God's actions is the preservation and display of his glory, and it is to this end that all Scripture points. Because all things are from God, through him, and to him, God's glory is exalted over all things (Rom. 11:36) and should be the goal of our lives (1 Cor. 10:31).

4. The Fulcrum (Sphere: Whom?)

Jesus Christ is the one to whom all salvation history points, and the one from whom all fulfillment comes. The entire Bible is centered on Jesus, who stands as the promised messianic deliverer and who secures reconciliation with God for all who believe in him as the divine, crucified, resurrected Messiah. A universal call to repentance and whole-life surrender is the natural overflow of Jesus' redemptive, kingdom work.

Frame	God reigns, saves, and satisfies (i.e., God's kingdom)
Form	through covenant
Focus	for God's glory
Fulcrum	in Christ.

Fig. 10.6. The Bible's Frame, Form, Focus, and Fulcrum

Stated succinctly, the ***Bible's message*** can be synthesized as *God reigns, saves, and satisfies through covenant for his glory in Christ.*[38] Or, put another way, the Bible calls Jews and Gentiles alike to magnify God as the supreme Sovereign, Savior, and Satisfier of the world through Messiah Jesus. The Old Testament provides the foundation for this message; the New Testament supplies the fulfillment.

38. I thank my friend and colleague Jason C. Meyer, who first presented to me the simple but profound multi-orbed synthesis of the Bible's message as "God's kingdom through covenant for his glory (What? How? Why?)." Since then, and since I originally published my Frame, Form, Focus, Fulcrum synthesis in *What the Old Testament Authors Really Cared About* (49–51), Gentry and Wellum have come out with their very helpful volume *Kingdom through Covenant*, using a similar title.

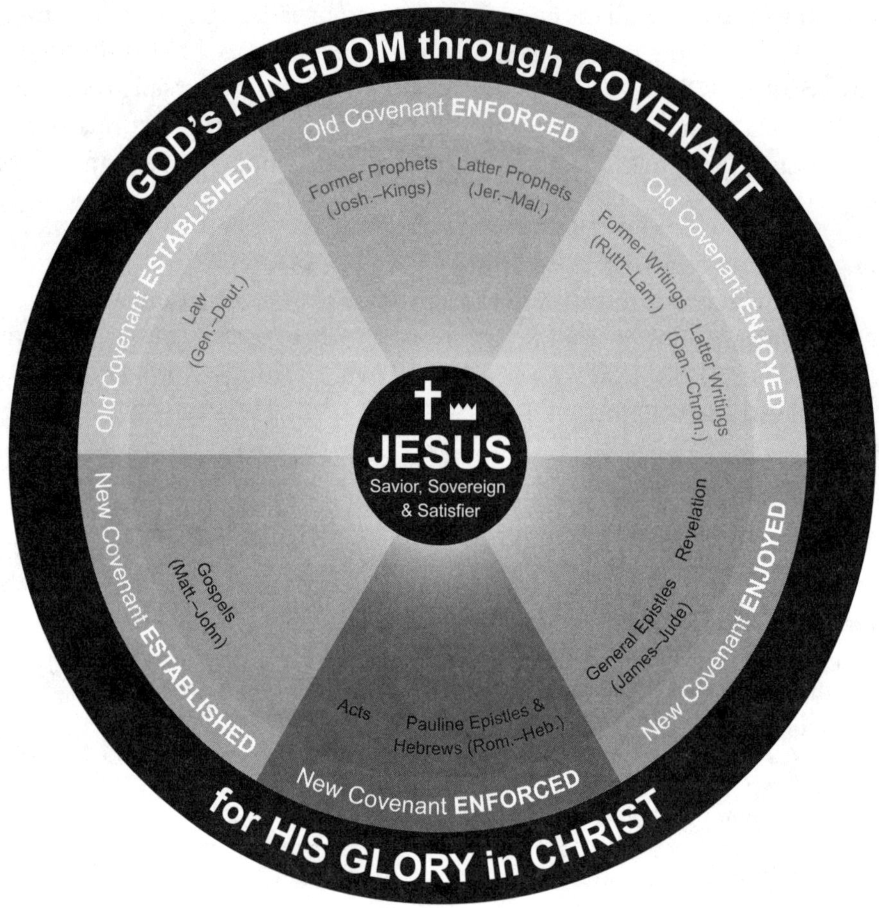

Fig. 10.7. A Synthesis of Scripture's Structure and Message[39]

An Example of Tracing a Theme—"A Kingdom of Priests" (Ex. 19:6)

As an example of doing whole-Bible theology on a single passage of Scripture, I want to look more intently at God's call for Israel to be a "kingdom of priests" in Exodus 19:6. This instruction builds on revelation already disclosed in Genesis and sets a theological trajectory for what will come in the rest of Scripture.

39. I thank my friend Miles V. Van Pelt, whose lectures and charts on Old Testament biblical theology at www.biblicaltraining.org initially sparked my vision for this diagram. This image originally appeared in DeRouchie, *What the Old Testament Authors Really Cared About*, 52. Used by permission.

1. Adam as God's Son, a Royal Priest

Exodus builds on the messianic and missiological plan set forth in Genesis, recalling the commission of Adam to image his heavenly Father for the global display of God's glory. In Genesis 2:7 the Lord commissions the first man to "serve" and "guard" the garden, terms used together outside Genesis 2–3 only in relation to the function of the Levites as servants and guardians of sacred space (Num. 3:4, 7–8; 8:26; 18:5–6; cf. Gen. 3:23–24). Adam was a *priest* of YHWH.

But God also charged the first man and woman to "subdue" the earth and to "have dominion" over its creatures (Gen. 1:28), royal language directly associated with Adam and Eve's role as imagers of God (1:26). Adam was also, then, a *king* under YHWH, commissioned to reflect, resemble, and represent his Father-Creator.

Genesis 5:1–3 identifies the close association of imageness and sonship when it writes: "When God created man, he made him in the likeness of God. Male and female he created them, and he blessed them and named them Man when they were created. When Adam had lived 130 years, he fathered a son in his own likeness, after his image, and named him Seth." In a way comparable to how human sons image their fathers, Adam imaged his God, and as God's son he was to operate as a royal priest, warding off evil and working to see God's sanctuary and presence extended through the world.

2. Israel as a New Adam, God's Son, a Royal Priest

In contrast to God's purposes for him, Adam sinned, failing to reflect, resemble, and represent his Father rightly. So the Sovereign of all things initiated his kingdom plan of salvation that would include a corporate royal-priest son who would in turn both give birth to and typologically anticipate an individual royal-Priest Son. The Lord anticipated the individual Son first when he announced in Genesis 3:15 that a male seed of the woman would ultimately render a deathblow to the serpent and his God-hostile ways. Following the flood, we learn that he would be a descendant of Shem (Gen. 9:26–27). Then, after having announced in Genesis 12:3 that Abraham would be the agent through whom the world would be blessed, Genesis 22:17b–18 detailed that the promised male deliverer would be in Abraham's line and that he would ultimately control enemy gates and bring worldwide blessing (cf. 24:60). We also learn in Genesis 49:8–10 that he would be a king in the line of Judah.

Into this context, YHWH announced in Exodus 4:22 that Israel is his "firstborn son," and then in Exodus 19:6 that he called this son to be "a kingdom of priests" in the midst of the whole world. Exodus 19:22, 24 tell us that at the time Israel had arrived at the mountain, the congregation already had priests who served as mediators between God and the people. These priests would serve as the primary teachers of God's Word (Lev. 10:10–11) and the primary offerors of sacrifices, by which right order would be reestablished and God's wrath against the people appeased (Lev. 4:1–6:7; 16:1–19; 1 Chron. 23:13). What is most amazing here is that Exodus 19:6 says not that Israel would have priests but that the entire nation was to be a kingdom of priests, mediating God's Word to the world through radical lives of surrender that would display the value and worth of the Lord. As Moses declares in Deuteronomy 4:6, "Keep [the statutes and the rules] and do them, for that will be your wisdom and your understanding in the sight of the peoples, who, when they hear all these statutes, will say, 'Surely this great nation is a wise and understanding people.'" Just as Moses would consecrate the Israelite priests by placing the blood of a sacrifice on them (Lev. 8:24), so in Exodus 24:8, "Moses took the blood and threw it on the people and said, 'Behold the blood of the covenant that the Lord has made with you in accordance with all these words.'" Thus the nation was set apart as God's royal-priest son, called to magnify his majesty in the world.

3. Israel's Loss of Priestly Status and God's Promise of Future Fulfillment

Like Adam, God's corporate son Israel rebelled, going his own way. Rather than praising and proclaiming God's name, the people profaned it. Moses had anticipated this in his prophetic prediction when he announced in Deuteronomy 32:5, "They have dealt corruptly with him; they are no longer his children because they are blemished; they are a crooked and twisted generation."

But in the midst of a sea of debauchery in the days of the Judges, God announced through Hannah, "The Lord will judge the ends of the earth; he will give strength to his king and exalt the power of his anointed" (1 Sam. 2:10). God still intended to raise up his king, whom he here called his "anointed." Then later in the chapter, a man of God announced, "I will raise up for myself a faithful priest, who shall do according to what is in my heart and in my mind. And I will build a sure house, and it shall go in and out before my anointed forever" (2:35, author's translation).[40] Now the anointed royal deliverer from Hannah's prediction is identified to also be a priest (cf. Zech. 6:13). At this point we expect that this priest-king will also be God's Son, and this is exactly what we are told in 2 Samuel 7 when God asserts that the throne of David will never end: "I will be to him a father, and he shall be to me a son. . . . And your house and your kingdom shall be made sure forever before me. Your throne shall be established forever" (2 Sam. 7:14, 16). In Hebrews 1:5, the author explicitly identifies God's royal Son from this text to be Jesus.

Not unexpectedly, when we get to Hosea, YHWH declares that he is removing his corporate son Israel from being his priest: "My people are destroyed for lack of knowledge; because you have rejected knowledge, I reject you from being a priest to me. And since you have forgotten the law of God, I also will forget your children" (Hos. 4:6). But though God declares corporate Israel's destruction, the prophet also promises, "After two days he will revive us; on the third day he will raise us up, that we may live before him" (6:2). This is one of the many Old Testament texts, I believe, that anticipate Jesus' resurrection and, with him, our own.

Hosea's words are part of a line of Old Testament prophetic announcements that the restored, new covenant people of God would effectively serve as YHWH's royal-priest sons, imaging YHWH's greatness to the world. Not only this, this new corporate

40. For this reading, see Kaiser, *The Messiah in the Old Testament*, 76. For an alternative possible reading, see Karl Deenick, "Priest and King or Priest-King in 1 Samuel 2:35," *WTJ* 73, 2 (2011): 325–39.

priesthood would include both redeemed Jews *and* Gentiles. We see this in numerous texts. For example, Isaiah wrote, "And they shall bring all your brothers from all the nations as an offering to the LORD . . . to my holy mountain Jerusalem, says the LORD, just as the Israelites bring their grain offering in a clean vessel to the house of the LORD. And some of them also I will take for priests and for Levites, says the LORD" (Isa. 66:20–21; cf. 56:6–7; 61:5–7). Similarly, Zephaniah predicted, "For at that time I will change the speech of the peoples to a pure speech, that all of them may call upon the name of the LORD and serve him with one accord. From beyond the rivers of Cush my worshipers, the daughter of my dispersed ones, shall bring my offering" (Zeph. 3:9–10). In both these passages, an international community engages in priestly service before the Lord.

Along with these texts, Psalm 110 also reasserts that the royal, anointed, divine Son of Psalm 2 is also YHWH's priest. God declares to him, "Rule in the midst of your enemies" (Ps. 110:2), and then he announces, "You are a priest forever after the order of Melchizedek" (110:4). This is the one who Psalm 72 declares will "have dominion from sea to sea" (72:8; cf. Zech. 9:9–10), whose name will "endure forever," and through whom the peoples of the nations will be blessed (Ps. 72:17). Building on Isaiah's vision of the suffering royal servant, Zechariah 3:8–9 treats the high priest Joshua as a type for the priest-king to come through whom God "will remove the iniquity of this land in a single day." In fulfillment of the hopes of 1 Samuel 2:35, the prophet also envisioned that this same messianic figure would bear "*royal* honor," be a "priest," and "sit and rule" on God's throne, with "the counsel of peace" being between them (Zech. 6:13).

4. Jesus the King-Priest and All in Him as Royal-Priest Sons and Daughters Forever

The angel Gabriel announced to Mary regarding Jesus, "He will be great and will be called the Son of the Most High. And the Lord God will give to him the throne of his father David, and he will reign over the house of Jacob forever, and of his kingdom there will be no end" (Luke 1:32–33). The wise men sought the "king of the Jews" (Matt. 2:2) and found Jesus (2:11), who later affirmed this as his identity (27:11). Through his ministry he proclaimed the nearness and good news of God's kingdom (4:17, 23; Mark 1:14–15), and the crowds recognized him to be the royal deliverer that the Old Testament had promised (Matt. 21:5). He establishes and upholds the throne of David with justice and with righteousness (Isa. 9:7). He lived in perfect accord with the Deuteronomic ideal for kingship (Deut. 17:14–20) in both his teaching and his actions (John 8:28; 15:10), and he brought justice to the broken and outcast (Matt. 12:18–21; Luke 4:18–19).

Along with being the king, he is the high priest in the line of Melchizedek who mediates the new covenant (1 Tim. 2:5; Heb. 9:15; 12:24), leading us into the very presence of the Lord (Heb. 5:6, 10; 6:20; 10:19–22). Christ "had to be made like his brothers in every respect, so that he might become a merciful and faithful high priest in the service of God, to make propitiation for the sins of the people" (2:17). He offered himself as a sacrifice in order to cleanse us from our sins and to secure us eternal salvation (Eph. 5:2; Heb. 9:11–12, 26; 10:12; 1 John 1:7). Now we can "with confidence draw near the throne of grace, that we may receive mercy and find grace to help in time of need" (Heb. 4:16).

Significantly, we who are in Christ have become royal-priestly sons and daughters of the living God, empowered to offer up sacrifices of praise (Rom. 12:1; Heb. 13:15–16; 1 Peter 2:5). As "a chosen race, a royal priesthood, a holy nation, a people for his own possession," we now "proclaim the excellencies of him who called you out of darkness into his marvelous light" (1 Peter 2:9). The task of being a kingdom of priests and a holy nation is no longer just a hope, for it is already being fulfilled in the church. The individual royal-Priest Son Christ has gone before us, doing what Adam and the nation of Israel were called to do. He represents us, and through him we are enabled to fulfill the calling of magnifying God's greatness among the nations.

Revelation 5:9–10 provides an apt stopping point for this biblical-theological survey. There, before the one called "the Lion of the tribe of Judah, the Root of David" (Rev. 5:5), and "the Lamb" (5:8), this song is sung: "Worthy are you to take the scroll and to open its seals, for you were slain, and by your blood you ransomed people for God from every tribe and language and people and nation, and you have made them a kingdom and priests to our God, and they shall reign on the earth" (5:9–10).

An Example of the Use of the Old Testament in the New—Hosea 11:1 in Matthew 2:15

One of the most challenging examples of the New Testament's use of the Old Testament is the appropriation of Hosea 11:1 in Matthew 2:15, which reads, "[Joseph] remained there [i.e., in Egypt] until the death of Herod. This was to fulfill what the Lord had spoken by the prophet, 'Out of Egypt I called my son.'" Here Matthew uses a fulfillment formula and direct quotation of Hosea 11:1 in order to clarify why God directed Joseph to take his family from Bethlehem to Egypt, returning to the Holy Land only after Herod's death.

Many scholars cite this text as a prime example of the New Testament's complete lack of respect for the meaning and context of the Old Testament. This is suggested because (1) Hosea 11:1 is simply a historical reflection, whereas Matthew reads it as prophecy fulfilled in Jesus, and (2) Hosea 11:1 refers to Israel the nation coming out of Egypt, but Matthew applies it to Christ. Building on the arguments of Duane A. Garrett, G. K. Beale, and others, I want to provide an overview of this interpretive challenge in order to highlight that Matthew is actually using the Old Testament in a way that is faithful to its original context broadly understood.[41] In order to do this, we will follow the pattern set forth by Beale and Carson in their *Commentary on the New Testament Use of the Old Testament.*

1. New Testament Context

Matthew 2 picks up after the birth of Christ (Matt. 1:18–25) and relates the events that led to his growing up in Nazareth. The visit of the wise men (2:1–12) arouses paranoia in King Herod (2:3–8) that results both in the holy family's temporary departure to Egypt (2:13–15) and in Herod's slaughter of the young of Bethlehem (2:16–18). Upon Herod's death, the holy family returns to the Holy Land but settles in Nazareth (2:19–23). Our particular quotation comes in the midst of a series of fulfillment texts reaching back to Micah 5:2 (Matt. 2:6), Hosea 11:1 (Matt. 2:15), and Jeremiah 31:15 (Matt. 2:18). Specifically, the quotation gives explanation for why the holy family left Bethlehem for Egypt before the narrative of their return.

2. Old Testament Context

Hosea 4–14 unpacks the nature of YHWH's lawsuit against Israel. The thesis statement is given in 4:1: "There is no faithfulness or steadfast love, and no knowledge of God in the land." Following a brief expansion on this point in 4:2–3, 4:4–6:3 unpacks "no knowledge," 6:4–11:11 clarifies "no steadfast love," and 11:12–14:8 details "no faithfulness/truth."

Hosea 11:1 comes at the end of the second of these units. The verse itself recalls the nation of Israel's feeble state when God first redeemed Israel from Egypt: "Out of Egypt I called my son." It then unpacks the Israelites'sustained covenant rebellion that will result in their exile to Assyria: "They shall not return to the land of Egypt, but Assyria shall be their king" (11:5).[42] Nevertheless, because of God's deep "compassion" (11:8), "they shall go after the Lord; he will roar like a lion; when he roars, his children shall come trembling from the west; they shall come trembling like birds from Egypt, and like doves from the land of Assyria, and I will return them to their homes, declares the Lord" (11:10–11).

What is clear here is that Hosea 11 begins with focusing on the first exodus (11:1; cf. 2:15b; 12:13; see also 12:9; 13:4) and ends by speaking of the return from Egypt and Assyria as a second exodus (11:10–11; cf. 7:11, 16b; 8:13b; 9:3, 6). The use of Egypt in 11:11 with respect to a fresh redemption recalls the first redemption and suggests that Hosea himself is interpreting the first exodus typologically,[43] following the pattern

41. See Duane A. Garrett, *Hosea, Joel*, NAC 19A (Nashville: Broadman & Holman, 1997), 222; Bass, *Hosea's Use of Scripture*, 217–24; Plummer, "Righteousness and Peace Kiss," 54–61; G. K. Beale, "The Use of Hosea 11:1 in Matthew 2:15: One More Time," *JETS* 55, 4 (2012): 697–715; Beale, "The Use of Hosea 11:1 in Matthew 2:15: Inerrancy and Genre," in *The Inerrant Word: Biblical, Historical, Theological, and Pastoral Perspectives*, ed. John MacArthur (Wheaton, IL: Crossway, 2016), 210–30.

42. Or: "Will they not return to the land of Egypt? And Assyria will be their king."

43. This view is all the more strengthened if Hosea 11:5 explicitly declares that Israel will *not* return to Egypt but will go to Assyria but then portrays her eschatological restoration as nothing less than returning from Egypt. For similar typological readings of Hosea 11 itself, see Garrett, *Hosea, Joel*, 222; Beale, "The Use of Hosea 11:1 in Matthew 2:15: One More Time," 703–5.

that Moses himself set for the exodus in Exodus 15:14–16. In these verses Moses and the people treat the future victory over the Canaanites as though it had already happened, simply because God had delivered them from the Egyptians (cf. Rom. 8:32). That is, Moses viewed the redemption from Egypt as a type of all future deliverances, the climax of which would be the work of the offspring of Abraham in overcoming all enemy gates and establishing global blessing (Gen. 22:17b–18; cf. 3:15).

Significantly, along with reading the original exodus as a type pointing to the future restoration as a second exodus, Hosea already linked that future restoration to a latter-day Davidic king: "Afterward the children of Israel shall return and seek the Lord their God, and David their king, and they shall come in fear to the Lord and to his goodness in the latter days" (Hos. 3:5). With this verse in mind, we must ask, "What role would the future David play in the second exodus?"

This question is further encouraged by a potential allusion to Numbers 23:21–24 and 24:7–9 in Hosea 11:10–11, the only passages where God's deliverance of Israel "from Egypt" is associated with the imagery of a "lion." Added to this is the fact that many scholars see the Old Testament background of the "king of the Jews" and "his star" in Matthew 2:2 to be Numbers 24:17: "I see him, but not now; I behold him, but not near: a star shall come out of Jacob, and a scepter shall rise out of Israel; it shall crush the forehead of Moab and break down all the sons of Sheth."

Hosea 11:10–11 reads, "They shall go after the Lord; he will roar *like a lion*; when *he roars*, his children shall come trembling from the west; they shall come trembling like birds *from Egypt*, and like doves from the land of Assyria, and I will return them to their homes, declares the Lord." At first glance, the "lion" appears to be YHWH, who delivers his trembling people from their adversity. Nevertheless, the close association of YHWH with his king (e.g., 3:5) suggests that God's roar could come through his royal human agent.

Numbers 23:21–24 treats the people of Israel in the first exodus as a lion, with the "king" most likely being YHWH, but possibly Moses (cf. Ex. 2:14; Acts 7:35):

> He has not beheld misfortune in Jacob, nor has he seen trouble in Israel. The Lord their God is with them, and the shout of a *king* is among them. God brings them *out of Egypt* and is for them like the horns of the wild ox. For there is no enchantment against Jacob, no divination against Israel; now it shall be said of Jacob and Israel, "What has God wrought!" Behold, a people! As a *lioness* it rises up and as a *lion* it lifts itself; it does not lie down until it has devoured the prey and drunk the blood of the slain.

In contrast, Numbers 24:7–9 points to a future exodus that will be led by YHWH's king, now called a lion. "God will bring him out of Egypt" and use him to crush either "Agag" (24:7), future king of the Amalekites (24:20; cf. 1 Sam. 15:3, 8) and image of God-hostility, or "Gog," the eschatological personification of evil (as rendered in the Septuagint; cf. Ezek. 38–39; Rev. 20:8):

> Water shall flow from his buckets, and his seed shall be in many waters; *his king* shall be higher than Agag [Gog?], and his kingdom shall be exalted. God brings him *out of Egypt* and is for him like the horns of the wild ox; he shall eat up the nations, his adversaries, and shall break their bones in pieces and pierce them through with his arrows. He crouched, he lay down like a *lion* and like a *lioness*; who will rouse him up? Blessed are those who bless you, and cursed are those who curse you."

Following the pattern set in Exodus 15:13–18, Numbers also appears to be treating the first exodus as typological of an eschatological exodus that will be led by a lion-king who represents his lion-people, under the guidance of YHWH.

3. Relevant Uses of the Old Testament Passage in Extrabiblical Jewish Literature

No clear passages in extrabiblical Jewish literature apply Hosea 11:1. We do find many second-exodus motifs, however.[44]

4. Textual Issues

Whereas the Septuagint uses the verb μετεκάλεω ("call to oneself, summon"), the New Testament simply employs καλέω ("call, summon").[45] Although the Septuagint uses a plural object with third masculine singular pronoun (τὰ τέκνα αὐτοῦ, "his children"), Matthew aligns with the MT, using a singular object with first common singular pronoun (τὸν υἱόν μου, "my son"). The LXX mentions "Israel's king," language that is not explicit in the MT but that is apparent in both Numbers 23:21 and 24:7 to which Hosea 11:10–11 alludes and in the context of Matthew 2:2, with reference to Jesus: "Where is he who has been born king of the Jews?"

Hosea 11:1	*Hosea 11:1*	*Matthew 2:15*
MT (*BHS/BHQ*)	LXX (Ziegler)[46]	NT (NA[28])[47]
כִּ֣י נַ֥עַר יִשְׂרָאֵ֖ל וָאֹהֲבֵ֑הוּ וּמִמִּצְרַ֖יִם קָרָ֥אתִי לִבְנִֽי׃	ὄρθρου ἀπερρίφησαν, ἀπερρίφη βασιλεὺς Ισραηλ. (1) Διότι νήπιος Ισραηλ, καὶ ἐγὼ ἠγάπησα αὐτὸν καὶ ἐξ Αἰγύπτου μετεκάλεσα τὰ τέκνα αὐτοῦ.	καὶ ἦν ἐκεῖ ἕως τῆς τελευτῆς Ἡρῴδου• ἵνα πληρωθῇ τὸ ῥηθὲν ὑπὸ κυρίου διὰ τοῦ προφήτου λέγοντος• ἐξ Αἰγύπτου ἐκάλεσα τὸν υἱόν μου.

Fig. 10.8. A Textual Comparison of Hosea 11:1 and Matthew 2:15

44. See T. R. Hatina, "Exile," *DNTB* 348–49.

45. Note that A′ 233 comparably uses ἐκάλεσα.

46. Joseph Ziegler, ed., *Septuagint, Vol. 13: Duodecim Prophetae*, 5th ed., Septuaginta: Vetus Testamentum Graecum Auctoritate Academiae Scientiarum Gottingensis editum 13 (Göttingen: Vandenhoeck & Ruprecht, 2014).

47. Barbara Aland et al., eds., *Novum Testamentum* Graece, 28th ed. (Stuttgart: Deutsche Bibelgesellschaft, 2012).

Hosea 11:1	*Hosea 11:1*	*Matthew 2:15*
ESV	**NETS**	**ESV**
When Israel was a child, I loved him, and out of Egypt I called my son.	At dawn they were cast out; Israel's king was cast out. (1) For Israel was an infant, and I loved him, and out of Egypt I recalled his children.	and [he] remained there until the death of Herod. This was to fulfill what the Lord had spoken by the prophet, "Out of Egypt I called my son."

Fig. 10.8. A Textual Comparison of Hosea 11:1 and Matthew 2:15 (cont.)

5. The New Testament Author's Textual and Hermeneutical Warrant for Using the Old Testament Text

Following the pattern of Hosea himself and Moses before him, Matthew appears to apply a typological hermeneutic that sees Hosea's reference to the first exodus as a type for the antitypical eschatological second exodus, ultimately led by Christ (cf. Luke 9:31). As the "king of the Jews," Jesus represents the nation, and his return from Egypt as a child was set forth as one more intermediary type in the progression of redemptive history that would climax in his bringing about the great second exodus on behalf of his people.

6. The New Testament Author's Theological and Rhetorical Use of the Old Testament Text

Matthew's use of Hosea 11:1 is but one of a whole series of Old Testament quotations designed to declare that Jesus, the Messiah-King, climactically fulfills the Old Testament. Hosea 11:1 was an ideal choice for a support text for at least three reasons. First, Hosea himself treats the first exodus of national Israel (God's "son") as typological of the eschatological second exodus.

Second, Hosea already employed imagery of corporate solidarity by tagging the nation as God's singular "son" (Hos. 11:1). His language recalls Exodus 4:22–23, where Israel the nation is first called God's "firstborn son." The Exodus text itself looks back to Genesis 5:1–3, where Adam himself is God's first son, and it anticipates texts such as 2 Samuel 7:14 and Psalm 2:7, which highlight Israel's messianic king as the Son of God. As with Adam, God called Israel, his corporate son, to display his image to the world as the people waited in hope for the (royal) offspring who would overcome evil and reconcile the world to God, thus restoring a state of blessing (Gen. 3:15; 22:17b–18; 49:8, 10). Like Adam, Israel the nation was placed into its own land-paradise, and like Adam, the people would lose it because of their sin. Yet the prophets are united in their conviction that the hope of the Messiah-led kingdom endured and that Israel's representative would one day rise, leading them out of bondage into freedom.

Third, Hosea already connected the antitypical second exodus with the reign of God and his Davidic royal Son. Hosea 3:5 reads, "Afterward the children of Israel shall return and seek the LORD their God, and David their king, and *they shall come in fear to the* Lord and to his goodness in the latter days." Then Hosea 11:10–11 states, "They shall go after the Lord; he will roar like a lion; when he roars, *his children shall come trembling* from the west; *they shall come trembling* like birds from Egypt, and like doves from the land of Assyria, and I will return them to their homes, declares the Lord." These parallels emphasize the close tie that Hosea saw between the ultimate second exodus and the Messiah's representative kingship.

Key Words and Concepts

Biblical theology
Salvation history
KINGDOM
Typology
Literary-canonical connections
Christotelic
The textual, epochal, and canonical horizons
The Bible's frame, form, focus, fulcrum, and message

Questions for Further Reflection

1. What does it mean to have a "canon within the canon"? What brings about this approach, and what negative effect does it have?
2. What does it mean that "Biblical theology makes organic connections with the whole of Scripture on its own terms"?
3. Offer some biblical support for the view that, in at least a high percentage of instances, the Old Testament authors were aware that they were making direct or typological predictions and recognized the nature of the fulfillment as the New Testament authors define it.
4. What is the six-step process to assess the New Testament's use of the Old Testament?
5. What is the danger of reading the Old Testament without focusing on Jesus? Consider using the metaphor of an answer key or a mystery novel in your answer.
6. What is the frame, form, focus, and fulcrum of the Bible?
7. The use of Hosea 11:1 in Matthew 2:15 has caused many scholars to conclude that the New Testament has no regard for the meaning and context of the Old Testament. After reading this chapter, how would you respond?

Resources for Further Study

For Teaching Kids the Story of Salvation History

Bruno, Chris. *The Whole Story of the Bible in 16 Verses*. Wheaton, IL: Crossway, 2015.
DeRouchie, Jason S., ed. Pages 30–40 in *What the Old Testament Authors Really Cared About: A Survey of Jesus' Bible*. Grand Rapids: Kregel, 2013.

DeYoung, Kevin. *The Biggest Story: How the Snake Crusher Brings Us Back to the Garden.* Wheaton, IL: Crossway, 2015.

Hamilton, James M., Jr. *The Bible's Big Story: Salvation History for Kids.* Illustrated by Tessa Janes. Fearn, Scotland: Christian Focus, 2013.

Helm, David. *The Big Picture Story Bible.* Wheaton, IL: Crossway, 2004.

Kaminski, Carol M. *Casket Empty Old Testament Timeline.* www.CasketEmpty.com.

Lloyd-Jones, Sally. *The Jesus Storybook Bible: Every Story Whispers His Name.* Illustrated by Jago. Grand Rapids: Zonderkidz, 2007.

Palmer, David L. *Casket Empty New Testament Timeline.* www.CasketEmpty.com.

Introduction, Methodology, and Survey

Adam, Peter. "Preaching and Biblical Theology." *NDBT* 104–12.

★ Alexander, T. Desmond. *From Eden to the New Jerusalem: An Introduction to Biblical Theology.* Grand Rapids: Kregel, 2008.

✪ Alexander, T. Desmond, and Brian S. Rosner, eds. *New Dictionary of Biblical Theology: Exploring the Unity and Diversity of Scripture.* Downers Grove, IL: InterVarsity Press, 2000.

Baker, David L. *Two Testaments, One Bible: The Theological Relationship between the Old and New Testaments.* 3rd ed. Downers Grove, IL: InterVarsity Press, 2010.

Balla, Peter. "Challenges to Biblical Theology." *NDBT* 20–27.

Bartholomew, Craig, Mary Healy, Karl Möller, and Robin Parry, eds. *Out of Egypt: Biblical Theology and Biblical Interpretation.* Scripture and Hermeneutics 5. Grand Rapids: Zondervan, 2004.

✪ Beale, G. K. "The Cognitive Peripheral Vision of Biblical Authors." *WTJ* 76, 2 (2014): 263–93.

———. *Handbook on the New Testament Use of the Old Testament: Exegesis and Interpretation.* Grand Rapids: Baker Academic, 2012.

———, ed. *The Right Doctrine from the Wrong Texts? Essays on the Use of the Old Testament in the New.* Grand Rapids: Baker Academic, 1994.

Beale, G. K., and D. A. Carson, eds. *Commentary on the New Testament Use of the Old Testament.* Grand Rapids: Baker Academic, 2007.

Beale, G. K., and Benjamin L. Gladd. *Hidden but Now Revealed: A Biblical Theology of Divine Mystery.* Downers Grove, IL: InterVarsity Press, 2014.

Beckwith, Roger T. "The Canon of Scripture." *NDBT* 27–34.

———. *The Old Testament Canon of the New Testament Church and Its Background in Early Judaism.* Grand Rapids: Eerdmans, 1985.

Berding, Kenneth, and Jonathan Lunde, eds. *Three Views on the New Testament Use of the Old Testament.* Counterpoints. Grand Rapids: Zondervan, 2008.

Blomberg, Craig L. "The Unity and Diversity of Scripture." *NDBT* 64–72.

✪ Bock, Darrell L. "Single Meaning, Multiple Contexts and Referents: The New Testament's Legitimate, Accurate, and Multifaceted Use of the Old." In *Three Views on the New Testament Use of the Old*, edited by Kenneth Berdin and Jonathan Lunde,

105–51. Responses to other contributors on pp. 90–95, 226–31. Counterpoints. Grand Rapids: Zondervan, 2008.

Carson, D. A. "The Bible and Theology." In *NIV Zondervan Study Bible*, edited by D. A. Carson, 2633–36. Grand Rapids: Zondervan, 2015.

———. "Biblical Theology." *DBCI* 35–41.

———. *Christ and Culture Revisited*. Grand Rapids: Eerdmans, 2007.

———. "Current Issues in Biblical Theology: A New Testament Perspective." *BBR* 5 (1995): 17–41.

✪ ———. "Mystery and Fulfillment: Toward a More Comprehensive Paradigm of Paul's Understanding of the Old and New." In *The Paradoxes of Paul*, 393–436. Vol. 2 of *Justification and Variegated Nomism*, edited by D. A. Carson, Peter T. O'Brien, and Mark A. Seifrid. 2 vols. WUNT 181. Grand Rapids: Baker Academic, 2004.

———. "Systematic Theology and Biblical Theology." *NDBT* 89–104.

Compton, Jared M. "Shared Intentions? Reflections on Inspiration and Interpretation in Light of Scripture's Dual Authorship." *Themelios* 33, 3 (2008): 23–33.

Enns, Peter. "Apostolic Hermeneutics and an Evangelical Doctrine of Scripture: Moving beyond a Modernist Impasse." *WTJ* 65, 2 (2003): 263–87.

Evans, Craig A. "New Testament Use of the Old Testament." *NDBT* 72–80.

France, R. T. "Relationship between the Testaments." *DTIB* 666–72.

Gaffin, Richard B. "Systematic Theology and Biblical Theology." *WTJ* 38, 3 (1976): 281–99.

Garrett, Duane A. "Type, Typology." *EDBT* 785–87.

Gentry, Peter J., and Stephen J. Wellum. Pages 21–126 in *Kingdom through Covenant: A Biblical-Theological Understanding of the Covenants*. Wheaton, IL: Crossway, 2012.

Glenny, W. Edward. "Typology: A Summary of the Present Evangelical Discussion." *JETS* 40, 4 (1997): 627–38.

Goldsworthy, Graeme. "Biblical Theology and Hermeneutics." *SBJT* 10, 2 (2006): 4–19.

———. *Christ-Centered Biblical Theology: Hermeneutical Foundations and Principles*. Downers Grove, IL: InterVarsity Press, 2012.

———. "Relationship of Old Testament and New Testament." *NDBT* 81–89.

Hafemann, Scott J., ed. *Biblical Theology: Retrospect and Prospect*. Downers Grove, IL: InterVarsity Press, 2002.

Hamilton, James M., Jr. "Biblical Theology and Preaching." In *Text Driven Preaching: God's Word at the Heart of Every Sermon*, edited by Daniel L. Akin, David L. Allen, and Ned L. Mathews, 193–218. Nashville: Broadman & Holman, 2010.

———. *What Is Biblical Theology? A Guide to the Bible's Story, Symbolism, and Patterns*. Wheaton, IL: Crossway, 2013.

Hasel, Gerhard F. "The Relationship between Biblical Theology and Systematic Theology." *TJ* 5, 2 (1984): 113–27.

Kaiser, Walter C., Jr. *The Uses of the Old Testament in the New*. Chicago: Moody, 1985.

Klink, Edward W., III, and Darian R. Lockett. *Understanding Biblical Theology: A Comparison of Theory and Practice*. Grand Rapids: Zondervan, 2012.

Köstenberger, Andreas J. "The Present and Future of Biblical Theology." *Themelios* 37, 3 (2012): 445–64.

———. "Testament Relationships." *DBCI* 350–52.

Kunjummen, Raju D. "The Single Intent of Scripture—Critical Examination of a Theological Construct." *GTJ* 7, 1 (1986): 81–110.

Lints, Richard. *The Fabric of Theology: A Prolegomenon to Evangelical Theology*. Grand Rapids: Eerdmans, 1993.

Moo, Douglas J., and Andrew David Naselli. "The Problem of the New Testament's Use of the Old Testament." In *The Enduring Authority of the Christian Scriptures*, edited by D. A. Carson, 702–46. Grand Rapids: Eerdmans, 2016.

Naselli, Andrew David. "D. A. Carson's Theological Method." *SBET* 29, 2 (2011): 245–74.

Osborne, Grant R. "The Old Testament in the New Testament" and "Biblical Theology." In *The Hermeneutical Spiral: A Comprehensive Introduction to Biblical Interpretation*, 323–44, 346–73. 2nd ed. Downers Grove, IL: InterVarsity Press, 2006.

———. "Type, Typology." *EDT* 1222–23.

———. "Typology." *ZEB* 5:952–54.

Payne, Philip B. "The Fallacy of Equating Meaning with the Human Author's Intention." *JETS* 20, 3 (1977): 243–52.

Plummer, Robert L. "Righteousness and Peace Kiss: The Reconciliation of Authorial Intent and Biblical Typology." *SBJT* 14, 2 (2010): 54–61.

Poythress, Vern S. "Dispensing with Merely Human Meaning: Gains and Losses from Focusing on the Human Author, Illustrated by Zephaniah 1:2–3." *JETS* 57, 3 (2014): 481–99.

———. "Kinds of Biblical Theology." *WTJ* 70, 1 (2008): 129–41.

———. "The Presence of God Qualifying Our Notions of Grammatical-Historical Interpretation: Genesis 3:15 as a Test Case." *JETS* 50, 1 (2007): 87–103.

Rosner, Brian S. "Biblical Theology." *NDBT* 3–11.

———. "Salvation, History of." *DTIB* 714–17.

Sailhamer, John. H. *Introduction to Old Testament Theology: A Canonical Approach*. Grand Rapids: Zondervan, 1995.

Schreiner, Thomas R. "Preaching and Biblical Theology." *SBJT* 10, 2 (2006): 20–29.

Schultz, Richard L. "Integrating Old Testament Theology and Exegesis: Literary, Thematic, and Canonical Issues." *NIDOTTE* 1:185–205.

Scobie, Charles H. H. "History of Biblical Theology." *NDBT* 11–20.

Taylor, Willard H. "Biblical Theology." *ZEB* 1:622–30.

Vanhoozer, Kevin J. "Exegesis and Hermeneutics." *NDBT* 52–64.

Yarbrough, Robert W. "Biblical Theology." *EDBT* 61–66.

———. "The Practice and Promise of Biblical Theology: A Response to Hamilton and Goldsworthy." *SBJT* 12, 4 (2008): 78–87.

Whole-Bible Biblical Theology: General

Alexander, T. Desmond. *From Eden to the New Jerusalem: An Introduction to Biblical Theology*. Grand Rapids: Kregel, 2008.

✪ Alexander, T. Desmond, and Brian S. Rosner, eds. *New Dictionary of Biblical Theology: Exploring the Unity and Diversity of Scripture*. Downers Grove, IL: InterVarsity Press, 2000.

Articles on Biblical Theology. In *NIV Zondervan Study Bible*, edited by D. A. Carson, 2629–96. Grand Rapids: Zondervan, 2015.

Beale, G. K., and Benjamin L. Gladd. *Hidden but Now Revealed: A Biblical Theology of Divine Mystery*. Downers Grove, IL: InterVarsity Press, 2014.

Bruno, Chris. *The Whole Story of the Bible in 16 Verses*. Wheaton, IL: Crossway, 2015.

Carson, D. A. Pages 193–314 in *The Gagging of God: Christianity Confronts Pluralism*. Grand Rapids: Zondervan, 1996.

———. *The God Who Is There: Finding Your Place in God's Story*. Grand Rapids: Baker, 2010.

———, ed. New Studies in Biblical Theology. Leicester: Apollos; Downers Grove, IL: InterVarsity Press, 1995–present. A master Scripture index for all the volumes in the series is available at http://www.theGospelCoalition.org/pages/nsbt.

Childs, Brevard S. *Biblical Theology of the Old and New Testaments: Theological Reflection on the Christian Bible*. Minneapolis: Fortress, 1993.

Clendenon, Ray, ed. NAC Studies in Bible and Theology. Nashville: Broadman & Holman, 2007–present.

Edwards, Jonathan. "A History of the Work of Redemption." In vol. 1 of *The Works of Jonathan Edwards*, edited by Edward Hickman, 532–619. Bellingham, WA: Logos Bible Software, 2008.

Elwell, Walter A., ed. *Evangelical Dictionary of Biblical Theology*. Grand Rapids: Baker, 1996.

Fuller, Daniel P. *The Unity of the Bible: Unfolding God's Plan for Humanity*. Grand Rapids: Zondervan, 1992.

★ Gentry, Peter J., and Stephen J. Wellum. *God's Kingdom through God's Covenants: A Concise Biblical Theology*. Wheaton, IL: Crossway, 2015.

✪ ———. *Kingdom through Covenant: A Biblical-Theological Understanding of the Covenants*. Wheaton, IL: Crossway, 2012.

Goldingay, John. *Biblical Theology: The God of the Christian Scriptures*. Downers Grove, IL: InterVarsity Press, 2016.

★ Goldsworthy, Graeme. *According to Plan: The Unfolding Revelation of God in the Bible*. Downers Grove, IL: InterVarsity Press, 1991.

———. *The Goldsworthy Trilogy*. Exeter, UK: Paternoster, 2000.

Hafemann, Scott J. *The God of Promise and the Life of Faith: Understanding the Heart of the Bible*. Wheaton, IL: Crossway, 2001.

Hafemann, Scott J., and Paul R. House, eds. *Central Themes in Biblical Theology*. Downers Grove, IL: InterVarsity Press, 2006.

Hamilton, James M., Jr. *God's Glory in Salvation through Judgment: A Biblical Theology*. Wheaton, IL: Crossway, 2010.

———. *What Is Biblical Theology? A Guide to the Bible's Story, Symbolism, and Patterns*. Wheaton, IL: Crossway, 2013.

Kaiser, Walter C., Jr. *The Promise-Plan of God: A Biblical Theology of the Old and New Testaments*. Grand Rapids: Zondervan, 2008.

———. *Recovering the Unity of the Bible: One Continuous Story, Plan, and Purpose*. Grand Rapids: Zondervan, 2009.

★ Lawrence, Michael. *Biblical Theology in the Life of the Church: A Guide for Ministry*. 9Marks. Wheaton, IL: Crossway, 2010.

Niehaus, Jeffrey J. *Ancient Near Eastern Themes in Biblical Theology*. Grand Rapids: Kregel, 2008.

Ortlund, Dane C., and Miles V. Van Pelt, eds. Short Studies in Biblical Theology. Wheaton, IL: Crossway, 2015–present.

Piper, John. "The Goal of God in Redemptive History." In *Desiring God: Meditations of a Christian Hedonist*, 308–21. 3rd ed. Sisters, OR: Multnomah, 2003.

★ Roberts, Vaughan. *God's Big Picture: Tracing the Storyline of the Bible*. Downers Grove, IL: InterVarsity Press, 2002.

★ Schreiner, Thomas R. *The King in His Beauty: A Biblical Theology of the Old and New Testaments*. Grand Rapids: Baker Academic, 2013.

VanGemeren, Willem A. *The Progress of Redemption: The Story of Salvation from Creation to the New Jerusalem*. Grand Rapids: Baker Academic, 1996.

Vos, Geerhardus. *Biblical Theology: Old and New Testaments*. Grand Rapids: Eerdmans, 1948.

Wellum, Stephen J., and Brent E. Parker, eds. *Progressive Covenantalism: Charting a Course between Dispensational and Covenant Theologies*. Nashville: Broadman & Holman, 2016.

Wright, Christopher J. H. *The Mission of God: Unlocking the Bible's Grand Narrative*. Downers Grove, IL: InterVarsity Press, 2006.

Whole-Bible Biblical Theology: Themes, Topics, Cross-Reference Lists

✪ Alexander, T. Desmond, and Brian S. Rosner, eds. *New Dictionary of Biblical Theology: Exploring the Unity and Diversity of Scripture*. Downers Grove, IL: InterVarsity Press, 2000.

★ Articles on Biblical Theology. In *NIV Zondervan Study Bible*, edited by D. A. Carson, 2629–96 and cross-references. Grand Rapids: Zondervan, 2015.

Bond, Steve, ed. *Holman Concise Topical Concordance*. Nashville: Holman, 1998.

Carson, D. A., ed. New Studies in Biblical Theology. Leicester: Apollos; Downers Grove, IL: InterVarsity Press, 1995–present. A master Scripture index for all the volumes in the series is available at http://www.theGospelCoalition.org/pages/nsbt.

Clendenon, Ray, ed. NAC Studies in Bible and Theology. Nashville: Broadman & Holman, 2007–present.

Clontz, T. E., and J. Clontz. *The Comprehensive Bible Cross References*. Castroville, TX: Cornerstone, 2011.

Davis, John Jefferson. *Handbook of Basic Bible Texts: Every Key Passage for the Study of Doctrine and Theology*. Grand Rapids: Zondervan, 1984.

Dennis, Lane T., and Wayne Grudem, eds. Cross-references in *ESV Study Bible.* Wheaton, IL: Crossway, 2008.

Elwell, Walter A., ed. *Evangelical Dictionary of Biblical Theology.* Grand Rapids: Baker, 1996.

———. *Topical Analysis of the Bible: A Survey of Essential Christian Doctrines.* Peabody, MA: Hendrickson, 2012.

Hafemann, Scott J., and Paul R. House, eds. *Central Themes in Biblical Theology.* Downers Grove, IL: InterVarsity Press, 2006.

Joy, Charles R. *Harper's Topical Concordance of the Bible.* 2nd ed. San Francisco: Harper & Row, 1976.

Nave, Orville J. *Nave's Topical Bible.* Peabody, MA: Hendrickson, 2002.

Ortlund, Dane C., and Miles V. Van Pelt, eds. Short Studies in Biblical Theology. Wheaton, IL: Crossway, 2015–present.

Smith, Jerome H., ed. *The New Treasury of Scripture Knowledge.* 2nd ed. Nashville: Thomas Nelson, 1992.

Thompson, Frank Charles, ed. *Thompson Chain-Reference Bible: New International Version.* Grand Rapids: Zondervan, 1983.

Topical concordances at the following websites:

- http://www.crosswalk.com/.
- http://www.biblestudytools.com/.
- http://www.studylight.org/.
- https://www.biblegateway.com/.

Torrey, R. A., and Timothy S. Morton. *The Treasury of Scripture Knowledge.* 3rd ed. Peabody, MA: Hendrickson, 2010.

VanGemeren, Willem A., ed. *New International Dictionary of Old Testament Theology and Exegesis.* 5 vols. Grand Rapids: Zondervan, 1997.

Viening, Edward. *The Zondervan Topical Bible.* Grand Rapids: Zondervan, 1969.

Old Testament Theology

Botterweck, G. Johannes, Helmer Ringgren, and Heinz-Josef Fabry, eds. *Theological Dictionary of the Old Testament.* 15 vols. Grand Rapids: Eerdmans, 1974–2006.

Brueggemann, Walter. *Theology of the Old Testament: Testimony, Dispute, Advocacy.* Minneapolis: Fortress, 2005.

Childs, Brevard S. *Old Testament Theology in a Canonical Context.* Philadelphia: Fortress, 1990.

Currid, John D. *Against the Gods: The Polemical Theology of the Old Testament.* Wheaton, IL: Crossway, 2013.

★ Dempster, Stephen G. *Dominion and Dynasty: A Biblical Theology of the Hebrew Bible.* NSBT 15. Downers Grove, IL: InterVarsity Press, 2003.

★ DeRouchie, Jason S., ed. *What the Old Testament Authors Really Cared About: A Survey of Jesus' Bible.* Grand Rapids: Kregel, 2013.

Dumbrell, William J. *Covenant and Creation: An Old Testament Covenant Theology.* 2nd ed. Milton Keynes, UK: Paternoster, 2013.

Eichrodt, Walther. *Theology of the Old Testament*. Translated by J. A. Baker. 2 vols. OTL. Philadelphia: Westminster, 1961, 1967.

Goldingay, John. *Israel's Faith*. Old Testament Theology 2. Downers Grove, IL: InterVarsity Press, 2006.

———. *Israel's Gospel*. Old Testament Theology 1. Downers Grove, IL: InterVarsity Press, 2003.

———. *Israel's Life*. Old Testament Theology 3. Downers Grove, IL: InterVarsity Press, 2009.

———. "Old Testament Theology and the Canon." *TynBul* 59, 1 (2008): 1–26.

Hasel, Gerhard F. *Old Testament Theology: Basic Issues in the Current Debate*. 4th ed. Grand Rapids: Eerdmans, 1991.

House, Paul R. *Old Testament Theology*. Downers Grove, IL: InterVarsity Press, 1998.

Kaiser, Walter C., Jr. "The Theology of the Old Testament." In *Introductory Articles*, edited by Frank E. Gaebelein, 283–305. Expositor's Bible Commentary 1. Grand Rapids: Eerdmans, 1979.

———. *Toward an Old Testament Theology*. Grand Rapids: Zondervan, 1978.

Kaminski, Carol M. *Casket Empty: God's Plan of Redemption through History—Old Testament Study Guide*. Salem, MA: Casket Empty Media, 2012.

———. *Casket Empty Old Testament Timeline*. www.CasketEmpty.com.

Kline, Meredith G. *Kingdom Prologue: Genesis Foundations for a Covenantal Worldview*. Overland Park, KS: Two Age, 2000.

Martens, Elmer A. "The Flowering and Floundering of Old Testament Theology." *NIDOTTE* 1:172–84.

———. *God's Design: A Focus on Old Testament Theology*. 4th ed. Eugene, OR: Wipf & Stock, 2015.

———. "Old Testament Theology Since Walter C. Kaiser Jr." *JETS* 50, 4 (2007): 673–91.

———. "Tackling Old Testament Theology." *JETS* 20, 2 (1977): 123–32.

McConville, J. G. *God and Earthly Power: An Old Testament Political Theology*. Edinburgh: T&T Clark, 2008.

Merrill, Eugene H. *Everlasting Dominion: A Theology of the Old Testament*. Nashville: Broadman & Holman, 2006.

Moberly, R. W. L. *The Old Testament of the Old Testament: Patriarchal Narratives and Mosaic Yahwism*. Eugene, OR: Wipf & Stock, 2001.

———. *Old Testament Theology: Reading the Old Testament as Christian Scripture*. Grand Rapids: Baker Academic, 2013.

———. "Theology of the Old Testament." In *The Face of Old Testament Studies: A Survey of Contemporary Approaches*, edited by David W. Baker and Bill T. Arnold, 452–78. Grand Rapids: Baker Academic, 2004.

Ollenberger, Ben C., ed. *Old Testament Theology: Flowering and Future*. 2nd ed. SBTS 1. Winona Lake, IN: Eisenbrauns, 2004.

Payne, J. Barton, and R. Alan Cole. "Old Testament Theology." *ZEB* 4:581–94.

Preuss, Horst Dietrich. *Old Testament Theology.* 2 vols. OTL. Louisville: Westminster John Knox, 1995.

Rad, Gerhard von. *Old Testament Theology.* 2 vols. OTL. Louisville: Westminster John Knox, 2001.

Rendtorff, Rolf. *The Canonical Hebrew Bible: A Theology of the Old Testament.* Leiden: Deo, 2005.

Sailhamer, John. H. *Introduction to Old Testament Theology: A Canonical Approach.* Grand Rapids: Zondervan, 1995.

———. *The Meaning of the Pentateuch: Revelation, Composition, and Interpretation.* Downers Grove, IL: InterVarsity Press, 2009.

Schultz, Richard L. "Integrating Old Testament Theology and Exegesis: Literary, Thematic, and Canonical Issues." *NIDOTTE* 1:185–205.

Smith, Ralph L. *Old Testament Theology: Its History, Method, and Message.* Nashville: Broadman & Holman, 1994.

✪ VanGemeren, Willem A., ed. *New International Dictionary of Old Testament Theology and Exegesis.* 5 vols. Grand Rapids: Zondervan, 1997.

★ Van Pelt, Miles V., ed. *A Biblical-Theological Introduction to the Old Testament: The Gospel Promised.* Wheaton, IL: Crossway, 2016.

Waltke, Bruce K., and Charles Yu. *An Old Testament Theology: A Canonical and Thematic Approach.* Grand Rapids: Zondervan, 2006.

Wright, Christopher J. H. *Old Testament Ethics for the People of God.* Downers Grove, IL: InterVarsity Press, 2004.

Zimmerli, Walther. *Old Testament Theology in Outline.* Atlanta: John Knox, 1978.

Zuck, Roy B., ed. *A Biblical Theology of the Old Testament.* Chicago: Moody, 1991.

New Testament Theology

✪ Beale, G. K. *A New Testament Biblical Theology: The Unfolding of the Old Testament in the New.* Grand Rapids: Baker Academic, 2011.

Bird, Michael F. "New Testament Theology Re-Loaded: Integrating Biblical Theology and Christian Origins." *TynBul* 60, 2 (2008): 265–91.

Carson, D. A. "New Testament Theology." *DLNT* 796–814.

Emerson, Matthew Y. *Christ and the New Creation: A Canonical Approach to the Theology of the New Testament.* Eugene, OR: Wipf & Stock, 2013.

Goppelt, Leonhard. *Theology of the New Testament.* Edited by Jürgen Roloff. Translated by John E. Alsup. 2 vols. Grand Rapids: Eerdmans, 1981.

Guthrie, Donald. *New Testament Theology.* Downers Grove, IL: InterVarsity Press, 1981.

Hasel, Gerhard F. *New Testament Theology: Basic Issues in the Current Debate.* Grand Rapids: Eerdmans, 1978.

Helyer, Larry R. *The Witness of Jesus, Paul, and John: An Exploration in Biblical Theology.* Downers Grove, IL: InterVarsity Press, 2008.

Kittel, Gerhard, and Gerhard Friedrich, eds. *Theological Dictionary of the New Testament.* Translated by Geoffrey W. Bromiley. 10 vols. Grand Rapids: Eerdmans, 1964–76.

★ Kruger, Michael J., ed. *A Biblical-Theological Introduction to the New Testament: The Gospel Realized*. Wheaton, IL: Crossway, 2016.

Ladd, George Eldon. *A Theology of the New Testament*. Edited by Donald A. Hagner. 2nd ed. Grand Rapids: Eerdmans, 1993.

Longenecker, Bruce W. "New Testament Theology." *ZEB* 4:474–81.

Marshall, I. Howard. *A Concise New Testament Theology*. Downers Grove, IL: InterVarsity Press, 2008.

———. *New Testament Theology: Many Witnesses, One Gospel*. Downers Grove, IL: InterVarsity Press, 2004.

Palmer, David L. *Casket Empty: God's Plan of Redemption through History—Old Testament Study Guide*. Salem, MA: Casket Empty Media, 2016.

———. *Casket Empty New Testament Timeline*. www.CasketEmpty.com.

Ridderbos, Herman N. *When the Time Had Fully Come: Studies in New Testament Theology*. Grand Rapids: Eerdmans, 1957.

Ryrie, Charles C. *Biblical Theology of the New Testament*. Chicago: Moody, 1959.

Schreiner, Thomas R. *Magnifying God in Christ: A Summary of New Testament Theology*. Grand Rapids: Baker Academic, 2010.

★ ———. *New Testament Theology: Magnifying God in Christ*. Grand Rapids: Baker Academic, 2008.

✪ Silva, Moisés, ed. *New International Dictionary of New Testament Theology and Exegesis*. 2nd ed. 5 vols. Grand Rapids: Zondervan, 2014.

Strecker, Georg. *Theology of the New Testament*. Louisville: Westminster John Knox, 2000.

Thielman, Frank. *Theology of the New Testament: A Canonical and Synthetic Approach*. Grand Rapids: Zondervan, 2005.

Witherington, Ben, III. *The Indelible Image: The Theological and Ethical Thought World of the New Testament*. 2 vols. Downers Grove, IL: InterVarsity Press, 2009.

Wright, N. T. *Jesus and the Victory of God*. Minneapolis: Fortress, 1997.

———. *The New Testament and the People of God*. Minneapolis: Fortress, 1992.

———. *Paul and the Faithfulness of God*. 2 vols. Minneapolis: Fortress, 2013.

———. *The Resurrection of the Son of God*. Minneapolis: Fortress, 2003.

Zuck, Roy B., ed. *A Biblical Theology of the New Testament*. Chicago: Moody, 1994.

Kingdom through Covenant

Baker, David L. "Covenant." In *Two Testaments, One Bible: The Theological Relationship between the Old and New Testaments*, 237–64. 3rd ed. Downers Grove, IL: InterVarsity Press, 2010.

Barrick, William D. "Inter-Covenantal Truth and Relevance: Leviticus 26 and the Biblical Covenants." *MSJ* 21, 1 (2010): 81–102.

———. "The Kingdom of God in the Old Testament." *MSJ* 23, 2 (2012): 173–92.

———. "The Mosaic Covenant." *MSJ* 10, 2 (1999): 213–32.

———. "New Covenant Theology and the Old Testament Covenants." *MSJ* 18, 2 (2007): 165–80.

Bateman, Herbert W., IV, ed. *Three Central Issues in Contemporary Dispensationalism: A Comparison of Traditional and Progressive Views*. Grand Rapids: Kregel, 1999.

Beckwith, Roger T. "The Unity and Diversity of God's Covenants." *TynBul* 38 (1987): 93–118.

Blaising, Craig A. "A Critique of Gentry and Wellum's *Kingdom through Covenant*: A Hermeneutical-Theological Response." *MSJ* 26, 1 (2015): 111–27.

Blaising, Craig A., and Darrell L. Bock, eds. *Dispensationalism, Israel and the Church: The Search for Definition*. Grand Rapids: Zondervan, 1992.

———. *Progressive Dispensationalism*. Grand Rapids: Baker, 1993.

Bock, Darrell L. "A Critique of Gentry and Wellum's *Kingdom through Covenant*: A New Testament Perspective." *MSJ* 26, 1 (2015): 139–45.

Brand, Chad Owen, ed. *Perspectives on Israel and the Church: 4 Views*. Nashville: Broadman & Holman, 2015.

Bright, John. *The Kingdom of God: The Biblical Concept and Its Meaning for the Church*. New York: Abingdon, 1953.

Chalmers, Aaron. "The Importance of the Noahic Covenant to Biblical Theology." *TynBul* 60, 2 (2009): 206–16.

Compton, R. Bruce. "Dispensationalism, the Church, and the New Covenant." *DBSJ* 8 (2003): 3–48.

Cowan, Christopher W. "The Warning Passages of Hebrews and the New Covenant Community." In *Progressive Covenantalism: Charting a Course between Dispensational and Covenant Theologies*, edited by Stephen J. Wellum and Brent E. Parker, 189–213. Nashville: Broadman & Holman, 2016.

Dean, David Andrew. "Covenant, Conditionality, and Consequence: New Terminology and a Case Study in the Abrahamic Covenant." *JETS* 57, 2 (2014): 281–308.

Decker, Rodney J. "The Church's Relationship to the New Covenant: Part 1." *BSac* 152 (1995): 290–305.

———. "The Church's Relationship to the New Covenant: Part 2." *BSac* 152 (1995): 431–56.

Dempster, Stephen G. *Dominion and Dynasty: A Biblical Theology of the Hebrew Bible*. NSBT 15. Downers Grove, IL: InterVarsity Press, 2003.

DeRouchie, Jason S. "Counting Stars with Abraham and the Prophets: New Covenant Ecclesiology in OT Perspective." *JETS* 58, 3 (2015): 445–85.

———. "Father of a Multitude of Nations: New Covenant Ecclesiology in OT Perspective." In *Progressive Covenantalism: Charting a Course between Dispensational and Covenant Theologies*, edited by Stephen J. Wellum and Brent E. Parker, 7–38. Nashville: Broadman & Holman, 2016.

———. "From Condemnation to Righteousness: A Christian Reading of Deuteronomy." *SBJT* 18, 3 (2014): 87–118.

———. Review of *Kingdom through Covenant: A Biblical-Theological Understanding of the Covenants*, by Peter J. Gentry and Stephen J. Wellum. *BBR* 23 (2013): 110–13.

Dumbrell, William J. *Covenant and Creation: An Old Testament Covenant Theology*. 2nd ed. Milton Keynes, UK: Paternoster, 2013.

———. "The Prospect of Unconditionality in the Sinaitic Covenant." In *Israel's Apostasy and Restoration: Essays in Honor of Roland K. Harrison*, edited by Avraham Gileadi, 141–55. Grand Rapids: Baker Academic, 1988.

Eichrodt, Walther. *Theology of the Old Testament*. Translated by J. A. Baker. 2 vols. OTL. Philadelphia: Westminster, 1961, 1967.

Feinberg, John S., ed. *Continuity and Discontinuity: Perspectives on the Relationship between the Old and New Testaments: Essays in Honor of S. Lewis Johnson Jr.* Westchester, IL: Crossway, 1988.

Fensham, F. Charles. "The Covenant as Giving Expression to the Relationship between Old and New Testament." *TynBul* 22 (1971): 82–94.

Fuller, Daniel P. *Gospel and Law: Contrast or Continuum—The Hermeneutics of Dispensationalism and Covenant Theology*. Grand Rapids: Eerdmans, 1980.

Gentry, Peter J., and Stephen J. Wellum. *God's Kingdom through God's Covenants: A Concise Biblical Theology*. Wheaton, IL: Crossway, 2015.

✪ ———. *Kingdom through Covenant: A Biblical-Theological Understanding of the Covenants*. Wheaton, IL: Crossway, 2012.

Gladd, Benjamin L., and Matthew S. Harmon. *Making All Things New: Inaugurated Eschatology for the Life of the Church*. Grand Rapids: Baker Academic, 2016.

Goldsworthy, Graeme. "Kingdom of God." *NDBT* 615–20.

Gray, Richard W. "A Comparison between the Old Covenant and the New Covenant." *WTJ* 4, 1 (1941): 1–30.

Grisanti, Michael A. "A Critique of Gentry and Wellum's *Kingdom through Covenant*: An Old Testament Perspective." *MSJ* 26, 1 (2015): 129–37.

———. "The Davidic Covenant." *MSJ* 10 (1999): 234–50.

Hafemann, Scott J. "The Covenant Relationship." In *Central Themes in Biblical Theology: Mapping Unity in Diversity*, edited by Scott J. Hafemann and Paul R. House, 20–65. Grand Rapids: Baker Academic, 2007.

———. "The Kingdom of God as the Mission of God." In *For the Fame of God's Name: Essays in Honor of John Piper*, edited by Sam Storms and Justin Taylor, 235–52. Wheaton, IL: Crossway, 2010.

Hahn, Scott. "Covenant in the Old and New Testaments: Some Current Research (1994–2004)." *CurBR* 3, 2 (2005): 263–92.

———. *Kinship by Covenant: A Canonical Approach to the Fulfillment of God's Saving Promises*. Anchor Yale Bible Reference Library. New Haven, CT: Yale University Press, 2009.

Horton, Michael. *Covenant and Eschatology: The Divine Drama*. Louisville: Westminster John Knox, 2002.

———. *God of Promise: Introducing Covenant Theology*. Grand Rapids: Baker, 2006.

———. "Law, Gospel, and Covenant: Reassessing Some Emerging Antitheses." *WTJ* 64, 2 (2002): 279–87.

———. *People and Place: A Covenant Ecclesiology*. Louisville: Westminster John Knox, 2008.

House, H. Wayne. "Creation and Redemption: A Study of Kingdom Interplay." *JETS* 35, 1 (1992): 3–17.

Hugenberger, Gordon P. *Marriage as a Covenant: Biblical Law and Ethics as Developed from Malachi*. Grand Rapids: Baker, 1998.

Johnston, Philip S., and Peter W. L. Walker, eds. *The Land of Promise: Biblical, Theological and Contemporary Perspectives*. Downers Grove, IL: InterVarsity Press, 2000.

Kaiser, Walter C., Jr. "The Unity of the Bible and Its Program: The Kingdom of God." In *Recovering the Unity of the Bible: One Continuous Story, Plan, and Purpose*, 127–40. Grand Rapids: Zondervan, 2009.

Kitchen, K. A. "The Fall and Rise of Covenant, Law, and Treaty." *TynBul* 40, 1 (1989): 118–35.

Kline, Meredith G. *Kingdom Prologue: Genesis Foundations for a Covenantal Worldview*. Overland Park, KS: Two Age, 2000.

———. *The Structure of Biblical Authority*. 2nd ed. Eugene, OR: Wipf & Stock, 1997.

Knoppers, Gary N. "Ancient Near Eastern Royal Grants and the Davidic Covenant: A Parallel?" *JAOS* 116, 4 (1996): 670–97.

Ladd, George Eldon. *Crucial Questions about the Kingdom of God*. Grand Rapids: Eerdmans, 1952.

———. *The Gospel of the Kingdom: Scriptural Studies in the Kingdom of God*. Grand Rapids: Eerdmans, 1959.

———. *The Presence of the Future: The Eschatology of Biblical Realism*. Grand Rapids: Eerdmans, 1974.

LaRondelle, Hans K. *The Israel of God in Prophecy: Principles of Prophetic Interpretation*. Andrews University Monographs; Studies in Religion 13. Berrien Springs, MI: Andrews University Press, 1983.

Marshall, I. Howard. "The Hope of a New Age: The Kingdom of God in the New Testament." *Themelios* 11, 1 (1985): 5–14.

———. "Kingdom of God (of Heaven)." *ZEB* 3:911–22.

Meade, John D. "Circumcision of Flesh to Circumcision of Heart: The Typology of the Sign of the Abrahamic Covenant." In *Progressive Covenantalism: Charting a Course between Dispensational and Covenant Theologies*, edited by Stephen J. Wellum and Brent E. Parker, 127–58. Nashville: Broadman & Holman, 2016.

✪ Meyer, Jason C. *The End of the Law: Mosaic Covenant in Pauline Theology*. NAC Studies in Bible and Theology 7. Nashville: Broadman & Holman, 2009.

Morgan, Christopher W., and Robert A. Peterson, eds. *The Kingdom of God*. Theology in Community. Wheaton, IL: Crossway, 2012.

Niehaus, Jeffrey J. "An Argument against Theologically Constructed Covenants." *JETS* 50, 2 (2007): 259–73.

———. *Biblical Theology*. Vol. 1, *The Common Grace Covenants*. Wooster, OH: Weaver, 2014.

———. "Covenant and Narrative, God and Time." *JETS* 53, 3 (2010): 535–59.

———. "Covenant: An Idea in the Mind of God." *JETS* 52, 2 (2009): 225–46.

———. *God at Sinai: Covenant and Theophany in the Bible and Ancient Near East*. SOTBT. Grand Rapids: Zondervan, 1995.

———. "God's Covenant with Abraham." *JETS* 56, 2 (2013): 249–71.

Payne, J. Barton. "Covenant (NT)." *ZEB* 1:1063–69.

———. "Covenant (OT)." *ZEB* 1:1051–63.

———. "Covenant, the New." *ZEB* 1:1071–76.

Pentecost, J. Dwight. *Thy Kingdom Come: Tracing God's Kingdom Program and Covenant Promises throughout History.* Grand Rapids: Kregel, 1995.

Robertson, O. Palmer. *The Christ of the Covenants.* Phillipsburg, NJ: Presbyterian and Reformed, 1987.

———. *The Israel of God: Yesterday, Today, and Tomorrow.* Phillipsburg, NJ: P&R Publishing, 2000.

Schreiner, Thomas R. "Part 1: The Fulfillment of God's Saving Promises: The Already-Not Yet." In *New Testament Theology: Magnifying God in Christ*, 39–116. Grand Rapids: Baker Academic, 2008.

Snoeberger, Mark A. "A Review Article: *Kingdom through Covenant: A Biblical-Theological Understanding of the Covenants.*" *DBSJ* 17 (2012): 99–103.

Stallard, Mike, ed. *Dispensational Understanding of the New Covenant: 3 Views.* Schaumburg, IL: Regular Baptist, 2012.

Stein, Robert H. "Kingdom of God." *EDBT* 451–54.

Strickland, Wayne G. "Preunderstanding and Daniel Fuller's Law-Gospel Continuum." *BSac* 144 (1987): 181–93.

Vlach, Michael J. *Has the Church Replaced Israel? A Theological Evaluation.* Nashville: Broadman & Holman, 2010.

———. "Have They Found a Better Way? An Analysis of Gentry and Wellum's *Kingdom through Covenant.*" *MSJ* 24, 1 (2013): 5–24.

———. "The Kingdom of God and the Millennium." *MSJ* 23, 2 (2012): 225–54.

———. "New Covenant Theology Compared with Covenantalism." *MSJ* 18 (2007): 201–19.

———. "What Does Christ as 'True Israel' Mean for the Nation Israel? A Critique of the Non-Dispensational Understanding." *MSJ* 23, 1 (2012): 43–54.

Waltke, Bruce K. "The Phenomenon of Conditionality within Unconditional Covenants." In *Israel's Apostasy and Restoration: Essays in Honor of Roland K. Harrison*, edited by Avraham Gileadi, 123–39. Grand Rapids: Baker Academic, 1988.

★ Wells, Tom, and Fred G. Zaspel. *New Covenant Theology: Description, Definition, Defense.* Frederick, MD: New Covenant Media, 2002.

Wellum, Stephen, J. "Baptism and the Relationship between the Covenants." In *Believer's Baptism: Sign of the New Covenant in Christ*, edited by Thomas R. Schreiner and Shawn D. Wright, 97–161. NAC Studies in Bible and Theology. Nashville: Broadman & Holman, 2007.

Wellum, Stephen J., and Brent E. Parker, eds. *Progressive Covenantalism: Charting a Course between Dispensational and Covenant Theologies.* Nashville: Broadman & Holman, 2016.

White, James R. "The Newness of the New Covenant: Better Covenant, Better Mediator, Better Sacrifice, Better Ministry, Better Hope, Better Promises (Part 1)." *RBTR* 1, 2 (2004): 144–68.

———. "The Newness of the New Covenant: Better Covenant, Better Mediator, Better Sacrifice, Better Ministry, Better Hope, Better Promises (Part 2)." *RBTR* 2, 1 (2005): 83–104.

Williamson, Paul R. "Covenant." *NDBT* 419–29.

———. *Sealed with an Oath: Covenant in God's Unfolding Purpose.* NSBT 23. Downers Grove, IL: InterVarsity Press, 2007.

Wright, N. T. *The Climax of the Covenant: Christ and the Law in Pauline Theology.* Minneapolis: Fortress, 1993.

Zaspel, Fred G. *The New Covenant and New Covenant Theology.* Frederick, MD: New Covenant Media, 2011.

For "Old Testament Law and the Christian" and "Seeing and Savoring Christ and the Gospel in the Old Testament," see the "Resources for Further Study" in chapter 12.

11

SYSTEMATIC THEOLOGY

Goal: Discern how your passage theologically coheres with the whole Bible, assessing key doctrines especially in direct relation to the gospel.

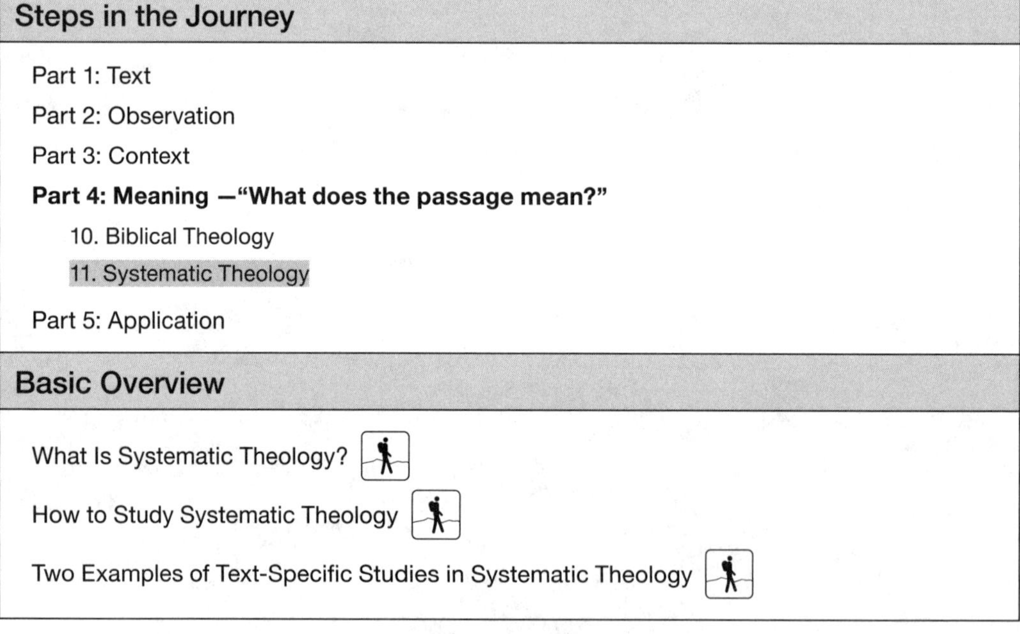

Steps in the Journey

Part 1: Text

Part 2: Observation

Part 3: Context

Part 4: Meaning —"What does the passage mean?"

- 10. Biblical Theology
- 11. Systematic Theology

Part 5: Application

Basic Overview

What Is Systematic Theology?

How to Study Systematic Theology

Two Examples of Text-Specific Studies in Systematic Theology

Fig. 11.1. Trail Guide to Chapter 11

What Is Systematic Theology?

Broadly speaking, ***systematic theology*** is the study of Bible doctrine designed to help us shape a proper worldview—what James Sire has defined as "a commitment, a fundamental orientation of the heart, that can be expressed as a story in a set of presuppositions . . . which we hold . . . about the basic constitution of reality, and that provides the foundation on which we live and move and have our being."[1] Systematic theology takes for granted that the Bible gets reality right, and it assumes Scripture's overarching unity, while affirming the progress of revelation and the development of redemptive history. In systematic theology, we seek to answer the question, "What does the whole Bible say about X?"

In the interpretive process, the stage considering systematic theology is asking more specifically, "How does our passage theologically cohere with the whole Bible?" Or, "What are those doctrines to which this passage contributes?"

Traditionally, systematic theology divides into at least ten categories:

- **Theology Proper** (the doctrine of *God*)
- **Bibliology** (the doctrine of *Scripture*)
- **Angelology** (the doctrine of *angels and demons*)
- **Anthropology** (the doctrine of *humanity*)
- **Hamartiology** (the doctrine of *sin*)
- **Christology** (the doctrine of *Christ*)
- **Soteriology** (the doctrine of *salvation*)
- **Pneumatology** (the doctrine of the *Holy Spirit*)
- **Ecclesiology** (the doctrine of the *church*)
- **Eschatology** (the doctrine of the *end times or last things*)

Different theological camps within the church arise from different perspectives on each of these topics. For example, Calvinists and Arminians disagree over theology proper, anthropology, hamartiology, and soteriology. Complementarians and egalitarians differ on anthropology and ecclesiology. Classic covenantalists, progressive covenantalists, and dispensationalists diverge primarily over ecclesiology and eschatology. And polity distinctions principally relate to ecclesiology.

1. James W. Sire, *The Universe Next Door: A Basic Worldview Catalog* (Downers Grove, IL: InterVarsity Press, 2004), 17.

It's important to recognize that not all doctrinal issues bear equal weight. Just as Jesus said that the law addressed some matters that were "weightier" than others (Matt. 23:23), so, too, Paul emphasized that the **gospel** he preached was of "first importance" (1 Cor. 15:3). Other teachings matter, but nothing is more fundamental than the good news that the reigning God saves and satisfies believing sinners through Christ Jesus' life, death, and resurrection.

Albert Mohler has termed the weighing out of different doctrines ***theological triage***.[2] The term *triage* is often used in medical contexts to address the assignment of degrees of urgency to wounds or illnesses in order to decide the order of treatment of a large number of patients or casualties. In systematic theology, theological triage involves assessing those doctrines that require the church's greatest attention. For the busy expositor, this means classifying your passage's doctrines as primary, secondary, or tertiary.

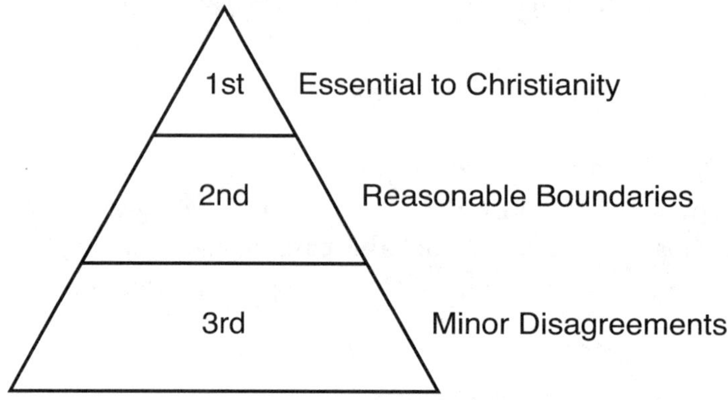

Fig. 11.2. Theological Triage

1. Level 1: Doctrines Essential to Christianity

First-level issues of doctrine are those most central and essential to Christianity. You can't deny these issues and still be a Christian. Mohler includes here doctrines such as the Trinity, the full deity and humanity of Jesus Christ, justification by faith, and the authority of Scripture.

2. Level 2: Doctrines That Generate Reasonable Boundaries

Second-level issues are usually those that distinguish denominations and local churches. These are issues that commonly spark the highest-level debates, that are usually grounded in some form of biblical interpretation, and that generate reasonable boundaries between Christians. Mohler includes among these the doctrines of the meaning and mode of baptism and views on the role of women in the home and

2. R. Albert Mohler Jr., "Confessional Evangelicalism," in *Four Views on the Spectrum of Evangelicalism*, ed. Andrew David Naselli and Collin Hansen, Counterpoints (Grand Rapids: Zondervan, 2011), 77–80; see also http://www.albertmohler.com/2005/07/12/a-call-for-theological-triage-and-christian-maturity/. Some refer to these levels as (1) dogma, (2) doctrine, and (3) differences; or (1) absolutes, (2) convictions, and (3) opinions and questions; or (1) essential, (2) important, or (3) nonessential.

church. To these I would add the questions of God's sovereignty in salvation and of divorce and remarriage. Level 2 differences do not identify someone as a Christian, but most local churches will struggle if their leaders disagree on these matters.

3. Level 3: Doctrines Addressing Minor Disagreements

Third-level issues are those doctrines over which Christians can disagree and easily remain in close fellowship, even within local congregations. At times these are matters of conscience or practice, such as "Should Christians participate in Halloween?" or "Is it best to educate children through public school, private school, private Christian school, or homeschool?" Other times they are matters of simple dispute that bear little influence on one's everyday life. In Romans 14:1–15:7, Paul addresses how Christians who are strong or weak in the faith with respect to food, wine, and holy days should not judge but welcome one another. He is here addressing disputable matters of conscience. Mohler includes among these questions about the millennium and those related to the timing and sequence of Christ's return.[3]

To say that certain doctrines are more important than others does *not* imply that Christians may take any biblical truth with less than full seriousness. There are no insignificant doctrines, but there are certain ones that are more fundamental—more foundational—than others and that undergird and inform the entire system of biblical truth. Furthermore, it is important to recognize that, regardless of the tier in which a given doctrine may fall, your conviction on that doctrine may influence your understanding of a doctrine in a different tier. For example, one's convictions about the nature of justification (a level 1 issue) will also impact one's understanding of the meaning of baptism (a level 2 issue).

As you work through your passage, be sure to ask how it theologically coheres with the whole Bible and what doctrines it addresses. Figure 11.3 identifies the key distinctions between biblical and systematic theology.[4]

	Biblical Theology	*Systematic Theology*
Base of Authority	Canonical Scripture	Canonical Scripture
Ordering Principles	1. Organic, historical, and canonical 2. Inductive, comparative, and as diachronic as possible, tracing out the salvation history that frames all Scripture	1. Ahistorical and universal 2. Topical, logical, hierarchical, and as synchronic as possible

Fig. 11.3. Biblical vs. Systematic Theology

3. The best book on identifying and working through these minor disagreements is Andrew David Naselli and J. D. Crowley, *Conscience: What It Is, How to Train It, and Loving Those Who Differ* (Wheaton, IL: Crossway, 2016). While we could easily multiply examples, they supply a list of twenty-seven for which Christians must seek to calibrate their consciences (80–81). They also supply a very helpful overview of theological triage (85–87).

4. For more on these differences, see D. A. Carson, "Systematic Theology and Biblical Theology," *NDBT* 102–03.

	Biblical Theology	*Systematic Theology*
Task and Shape	1. Inductive and descriptive, earning normative power by the credibility of its results 2. A little further from culture but closer to the biblical text 3. Seeks out the rationality and communicative genius of each literary genre or canonical unit	1. Rearticulates what the Bible says with a mind toward engaging and even confronting culture 2. A little closer to culture with highest influence on all other areas (exegesis, biblical theology, historical theology) because of its worldview-shaping nature 3. Integrates the Bible's diverse rationalities in its pursuit of a large-scale, worldview-forming synthesis
Nature	Bridge discipline	Culminating discipline

Fig. 11.3. Biblical vs. Systematic Theology (cont.)

How to Study Systematic Theology[5]

Approaching the Bible's doctrines is no light matter, for we are seeking to grasp all that God has revealed in Scripture on a given topic. I propose the following approach to the study of systematic theology.

1. Ask God to supply both insight with reason and humility with love.

There are at least two reasons why all pursuit of doctrine must begin with prayer. First, we do not want to be ashamed of failing in rigorous, God-dependent thinking. Paul charged the Corinthians, "Be infants in evil, but in your thinking be mature" (1 Cor. 14:20). Similarly, he told Timothy, "Think over what I say, for the Lord will give you understanding in everything. . . . Do your best to present yourself to God as one approved, a worker who has no need to be ashamed, rightly handling the word of truth" (2 Tim. 2:7, 15). These texts stress that the quest for right doctrine will include

5. Some of the shape of this section is adapted from Wayne A. Grudem, *Systematic Theology: An Introduction to Biblical Doctrine* (Grand Rapids: Zondervan, 1994), 32–37.

God-dependent, rigorous thought, directed toward God's Book. The danger of failing at this point is serious. As Peter notes, "There are some things in [Paul's letters] that are hard to understand, which the ignorant and unstable twist to their own destruction, as they do the other Scriptures" (2 Peter 3:16). Destruction comes to those who mishandle God's Word, and because the quest is so serious and because it necessitates rigorous, God-dependent thought, we must pray that God will "open our eyes that we may behold wonderful things in your law" (Ps. 119:18).

Second, we need the Spirit's aid to gain the experiential knowledge that the Bible demands. James warns us: "Be doers of the word, and not hearers only, deceiving yourselves. . . . Religion that is pure and undefiled before God, the Father, is this: to visit orphans and widows in their affliction, and to keep oneself unstained from the world" (James 1:22, 27; cf. Rom. 2:13). Far too often, great knowledge of God, his ways, and his world creates kings rather than servants and leads to pride rather than to love (1 Cor. 8:1). "God opposes the proud but gives grace to the humble" (1 Peter 5:5), and in the Lord's economy, "he who is least . . . is the one who is great" (Luke 9:48). James charged:

> Who is wise and understanding among you? By his good conduct let him show his works in the meekness of wisdom. . . . But the wisdom from above is first pure, then peaceable, gentle, open to reason, full of mercy and good fruits, impartial and sincere. And a harvest of righteousness is sown in peace by those who make peace. (James 3:13, 17–18)

This kind of experiential knowledge of God is only "spiritually discerned" (1 Cor. 2:14; cf. Eph. 1:17–19), and because of this, our quest to grasp Bible doctrine must be saturated with prayer. We must pray, "Incline our hearts to your testimonies" (Ps. 119:36); "Unite my heart to fear your name" (86:11); and "Satisfy us this morning with your steadfast love, that we may rejoice and be glad all our days" (90:14).

2. Catalogue and synthesize all the relevant passages.

After praying, the first thing you need to do is to collect the most relevant passages related to the topic with which you are wrestling. The best tool here is a concordance (see "An Overview of Concordances, Lexicons, and Theological Wordbooks" in chapter 7), which will allow you to look up key words or concepts to find where the Bible treats your subject. For example, if you were studying Moses' intercessory prayer in Deuteronomy 9:25–29 and wanted to know more about the Bible's teaching on prayer and what your passage contributes to it, you would want to look not only for instances of *pray* and *prayer* but also for occurrences of terms such as *confess*, *intercede*, *petition*, and *supplication* and even words such as *prostrate*. You should also investigate other intercessory prayers, such as Moses' parallel prayer in Exodus 32:11–13, his prayer in Numbers 14:13–19, and those in Daniel 9, Ezra 9, and Nehemiah 9. Systematic theologies can serve you here, making you aware of texts that you may have never thought of.

Once you have identified the most relevant texts, the next step is to classify them. This process entails reading all the texts carefully, summarizing their points, and organizing them into groups based on distinct patterns or features.

The final step is to synthesize in one or more points what the Bible teaches on your topic and then to identify how your passage contributes to this understanding. If your passage were not present in Scripture, would some crucial knowledge about your topic be missing?

3. Consider what others have said.

At this point, it can be helpful to consider what others have said on the topic. The Lord has given the church pastors and teachers (1 Cor. 12:28; Eph. 4:11), so we should not hesitate to use them in our quest for understanding Bible doctrine. Once you have catalogued and synthesized what you believe the Bible has to say about your topic and how your passage contributes to this understanding, make use of systematic theologies and other books and talk with your shepherds regarding what you are learning and thinking. The very greatest individuals in human history were standing on the shoulders of others, and we must humbly seek critique and shaping from our peers and from those who are further along than we are. Very often other perspectives will guard us from error and keep us more faithful.

4. Praise the Lord for his truth and act accordingly.

The final step is to praise God for his illumination and to act in accordance with the truths we have gained. Study of doctrine cannot be a dispassionate exercise, for we are engaging in the highest pursuit—knowing God and his ways. We must declare with the psalmists, "How sweet are your words to my taste" (Ps. 119:103) and "How precious to me are your thoughts, O God!" (139:17). Then we must act—speaking "as one who speaks oracles of God" and serving "as one who serves by the strength that God supplies—in order that in everything God may be glorified through Jesus Christ. To him belong glory and dominion forever and ever" (1 Peter 4:11; cf. 1 Cor. 15:10; Phil. 2:12–13; Col. 1:29).

Two Examples of Text-Specific Studies in Systematic Theology

Soteriology and Missiology in Exodus 19:4–6

We have seen how a lot of later Scriptures build on Exodus 19:4–6 and how this passage supplies a helpful synthesis of the revealed purpose of the old covenant. Now

I want to consider how this passage contributes to our understanding of Christian doctrine. We are going to look at soteriology in this section and then missiology in the next.

1. Soteriology

None can miss that Exodus 19:4 addresses the most foundational redemptive act of the old covenant period. Advocates of the new perspective on Paul have ever been quick to note that YHWH saved Israel *before* he ever gave them the law at Sinai. Thus the law was never about getting into relationship; it was about staying in. God ransomed before he required; he freed before he called his people to follow. The indicative of redemption accomplished precedes the imperative of redemption enjoyed, and this is the same pattern in the new covenant. God converts and then calls us to follow. In the classic sense, justification gives rise to sanctification. Faith is the root; obedience is the fruit. To put works first makes us legalists who trust in our own merits rather than in the merits of Christ. There is therefore a similar *structure of grace* in both the old and new covenants: gracious redemption precedes gracious lawgiving. Christ's saving work secures pardon and purchases power so that we can respond with his help in obedience.

While this is true, we must not miss what most advocates of the new perspective on Paul seem to miss. Namely, while the structure of grace between the old and new covenants may be the same, the *nature of grace* is entirely different. Old covenant grace was external; new covenant grace is internal. In the old covenant, YHWH delivers the Israelites from physical slavery in Egypt, but for the majority their bondage to sin remained. As Moses asserted forty years after the exodus: "Know, therefore, that the Lord your God is not giving you this good land to possess because of your righteousness, for you are a stubborn people. Remember and do not forget how you provoked the Lord your God to wrath in the wilderness. From the day you came out of the land of Egypt until you came to this place, you have been rebellious against the Lord" (Deut. 9:6–7). The rest of Deuteronomy and redemptive history note how this rebellion would persist until the prophet greater than Moses would arise and establish a new covenant based on better promises and God-wrought inward transformation. *Nothing* in the old covenant itself secured eternal life for all its members.

Along with saving only externally, YHWH revealed his will at Sinai in a way that did not reach the hearts of the majority. They saw but didn't really see; they heard but didn't really hear. As Moses would later assert, "You have seen all that the Lord did before your eyes in the land of Egypt, to Pharaoh and to all his servants and to all his land, the great trials that your eyes saw, the signs, and those great wonders. But to this day the Lord has not given you a heart to understand or eyes to see or ears to hear" (Deut. 29:2–4[H1–3]). Rather than having God's law written on their hearts, Jeremiah tells us, "the sin of Judah is written with a pen of iron; with a point of diamond it is engraved on the tablet of their heart" (Jer. 17:1).

In contrast, whereas most of those in the old covenant were rebels, all in the new covenant would be remnant. With circumcised hearts, those in the transformed community would, in Moses' words, "turn and listen unto the voice of the Lord and do all his commandments that I am commanding you today" (Deut. 30:8, author's translation). The prophet also asserted that in that day, "the word will be very near you; it will be in your mouth and in your heart so that you can do it" (30:14, author's translation).[6] Paul says in Romans 10:8 that this is fulfilled in Christ. Through Jeremiah YHWH also predicted, "I will put my law within them, and I will write it on their hearts. . . . And no longer shall each one teach his neighbor and each his brother, saying, 'Know the Lord,' for they shall all know me, from the least of them to the greatest, declares the Lord. For I will forgive their iniquity, and I will remember their sin no more" (Jer. 31:33–34).

Even though external salvation preceded external lawgiving in the old covenant, because Israel's sin remained undealt with, all its outward alignment with the law was unacceptable to God and equivalent to seeking salvation by works. Because the nation lost sight of its inability and need for repentance and a substitute, the people's outward pursuits of righteousness did not allow them to attain the life that the law promised. "What shall we say, then? That Gentiles who did not pursue righteousness have attained it, that is, a righteousness that is by faith; but that Israel who pursued a law that would lead to righteousness did not succeed in reaching that law. Why? Because they did not pursue it by faith, but as if it were based on works. They have stumbled over the stumbling stone" (Rom. 9:30–32).

In Exodus 19:4–6 we read that the revealed purpose of the old covenant was that the nation would, through a surrendered pursuit of God and his ways, stand as a kingdom of priests and a holy nation amid the world. But the revealed purposes of God for the old covenant were not his sovereign purposes: "Now the law came in to increase the trespass, but where sin increased, grace abounded all the more" (Rom. 5:20). Paul says that the old covenant bore "a ministry of condemnation"; only the new covenant would bear a "ministry of righteousness" (2 Cor. 3:9). In the old covenant, God commanded but did not enable. He changed Israel's outward status but did not alter the people's souls. He disclosed to them his law but did not give them the desire to keep it. And he did so in order to highlight the beauty and centrality of Christ: "What if God, desiring to show his wrath and to make known his power, has endured with much patience vessels of wrath prepared for destruction, in order to make known the riches of his glory for vessels of mercy, which he has prepared beforehand for glory—even us whom he has called, not from the Jews only but also from the Gentiles?" (Rom. 9:22–24).

To Israel God gave the adoption, the glory, the covenants, the law, the worship, the promises, the patriarchs, and the Messiah (Rom. 9:4–5). But if, after receiving so much, the nation was unable to live for God, how much more would the rest of humanity stand culpable before God and in need of a Savior, having never received the law.

6. For more on reading Deuteronomy 30:11–14 as *future*, see Steven R. Coxhead, "Deuteronomy 30:11–14 as a Prophecy of the New Covenant in Christ," *WTJ* 68, 2 (2006): 305–20.

> Now we know that whatever the law says it speaks to those who are under the law, so that every mouth may be stopped, and the whole world may be held accountable to God. For by works of the law no human being will be justified in his sight, since through the law comes knowledge of sin. But now the righteousness of God has been manifested apart from the law, although the Law and the Prophets bear witness to it—the righteousness of God through faith in Jesus Christ for all who believe. (Rom. 3:19–22)

When we read that salvation grounded Israel's calling, we must not equate it with the salvation that we enjoy today. The exodus served as a type of the second exodus that was accomplished in Christ. The first exodus was but a picture of, a predictive pointer to, the more ultimate deliverance that Jesus accomplishes on behalf of his elect.

2. Missiology—A Subset of Ecclesiology

Back in chapter 6, I summarized the main idea of Exodus 19:4–6: "In response to God's gracious redemption, the Lord calls his people to a God-exalting task of mediating and displaying his greatness and worth to the world through radical God-centered living." Israel's God-honoring calling is the central thrust of the passage. We must ask, however, how this task relates to the church's great commission that Jesus gave after his resurrection (Matt. 28:18–20). Did old covenant Israel bear a mission to cross-culturally evangelize the lost as Christians do in the new covenant?

There is very little potential support from the Old Testament that within the old covenant period Israel bore a normative responsibility to be a "go and tell" people, seeking the conversion of the nations. Certainly Exodus 12 clarified how a resident alien or "sojourner" (גֵּר) could become like a native-born Israelite and thus be freed to partake in the nation's various holy days (Ex. 12:43–49). This "mixed multitude" (12:38), however, was still counted as the single nation of Israel (12:19, 48). Similarly, within the framework of Israel's history, people such as Rahab the Canaanite, Ruth the Moabite, and Uriah the Hittite could, by their own choosing, become Israelites. Yet even so, Abraham was still considered the father of a single nation. The shift to his being "the father of a multitude of nations" (Gen. 17:4–5) would come only when the single, male deliverer would rise, overcoming enemy powers and reversing the Adamic curse: "And your offspring shall possess the gate of his enemies, and in your offspring shall all the nations of the earth be blessed" (22:17b–18; cf. 3:15; 24:60). It was in his day alone "that repentance and forgiveness of sins should be proclaimed in his name to all nations, beginning from Jerusalem" (Luke 25:47; cf. Acts 3:25–26; Gal. 3:8, 14, 16, 29).

Not even in the book of Jonah do we find evidence of a normative mandate for global missions in the old covenant period. Jonah's prophetic role was first not to convert the Ninevites but to "call out against" them, declaring to them that they had sinned against YHWH and warning them of punishment (Jonah 1:2). Many prophets wrote oracles against the nations (e.g., Isa. 13–23; Jer. 46–51; Ezek. 25–32; Obad. 1–21; Zeph. 2:5–3:7), but Jonah is the only one we know of who confronted a foreign power directly. YHWH would later declare through Jeremiah, "If at any time I declare concerning a nation or a kingdom, that I will pluck up and break down and destroy it, and if that nation, concerning which I have spoken, turns from its evil, I will relent of the disaster that I intended to do to it" (Jer. 18:7–8). Jonah says that the reason he fled to Tarshish was that he "knew that you are a gracious God and merciful, slow to anger and abounding in steadfast love, and relenting from disaster" (Jonah 4:2). The prophet of YHWH did not like the character of YHWH. Certainly the book of Jonah reminds the reader that Israel's long-range mission through its Messiah would be to see the curse against all the families of the earth overcome by divine blessing (Gen. 22:18; cf. 12:3 with 10:32, where the ESV's "clans" is the same word for "families"). Yet the book focuses not on the need to evangelize our neighbors but on the proper disposition that God's people are to maintain toward YHWH and his world. Jonah delighted in God's mercy so long as he was its recipient, but he did not celebrate seeing this mercy extended to those outside Israel.

YHWH is both right and committed to bestow mercy on whomever he wills (Ex. 33:19; Rom. 9:15), and he calls his people to celebrate that he is this kind of God. He also promised that his anointed king and his followers would proclaim his glories to the nations. As Paul notes, quoting Psalm 18:49 and 117:1, "Christ became a servant to the circumcised to show God's truthfulness, in order . . . that the Gentiles might glorify God for his mercy. As it is written, 'Therefore I will praise you among the Gentiles, and sing to your name.' . . . And again, 'Praise the Lord, all you Gentiles, and let all the peoples extol him'" (Rom. 15:8–9, 11; cf. Pss. 9:11[H12]; 66:8; 96:3, 8). Similarly, speaking of the time when "the nations [will] inquire" of the royal servant and when "the Lord will extend his hand yet a second time to recover the remnant that remains of his people" (Isa. 11:10–11), Isaiah declared that "in that day" the redeemed will say, "Give thanks to the LORD, call upon his name, make known his deeds among the peoples, proclaim that his name is exalted" (12:4). Nevertheless, I am not aware of texts within the old covenant itself that called Israel to urge the nations to respond to the news of global salvation.

Instead, the Israelites were to live in their land as mediators of God's tabernacling greatness. By their encountering his presence at the temple/tabernacle (Ex. 33:16), reverent fear would be generated that would lead to holiness (20:20). And by heeding his voice, keeping his covenant, and existing as his treasured possession, Israel would serve as a God-exalting witness in the midst of the world (19:5–6). The people's righteous lives would attract the nations to YHWH's uniqueness as those outside saw their righteous deeds and were directed to YHWH's wonders. Thus Deuteronomy 4:6–8 asserted:

> Keep . . . and do [the statutes and rules], for that will be your wisdom and your understanding in the sight of the peoples, who, when they hear all these statutes, will say, "Surely this great nation is a wise and understanding people." For what great nation is there that has a god so near to it as the LORD our God is to us, whenever we call upon him? And what great nation is there, that has statutes and rules so righteous as all this law that I set before you today?

There was expectation within the old covenant that foreigners from faraway lands would hear of YHWH's fame, come to the temple and pray toward to the God of heaven, and receive their requests "in order that all the peoples of the earth may know your name and fear you" (1 Kings 8:41–43). Evidence that this pattern actually happened is minimal, but we do see it in 1 Kings 10 when the queen of Sheba journeys to Jerusalem and YHWH's temple because she has "heard of the fame of Solomon concerning the name of the LORD" (10:1). When she saw the glories of Solomon and of YHWH's house, "there was no more breath in her" (10:5), and she declared, "Blessed be the LORD your God, who has delighted in you and set you on the throne of Israel! Because the LORD loved Israel forever, he has made you king" (10:9).

What is important to recognize is that once Israel arrived into the Promised Land, the old covenant focused attention on Jerusalem, its temple, and its king. YHWH's call for Israel to be a God-honoring witness was *not* a directive to evangelize her neighbors but was a summons for Israel to live in a way so that others would want to *come and see.*

In the days of the Old Testament, the gospel of the kingdom was still only a *future* hope and not a present reality. Isaiah 40–66 stresses this very point when it highlights the salvation-historical shift from a hope for good news to the intrusion of good news through the messianic servant. YHWH would give comfort to his despondent Jerusalem (Isa. 40:1–3; cf. Matt. 3:3; Mark 1:3; Luke 3:4; John 1:23) through the news of the herald who proclaims, "Behold your God!" (40:9). Only in this future day, now realized in Christ, does the messenger "publish peace" and "salvation," declaring the "good news" that "your God reigns" (52:7). And the one leading the global testimony is the royal deliverer himself, who declares, "The Spirit of the Lord GOD is upon me, because the LORD has anointed me to bring good news to the poor; he has sent me to bind up the brokenhearted, to proclaim liberty to the captives, and the opening of the prison to those who are bound; to proclaim the year of the LORD's favor, and the day of vengeance of our God" (61:1–2; cf. 11:2–5; Luke 4:18–19).

Within the old covenant, YHWH called his servant nation Israel to live in a way that pointed to the Lord's greatness in the midst of the world. By God-dependent obedience the Israelites would serve as a kingdom of priests and a holy nation (Ex. 19:5–6), attracting other nations to come and see the display of YHWH's glory in and through his people. But the old covenant law could only clarify what Israel *ought* to do; it could not empower her to do it (Rom. 8:3) (for more on this, see "Old Testament Law and the Christian" in chapter 12). Thus, the Israelites failed miserably at representing YHWH's worth, and this sin ultimately resulted in their misrepresenting God's name among the nations (Ezek. 36:20). But stage 1 of the Abrahamic covenant (i.e., the Mosaic covenant) was never portrayed as the end of God's kingdom-building purposes (see "An Example of Text Grammar—Genesis 12:1–3" in chapter 5). Indeed, YHWH predicted the rise of an obedient son who would "be a blessing" perfectly, and through this open the door for "all the families of the ground" to be blessed (Gen. 12:2–3, author's translation; cf. 22:17b–18).

The old covenant remnant longed for the day when God's individual servant—the royal representative king—would succeed through his priestly obedience unto death (Isa. 52:13–53:12; 55:3). Not only this, he would go beyond what the Israelites themselves were ever called to by fulfilling that for which they and the world hoped—through him the nations would enjoy God's blessing (cf. Ps. 72:17). The servant's atoning work would open the door for the salvation of all who believe from both Jews and Gentiles, and he would establish a new covenant that would include light, law, and justice for the nations (Isa. 42:1, 6; 49:6, 8; 51:4–5). The individual servant's work would birth multiple servants who would carry out his redemptive purposes. Ultimately, fulfilling the promise of Isaiah 49:6, the individual royal servant "[Christ] would proclaim light" and salvation to both Jews and Gentiles (Acts 26:23) *through* his commissioned servants (13:47), as the gospel message of the beautiful one (Isa. 52:7) would become the gospel message of the beautiful ones (Rom. 10:15).

In summary, the nation of Israel's old covenant call to be a kingdom of priests addressed only the immediate witness of the people's lives and not an intentional outward evangelistic proclamation of the gospel. The old covenant community was simply to urge others to "come and see" by the testimony of their surrendered lives, as they enjoyed the sustained presence of God at the temple.

Christ's coming marks a salvation-historical shift from a "come and see" to a "come and see and *go and tell*" community. As for the "come and see" element, the church is now empowered to stand as a kingdom of priests and a holy nation, faithfully (though imperfectly) proclaiming "the excellencies of him who called [us] out of darkness into his marvelous light" (1 Peter 2:9). With God's help, we heed the call, "Let your light shine before others, so that they may see your good works and give glory to your Father who is in heaven" (Matt. 5:16). We bear the fruits of the Spirit in our daily lives (Gal. 5:22–23), and we seek "to maintain the unity of the Spirit in the bond of peace" (Eph. 4:3; cf. 4:13; 1 Peter 3:8).

Furthermore, enjoying Christ's tabernacling presence (John 1:14; cf. 2:21) by his Spirit (Acts 1:8), the church as God's temple (1 Cor. 3:16; 2 Cor. 6:16) has now expanded to fill the whole earth (Acts 13:47; Col. 1:23). Worship is no longer localized in one geographical place (John 4:20–24) because Jesus' "kingdom is not from the world" (18:36). Now the church is bearing witness to Christ from "Jerusalem and in all Judea and Samaria, and to the end of the earth" (Acts 1:8), proclaiming the good news that the reigning God saves and satisfies believing sinners through Christ Jesus' life, death, and resurrection. This "gospel" is of first importance (1 Cor. 15:3–5), and its proclamation marks the "go and tell" element that is new to the new covenant. The divine presence of the heavenly Jerusalem (Gal. 4:26; Heb. 12:22) is more accessible to the world than ever before, for it is not localized in a building but embodied in the lives of a new covenant community that has spread out to every corner of the globe (Isa. 2:1–4; Jer. 3:16–18). As the gospel advances, the church grows, with peoples from every tribe and language and people and nation being gathered into the one people of God, who together have become "a kingdom and priests to our God" and who together "shall reign on the earth" (Rev. 5:9–10). Because Christ now enjoys all authority in heaven and on earth, we are commissioned to make new covenant disciples not only within our own families and neighborhoods but also across cultures among the nations. Others will not know unless they are told (Rom. 10:13–15), so we live and we evangelize for the fame of God's name in Christ.[7]

Ecclesiology and Eschatology in Zephaniah 3:9–10

YHWH declares in Zephaniah 3:9–10: "For at that time I will change the speech of the peoples to a pure speech, that all of them may call upon the name of the LORD and serve him with one accord. From beyond the rivers of Cush my worshipers, the daughter of my dispersed ones, shall bring my offering." In the previous verse, YHWH had commanded the believing remnant in Judah to continue waiting on him in faith, looking through to the day-of-the-Lord judgment in hope. Verses 9–10 then provide one of the reasons why they must persist in their Godward trust.

On the very day of his judicial sentencing of the world ("at that time," Zeph. 1:9) the Lord will cleanse the surviving peoples' "speech" (שָׂפָה), which the LXX renders γλῶσσα ("tongue"). This speech transformation will in turn generate a unified profession that will result in a unified service: they will "call upon the name of the LORD and serve him with one accord" (Zeph. 3:9; cf. Rev. 7:9–10). The imagery of speech purification implies the overturning of judgment (Ps. 55:9[H10]) and likely alludes to a reversal of the Tower of Babel episode, in which a communal pride against God resulted in his confusing "language/speech" and his "dispersing" the rebels across the globe (Gen. 11:7, 9). To call on the name of YHWH is to outwardly express worshipful dependence on him as the Sovereign, Savior, and Satisfier (Ps. 116:4, 13, 17). In Joel 2 the prophet similarly connected this phenomenon with the day of the Lord (Joel 2:28–32[H3:1–5]).

"Cush" was ancient Ethiopia, the center of black Africa and located in modern Sudan. Its rivers were likely the White and Blue Nile (see Isa. 18:1–2). As if following the rivers of life back up to the garden of Eden for fellowship with the great King (Gen. 2:13; cf. Rev. 22:1–2), the prophet envisions that even the most distant lands on which the

7. John Piper rightly notes how, in God's providence, the use of Hebrew in the Old Testament and Greek in the New Testament contributed to the distinctions in witness and mission between the old and new covenants (*Let the Nations Be Glad: The Supremacy of God in Missions*, 3rd ed. [Grand Rapids: Baker Academic, 2010], 29–30). The mere fact that the Old Testament was written in Hebrew, a Canaanite dialect, limited the scope of its message, for Israel was the only people group in the ancient Near East that used it as their primary language (known in Scripture as "the language of Canaan" [Isa. 19:18] or "the language of Judah" [2 Kings 18:26, 28 = Isa. 36:13 = 2 Chron. 32:18; Isa. 36:11; Neh. 13:24). In contrast, God purposed that the New Testament be written in Greek, the common language of the day, so that its message could be spread throughout the entire Roman Empire.

Lord has poured his wrath (Zeph. 2:11–12) will have a remnant of "worshipers" whom God's presence will compel to Jerusalem. Those gathered before God's presence would be a worldwide, multiethnic community descending from the seventy families that the Lord once "dispersed" in judgment at Babel after the flood (Gen. 11:8–9). Indeed, even some from Cush, Zephaniah's own heritage (Zeph. 1:1), would gain new birth certificates declaring that they were born in Zion (Ps. 87:4).

As we assess this text from the perspective of systematic theology, I believe it informs both our eschatology and ecclesiology. As for the doctrine of the last things, Zephaniah envisions that the new creation community will be born "at that time" (Zeph. 3:9) when God rises as Judge and executes his punishment on the world (3:8). What is significant here is that the New Testament authors view Jesus' death to be an intrusion of the future judgment on behalf of the elect, and that therefore his resurrection already inaugurates the new creation: "Since, therefore, we have now been justified by his blood, much more shall we be saved by him from the wrath of God" (Rom. 5:9). "If anyone is in Christ, he is a new creation. The old has passed away; behold, the new has come. . . . For our sake [God] made [Christ] to be sin who knew no sin, so that in him we might become the righteousness of God" (2 Cor. 5:17, 21).

With respect to the doctrine of the church, Zephaniah speaks to both the disposition and international makeup of a community that will be preserved through judgment. If Jesus has already borne the day-of-the-Lord judgment anticipated in 3:8, it seems likely that the multiethnic community of worshipers he describes in 3:9–10 is indeed the church of Christ Jesus. Certainly the depiction fulfills the hopes of the Abrahamic covenant (Gen. 12:3), and it finds support in the way in which the New Testament sees the messianic new covenant community to be made up of Jews and Gentiles in Christ who are now one flock (John 10:16; cf. 11:51–52; 12:19–20), a single olive tree (Rom. 11:17–24), and one new man (Eph. 2:11–22).

In support of this view is the way in which Luke describes the beginnings of the church at Pentecost. The outpouring of the Spirit of Christ on the saints in Jerusalem inaugurated the change of speech and unity that Zephaniah predicted (Zeph. 3:9–10). Not only does the early church speak in new "tongues" (fem. pl. of γλῶσσα) (Acts 2:4, 11; cf. 10:46; 19:6), but its people also call on the name of Lord Jesus (2:21, 38) and devote themselves together "to the apostles' teaching and the fellowship, to the breaking of bread and the prayers" (2:42). Through Christ's atoning death, the blessing of God moves from "Jerusalem . . . to the end of the earth" (1:8; cf. Luke 24:47), reaching even into ancient Ethiopia/Cush, as the story of the Ethiopian eunuch testifies (Acts 8:26–40).

Now bringing together eschatology and ecclesiology, we can mark initial fulfillment of Zephaniah's hopes and say that already the Lord is shaping "a kingdom and priests" "from every tribe and language and people and nation" (Rev. 5:9–10; cf. 7:9–10). To this we can add that already as priests we are offering sacrifices of praise (Rom. 12:1; Heb. 13:15–16; 1 Peter 2:5) at "Mount Zion and . . . the city of the living God, the heavenly Jerusalem" (Heb. 12:22; cf. Isa. 2:2–3; Zech. 8:20–23). Nevertheless, we are still awaiting the day when "the holy city, new Jerusalem," will descend from heaven as the new earth (Rev. 21:2) and when our daily journey to find rest in Christ's supremacy and sufficiency (Matt. 11:28–29; John 6:35) will be consummated in a place where the curse is no more (Rev. 21:24–22:5; cf. Isa. 60:3; Heb. 4:1, 9–11). Thus I believe that we can see Zephaniah's prophetic prediction already being fulfilled today in the church of Jesus, even as we the saints await its full realization.

Key Words and Concepts

Systematic theology
Gospel
Theological triage

Questions for Further Reflection

1. What general question does systematic theology answer, and what specific question do we ask when relating a specific passage's teaching to systematic theology?
2. Draw figure 11.2, "Theological Triage," on a separate piece of paper. Take five minutes to classify as many doctrines as you can, fitting each within one of these tiers. Prayerfully consider your selection. What is the danger of placing a doctrine in the wrong slot? Defend any placements that you consider controversial. Now acquire a copy of your church's statement of faith, and assess whether your own theological tradition has chosen to major on level 1, 2, or 3 doctrines.
3. Using figure 11.3, what are the differences between systematic and biblical theology?
4. Why is prayer so vitally important when trying to understand biblical truth?
5. Using one of the two sample passages in this chapter, show how the text contributes to a larger doctrine.

Resources for Further Study

Bavinck, Herman. *Reformed Dogmatics*. Edited by John Bolt. Translated by John Vriend. 4 vols. Grand Rapids: Baker Academic, 2003–8.

Berkhof, Louis. *Systematic Theology*. 4th ed. Grand Rapids: Eerdmans, 1938.

The Bethlehem Baptist Church *Elder Affirmation of Faith*. Minneapolis: Bethlehem Baptist Church, 2003. http://www.hopeingod.org/document/elder-affirmation-faith.

Bird, Michael F. *Evangelical Theology: A Biblical and Systematic Introduction*. Grand Rapids: Zondervan, 2013.

Bloesch, Donald G. Christian Foundations. 7 vols. Downers Grove, IL: InterVarsity Press, 1992–2009.

Bray, Gerald, ed. Contours of Christian Theology. 8 vols. Downers Grove, IL: InterVarsity Press, 1993–2002.

- Bray, Gerald. *The Doctrine of God*. 1993.
- Letham, Robert. *The Work of Christ*. 1993.

- Helm, Paul. *The Providence of God*. 1994.
- Clowney, Edmund P. *The Church*. 1995.
- Ferguson, Sinclair B. *The Holy Spirit*. 1996.
- Sherlock, Charles. *The Doctrine of Humanity*. 1996.
- Macleod, Donald. *The Person of Christ*. 1998.
- Jensen, Peter. *The Revelation of God*. 2002.

———. *God Is Love: A Biblical and Systematic Theology*. Wheaton, IL: Crossway, 2012.

Calvin, John. *Institutes of the Christian Religion*. Edited by John T. McNeill. Translated by Ford Lewis Battles. 2 vols. Library of Christian Classics. Philadelphia: Westminster, 1960.

Carson, D. A. "The Bible and Theology." In *NIV Zondervan Study Bible*, edited by D. A. Carson, 2633–36. Grand Rapids: Zondervan, 2015.

———. *Christ and Culture Revisited*. Grand Rapids: Eerdmans, 2007.

———. "Logical Fallacies." In *Exegetical Fallacies*, 87–123. 2nd ed. Grand Rapids: Baker Academic, 1996.

———. "Systematic Theology and Biblical Theology." *NDBT* 89–104.

Carson, D. A., and Timothy Keller, eds. *The Gospel as Center: Renewing Our Faith and Reforming Our Ministry Practices*. Wheaton, IL: Crossway, 2012. Unpacks The Gospel Coalition's "Confessional Statement" (http://www.thegospelcoalition.org/about/foundation-documents/confessional-statement).

Carter, Charles W. *A Contemporary Wesleyan Theology: Biblical, Systematic, and Practical*. 2 vols. Grand Rapids: Francis Asbury, 1983.

Chafer, Lewis Sperry. *Systematic Theology*. 8 vols. Grand Rapids: Kregel, 1948.

Davis, John Jefferson. *Handbook of Basic Bible Texts: Every Key Passage for the Study of Doctrine and Theology*. Grand Rapids: Zondervan, 1984.

———. *Theology Primer: Resources for the Theological Student*. Grand Rapids: Baker, 1981.

Elwell, Walter A., ed. *Evangelical Dictionary of Theology*. 2nd ed. Grand Rapids: Baker Academic, 2001.

Erickson, Millard J. *Christian Theology*. 3rd ed. Grand Rapids: Baker Academic, 2013.

Feinberg, John S., ed. Foundations of Evangelical Theology. Wheaton, IL: Crossway, 1997–present.

- Demarest, Bruce. *The Cross and Salvation: The Doctrine of Salvation*. 1997.
- Feinberg, John S. *No One like Him: The Doctrine of God*. 2001.
- Clark, David K. *To Know and Love God: Method for Theology*. 2003.
- Cole, Graham A. *He Who Gives Life: The Doctrine of the Holy Spirit*. 2007.
- Allison, Gregg R. *Sojourners and Strangers: The Doctrine of the Church*. 2012.
- Wellum, Stephen J. Forthcoming on Christology.
- McCall, Tom. Forthcoming on Sin.
- VanGemeren, Willem. Forthcoming on Eschatology.

Frame, John M. *Apologetics: A Justification of Christian Belief*. Edited by Joseph E. Torres. 2nd ed. Phillipsburg, NJ: P&R Publishing, 2015.

———. *Salvation Belongs to the Lord: An Introduction to Systematic Theology.* Phillipsburg, NJ: P&R Publishing, 2006.

✪ ———. *Systematic Theology: An Introduction to Christian Belief.* Phillipsburg, NJ: P&R Publishing, 2013.

Gaffin, Richard B. "Systematic Theology and Biblical Theology." *WTJ* 38, 3 (1976): 281–99.

Geisler, Norman L. *Systematic Theology: In One Volume.* Minneapolis: Bethany House, 2011.

Green, Joel B., and Max Turner, eds. *Between Two Horizons: Spanning New Testament Studies and Systematic Theology.* Grand Rapids: Eerdmans, 2000.

Grudem, Wayne A. *Bible Doctrine: Essential Teachings of the Christian Faith.* Edited by Jeff Purswell. Grand Rapids: Zondervan, 1999.

———. *Christian Beliefs: Twenty Basics Every Christian Should Know.* Edited by Elliot Grudem. Grand Rapids: Zondervan, 2005.

★ ———. *Systematic Theology: An Introduction to Biblical Doctrine.* Grand Rapids: Zondervan, 1994.

Hasel, Gerhard F. "The Relationship between Biblical Theology and Systematic Theology." *TJ* 5, 2 (1984): 113–27.

Hodge, Charles. *Systematic Theology.* 3 vols. New York: Scribner's, 1887; repr., Peabody, MA: Hendrickson, 1999.

✪ Horton, Michael. *The Christian Faith: A Systematic Theology for Pilgrims on the Way.* Grand Rapids: Zondervan, 2011.

★ ———. *Pilgrim Theology: Core Doctrines for Christian Disciples.* Grand Rapids: Zondervan, 2013.

Lints, Richard. *The Fabric of Theology: A Prolegomenon to Evangelical Theology.* Grand Rapids: Eerdmans, 1993.

MacArthur, John, and Richard Mayhue, eds. *Biblical Doctrine: A Systematic Summary of Bible Truth.* Wheaton, IL: Crossway, 2017.

McCune, Rolland. *A Systematic Theology of Biblical Christianity.* 3 vols. Allen Park, MI: Detroit Baptist Theological Seminary, 2009–10.

McGrath, Alister E. *Christian Theology: An Introduction.* 5th ed. Malden, MA: Wiley-Blackwell, 2011.

Oden, Thomas C. *Classic Christianity: A Systematic Theology.* 2nd ed. New York: HarperOne, 2009.

Packer, J. I. *Concise Theology: A Guide to Historic Christian Beliefs.* Wheaton, IL: Tyndale House, 1995.

Ryrie, Charles C. *Basic Theology: A Popular Systematic Guide to Understanding Biblical Truth.* 2nd ed. Chicago: Moody, 1999.

Thiselton, Anthony C. *Systematic Theology.* Grand Rapids: Eerdmans, 2015.

Weston, Anthony. *A Rulebook for Arguments.* 4th ed. Indianapolis: Hackett, 2008.

Wiley, H. Orton. *Christian Theology.* 5th ed. 3 vols. Kansas City: Beacon Hill, 1940.

PART 5

APPLICATION—"WHY DOES THE PASSAGE MATTER?"

12

PRACTICAL THEOLOGY

Goal: Apply the text to yourself, the church, and the world, stressing the centrality of Christ and the hope of the gospel.

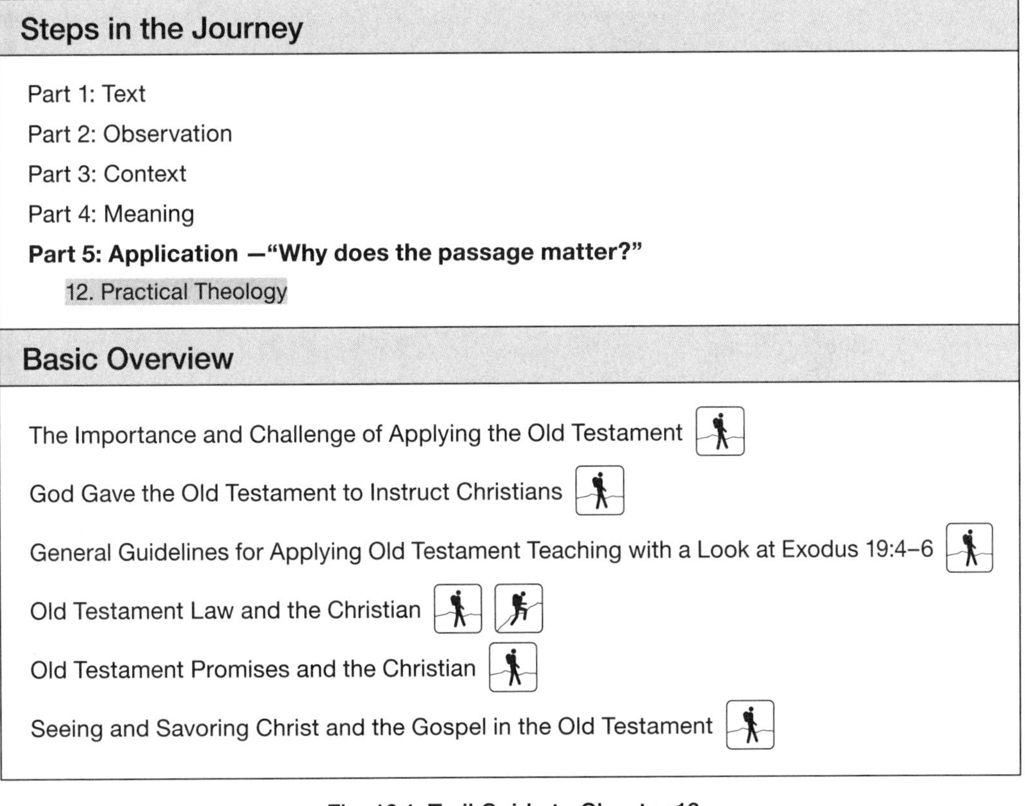

Steps in the Journey

Part 1: Text
Part 2: Observation
Part 3: Context
Part 4: Meaning
Part 5: Application —"Why does the passage matter?"
12. Practical Theology

Basic Overview

The Importance and Challenge of Applying the Old Testament
God Gave the Old Testament to Instruct Christians
General Guidelines for Applying Old Testament Teaching with a Look at Exodus 19:4–6
Old Testament Law and the Christian
Old Testament Promises and the Christian
Seeing and Savoring Christ and the Gospel in the Old Testament

Fig. 12.1. Trail Guide to Chapter 12

The Importance and Challenge of Applying the Old Testament

Before the priest-scribe Ezra ever set his heart to teach God's Word, he first studied the Word and *practiced* it (Ezra 7:10). That is, he first set himself to observe what was there in the text, to understand it rightly, and to evaluate it fairly. Then, having studied, he sought to feel appropriately in accordance with the nature of the truth that was studied and to act—to act in dependence, in submission, in obedience, following and treasuring God in accordance with his worth and instruction disclosed in the Book.

We have come to the last stage in the interpretive process before actually heralding the Word. Having exegeted the text and grasped God's intended meaning, we now endeavor to do ***practical theology***, seeking to capture in our own lives and the lives of others the author's intended effect.

When it comes to applying the Old Testament, we are faced with a dilemma: that the Old Testament was written in the context of the old covenant, yet we as Christians are part of the new covenant. The challenge is to discern rightly how Christians are to relate with and respond to Old Testament instructions and Old Testament promises. Are we to obey the laws of the old covenant? Are we to claim old covenant blessings and curses as relevant today? These are difficult questions, but we must engage them if we are to shape Christian practical theology from the Old Testament.

In the coming sections, I intend to summarize a Christian's approach to applying the Old Testament. Naturally, this will require a lot of biblical theology, and it is your responsibility to be like those in Berea and "examine the Scriptures" to see whether my assertions are correct (Acts 17:11)—to be like Timothy and "think over" what I say, trusting that the Lord will give you understanding in everything (2 Tim. 2:7).

God Gave the Old Testament to Instruct Christians

I first want to highlight a number of texts that stress that God gave the Old Testament to instruct *Christians*. Indeed, as we will see, even the Old Testament prophets understood that what they were writing in the Old Testament was often less for their contemporaries and more for us, living on this side of the cross.

1. New Testament Reflections on the Main Audience of Old Testament Instruction

Paul believed that God gave the Old Testament for *new* covenant believers. Referring to the statement in Genesis 15:6 that Abram's faith was "counted to him as righteousness," Paul asserted that "the words 'it was counted to him' were *not written for his sake alone, but for ours also*" (Rom. 4:23–24). Similarly, just after identifying Christ as the referent in Psalm 69, the apostle emphasized, "For *whatever was written in former days was written for our instruction*, that through endurance and through the encouragement of the Scriptures we might have hope" (15:4). Finally, upon recalling Israel's history in the wilderness, Paul said, "Now these things happened to them as an example, but *they were written down for our instruction*, on whom the end of the ages has come" (1 Cor. 10:11). Paul's point in these three texts was that at least part of the divine purpose in giving the Old Testament was to teach and guide those living on this side of the cross.

Peter says more:

> Concerning this salvation, the prophets who prophesied about the grace that was to be yours searched and inquired carefully, inquiring what person or time the Spirit of Christ in them was indicating when he predicted the sufferings of Christ and the subsequent glories. It was revealed *to them* that they were serving not themselves but you, in the things that have now been announced to you through those who preached the good news to you by the Holy Spirit sent from heaven, things into which angels long to look. (1 Peter 1:10–12)

Peter emphasizes that the inspired authors themselves knew that their words revealed in the Old Testament were principally for us, not them. Therefore, far from being not applicable for believers, the Old Testament is actually *more relevant* to Christians today than it was for the majority in the old covenant. Let's consider a number of texts. We will look at quotations from Moses, Isaiah, Jeremiah, and Daniel.

2. Old Testament Reflections on the Main Audience of Old Testament Instruction

First, Moses' three favorite words to characterize Israel were "stubborn" (Deut. 9:6, 13; 10:16; 31:27), "unbelieving" (1:32; 9:23; cf. 28:66), and "rebellious" (9:7, 24; 31:27; cf. 1:26, 43; 9:23). His audience was wicked (9:4–6, 27), and God promised that after the prophet's death, the people's defiance would only continue: "This people will rise and whore after the foreign gods among them in the land that they are entering, and they will forsake me and break my covenant that I have made with them" (31:16). This God-hostility would result in God's pouring out his covenant curses on them (31:17, 29; cf. 28:15–68). Deuteronomy 29:4[H3] tells us that God did not give Moses' generation "a heart to understand or eyes to see or ears to hear." And he would not overcome their crookedness and twistedness (Deut. 32:5; Acts 2:40; Phil. 2:15) until the prophet like Moses would rise to whom we are told they would listen (Deut. 18:5; cf. Matt. 17:5). In the age of restoration, God would change the remnant's hearts and enable their love: "The Lord your God will circumcise your heart . . . so that you will love the Lord your God with all" (Deut. 30:6). In this day, the day we now identify with the new covenant and church age (cf. Rom. 2:29; 2 Cor. 3:6), Moses' message in Deuteronomy would finally be heard and heeded: "And you will turn and you will hear the voice of the Lord and do all his commandments that I am commanding you today" (Deut. 30:8, author's translation).

Second, Israel's spiritual disability was apparent in the days of Isaiah, who was called to preach, "Keep on hearing, but do not understand; keep on seeing, but do not perceive" (Isa. 6:9). YHWH chose to let Israel's history be characterized by "deep sleep" and the inability to "read" the Word; it was as though the Bible were a sealed book to them. Isaiah writes in 29:9–11:

> Astonish yourselves and be astonished;
>   blind yourselves and be blind!
> . . . .
> For the Lord has poured out upon you
>   a spirit of deep sleep,
> and has closed your eyes (the prophets),
>   and covered your heads (the seers).
>
> And the vision of all this has become to you like the words of a book that is sealed. When men give it to one who can read, saying, "Read this," he says, "I cannot, for it is sealed."

Isaiah's audience could not fully understand God's Word. Nevertheless, YHWH promised a day when "the deaf shall hear the words of a book, and . . . the eyes of the blind see" (Isa. 29:18). Because God instructed Isaiah to write his words in a book for a perpetual witness, because his own audience could not grasp these words, his book-writing was principally for the later generation that would have eyes to see: "And now, go, write it before them on a tablet and inscribe it in a book, that it may be for the time to come as a witness forever" (30:8). These future generations would all "be taught by the Lord" (54:13), which Jesus stressed God was fulfilling in drawing people to him (John 6:44–45). To these would be given "the secret of the kingdom of God, but for those outside everything is in parables, so that 'they may indeed see but not perceive, and may indeed hear but not understand, lest they should turn and be forgiven'" (Mark 4:11–12, quoting Isa. 6:9–10).

Third, YHWH told Jeremiah that his writing was specifically intended for the restored community of God: "Thus says the Lord, the God of Israel: Write in a book all the words that I have spoken to you. *For* [כִּי] behold, days are coming, declares the Lord, when I will restore the fortunes of my people, Israel and Judah, says the Lord, and I will bring them back to the land that I gave to their fathers, and they shall take possession of it" (Jer. 30:2–3). Jeremiah needed to write his words in a book because the future generations would need them. He further notes that only in the latter days would they truly comprehend what he was writing: "The fierce anger of the Lord will not turn back until he has executed and accomplished the intentions of his mind. *In the latter days you will understand this*. 'At that time, declares the LORD, I will be the God of all the clans of Israel, and they shall be my people'" (Jer. 30:24–31:1). The repetition of the last clause in 31:33 shows that the "latter days" are none other than those associated with the new covenant, the age of the church: "For this is the [new] covenant that I will make with the house of Israel after those days, declares the LORD: I will put my law within them, and I will write it on their hearts. And I will be their God, and they shall be my people" (31:33). In this day, the forgiveness of all in the covenant would mean that "no longer shall each one teach his neighbor and each his brother, saying, 'Know the LORD,' for they shall all know me, from the least of them to the greatest" (31:34). In Jeremiah, knowledge of God relates to an experiential involvement in the Lord's commitment to steadfast love, justice, and righteousness (9:24; 22:15–16). John stresses how this knowledge is enjoyed by *all* who are in Christ (1 John 2:20–21, 27–29).

Fourth, God told Daniel that all the kingdom revelation that he received he was to seal up in a book until the appointed time of disclosure to the wise:

> But you, Daniel, shut up the words and seal the book, until the time of the end. Many shall run to and fro, and knowledge shall increase. . . . Go your way, Daniel, for the words are shut up and sealed until the time of the end. Many shall purify themselves and make themselves white and be refined, but the wicked shall act wickedly. And none of the wicked shall understand, but those who are wise shall understand. (Dan. 12:4, 9–10)

Daniel envisioned that only at "the time of the end," which the Old Greek in the rest of Daniel describes as the last "hour" (Dan. 8:17, 19; 10:14; 11:35, 40; 12:1), would people grasp the meaning of his revelations regarding God's kingdom. From a New Testament perspective, the first coming of Christ has inaugurated this period of eschatological realization (see Mark 13:11; John 4:23; 5:25; 12:23; 16:32; 17:1; 1 John 2:18; cf. Acts 2:17; 1 Cor. 10:11; Heb. 1:2; 9:26; 1 Peter 1:20).[1]

These Old Testament texts from Deuteronomy, Isaiah, Jeremiah, and Daniel all suggest that the Old Testament prophets knew that the rebel majority would neither hear nor heed their messages. They were able to physically hear and read the words, but something in their own hearts caused them to not encounter God through them. They were hardened, and because of this, they didn't grieve over their sins; they didn't feel the need to hope in the Messiah; they didn't long to encounter God's glory and kingdom. God's Word remained distant.

This is partly what Paul meant in Romans 11:25 when he said, "I do not want you to be unaware of this mystery, brothers: a partial hardening has come upon Israel, until the fullness of the Gentiles has come in." God purposed that a proper interpretation of the Old Testament would come only through the revelation of Jesus, and those who fail to embrace Christ will ever fail to grasp the message of the Old Testament fully (2 Cor. 3:14).

1. See G. K. Beale, "The Old Testament Background of the 'Last Hour' in 1 John 2,18," *Bib* 92, 2 (2011): 231–54.

3. New Testament Reflections on Christ as the Key to Understanding the Old Testament

God closed off the message of the Old Testament itself from the majority of those in the old covenant. This blindness continued forward into the days of Christ. Jesus' audience failed to "see" and grasp the significance of his coming. As Jesus asserted to the religious leaders, "You search the Scriptures because you think that in them you have eternal life; and it is they that bear witness about me, yet you refuse to come to me that you may have life" (John 5:39–40).

In Romans 11:7–8, Paul brings together Isaiah 29:9–12 and the "unto this day" of Deuteronomy 29:4[H3], highlighting the sustained deafness of his people: "Israel failed to obtain what it was seeking. The elect obtained it, but the rest were hardened, as it is written, 'God gave them a spirit of stupor, eyes that would not see and ears that would not hear, down to this very day.'" God hardened generations of Israelites in order that we today might magnify all the more the mercy and majesty of Christ: "What if God, desiring to show his wrath and to make known his power, has endured with much patience vessels of wrath prepared for destruction, in order to make known the riches of his glory for vessels of mercy, which he has prepared beforehand for glory" (Rom. 9:22–23).

Israel's spiritual blindness and deafness would be healed only through Jesus. "The [Jews'] minds were hardened. For to this day, when they read the old covenant, that same veil remains unlifted, because only through Christ is it taken away" (2 Cor. 3:14). In 2 Corinthians 3, Moses' veil that he wore after encountering the divine presence served as a parable of the people's spiritual hardness. Apart from Jesus, the Jews could not fully see and savor the beauty of God in the Old Testament, but with the coming of Christ, the veil is lifted and the glory that was always there is now revealed.

This is what I believe Paul means in Romans 16:25–26 when he speaks of the mystery of the gospel of Christ: "Now to him who is able to strengthen you according to my gospel and the preaching of Jesus Christ, according to *the revelation of the mystery that was kept secret for long ages but has now been disclosed and through the prophetic writings has been made known* to all nations, according to the command of the eternal God, to bring about the obedience of faith."[2] The message of the good news of Jesus is disclosed and made known in the Old Testament—the prophetic writings make it known. Yet for most the true meaning of the Old Testament remained a mystery hidden through the ages. It was always there but was never broadly appreciated until Christ came and began to transform hearts and eyes to embrace the truth. Consider two passages:

> The Jews then said, "It has taken forty-six years to build this temple, and will you raise it up in three days?" But [Jesus] was speaking about the temple of his

2. See D. A. Carson, "Mystery and Fulfillment: Toward a More Comprehensive Paradigm of Paul's Understanding of the Old and New," in *The Paradoxes of Paul*, vol. 2 of *Justification and Variegated Nomism*, ed. D. A. Carson, Peter T. O'Brien, and Mark A. Seifrid, 2 vols., WUNT 181 (Grand Rapids: Baker Academic, 2004), 393–436; G. K. Beale and Benjamin L. Gladd, *Hidden but Now Revealed: A Biblical Theology of Divine Mystery* (Downers Grove, IL: InterVarsity Press, 2014).

> body. When therefore he was raised from the dead, his disciples remembered that he had said this, and they believed the Scripture and the word that Jesus had spoken. (John 2:20–22)

> So they took branches of palm trees and went out to meet him, crying out, "Hosanna! Blessed is he who comes in the name of the Lord, even the King of Israel!" And Jesus found a young donkey and sat on it, just as it is written, "Fear not, daughter of Zion; behold, your king is coming, sitting on a donkey's colt!" His disciples did not understand these things at first, but when Jesus was glorified, then they remembered that these things had been written about him and had been done to him. (John 12:13–16)

To say that the full message of the Old Testament was hidden from the majority in the Old Testament period does not mean that the Old Testament prophets themselves did not foresee the glories of Christ, for indeed they did. Jesus said, "Your father Abraham rejoiced that he would see my day. He saw it and was glad" (John 8:56). Similarly, the writer of Hebrews stressed, "These all died in faith, not having received the things promised, but having seen them and greeted them from afar" (Heb. 11:13; cf. 11:39). Paul likewise says that he was "set apart for the gospel of God, which he promised beforehand through his prophets in the holy Scriptures, concerning his Son" (Rom. 1:1–3). And Peter wrote: "Concerning this salvation, the prophets who prophesied about the grace that was to be yours searched and inquired carefully, inquiring what person or time the Spirit of Christ in them was indicating when he predicted the sufferings of Christ and the subsequent glories. It was revealed to them that they were serving not themselves but you" (1 Peter 1:10–12; cf. Luke 18:31–33; Acts 3:18, 24; 10:43).

Peter stresses that the Old Testament prophets were studiers of all earlier revelation. Under the guiding hand of the Spirit, they "searched and inquired carefully" to know both *who* the Messiah would be and *when* he would appear. Out of this context they predicted Christ's sufferings and the days of the church. These statements strongly suggest that often the Old Testament prophets envisioned the very form that we now enjoy. They saw not only the shadow but also the substance that is Christ (Col. 2:16–17; cf. Heb. 8:5; 10:1).

At other times, however, they may have seen only the acorn, with little grasp of how glorious the oak would be that you and I now visualize. And at still other times, they may not have even recognized that the person, event, or institution they were recounting foreshadowed a greater antitype.[3]

What is clear is that while a remnant few rightly grasped that the entire Old Testament was a messianic document designed to instill messianic hope, the majority did not truly hear God's Word in any way. To them, the Lord's gracious instruction did not serve as a guide, and his gracious promises did not motivate hearts of dependence.

3. While I believe the norm was that the Old Testament prophets grasped at least the seed of what they were proclaiming, they may not have always understood—much as the disciples themselves failed to grasp Christ's statements about his passion until after his death and resurrection (Mark 6:51–52; Luke 2:50; 9:45; 18:31–34; 24:16; John 12:16).

But in Christ, all this changes. In him the Lord has disclosed the mystery of the gospel bound up in the Old Testament. These ancient Scriptures can be compared to a dark room filled with furniture. While objects filled the space, their shape and number remained unclear. But the light of Christ enables us to see what was there in the Old Testament all along. We must interpret and apply the Old Testament in light of the finished work of Jesus. If we attempt to read the old covenant materials apart from him, it's as though the veil were still on our eyes (2 Cor. 3:14). But through Jesus, the veil is lifted! Let's now consider more deeply what it means to engage the initial three-fourths of our Bibles while living in the age of fulfillment.

General Guidelines for Applying Old Testament Teaching with a Look at Exodus 19:4–6

In his book *Old Testament Exegesis*, Douglas Stuart offers some helpful guidelines for applying biblical texts.[4] I am going to summarize and somewhat adapt them here, using Exodus 19:4–6 to illustrate the process. I will set out my translation of the text to begin, but you may want to have your Bible open to help you track the discussion. Later in the chapter I will address the thorny challenges related to Christians' applying the Old Testament laws and promises, both of which demand special guidance.

> 4 You [mp] have seen what I did to Egypt, and how I lifted you [mp] on eagles' wings and brought you [mp] to myself. 5 And now, if you [mp] will indeed listen unto my voice and keep my covenant and be to me a treasured possession from all the peoples, for all the earth is mine, 6 then you [mp] will be to me a kingdom of priests and a holy nation.
>
> *mp = masculine plural

Fig. 12.2. DeRouchie's Translation of Exodus 19:4–6

1. Establish the original revealed application.

a. Identify the audience of the application.

Does the passage target individuals, groups, or institutions? If such a differentiation cannot be made, why not? If the object is individuals, what kind (e.g., believing

4. Douglas Stuart, *Old Testament Exegesis: A Handbook for Students and Pastors*, 4th ed. (Louisville: Westminster John Knox, 2009), 25–29.

remnant or faithless rebel, parents or children, powerful or weak)? If the object is a group, what kind (e.g., the community of faith, a nation, clergy, a profession)?

The second masculine plural "you" throughout Exodus 19:4–6 suggests that the target is every individual within the entire community. It was the nation as a whole that was considered God's "son" (Ex. 4:22–23), and it was the nation as a whole that he redeemed. Certainly the plural requires individuals to act, but it also highlights that the task will be accomplished only in the context of corporate solidarity.

b. List the external life issues of application.

Here we consider: What aspects of life is the passage most concerned with? What do we encounter that is similar to or at least closely related to what the passage deals with? Is the application directed toward matters that are more interpersonal in nature? Is the concern social, economic, religious, spiritual, familial, financial, or something else? Does the passage relate directly to the people's relationship with God?

With respect to Exodus 19:4–6, we see the personal experience of communal deliverance in verse 4, the daily pursuit of God in community in verse 5, a political context in which Israel is distinct from surrounding nations in verse 5, and a sense of life's purpose in verse 6. The church, too, has experienced a communal deliverance, but ours is from bondage to sin and salvation from God's wrath. Unlike Israel, the church has no geopolitical affiliation; the church is not a theocracy but is rather a transcultural, transnational people united in Christ with a similar call to daily pursue God in community for the display of his glory.

Furthermore, Exodus 19:4–6 is calling for daily witness of YHWH's greatness by every member of the community. This text covers the foundation, makeup, and ultimate goal of Israel's relationship with God. Sadly, Israel's redemption was external and its law-keeping only skin-deep, so the people never had the impact on the nations that God promised would come through whole-life surrender. Nevertheless, a lasting point of the texts is that the Lord's gracious redemption requires living exclusively for him in every area, whether in our social engagements, our work, our personal and corporate worship, our family life, or our finances. The freedom we experience must lead to radical following, which will overflow in lives that testify to God's majesty.

c. Clarify the nature of the application.

Some passages inform the mind, supplying information, whereas others direct the will, giving instruction. Still others focus on the root of faith, whereas others address the fruit of action. One passage may describe some aspect of the love of God (i.e., inform), while another may command the reader to love God wholeheartedly (i.e., direct). One may identify the nature of trust (i.e., faith), while another clarifies the nature of deeds. Often these two pairs come in packages, so that informing leads to directing and believing leads to obeying. Ask, "Does this passage supply an indicative or an imperative? Does it focus more on the heart and head or the hands?"

On the surface, Exodus 19:4–6 recalls God's gracious past redemption and informs Israel of its future responsibility and calling. Implicitly, the text says more, for it calls the people to Godward allegiance for the sake of mediating and displaying God's glory to the nations. That Israel recognizes the necessity for response is clear from the elders' reply to Moses in 19:8: "All that the LORD has spoken we will *do*." Nevertheless, the rest of the narrative also reveals that Israel's commitment meant little, because the people's stubborn hearts resulted in lack of faith and rebellion (Deut. 9:6–7; 29:4[H3]).

Exodus 19:4–6 also most explicitly addresses action and state of being, calling Israel to "hear" and "keep" and "be" (v. 5). Nevertheless, because these charges are couched as the means for seeing Israel's God-exalting, world-influencing calling accomplished, faith in God's promises is the generator for the nation's obedience. Only to the level at which the people *desire* the promise of being a kingdom of priests and a holy nation and *believe* that the promise-maker can act will they be motivated to heed his voice, keep his covenant, and intentionally seek to live as his treasured possession.

d. Determine the time focus of the application.

Does the passage call for present faith or action? Does it look back to something in the past or ahead to something in the future?

We can see that Exodus 19:4–6 called Israel to make an immediate response. And for every future generation in the old covenant, God's revelation remained the same. He had set Israel apart to express his worth in the world. Through this single nation the world would be blessed, and the Israelites' lives of surrender would parade God's upright character until the promised deliverer would overcome the world's curse with blessing.

e. Fix the limits of the application.

Does the passage function more as background or support? Is it part of a larger passage that suggests a clearer application than your passage does? Is it one of several passages that all function together to suggest a given application that none of them individually would quite have? Does the passage call for a response that could be misunderstood or taken too far? In what ways does the passage not apply?

Exodus 19:4–6 is perhaps the most foundational synthesis of the revealed purpose of the old covenant that we have in Scripture. It looks back to the Abrahamic covenant promises and directly anticipates God's revelation of his person and Word at Sinai. It expresses God's revealed will for Israel, but it does not address the implications of failure.

f. Summary

When it comes to establishing the original revealed application of Exodus 19:4–6, we can say that the text supplies a synthesis of the old covenant by addressing the nation of Israel's redemption and life calling in relation to the world. It explicitly informs but also implicitly directs, calling for action and motivating this call by the promise of global impact. The words target every member of the community and address a surrender to YHWH that impacts every facet of life in every present and future generation.

2. Determine the theological significance of the passage.[5]

a. Clarify what the passage tells us about God and his ways.

Our wrestling with biblical and systematic theology should have already highlighted numerous elements in the passage that disclose something about God and his ways. When applying the Old Testament, it is vitally important to recall what we have learned about God's unchanging character, desires, values, concerns, and standards, and what our passage says about the Lord's purposes in redemption.

Exodus 19:4–6 portrays YHWH as one who delivers in order to create people who can in turn display his excellencies. With respect to his character and actions, he is an able warrior-God who redeemed Israel from the grip of an imperial power (v. 4). He is also a God who commands, establishes covenants, and treasures some more than others (v. 5). Finally, he is a God who motivates through promises and who desires his people to mediate and display his greatness to the world (v. 6). All of these are features from which solid application could be made, for his work in the new covenant is very analogous.

As for his desires, God intends that his people hear his voice, heed his covenant, and be his treasured possession (Ex. 19:5) (see "Determining the Protasis and Apodosis in Exodus 19:5–6" in chapter 5 for my view on the placement of the apodosis). All these activities will supply the means for Israel's serving as a kingdom of priests and a holy nation (v. 6).

b. Assess how Christ's fulfillment of the Old Testament impacts our application of this passage.[6]

Some of the questions we can ask here are as follows: Does the passage speak directly to old covenant structures that get transformed in the new? How has the progress of salvation history influenced how we hear and may apply this text? How does the passage anticipate Jesus' life and work, the church age, or the consummation? Does the text express time-bound or culturally bound elements that can no longer relate to us on this side of the cross? Does the New Testament quote or allude to the particular text in a way that clarifies its lasting value for Christians?

Christ's work fulfills Exodus 19:4–6 in at least three ways: First, the initial exodus typologically anticipated a greater, more universal second exodus that Jesus himself embodies. In Exodus 19:4, YHWH highlights his defeat of Egypt and his deliverance of Israel from the bonds of slavery. Moving ahead in redemptive history, Christ's death and resurrection initiates for all believers the antitypical exodus, the ultimate redemption to which Israel's liberation from Egypt's clutches only pointed. The Old Testament prophets foresaw this second exodus (e.g., Isa. 11:16–12:6; Jer. 16:14–15; 23:7–8; Hos. 11:10–11), which Jesus accomplished in Jerusalem (Luke 9:31).

5. Douglas Stuart, whose general process I am following here, does not explicitly stress the need to recall what we have learned about the theological significance of the passage when making application. I believe, however, that considering both what the passage tells us about God and his ways and how Christ's fulfillment of the Old Testament impacts our passage is vital for accurately establishing the lasting significance of an Old Testament text.

6. For a more developed discussion of Christ's law-fulfillment, see "How to Apply Old Testament Law" below.

Second, Christ fulfilled the charge of this text as the perfect royal priest, bringing us to God and empowering us to serve him. The Israelites' fleshly, rebellious hearts were hostile to God, making it impossible for them to submit to God's law or to please him (Deut. 29:4[H3]; Rom. 8:7–8; 11:7–8). They therefore never operated as the kingdom of priests and the holy nation for which Exodus 19:4–6 called. But where God's corporate "son" failed, his individual Son, Jesus, as Israel's royal and priestly representative, succeeded. Christ's perfect life embodied the ideals of righteousness that the law requires (Rom. 5:18–19; 8:4), and by this he was able to serve as the perfect royal priest (Heb. 4:15), satisfying the Lord's wrath against sinners through his substitutionary death and proving through his resurrection that every believer incorporated into him can enjoy right standing with God. The Lord imputes our sins to Christ and Christ's righteousness to us, thus securing both our pardon (Rom. 5:18–19; 2 Cor. 5:21; Phil. 3:9) and amazing promises (2 Cor. 1:20), which together become power for our salvation—past (Eph. 2:8), present (1 Cor. 1:18), and future (Rom. 5:9). Thus, through Christ's law-fulfillment, we as the new covenant community of faith are not only charged but also empowered to fulfill the law of Christ (Rom. 2:26, 29; 13:8–10; 1 Cor. 9:21; Gal. 6:2), which includes applying the Old Testament laws in light of Christ's fulfillment (Matt. 5:17–19).

Third, Christ represented the nation of Israel, succeeding where it failed and by this magnifying God (see esp. Isa. 49:1–6). Jesus said, "Whoever has seen me has seen the Father" (John 14:9). As the holy king-priest, Jesus perfectly represented Israel and reflected God's holiness. As Hebrews 1:3 says, "[God's Son] is the radiance of the glory of God and the exact imprint of his nature." And now, for those of us in him, "we all, with unveiled face, beholding the glory of the Lord, are being transformed into the same image from one degree of glory to another" (2 Cor. 3:18). That is, in Christ God has, as Peter asserts, made us "a chosen race, a royal priesthood, a holy nation, a people for his own possession, that [we] may proclaim the excellencies of him who called [us] out of darkness into his marvelous light" (1 Peter 2:9).

3. Summarize the lasting significance of the passage for today.

Using your answers to all the questions above, summarize your application of the passage for today. Most probably, it will be related to your main-idea statement that you originally drafted when crafting your exegetical outline (see "Step 2: Exegetical Outlining" and "How to Draft an Exegetical Outline" in chapter 6). Try to decide on one application that is most central to and follows naturally from the passage. Keeping in mind God's unchanging nature and his progressive purposes, and reading the passage in light of the new covenant work of Jesus, what is God calling for in this passage?

With respect to Exodus 19:4–6, I believe the simplest synthesis of what this passage calls for through Jesus is that the church is to live as a royal priesthood and holy people, proclaiming through our life-witness the worth and majesty of God (1 Peter 2:9). In chapter 6, I summarized the main idea of Exodus 19:4–6 as this: "In response to God's gracious redemption, the Lord calls his people to a God-exalting task of mediating and displaying his greatness and worth to the world through radical God-centered living."

Our unchanging Lord is consistent in what he requires, in what he intends, and in the way he uses promises to motivate obedience. Like the nation of Israel, the church is called to follow the instruction of our chief, new covenant Mediator: "Make disciples of all nations, . . . teaching them to obey all that I have commanded" (Matt. 28:20). Also, God uses promises to motivate holiness and to keep us from evil: "He has granted to us his precious and very great promises, so that through them you may become partakers of the divine nature, having escaped from the corruption that is in the world because of sinful desire" (2 Peter 1:4). Finally, God's purpose ever remains that others "may see [our] good works and give glory to [our] Father who is in heaven" (Matt. 5:16).

Old Testament Law and the Christian

Establishing the Law's Relevance for Christians

Paul stressed that "whatever was written in former days was written for *our* instruction" (Rom. 15:4). Similarly, immediately after stressing how the sacred *Jewish* writings "are able to make you wise for salvation through faith in Christ Jesus," he stressed that "all Scripture is . . . profitable for teaching, for reproof, for correction, and for training in righteousness" (2 Tim. 3:15). In the apostle's mind, we should be able to direct Christians back into a path of godliness from the Old Testament. Yet how do we do this faithfully when we know that so much has changed with the coming of Christ? Before setting out a method for applying Old Testament law Christianly, I want to state and unpack three principles that guide my Christian approach to Old Testament law.

1. Christians are part of the new covenant, not the old.

Jesus said that "all the Prophets and the Law prophesied until John [the Baptist]," but since his coming we have moved into the age of fulfillment in which centuries of Old Testament hopes are now being realized (Matt. 11:13; cf. Luke 16:16). The grace of the Mosaic law has now been superseded by the grace and truth coming to us through Jesus Christ (John 1:16–17).

As new covenant believers, Christians are not "under [old covenant] law but under grace" (Rom. 6:14–15; cf. 1 Cor. 9:20–21; Gal. 5:18). For Paul, the Mosaic law represented an era of enslavement and death, and the old covenant bore a "ministry of condemnation" in contrast to the new covenant's "ministry of righteousness" (2 Cor. 3:9). Moses would have fully agreed, because he affirmed both Israel's innate stubbornness and its future destruction (Deut. 9:6–7; 31:27–29).[7] Christians' "release from the law" (Rom. 7:6) in part means that the Mosaic law is no longer the direct and immediate guide or judge of the conduct of God's people.[8] The age of the Mosaic law covenant has come to an end in Christ, so the law itself has ceased having a central and determinative role among God's people (2 Cor. 3:4–18; Gal. 3:15–4:7).[9] "Christ is the end of the law for righteousness to everyone who believes" (Rom. 10:4). Not one of the 613 stipulations in the Mosaic law covenant, as a written legal code, is directly binding on Christians (cf. Acts 15:10; Gal. 4:5; 5:1–12; Eph. 2:14–16).

The old covenant brought forth an age of death to the majority of the Israelites who retained hard hearts, and the eschatological, new covenant work of Christ transcends and supersedes this law covenant. In Paul's words, "Before faith came, we were held captive under the law, imprisoned until the coming faith would be revealed. So then, the law was our guardian until Christ came, in order that we might be justified by faith. But now that faith has come, we are no longer under a guardian" (Gal. 3:23–25). Similarly, the writer of Hebrews said, "Christ has obtained a ministry that is as much more excellent than the old as the covenant he mediates is better, since it is enacted on better promises. . . . In speaking of a new covenant, he makes the first one obsolete. And what is becoming obsolete and growing old is ready to vanish away" (Heb. 8:6, 13; cf. 7:12; 10:9). Christians are part of the new covenant, not the old.

2. Christ fulfills the Mosaic law, and we appropriate it only through his fulfillment.

Jesus stressed that he came not "to abolish the Law and the Prophets" but "to fulfill them" (Matt. 5:17). By his ***"fulfilling" the Old Testament***, I believe he meant that he supplies the "eschatological actualization" of all that the Old Testament predicted, whether through direct or typological prophecy or through the overarching salvation-historical trajectory.[10] In other words, Jesus stood as the goal and end of Old Testament hopes and shadows.[11] All of us can easily recognize how Christ—being the last Adam (1 Cor. 15:45;

7. For more on Moses' conviction that his ministry was one of condemnation as he awaited a greater prophet who would mediate a better covenant, see Jason S. DeRouchie, "From Condemnation to Righteousness: A Christian Reading of Deuteronomy," *SBJT* 18, 3 (2014): 87–118.

8. So too Douglas J. Moo, "The Law of Christ as the Fulfillment of the Law of Moses: A Modified Lutheran View," in *Five Views on Law and Gospel*, ed. Wayne G. Strickland, Counterpoints (Grand Rapids: Zondervan, 1999), 343; cf. 375.

9. Ibid., 359.

10. Tom Wells and Fred G. Zaspel, *New Covenant Theology: Description, Definition, Defense* (Frederick, MD: New Covenant Media, 2002), 115; cf. 77–159. For an exceptional word study on πληρόω ("to fulfill"), see Vern S. Poythress, *The Shadow of Christ in the Law of Moses* (Phillipsburg, NJ: Presbyterian and Reformed, 1991), 363–77; cf. 267. For similar approaches to Matthew 5:17–19, see Douglas J. Moo, "Jesus and the Authority of the Mosaic Law," *JSNT* 7, 20 (1984): 23–28; Moo, "Law," *DJG* 456–58; Moo, "The Law of Christ as the Fulfillment of the Law of Moses," 347–53; Poythress, *The Shadow of Christ in the Law of Moses*, 263–69; D. A. Carson, "Matthew," in *Matthew & Mark*, 2nd ed., Expositor's Bible Commentary 9 (Grand Rapids: Zondervan, 2010), 172–79.

11. Poythress helpfully writes, "Jesus does not assert merely a static continuation of the force of the law, but rather a dynamic advance—in fact, the definitive fulfillment. What was temporary and shadowy in the form of the Old Testament law is superseded, now that God's glory and kingly power are being manifested in the very

cf. Rom. 5:14), the representative of Israel (Isa. 49:1–6; Matt. 21:9; Luke 1:32–33), the true Passover Lamb (John 1:29; 1 Cor. 5:7), the true temple (John 2:21), and so on—is the substance of all old covenant shadows (Col. 1:16–17; Heb. 8:5; 10:1). Yet the Mosaic law also anticipated Jesus in the way it identified and multiplied sin (Rom. 3:20; 5:20; cf. 7:7–12; Gal. 3:19), imprisoned the sinful (Rom. 3:19–20; 8:2–3; Gal. 3:10, 13, 22), and by these disclosed everyone's need for atonement in Christ. The law, in this sense, predicted Christ, who is "the end of the law for righteousness to everyone who believes" (Rom. 10:4). As Paul states elsewhere: "By works of the law no human being will be justified in [God's] sight, since through the law comes knowledge of sin. But now the righteousness of God has been manifested apart from the law, although the Law and the Prophets bear witness to it—the righteousness of God through faith in Jesus Christ for all who believe" (Rom. 3:20–22).

Every Old Testament ethical ideal pointed ahead to Christ's perfect righteousness on behalf of his elect (Rom. 5:18–19; 8:3–4; Phil. 2:8), a point that I will take up further in the next unit. Furthermore, Jesus' role as teacher and covenant Mediator also fulfills Moses' own eschatological hopes for a "prophet" like him—one who would know God face to face, who would perform great signs and wonders, and to whom people would listen (Deut. 18:15; 34:10–12; cf. Luke 7:16; 9:35; Acts 3:22–26; 7:37).

Significantly, Jesus fulfilled the law in such a way as to maintain the lasting relevance of each part. Christ said, "The Law and the Prophets were until John [the Baptist]; since then the good news of the kingdom of God is preached . . . . But it is easier for heaven and earth to pass away than for one dot of the Law to become void" (Luke 16:16–17). In these verses we see both *continuity* (all the Law remains part of Christian Scripture and is therefore instructive) and *discontinuity* (the Old Testament age of prediction has given rise to fulfillment).

A similar tension is present in Matthew 5:17–19, which we will now quote in whole. Here Jesus stresses that all the commanding parts of the Mosaic law are still instructive for his followers, but *only when read in the light of his law-fulfillment*:

> Do not think that I have come to abolish the Law or the Prophets; I have not come to abolish them but to fulfill them. For truly, I say to you, until heaven and earth pass away, not an iota, not a dot, will pass from the Law until all is accomplished. Therefore whoever relaxes one of the least of these commandments and teaches others to do the same will be called least in the kingdom of heaven, but whoever does them and teaches them will be called great in the kingdom of heaven.

By "these commandments," Jesus most likely refers to the directives and prohibitions of the Mosaic law itself.[12] He thus affirms that the Mosaic law remains a relevant guide for

---

person of Jesus and in his ministry. The promise of the kingdom of heaven involves the intensification of all that served to manifest God in the Old Testament. All is transformed by the supremacy and weightiness of God Himself coming to save" (*The Shadow of Christ in the Law of Moses*, 265).

12. So too Moo, "Jesus and the Authority of the Mosaic Law," 28; Moo, "Law," 458; Moo, "The Law of Christ as the Fulfillment of the Law of Moses," 353; Poythress, *The Shadow of Christ in the Law of Moses*, 267–69; Wells and Zaspel, *New Covenant Theology*, 127; Carson, "Matthew," 179.

believers, but *only* when we engage it through his law-fulfillment, which could result in the intensifying, transforming, extending, or annulling of any given law. The "law of Christ" that we live out (Isa. 42:4; Matt. 28:20; 1 Cor. 9:21) is the law as fulfilled by Jesus, which is the eschatological realization of the Mosaic law in its original form. Thus, our keeping the law of Christ fulfills Moses' prediction that in the day when God would circumcise hearts and empower love (Deut. 30:6)—something that we are experiencing today in Christ and the new covenant (Rom. 2:29)—God's people would heed all the commands Moses gave *in Deuteronomy*: "And you shall turn and heed the voice of the Lord and keep *all his commandments that I command you today*" (Deut. 30:8, author's translation).

While Christians are not directly legally bound to the Mosaic law, we do not throw out the law itself. Instead, we follow the pattern of the New Testament authors, viewing all the Old Testament laws as profitable and instructive (e.g., Rom. 13:9; 1 Cor. 9:7–9; Eph. 6:1–3; 1 Tim. 5:18; 1 Peter 1:15–16; cf. Rom. 4:23; 15:4; 1 Cor. 10:11), yet only through the mediation of Christ. And because Jesus fulfills different laws in different ways, we must consider each law on its own in light of Christ's work. The end result after doing such work is what Paul terms the "***law of Christ***" (1 Cor. 9:21; Gal. 6:2).

When Jesus is viewed as the lens for considering the lasting validity of Moses (fig. 12.3), we recognize that some laws come straight through him (e.g., maintain gender distinction and never commit adultery, murder, theft, etc.), looking the same within the law of Christ as they did in the law of Moses. For example, when Christ fulfills the Mosaic law related to gender distinction (e.g., Deut. 22:5), he *maintains* all gender distinction. We could say similar things regarding the prohibitions against adultery, murder, theft, and so on. At one level, even these laws are intensified in that Jesus' own life supplies believers with an unparalleled pattern for living the Godward life (Phil. 2:5–7; Heb. 12:1–3; 1 Peter 2:21; 1 John 2:6) and an unparalleled power to do so (Rom. 1:16; 1 Cor. 1:18), specifically through his blood-bought pardon (Rom. 6:6–7, 22; 8:10) and promises (Rom. 8:32; 2 Cor. 1:20; 2 Peter 1:4). Nevertheless, Christian obedience to these instructions is very comparable to what Old Testament believers would have looked like in carrying out the laws. In contrast, when other laws hit the lens of Christ, they get "bent" in various ways. Consider these examples:

- When Christ fulfills the Mosaic law of the Sabbath (e.g., Deut. 5:12), he *transforms* it into sustained rest for the people of God. In Jesus, the kingdom rest to which the Sabbath pointed reaches its eschatological realization.
- Similarly, when Christ fulfills the Mosaic law regarding parapet-building (Deut. 22:8), we find the application *extended* in a way that necessitates care for neighbor in every area of one's home-building.
- Finally, when Christ fulfills the Mosaic law associated with unclean food (e.g., Lev. 20:25–26), he *annuls* it, declaring all foods clean. Even though he rescinded the earlier diet restrictions, we can still benefit from these commands by considering what they tell us about God and how they magnify Jesus' work. Nevertheless, we do not keep these laws in any way.

We must assess every law on its own terms in order to properly discern how it applies today. In the pages that follow, I will illustrate how Jesus fulfills four distinct laws in different ways, whether by maintaining it (gender distinction), transforming it (Sabbath), extending it (parapet-building), or annulling it (unclean food).

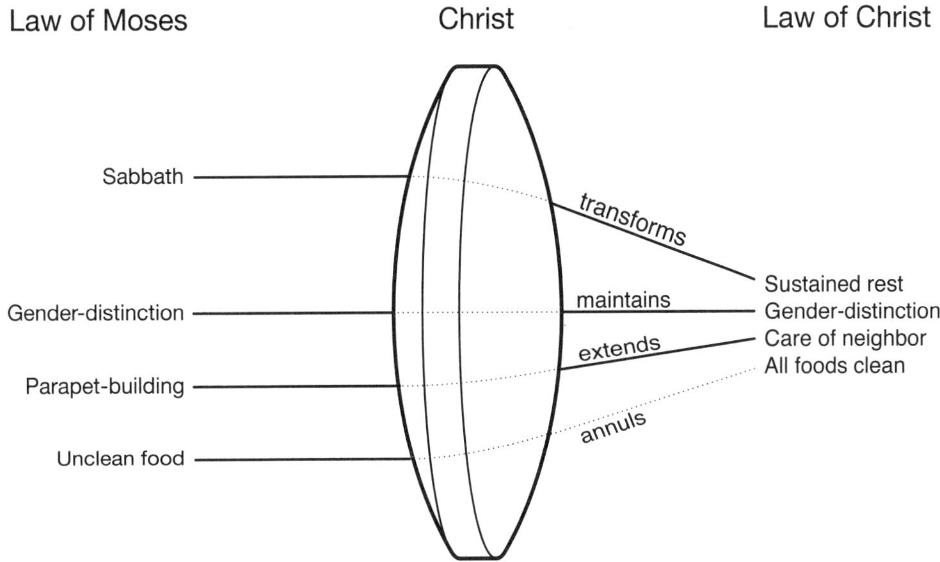

Fig. 12.3. The Law's Fulfillment through the "Lens" of Christ[13]

Another way to grasp our relationship to Old Testament law is to visualize two riverbanks separated at varying distances by water (fig. 12.4). The two sides symbolize the old and new covenant laws, and Jesus is the "bridge" over which we move from one side to the other. The length of the bridge and our distance from the specific Mosaic legislation changes depending on the nature of the law itself. The distance is always great enough that we can't access the other side apart from Christ, but some laws are so similar on each side of the bridge that the distance seems almost nonexistent (gender distinction, adultery, theft, etc.). Other laws, however, disclose substantial distance or changes (Sabbath, food laws, etc.).

13. I thank my student Benjamin Holvey, who initially inspired this lens illustration.

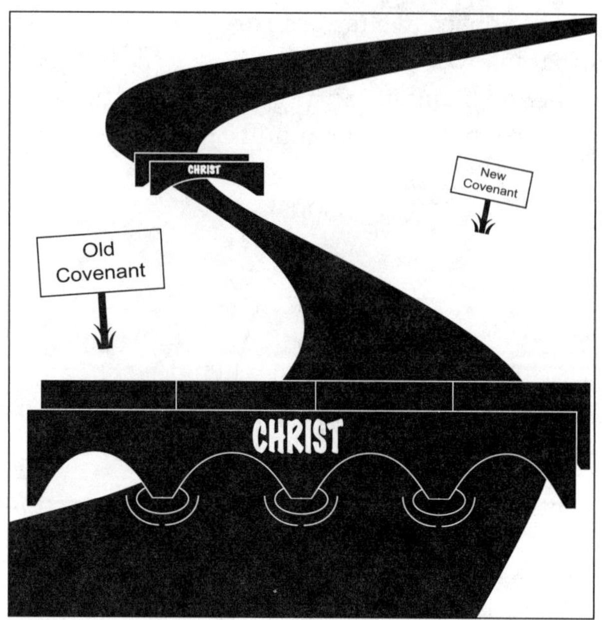

Fig. 12.4. The Law's Fulfillment over the "Bridge" of Christ

Regardless, when we approach the Old Testament through the lens of Christ, everything in the Old Testament operates as Christian Scripture written "for our instruction" (Rom. 15:4; cf. 4:23; 1 Cor. 10:11) and remains "profitable for teaching, for reproof, for correction, and for training in righteousness" (2 Tim. 3:16). We access and apply the Mosaic law only through Christ and in light of the teaching of his apostles, which together alone ground and sustain the church (Acts 2:42; Eph. 2:20; cf. Matt. 7:24–27; 17:5; 28:20; John 16:12–14; 17:8, 18, 20; 2 Thess. 2:15; Heb. 1:1–2).[14]

14. For more on this redemptive-historical approach to a Christian's relationship to Old Testament law, see David A. Dorsey, "The Law of Moses and the Christian: A Compromise," *JETS* 34, 3 (1991): 321–34; Poythress, *The Shadow of Christ in the Law of Moses*, 251–86; Moo, "The Law of Christ as the Fulfillment of the Law of Moses," 317–76; Wells and Zaspel, *New Covenant Theology*, 77–160, esp. 126–27, 157–60; Daniel M. Doriani, "A Redemptive-Historical Model," in *Four Views on Moving beyond the Bible to Theology*, ed. Gary T. Meadors, Counterpoints (Grand Rapids: Zondervan, 2009), 75–121, responses to other contributors on pp. 51–56, 205–9, 255–61; Jason C. Meyer, *The End of the Law: Mosaic Covenant in Pauline Theology*, NAC Studies in Bible and Theology 7 (Nashville: Broadman & Holman, 2009); Meyer, "The Mosaic Law, Theological Systems, and the Glory of Christ," in *Progressive Covenantalism: Charting a Course between Dispensational and Covenant Theologies*, ed. Stephen J. Wellum and Brent E. Parker (Nashville: Broadman & Holman, 2016), 69–99; Thomas R. Schreiner, *40 Questions about Christians and Biblical Law*, 40 Questions (Grand Rapids: Kregel, 2010); Jason S. DeRouchie, "Making the Ten Count: Reflections on the Lasting Message of the Decalogue," in *For Our Good Always: Studies on the Message and Influence of Deuteronomy in Honor of Daniel I. Block*, ed. Jason S. DeRouchie, Jason Gile, and Kenneth J. Turner (Winona Lake, IN: Eisenbrauns, 2013), 415–40; Brian S. Rosner, *Paul and the Law: Keeping the Commandments of God*, NSBT 31 (Downers Grove, IL: InterVarsity Press, 2013); William W. Combs, "Paul, the Law, and Dispensationalism," *DBSJ* 18 (2013): 19–39; Stephen J. Wellum, "Progressive Covenantalism and Doing Ethics," in *Progressive Covenantalism: Charting a Course between Dispensational and Covenant Theologies*, ed. Stephen J. Wellum and Brent E. Parker (Nashville: Broadman & Holman, 2016), 218–21.

3. The Old Testament law portrays the character of God, anticipates Christ, and clarifies the makeup of love and wise living.

I have argued that, through Jesus, "every detail" of the Mosaic law matters for Christians. This is so for at least three reasons: The old covenant law (a) clarifies for believers the character of God, (b) serves as a prophetic witness to Christ, and (c) identifies how deep and wide love for God and neighbor goes.

a. The law portrays the character of God.

The Mosaic law is an expression of the character of God. The Lord asserted, "You shall . . . be holy, for I am holy" (Lev. 11:45), and Israel would fulfill this charge by heeding God's words. "Now therefore, if you will indeed obey my voice and keep my covenant, . . . you shall be to me a kingdom of priests and a holy nation" (Ex. 19:5–6). And again, "So you shall remember and do all my commandments, and be holy to your God" (Num. 15:40). Paul stressed that "the law is holy, and the commandment is holy and righteous and good" (Rom. 7:12). When we read the law of Moses, we get a glimpse into the very character of our great God.

b. The law anticipates Christ.

Along with portraying God's character, the law points us to Christ, a note already stressed in the discussion on Christ's law-fulfillment. Here I want to highlight the fact that every Old Testament ethical ideal finds embodiment in the divine Son of God. So Christians can use the Old Testament laws to move us to magnify all that God is for us in Jesus. We see this anticipated first in Deuteronomy 17:18–20, where the Lord gives parameters for kingship in Israel. The monarch will be a man of the book, never replacing YHWH but representing him perfectly as he lives out the law. He will have his own copy of Moses' words, and he will read them daily, which will generate fear leading to obedience, humility, and a lasting kingdom. Jesus is the embodiment of this ideal.

Similarly, the divine servant is able to make "many to be accounted righteous" only because he himself is "righteous" and bears the iniquity of the guilty (Isa. 53:11; cf. 1 John 1:9–2:1). He was perfectly obedient (Rom. 5:19; Phil. 2:8; Heb. 5:8) and sinless (John 8:46; 14:30; Heb. 7:26; 1 Peter 2:22; 1 John 3:5), and for those in him, his life of perfect surrender provides freedom from the law's condemning power and supplies for us all the righteousness that the law required. At the cross, God canceled "the record of debt that stood against us with its legal demands" (Col. 2:13–14; cf. Gal. 3:13). This he accomplished by counting our sins to Jesus, by pouring out his wrath against Jesus in our stead, and by counting Jesus' righteousness as ours: "For our sake [God the Father] made [Christ] to be sin who knew no sin, so that in him we might become the righteousness of God" (2 Cor. 5:21; cf. Rom. 5:18–19; Heb. 9:28). Through Jesus, God "condemned sin in the flesh, in order that the righteous requirement of the law might be fulfilled in us" (Rom. 8:3–4). I believe the latter text means that Christ's perfect statute-keeping is applied to all who are in him, the proof of which is that we now walk by the Spirit.[15]

15. The singular use of δικαίωμα ("righteous requirement") in Romans 5:18 strongly suggests that the singular use of the same term in 8:4 refers to *Christ's* perfect obedience—his righteousness—counted as ours through our

c. The law clarifies the makeup of love and wise living.

Jesus said that "all the Law and the Prophets" depend on the dual commands to love God and love neighbor (Matt. 22:37–40). Stressing how love for neighbor really proves whether we love God, Jesus went further, saying, "Whatever you wish that others would do to you, do also to them, for this is the Law and the Prophets" (7:12). Similarly, Paul stressed that "the whole law is fulfilled in one word: 'You shall love your neighbor as yourself'" (Gal. 5:14). Significantly, not just a "moral" subset of the law but all the law—every commandment—is fulfilled in the call to love:

> Owe no one anything, except to love each other, for the one who loves another has fulfilled the law. For the commandments, "You shall not commit adultery, You shall not murder, You shall not steal, You shall not covet," and any other commandment, are summed up in this word: "You shall love your neighbor as yourself." Love does no wrong to a neighbor; therefore love is the fulfilling of the law. (Rom. 13:8–10)

In both the old and new covenants, love is *what* God's people are to do. All the other commandments simply clarify *how* to do it. From this perspective, while the Mosaic law does not bear direct or immediate guidance in a Christian's life, it does supply us with a pattern for how deeply and widely love for God and neighbor is to impact our lives.[16]

Indeed, even within ancient Israel, the familial, social, economic, and political structures as revealed in the Old Testament bore a testimonial purpose and were intended to provide a contextual paradigm of the values God desires for all peoples and in all times. We first see evidence of this fact in the life of Abraham, who YHWH says "obeyed my voice and kept my charge, my commandments, my statutes, and my laws" (Gen. 26:5). Using the very language of the Mosaic covenant (see Deut. 30:10; 1 Kings 2:3; 2 Kings 17:13, 34) to describe Abraham's life of dependence identifies the paradigmatic nature of the Mosaic law.

If the Israelites would heed God's voice, keep his covenant, and be his treasured possession, they would bear witness to YHWH's greatness in the midst of the world (Ex. 19:5–6). By their living out the statutes and rules, the nations would see the uprightness

---

incorporation into him rather than to the Christian's keeping of the law. On this, I agree with Douglas J. Moo, *Romans*, NICNT (Grand Rapids: Eerdmans, 1996), 483–84. Our walking by the Spirit is in turn evidence that we are justified, and Paul speaks of this walking both as fulfilling the law (Rom. 13:8, 10) and as keeping the law's "righteous requirements" (δικαίωματα, plural accusative of δικαίωμα) through a circumcised heart and by the power of the Spirit (2:26; cf. Ezek. 36:27; Rom. 2:29). For an alternative view of Romans 8:4 that sees the "righteous requirement" as something that we are empowered to do instead of what Christ did for us, see Thomas R. Schreiner, *Romans*, BECNT 6 (Grand Rapids: Baker Academic, 1998), 404–8, 690–95; Kevin W. McFadden, "The Fulfillment of the Law's *Dikaiōma*: Another Look at Romans 8:1–4," *JETS* 52, 3 (2009): 483–97.

16. For examples of a principlizing approach to Old Testament law, see Walter C. Kaiser Jr., *Toward Old Testament Ethics* (Grand Rapids: Zondervan, 1983); Kaiser, "A Principlizing Model," in *Four Views on Moving beyond the Bible to Theology*, ed. Gary T. Meadors, Counterpoints (Grand Rapids: Zondervan, 2009), 19–50; J. Daniel Hays, "Applying the OT Law Today," *BSac* 158, 1 (2001): 21–35; Jerram Barrs, *Delighting in the Law of the Lord: God's Alternative to Legalism and Moralism* (Wheaton, IL: Crossway, 2013), 315–26. In my view, we must include a redemptive-historical lens in order to engage in a principlizing approach faithfully.

of God's law and view Israel as both wise and understanding (Deut. 4:5–8). The Mosaic law, therefore, served to shape for the world a clear picture of righteous living.[17]

4. Summary

None of the old covenant law is directly or immediately legally binding on God's people, for Moses' commands are part of a covenant that has come to an end and of which we are not a part: "The law was our guardian until Christ came. . . . But now that faith has come, we are no longer under a guardian" (Gal. 3:24–25). Nevertheless, Christians benefit from the Mosaic law in the way it portrays the character of God, anticipates Christ, and clarifies the nature of love and wise living. So while the Mosaic law does not serve as a direct or immediate legal judge or guide on the Christian, when we read it in light of Christ's law-fulfillment, it continues to impact us in both a revelatory and pedagogical way.[18] This perspective led Paul to say, "Do we then overthrow the law by this faith? By no means! On the contrary, we uphold the law" (Rom. 3:31).

Moses looked ahead to the eschatological age when God's transformed people would "keep all his commandments that I command you today" (Deut. 30:8). Similarly, Jeremiah envisioned that in the new covenant era, some who had once been evil neighbors—the Gentiles—would "diligently learn the ways" of God's people and by this "be built up" into their midst (Jer. 12:16). Ezekiel, too, said that when the Lord would pour out his Spirit, he would cause his people to "walk in my statutes [LXX = pl. of δικαίωμα] and be careful to obey my rules" (Ezek. 36:27). It is the fulfillment of these anticipations that Paul describes in Romans 2:26, 29 when he says that Christian Gentiles were actually keeping "the precepts [pl. of δικαίωμα] of the law" by means of their circumcised hearts and by the power of the Spirit.[19] It is also this law-fulfillment that the apostle says we accomplish when we love our neighbor (Rom. 13:8, 10). All of these texts identify levels of continuity between the "law of Moses" and the "law of Christ."

Isaiah, however, identified a level of discontinuity through progression, for in the messianic era the nations would gather to the new Jerusalem to hear YHWH's law as declared *through his royal servant* (Isa. 2:3; 42:4; 51:4). The Mosaic law finds fulfillment in and informs "the law of Christ" (1 Cor. 9:20–21; Gal. 6:2), which is also called "the perfect law," "the law of liberty," and "the royal law" (James 1:25; 2:8, 12). The Old

17. For more on the principlizing-paradigmatic approach to the Mosaic law, see Christopher J. H. Wright, *Old Testament Ethics for the People of God* (Downers Grove, IL: InterVarsity Press, 2004), 62–74, 182–211, 314–25; cf. Waldemar Janzen, *Old Testament Ethics: A Paradigmatic Approach* (Louisville: Westminster John Knox, 1994); Elmer A. Martens, "How Is the Christian to Construe Old Testament Law?," *BBR* 12, 2 (2002): 199–216; Peter T. Vogt, *Interpreting the Pentateuch: An Exegetical Handbook*, Handbooks for Old Testament Exegesis (Grand Rapids: Kregel, 2009), 42–48; Daniel I. Block, "Preaching Old Testament Law to New Testament Christians," in *The Gospel according to Moses: Theological and Ethical Reflections on the Book of Deuteronomy* (Eugene, OR: Cascade, 2012), 104–46, esp. 133–36; orig. published in *Hiphil (Scandinavian Evangelical E-Journal)* 3 (2006) 1–24, and subsequently published in three parts in *Ministry* 78, 5 (2006): 5–11; 78, 7 (2006): 12–16; 78, 9 (2006): 15–18. In my view, we must employ a redemptive-historical, Christological lens if we are to engage faithfully in the principlizing-paradigmatic approach.

18. On these distinctions, see Dorsey, "The Law of Moses and the Christian," 325, 331.

19. For this reading of Romans 2, see Simon J. Gathercole, "A Law unto Themselves: The Gentiles in Romans 2.14–15 Revisited," *JSNT* 24, 3 (2002): 27–49; Ardel B. Caneday, "Judgment, Behavior, and Justification according to Paul's Gospel in Romans 2," *JSPHL* 1, 2 (2011): 153–92; cf. Schreiner, *Romans*, 136–45.

Testament law gives us fresh glimpses of God's character and the perfect righteousness of Christ and helps Christians better understand what a loving life looks like. In this way, the Old Testament law becomes useful "for teaching, for reproof, for correction, and for training in righteousness" (2 Tim. 3:16; cf. Matt. 5:17–20; 28:20; John 14:15; 1 Cor. 7:19; Titus 2:14; 1 John 2:3; 5:3).

Assessing the Threefold Division of the Law

In echo of what I have already argued above, Brian Rosner has asserted that Paul repudiated the Mosaic law as a law covenant, replaced the Mosaic law with the law of Christ, and reappropriated the Mosaic law both as prophecy that anticipates the gospel of Jesus and as wisdom intended to guide New Testament saints in our pursuit of God.[20] This seems right to me.

In minimal contrast to this approach, it is very common in evangelical circles, especially those related to covenant theology, to speak of three kinds of Mosaic laws:[21]

- ***Moral laws*** are those fundamental ethical principles that are eternally applicable, regardless of the time or covenant.
- ***Civil laws*** are related to Israel's political and social structures in the land and are time-bound.
- ***Ceremonial laws*** are those symbolic requirements related to Israel's religious ceremonies and cult worship that find their typological end in Christ.

In this view, as salvation history progresses through Christ, only the moral laws of the Mosaic legislation remain legally binding on Christians.

I appreciate this attempt to retain the lasting validity of at least some of God's old covenant instruction. I affirm that the coming of Christ clearly changes some laws more than others and that the commands of the law that Christians "fulfill" (see Rom. 13:8, 10; Gal. 5:14; cf. 6:2) in a fashion most similar with their function within the old covenant are those normally tagged as "moral."[22] But I do not think that this particular approach is the most biblically faithful or devotionally helpful.[23]

20. Rosner, *Paul and the Law.*

21. For an affirmation of this view, see Westminster Confession of Faith 19.3–5. These are *theological* categories, in contrast to the *content* distinctions of criminal, civil, family, cultic/ceremonial, compassion (see figs. 1.8 and 12.4).

22. Carson affirms these same two points in "Mystery and Fulfillment," 429.

23. Some in the classic Reformed tradition affirm this fact. For example, Vern S. Poythress, professor of New Testament interpretation at Westminster Theological Seminary, reflects on the proposed division of the Old

1. The Bible never differentiates laws in this way but treats the law as a singular entity.

The Old Testament includes different types of laws based on content (i.e., criminal, civil, family, ceremonial, and compassion laws; see fig. 1.8 in chap. 1). Within this framework, the call to love was always considered more foundational than ritual (e.g., Deut. 6:5; 10:12; 1 Sam. 15:22–23; Isa. 1:11–17; Hos. 6:6; Amos 5:21–24; Mic. 6:8). At times, people applied the law in fresh ways (1 Chron. 15:12–15 with Num. 7:9; Deut. 10:8; 2 Chron. 30:2–3 with Num. 9:9–13), adapted it to new contexts (2 Chron. 29:34, 36 with Lev. 1:5–6; 2 Chron. 30:17–20; 35:5–6 with Ex. 12:21), or even developed it (2 Chron. 8:12–15; 29:25–30). We even have instances in which people failed to fulfill ceremonial obligations (Lev. 10:16–20) or engaged in ceremonially unlawful activity (1 Sam. 21:3–6; cf. Lev. 22:10; Matt. 12:4), and yet God did not hold them guilty.

Nevertheless, the Old Testament never distinguishes moral, civil, and ceremonial laws, and all laws remained binding. Leviticus 19, for example, shows little distinction between laws, mixing calls to love one's neighbor (vv. 11–12, 17–18) with various commands related to family (vv. 3a, 29), worship (vv. 3b–8, 26–28, 30–31), business practice (vv. 9–10, 13b, 19a, 23–25, 34b–36), care for the needy and disadvantaged (vv. 9–10, 13–14, 33–34), criminal and civil disputes (vv. 15–16, 35a), and ritual matters (v. 19b). No attempt is made to elevate certain laws over others.

Following the Old Testament prophets before him, Jesus did distinguish "weightier" and "lighter" matters of the law (Matt. 23:23; cf. 9:13; 12:7). Yet while he tagged as hypocritical those who were willing to tithe on their spice rack but unwilling to engage in the more difficult tasks of "justice and mercy and faithfulness," he emphasized, "These you ought to have done, without neglecting the others." That is, he is not here saying that the "lighter matters" bear no lasting value. Instead, his focus was the overarching principles and purposes of the whole law and the underlying principles and purposes of the individual laws.

Furthermore, whether addressing the law's repudiation, replacement, or reappropriation, the New Testament consistently speaks of the whole law as a unit. Paul

---

Testament law into moral, civil, and ceremonial: "No simple and easy separation between types of law will do justice to the richness of Mosaic revelation. . . . The entirety of this Mosaic revelation simultaneously articulates general moral principles and symbolic particulars: it points forward to Christ as the final and permanent expression of righteousness and penal substitution (with moral overtones) but is itself, in that very respect, a shadow (with ceremonial overtones)" (*The Shadow of Christ in the Law of Moses*, 283). Similarly, Jerram Barrs, professor of Christian studies and contemporary culture at Covenant Theological Seminary, writes, "These divisions [between moral, civil, and ceremonial] are not hard and fast. For example, many of the ceremonial laws include moral and civil aspects. Many of the civil laws include moral aspects. A problematic consequence in this view, if it is held with systematic rigor, is that the beauties of the ceremonial and civil aspects of the law become lost to us during this present age" (*Delighting in the Law of the Lord*, 314). For further reflections on why dividing the law into these categories is not preferable, see Dorsey, "The Law of Moses and the Christian," 329–31; D. A. Carson, "The Tripartite Division of the Law: A Review of Philip Ross, *The Finger of God*," in *From Creation to New Creation: Biblical Theology and Exegesis: Essays in Honor of G. K. Beale*, ed. Daniel M. Gurtner and Benjamin L. Gladd (Peabody, MA: Hendrickson, 2013), 223–36; Combs, "Paul, the Law, and Dispensationalism," 26–28; Rosner, *Paul and the Law*, 36–37; Meyer, "The Mosaic Law, Theological Systems, and the Glory of Christ," 87–89; Wellum, "Progressive Covenantalism and Doing Ethics," 218–21.

says, "The commandments, 'You shall not commit adultery, You shall not murder, You shall not steal, You shall not covet,' and *any other commandment*, are summed up in this word: 'You shall love your neighbor as yourself'" (Rom. 13:9). The call to love neighbor synthesizes not just a group of "moral" laws but every commandment. Jesus, too, spoke broadly when he asserted, "Therefore whoever relaxes one of the least of these commandments and teaches others to do the same will be called least in the kingdom of heaven, but whoever does them and teaches them will be called great in the kingdom of heaven" (Matt. 5:19). There is no special categorizing of laws here. James said, "Whoever keeps *the whole law* but fails in one point has become accountable for all of it" (James 2:10). Similarly, earlier Paul stressed that the whole "law" brought curse to all (Gal. 3:10), that in Christ we are no longer under the law covenant as a guardian (3:24–25), and that "every man who accepts circumcision . . . is obligated to keep the whole law" (5:3).

The New Testament repudiates *all* the Mosaic law, sees *all* the law replaced with the law of Christ, and reappropriates *all* the law as both a pointer to Christ and a guide for wise Christian living. The tripartite division of the law is simply not taught in Scripture.

2. All the laws express moral principles, and most of the so-called moral laws contain temporally or culturally bound elements.

The so-called civil laws simply provide examples of moral principles working their way out in Late Bronze and Iron Age culture. Also, the so-called ceremonial laws illustrate ethical or moral elements through symbolism, and by distinguishing itself from its pagan neighbors, Israel pointed to the uniqueness of YHWH over all, which is the greatest act of love that one could give. With this, we see many culturally bound features in the Ten Commandments, which are considered the chief example of "moral law":[24]

- The prologue identifies Israel as a people whom YHWH redeemed from slavery in Egypt (Deut. 5:6), and this element also grounds the call to rest in the Sabbath command (5:14–15).
- The idolatry command assumes a religious system that includes carved images (Deut. 5:8).
- The Sabbath command presumes the context of ancient Near Eastern bond service, geographically limited animals, and cities with gates (5:14); its use of גֵּר ("sojourner") (5:14) implies the existence of the politically defined nation of Israel.
- The command to honor one's parents directly points to the existence of the nation of Israel in the land of Canaan (5:16).

24. The initial five of these are taken from Dorsey, "The Law of Moses and the Christian," 330; the last is noted in Daniel I. Block, "'You Shall Not Covet Your Neighbor's Wife': A Study in Deuteronomic Domestic Ideology," *JETS* 53, 3 (2010): 449–74.

- The coveting commands assume a people acquainted with ancient Near Eastern bond service and with animals common in the Mediterranean world (5:21).
- The commands principally address household heads who enjoy wives, children, household servants, and property—all of which point to Israel's patricentric society.[25]

This list should caution those who want to identify the Ten Commandments as moral law in distinction from civil or ceremonial.

3. We are to gain benefit from *all* the Old Testament, not just the moral portions. Most theologians holding to the tripartite division of the Mosaic law affirm the lasting value of *all* Scripture. But the stress on the lasting relevance of the moral law in distinction to the secondary nature of the civil and ceremonial has moved many laymen to see books such as Leviticus as having little lasting relevance for Christians. Yet Paul drew pastoral insight from the instructions on temple service (1 Cor. 9:13–14), and he stressed that "all Scripture is . . . profitable" for Christians (2 Tim. 3:16). Are we not on firmer ground to emphasize how *every* commandment in all the law is fulfilled in our love of neighbor (Rom. 13:8, 10), rather than narrowing attention to only some of the law?

In light of these observations and my earlier arguments, I think it is best to see *none* of the Mosaic law as directly binding on Christians in a *legal* way but *all* the Mosaic law as significant for believers in a *revelatory* and *pedagogical* way, when read in light of Christ's fulfillment of the law. The old covenant law is not our legal code, but it was still written *for* us in order to portray the Lord's character, to direct our eyes to Jesus, and to clarify how deeply and widely love for God and neighbor should consume our lives.

How to Apply Old Testament Law

In this section I want to focus on the role of the Mosaic law as wisdom for Christians. How should a Christian go about reappropriating the Mosaic law in light of the fulfillment secured by Jesus? I here adopt the three general principles I set forth earlier in this chapter (see "General Guidelines for Applying Old Testament Teaching"), but now address them specifically to applying Old Testament law.[26]

25. On the biblical vision of Israelite society's being centered on the father as servant leader (i.e., patricentric) as opposed to dominated by a father as self-exalting dictator (i.e., patriarchal), see Daniel I. Block, "Marriage and Family in Ancient Israel," in *Marriage and Family in the Biblical World*, ed. Ken M. Campbell (Downers Grove, IL: InterVarsity Press, 2003), 33–102.

26. Some of this material is adapted from Wright, *Old Testament Ethics for the People of God*, 314–24; and Dorsey, "The Law of Moses and the Christian," 332–33.

1. Establish the original revealed meaning and application of the law. This includes three parts with respect to Old Testament laws.

a. Type

Recalling that this particular law was not given to us but to old covenant Israel, define the type of law it is in accordance with the five types I laid out in our discussion on the prophetic genre: criminal, civil, family, cultic/ceremonial, or compassion (fig. 1.8 in chap. 1).

Criminal	Laws governing crimes or offenses that put the welfare of the whole community at risk; the offended party is the state or national community, and therefore the punishment is on behalf of the whole community in the name of the highest state authority, which in Israel meant YHWH. *SAMPLE ISSUES*: Kidnapping and homicide; false prophecy and witchcraft; adultery and rape.
Civil	Laws governing private disputes between citizens or organizations in which the public authorities are appealed to for judgment or called on to intervene; the offended party is not the state or national community. *SAMPLE ISSUES*: Accidental death and assault; theft and destruction of property; limited family issues such as premarital unchastity, postdivorce situations, and the mistreatment of slaves.
Family	Noncivil, domestic laws governing the Israelite household. *SAMPLE ISSUES*: Marriage and inheritance; the redemption of land and persons; family discipleship; care of slaves.
Cultic/ Ceremonial	Laws governing the visible forms and rituals of Israel's religious life. *SAMPLE ISSUES*: The sacred sacrifice, the sacred calendar, and various sacred symbols such as the tabernacle, priesthood, and ritual purity that distinguished Israel from the nations and provided parables of more fundamental truths about God and relating to him.
Compassion	"Laws" dealing with charity, justice, and mercy toward others. These are not exactly the kinds of laws that can be enforced in court, but God knows the heart. *SAMPLE ISSUES*: Protection and justice for the weak; impartiality and generosity; respect for persons and property.
For a more detailed overview, see figure 1.8 in chapter 1. Prepared by both Jason S. DeRouchie and Kenneth J. Turner. Originally published in DeRouchie, ed., *What the Old Testament Authors Really Cared About*, 466–67. Used by permission. The five main categories are taken from Christopher J. H. Wright, *Old Testament Ethics for the People of God* (Downers Grove, IL: InterVarsity Press, 2004), 288–301, which he adapted from Anthony Phillips, *Ancient Israel's Criminal Law: A New Approach to the Decalogue* (New York: Schocken Books, 1970), 2, 13.	

Fig. 12.5. Types of Old Testament Laws by Content

b. Original Meaning and Significance

Assess the makeup of the law in its original context. Clarify its social function and relative status. Is it central or peripheral to the dominant themes and social objectives that we find in the rest of the material? Is it a primary expression of YHWH's values and priorities, or is it more secondary, reinforcing and supplying an example of a more primary law?

c. Original Purpose

We now consider the role that the law was intended to play in Israelite society, asking: Who? What? When? Where? Why? How? How often? To what extent? For example:

- What kind of situation was this law trying to promote or prevent?
- Whose interests was this law aiming to protect?
- Who would have benefited from this law, and why?
- Whose power was this law trying to restrict, and how did it do so?
- What rights and responsibilities were embodied in this law?
- What kind of behavior did this law encourage or discourage?
- What vision of society motivated this law?
- What moral principles, values, or priorities did this law embody or initiate?
- What motivation did this law appeal to?
- What sanction or penalty (if any) was attached to this law, and what does that show regarding its relative seriousness or moral priority?

2. Determine the theological significance of the law.

a. Clarify what the law tells us about God and his ways.

What does the law disclose to us about God's unchanging character, desires, values, concerns, or standards? We learn about God through his law, and meditating on the Mosaic law should move us to worship him and to recognize and grieve over lawlessness as a direct affront to his person. It should also move us to celebrate his provision of Christ as the perfect law-keeper and righteousness-supplier.

b. Assess how Christ's law-fulfillment impacts the law.

God's character remains unchanged, which means that every expression of his eternal law at different times in the progress of salvation history can instruct every other age and culture. This is true even if the specific legislation is no longer binding because of the changes in covenant and historical-cultural context. The person and work of Christ completely embody the call to love God and neighbor, and he fulfills the law not only in the way that he perfectly met the law's demands but also in the way that he is the substance of all old covenant shadows (Col. 2:16–17). That is, he is the ultimate reality to which all the Old Testament types pointed, whether persons, events, or institutions. As we consider how the Mosaic law informs the law of Christ, some new covenant instructions look identical to the teaching of Moses, whereas other laws get transformed (e.g., Sabbath), extended (e.g., adultery includes lust), or annulled (e.g., sacrifices). Homosexuality is as wrong today as it was in the old covenant (Rom.

1:26–27; 1 Cor. 6:9), but unlike the Israelites, Christians are free to eat bacon because Jesus' kingdom work rendered all foods clean (Mark 7:19; Acts 10:13–15). Because most often the various types of laws are all mixed up in the Pentateuch, we have to deal with each law on its own, considering how Christ's fulfillment impacts any given law.

Significantly, no laws from the old covenant come to us directly. We do not obey the Ten Commandments, for example, simply because they are the Ten Commandments. Rather, each of the Ten Words meets us only through the lens of Christ, and every one of the Ten Words gets focused through him (see fig. 12.1). Even a command such as "Do not commit adultery" gains a new *pattern* in the life of Jesus (Phil. 2:5–7; Heb. 12:1–3; 1 Peter 2:21; 1 John 2:6) and a new *power* through his work (Rom. 1:16; 1 Cor. 1:18). Christ embodies for us a perfect example of what living out the law of Christ looks like in the way he treated women and controlled his own desires with the aid of the Spirit, and he secures power for our own pursuit of holiness through his blood-bought pardon (Rom. 6:6–7, 22; 8:10) and blood-bought promises (Rom. 8:32; 2 Cor. 1:20; 2 Peter 1:4). Every law finds focus if not complete transformation in Christ—even those that his law-fulfillment does not change in nature.

c. State in a single sentence the love principle behind the law.

If indeed love is what God called the people to do and all the other commandments simply clarify how to do it (Matt. 7:12; 22:37–40; Rom. 13:8, 10; Gal. 5:14), we should be able to boil down every law into a ***principle of love***. Being as detailed as possible, complete the following statement for every law: The call to love God/neighbor means/implies/impacts/necessitates ____________________.

3. Summarize the lasting significance of the law for today.

Here we preserve both the portrait of God and the love principle behind the law but change the context, all in light of Christ's new covenant work. We consider the practical implications of the theological insights gained from this law for our own new covenant context. God's nature is unchanging, but his purposes progress over time. Furthermore, we must consider not only living in light of the *pattern* that Christ set for us but also living by his gospel *power*. As similar as the old and new covenants are in many respects, the internalization of grace in all members marks the new covenant as a massive progression within salvation history.

Below I supply four examples that represent different ways in which Christ's law-fulfillment impacts the application of Old Testament law to Christians. As noted, we must examine every law on its own terms in order to rightly understand its lasting significance in the new covenant. No preset categories (such as moral, civil, and ceremonial) determine whether certain laws are extended (Deut. 22:8), operate identically (22:5), are transformed (5:12), or are annulled (Lev. 20:25–26).

House-Building with Love in Deuteronomy 22:8

My first example of applying Old Testament law is a "slow-pitch, easy-hitter." It illustrates how some laws get extended into new spheres as times and culture change.

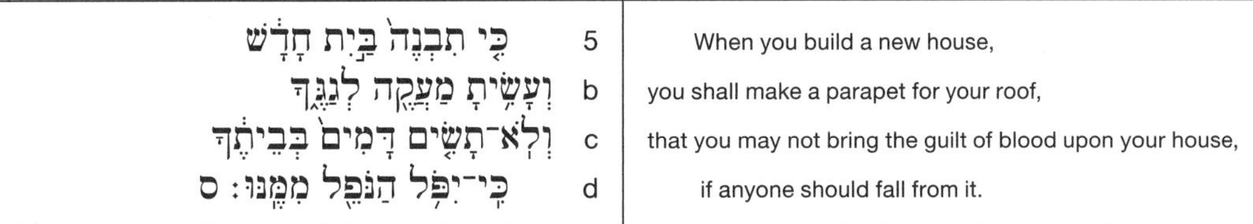

MT		ESV
כִּ֤י תִבְנֶה֙ בַּ֣יִת חָדָ֔שׁ	5	When you build a new house,
וְעָשִׂ֥יתָ מַעֲקֶ֖ה לְגַגֶּ֑ךָ	b	you shall make a parapet for your roof,
וְלֹא־תָשִׂ֤ים דָּמִים֙ בְּבֵיתֶ֔ךָ	c	that you may not bring the guilt of blood upon your house,
כִּֽי־יִפֹּ֥ל הַנֹּפֵ֖ל מִמֶּֽנּוּ׃ ס	d	if anyone should fall from it.

Fig. 12.6. Deuteronomy 22:8 in MT and ESV

1. Establish the original revealed meaning and application of the law.

The conditional nature of the law suggests that it stands as a secondary application of a more fundamental principle. Flat roofs were and are common throughout the Middle East, for in the Mediterranean climate, the roof supplies an extra living space. A parapet is the low wall that surrounds the roof and that protects folks from accidentally falling off. Here we learn that a homeowner is responsible to build his house with a parapet to guard against the accidental death of others. The principal purpose of the law was clearly to minimize the number of domestic deaths brought about by avoidable accidents, negligence, or carelessness. Causing accidental death from negligence was a criminal act that could be curbed only by the offending party's fleeing to a city of refuge (Ex. 21:13; Num. 35:9–15; Deut. 19:1–10). Deuteronomy 19:10 warns that if innocent blood is shed and the manslayer does not take the prescribed actions, "the guilt of the bloodshed" will remain on the people, thus incurring the wrath of God.

2. Determine the theological significance of the law.

We have a God who treasures the display of his image in humans and who calls us to value this display in others. If we take human life lightly, we are declaring that we take God lightly and will be judged. We see in Deuteronomy 22:8 a very gracious Lord who warns against dangers that could ultimately result in the harm of others and, by this, our harm.

Similarly, when Jesus used a coin to highlight the way in which God owns every person, he declared the lasting importance of God's image in others: "Jesus said to them, 'Whose likeness and inscription is this?' They said, 'Caesar's.' Then he said to them, 'Therefore render to Caesar the things that are Caesar's, and to God the things that are God's'" (Matt. 22:20–21). The Lord's image is on us, and therefore we owe him our lives.

Building on his value of God's image, Christ called for the application of love of neighbor in all contexts: "So whatever you wish that others would do to you, do also to them, for this is the Law and the Prophets" (Matt. 7:12). This Golden Rule is evident in our passage, and it suggests that Christ's followers today must maintain the call to love others in the most practical of ways—including how we ready our living space for guests. I summarize the main love principle of Deuteronomy 22:8: *Loving others means that we will make our living environment safe for them, removing all dangers and respecting God's image displayed in every life.*

3. Summarize the lasting significance of the law for today.

All homeowners bear the responsibility to watch out for the well-being of everyone who comes under their roofs. While many climates do not allow for houses with parapets, the teaching of Deuteronomy 22:8 is naturally extended to include building a fence around a pool or raised deck, placing a protective gate above a stairwell where toddlers are present, or shoveling a sidewalk after a snowstorm. Love for neighbor is to impact even the littlest details of our everyday lives, as we live under the supremacy of God in Christ. We love our neighbors in these small particulars of love because of the way that God has first loved us in Christ (1 John 4:11, 19). We must ever care for others' welfare, valuing God's image in them. This means that we will make our homes into places where others can thrive without undue safety risks.

Gender Confusion in Deuteronomy 22:5

The West is in the midst of a gender-identity crisis, and the brokenness that it is causing in our culture is tragic. I know that some of you reading this study have yourselves wrestled with gender identity or have been the victim of another's gender-identity crisis. I ache for you, and I long for you to know the healing that only Jesus can bring.

In light of what can be called a transgender storm, I want to consider the lasting relevance of Deuteronomy 22:5 for the church. As we will see, our alignment with this law should look today much as it did for Moses and the Israelites.[27]

27. For a more expansive discussion of this text that attempts to model how to handle such a personal and difficult issue exegetically, theologically, and pastorally, see Jason S. DeRouchie, "Confronting the Transgender Storm: New Covenant Reflections on Deuteronomy 22:5," *JBMW* 21, 1 (2016): 58–69. I have adapted the material that follows from this study.

לֹא־יִהְיֶה כְלִי־גֶבֶר עַל־אִשָּׁה	5	A woman shall not wear a man's garment,
וְלֹא־יִלְבַּשׁ גֶּבֶר שִׂמְלַת אִשָּׁה	b	nor shall a man put on a woman's cloak,
כִּי תוֹעֲבַת יְהוָה אֱלֹהֶיךָ כָּל־עֹשֵׂה אֵלֶּה׃ פ	c	for whoever does these things is an abomination to the LORD your God.

Fig. 12.7. Deuteronomy 22:5 in MT and ESV

1. Establish the original revealed meaning and application of the law.

While the law bears lasting import for new covenant believers (Deut. 30:8; Rom. 15:4), Moses originally wrote it to Israel, and our assessment must begin within this context. We can immediately note that the prohibition in Deuteronomy 22:5 appears less a core principle and more a secondary application of a more fundamental truth. On the surface, the verse relates to what could be called *gender expression*; yet the law assumes a more fundamental rule: that there are two biological sexes (male and female) and that what is gender-normative in God's world is that one's biological sex governs both one's gender identity and its expression. Before divine wrath is poured out, this text provides a kind of corrective to gender confusion and transgender identity.

Deuteronomy 22:5 stands independent of its context and simply comes to us as two prohibitions followed by a single motivation clause. In Hebrew, there are two types of negative commands—immediate (אַל־) and durative (לֹא־), and God chose to frame these prohibitions as durative, so that we should read the "not" as a "never": "A woman shall *never* wear a man's garment, nor shall a man *ever* put on a woman's cloak." From God's perspective, there is never a permissible time for the type of cross-dressing that this passage addresses.

Digging deeper into this law, we should note that the term translated "man" is גֶּבֶר ("strong man") and not the more common אִישׁ. Some have suggested that גֶּבֶר means "warrior" here (cf. 2 Sam. 1:27; Ezek. 32:27),[28] but this meaning is more closely associated with the adjective גִּבּוֹר ("mighty one," cf. Gen. 10:8–9; Deut. 10:17). Furthermore, within the Pentateuch all other instances of גֶּבֶר simply overlap in meaning with אִישׁ, showing up in contexts that distinguish the men from the young (Ex. 10:7, 11) or from women and children (12:37).[29] The clear difference between גֶּבֶר and אִישׁ is that, when paralleled with "woman" (אִשָּׁה) the term אִישׁ can often mean "husband," whereas גֶּבֶר never does in any of its twenty-four Old Testament uses. At the very least, then, this law concerning male-female relationships is not restricted to husbands and wives and thus family law but speaks to the broader society and community. *From God's perspective, the fact of maleness and femaleness bears implications beyond the home or gathered worshiping community. It also impacts daily life in society.*

28. E.g., J. Gordon McConville, *Deuteronomy*, ApOTC (Downers Grove, IL: InterVarsity Press, 2002), 336–37.
29. "I גֶּבֶר," *HALOT*, 1:175.

The term used here for the woman's "cloak" (שִׂמְלָה) is restrictive, pointing specifically to the outer wrapper or mantle that a female would wear.[30] In contrast, the term rendered "garment" (כְּלִי) in relation to a man is broader and suggests any object associated with men—whether clothing (1 Sam. 21:5[H6]), vessel (1 Kings 10:21), ornament (Gen. 24:53), or piece of equipment (Num. 19:18) that was specifically associated with men.[31] This could even include weapons of war (Gen. 49:5; Deut. 1:41; Judg. 9:54), but it was in no way limited here.

Within Israelite culture, therefore, certain styles of dress, ornaments, or items distinguished men and women. Thus, two things appear to be at stake in this law:

- Everyone needed to let individual gender expression align with one's biological sex; and
- Everyone needed to guard against gender confusion, so that others would not wrongly perceive a man to be a woman and a woman to be a man based on dress.

Whether arising from pagan religious activity or from a desire to engage in roles restricted to the opposite sex, such practices opposed any form of godliness.[32]

The fact that this type of cross-dressing is here called an "abomination to the Lord" highlights the gravity of the offense and associates it with not only the crimes of idolatry (Deut. 13:14; 17:4) and witchcraft (18:12) but also the sin of dishonest gain, which could relate at the level of criminal, civil, or family law (25:16). What is it about idolatry, witchcraft, and dishonesty that make them abominable to the Lord? Idolatry gives glory to someone other than YHWH; witchcraft looks to means other than God's Word to discern the future or his will; dishonest gain diminishes the value of God's image in others. We must conclude, therefore, that something about cross-dressing and gender confusion directly counters the very nature of God.

This raises the likelihood that what makes transgenderism abominable is that it maligns humanity's ability to reflect, resemble, and represent God rightly in this world. The possibility that it is also a criminal offense suggests that the sin actually endangers the welfare of the entire community. The clear distinctions between men and women laid out in Genesis 1 and 2 and maintained throughout the Pentateuch further suggest that this law bears a symbolic element. Those born boys are to live and thrive as boys, and those born girls are to live and thrive as girls. When

30. "שִׂמְלָה," *HALOT*, 3:1337.

31. "כְּלִי," *HALOT*, 2:478.

32. Harry A. Hoffner Jr. argues that the transgender practices evidenced here were potentially connected to the pagan religious rites or magical practices of Israel's neighbors ("Symbols for Masculinity and Femininity," *JBL* 85, 3 [1966]: 326–34). While that is possible, nothing in Deuteronomy 22 explicitly links the text to cultic ritual (so too P. J. Harland, "Menswear and Womenswear: A Study of Deuteronomy 22:5," *ExpTim* 110, 3 [1998]: 74–75). For further reflections on ancient Israel's problem of cross-dressing, see Nili S. Fox, "Gender Transformation and Transgression: Contextualizing the Prohibition of Cross-Dressing in Deuteronomy 22:5," in *Mishneh Todah: Studies in Deuteronomy and Its Cultural Environment in Honor of Jeffrey H. Tigay*, ed. Nili S. Fox, David A. Glatt-Gilad, and Michael J. Williams (Winona Lake, IN: Eisenbrauns, 2009), 49–71.

corrupt desires are leading us to deviate from this course, we must choose with God's help the path that best magnifies the majesty of God, and that path is defined in Deuteronomy 22:5.

As for the purpose of the law, its objective appears to have been to maintain divinely created gender distinctions within the community of faith. The goal of this pursuit was to nurture an environment that properly displays the supremacy of God and the ever-present Head-helper distinction between God and the people he is creating for himself.

2. Determine the theological significance of the law.

Deuteronomy 22:5 is the fruit of this truth: YHWH is ever passionate to preserve and display right order in his world. This is the essence of his righteousness, and maintaining gender distinctions is an important part of this order. The stress in Genesis 1–2 on the way in which males and females image God and the Pentateuch's depiction of YHWH's relationship with Israel as a marriage push readers to view our biological sex and gender identity and expression as being first and foremost about God. The rest of the Old Testament highlights this parabolic purpose of sex and gender distinctions in books such as Hosea (chaps. 1–3; cf. Judg. 2:16–17; Isa. 1:21; 57:3; Jer. 2:2, 20; 3:1, 8–11; 31:31–32), and then the same idea is carried into the New Testament (see Matt. 9:15; 12:38–39; 16:1–4; Mark 2:19; 8:38; Luke 5:34), most clearly where Paul portrays the church as Christ's bride (Eph. 5:22–27; cf. Rev. 19:7–9; 21:9). To the level that we flatten the inborn distinctions between maleness and femaleness, we flatten the distinctions between the sovereign Savior and the saved, between the exalted and the needy, between the Blameless One and the sinner. We take glory away from God and his Christ when we act as though distinctions between men and women were nonexistent. And we hurt the entire community both in the way that we fail to point them to gospel righteousness and in the way that we open them up for God's just wrath.

How does Christ's law-fulfillment affect this law? We can first say that Christ and his followers continued to distinguish men from women. Indeed, Jesus perfectly exemplified maleness in the way that he deeply respected femaleness, standing as the ultimate provider and protector and leader in servant-hearted love. Jesus:

- Respected his parents (Luke 2:41–52; John 2:1–11);
- Had female disciples (Luke 8:1–3);
- Sought to protect women from male abuses (Matt. 5:27–32; 19:3–12; Luke 7:36–50);
- Portrayed women as models of faith (Matt. 25:1–13; Mark 7:24–30; Luke 4:24–26; 11:31; 18:1–8; 21:1–4);
- Extended care and healing to marginalized female sufferers (Mark 1:30–31; 5:25–43; 7:24–30; Luke 7:11–17; 13:10–17; John 4:1–42; 7:53–8:11; 11:1–44);
- Received anointing from women (Luke 7:36–50; John 12:1–8); and
- Disclosed himself first to women after his resurrection (Matt. 28:9; John 20:14–18).

Christ is the substance to which all biblical symbols point, but unlike some pictures such as the temple and clean and unclean laws, which have reached their terminus in Christ's first appearing, the distinction between males and females will continue at least to the consummation (as is clear in texts such as Ephesians 5:22–33 and 1 Timothy 3:4–5). And even then, while earthly marriage will be no more (Matt. 22:30)—the picture being overcome by the reality—there is no reason to think that the distinction between men and women, heads and helpers within the community of faith, will alter in the new heavens and earth (cf. Rev. 21:24, where "kings" are distinguished). Maleness and femaleness will most likely provide an eternal reminder of God's order in reality, in which he is supreme over all.

Along with this, new covenant teaching maintains role distinctions between men and women, most explicitly in its instructions to husbands and wives (e.g., Eph. 5:22–32; 1 Peter 3:1–7) and to local churches regarding their corporate worship, teaching, and leadership (1 Cor. 11:1–16; 14:33–35; 1 Tim. 2–3; Titus 1:5–16). It also calls for men to live as men, for women to live as women, and for the young to be trained to live out the gender role related to their God-given sex (Titus 2:2–6). Paul exhorted Timothy to respect and encourage older men as fathers, younger men as brothers, older women as mothers, and younger women as sisters, in all purity (1 Tim. 5:1–2). All this instruction assumes that we can rightly identify those who are men and those who are women.

Paul asserted that every Old Testament commandment is summarized in the call to love our neighbor (Rom. 13:8, 10). Jesus, too, said that "whatever you wish that others would do to you, do also to them, for this is the Law and the Prophets" (Matt. 7:12). With every law in the Old Testament, we should therefore be able to boil it down into a single principle of love. In Deuteronomy 22:5, *loving others and God means that people will maintain a gender identity that aligns with their biological sex and will express this gender in a way that never leads to gender confusion in the eyes of others.* We should always be able to distinguish boys as boys and girls as girls. When our biological sex aligns with our gender identity and our gender expression, we express love for both God and our neighbor.

3. Summarize the lasting significance of the law for today.

Deuteronomy 22:5 was not originally given to the church, but it contains a portrait of God and a principle of love that can guide the church today when read in light of the finished work of Christ. In Jesus we have a perfect pattern for maleness in relation to femaleness. With this, in Jesus we are supplied with unmatched power for our pursuit of rightly ordered living. The power comes through the pardon that Jesus secured at the cross and the promises that he purchased there. The gender-identity crisis that we are facing today can be rightly confronted only in the context of past and future grace.

We have already noted that God's passion for right order has not changed in the new covenant, for it is part of his very being. With this, the physical and role distinctions between men and women have not changed this side of the cross. God's righteousness is unswerving, and we must be ever concerned to display the magnificence of Christ's love for his church in every situation of life.

This affirmed, Deuteronomy 22:5 becomes instructive for the church in helping us recognize the appropriate path for gender expression and the sinfulness of gender confusion, which includes cross-dressing and transgender practice. Clothing stores in the West still distinguish men's and women's clothing, and there are certainly styles that are more masculine or more feminine than others. As believers, we should be among those who celebrate men's being masculine and women's being feminine, even in the way we dress. Furthermore, it is noteworthy that in our present culture, ladies can wear slacks, collars, and even ties (in a context such as serving in a restaurant), with none questioning their femaleness. The church needs to account for this. What was at stake in Moses' law was gender confusion, and from this perspective our outward apparel matters.

Because the law is focused on adults and also because it addresses gender *confusion*, the law itself would not directly dissuade a young girl from dressing up with a mustache in a kids' play or a little boy's putting on a girl's dress after ransacking the dress-up box. No viewer of this "cuteness" would be confused regarding the child's gender. Nevertheless, we must be cautious here, because we are always guiding our children into what is appropriate, and we are now living in a society that acts as though gender were a matter of choice rather than providence. This is abominable, and Deuteronomy 22:5 speaks directly against this perspective.

As I close this section, I call the church to be mindful of those broken in this gender-identity crisis and to care deeply for the violators and the violated. One's self-identity will be forever maligned so long as we are looking at a mirror and not into the face of Jesus Christ. We need to help those struggling with transgender identity find a new identity in Christ, and we need to help those who have been hurt by others find the healing and relief that only Jesus brings. He alone is the Savior. He alone is the Healer.

Keeping the Sabbath in Deuteronomy 5:12

My next example of applying old covenant law on this side of the cross relates to the Sabbath command, one of the disputable matters that Christians must not allow to separate us, even while we seek to become increasingly strong in faith with consciences that are calibrated to the truth of Scripture (Rom. 14:1–15:7, esp. 14:5).[33] This law will show us how important it is to consider Christ's law-fulfillment, which in this instance we will see fully transforms the law.

33. For a helpful discussion of how fellow Christians should relate when their consciences disagree about disputable matters, see Andrew David Naselli and J. D. Crowley, *Conscience: What It Is, How to Train It, and Loving Those Who Differ* (Wheaton, IL: Crossway, 2016), 84–117.

שָׁמ֛וֹר אֶת־י֥וֹם הַשַּׁבָּ֖ת לְקַדְּשׁ֑וֹ	12	Observe the Sabbath day, to keep it holy,
כַּאֲשֶׁ֥ר צִוְּךָ֖ ׀ יְהוָ֥ה אֱלֹהֶֽיךָ	b	as the LORD your God commanded you.

Fig. 12.8. Deuteronomy 5:12 in MT and ESV

1. Establish the original revealed meaning and application of the law.

That Numbers 15:32–36 declares death on the high-handed Sabbath-breaker identifies the Sabbath instruction as criminal law. There was something about maintaining the weekly 6 + 1 rhythm of life that impacted the entire community for good, yet failure would impact them negatively.

Along with being identified with criminal law, the Sabbath appears to have also been linked with ceremonial law, for it bears a lot of symbolism. Within the context of the Ten Commandments, the purpose of the law is explicit—to ensure that household heads would supply every household member, including the servants, with a day of rest (Deut. 5:14). Within the context of the whole Pentateuch, however, the law's objective appears to be broader.

YHWH tagged the Sabbath as the "sign" (אוֹת) of the Mosaic covenant, which suggests that the law was primary and fundamental rather than secondary and illustrative. We are told that the purpose of the covenant sign was that Israel might "know that I, the LORD, sanctify you" (Ex. 31:13; cf. 31:17). In the Israelites' journey from Egyptian slavery to Mount Sinai, they learned that the Sabbath would test their obedience and nurture trust in YHWH as the great provider (16:4–5, 23–26). By not working one day a week and by trusting God to supply their daily bread, the people's keeping the Sabbath would result in their growth in holiness.

Yet the sign of the Sabbath also served to remind Israel of her identity and purpose as a people in relation to the whole world. The Exodus version of the Sabbath command grounds it in the original creation week (20:11; 31:17), whereas the version in Deuteronomy links it to the exodus (Deut. 5:15). The Sabbath is therefore explicitly connected with the two greatest Old Testament initiatory acts: God's creation of the world and his creation/redemption of a people for himself.

For God, the culmination of the creation week was a rest born not of laziness but of sovereignty, in which the Great King, having established the sacred space of his kingdom, sat enthroned, enjoying peace with all that he had made (Gen. 2:1–3; cf. Ps. 132:7–8, 13–14). While mankind's rebellion at the fall did not remove God's right and authority over all things, it did alter the state of universal peace or rest. Thus, within the Pentateuch, the 6 + 1 pattern of creation is used not simply as a portrait of what was but as an image of what should be, and this ideal becomes directly attached to the Israelites' commission to honor God among the nations (Ex. 19:4–6; Deut. 4:5–8; 26:18–19) and for their royal representative to operate as the instrument of curse-reversal and global blessing (Gen. 12:3; 18:18; 22:17b–18; 26:4; 28:14). The Sabbath was to serve as a weekly reminder to the community that Israel's calling (as a people and, ultimately, through the Messiah) was to stand as the agent through whom God's sovereignty would be celebrated once again on a global scale. It is in this context that Moses stresses in the Ten Words that "the seventh day is a Sabbath *to the Lord*" (Deut. 5:14); it was ultimately kept in order to see God exalted over all. For Israel, then, the Sabbath represented a future reality to which both Israel and the world were to hope.

2. Determine the theological significance of the law.

We learn a number of things about God from the Sabbath command: (a) YHWH is a God who ever watches out for the least. He shows no partiality and emphasizes the need for regular rest for ourselves and those in our care. (b) YHWH is a God who sanctifies by providing means in our daily lives to test our trust and to develop our dependence. The weekly Sabbath did this for Israel. (c) The Sabbath teaches us that YHWH is a God who is passionate to restore and display right order in his world, in which he is exalted as sovereign over all. He created Israel for the sake of reconciling the world, and Israel's weekly Sabbath was to ever remind the people of their purpose of seeing the ultimate Sabbath restored on a global scale. This is what it means that the Sabbath was kept "to the Lord" (Deut. 5:14).

As we consider Christ's law-fulfillment, we recall that Jesus saw himself as establishing God's kingdom and as the source of mankind's ultimate rest. We read in Matthew 11:27–30: "All things have been handed over to me by my Father . . . . Come to me, all who labor and are heavy laden, and I will give you rest. Take my yoke upon you, and learn from me, for I am gentle and lowly in heart, and you will find rest for your souls. For my yoke is easy, and my burden is light." Significantly, it is directly after this assertion that Matthew includes the story of Jesus' allowing his disciples to pluck heads of grain on the Sabbath and then declaring himself both "greater than the temple" (12:6) and "lord of the Sabbath" (12:8). Such a testimony was an overflow of the fact that not only was "the kingdom of heaven . . . at hand" (10:7), but also "the kingdom of God has come upon you" (12:28; cf. Luke 17:21).

In contrast to the views of some, I do not believe that the divine Sabbath of the original creation week continued after the fall. As Jesus asserted directly after healing a lame man on the Sabbath, "My Father is working until now, and I am working" (John 5:17). Jesus' redeeming work brought Israel's global Sabbath mission to fulfillment. He is the one through whom the world is blessed (Gen. 22:17b–18; Acts 3:25–26; Gal. 3:8, 14), and by his victorious resurrection he inaugurated the end-times Sabbath rest as a culmination of his new-creation work. Jesus stands superior to Moses (Heb. 3:1–6), and those of us in him have already entered rest, even though we await its full consummation (4:3–10).

A love principle stands behind the Sabbath command in Deuteronomy 5:12–15. I would summarize it as follows: *Loving God and neighbor requires carrying out the 6 + 1 pattern of life as a witness to the kingdom hope of ultimate rest.*

3. Summarize the lasting significance of the law for today.

Until the final judgment, God will ever retain his commitment to his kingdom community, even those whom the world considers "least." As believers look out for the marginalized among the people of God, we serve King Jesus (Matt. 25:31–40). This is a sustained application of the old covenant Sabbath command on this side of the cross.

Not only this, the Old Testament command to keep the Sabbath teaches us of our own need as humans to rest, both to restore energy and to nurture increased dependence on God. "It is in vain that you rise up early and go late to rest, eating the bread of anxious toil; for he gives to his beloved sleep" (Ps. 127:2). Resting is a key means of divine grace to counter human tendencies toward workaholism and to nurture deeper levels of trust in God. God opposes the proud but gives grace to the humble (James 4:6; 1 Peter 5:5), and therefore he continues to mercifully humble us so that we might enjoy more grace. These, too, are general applications of the Sabbath command that continue today.

We must wrestle directly, however, with the place of the Sabbath in the Christian's life. As the sign of the old covenant, the Sabbath was by nature teleological, pointing toward a goal. It stood at the end of every Israelite's week and symbolized sovereign rest as the goal of life. In contrast, for the believer in Christ Jesus, fulfillment of God's sovereign rest has already been inaugurated, the "shadow" finding its "substance" in Christ (Col. 2:16–17). As representative of national Israel, Jesus fulfills its Sabbath-generating mission, and through him the kingdom authority of God is once again realized on a global scale, moving out through the church from Jerusalem to Judea and Samaria to the ends of the earth (Acts 1:8).

Jesus declared, "All authority in heaven and on earth has been given to me" (Matt. 28:18), and we must affirm that God has already put "everything in subjection to him," leaving "nothing outside his control," though "we do not yet see everything in subjection to him" (Heb. 2:8). In this church age, believers are enjoying Sabbath rest under the lordship of God in Christ all seven days of the week (Matt. 11:28–29; Heb. 4:8–11; cf. Rom. 15:5–6). Because we already "share in Christ" (Heb. 3:14), we have already entered the Sabbath rest he secures (4:9–10). We are no longer striving to confirm our eternal destiny but are resting, certain that what Christ has already accomplished will be fully revealed at the future consummation.

In the new covenant there is not one specific day as opposed to others that marks the Sabbath. Christ's resurrection initiates an eschatological shift from old creation to new creation (2 Cor. 5:17; Gal. 6:15), from Sabbath-anticipation to Sabbath-fulfillment. Now seven days a week, those in Christ live in the context of Sabbath rest.

Like the early church, our corporate worship follows a 1 + 6 rather than 6 + 1 pattern, gathering on the first day of the week, not the last (Acts 20:7; 1 Cor. 16:2). Why? All the Gospel writers highlight that Jesus rose on Sunday (Matt. 28:1; Mark 16:2, 9; Luke 24:1; John 20:1), and by this they identify that Israel's vision of seeing Sabbath realized was accomplished on that resurrection Lord's Day (Rev. 1:10). On that first day of the week, light dawned over the darkness, new creation was initiated, and God's kingdom in Christ began to be realized. Sunday worship reflects that inaugurated nature of our rest that we enjoy all the rest of the week. It also nurtures within us hope for the day when our faith will become sight (2 Cor. 5:7) and when the rest that we already taste will be completed through the removal of all evil, pain, and death when we see our Savior face to face (Rev. 21:4; 22:3). As we currently enjoy Sabbath rest every day of the week, we magnify the curse-overcoming work of Christ, even as we continue to pray, "Your kingdom come . . . on earth as it is in heaven" (Matt. 6:10).

In the end, the Old Testament call to keep the Sabbath establishes a sustained principle of rest for believers—resting so that we can run. We need to take breaks to refuel for our divine service, and sleep serves as a means of God's grace to nurture sustained dependence and surrender in our souls (Ps. 127:2). Nevertheless, in Christ no single day is more important than another, and God-dependent work on any day of the week is sanctified to the Lord. We must maintain a pattern of corporate worship (Heb. 10:25), and Sunday is a natural time for this (Acts 20:7; 1 Cor. 16:2) because of its eschatological significance of being the day on which God initiated his new-creation kingdom (Acts 26:23; Rom. 6:4; 1 Cor. 15:20, 23; 2 Cor. 5:17; 2 Thess. 2:13; Rev. 14:4). But corporate worship on another day of the week is not sin, nor is it necessarily wrong to paint your house, weed your garden, study for an exam, or engage in sports on a Sunday—so long as you work hard, as on every other day, in a way that never replaces grace (1 Cor. 15:10; Phil. 2:12–13; Col. 1:29). In all times and in all ways we must live and labor by faith in the one from whom, through whom, and to whom are all things (Rom. 11:36), so that "in everything God may be glorified through Jesus Christ" (1 Peter 4:11).[34]

Forbidden Food in Leviticus 20:25–26

My final illustration of the lasting significance of Old Testament law for Christians addresses a command that Christ's coming annuls, yet in a way in which we can still find significant Godward benefit from the law itself while celebrating the progressions in salvation history.

34. For more on this approach to the Sabbath command, see Wells and Zaspel, *New Covenant Theology*, 215–36; Thomas R. Schreiner, "Good-Bye and Hello: The Sabbath Command for New Covenant Believers," in *Progressive Covenantalism: Charting a Course between Dispensational and Covenant Theologies*, ed. Stephen J. Wellum and Brent E. Parker (Nashville: Broadman & Holman, 2016), 159–88.

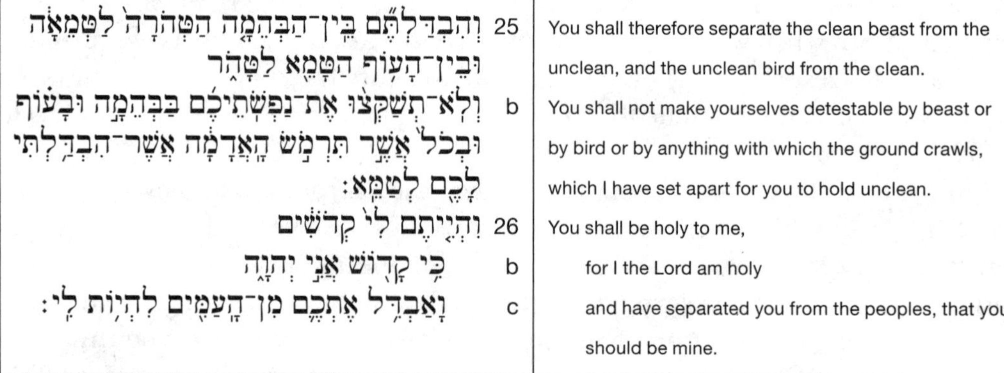

וְהִבְדַּלְתֶּם בֵּין־הַבְּהֵמָה הַטְּהֹרָה לַטְּמֵאָה וּבֵין־הָעוֹף הַטָּמֵא לַטָּהֹר	25	You shall therefore separate the clean beast from the unclean, and the unclean bird from the clean.
וְלֹא־תְשַׁקְּצוּ אֶת־נַפְשֹׁתֵיכֶם בַּבְּהֵמָה וּבָעוֹף וּבְכֹל אֲשֶׁר תִּרְמֹשׂ הָאֲדָמָה אֲשֶׁר־הִבְדַּלְתִּי לָכֶם לְטַמֵּא׃	b	You shall not make yourselves detestable by beast or by bird or by anything with which the ground crawls, which I have set apart for you to hold unclean.
וִהְיִיתֶם לִי קְדֹשִׁים	26	You shall be holy to me,
כִּי קָדוֹשׁ אֲנִי יְהוָה	b	for I the Lord am holy
וָאַבְדִּל אֶתְכֶם מִן־הָעַמִּים לִהְיוֹת לִי׃	c	and have separated you from the peoples, that you should be mine.

Fig. 12.9. Leviticus 20:25–26 in MT and ESV

1. Establish the original revealed meaning and application of the law.

Distinguishing between "the holy and the common, and between the unclean and the clean," was vital within Israel's religious life (Lev. 10:10; cf. 11:46–47; 20:25–26). I define God's holiness as *the reality and value of his divine fullness, expressed in his self-sustainability, his absoluteness and sole-ness, his excellence and worth, and the beautiful harmony of all his acts with that fullness.* Divine holiness is the embodiment of what it means to be God, and the Lord called his people to image his unique excellence and beauty to the world: "You shall be holy to me, for I the Lord am holy and have separated you from the peoples, that you should be mine" (Lev. 20:26).

Within the old covenant, *holy* and *common* related to a person, object, space, or time's state or status in relation to the Lord; everything not holy was common. Similarly, *unclean* and *clean* were distinct conditions associated with the ritual or moral standing of people, food, and space. What was clean could be either holy or common, and what was common could be either clean or unclean. (These relationships are represented by the adjoining boxes in figure 12.10.) What was holy, however, was neither to come in contact with what was unclean (= contamination) nor to be treated as if it were unclean (= desecration). (In figure 12.10, their boxes do not touch.)

Holiness and uncleanness were also dynamic, in that the particular state or condition sought to influence and overcome its parallel state or condition. (Figure 12.10 highlights this by the dotted lines, directional arrows, and bold-italics font.) But the common and clean were static, unable to transfer their state or condition, and they were understood only in relation to their partner: cleanness was the absence of uncleanness, and commonness was the absence of holiness.

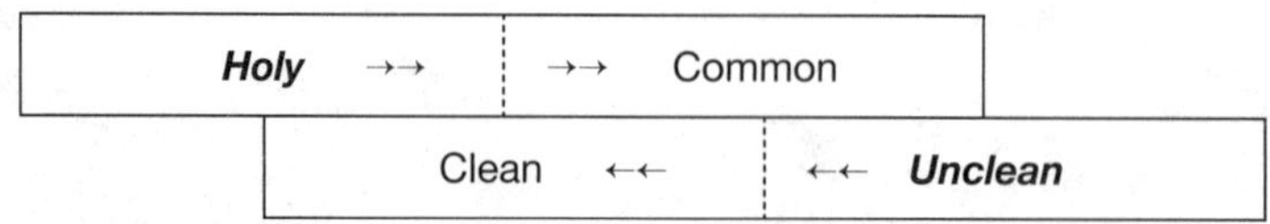

Fig. 12.10. The Holiness Continuum[35]

35. For this basic understanding of the holiness continuum in Leviticus, see John E. Hartley, "Holy and Holiness,

What was it about certain foods that made them unclean? Scholars have offered different answers,[36] but in my view the best response is that all unclean animals symbolically bore some association with the God-hostility or curse of the serpent in Genesis 3.[37]

The first explicit distinction between clean and unclean animals occurs in the narrative of Noah's flood, when YHWH directed Noah to take "seven pairs of all clean animals, the male and his mate, and a pair of the animals that are not clean, the male and his mate, and seven pairs of the birds of the heavens also, male and female, to keep their offspring alive on the face of all the earth" (Gen. 7:2–3; cf. v. 8). Noah then used "some of every clean animal and some of every clean bird" when he offered burnt offerings to the Lord following the deluge (8:20). Significantly, the account contains no clear instruction regarding the clean-unclean distinction. Noah appears to have already been well aware of this dichotomy, and Moses assumes that we as readers of the Pentateuch will make the necessary connections. Before the flood story, the place where forbidden food and animals are most clearly discussed is in the fall narrative of Genesis 3, so the reader is pushed back there to find answers.

Within this framework, the division between clean and unclean animals is most naturally understood as a result of the Adamic curse. I propose that the ancients considered as unclean those animals most closely associated with either the murderous activity of the serpent or the divine punishment against him. The serpent was "more crafty than any other beast of the field" (Gen. 3:1), moved the man and woman to eat what God had forbidden (2:17; 3:1–7), and was cursed more than "all livestock and all beasts of the field" (3:14). The beasts most imaging the serpent's "craftiness" are those predatory in nature (those with a will to kill), all of which were "unclean." Those animals most identified with the serpent's dust-eating, death-culminating curse would be bottom-feeders (the realm of dust) and those linked in any way to the realms of death and waste, all of which were "unclean."

More specifically, Leviticus 11 distinguishes the land, water, and air animals. Not all the associations with Genesis 3 are easy to assess, but a general pattern does seem clear. Naturally, we are having to "read between the lines," but I offer this schema as an alternative to other less biblically grounded proposals that scholars have suggested.

Among the terrestrial creatures, the clean include those that are both split-hooved and cud-chewing (Lev. 11:2–8). Hooved animals are ungulates, animals that use the tip of their toe (or hoof) to support the weight of their bodies. They thus touch as little of the *dust* as possible, their weight resting on the hard or rubbery sole and a hard wall formed by a thick nail rolled around the tip of the toe. Clean animals had to be both

---

Clean and Unclean," *DOT:P* 420–31; Jacob Milgrom, "Holy, Holiness, OT," *NIDB* 2:850–58. For an alternative view, see Gordon J. Wenham, *The Book of Leviticus*, NICOT (Grand Rapids: Eerdmans, 1979), 26.

36. For a survey, see Hartley, "Holy and Holiness, Clean and Unclean," 428–29; cf. Walter Houston, *Purity and Monotheism: Clean and Unclean Animals in Biblical Law*, JSOTSup 140 (Sheffield, UK: Sheffield Academic, 1993), 68–123.

37. Jacob Milgrom does not make this point, but he does suggest that the underlying principle between clean and unclean was the life-death nexus, in which clean is connected to life, and unclean to death (*Leviticus 1–16: A New Translation with Introduction and Commentary*, AB 3 [New Haven, CT: Yale University Press, 1998], 1001–3). Milgrom sees a level of randomness in the distinction between clean and unclean beasts, but he notes that Scripture promotes reverence for blood and life by limiting Israel's flesh intake to a minimal number of animals—herbivores from domesticated cattle and some wild game, fish, birds, and locusts.

split-hooved (double protection from the cursed dust) and cud-chewing, the latter of which means that they were ruminants—herbivores that spend extra time "ruminating" (or meditating) on the food that God supplies. No clean land animal was a predator. The unclean land animals were those that do not align with both the features above. They were animals with paws—those walking directly on the ground with no "protection" (11:27). They were also all the swarming creatures, which surround and infest (11:29–31) or which have multiple legs and crawl on their bellies in the dust (11:41–43).

As for the water creatures, clean animals were those with both fins and scales (11:9–12). Fins propel and give balance, whereas scales shield or guard. The unclean subterranean creatures were those that lacked this type of stability or protection—features also missing from Adam's leadership in the garden.

Finally, Leviticus gives no specific criteria to distinguish clean flying animals, though it does list nonpermitted birds and insects (11:13–23). Those bugs that hop on the ground (perhaps portraying the defeat of the curse) are clean. In contrast, all birds of prey that thrive on consuming flesh are unclean, as are all winged insects that do not hop on the ground but rest there.

Before the fall, God forbade the eating of a certain food (the tree of knowledge related to good and evil) in order to supply a context for mankind to mature in wisdom (Gen. 2:17; cf. 3:5). Adam and Eve failed to obey, still gaining knowledge of good and evil but by the wrong means (3:22). The result was that God cursed the world, and from this he also forbade a new food—unclean animals (7:2–3). This group of creatures were most likely identified by some commonality with the death-causing activities of the serpent or the curse connected with him.

Leviticus 20:25–26 identifies that one purpose of the clean- and unclean-food laws was to separate Israel from the nations. Because Israel's pagan neighbors were part of the serpent's offspring and represented the chaos, disorder, and death associated with him, the meaning Israel associated with unclean food paralleled the makeup of the nations themselves. So the Israelites' diet symbolically distinguished them from the peoples around them. It also set them up to point the world to YHWH's uniqueness (Ex. 19:5–6; Deut. 4:5–8), ultimately as the only Savior who could overcome curse with blessing (Gen. 12:3; 22:18).

2. Determine the theological significance of the law.

We have a God who is holy and whom we and the world should see and celebrate for who he is. John Hartley notes that within the old covenant, the rules dealing with clean and unclean animals "made the Israelites conscious at every meal that they were to order their lives to honor the holy God with whom they were in covenant."[38] For example, the ancient call to not eat pork served to heighten awe of YHWH's nature and worth and to distinguish God's people from those outside the covenant. We are told that pig's flesh was unclean because these animals do not chew their cud (Lev.

38. Hartley, "Holy and Holiness, Clean and Unclean," 429. The truth of this statement is heightened by the fact that the call to be holy as God is holy is directly associated with food regulations in three spots (Lev. 11:44–45; 20:25–26; Deut. 14:21; cf. Ex. 22:31).

11:7–8). Some propose that the lack of this activity symbolized a failure to appreciate God's provision[39]—much as Adam and Eve failed to value God's provision in the garden. Pigs are indiscriminate with respect to their diet, not only in the way that they will eat meat, vegetables, and even garbage but also in the way that females at times attack and even consume their own young. These features may further identify why the Lord tagged them as unclean.

Today, however, with the progression of redemptive history, Jesus has "declared all foods clean" (Mark 7:19), stressing that it's not what goes into a person's mouth but what comes out of a person's heart that defiles him (7:18–23).[40] Paul designates sin as impurity (Rom. 6:19; 2 Cor. 12:21; Eph. 5:3; 1 Thess. 4:7), and he calls us as Christians to "cleanse ourselves from every defilement of body and spirit" (2 Cor. 7:1). We are to be pure *in heart* (Matt. 5:8; cf. 2 Tim. 2:22) and to have a clean conscience (1 Tim. 1:5; 3:9; 2 Tim. 1:3). Nevertheless, with respect to foods, there is nothing unclean anymore. The Lord gave Peter a vision of unclean animals, commanded him, "Rise, Peter; kill and eat," and then asserted, "What God has made clean, do not call common" (Acts 10:10–15). From this Peter inferred that God would have believers in Christ no longer "call any person common or unclean" (Acts 10:28). This was the natural implication in light of the way in which unclean foods separated the Lord's people from the nations in the old covenant (Lev. 20:25–26). Jesus "has broken down in his flesh the dividing wall of hostility [between Jews and Gentiles] by abolishing the law of commandments expressed in ordinances, that he might create in himself one new man in place of the two, so making peace" (Eph. 2:14–15). Sadly, Peter himself was inconsistent in his application of this change, and Paul had to confront him (Gal. 2:11–14).

Now we must ask, "What exactly happened in salvation history to make all foods clean?" Paul states that the change directly relates to what Jesus did "through the cross" (Eph. 2:16)—Christ "disarmed the rulers and authorities and put them to open shame, by triumphing over them" (Col. 2:15). That is, in Jesus' first coming "the great dragon was thrown down, that ancient serpent, who is called the devil and Satan" (Rev. 12:9).[41] Unclean foods represented the God-hostility and curse identified with the first creation and fall. In Christ, however, the new creation is inaugurated (2 Cor. 5:17; Gal. 6:15), the curse is overcome by blessing (Gal. 3:13–14), and all foods are now symbolically clean.[42]

39. Mary Douglas, *Purity and Danger: An Analysis of Concepts of Pollution and Taboo* (New York: Praeger, 1966), 54.

40. That no food is "common" suggests that all food is also "holy" (Acts 10:14–15).

41. An amillennialist would further hold that this is the exact eschatological reality spoken about in Revelation 20:2: "And he seized the dragon, that ancient serpent, who is the devil and Satan, and bound him for a thousand years."

42. William N. Wilder argues that God's goal for Adam and Eve was always for them to enjoy both wisdom and kingship ("Illumination and Investiture: The Royal Significance of the Tree of Wisdom in Genesis 3," *WTJ* 68, 1 [2006]: 51–69). Their nakedness was a sign of immaturity that would have been replaced with investiture had they grown in the way and time that the Lord intended. This raises the possibility that the tree of the knowledge related to good and evil was a temporary prohibition and that the first couple would have had freedom to enjoy its fruit once they came of age. (A challenge here is that Genesis 2:17 uses לֹא + *yiqtol*, which usually expresses permanent prohibitions [see "The Nonindicative *Yiqtol* and *Weyiqtol*" in chapter 5].) In this light, one wonders whether the prohibition against unclean foods would have been understood as equally temporary, with complete

In Paul's words, "I know and am persuaded in the Lord Jesus that nothing is unclean in itself. . . . Everything is indeed clean, but it is wrong for anyone to make another stumble by what he eats" (Rom. 14:14, 20; cf. 1 Cor. 8:7–13). And again, "Everything created by God is good, and nothing is to be rejected if it is received with thanksgiving" (1 Tim. 4:4).

What, then, was the love principle behind Leviticus 20:25–26? Within the original Old Testament context, the call to not eat unclean food identified that *love of neighbor means that the Israelites were to maintain a display of God's holy animosity toward sin and the curse even in their diet.*

3. Summarize the lasting significance of the law for today.

God is forever holy, and his holiness continues to affect the ethical obligations of his people: "Be holy in all your conduct, since it is written, 'You shall be holy, for I am holy'" (1 Peter 1:15–16). Peter here echoes the truth of Leviticus 20:26, and he later highlights that what the Lord commanded Israel is now being fulfilled in the church: "But you are a chosen race, a royal priesthood, a holy nation, a people for his own possession, that you may proclaim the excellencies of him who called you out of darkness into his marvelous light" (1 Peter 2:9).

From Genesis 3:15 forward, the reader of Scripture anticipates a male deliverer, a serpent-slayer, who would triumph through tribulation, restoring order and bringing life. Jesus fulfills the Old Testament's prohibitions against unclean foods in this way. The food laws captured a portrait of God's wrath against rebellion and of his animosity against the works of Satan. Clean foods certainly pointed to the cleanness that Christ would win for all in him (John 13:10; 15:3; Heb. 10:22), but the unclean foods, too, were part of the shadow for which Christ is the substance (Col. 2:16–17; Heb. 10:1). The unclean was part of the curse that Christ bore at the cross, bearing the shame and guilt of all that is hostile to God (Gal. 3:13; 1 Peter 2:24). In Jesus, every promise is already "Yes" (2 Cor. 1:20), the new creation is already initiated (2 Cor. 5:17; Gal. 6:15), and the new covenant is already enacted (Heb. 8:6), rendering the old covenant already obsolete (8:13; 10:9; cf. Gal. 3:23–26). Many who were once enemies have now been "reconciled to God by the death of his Son," and these same ones "shall be saved by his life" (Rom. 5:10).

Significantly, the New Testament teaches that the purity that Christ has secured for believers should bear fruits of love for one another (1 Peter 1:22). As we consider what love of neighbor means today with respect to food, we must view it from two angles. First, love of neighbor means that those who are strong in faith, having full freedom in their consciences to eat and drink anything, must be careful not to judge or to cause to stumble those believers who are weaker in faith and who choose to abstain from eating certain things:

> One person believes he may eat anything, while the weak person eats only vegetables. . . . Let us not pass judgment on one another any longer, but rather

---

freedom to eat all foods after YHWH's "son" (Ex. 4:22–23) came of age, no longer being "under a guardian" or "enslaved to the elementary principles of the world" (Gal. 3:23–4:7).

> decide never to put a stumbling block or hindrance in the way of a brother. I know and am persuaded in the Lord Jesus that nothing is unclean in itself, but it is unclean for anyone who thinks it unclean. For if your brother is grieved by what you eat, you are no longer walking in love. (Rom. 14:2, 13–15)

Second, love of neighbor means that we will *not* stop proclaiming that Christ has triumphed on our behalf, opening the door for all peoples to stand reconciled to him. One way in which we can do this is by eating the foods that God once prohibited. Just as Old Testament believers *abstained* from these foods in order to proclaim and mirror God's holiness, so also New Testament believers *partake* of them for the same purpose—"So, whether you eat or drink, or whatever you do, do all to the glory of God" (1 Cor. 10:31). Within this framework, *bacon is victory food*!

Christians can now enjoy food that was once unclean as a testimony that Christ has defeated the serpent and with that the curse. The cultural distinctions that set Israel apart from the nations are now abolished. We still await the consummation when "the God of peace will soon crush Satan under your feet" (Rom. 16:20). Nevertheless, the eschatological shift from the old age of death to the new age of life has *already* begun, and the war against the serpent is decisively over. This means that we can rest in confidence, awaiting the day when the unclean will be fully cast out and the evidence of the curse will be no more (Rev. 21:27; 22:3).[43]

43. For centuries, many Jewish believers who cherish Christ (i.e., messianic Jews) have chosen to follow the clean-unclean food distinctions as a matter of Jewish cultural identity, recognizing this as a free choice and not an obligation. Paul would have been fine with this practice, especially when driven by a heart to win more Jews to Jesus (1 Cor. 9:20; cf. Acts 16:3 vs. Gal. 2:3). Yet a growing number of professing Christians in what some term the Hebrew Roots Movement claim that faithful Christians *ought* to follow the Old Testament law as much as is possible without the temple, including the keeping of the various holy days and food regulations. Like the Judaizers in Galatia who sought to "submit again to a yoke of slavery" (Gal. 5:1), these folks "*require* abstinence from foods that God created to be received with thanksgiving" (1 Tim. 4:3). Paul said that such teachers would arise "in later times," and he also characterized them as departing "from the faith by devoting themselves to deceitful spirits and teachings of demons" (4:1–2). Whether dealing with food (Gal. 2:11–14), the observance of holy days (4:10), or circumcision (5:2), all who *require* following the Old Testament law as though Christ had not changed everything "are severed from Christ" and "have fallen away from grace" (5:4). What matters today is faith in Christ working through love (5:6). We cannot keep the whole law (5:3; cf. Acts 15:10), so we must trust Christ, who fulfilled the law on behalf of his elect (Rom. 5:18; 8:4) and who fulfills the law through us by his Spirit as we live a life of love (Gal. 5:14; Rom. 2:26–29; 13:8–10).

Old Testament Promises and the Christian

The Challenge and Need for Christians to Claim Old Testament Promises

1. The importance of God's promises in the believer's life

The psalmist declared, "This is my comfort in my affliction, that your promise gives me life" (Ps. 119:50). This is even more true today than it was then in light of Christ's resurrected life, on which our future rests (1 Cor. 15:17–20). When we face suffering, God's promises in Scripture supply one of the bulwarks of hope for Christians. I say "*one* of the bulwarks of hope," because God's character and disposition toward the broken also give us hope: "O Israel, hope in the Lord! For with the Lord there is steadfast love, and with him is plentiful redemption" (Ps. 130:7; cf. Ex. 32:6–7; Deut. 10:17–18). Nevertheless, with respect to his promises, we trust that God *will* be faithful to his Word and that in his good time he *will* act.

God's promises do not merely supply comfort. They are one of the Lord's key provisions for helping us defeat sin in our pursuit of holiness. As Peter notes, "[The Lord] has granted to us his precious and very great promises, so that *through them* you may become partakers of the divine nature, having escaped from the corruption that is in the world because of sinful desire" (2 Peter 1:4; cf. 2 Cor. 7:1; 1 John 3:2–3).

We wage war against lust by recalling that "the pure in heart . . . shall see God" (Matt. 5:8). We also remember Jesus' warning that "it is better that you lose one of your members than that your whole body be thrown into hell" (5:29–30). We turn from anxiety and toward prayer and supplication with thanksgiving because we believe that when we do, "the peace of God, which surpasses all understanding, will guard [our] hearts and [our] minds in Christ Jesus" (Phil. 4:7). When we lose a job or face massive loss, we hold fast to the hope that "my God will supply every need of [ours] according to his riches in glory in Christ Jesus" (4:19). And when death's shadow draws near, we declare, "To me to live is Christ, and to die is gain" (1:21), trusting all the while that "the Lord is my shepherd . . . [and] even though I walk through the valley of the shadow of death, I will fear no evil, for you are with me" (Ps. 23:1, 4).

2. Which promises are for Christians?

This last text raises a question, though, for Psalm 23 is a song from the period of the old covenant. Paul declares in 2 Corinthians 1:20 that "all the promises of God find their Yes in [Jesus]." But was he talking about the old covenant promises, too—those that the Lord gave directly to national Israel? Can we as Christians claim as our own the various promises given before the time of Jesus? Should we have our kids sing these words?

> *Every* promise in the Book is mine,
> *Every* chapter, every verse, and every line.
> All the blessings of his love, divine—
> Every promise in the Book is mine.[44]

The "prosperity gospel" has quickly answered, "Yes," claiming that if Christians have enough faith, God will reward them today with all the spiritual *and* material prosperity detailed in the old covenant blessings.

> And if you faithfully obey the voice of the Lord your God, . . . blessed shall you be in the city, and blessed shall you be in the field. Blessed shall be the fruit of your womb and the fruit of your ground and the fruit of your cattle, the increase of your herds and the young of your flock. Blessed shall be your basket and your kneading bowl. Blessed shall you be when you come in, and blessed shall you be when you go out. (Deut. 28:1, 3–6; cf. 30:16)

Are these blessings from Deuteronomy something that we in Christ can or even should claim as ours today, already, by faith?[45]

Health-and-wealth teachers rightly affirm that "those who are of faith are blessed along with Abraham, the man of faith" (Gal. 3:9), and that "though [our Lord Jesus Christ] was rich, yet for your sake he became poor, so that you by his poverty might become rich" (2 Cor. 8:9). What is missed, however, is that Paul's "blessing" in Galatians 3:9 is focused on our receiving "the promised *Spirit* through faith" (Gal. 3:14) and that Abraham was among those who "died in faith, not having received the things promised" (Heb. 11:13). Furthermore, because the "poverty" of Christ in 2 Corinthians 8:9 is focused not on an abject material lack but on his incarnation (Phil. 2:6–8), our "riches" point not directly to material prosperity but to salvation and all its benefits (1 Cor. 1:4–8). How much these "benefits" relate to health and wealth in this life is what this section seeks to address.

44. The Sensational Nightingales, "Every Promise in the Book Is Mine," *Let Us Encourage You* (Malco Records, 2005; orig. 1957).

45. By "prosperity gospel" I do *not* mean speaking and working to see people move from material, social, emotional, and spiritual poverty to prosperity, for such a desire is God-honoring and stands as a natural fruit of the gospel in one's life (see Timothy Keller, "The Gospel and the Poor," *Themelios* 33, 3 [2008]: 8–22; cf. Craig L. Blomberg, *Neither Poverty nor Riches: A Biblical Theology of Possessions*, NSBT 7 [Downers Grove, IL: InterVarsity Press, 1999]; Steve Corbett and Brian Fikkert, *When Helping Hurts: How to Alleviate Poverty without Hurting the Poor—and Yourself*, 2nd ed. [Chicago: Moody Press, 2012]; Wayne Grudem and Barry Asmus, *The Poverty of Nations: A Sustainable Solution* [Wheaton, IL: Crossway, 2013]; Brian Fikkert and Russell Mask, *From Dependence to Dignity: How to Alleviate Poverty through Church-Centered Microfinance* [Grand Rapids: Zondervan, 2015]). Instead, what I mean by "prosperity gospel" is a type of teaching that replaces with worldliness the true good news that the reigning God saves and satisfies believing sinners by Christ Jesus' life, death, and resurrection. For more, see the next footnote.

3. The New Testament's application of Old Testament promises to Christians

As noted, my macro-purpose in this discussion is not to critique the health-and-wealth teaching but rather to equip Christians to think through the lasting significance of Old Testament promises.[46] In responding to prosperity teachers or in grasping for ourselves how Old Testament promises relate to believers, it is not enough to say simply, "We are part of the new covenant, and therefore old covenant promises do not apply to the church," for the New Testament apostles are very quick to cite Old Testament promises and to apply lasting significance to them!

For example, consider Romans 12:19, where Paul charges: "Never avenge yourselves, but leave it to the wrath of God, for it is written, 'Vengeance is mine, I will repay, says the Lord.'" Here the apostle quotes the promise from Deuteronomy 32:35, which YHWH asserts over all who would oppress his people: "Vengeance is mine. I will repay!" (cf. Heb. 10:30). Paul says that as Christians, we gain power to love our enemies in the present because we can rest assured that God will indeed judge rightly in the future. And we believe this because of an Old Testament promise.

Similarly, Hebrews 13:5–6 declares: "Keep your life free from love of money, and be content with what you have, for he has said, 'I will never leave you nor forsake you.'

46. For two helpful, balanced, recent critiques of the prosperity gospel, see John Piper, "Introduction to the Third Edition: New Realities in World Christianity and Twelve Appeals to Prosperity Preachers," in *Let the Nations Be Glad! The Supremacy of God in Missions*, 3rd ed. (Grand Rapids: Baker, 2010), 15–32; Michael Otieno Maura, Conrad Mbewe, Ken Mbugua, John Piper, and Wayne Grudem, *Prosperity? Seeking the True Gospel* (Nairobi: Africa Christian Textbooks Registered Trustees in partnership with The Gospel Coalition, 2015). As an initial response, I would say that a conscious or unconscious imbalanced belief in retribution theology—"what you sow you will reap in the here and now"—often bears devastating effects. The worldliness of prosperity theology is seen at least in the ways in which it (1) nurtures an entitlement mentality, (2) places undue guilt, (3) misrepresents God's character, and (4) minimizes Christ's saving work while exalting some at the expense of others. *First*, in my life and in the lives of many others who are part of Western evangelical churches, prosperity-gospel perspectives show up when we have wealth or health, expect to keep it, and get angry at God or at least very anxious when he takes it away. We feel entitled to a certain level of physical provision and protection right now. Oh, that we with Paul would live out the truth, "In any and every circumstance, I have learned the secret of facing plenty and hunger, abundance and need. I can do all things through him who strengthens me" (Phil. 4:12–13). *Second*, another subtle version of health-and-wealth thinking occurs when parishioners carry unjustified guilt or burden because they believe that their hardship or ailment must be due to their own lack of spiritual fervor. While possible (e.g., 1 Cor. 11:29–30), both the story of Job and Jesus' own teaching stress that some brokenness has nothing to do with our sin or the sins of our parents (Job 2:3; John 9:2–3). *Third*, prosperity preaching becomes full grown when popular personalities in North America, South America, Africa, and parts of Asia become rich by promoting a shallow, paralyzing, unqualified health-and-wealth message. They promise material riches or bodily wholeness for the here and now, if one has enough faith. But in doing so, as with idolatry in the Old Testament age, they misrepresent God's character and commitments, treating him as one whom we can manipulate and viewing material blessing as a wage earned (e.g., Hos. 2:12; 9:1; Mic. 1:7) (somewhat comparable to the Eastern religious principle of karma). In contrast, the Lord "is not partial and takes no bribe," and he "executes justice for the fatherless and the widow, and loves the sojourner, giving him food and clothing" (Deut. 10:17–18). *Fourth*, health-and-wealth teaching often fails to address the true core of the gospel—that the reigning God saves and satisfies believing sinners by Christ Jesus' life, death, and resurrection. In failing to address sin and the need for a Savior, they fail to clarify the only means of relief from eternal suffering. And in the end, the worldview repays little, except into the pockets of those who are not at all grieved over the ruin before them (Amos 6:6). God is not pleased with these destructive teachers, and to such as these he declared through Amos, "Prepare to meet your God" (4:12); "Woe to you who desire the day of the LORD! Why would you have the day of the LORD? It is darkness, and not light" (5:18).

So we can confidently say, 'The Lord is my helper; I will not fear; what can man do to me?'" Here the author quotes one Old Testament promise from Joshua 1:5 and one Old Testament expression of confidence from Psalm 118:6. This New Testament author sees his Old Testament Scriptures as lastingly relevant for the church. The psalmist proclaims Godward trust during a time of distress, and the author of Hebrews asserts that every believer can rest assured with the same truths. As for the promise, the author claims that we should not look to money for security *because* God has promised to always be with us! He cites the pledge that YHWH gave to Joshua just before Israel's conquest of Canaan: "No man shall be able to stand before you all the days of your life. Just as I was with Moses, so I will be with you. I will not leave you or forsake you" (Josh. 1:5). Somehow we can legitimately use this promise to help us battle giants such as covetousness in our own lives.

As Christians, we must have a framework for helping the church benefit from God's ancient promises such as these, yet in a way that does not produce abuses. In the discussion that follows, we will look at some key verses that should guide our thinking, and then I will propose some biblical-theological guidelines for the Christian's application of Old Testament promises.

Five Foundational Texts for a Biblical Theology of God's Promises

I have noted the challenge and necessity for Christians to claim Old Testament promises. Now I want to focus on five key texts that have helped me assess how Old Testament promises relate to new covenant believers.

1. Deuteronomy 30:6–7

The first passage comes from Deuteronomy 30:6–7: "And the Lord your God will circumcise your heart and the heart of your offspring, so that you will love the Lord your God with all your heart and with all your soul, that you may live. And the Lord your God will put all these curses on your foes and enemies who persecuted you." Notice here that in the age of new covenant heart circumcision (already being realized in the church, Rom. 2:28–29), God will take the curses of Deuteronomy—the very curses that served as warnings to old covenant national Israel—and will pour them out on the enemies of the restored community. This suggests that the old covenant curses become new covenant curses, which God brings not on the members of the new covenant but on their enemies. As in the Abrahamic covenant, under which YHWH promised to curse anyone who dishonored the patriarch and those he represented (Gen. 12:3), so, too, the Lord will confront those who spurn his new covenant community. We see this reaffirmed in both Romans 12:19 and Hebrews 10:30, which recall Deuteronomy 32:35–36: "'Vengeance is mine, and recompense, for the time when their foot shall slip; for the day of their calamity is at hand, and their doom comes swiftly.' For the LORD will vindicate his people and have compassion on his servants."

2. 2 Corinthians 6:16

As I set out in my discussion on Old Testament prophecy in chapter 1, Moses originally motivated those in the old covenant to loyalty by distinguishing blessings that would come for obedience (Lev. 26:3–13; Deut. 28:1–14) and curses that would result from disobedience (Lev. 26:14–39; Deut. 28:15–68). Being certain that Israel's stubbornness would produce its destruction (e.g., Deut. 4:25–28; 31:16–18, 27–29), the prophet also looked beyond curse to restoration blessings, fulfilled in the period that we now know as the new covenant (Lev. 26:40–45; Deut. 4:29–31; 30:1–14; cf. Jer. 31:31–34).

Drawing on this framework, Paul declared in 2 Corinthians 6:16: "What agreement has the temple of God with idols? For we are the temple of the living God; as God said, 'I will make my dwelling among them and walk among them, and I will be their God, and they shall be my people.'" What is significant here is that one of the Old Testament texts that Paul used to justify the idea that the members of the church are indeed God's temple is an original old covenant blessing and *not* a restoration blessing: "If you walk in my statutes and observe my commandments and do them, . . . I will make my dwelling among you, and my soul shall not abhor you. And I will walk among you and will be your God, and you shall be my people" (Lev. 26:3, 11–12). Paul is likely also citing Ezekiel 37:27, which is a new covenant restoration blessing that is more in line with the type of promise that we would expect: "My dwelling place shall be with them, and I will be their God, and they shall be my people." But because Leviticus 26:12 mentions the Lord's commitment to "walk" among his people, Paul likely has both Old Testament texts in mind.

I draw two important observations from the use of these texts: (a) The restoration blessings of the old covenant include all the original blessings, but in escalation and with never the chance of loss. This fact is suggested in the way that Ezekiel's new covenant promise reasserts the original old covenant blessings from Leviticus 26. (b) The original old covenant blessings *and* the restoration blessings have direct bearing on Christians. Paul appears to draw together both texts, suggesting not only their close tie in the Old Testament but also that, with the new covenant restoration blessings, the original old covenant blessings do indeed relate to believers.

Paul is applying to the church of Jesus one of the old covenant blessings that was contingent on perfect obedience: "If you walk in my statutes and observe my commandments and do them, . . . I will make my dwelling among you" (Lev. 26:3, 11). Most likely, he is seeing Christ's perfect obedience to be wholly meeting for his elect the required loyalty needed to enjoy God's blessing (cf. John 15:10; Rom. 5:18–19; 8:4; Phil. 2:8; Heb. 5:8). We as the church are delighting in the presence of God today because of what Jesus has done on our behalf and not because we have kept the law perfectly.

3. Ephesians 1:3, 13–14

Paul highlighted in Ephesians 1:3, 13–14:

> Blessed be the God and Father of our Lord Jesus Christ, who has blessed us in Christ with every spiritual blessing in the heavenly places . . . . In him you also, when you heard the word of truth, the gospel of your salvation, and believed in him, were sealed with the promised Holy Spirit, who is the guarantee of our inheritance until we acquire possession of it, to the praise of his glory.

Most scholars think that the "spiritual blessings in the heavenly places" are all the blessings that the Spirit of Christ secures for the saints—both those *already* enjoyed, such as election, adoption to sonship, redemption, forgiveness, and sealing, and those *not yet* enjoyed, such as the full inheritance (Eph. 4:4–14). All of these are the eschatological realization of the Old Testament's hopes related to new covenant restoration blessings (e.g., Deut. 30:6; Isa. 53:11; Jer. 31:33–34; 32:40; Ezek. 36:27; Dan. 9:24). Therefore, while *all* of God's promises find their "Yes" in Christ (2 Cor. 1:20), we enjoy some *already*, while others remain for the future. "[He] has also put his seal on us and given us his Spirit in our hearts as a guarantee" (1:22).

4. Hebrews 6:7–12

My fourth text serves as a launching point for a broader discovery I have made in the book of Hebrews that addresses the role of Christian obedience for receiving what God has promised. The author reasons that every person—represented by the imagery of old covenant land—"that has drunk the rain that often falls on it, and produces a crop useful to those for whose sake it is cultivated, receives a blessing from God. But if it bears thorns and thistles, it is worthless and near to being cursed, and its end is to be burned" (Heb. 6:7–8). He then asserts, however, "Though we speak in this way, yet in your case, beloved, we feel sure of better things—things that belong to salvation. For God is not unjust so as to overlook your work and the love that you have shown for his name in serving the saints, as you still do" (6:9–10). Finally he charges, "We desire each one of you to show the same earnestness to have the full assurance of hope until the end, so that you may not be sluggish, but imitators of those who through faith and patience inherit the promises" (6:11–12).

Because in the very next verse the author speaks of "when God made a promise to Abraham" (Heb. 6:13), we know that the promises to which he refers in verse 12 include those in the Old Testament. The only ones who will inherit these promises are those who persevere until the end, maintaining a believing heart and not falling away by giving into sin's deceitfulness (3:12–13). These alone are truly part of the new covenant, for it is these who truly share in the work of the new covenant Mediator:

"For we have come to share in Christ, if indeed we hold our original confidence firm to the end" (3:14; cf. 8:6–7, 13; 9:15).

Like other New Testament teachers (e.g., Matt. 5:8; 2 Cor. 7:1; Rev. 21:27), the author of Hebrews emphasizes that "without [holiness] no one will see the Lord" (Heb. 12:14). Persevering loyalty is a necessary condition to enjoy the future inheritance, for future judgment will be in accord with (though not on the basis of) deeds we do in this life (Matt. 16:27; Rom. 2:6; 2 Cor. 5:10; 1 Peter 1:17; Rev. 2:23; 20:12). Thus Paul can urge Timothy, "Keep a close watch on yourself and on the teaching. Persist in this, for by so doing you will save both yourself and your hearers" (1 Tim. 4:16). And elsewhere he can stress, "If you live according to the flesh you will die, but if by the Spirit you put to death the deeds of the body, you will live" (Rom. 8:13; cf. 1 Cor. 6:9–10; Gal. 5:19–24; Eph. 5:5).

But this new covenant call to persevere in faith is *not like* the old covenant's call to obey in order to live: "If a person does [my statutes and rules], he shall live by them: I am the LORD" (Lev. 18:5; cf. Rom. 10:5; Gal. 3:12). Speaking predominantly to the unregenerate, the old covenant charged Israel to pursue righteousness (Deut. 16:20), and it declared that the people would be counted righteous and secure life only *if* they met *all* of the covenant's demands (6:25; 8:1; cf. 4:1). Yet for Paul, "the very commandment that promised life proved to be death" (Rom. 7:10). "The law is holy, and the commandment is holy and righteous and good" (7:12). Yet the majority in "Israel who pursued a law that would lead to righteousness did not succeed in reaching that law . . . because they did not pursue it by faith, but as if it were based on works" (9:31–32). Paul can thus declare that "Christ is the end of the law for righteousness to everyone who believes" (10:4), because by Christ's perfect obedience in life and death God frees those who believe from sin's condemning power (5:18–19; 8:1; Col. 2:14) and declares us righteous and reconciled (Rom. 5:9–10; 2 Cor. 5:21). That is, in the new covenant, righteousness and life become the foundation and not just the goal.

From the perspective of Hebrews, Christ's priestly work as new covenant Mediator provides an unprecedented "sure and steadfast anchor of the soul" (Heb. 6:19) and "a better hope" than that of the old covenant (7:19). This is so for at least two reasons. First, unlike the sinful old covenant priests who themselves died, "[the high priest Jesus] always lives to make intercession" for those he saves (7:25), which means that we can "with confidence draw near to the throne of grace," expecting to "receive mercy and find grace to help in time of need" (4:16). The one with all authority in heaven and on earth has our back! Furthermore, by his death he not only "redeems [all his saints] from the transgressions committed under the first covenant" (9:15) but also "has perfected for all time those who are being sanctified" (10:14). Those in the new covenant *start* from the basis of being completely forgiven for all time (10:17–18), and this places our pursuit of holiness on a completely different footing from that of the old covenant. With this, God now writes his laws on our minds (10:16), moving us to follow his ways. Stated another way, because through Christ's single sacrifice "we have been sanctified" (10:10) "with our hearts sprinkled clean from an evil conscience and our bodies washed with pure water" (10:22), we can now "hold fast the confession of our hope without wavering" (10:23), knowing that God is *already* 100 percent for us in Jesus (13:5) and that "he who promised is faithful" (10:23). We have already "come to Mount Zion and to the city of the living God, the heavenly Jerusalem" (12:22), and he will "equip [us] with everything good that [we] may do his will, working in us that which is pleasing in his sight, through Jesus Christ, to whom be glory forever and ever" (13:21).

All sins that true saints seek to conquer are ones that God has already forgiven in Christ. We will receive our future inheritance on the basis of Christ's new covenant sacrifice alone. We must persevere and enjoy "the holiness without which no one will see the Lord" (Heb. 12:14). But by means of our past pardon, Christ's present intercession, and the promises of future reward for the faithful and of future punishment for those who fall away, God generates persevering faith, hope, and love and thus makes certain the endurance of all members of the new covenant.

5. 1 Peter 3:9–12

The final foundational text I want to address is 1 Peter 3:9–12, in which Peter claims the promise of divine favor in Psalm 34:12–16 as lastingly relevant for the church:

> Do not repay evil for evil or reviling for reviling, but on the contrary, bless, for to this you were called, that you may obtain a blessing. For
>
> "Whoever desires to love life
> and see good days,
> let him keep his tongue from evil
> and his lips from speaking deceit;
> let him turn away from evil and do good;
> let him seek peace and pursue it.
> For the eyes of the Lord are on the righteous,
> and his ears are open to their prayer.
> But the face of the Lord is against those who do evil."

Psalm 34 holds out a vision of eschatological blessing for the righteous ones (plural) who pursue good and not evil, and Peter here claims that this hope still exists for believers today. The retribution principle that stands behind the psalm appears to build on the covenantal blessing-curse structure of Leviticus 26 and Deuteronomy 28, yet it colors these promises in eschatological hues. This future orientation is clear in the fact that the psalmist knew that in the present many afflictions would come to God's followers, and yet he was confident that "the LORD hears and delivers them out of all their troubles" (Ps. 34:17[H18]) and that those who serve YHWH and take refuge in him will not be condemned (34:22[H23]). In contrast, those who hate the righteous one (singular), which I believe is shorthand for the messianic king, will be condemned (34:21[H22]; cf. 2:12). Peter, too, clearly recognized that obedient Christians suffer

(1 Peter 2:19–23; 3:14, 17; 4:12–19), and he, too, remained certain that in time God would "restore, confirm, strengthen, and establish you" (5:10).

At one level, the "blessing" that is sought in 1 Peter 3:9 appears to be something that God-followers can *already* enjoy in light of its connection to the "living hope" into which saints are already born (1:3; cf. 1:22–24; 5:1). We see the present nature of "blessing" in 4:14, where the apostle stresses, "If you are insulted for the name of Christ, *you are blessed*, because the Spirit of glory and of God rests upon you." From this perspective, Peter stresses that we experience numerous present expressions of divine favor as we pursue right conduct by faith and in God's power (1:5).[47]

At a greater level, however, most of the "blessing" that we seek appears to remain *not yet*, for it relates to the future "inheritance that is imperishable, undefiled, and unfading, kept in heaven for you" (1 Peter 1:4). It relates to the hope that our faith may result "in praise and glory and honor at the revelation of Jesus Christ" (1:7) and to "the unfading crown of glory" that we long to receive (5:4). We see this future orientation in 3:14, which reads, "But even if you should suffer for righteousness' sake, *you will be blessed*."

From Peter's perspective, the pursuit of "blessing" is in no way works-righteousness, for Christ's work on the cross purchased not only our justification but also our sanctification. By God's "great mercy, *he has caused* us to be born again to a living hope through the resurrection of Jesus Christ from the dead" (1 Peter 1:3). We "*by God's power* are being guarded through faith for a salvation ready to be revealed in the last time" (1:5). We serve "*by the strength that God supplies*—in order that in everything God may be glorified through Jesus Christ" (4:11). Our faithful pursuit of blessing today, therefore, is a fruit that points to the Lord's work in our lives.

Guidelines for the Christian's Application of Old Testament Promises

With these texts in hand, I want to offer some guidelines for the Christian's application of Old Testament promises.

47. Wayne A. Grudem (*1 Peter*, TNTC 17 [Downers Grove, IL: InterVarsity Press, 1988], 157) finds no less than ten "blessings" in this life that Peter stressed result from a Christian's right conduct: (1) loving Christ leads to unutterable joy (1:8); (2) continuing faith leads to more benefits of salvation (1:9); (3) holy life with fear leads to avoiding God's fatherly discipline (1:17); (4) partaking of spiritual milk leads to growing up toward salvation (2:2); (5) trusting God and obeying him leads to his approval (2:19–20); (6) submitting to husbands leads to husbands won for Christ (3:1–2); (7) living considerately with one's wife leads to a husband's unhindered prayers (3:7); (8) enduring reproach for the name of Christ leads to a spirit of glory and of God's resting on you (4:14); (9) casting one's cares on God leads to his caring for one's needs (5:7); and (10) resisting the devil leads to God's restoring, confirming, strengthening, and establishing you (5:9–10). To these I would add that humility before God leads to enjoyment of his grace (5:5).

1. Recognize the importance of God's promises for our pursuit of holiness.

Faith in God's promises creates hope or dread, and what we anticipate tomorrow changes who we are today. Notice how Peter stresses the central importance of God's promises in our pursuit of godliness: "He has granted to us his precious and very great promises, so that through them you may become partakers of the divine nature, having escaped from the corruption that is in the world because of sinful desire" (2 Peter 1:4; cf. Rom. 4:18–21; 15:13). Both Paul and John make similar statements: "Since we have these promises, beloved, let us cleanse ourselves from every defilement of body and spirit, bringing holiness to completion in the fear of God" (2 Cor. 7:1). "Beloved, we are God's children now, and what we will be has not yet appeared; but we know that when he appears we shall be like him, because we shall see him as he is. And everyone who thus hopes in him purifies himself as he is pure" (1 John 3:2–3).

A fundamental way that we as Christians are to fight sin and to pursue holiness is by overcoming sinful desire by embracing higher, more beautiful desires. Sin makes deceitful promises that lure us away from God, and we battle the desires of the flesh by trusting God's promises for a better tomorrow. We put our faith in the Lord's promise of future grace, and in doing so we gain fresh power in our pursuit of godliness.[48] God's promises confront a whole host of sins.

If our struggle is with *anxiety*, we turn from worry and heed Jesus' call to "seek first the kingdom of God and his righteousness," confident that "all these things will be added to you" (Matt. 6:33). We engage in "prayer and supplication with thanksgiving," trusting that God's peace "will guard your hearts and your minds in Christ Jesus" (Phil. 4:6–7). When *covetousness* rises in our soul, we nurture contentment and keep our lives free from the love of money by recalling such promises as "I will never leave you nor forsake you" (Heb. 13:5) and "My God will supply every need of yours according to his riches in glory in Christ Jesus" (Phil. 4:19). Jesus used God's promises to motivate his followers to fight *lust* in pursuit of sexual purity: "Blessed are the pure in heart, for they shall see God" (Matt. 5:8; cf. 5:29–30). Similarly, to overcome seeds of *bitterness*, Jesus warned, "If you do not forgive others their trespasses, neither will your Father forgive your trespasses" (6:15). Also, Paul motivates his readers to follow his charge to "repay no one evil for evil" and to "never avenge yourselves" by promising that God takes seriously all sins against his own people and will repay: "Leave it to the wrath of God, for it is written, 'Vengeance is mine, I will repay, says the Lord'" (Rom. 12:17, 19). According to Jesus, we battle *fear of man* by heightening our fear of God, recalling how valuable we are to him and recognizing that the consequence of not living for his pleasure is far greater than anything that man can do to us: "And do not fear those who kill the body but cannot kill the soul. Rather fear him who can destroy both soul and body in hell. Are not two sparrows sold for a penny? And not one of them will fall to the ground apart from your Father. But even the hairs of your head are all numbered.

48. For an entire book addressing this topic, see John Piper, *Future Grace: The Purifying Power of the Promises of God*, 2nd ed. (Colorado Springs: Multnomah, 2012).

Fear not, therefore; you are of more value than many sparrows" (Matt. 10:28–31). Assurance that God is already 100 percent for us in Christ is fundamental to battling *fear of condemnation* and to pursuing holiness. The only sins that we can overcome are forgiven ones, for we must move ahead in the power of blood-bought grace. Those in Christ Jesus trust that "there is . . . now no condemnation" (Rom. 8:1), for "Christ Jesus is the one who died—more than that, who was raised—who is at the right hand of God, who indeed is interceding for us" (8:34; cf. 8:32; John 10:27–30). Finally, to battle *fear of failure*, we believe promises such as "He who began a good work in you will bring it to completion at the day of Jesus Christ" (Phil. 1:6; cf. Jer. 32:40; 1 Thess. 5:23–24).

Our trust in God's future grace is a fundamental way that the Lord intends for believers to become more like him. Christians must recognize the importance of God's promises for our pursuit of holiness.

2. Celebrate that in Christ, all of God's promises are *already* "Yes"—both blessings and curses.

Paul stressed that "all the promises of God find their Yes in [Jesus Christ]" (2 Cor. 1:20). This would include both the old covenant's original blessings and curses and its restoration blessings and curses, the latter of which include the former and are the blessings and curses of the new covenant.

With respect to *blessings*, all the old covenant blessings and restoration blessings from Leviticus 26 and Deuteronomy 28 and 30 are the new covenant blessings that are *already* "Yes" in Christ (for a full list, see fig. 1.6 in chap. 1). As Paul notes, God has already "blessed us in Christ with every spiritual blessing in the heavenly places" (Eph. 1:3; cf. 2 Cor. 1:22).

As for *curses*, Christ bears on himself God's curse against all believers: "Christ redeemed us from the curse of the law by becoming a curse for us" (Gal. 3:13; cf. John 3:14–15; 2 Cor. 5:17; 1 Peter 2:24). This means that true new covenant members will not experience curse in a punitive way. We can still experience God's immediate "wrath" through human authorities (Rom. 13:4), forms of his "judgment" (1 Cor. 11:29–32), and his fatherly "discipline" (Heb. 12:7–11; Rev. 3:19). All of these carry out the revealed purpose of biblical curses—to move people to repentance and to grow them in holiness (Lev. 26:18, 21, 23, 27). Nevertheless, "since . . . we have now been justified by his blood, much more shall we be saved by him from the [ultimate] wrath of God" (Rom. 5:9; cf. John 3:36). No level of earthly discipline or consequence calls into question the eternal security of any believer.

Old covenant curses become the new covenant's curses (Deut. 30:7) and are visible within the New Testament as warnings of punishment against apostasy and against all who stand at odds with God and his people. For example, new covenant curses are evident in (a) Jesus' parable of the "sheep and goats" (Matt. 25:31–46), (b) Jesus' "blessings and woes" in the Sermon on the Plain (Luke 6:20–26), and (c) the numerous warning passages that dot the New Testament, especially in Paul's letters, Hebrews, and Revelation. For example, Paul said, "If we endure, we will also reign with him;

if we deny him, he also will deny us" (2 Tim. 2:12). Finally, Hebrews emphasizes that "if we go on sinning deliberately after receiving the knowledge of the truth, there no longer remains a sacrifice for sins, but a fearful expectation of judgment, and a fury of fire that will consume the adversaries" (Heb. 10:26–27).[49]

Within the new covenant, the old covenant curses are renewed for two reasons. First, they serve as a means of grace to the elect in order to generate within them reverent fear of God leading to greater holiness. Every sinner deserves death, and any experience of divine forbearance or even lesser punishment is designed to lead us to repentance (Lev. 26:18, 21, 23, 27; Rom. 2:4). When God disciplined in the old covenant, it was met by hardness rather than repentance (e.g., Amos 4:6–11), so YHWH declared, "Prepare to meet your God" (4:12). The new covenant Scriptures are loaded with warnings, and failure to trust and obey God's revelation would result in curse. Nevertheless, the author of Hebrews could declare of his audience, "We feel sure of better things—things that belong to salvation" (Heb. 6:9). Indeed, whereas in the old covenant the majority never heeded God's word, all true new covenant members will heed God's warnings (not perfectly, but truly, in Christ), thus identifying their true connection with the new covenant Mediator. "For we have come to share in Christ, if indeed we hold our original confidence firm to the end" (Heb. 3:14; cf. 6:11–12 with 8:6–7, 13; 9:15).[50]

Second, old covenant curses are renewed in the new covenant in order to declare lasting punishment on all apostates and those who stand against the Lord and his people (cf. Gen. 12:2; Deut. 30:7). This role is very clear in the warning passages of Hebrews, where the author quotes the new covenant curse text in Deuteronomy 32:35 and declares punishment on apostates who for a while looked as though they were a part of the new covenant but then turned on God: "How much worse punishment, do you think, will be deserved by the one who has trampled underfoot the Son of God, and has profaned the blood of the covenant by which he was sanctified, and has outraged the Spirit of grace? For we know him who said, 'Vengeance is mine; I will repay'" (Heb. 10:29–30; cf. 2 Peter 2:1).

3. Affirm that while all of the Bible's promises are already "Yes" in Christ, they are *not yet* all fully realized.

As highlighted, Paul affirms that God has already "blessed us in Christ with every spiritual blessing in the heavenly places" (Eph. 1:3). He stresses that the "blessing" is "in the heavenly places" and that the full inheritance is not yet ours, though it is secured.

49. For more examples of new covenant curses, see Matt. 6:15; Rom. 8:13; 11:22; 1 Cor. 6:9–11; Gal. 5:4, 19–21; Heb. 2:3; 6:4–8; 10:28–31; 12:15; Rev. 2:5, 16, 22–23; 22:19.

50. For this view of the warning passages in Hebrews, see Christopher W. Cowan, "The Warning Passages of Hebrews and the New Covenant Community," in *Progressive Covenantalism: Charting a Course between Dispensational and Covenant Theologies*, ed. Stephen J. Wellum and Brent E. Parker (Nashville: Broadman & Holman, 2016), 189–213; cf. Cowan, *"Confident of Better Things": Assurance of Salvation in the Letter to the Hebrews* (Ph.D. diss., The Southern Baptist Theological Seminary, 2012); Thomas R. Schreiner and Ardel B. Caneday, *The Race Set before Us: A Biblical Theology of Perseverance and Assurance* (Downers Grove, IL: InterVarsity Press, 2001); Thomas R. Schreiner, *Run to Win the Prize: Perseverance in the New Testament* (Wheaton, IL: Crossway, 2010).

He says that the Spirit of Christ in us "is the guarantee of our inheritance until we acquire possession of it" (1:14; cf. 2 Cor. 1:20, 22).

Of all the blessings in Leviticus 26:3–12, verses 11–12 alone focus on the presence of God. The rest address various physical, material blessings of provision and protection. While Paul's use of Leviticus 26 in 2 Corinthians 6:16 (see above) suggests that indeed old covenant blessings matter for Christians, the fact that the apostle focused only on the blessing related to God's Spirit in the midst of his people highlights that the material blessings are still to come in the new earth. They are ***already*** our inheritance but ***not yet*** ours to enjoy in the fullness that we will have in the age to come.

God does promise to "supply every need of yours according to his riches in glory in Christ Jesus" (Phil. 4:19). Yet as Paul stresses earlier, we must be willing to let the Lord define our needs, learning how "to be brought low and . . . how to abound" (4:12). Today we look to the Lord for daily bread (Matt. 6:11), trusting that he values his people and will give food, drink, and clothing in due measure to those who "seek first the kingdom of God and his righteousness" (6:25–26, 31–33). We also rest confident in Jesus' command and promise, "Give, and it will be given to you. Good measure, pressed down, shaken together, running over, will be put into your lap" (Luke 6:38). Yet as was clear in Paul's own life, having great faith in the truth of these promises does not secure a life free of beatings, stonings, shipwrecks, dangers, toil and hardship, sleepless nights, hunger and thirst, and cold and exposure (2 Cor. 11:23–28).

Similarly, Jesus often healed physical sickness and charged his disciples to do the same (Matt. 4:23; 10:6–8; Mark 2:8–12). Nevertheless, in his first coming he mostly restricted his ministry to the Jews (Matt. 10:6–8), he raised only three people from the dead (i.e., the ruler's daughter, Mark 5:35–36, 41–43; the son of the widow of Nain, Luke 7:12–15; Lazarus, John 11:38–46), and he did not right all wrongs or relieve all pains (Luke 4:16–21; 7:18–23). There is a tension that we must hold in this "already-but-not-yet" period: "Truly, I say to you, there is no one who has left house or brothers or sisters or mother or father or children or lands for my sake and for the gospel, who will not receive a hundredfold *now in this time*, houses and brothers and sisters and mothers and children and lands, *with persecutions*, and *in the age to come* eternal life" (Mark 10:29–30). We must live today recognizing the truth of Christ's declaration that "some of you they will put to death," while always trusting, "But not a hair of your head will perish" and "by your endurance you will gain your lives" (Luke 21:16, 18–19).

Paul, too, healed only sporadically and does not appear to have expected that all would be healed in this age. He healed the crippled man in Lystra (Acts 14:10), the demonized girl in Philippi (16:18), many people in Ephesus (19:12), and Eutychus when he was taken up dead after falling out of a window (20:9–10). But he couldn't gain relief from his "thorn," whether it was sickness or persecution (2 Cor. 12:7), and he couldn't heal himself of the ailment that he had when he preached in Galatia (Gal. 4:13–14). He also evidently couldn't heal Epaphroditus of his life-threatening sickness (Phil. 2:26–27), Timothy of his stomach ailments (1 Tim. 5:23), or Trophimus, whom he "left . . . ill, at Miletus" (2 Tim. 4:20).

My point in all of this is to stress that the "living hope" into which God has caused us to be born relates "to an inheritance that is imperishable, undefiled, and unfading, kept in heaven for you" (1 Peter 1:3–4). The Spirit is *already* ours, but the full inheritance is *not yet* (Eph. 1:3, 13–14; cf. 2 Cor. 1:22). Prosperity-gospel advocates are wrong in thinking that more faith will bring health and wealth today. They are also wrong not because they assert that old covenant blessings apply to Christians but because their eschatology is overrealized. They are wanting to bring the future into the present too quickly.

In this overlap of the ages, our future destiny is secure in Christ, but our physical bodies still rest firmly in the old, cursed creation. Nevertheless, for believers, experiencing the effects of the old age's curse is now holiness-generating rather than destructive.

- The battle with sin is still evident, but God has freed believers from sin's enslavement and condemnation. Furthermore, rather than being "given over" (παραδίδωμι) to rebellion and a debased mind (Rom. 1:24, 26, 28), God now "gives us over" (παραδίδωμι) to obedience and a renewed mind (6:16–18; 12:2; cf. 7:22–23, 25).
- The battle with brokenness and decay is very apparent with every cold and every struggle with cancer, but such sufferings only develop our dependent faith in God and heighten our longing for the future (Rom. 8:20–23; 2 Cor. 4:16–18).
- The battle with death looms over all of us, but in Christ the sting is removed and death becomes the channel to great reward: "For to me to live is Christ, and to die is gain" (Phil. 1:21; cf. Rom. 5:17; 6:23; Rev. 22:4).

The New Testament is clear that believers in this age are to expect suffering, tribulation, and affliction of all sorts. Jesus said, "If they persecuted me, they will also persecute you" (John 15:20). He also stressed, "In the world you will have tribulation. But take heart; I have overcome the world" (John 16:33). Discipleship comes at great cost (Luke 14:33; John 12:25). Just as Christ had to endure the cross before enjoying his resurrection body, so, too, the church as the body of Christ must carry our cross, identifying with Christ in his suffering, before receiving our resurrection bodies (Mark 8:34; 1 Peter 4:13). God's discipline in our lives nurtures holiness and righteousness (Heb. 12:7–11), and we endure today knowing that something better is coming tomorrow (10:34; 13:12–14; 1 Peter 1:6–7).

Paul said, "Through many tribulations we must enter the kingdom of God" (Acts 14:22). God has granted that we "should not only believe in [Christ] but also suffer for his sake" (Phil. 1:29). We are "destined" for "afflictions" (1 Thess. 3:3), and "all who desire to live a godly life in Christ Jesus will be persecuted" (2 Tim. 3:12). Paul himself experienced trials far broader than persecution—"afflictions, hardships, calamities, beatings, imprisonments, riots, labors, sleepless nights, hunger" (2 Cor. 6:4–5; cf. 11:23–28). As he did, he said, "In any and every circumstance, I have learned the secret of facing plenty and hunger, abundance and need. I can do all things through him who strengthens me" (Phil. 4:12–13).

If you are a believer, I encourage you to boldly claim the promises of God in *all* of Scripture, following the pattern of the New Testament authors. Any promise related to God's presence, favor, power, or pleasure is *already* something that we can enjoy, for it comes to us today by the Spirit of Christ. All other promises addressing more physical, material provision and protection will indeed be realized, but such blessings are certain only at the consummation of the new heavens and new earth when we will receive our resurrection bodies and when there will be no more tears, death, mourning, crying, or pain (Rev. 21:4).

"With the LORD there is steadfast love, and with him is plentiful redemption" (Ps. 130:7). In light of his character, God may still be pleased at any moment to bring our future hope into the present through a miracle act of power. We must therefore continue to seek that others be relieved of poverty (Deut. 10:17–19; 15:11; Ps. 41:1; Gal. 2:10; 1 John 3:17) and to pray that God would heal those sick and suffering (James 5:13–15; cf. 1 Cor. 12:9), all for God's glory and his kingdom's advance. God is pleased to magnify his power, but he can do this either by removing the pain or by sustaining us through it. The Lord will bring relief according to his timetable, manner, and degree, but we can trust that he will work out all things for our good (Rom. 8:28) and that the day is coming when all will be restored and God's people will never again hunger or thirst (Rev. 7:16).

4. Consider how Christ's fulfillment of Old Testament hopes influences our appropriation of Old Testament promises.

Jesus highlighted how he came not "to abolish" the Law or the Prophets but "to fulfill them" (Matt. 5:17), actualizing what Scripture anticipated and achieving what God promised and predicted. Similarly, Paul emphasized that *Christ* alone is the means by which all promissory hopes come to fruition: "All the promises of God find their Yes *in him*" (2 Cor. 1:20); "[God] has blessed us *in Christ* with every spiritual blessing in the heavenly places" (Eph. 1:3). The Old Testament promises become operative for believers only through Jesus.[51]

As when wrestling with the lasting significance of the Mosaic law for Christians (see earlier in this chapter), I find it useful to view Christ as the filter or "lens" through which we consider the contemporary relevance of Old Testament promises. His death and resurrection give living hope that every promise will indeed come to pass (1 Peter 1:3–4), and his Spirit supplies the "guarantee" of our future inheritance (2 Cor. 1:22; Eph. 1:14). These things noted, the way Jesus fulfills the various promises of the Old Testament results in some being maintained for the church in much the same way as they were originally given, while other promises are completed, transformed, or extended. In order to faithfully establish any Old Testament promise's relationship to believers, we must carefully consider its original historical and literary context and then assess how Christ's salvation-historical work informs our appropriation.

51. This is so because through his death and resurrection Christ purchased both common grace (Gen. 8:20–21; Rom. 2:4) and saving grace (Rom. 3:24; 5:8–9), justifying every expression of God's kindness, forbearance, and patience toward sinners and identifying his just severity toward them (3:25–26).

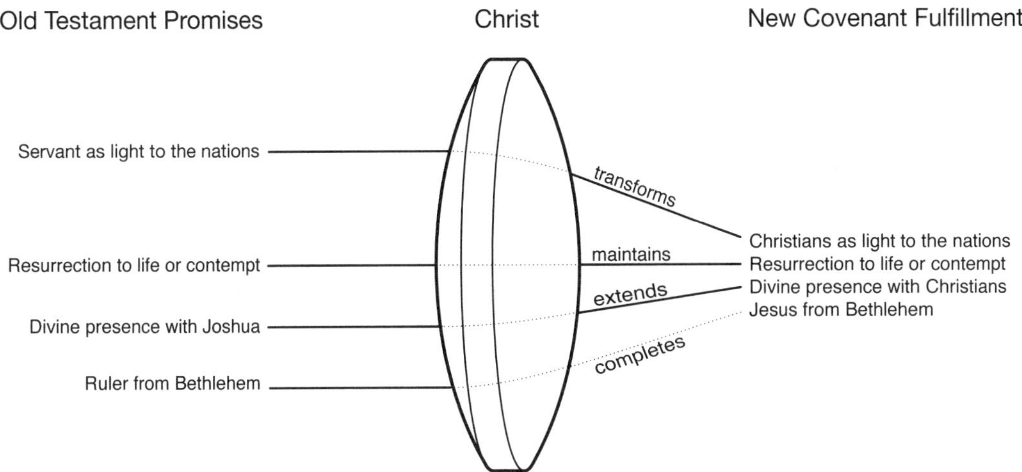

Fig. 12.11. The Fulfillment of Old Testament Promises through the "Lens" of Christ

a. Old Testament Promises Maintained

Many of the promises that are *maintained* are those that were already explicitly restoration promises, which YHWH promised would be realized after Israel's exile. Consider, for example, Daniel 12:2: "And many of those who sleep in the dust of the earth shall awake, some to everlasting life, and some to shame and everlasting contempt." Likely alluding to this text, Jesus asserted, "An hour is coming when all who are in the tombs will hear [the Son of Man's] voice and come out, those who have done good to the resurrection of life, and those who have done evil to the resurrection of judgment" (John 5:28–29; cf. 11:11). Similarly, Paul said, "We shall not all sleep, but we shall all be changed. . . . For the trumpet will sound, and the dead will be raised imperishable, and we shall be changed" (1 Cor. 15:51–52). Christians can hope in the future resurrection, claiming the promise of Daniel 12:2 as our own! We do so, however, recognizing that we will rise only because Christ was first raised—"the firstfruits of those who have fallen asleep" (1 Cor. 15:20). The Old Testament identifies that the Messiah's resurrection would precede and facilitate our own.

Luke asserted, "Thus *it is written*, that the Christ should suffer and on the third day rise from the dead" (Luke 24:46). Paul, too, claimed "that Christ died for our sins in accordance with the Scriptures, that he was buried, that he was raised on the third day *in accordance with the Scriptures*, and that he appeared to Cephas, then to the twelve" (1 Cor. 15:3–5). The Old Testament portrays YHWH as one who would raise the dead: "I kill and I make alive; I wound and I heal" (Deut. 32:39). Speaking to a people that God had already torn and struck down, Hosea said, "After two days he will revive us; on the third day he will raise us up, that we may live before him" (Hos. 6:2). The resurrection of God's people would come *on the third day*. On this basis, YHWH questioned, "Shall I ransom them from the power of Sheol? Shall I redeem them from Death?" And he responded, "O Death, where are your plagues? O Sheol, where is your sting?" (Hos. 13:14; cf. 1 Cor. 15:55). Earlier, in the very context in which Hannah prophesied that God would "give strength to his king and exalt the power of his anointed," she proclaimed, "The LORD kills and brings to life; he brings down to Sheol and raises up" (1 Sam. 2:6; cf. 2:10).

David, too, captured the Messiah's journey through tribulation unto triumph in Psalm 22, which opens with the king crying, "My God, my God, why have you forsaken me?" (Ps. 22:1; cf. Matt. 27:46). He is "scorned by mankind and despised by the people," with some mocking him and wagging their heads (Ps. 22:6–8; cf. 2:1; Matt. 27:39, 43). His strength and mouth are dried up (Ps. 22:15; John 19:28). He is encircled by evildoers who pierce his hands and feet and then cast lots for his clothing (Ps. 22:16–18; cf. Matt. 27:35; Luke 24:39–40; John 19:24), yet not one of his bones is broken (Ps. 22:17; 34:20; John 19:36). He declares, "You lay me in the dust of death" (Ps. 22:15), but he then proclaims, "You have rescued me from the horns of the wild oxen! I will tell of your name to my brothers" (22:21–22; cf. Matt. 28:10; Heb. 2:10–12).

Isaiah 52:13–53:12 comparably promises the royal servant's victory over death. Isaiah asserts:

> Yet it was the will of the LORD to crush him;
> he has put him to grief;
> when his soul makes an offering for guilt,
> he shall see his offspring; he shall prolong his days;
> the will of the LORD shall prosper in his hand.
> Out of the anguish of his soul he shall see and be satisfied;
> by his knowledge shall the righteous one, my servant,
> make many to be accounted righteous,
> and he shall bear their iniquities. (Isa. 53:10–11)

Our right standing with God and our hope is built solely on the death and resurrection of the Christ, who suffered as a sacrifice but who now sees and is satisfied in his saints.

The resurrection from the dead and eternal judgment are two of "the elementary doctrine[s] of Christ" (Heb. 6:1–2). Daniel 12:2 gives Christians hope because Christ, who rose from the dead, has claimed us as his own. "For if we have been united with him in a death like his, we shall certainly be united with him in a resurrection like his" (Rom. 6:5).

b. Old Testament Promises Completed

There are some Old Testament promises whose fulfillment is already fully *completed* in Christ. Their lasting relevance for us, therefore, comes only in the way in which they nurture present confidence in God's faithfulness and, at times, in the way in which the fulfillment bears a continuing impact. We see one such example in the prophet Micah's prediction that a long-prophesied ruler in Israel would rise from Bethlehem (Mic. 5:2), which Matthew identifies is fulfilled in Christ's birth (Matt. 2:6). There is only one Christ, and he was born only once. Nevertheless, his birth was to spark a global return of "his brothers," and as king he would "shepherd his flock in the strength of the LORD," establishing lasting security and peace and enjoying a great name (Mic. 5:3–5). All these added promises continue to give Christians comfort and hope, and Christ's birth in Bethlehem validates for us the certainty of his permanent and global exaltation.

Another example is YHWH's promise to Solomon that because he asked for wisdom rather than long life or riches or punishment on his enemies, God would give him both wisdom *and* riches and honor (1 Kings 3:11–13). This promise was Yes in Christ in that on the cross Jesus purchased every divine bestowal of kindness, forbearance, and patience experienced in the realm of common grace (Gen. 8:20–21; Rom. 2:4; 3:25–26). Nevertheless, the specificity of the promise itself, being contingent on one man's request and including blessing related to one man's specific reign, identifies that this is not a promise that any person and at any time enjoys. Unlike YHWH's promise to Joshua in Joshua 1:5, which was true for all who followed him (see below), this promise was unique to Solomon himself, with others benefiting only from the wisdom, riches, and honor that he himself enjoyed.

c. Old Testament Promises Transformed

Isaiah 49:6 supplies an example of an Old Testament promise that Christ's fulfillment *transforms*. In this third servant song, Isaiah portrays the coming royal deliverer as speaking in first person. He says that the Lord called him from the womb, named him "Israel," and commissioned him as "his servant, to bring Jacob back to him; and that Israel might be gathered to him" (49:1, 3, 5). This is perhaps the clearest Old Testament text that *Jesus is Israel*, the one representing the many in every way. Then in 49:6 we read YHWH's declaration, "It is too light a thing that you should be my servant to raise up the tribes of Jacob and to bring back the preserved of Israel; I will make you as a light for the nations, that my salvation may reach to the end of the earth." Through the coming Messiah, God would save not only ethnic Israelites but also some from the nations, thus fulfilling his earlier promises to Abraham (Gen. 12:3; 22:18).

As we enter the New Testament, we find Simeon, who was "waiting for the consolation of Israel" (Luke 2:25), declaring by the Holy Spirit that Jesus was none other than God's "salvation," which he "prepared in the presence of all peoples, a light for revelation to the Gentiles, and for glory to your people Israel" (2:30–32). Similarly, Paul emphasized that both the prophets and Moses said that the Messiah, following his death and resurrection, "would proclaim light both to our people and to the Gentiles" (Acts 26:23). Both these texts allude to Isaiah 49:6 and identify Christ as the direct fulfillment of this promise.

The transformation of this promise comes in Paul's earlier words to the Jews at Antioch in Pisidia, where he declares with reference to himself and Barnabas, "The Lord has commanded us, saying, 'I have made you a light for the Gentiles, that you may bring salvation to the ends of the earth'" (Acts 13:47). What was a promise related to the servant Christ has now become a commission for all identified with him. As Isaiah himself anticipated, following the work of the one servant-king (singular) (Isa.

42:1; 49:3, 5–7; 50:10; 52:13; 53:11; cf. Acts 4:27–30), God would commission many priestly "servants" (plural) from both Jews and Gentiles to carry on the work of the Messiah (e.g., Isa. 54:17; 56:6; 63:17; 65:8–9, 13–15; 66:14). Paul saw himself as one of these ambassadors (Isa. 42:6–7 with Acts 26:15–18, 22–23; Isa. 49:6 with Acts 13:45–48; Isa. 49:8 with 2 Cor. 6:1–4). Jesus' cross-work had purchased Paul's rescue from sin and God's wrath, and now the apostle was bound as "a servant" of his Savior (cf. Rom. 1:1 with 6:20, 22).

As a further example of a transformed promise, we can assess Leviticus 26:3, 11–12, which I quoted above. It's an old covenant blessing (not a restoration blessing), conditioned on the nation's obedience: "If you walk in my statutes and observe my commandments and do them, . . . I will make my dwelling among you, and my soul shall not abhor you. And I will walk among you and will be your God, and you shall be my people." Paul in turn quotes this text as support for his claim that "we [the church] are the temple of the living God" (2 Cor. 6:16). The promise stands, but through Christ its meaning has been transformed. Let me explain.

In the days of Leviticus, YHWH was already inhabiting the material tabernacle, in which he "walked" with Israel through the wilderness (Deut. 23:14). What Leviticus 26:11–12 portrays as *future* promise, therefore, likely points to a reality beyond the physical dwelling place (whether tabernacle or temple) to a grander manifestation on earth of the ultimate heavenly temple that served as the earthly tent's pattern (Ex. 25:9, 40; 26:30; 27:8; cf. Acts 7:44). Because what Moses, and later Solomon and Zerubbabel, built on earth was only a model of a heavenly reality (cf. 1 Chron. 28:11–12, 18–19), the earthly "picture" bore a built-in obsolescence. The author of Hebrews touches on this fact when he writes, "[The old covenant priests] serve a copy and shadow of the heavenly things. For when Moses was about to erect the tent, he was instructed by God, saying, 'See that you make everything according to the pattern that was shown you on the mountain.'. . . Christ has entered, not into holy places made with hands, which are copies of the true things, but into heaven itself, now to appear in the presence of God on our behalf" (Heb. 8:5; 9:24; cf. 9:11–12). Moses' words in Leviticus 26:11–12 appear to anticipate that the pictoral earthly structure would be superseded when God's obedient "son" would fulfill his covenant obligations.

The temporary quality of the earthly sanctuary is highlighted in the way in which the movable tabernacle gives rise to a stationary temple. Then, after God's presence departs from Jerusalem (Ezek. 8–11), he lets the temple itself be destroyed (33:21; cf. 2 Kings 25). Yet the prophet also anticipated a day when the Lord would again dwell in the midst of his people, declaring that the transformed city would be called "The Lord Is There" (Ezek. 48:35). Echoing Leviticus 26:11–12, now shaped as a restoration blessing, YHWH stated in Ezekiel 37:27–28, "My dwelling place shall be with them, and I will be their God, and they shall be my people. Then the nations will know that I am the Lord who sanctifies Israel, when my sanctuary is in their midst forevermore." Associated with this promise is that "David my servant shall be their prince forever" (37:25) and that the people themselves would operate as God's temple, enjoying his indwelling presence and giving witness to God's greatness before the eyes of the onlooking nations: "And I will put my Spirit within you, and you shall live" (37:14), and again, "The nations will know that I am the Lord, declares the Lord God, when through you I vindicate my holiness before their eyes. . . . I will put my Spirit within you, and cause you to walk in my statutes and be careful to obey my rules" (36:23, 27). Earlier Isaiah had equated the people with the city of Jerusalem when he wrote, "And they shall be called The Holy People, The Redeemed of the Lord; and you shall be called Sought Out, A City Not Forsaken" (Isa. 62:12). Similarly, Jeremiah identified the new Zion with both the temple and people when he predicated that one day all Jerusalem would be God's throne (and not just the ark of the covenant), and that gathered there would be the redeemed from both the nations and a reunited house of Israel (Jer. 3:16–18).

While Zerubbabel helped oversee the building of a second temple, Haggai looked further ahead to a greater glory, suggesting that the earthly temple would be transformed: "The latter glory of this house shall be greater than the former, says the Lord of hosts. And in this place I will give peace" (Hag. 2:9). Even more, Zechariah said that the coming Messiah would build this temple with the aid of "those who are far off" (Zech. 6:15) and would serve as God's priest-king, reigning from God's temple-throne: "It is he who shall build the temple of the Lord and shall bear royal honor, and shall sit and rule on his throne. And there shall be a priest on his throne, and the counsel of peace shall be between them both" (6:13). YHWH's return of his presence to the temple would happen at the day of the Lord (Mal. 3:2).

As noted, the future tabernacling presence to which Leviticus 26:11–12 points was conditioned on the obedience of God's covenant "son." This conditional structure echoes YHWH's earlier declaration: "Be a blessing, so that I may bless those who bless you . . . with the result that in you all the families of the ground may be blessed" (Gen. 12:2–3, author's translation). Israel, as God's corporate "son" (Ex. 4:22–23), "dealt corruptly" with the Lord, so Moses declared that the Israelites "are no longer his children because they are blemished; they are a crooked and twisted generation" (Deut. 32:5; cf. Acts 2:40; Phil. 2:15). Because the Israelites failed to reflect, resemble, and represent God as a true son should, displaying his image and likeness (Gen. 5:1–3), the Lord promised to curse them, asserting, "You were unmindful of the Rock that bore you, and you forgot the God who gave you birth" (Deut. 32:18).

Nevertheless, YHWH had already identified that he would defeat the evil one that originally separated mankind from his tabernacling presence in the garden of Eden (Gen. 3:8). He would do this, however, *not* by his corporate son (the nation) but by a single, male, royal son. A male offspring of the woman would crush the skull of the serpent (3:15). He would be a Shemite (9:26–27) in the lines of Abraham (22:17b–18) and Judah (49:8–10), and only in his day would the enemy gates be brought down and God's blessing extend to the world (22:17b–18; cf. 17:4–6). As God's ideal king, he would live righteously, embodying God's character portrayed in his law (Deut. 17:18–20; Isa. 11:5 with 59:17). His exalted reign would make his people like a restored garden of Eden (Num. 24:5–7) because his own new creational sprouts (Isa. 6:13; 11:1; 53:2) would produce fruit (61:3, 11). As king, he would represent the people (cf. Num. 23:24; 24:9), even bearing their name "Israel" (Isa. 49:3, 5). He would "crush the forehead" of his enemies (Num. 24:17), and those who blessed him would be blessed, whereas those who cursed him would be cursed (24:9; cf. Gen. 12:3).

This royal "son" of God (2 Sam. 7:14; Ps. 2:7) would be intimately identified with YHWH himself. The son's "law" (Isa. 42:4) would be YHWH's law (2:3; 51:4); he would be the Lord's very "arm" working salvation (53:1; 59:16); and his royal name would be "Wonderful Counselor, Mighty God, Everlasting Father, Prince of Peace" (9:6). Even more, like the ark in the temple's Most Holy Place, "the Spirit of the LORD shall rest upon him, the Spirit of wisdom and understanding, the Spirit of counsel and might, the Spirit of knowledge and the fear of the LORD" (11:2; cf. 42:1; 61:1). Isaiah seems to envision that the presence of God that once stood separated from the people in the central sanctuary would now be connected to the people through this unique servant-son.

Filling up all these Old Testament hopes, God's "Word became flesh and dwelt among us, and we have seen his glory, glory as of the only Son from the Father, full of grace and truth" (John 1:14). Jesus identified himself as "the temple," and the disciples recognized this fact after his resurrection (2:19–22). With this, all who believe become "members of the household of God, built on the foundation of the apostles and prophets, Christ Jesus himself being the cornerstone, in whom the whole structure, being joined together, grows into a holy temple in the Lord" (Eph. 2:19–21). Indeed, with potential echo of Leviticus 26:11, we become "a dwelling place for God by the Spirit" (Eph. 2:22). As Christ is the temple, so all who are in him become God's temple (1 Cor. 3:16; 2 Cor. 6:16; cf. 1 Peter 2:5) and operate as priests who proclaim light and life in the dark world (1 Peter 2:9). Already we have come to the heavenly Jerusalem (Gal. 4:26; Heb. 12:22), but we still await the day when the holy city itself will come down from heaven, when "the dwelling place of God is with man" (Rev. 21:2–3). Then the Most Holy Place will be all that we enjoy, for the temple of the city will be "the Lord God the Almighty and the Lamb" (21:22). Then God will have made some "from every tribe and language and people and nation" into "a kingdom and priests to our God, and they shall reign on the earth" (5:9–10).

d. Old Testament Promises Expanded

We find an example of an *expanded* promise in the way that the author of Hebrews 13:5 applies to all Christians battling coveteousness the promise of God's presence given to Joshua regarding the conquest in Joshua 1:5. The Lord said to Moses' successor, "Just as I was with Moses, so I will be with you. I will not leave you or forsake you. Be strong and courageous, for you shall cause this people to inherit the land that I swore to their fathers to give them" (Josh. 1:5–6). In Hebrews, the Old Testament's wilderness and conquest narratives play an important role in magnifying the way in which Christ and the new covenant are better. Moses was faithful to God "as a servant," whereas Christ was faithful "as a son" (Heb. 3:5–6). Most in the exodus generation rebelled, hardening their hearts in unbelief, and because of this YHWH declared, "They shall not enter my rest" (3:7–11). Some like Joshua believed that God was able to secure rest, but all others died because of unbelief (4:2). Later Joshua did lead Israel into the Promised Land, but the rest he secured was only temporary and predictive of the greater rest that the more supreme Joshua (i.e., Jesus) secured for all (4:8).

Within this framework, if the Lord was with the first Joshua, how much more can we be assured that he will be with those identified with the greater Joshua! The original promise given to one man expands to be a promise given to all in Christ. We already share in Christ Jesus (Heb. 3:14) but have not yet inherited the promises (6:12). But because God has promised, "I will never leave you nor forsake you" (13:5), we can rest secure, knowing that our full inheritance will come. We are thus freed to live radically for God in the present, unencumbered by the "love of money" and finding contentment with all we have (13:5). Knowing that God is for us and with us helps us "lay aside every weight, and sin which clings so closely" (12:1). We look "to Jesus, the founder and perfecter of our faith, who for the joy that was set before him endured the cross, despising the shame, and is seated at the right hand of the throne of God" (12:2). And as we consider "him who endured from sinners such hostility against himself," we are helped to "not grow weary or fainthearted" (12:3). God's presence and favor are our hope and our security. "For you had compassion on those in prison, and you joyfully accepted the plundering of your property, since you knew that you yourselves had a better possession and an abiding one" (10:34).

Seeing and Savoring Christ and the Gospel in the Old Testament

For Old Testament interpretation to be considered Christian, it must follow the teaching and exegesis of Christ and the apostles, on which the church is built (Acts 2:42; Eph. 2:20; cf. Matt. 7:24–27; 17:5; 28:20; John 16:12–14; 17:8, 18, 20; 2 Thess. 2:15; Heb. 1:1–2). If a nonbelieving Jew were present during an Old Testament sermon in your church, I don't believe that he should feel comfortable, for we must magnify Christ in all Old Testament interpretation. We should be able to say of *all* our biblical teaching, "I decided to know nothing among you except Jesus Christ and him crucified" (1 Cor. 2:2). This kind of Christ-centrality does not require that we think every Old Testament passage is *about* Christ, but it does necessitate that we consider how every one *points* to him. The gospel is not the only thing that is important, but it is of "first importance" (15:3). Necessarily, considering how to magnify Christ faithfully requires humility, prayerfulness, and solid biblical interpretation that draws on the cultural-historical setting, the linguistic data, the immediate literary context, and the broader canonical context of every passage we consider.

As I have already shown earlier (see "The Centrality of Christ" in chapter 10 and "Establishing the Law's Relevance for Christians" above), Jesus believed that the Old Testament pointed to him (Luke 24:27; John 5:39) and that his role was to fulfill all of the Old Testament's eschatological hopes and trajectories (Matt. 5:17; Luke 24:44; Acts 3:18). Much of what precedes is shadow, whereas Christ is the substance (Col. 3:16–17; Heb. 8:5–6; 10:1). Jesus is the end and goal of the Old Testament's instruction and should be central in all our biblical study, practice, and teaching.

In this section, I want to propose seven different ways that we can encounter and ultimately proclaim Christ and the gospel from the Old Testament. In order to do this, I will consider how Christ fulfills the Old Testament in light of the progress of salvation history (for more on Christ's fulfillment of the Old Testament, see "Establishing the Law's Relevance for Christians" above). Jesus' fulfillment of the Law and the Prophets is not uniform. Christ "fills up" or realizes the Old Testament's eschatological anticipations in numerous ways, and each of these provides avenues by which we can exalt Christ and the gospel through our biblical interpretation.[52]

1. Christ fulfills the Old Testament by standing as the physical embodiment of YHWH.

Because Jesus asserts that "no one has ever seen God" the Father except the Son (John 1:18; 6:46), every Old Testament manifestation of YHWH in human form was most likely the preincarnate Son. We see this figure in the stories of Abraham's third guest (Gen. 18), Joshua's "commander of the army of YHWH" (Josh. 5:13–15), Ezekiel's exalted king (Ezek. 1:26), Daniel's "son of man" (Dan. 7:13–14), and the numerous manifestations of the "angel/messenger of YHWH" (e.g., Gen. 16:7–13; 22:11–18; Ex. 3:2; Num. 20:16; 22:22–35; Judg. 2:1–4; 5:23; 6:11–12, 21–22; 13:3, 13–21; 2 Sam. 24:16; 1 Kings 19:7; 2 Kings 1:3, 15; 19:35; Dan. 3:24, 28). On this latter image Isaiah is perhaps the most explicit, for after declaring that "[YHWH] became [Israel's] Savior"—treating the future eschatological deliverance as though already accomplished—he writes in language similar to Isaiah 53:3–5, "In all their affliction he was afflicted, and the angel of his presence saved them" (63:9). Comparable equations are made by tagging this same person as YHWH's "arm" (63:12), which through Isaiah connects the Lord himself (59:16; 63:5) with his Suffering Servant (53:1). Significantly, in speaking of Isaiah's vision of the Lord seated on the throne in Isaiah 6, John asserts that the prophet "saw [Jesus'] glory and spoke of him" (John 12:41). Each of these revelations anticipates the coming of the Son as the God-man, and we can preach them in this light.

Not only this, often the New Testament interprets Old Testament texts that describe God or YHWH as referring to Jesus. For example, anticipating the messianic era, Isaiah declared, "A voice cries: 'In the wilderness prepare the way of the LORD [i.e., YHWH]" (Isa. 40:3), and each of the Gospel writers identifies this with John the Baptist's pointing

52. For some similar reflections, see Sidney Greidanus, *Preaching Christ from the Old Testament* (Grand Rapids: Eerdmans, 1999), 203–77. For other books on finding Christ and the gospel in the Old Testament, see the "Resources for Further Study" at the end of this chapter.

to the coming of *Jesus* (Matt. 3:3; Mark 1:3; Luke 3:4; John 1:23). Similarly, Joel proclaimed, "Everyone who calls on the name of the LORD [i.e., YHWH] shall be saved" (Joel 2:32), and Paul applies this verse to *Jesus* in Romans 10:13. Finally, Malachi asserted that a new Elijah would come before the day of YHWH when "the Lord whom you seek will suddenly come to his temple" (Mal. 3:1; 4:5[H3:23]). Jesus claimed that John the Baptist was this Elijah (Matt. 11:11–15; 17:10–13), who himself pointed to Christ as the anticipated Lord (3:11–12), whom we know from elsewhere was also God's tabernacling presence (John 1:14; 2:21).

Jesus said that if we have seen him, we have seen the Father (John 14:9), for he does only what the Father is doing (5:19). This close identity between YHWH and his royal servant is already anticipated in texts such as Isaiah 42, where both bear influence among the coastlands (Isa. 42:4, 10, 12), redeem the blind (42:7, 16), serve as guides (42:4, 16), overcome darkness with light (42:6–7, 16), and put to shame carved idols (42:8, 17). The servant would be nothing less than "the arm of the LORD" (53:1; cf. 51:9; 59:16), the Spirit-endowed agent of God (42:1; cf. 11:2; 61:1; Luke 4:18), who would embody the presence of God (Isa. 7:6; Matt. 1:23), bear the character of God (Isa. 9:6; cf. 10:21; 28:29; 63:16; 66:12), bear the armor of God (11:3–5; 59:16–17), and establish God's reign on the earth (9:7; 52:7; 53:10). When John the Baptist asked Jesus, "Are you the one who is to come, or shall we look for another?," Jesus replied, "Go and tell John what you hear and see: the blind receive their sight and the lame walk, lepers are cleansed and the deaf hear, and the dead are raised up, and the poor have good news preached to them" (Matt. 11:3–5; cf. Isa. 35:4–6; 61:1–4).

The words of Christ bear unparalleled authority (Mark 1:22), and he did what only God can do—commanding demons and healing the sick (1:34; 3:10–11, 22), forgiving sins (2:7, 10–11), and raising the dead (5:35–36, 41–43). Every Old Testament manifestation of God's punishment and pardon, retribution and reconciliation, directly foreshadows and ultimately flows from the work of God's Son, "whom he appointed the heir of all things, through whom he created the world," who "is the radiance of the glory of God and the exact imprint of his nature," and who "upholds the universe by the word of his power" (Heb. 1:2–3).

2. Christ fulfills the Old Testament by bringing us the righteousness to which the Old Testament bears witness.

The Old Testament is filled with stories of sinners who needed a Savior. The Mosaic law pointed to the importance of Christ in the way it identified and multiplied sin (Rom. 3:20; 5:20; cf. 7:7–12; Gal. 3:19), imprisoned the sinful (Rom. 3:19–20; 8:2–3; Gal. 3:10, 13, 22), and showed everyone's need for atonement. The law by its nature, therefore, predicted Christ as "the end of the law for righteousness to everyone who believes" (Rom. 10:4).

Jesus is the perfect embodiment of God's character and the ideal image of faith, law-keeping, and wisdom. Paul stressed both that in the law we have "the embodiment of knowledge and truth" (Rom. 2:20) and that "the law is holy, and the commandment is holy and righteous and good" (7:12). The same can be said of Christ, who remained sinless (2 Cor. 5:21; Heb. 4:15; 1 Peter 2:22; 1 John 3:5) and "became to us wisdom from God, righteousness and sanctification and redemption" (1 Cor. 1:30).

Paul stressed, "But now the righteousness of God has been manifested apart from the law, although the Law and the Prophets bear witness to it—the righteousness of God through faith in Jesus Christ for all who believe" (Rom. 3:21–22). Figures such as Moses, David, and Isaiah anticipated the righteousness displayed through the gospel (1:16–17). It's bound up in Christ's perfect obedience climaxing in his death on the cross (3:22–26; Phil. 2:8), through which we are justified by faith (Rom. 3:27–30; 5:1). Jesus incarnated the portrait of the worshiping sufferer and victorious king of the Psalms. He perfectly kept his Father's commandments and abided in his love (John 15:10). Through Christ's substitutionary work, God canceled "the record of debt that stood against us with its legal demands" (Col. 2:14). He "condemned sin in the flesh, in order that the righteous requirement of the law might be fulfilled in us" (Rom. 8:3–4).

As God's Word made flesh, Jesus manifests in his person the essence of every ethical ideal aligned with YHWH's revealed will, and it is this perfection that is then imputed to believers: "Therefore, as one trespass led to condemnation for all men, so one act of righteousness leads to justification and life for all men. For as by the one man's disobedience the many were made sinners, so by the one man's obedience the many will be made righteous" (Rom. 5:18–19; cf. 8:4). "For our sake he made him to be sin who knew no sin, so that in him we might become the righteousness of God" (2 Cor. 5:21; cf. Phil. 3:8–9). With every law and every wise saying in the Old Testament, we find pointers that magnify the greatness of Christ and his work on our behalf.

3. Christ fulfills the Old Testament by supplying us the power to love and thus fulfill the law.

Paul says that "all the promises of God find their Yes in [Christ]" (2 Cor. 1:20). These include the Old Testament promises related to new covenant believers' living out God's law. For instance, Moses promised, "The Lord your God will circumcise your heart and the heart of your offspring, so that you will love the Lord your God with all your heart and with all your soul" (Deut. 30:6; cf. 6:5). He also envisioned that this same people would "obey the voice of the Lord and keep all the commandments that I command you today" (30:8). Deuteronomy would continue its relevance in the day of heart change. Similarly, through Ezekiel God promised, "I will put my Spirit within you, and cause you to walk in my statutes and be careful to obey my rules" (Ezek. 36:27; cf. Jer. 12:16). In this day of restoration, all the children "shall be taught by the Lord" (Isa. 54:13; cf. John 6:44–45). Having the law written on their hearts, "they shall all know [the Lord], from the least of them to the greatest" (Jer. 31:33–34; cf. 1 John 2:20–21, 27).

Both Moses and Ezekiel predicted an eschatological day when God's people would keep the Lord's "statutes" (LXX = plural of δικαίωμα) (Deut. 30:10; Ezek. 36:27). Through his one "act of righteousness" (singular of δικαίωμα), Jesus secures our justification (Rom. 5:18), fulfilling this "righteous requirement" (singular of δικαίωμα) in us (8:4) and by this moving us to live by the Spirit (8:13; Gal. 5:25).[53] We who are in Christ are now empowered to keep the "precepts" (plural of δικαίωμα) of the law, as we live with circumcised hearts by the power of the Spirit (Rom. 2:26, 29). We fulfill the law as we love our neighbor (13:8–10; cf. Matt. 7:12; Gal. 6:2). Christ is our teacher (Isa. 42:4; 51:4; Matt. 17:5; 28:20), and his own law-fulfillment now clarifies for us what it means to follow God (Matt. 5:17–19; cf. 1 Cor. 9:21; James 1:25; 2:8, 12).

4. Christ fulfills the Old Testament by operating as the object of direct Old Testament messianic predictions.

Peter stressed that "what God foretold by the mouth of *all* the prophets, that his Christ would suffer, he thus fulfilled" (Acts 3:18). Every one of the prophets from Moses onward anticipated the work of the Messiah and the mission he would spark (3:22–24; 10:43). The Old Testament is loaded with these predictions. YHWH promised Abraham that a single, male offspring would "possess the gate of his enemies" and that in him "all the nations of the earth [would] be blessed" (Gen. 22:17b–18). Paul then notes that the gospel of international blessing that God promised Abraham came to the Gentiles in Christ Jesus (Gal. 3:8, 14). Indeed, "the promises were made to Abraham and to his offspring . . . , who is Christ. . . . And if you are Christ's, then you are Abraham's offspring, heirs according to promise" (3:16, 29). Similarly, YHWH promised through Ezekiel, "I will set up over them one shepherd, my servant David, and he shall feed them" (Ezek. 34:23). Then in John 10, Jesus declared, "I am the good shepherd" (John 10:11), and again, "There will be one flock, one shepherd" (10:16). At times, the element of prediction-fulfillment is even more pronounced, as when Micah 5:2 foretells that the royal deliverer would be born in Bethlehem, and then Matthew 2:6 explicitly asserts that it happened just as the prophet wrote. Christ fulfills the Old Testament as the specific focus or goal of direct Old Testament messianic predictions and redemptive-historical hopes.

5. Christ fulfills the Old Testament by serving as the climax of all salvation-historical trajectories.

The Old and New Testaments are framed by the narrative of redemption—a historical plot designed to magnify the truth that God reigns, saves, and satisfies through covenant for his glory in Christ. The entire story line progresses from creation to the fall to redemption to consummation and highlights the work of Jesus as the decisive turning point in salvation history. The Old Testament provides foundation, the New Testament fulfillment. I have attempted to capture the basic plotline through the acronym KINGDOM (for more, see "Salvation-Historical Connections" in chapter 10).

53. I noted earlier under "Establishing the Law's Relevance for Christians" that I now side with Moo on his reading of Romans 8:4 as pointing to *Christ's* fulfillment of the righteous requirement of the law in us (i.e., positive imputation) (see *Romans*, 483–84). Nevertheless, I still see a place for Christians' fulfilling the law—just not in this text (see Rom. 2:26; 13:8–10). So although I disagree with McFadden's reading of Romans 8:4, I do agree with him that our imperfect loving of others today truly fulfills the law, but only because the Spirit's liberating work will become completed at the resurrection, at which time we will fulfill the law's righteous requirement perfectly (see "The Fulfillment of the Law's *Dikaiōma*," 483–97, esp. 491–94).

Old Testament Narrative Foundation	**K**	1. Kickoff and rebellion	Creation, fall, and flood
	I	2. Instrument of blessing	Patriarchs
	N	3. Nation redeemed and commissioned	Exodus, Sinai, and wilderness
	G	4. Government in the land	Conquest and kingdoms
	D	5. Dispersion and return	Exile and initial restoration
New Testament Narrative Fulfillment	**O**	6. Overlap of the ages	Christ's work and the church age
	M	7. Mission accomplished	Christ's return and kingdom consummation

Fig. 12.12. God's KINGDOM Plan

The biblical authors highlight the progression of salvation history many times, always with Christ as the center. "The Law and the Prophets were until John [the Baptist]; since then the good news of the kingdom of God is preached" (Luke 16:16). "Christ is the end of the law for righteousness to everyone who believes" (Rom. 10:4). "The law was our guardian until Christ came, in order that we might be justified by faith. But now that faith has come, we are no longer under a guardian, for in Christ Jesus you are all sons of God, through faith" (Gal. 3:24–26).

Each of the five major salvation-historical covenants finds its terminus in Christ:

- In fulfillment of the *Adamic-Noahic covenant*, Jesus is the Son of Man, last Adam, and image of God (Mark 10:45; 14:62; 1 Cor. 15:45; 2 Cor. 4:4).
- In fulfillment of the *Abrahamic covenant*, Jesus is the offspring of Abraham and agent of universal blessing (Gen. 22:17b–18; Acts 3:25–26; Gal. 3:16).
- In fulfillment of the *Mosaic (old) covenant*, Jesus represents Israel and stands as God's Son, YHWH's servant, the embodiment of wisdom, the one who fulfilled the law's demands, and the substance of all covenant shadows (Ex. 4:22–23; Isa. 49:3, 5–6; Matt. 3:17; 11:2, 19; 12:42; 13:54; John 2:19–21; Acts 3:25–26; Rom. 5:19; Col. 2:17; Heb. 9:9–12; 10:1).
- In fulfillment of the *Davidic covenant*, Jesus is the King of the Jews and Son of David (Matt. 2:1; 21:9; Luke 1:32–33).
- In fulfillment of the *new covenant* promises, Jesus is the prophet like Moses who was to come and the only true Mediator between God and man (Deut. 18:15, 18; Luke 7:16; 22:20; Acts 3:22–26; 7:37; 1 Tim. 2:5; Heb. 8:6; 9:15; 12:24).

We also see that various themes develop or progress as God gradually reveals more of himself and his ways through biblical revelation. Some of the main ones include covenant, God's kingdom, law, temple and God's presence, atonement, and mission, all of which find focus in Jesus. Christ fulfills all of the Old Testament's salvation-historical trajectories.

6. Christ fulfills the Old Testament by both similarity and contrast.

The progress of the biblical covenants and the history of redemption display numerous points of similarity and contrast, many of which are centered in the person of Christ. Many of the analogies and differences come in type-antitype relationships, which I unpack in the next unit. Another major similarity comes in the old and new covenants' structure of grace, both having a gracious redemption give rise to a gracious lawgiving. The pattern in both covenants is that obedience follows deliverance and not vice versa. In light of this, the preacher can build numerous analogies between the surface features of the old and new covenants, identifying similarities and then magnifying Christ as the one who now supplies the pattern, pardon, and promise for living God's way for God's glory.

In the way of contrast, the nature of grace between the old and new covenants is different, for whereas the new covenant supplies freedom from sin and power for obedience to *all* covenant members, there was nothing organic to the old covenant itself that changed hearts. Under Moses, the redemption and giving of the law remained external for the majority, whereas the redemption and law in the new covenant are both internalized in all members by the eschatological work of the Spirit of Christ.

Numerous other points of contrast (or progression) are also apparent. For example, whereas Adam disobeyed and brought death to all, Christ obeys and brings life to many (Rom. 5:18–19). Whereas God used the blood of bulls and goats to picture atonement in the old covenant, Christ's own substitutionary sacrifice provides the ground for eternal redemption (Heb. 9:11–14). Whereas access to YHWH's presence in the temple was restricted to the high priest on the Day of Atonement, Christ's priestly work opens the way for all in him to enjoy God's presence (9:24–26; 10:19–22). Whereas the nations needed to come to the tabernacle/temple to encounter the Lord's presence in the old covenant, the Spirit of Christ now empowers the church in its witness to the nations from Jerusalem to the ends of the earth (Matt. 28:18–20; Acts 1:8).

The work of Jesus creates both continuities and discontinuities. We can celebrate his work more fully by identifying the patterns and transformations.

7. Christ fulfills the Old Testament by functioning as the antitype of all types.

In the words of the author of Hebrews, the Old Testament law was but "a shadow of good things to come" (Heb. 10:1). Clean- and unclean-food laws, the various Jewish festivals and monthly sacrificial calendar, and even the Sabbath were all "a shadow of the things to come, but the substance belongs to Christ" (Col. 2:16–17). God structured the progressive development of salvation history in such a way that various Old

Testament persons, events, or institutions predictively anticipate later persons, events, or institutions, all of which escalate and culminate in the life and work of Jesus Messiah. Without attempting to be exhaustive, here are some examples of Old Testament types that find their terminus in Christ.

a. *Typological persons*:
   - Adam was a type of Christ as the ultimate human (Rom. 5:12–21; 1 Cor. 15:45–49).
   - Melchizedek was a type for Christ's eternal royal priesthood (Gen. 14:18–24; Heb. 5:5–9; 6:20; 7:1–10, 17).
   - Moses was a type for Christ's prophetic role (Deut. 18:15–19; Acts 3:19–26) and faithfulness (Heb. 3:1–6).
   - Aaron was a type for Christ's high priesthood (Heb. 5:1–5).
   - Jonah's time in and departure from the belly of the fish made him a type for Christ's death, burial, and resurrection (Jonah 2; Matt. 12:40).

b. *Typological events or acts*:
   - Every one of God's major creative or redemptive acts in the Old Testament anticipates Christ's salvific work. Creation gives rise to new creation; the original exodus points to the second exodus; the destruction of Samaria and Jerusalem on the day of the Lord find culmination at the cross and final day of judgment; the initial restoration to the land prepares for the ultimate reconciliation with God.
   - The elevation of the bronze serpent typified the crucifixion of Christ (when he became sin and bore our curse) and its resulting benefits (Num. 21:4–9; John 3:14).
   - The flood and Red Sea deliverances typified baptism (1 Cor. 10:2; 1 Peter 3:20–21).
   - The smiting of the rock typified Christ's substitutionary, life-giving sacrifice (1 Cor. 10:4).
   - Other events in Israel's wilderness years were types to benefit Christians (1 Cor. 10:11).

c. *Typological institutions*:
   - The earthly tabernacle and all its furniture (Ex. 25:9, 40) were but "a copy and shadow of the heavenly things" (Heb. 8:5; cf. Acts 7:24; Heb. 8:2; 9:11). This included "the mercy seat" (Ex. 25:21–22; Lev. 16:14–15) that points directly to Christ as the one upon whom atonement is realized (Rom. 3:24–26).
   - The earthly temple typified Christ (John 2:19–21; cf. 1:14) and his church (1 Cor. 6:19).
   - The Old Testament priesthood (Zech. 3:8) anticipated Christ as the high priest (Heb. 2:17; 9:11; cf. 9:24) and the church as priests (1 Peter 2:5, 9).
   - The Passover lamb (Ex. 12:3) typified Christ's substitutionary death (Isa. 53:7; John 1:29; Acts 8:32; 1 Cor. 5:7; 1 Peter 1:19).

- The substitutionary sacrifices in Leviticus typified Christ's own substitutionary sacrifice (Isa. 53:4–5, 8, 10–12; Heb. 9:12–14; 10:1–4, 10; 1 John 1:9–2:2; 10; cf. Col. 2:13–14).
- Clean- and unclean-food laws and the various Jewish festivals and monthly sacrificial calendar typologically pointed to Christ (Col. 2:16–17).
- The Sabbath typologically anticipated the rest that Christ's resurrection inaugurated (Matt. 11:28–12:8; Col. 2:16–17; Heb. 4:1–11).

8. Summary

I have given seven ways that Christ fulfills the eschatological hopes of the Old Testament. Each of these provides readers and teachers of Scripture with fresh avenues for seeing, savoring, and proclaiming Christ and the gospel from the Old Testament. Engage the initial three-fourths of our Christian Bible for the glory of Christ. In doing so, you will honor God, feed yourself, and serve the church.

Key Words and Concepts

Practical theology
Christ's "fulfilling" the Old Testament
Law of Christ
Moral, civil, and ceremonial law
Love principle
Already but not yet

Questions for Further Reflection

1. Argue for the statement that "the Old Testament is actually *more relevant* to Christians today than it was for the majority in the old covenant." Be sure to include Scripture in your answer.
2. In every chapter of this book, we have progressively sought to grasp the lasting message of Exodus 19:4–6. What effect does this passage have on you now? How can you apply it to your life?
3. What does it mean that Christ "fulfilled" the law instead of abolishing it? How does that affect Christians' "doing and teaching" (Matt. 5:19), "upholding" (Rom. 3:31), and "fulfilling" (13:8, 10) the law?
4. Using the analogy of a lens, explain how the law of Moses relates to the law of Christ.
5. Why might one be cautious about dividing the Mosaic law into moral, civil, and ceremonial laws?
6. What steps does a Christian need to take in order to apply an Old Testament law, and why is it important to include every step and to follow the process in order?

7. Which of the examples of applying the Old Testament today did you find most edifying and why? What did you find particularly insightful? What surprised you in the discussion, and what questions did the examples spark?
8. What factors should a Christian consider when claiming Old Testament promises today?
9. How can God's promises of blessing and curse serve to produce holiness in believers today? Give some examples.
10. Pick three of the following twelve passages and consider how one might encounter Christ and the gospel from them. Which of the seven categories supply the best lens by which to encounter and proclaim the good news from the various texts? Write down your answer. Exodus 40:34–38; Numbers 24:15–19; Deuteronomy 6:20–25; Joshua 5:13–15; Ruth 4:18–22; 1 Samuel 2:1–10; 2 Kings 17:6–23; 2 Chronicles 20:1–30; Psalm 3; Proverbs 3:13–18; Isaiah 49:1–6; Habakkuk 3:17–19.

Resources for Further Study

General Works on Application

Casillas, Ken. *Beyond Chapter and Verse: The Theology and Practice of Biblical Application.* Forthcoming.

★ Doriani, Daniel M. *Putting the Truth to Work: The Theory and Practice of Biblical Application.* Phillipsburg, NJ: P&R Publishing, 2001.

Duvall, J. Scott, and Verlyn D. Verbrugge, eds. *Devotions on the Greek New Testament: 52 Reflections to Inspire and Instruct.* Grand Rapids: Zondervan, 2012.

Eng, Milton, and Lee M. Fields, eds. *Devotions on the Hebrew Bible: 54 Reflections to Inspire and Instruct.* Grand Rapids: Zondervan, 2015.

Klein, William W., Craig L. Blomberg, and Robert L. Hubbard Jr. "Application." In *Introduction to Biblical Interpretation*, 477–504. 2nd ed. Dallas: Word, 2004.

Life Application Study Bible: NIV. Carol Stream, IL: Tyndale House, 2012.

Mathis, David. *Habits of Grace: Enjoying Jesus through the Spiritual Disciplines.* Wheaton, IL: Crossway, 2016.

Meadors, Gary T., ed. *Four Views on Moving beyond the Bible to Theology.* Counterpoints. Grand Rapids: Zondervan, 2009: (1) Walter Kaiser, "A Principlizing Model," (2) Dan Doriani, "A Redemptive-Historical Model," (3) Kevin Vanhoozer, "A Drama-of-Redemption Model," and (4) Bill Webb, "A Redemptive-Movement Model."

Muck, Terry C., ed. NIV Application Commentary. 42 vols. Grand Rapids, Zondervan, 1994–2012.

Ortlund, Dane C., Erika Allen, and Bill Deckard, eds. *ESV Women's Devotional Bible.* Wheaton, IL: Crossway, 2014.

Piper, John. *Desiring God: Meditations of a Christian Hedonist.* 4th ed. Colorado Springs: Multnomah, 2011.

———. *Future Grace: The Purifying Power of the Promises of God*. 2nd ed. Colorado Springs: Multnomah, 2012.

———. *The Pleasures of God: Meditations on God's Delight in Being God*. 2nd ed. Sisters, OR: Multnomah, 2000.

Storms, Sam, and Dane C. Ortlund, eds. *ESV Men's Devotional Bible*. Wheaton, IL: Crossway, 2015.

Strauss, Mark L. *How to Read the Bible in Changing Times: Understanding and Applying God's Word Today*. Grand Rapids: Baker, 2011.

Whitney, Donald S. *Spiritual Disciplines for the Christian Life*. 2nd ed. Colorado Springs: NavPress, 2014.

Old Testament Law and the Christian

Barker, William S., and W. Robert Godfrey, eds. *Theonomy: A Reformed Critique*. Grand Rapids: Zondervan, 1991.

Block, Daniel I. "Preaching Old Testament Law to New Testament Christians." In *The Gospel according to Moses: Theological and Ethical Reflections on the Book of Deuteronomy*, 104–46. Eugene, OR: Cascade, 2012. Originally published in *Hiphil (Scandinavian Evangelical E-Journal)* 3 (2006): 1–24. Subsequently published in three parts in *Ministry* 78, 5 (2006): 5–11; 78, 7 (2006): 12–16; 78, 9 (2006): 15–18.

Casillas, Ken. *The Law and the Christian: God's Light within God's Limits*. Biblical Discernment for Difficult Issues. Greenville, SC: Bob Jones University Press, 2007.

✪ Combs, William W. "Paul, the Law, and Dispensationalism." *DBSJ* 18 (2013): 19–39.

DeRouchie, Jason S. "Confronting the Transgender Storm: New Covenant Reflections on Deuteronomy 22:5." *JBMW* 21, 1 (2016): 58–69.

———. "From Condemnation to Righteousness: A Christian Reading of Deuteronomy." *SBJT* 18, 3 (2014): 87–118.

———. "Making the Ten Count: Reflections on the Lasting Message of the Decalogue." In *For Our Good Always: Studies on the Message and Influence of Deuteronomy in Honor of Daniel I. Block*, edited by Jason S. DeRouchie, Jason Gile, and Kenneth J. Turner, 415–40. Winona Lake, IN: Eisenbrauns, 2013.

Doriani, Daniel M. "A Redemptive-Historical Model." In *Four Views on Moving beyond the Bible to Theology*, edited by Gary T. Meadors, 75–121. Responses to other contributors on pp. 51–56, 205–9, 255–61. Counterpoints. Grand Rapids: Zondervan, 2009.

⋆ Dorsey, David A. "The Law of Moses and the Christian: A Compromise." *JETS* 34, 3 (1991): 321–34.

———. "The Use of the OT Law in the Christian Life: A Theocentric Approach." *EJ* 17, 1 (1999): 1–18.

Ferguson, Sinclair B. *The Whole Christ: Legalism, Antinomianism, and Gospel Assurance—Why the Marrow Controversy Still Matters*. Wheaton, IL: Crossway, 2016.

Hays, J. Daniel. "Applying the OT Law Today." *BSac* 158, 1 (2001): 21–35.

House, H. Wayne, and Thomas Ice. *Dominion Theology: Blessing or Curse? An Analysis of Christian Reconstructionism*. Portland, OR: Multnomah, 1988.

Janzen, Waldemar. *Old Testament Ethics: A Paradigmatic Approach*. Louisville: Westminster John Knox, 1994.

Jones, Mark. *Antinomianism: Reformed Theology's Unwelcome Guest?* Phillipsburg, NJ: P&R Publishing, 2013.

Kaiser, Walter C., Jr. "A Principlizing Model." In *Four Views on Moving beyond the Bible to Theology*, edited by Gary T. Meadors, 19–50. Responses to other contributors on pp. 121–25, 200–4, 249–54. Counterpoints. Grand Rapids: Zondervan, 2009.

———. *Toward Old Testament Ethics*. Grand Rapids: Zondervan, 1983.

Keller, Timothy. *Generous Justice: How God's Grace Makes Us Just*. New York: Dutton, 2010.

Martens, Elmer A. "How Is the Christian to Construe Old Testament Law?" *BBR* 12, 2 (2002): 199–216.

Meadors, Gary T., ed. *Four Views on Moving beyond the Bible to Theology*. Counterpoints. Grand Rapids: Zondervan, 2009.

Meyer, Jason C. *The End of the Law: Mosaic Covenant in Pauline Theology*. NAC Studies in Bible and Theology 7. Nashville: Broadman & Holman, 2009.

———. "The Mosaic Law, Theological Systems, and the Glory of Christ." In *Progressive Covenantalism: Charting a Course between Dispensational and Covenant Theologies*, edited by Stephen J. Wellum and Brent E. Parker, 66–99. Nashville: Broadman & Holman, 2016.

✪ Moo, Douglas J. "The Law of Christ as the Fulfillment of the Law of Moses: A Modified Lutheran View." In *Five Views on Law and Gospel*, edited by Wayne G. Strickland, 319–76. Responses to other contributors on pp. 83–90, 165–73, 218–25, 309–15. Counterpoints. Grand Rapids: Zondervan, 1999.

———. "The Law of Moses or the Law of Christ." In *Continuity and Discontinuity: Perspectives on the Relationship between the Old and New Testaments: Essays in Honor of S. Lewis Johnson Jr.*, edited by John S. Feinberg, 203–18, 373–76. Westchester, IL: Crossway, 1988.

★ Poythress, Vern S. Pages 251–86 in *The Shadow of Christ in the Law of Moses*. Phillipsburg, NJ: Presbyterian and Reformed, 1991.

Rosner, Brian S. *Paul and the Law: Keeping the Commandments of God*. NSBT 31. Downers Grove, IL: InterVarsity Press, 2013.

★ Schreiner, Thomas R. *40 Questions about Christians and Biblical Law*. 40 Questions. Grand Rapids: Kregel, 2010.

———. "The Law and Salvation History." In *New Testament Theology: Magnifying God in Christ*, 617–72. Grand Rapids: Baker Academic, 2008.

Strickland, Wayne G., ed. *Five Views on Law and Gospel*. Grand Rapids: Zondervan, 1999.

Todd, James M., III. *Sinai and the Saints: Reading Old Covenant Laws for the New Covenant Community*. Downers Grove, IL: InterVarsity Press, 2017.

★ Wells, Tom, and Fred G. Zaspel. Pages 77–160 in *New Covenant Theology: Description, Definition, Defense*. Frederick, MD: New Covenant Media, 2002.

★ Wellum, Stephen J. "Progressive Covenantalism and Doing Ethics." In *Progressive Covenantalism: Charting a Course between Dispensational and Covenant Theologies*, edited by Stephen J. Wellum and Brent E. Parker, 215–33. Nashville: Broadman & Holman, 2016.

Wright, Christopher J. H. *Old Testament Ethics for the People of God*. Downers Grove, IL: InterVarsity Press, 2004.

Old Testament Promises and the Christian

Alcorn, Randy. "Prosperity Theology: The Gospel of Wealth." In *Money, Possessions, and Eternity*, 75–92. 2nd ed. Wheaton, IL: Tyndale House, 2003.

Barrett, Matthew. "'Bigger Is Better': When the Prosperity Gospel Creeps into the Evangelical Church." *Credo* 4, 2 (2014): 27–29.

Beale, G. K. "Eschatology." *DLNT* 330–45.

Evans, Mary J. "Blessing/Curse." *NDBT* 397–401.

Fee, Gordon D. *The Disease of the Health and Wealth Gospels*. Vancouver: Regent College, 2006.

Gladd, Benjamin L., and Matthew S. Harmon. *Making All Things New: Inaugurated Eschatology for the Life of the Church*. Grand Rapids: Baker Academic, 2016.

Hollifield, Gregory K. "Does God Want You to Be Rich? A Practical Theologian's Response to the Gospel of Prosperity." *JMT* 15, 2 (2011): 25–53.

Jones, David W., and Russell S. Woodbridge. *Health, Wealth and Happiness: Has the Prosperity Gospel Overshadowed the Gospel of Christ?* Grand Rapids: Kregel, 2011.

Keller, Timothy. *Counterfeit Gods: The Empty Promises of Money, Sex, and Power, and the Only Hope That Matters*. New York: Dutton, 2009.

Leeman, Jonathan, ed. *9Marks Journal [Prosperity Gospel]*. 2014. https://9marks.org/journal/prosperity-gospel/.

Lioy, Dan. "The Heart of the Prosperity Gospel: Self or the Savior?" *Conspectus* 4 (2007): 41–64.

Maura, Michael Otieno, Conrad Mbewe, Ken Mbugua, John Piper, and Wayne Grudem. *Prosperity? Seeking the True Gospel*. Nairobi: Africa Christian Textbooks Registered Trustees in partnership with The Gospel Coalition, 2015.

Piper, John. *Future Grace: The Purifying Power of the Promises of God*. 2nd ed. Colorado Springs: Multnomah, 2012.

———. "Introduction to the Third Edition: New Realities in World Christianity and Twelve Appeals to Prosperity Preachers." In *Let the Nations Be Glad! The Supremacy of God in Missions*, 15–34. 3rd ed. Grand Rapids: Baker, 2010.

Sarles, Ken L. "A Theological Evaluation of the Prosperity Gospel." *BSac* 143 (1986): 329–50.

Schreiner, Thomas R., and Ardel B. Caneday. *The Race Set before Us: A Biblical Theology of Perseverance and Assurance*. Downers Grove, IL: InterVarsity Press, 2001.

Seeing and Savoring Christ and the Gospel in the Old Testament

Adam, Peter. "Preaching and Biblical Theology." *NDBT* 104–12.

Barrett, Michael P. V. "Christ in the Covenants." In *Beginning at Moses: A Guide to Finding Christ in the Old Testament*, 109–44. Greenville, SC: Ambassador-Emerald International, 1999.

Bateman, Herbert W., IV, Darrell L. Bock, and Gordon H. Johnston. *Jesus the Messiah: Tracing the Promises, Expectations, and Coming of Israel's King*. Grand Rapids: Kregel, 2012.

Carson, D. A., ed. *The Scriptures Testify about Me: Jesus and the Gospel in the Old Testament*. Wheaton, IL: Crossway, 2013.

Chapell, Bryan. *Christ-Centered Preaching: Redeeming the Expository Sermon*. 2nd ed. Grand Rapids: Baker Academic, 2005.

———. *Christ-Centered Sermons: Models of Redemptive Preaching*. Grand Rapids: Baker Academic, 2013.

———, ed. *Gospel Transformation Bible: English Standard Version*. Wheaton, IL: Crossway, 2013.

Clowney, Edmund P. *Preaching Christ in All of Scripture*. Wheaton, IL: Crossway, 2003.

★ ———. *The Unfolding Mystery: Discovering Christ in the Old Testament*. Phillipsburg, NJ: Presbyterian and Reformed, 1988.

Davis, Dale Ralph. *The Word Became Fresh: How to Preach from Old Testament Narrative Texts*. Fearn, Scotland: Mentor, 2006.

DeRouchie, Jason S., ed. *What the Old Testament Authors Really Cared About: A Survey of Jesus' Bible*. Grand Rapids: Kregel, 2013.

Duguid, Ian M. *Is Jesus in the Old Testament? Basics of the Faith*. Phillipsburg, NJ: P&R Publishing, 2013.

Ferguson, Sinclair B. *Preaching Christ from the Old Testament*. Proclamation Trust Media Paper 2. London: Proclamation Trust Media, 2002.

France, R. T. *Jesus and the Old Testament: His Application of Old Testament Passages to Himself and His Mission*. Downers Grove, IL: InterVarsity Press, 1971.

Goldsworthy, Graeme. *Gospel-Centered Hermeneutics: Foundations and Principles of Evangelical Biblical Interpretation*. Downers Grove, IL: InterVarsity Press, 2006.

———. *Preaching the Whole Bible as Christian Scripture: The Application of Biblical Theology to Expository Preaching*. Grand Rapids: Eerdmans, 2000.

★ Greidanus, Sidney. *Preaching Christ from the Old Testament*. Grand Rapids: Eerdmans, 1999.

Guthrie, Nancy. Seeing Jesus in the Old Testament. Wheaton, IL: Crossway, 2014–present.

- *The Promised One: Seeing Jesus in Genesis* (2011).
- *The Lamb of God: Seeing Jesus in Exodus, Leviticus, Numbers, and Deuteronomy* (2012).
- *The Wisdom of God: Seeing Jesus in the Psalms and Wisdom Books* (2012).
- *The Son of God: Seeing Jesus in the Historical Books* (2013).
- *The Word of God: Seeing Jesus in the Prophets* (2014).

Hamilton, James M., Jr. "Biblical Theology and Preaching." In *Text Driven Preaching: God's Word at the Heart of Every Sermon*, edited by Daniel L. Akin, David L. Allen, and Ned L. Mathews, 193–218. Nashville: Broadman & Holman, 2010.

Johnson, Dennis E. *Him We Proclaim: Preaching Christ from All the Scriptures*. Phillipsburg, NJ: P&R Publishing, 2007.

★ ———. *Walking with Jesus through His Word: Discovering Christ in All the Scriptures*. Phillipsburg, NJ: P&R Publishing, 2015.

✪ Kaiser, Walter C., Jr. *The Messiah in the Old Testament*. SOTBT. Grand Rapids: Zondervan, 1995.

Kim, Julius J. *Preaching the Whole Counsel of God: Design and Deliver Gospel-Centered Sermons*. Grand Rapids: Zondervan, 2015.

Lawrence, Michael. *Biblical Theology in the Life of the Church: A Guide for Ministry*. 9Marks. Wheaton, IL: Crossway, 2010.

Marshall, I. Howard. "Jesus Christ." *NDBT* 592–602.

Meyer, Jason C. *Preaching: A Biblical Theology*. Wheaton, IL: Crossway, 2013.

Motyer, J. Alec. *Look to the Rock: An Old Testament Background to Our Understanding of Christ*. Downers Grove, IL: InterVarsity Press, 1996.

Murray, David. *Jesus on Every Page: 10 Simple Ways to Seek and Find Christ in the Old Testament*. Nashville: Thomas Nelson, 2013.

Piper, John. *Seeing and Savoring Jesus Christ*. Wheaton, IL: Crossway, 2004.

✪ Poythress, Vern S. *The Shadow of Christ in the Law of Moses*. Phillipsburg, NJ: Presbyterian and Reformed, 1991.

✪ Rydelnik, Michael. *The Messianic Hope: Is the Hebrew Bible Really Messianic?* NAC Studies in Bible and Theology 9. Nashville: Broadman & Holman, 2010.

Sailhamer, John H. "The Messiah and the Hebrew Bible." *JETS* 44, 1 (2001): 5–23.

Satterthwaite, Philip E., Richard S. Hess, and Gordon J. Wenham, eds. *The Lord's Anointed: Interpretation of Old Testament Messianic Texts*. Exeter, UK: Paternoster, 1995.

Schreiner, Thomas R. "Preaching and Biblical Theology." *SBJT* 10, 2 (2006): 20–29.

Van Pelt, Miles V. "Introduction." In *A Biblical-Theological Introduction to the Old Testament: The Gospel Promised*, edited by Miles V. Van Pelt, 23–42. Wheaton, IL: Crossway, 2016.

Williams, Michael. *How to Read the Bible through the Jesus Lens: A Guide to Christ-Focused Reading of Scripture*. Grand Rapids: Zondervan, 2012.

Wright, Christopher J. H. *How to Preach and Teach the Old Testament for All Its Worth*. Grand Rapids: Zondervan, 2016.

———. *Knowing Jesus through the Old Testament*. 2nd ed. Downers Grove, IL: InterVarsity Press, 2014.

CONCLUSION

A FINAL WORD ON WALKING IN THE DARK

"Your word is a lamp to my feet and a light to my path."
(Psalm 119:105)

YOUR JOURNEY OF discovery and divine encounter in God's Word is only beginning. You should now be more aware of some of the interpretive dangers that naturally arise while living in this dark and cursed world. Yet I hope you are also energized and more equipped to trek further in and higher up in pursuit of knowing God through his sacred text. In it you will find treasures of greater worth than gold or jewels—riches for which nothing else you desire can compare (Prov. 3:15; cf. Ps. 19:10; 2 Cor. 4:7). In the Scripture you will discover "the light of the knowledge of the glory of God in the face of Jesus Christ" (2 Cor. 4:6).

Your search to see and savor this beauty will be filled with a mixture of suffering and satisfaction—"sorrowful, yet always rejoicing" (2 Cor. 6:10). Yet know that God's Word will illumine your path, guiding by its commands and motivating by its promises. You will taste and see the goodness of the Lord (Ps. 34:8[H9]), but your quest for more will never end. Indeed, you will never scour all the depths of divine splendor in Scripture, nor will you ever run out of vistas from which to "behold the king in his beauty" (Isa. 33:17). But I dare you to try!

In this book we have examined twelve steps from exegesis to theology. In the process we have traveled through TOCMA—from *Text* to *Observation* to *Context* to *Meaning* to *Application*.

Part 1: TEXT—"What is the makeup of the passage?"

1. **Genre:** Determine the literary form, subject matter, and function of the passage, compare it to similar genres, and consider the implications for interpretation.

2. **Literary units and text hierarchy:** Determine the limits and basic structure of the passage.
3. **Text criticism:** Establish the passage's original wording.
4. **Translation:** Translate the text and compare other translations.

Part 2: OBSERVATION—"How is the passage communicated?"

5. **Clause and text grammar:** Assess the makeup and relationship of words, phrases, clauses, and larger text units.
6. **Argument-tracing:** Finish tracing the literary argument and create a message-driven outline that is tied to the passage's main point.
7. **Word and concept studies:** Clarify the meaning of key words, phrases, and concepts.

Part 3: CONTEXT—"Where does the passage fit?"

8. **Historical context:** Understand the historical situation from which the author composed the text and identify any historical details that the author mentions or assumes.
9. **Literary context:** Comprehend the role that the passage plays in the whole book.

Part 4: MEANING—"What does the passage mean?"

10. **Biblical theology:** Consider how your passage connects to the Bible's overall story line or message and points to Christ.
11. **Systematic theology:** Discern how your passage theologically coheres with the whole Bible, assessing key doctrines especially in direct relation to the gospel.

Part 5: APPLICATION—"Why does the passage matter?"

12. **Practical theology:** Apply the text to yourself, the church, and the world, stressing the centrality of Christ and the hope of the gospel.

Now, may you increasingly read God's living and abiding Word for depth and not just distance. May you study, practice, and teach God's Word—in that order. May you approach the Old Testament as *Christian* Scripture with a submissive heart. And as you do, may you say with Philip, "We have found him of whom Moses in the Law and also the prophets wrote, Jesus of Nazareth" (John 1:45)! Jesus said, "You search the Scriptures because you think that in them you have eternal life; and it is they that bear witness about me" (5:39). May your text work, literary and historical analysis, and theology move you to worship the exalted God who has so beautifully and mercifully revealed himself to us through Scripture and ultimately in the face of Christ.

APPENDIX

THE KINGDOM BIBLE READING PLAN

ONLY BY *READING* God's Word do we *hear* the Lord in a way that moves us to *fear* him, so that we *follow* him (Deut. 31:12–13; cf. 6:1–3; 17:19–20; John 6:44–45). "[Scripture] is no empty word for you, but your very life" (Deut. 32:47). Only through an encounter with God's pure, perfect, true, and abiding Word (Pss. 12:6; 119:96, 160) can people be:

- Reborn in Christ (Ps. 119:93; Rom. 10:17; James 1:18; 1 Peter 1:23);
- Empowered for holiness (Ps. 119:50; John 17:17; 2 Tim. 3:17; 2 Peter 1:4);
- Sustained to glory (Deut. 8:3; Rom. 1:16; 2 Tim. 3:15); and
- Satisfied always (Pss. 1:2; 19:10; 1 Peter 2:3).

Man lives through "every word that comes from the mouth of God" (Matt. 4:4; cf. Deut. 8:3), so we must saturate ourselves in God's Book (Deut. 6:7; Josh. 1:7–8; Pss. 1:3; 78:5–8). We must seek its truths like silver, think deeply over its teachings, and passionately desire our study to generate reverence, dependence, and obedience and to overflow in proclamation—all in a way that points to the worth of the one who has revealed himself in it (Ezra 7:10; Prov. 2:4; Isa. 66:2; 2 Tim. 2:7, 15; 1 Peter 4:11).

As God's disclosure of himself and his purposes in a way we can understand, the Bible is about the good news of God's kingdom in which he reigns, saves, and satisfies through covenant for God's glory in Christ (Luke 4:43; 24:44–47; Acts 1:3; 20:25; 26:22–23; 28:23, 31). The KINGDOM Bible Reading Plan derives its name from the Bible's kingdom framework. The plan is distinguished by the following features:

1. The plan gives proportionate weight to the Old and New Testaments in view of their relative length, the Old receiving three readings per day and the New getting one reading per day.
2. The Old Testament readings follow the arrangement of Jesus' Bible (Luke 24:44—Law, Prophets, Writings), with one reading coming from each portion per day.
3. In a single year, one reads through Psalms twice and all other biblical books once; the second reading of Psalms (highlighted in gray) supplements the readings through the Law (Genesis–Deuteronomy). Dividing lines separate the Psalter's five "books."
4. The plan slates only twenty-five readings per month in order to provide more flexibility in daily devotions.
5. You can start the plan at any time of the year, and if four readings per day are too much, you can simply stretch the plan to two or more years (reading from one, two, or three columns per day).

JANUARY			
OT Law (& Pss.)	OT Prophets	OT Writings	NT
Gen.	***Josh.***	***Ruth***	***Matt.***
1. ☐ ☐ 1:1-2:3	☐ 1-2	☐ 1	☐ 1
2. ☐ 2:4-25	☐ 3-4	☐ 2	☐ 2
3. ☐ 3	☐ 5-6	☐ 3-4	☐ 3
		Pss.	
4. ☐ 4	☐ 7	☐ 1-2	☐ 4
5. ☐ 5:1-6:8	☐ 8	☐ 3-4	☐ 5:1-20
6. ☐ 6:9-7:24	☐ 9	☐ 5-6	☐ 5:21-48
7. ☐ 8	☐ 10	☐ 7-8	☐ 6
8. ☐ 9	☐ 11-12	☐ 9	☐ 7
9. ☐ 10:1-11:9	☐ 13-14	☐ 10	☐ 8
10. ☐ 11:10-32	☐ 15-16	☐ 11-12	☐ 9
11. ☐ 12	☐ 17-18	☐ 13-14	☐ 10
12. ☐ 13	☐ 19	☐ 15-16	☐ 11
13. ☐ 14	☐ 20-21	☐ 17	☐ 12:1-21
14. ☐ 15	☐ 22	☐ 18	☐ 12:22-50
15. ☐ 16	☐ 23-24	☐ 19	☐ 13:1-30
	Judg.		
16. ☐ 17	☐ 1	☐ 20-21	☐ 13:31-58
17. ☐ 18	☐ 2	☐ 22	☐ 14
18. ☐ 19	☐ 3	☐ 23-24	☐ 15
19. ☐ 20	☐ 4	☐ 25	☐ 16
20. ☐ 21	☐ 5	☐ 26	☐ 17
21. ☐ 22	☐ 6	☐ 27	☐ 18
22. ☐ 23	☐ 7	☐ 28-29	☐ 19
23. ☐ 24:1-28	☐ 8	☐ 30	☐ 20
24. ☐ 24:29-67	☐ 9	☐ 31	☐ 21:1-22
25. ☐ 25	☐ 10-11	☐ 32-33	☐ 21:23-46

FEBRUARY			
OT Law (& Pss.)	OT Prophets	OT Writings	NT
Gen.	***Judg.***	***Pss.***	***Matt.***
1. ☐ 26	☐ 12-13	☐ 34	☐ 22
2. ☐ 27	☐ 14-15	☐ 35	☐ 23
3. ☐ 28	☐ 16	☐ 36	☐ 24:1-28
4. ☐ 29	☐ 17-18	☐ 37	☐ 24:29-51
5. ☐ 30	☐ 19	☐ 38	☐ 25
6. ☐ Pss. 1-2	☐ 20	☐ 39	☐ 26:1-35
7. ☐ Pss. 3-4	☐ 21	☐ 40	☐ 26:36-75
	1 Sam.		
8. ☐ 31:1-24	☐ 1:1-2:11	☐ 41	☐ 27:1-31
9. ☐ 31:25-55	☐ 2:12-36	☐ 42-43	☐ 27:32-66
10. ☐ 32	☐ 3-4	☐ 44	☐ 28
			Mark
11. ☐ 33	☐ 5-6	☐ 45	☐ 1:1-20
12. ☐ Pss. 5-6	☐ 7-8	☐ 46-47	☐ 1:21-45
13. ☐ Pss. 7-8	☐ 9	☐ 48	☐ 2
14. ☐ 34	☐ 10-11	☐ 49	☐ 3
15. ☐ 35	☐ 12	☐ 50	☐ 4
16. ☐ 36:1-37:1	☐ 13	☐ 51	☐ 5
17. ☐ Pss. 9-10	☐ 14	☐ 52-54	☐ 6:1-29
18. ☐ Pss. 11-13	☐ 15	☐ 55	☐ 6:30-56
19. ☐ 37:2-36	☐ 16	☐ 56	☐ 7
20. ☐ 38	☐ 17	☐ 57	☐ 8:1-9:1
21. ☐ 39	☐ 18	☐ 58	☐ 9:2-29
22. ☐ 40	☐ 19	☐ 59	☐ 9:30-50
23. ☐ Pss. 14-16	☐ 20	☐ 60-61	☐ 10:1-31
24. ☐ Ps. 17	☐ 21-22	☐ 62	☐ 10:32-52
25. ☐ Ps. 18	☐ 23-24	☐ 63-64	☐ 11

MARCH			
OT Law (& Pss.)	OT Prophets	OT Writings	NT
Gen.	***1 Sam.***	***Pss.***	***Mark***
1. ☐ 41:1-36	☐ 25	☐ 65	☐ 12:1-17
2. ☐ 41:37-57	☐ 26-27	☐ 66-67	☐ 12:18-44
3. ☐ 42	☐ 28-29	☐ 68	☐ 13
4. ☐ Ps. 19	☐ 30-31	☐ 69	☐ 14:1-31
	2 Sam.		
5. ☐ Pss. 20-21	☐ 1	☐ 70-71	☐ 14:32-72
6. ☐ 43	☐ 2	☐ 72	☐ 15
7. ☐ 44	☐ 3	☐ 73	☐ 16
			Luke
8. ☐ 45	☐ 4-5	☐ 74	☐ 1:1-38
9. ☐ 46	☐ 6	☐ 75-76	☐ 1:39-80
10. ☐ 47	☐ 7	☐ 77	☐ 2:1-21
11. ☐ Ps. 22	☐ 8-9	☐ 78:1-39	☐ 2:22-52
12. ☐ Pss. 23-24	☐ 10-11	☐ 78:40-72	☐ 3
13. ☐ 48	☐ 12	☐ 79	☐ 4:1-30
14. ☐ 49	☐ 13	☐ 80	☐ 4:31-44
15. ☐ 50	☐ 14	☐ 81-82	☐ 5
16. ☐ Ps. 25	☐ 15	☐ 83	☐ 6:1-16
17. ☐ Ps. 26	☐ 16	☐ 84	☐ 6:17-49
Ex.			
18. ☐ 1-2	☐ 17	☐ 85	☐ 7:1-35
19. ☐ 3:1-4:17	☐ 18	☐ 86-87	☐ 7:36-50
20. ☐ 4:18-5:23	☐ 19	☐ 88	☐ 8:1-25
21. ☐ 6	☐ 20	☐ 89	☐ 8:26-56
22. ☐ 7	☐ 21	☐ 90	☐ 9:1-27
23. ☐ Ps. 27	☐ 22	☐ 91	☐ 9:28-62
24. ☐ Pss. 28-29	☐ 23	☐ 92-93	☐ 10:1-20
25. ☐ Ps. 30	☐ 24	☐ 94	☐ 10:21-42

APRIL			
OT Law (& Pss.)	OT Prophets	OT Writings	NT
Ex.	***1 Kings***	***Pss.***	***Luke***
1. ☐ 8	☐ 1	☐ 95	☐ 11:1-26
2. ☐ 9	☐ 2	☐ 96	☐ 11:27-54
3. ☐ 10-11	☐ 3	☐ 97	☐ 12:1-21
4. ☐ Ps. 31	☐ 4-5	☐ 98-99	☐ 12:22-59
5. ☐ Ps. 32	☐ 6	☐ 100-101	☐ 13
6. ☐ 12:1-28	☐ 7	☐ 102	☐ 14
7. ☐ 12:29-51	☐ 8	☐ 103	☐ 15
8. ☐ 13	☐ 9	☐ 104	☐ 16
9. ☐ 14	☐ 10	☐ 105	☐ 17
10. ☐ 15	☐ 11	☐ 106	☐ 18
11. ☐ Ps. 33	☐ 12	☐ 107	☐ 19:1-27
12. ☐ Ps. 34	☐ 13	☐ 108	☐ 19:28-48
13. ☐ Ps. 35	☐ 14	☐ 109	☐ 20:1-26
14. ☐ 16	☐ 15	☐ 110-111	☐ 20:27-47
15. ☐ 17	☐ 16	☐ 112-114	☐ 21
16. ☐ 18	☐ 17	☐ 115	☐ 22:1-38
17. ☐ Ps. 36	☐ 18	☐ 116-117	☐ 22:39-71
18. ☐ Ps. 37	☐ 19	☐ 118	☐ 23:1-25
19. ☐ 19	☐ 20	☐ 119:1-40	☐ 23:26-56
20. ☐ 20	☐ 21	☐ 119:41-72	☐ 24:1-12
21. ☐ 21	☐ 22	☐ 119:73-104	☐ 24:13-53
	2 Kings		***John***
22. ☐ 22	☐ 1–2	☐ 119:105-136	☐ 1:1-28
23. ☐ 23	☐ 3	☐ 119:137-176	☐ 1:29-51
24. ☐ Ps. 38	☐ 4	☐ 120-122	☐ 2
25. ☐ Ps. 39	☐ 5	☐ 123-125	☐ 3

MAY			
OT Law (& Pss.)	OT Prophets	OT Writings	NT
Ex.	*2 Kings*	*Pss.*	*John*
1. □ 24	□ 6	□ 126-128	□ 4
2. □ 25	□ 7	□ 129-131	□ 5
3. □ Ps. 40	□ 8	□ 132-133	□ 6:1-40
4. □ Ps. 41	□ 9	□ 134-135	□ 6:41-71
5. □ 26	□ 10	□ 136	□ 7:1-24
6. □ 27	□ 11-12	□ 137-138	□ 7:25-52
7. □ 28	□ 13	□ 139	□ 7:53-8:30
8. □ Pss. 42-43	□ 14	□ 140	□ 8:31-59
9. □ Ps. 44	□ 15	□ 141-142	□ 9
10. □ Ps. 45	□ 16	□ 143	□ 10
11. □ 29	□ 17	□ 144	□ 11:1-27
12. □ 30	□ 18	□ 145	□ 11:28-57
13. □ 31	□ 19	□ 146	□ 12:1-19
14. □ Pss. 46-47	□ 20	□ 147	□ 12:20-50
15. □ Ps. 48	□ 21	□ 148	□ 13
16. □ Ps. 49	□ 22	□ 149-150	□ 14
		Job	
17. □ 32	□ 23	□ 1	□ 15
18. □ 33	□ 24	□ 2	□ 16
19. □ 34	□ 25	□ 3	□ 17
	Jer.		
20. □ Ps. 50	□ 1	□ 4	□ 18
21. □ Ps. 51	□ 2	□ 5	□ 19
22. □ Pss. 52-54	□ 3	□ 6	□ 20
23. □ 35	□ 4	□ 7	□ 21
			Acts
24. □ 36	□ 5	□ 8	□ 1
25. □ 37	□ 6	□ 9	□ 2:1-41

JUNE			
OT Law (& Pss.)	OT Prophets	OT Writings	NT
Ex.	*Jer.*	*Job*	*Acts*
1. □ 38	□ 7	□ 10	□ 2:42-3:26
2. □ 39	□ 8	□ 11	□ 4
3. □ 40	□ 9	□ 12	□ 5
4. □ Ps. 55	□ 10	□ 13	□ 6
5 □ Ps. 56	□ 11-12	□ 14	□ 7:1-29
6. □ Ps. 57	□ 13	□ 15	□ 7:30-60
Lev.			
7. □ 1-2	□ 14	□ 16	□ 8
8. □ 3-4	□ 15-16	□ 17	□ 9:1-19
9. □ 5:1-6:7	□ 17	□ 18	□ 9:20-43
10. □ 6:8-30	□ 18	□ 19	□ 10
11. □ 7	□ 19-20	□ 20	□ 11
12. □ Ps. 58	□ 21	□ 21	□ 12
13. □ Ps. 59	□ 22	□ 22	□ 13:1-12
14. □ Pss. 60-61	□ 23	□ 23	□ 13:13-52
15. □ 8	□ 24-25	□ 24	□ 14
16. □ 9	□ 26	□ 25-26	□ 15
17. □ 10	□ 27	□ 27	□ 16
18. □ Pss. 62-63	□ 28	□ 28	□ 17
19. □ Pss. 64-65	□ 29	□ 29	□ 18
20. □ Pss. 66-67	□ 30	□ 30	□ 19
21. □ 11	□ 31	□ 31	□ 20
22. □ 12:1–13:37	□ 32	□ 32	□ 21
23. □ 13:38–59	□ 33	□ 33	□ 22
24. □ Ps. 68	□ 34	□ 34	□ 23
25. □ Ps. 69	□ 35	□ 35	□ 24

JULY			
OT Law (& Pss.)	OT Prophets	OT Writings	NT
Lev.	*Jer.*	*Job*	*Acts*
1. □ 14	□ 36	□ 36	□ 25
2. □ 15	□ 37	□ 37	□ 26
3. □ 16	□ 38	□ 38	□ 27
4. □ Pss. 70-71	□ 39-40	□ 39	□ 28
			Rom.
5. □ Ps. 72	□ 41-42	□ 40	□ 1
6. □ 17	□ 43-45	□ 41	□ 2
7. □ 18	□ 46-47	□ 42	□ 3
		Prov.	
8. □ 19	□ 48	□ 1	□ 4
9. □ 20	□ 49	□ 2	□ 5
10. □ Ps. 73	□ 50	□ 3	□ 6
11. □ Ps. 74	□ 51	□ 4	□ 7
12. □ Pss. 75-76	□ 52	□ 5	□ 8
	Ezek.		
13. □ 21	□ 1	□ 6	□ 9
14. □ 22	□ 2-3	□ 7	□ 10
15. □ 23	□ 4-5	□ 8	□ 11
16. □ 24	□ 6-7	□ 9	□ 12
17. □ Ps. 77	□ 8-9	□ 10	□ 13
18. □ Ps. 78:1-39	□ 10-11	□ 11	□ 14
19. □ Ps. 78:40-72	□ 12	□ 12	□ 15
20. □ 25:1-46	□ 13	□ 13	□ 16
			1 Cor.
21. □ 25:47-26:13	□ 14-15	□ 14	□ 1
22. □ 26:14-46	□ 16	□ 15	□ 2
23. □ 27	□ 17	□ 16	□ 3
24. □ Ps. 79	□ 18-19	□ 17	□ 4
25. □ Ps. 80	□ 20	□ 18	□ 5

AUGUST			
OT Law (& Pss.)	OT Prophets	OT Writings	NT
Num.	*Ezek.*	*Prov.*	*1 Cor.*
1. □ 1	□ 21	□ 19	□ 6
2. □ 2	□ 22	□ 20	□ 7
3. □ 3	□ 23	□ 21	□ 8
4. □ Pss. 81-82	□ 24	□ 22	□ 9
5. □ Ps. 83	□ 25-26	□ 23	□ 10
6. □ 4	□ 27	□ 24	□ 11
7. □ 5	□ 28	□ 25	□ 12
8. □ 6	□ 29	□ 26	□ 13
9. □ Ps. 84	□ 30	□ 27	□ 14
10. □ Ps. 85	□ 31	□ 28	□ 15:1-34
11. □ 7:1-41	□ 32	□ 29	□ 15:35-58
12. □ 7:42-89	□ 33	□ 30	□ 16
			2 Cor.
13. □ 8	□ 34-35	□ 31	□ 1
		Eccl.	
14. □ Pss. 86-87	□ 36	□ 1	□ 2
15. □ Ps. 88	□ 37	□ 2	□ 3
16. □ Ps. 89	□ 38	□ 3	□ 4
17. □ 9	□ 39	□ 4	□ 5
18. □ 10	□ 40	□ 5	□ 6
19. □ 11	□ 41-42	□ 6	□ 7
20. □ Ps. 90	□ 43	□ 7	□ 8
21. □ Ps. 91	□ 44	□ 8	□ 9
22. □ Pss. 92-93	□ 45	□ 9	□ 10
23. □ 12-13	□ 46	□ 10	□ 11
24. □ 14:1-19	□ 47	□ 11	□ 12
25. □ 14:20-45	□ 48	□ 12	□ 13

SEPTEMBER			
OT Law (& Pss.)	OT Prophets	OT Writings	NT
Num.	***Isa.***	***Song***	***Gal.***
1. ☐ 15	☐ 1	☐ 1	☐ 1
2. ☐ 16:1-24	☐ 2	☐ 2	☐ 2
3. ☐ 16:25-50	☐ 3-4	☐ 3	☐ 3
4. ☐ 17	☐ 5	☐ 4	☐ 4
5. ☐ Ps. 94	☐ 6-7	☐ 5	☐ 5
6. ☐ Ps. 95	☐ 8	☐ 6	☐ 6
			Eph.
7. ☐ Ps. 96	☐ 9	☐ 7	☐ 1
8. ☐ 18	☐ 10	☐ 8	☐ 2
		Lam.	
9. ☐ 19	☐ 11-12	☐ 1	☐ 3
10. ☐ 20	☐ 13	☐ 2	☐ 4
11. ☐ Ps. 97	☐ 14	☐ 3	☐ 5
12. ☐ Pss. 98-99	☐ 15-16	☐ 4	☐ 6
			Phil.
13. ☐ Pss.100-101	☐ 17-18	☐ 5	☐ 1
		Dan.	
14. ☐ 21	☐ 19-20	☐ 1	☐ 2
15. ☐ 22	☐ 21	☐ 2	☐ 3
16. ☐ 23	☐ 22	☐ 3	☐ 4
			Col.
17. ☐ Ps. 102	☐ 23	☐ 4	☐ 1
18. ☐ Ps. 103	☐ 24	☐ 5	☐ 2
19. ☐ 24	☐ 25-26	☐ 6	☐ 3
20. ☐ 25	☐ 27	☐ 7	☐ 4
			1 Thess.
21. ☐ 26	☐ 28	☐ 8	☐ 1
22. ☐ 27	☐ 29	☐ 9	☐ 2
23. ☐ Ps. 104	☐ 30	☐ 10	☐ 3
24. ☐ Ps. 105	☐ 31-32	☐ 11	☐ 4
25. ☐ Ps. 106	☐ 33	☐ 12	☐ 5

OCTOBER			
OT Law (& Pss.)	OT Prophets	OT Writings	NT
Num.	***Isa.***	***Esther***	***2 Thess.***
1. ☐ 28	☐ 34-35	☐ 1	☐ 1
2. ☐ 29	☐ 36	☐ 2	☐ 2
3. ☐ 30	☐ 37	☐ 3-4	☐ 3
			1 Tim.
4. ☐ Ps. 107	☐ 38-39	☐ 5-6	☐ 1
5. ☐ Ps. 108	☐ 40	☐ 7-8	☐ 2
6. ☐ Ps. 109	☐ 41	☐ 9-10	☐ 3
		Ezra	
7. ☐ 31	☐ 42	☐ 1-2	☐ 4
8. ☐ 32	☐ 43	☐ 3-4	☐ 5
9. ☐ 33	☐ 44	☐ 5	☐ 6
			2 Tim.
10. ☐ Pss.110-112	☐ 45	☐ 6	☐ 1
11. ☐ Pss.113-114	☐ 46-47	☐ 7	☐ 2
12. ☐ Ps. 115	☐ 48	☐ 8	☐ 3
13. ☐ 34	☐ 49	☐ 9	☐ 4
			Titus
14. ☐ 35	☐ 50	☐ 10	☐ 1
		Neh.	
15. ☐ 36	☐ 51	☐ 1-2	☐ 2
16. ☐ Pss.116-117	☐ 52-53	☐ 3	☐ 3
			Philem.
17. ☐ Ps. 118	☐ 54-55	☐ 4	☐ 1
Deut.			***Heb.***
18. ☐ 1:1-18	☐ 56	☐ 5-6	☐ 1
19. ☐ 1:19-46	☐ 57	☐ 7	☐ 2
20. ☐ 2	☐ 58	☐ 8	☐ 3
21. ☐ 3	☐ 59	☐ 9	☐ 4
22. ☐ 4:1-43	☐ 60-61	☐ 10	☐ 5
23. ☐ Ps. 119:1-40	☐ 62-63	☐ 11	☐ 6
24. ☐ Ps. 119:41-72	☐ 64-65	☐ 12	☐ 7
25. ☐ Ps. 119:73-104	☐ 66	☐ 13	☐ 8

NOVEMBER			
OT Law (& Pss.)	OT Prophets	OT Writings	NT
Deut.	***Hos.***	***1 Chron.***	***Heb.***
1. ☐ 4:44-6:3	☐ 1	☐ 1	☐ 9
2. ☐ 6:4-25	☐ 2-3	☐ 2	☐ 10:1-18
3. ☐ 7	☐ 4	☐ 3-4	☐ 10:19-39
4. ☐ 8	☐ 5-6	☐ 5	☐ 11:1-22
5. ☐ Ps. 119:105-136	☐ 7	☐ 6	☐ 11:23-40
6. ☐ Ps. 119:137-176	☐ 8	☐ 7	☐ 12
7. ☐ Pss. 120-122	☐ 9	☐ 8	☐ 13
			James
8. ☐ 9	☐ 10	☐ 9-10	☐ 1
9. ☐ 10	☐ 11-12	☐ 11	☐ 2
10. ☐ 11	☐ 13-14	☐ 12	☐ 3
	Joel		
11. ☐ Pss. 123-125	☐ 1	☐ 13-14	☐ 4
12. ☐ Pss. 126-128	☐ 2	☐ 15	☐ 5
			1 Peter
13. ☐ 12	☐ 3	☐ 16	☐ 1
	Amos		
14. ☐ 13	☐ 1	☐ 17	☐ 2
15. ☐ 14	☐ 2	☐ 18-19	☐ 3
16. ☐ 15	☐ 3	☐ 20-21	☐ 4
17. ☐ Pss. 129-131	☐ 4	☐ 22	☐ 5
			2 Peter
18. ☐ Pss. 132-134	☐ 5	☐ 23	☐ 1
19. ☐ 16	☐ 6	☐ 24-25	☐ 2
20. ☐ 17	☐ 7	☐ 26	☐ 3
			1 John
21. ☐ 18	☐ 8	☐ 27	☐ 1
22. ☐ Ps. 135	☐ 9	☐ 28	☐ 2
	Obad.		
23. ☐ Ps. 136	☐ 1	☐ 29	☐ 3
	Jonah	***2 Chron.***	
24. ☐ 19	☐ 1-2	☐ 1-2	☐ 4
25. ☐ 20	☐ 3-4	☐ 3-4	☐ 5

DECEMBER			
OT Law (& Pss.)	OT Prophets	OT Writings	NT
Deut.	***Mic.***	***2 Chron.***	***2 John***
1. ☐ 21	☐ 1	☐ 5:1-6:11	☐ 1
			3 John
2. ☐ 22	☐ 2	☐ 6:12-42	☐ 1
			Jude
3. ☐ 23	☐ 3	☐ 7	☐ 1
			Rev.
4. ☐ Pss. 137-138	☐ 4	☐ 8	☐ 1
5. ☐ Ps. 139	☐ 5	☐ 9	☐ 2
6. ☐ 24	☐ 6	☐ 10-11	☐ 3
7. ☐ 25	☐ 7	☐ 12-13	☐ 4
	Nah.		
8. ☐ 26	☐ 1-2	☐ 14-15	☐ 5
9. ☐ Ps. 140	☐ 3	☐ 16-17	☐ 6
	Hab.		
10. ☐ Pss. 141-142	☐ 1	☐ 18-19	☐ 7
11. ☐ 27:1-28:14	☐ 2	☐ 20	☐ 8
12. ☐ 28:15-29:1	☐ 3	☐ 21	☐ 9
	Zeph.		
13. ☐ Ps. 143	☐ 1	☐ 22-23	☐ 10
14. ☐ Ps. 144	☐ 2	☐ 24	☐ 11
15. ☐ Ps. 145	☐ 3	☐ 25	☐ 12
	Hag.		
16. ☐ 29:2–29	☐ 1-2	☐ 26	☐ 13
	Zech.		
17. ☐ 30	☐ 1-2	☐ 27-28	☐ 14
18. ☐ 31:1-29	☐ 3-5	☐ 29	☐ 15
19. ☐ Ps. 146	☐ 6-7	☐ 30	☐ 16
20. ☐ Ps. 147	☐ 8	☐ 31	☐ 17
21. ☐ 31:30-32:52	☐ 9-10	☐ 32	☐ 18
22. ☐ 33	☐ 11-12	☐ 33	☐ 19
23. ☐ 34	☐ 13-14	☐ 34	☐ 20
	Mal.		
24. ☐ Ps. 148	☐ 1-2	☐ 35	☐ 21
25. ☐ Pss. 149-150	☐ 3-4	☐ 36	☐ 22

GLOSSARY

accidental changes. Textual errors due to the physical deterioration of a manuscript. (chap. 3)

Aktionsart (German "kind of action"). A lexical feature of language that relates to the actual (and not just portrayed) procedural characteristics attributed to a verb phrase. *Dynamicity* (dynamic vs. stative), *durativity* (durative vs. punctiliar), and *telicity* (telic vs. atelic) are all features of *Aktionsart*. (chap. 5)

already but not yet. An eschatological expression identifying the inaugurated yet unconsummate nature of God's kingdom. With respect to God's promises, it means that while all the kingdom blessings for believers are *already* secured in Jesus, we enjoy only some of them now, while others await future enjoyment in the consummated new heavens and earth. (chap. 12)

anticipatory discourse. The **text type** that predicts or promises forthcoming events, at times in contingent succession; usually future **tense**. The default pattern is the ***weqatal* clause**. Cf. **directive discourse** and **historical discourse**. (chap. 2)

apodictic laws. A formal category identifying laws that are base principles, being stated in a way that allows for no qualification or exception. Cf. **casuistic laws**. (chap. 1)

apodosis. The concluding or "then" portion of a two-part syntactic construction ("if-then," "when-then," "because-therefore"). Cf. **protasis**. (chaps. 2, 5)

aspect. The way in which a speaker represents or portrays an action; the primary aspects in Hebrew are **perfective** and **imperfective**. (chap. 5)

asyndeton. The absence of a connector. At the front of a **clause**, asyndeton usually signals either (1) a fresh beginning (i.e., the start of a new discourse unit or **text block**) or (2) explication (i.e., the restatement, clarification, or support of a previous text unit). (chap. 2)

autograph. The original document as penned by the biblical writers. (chap. 3)

Bible's focus. God's glory. (chap. 10)

Bible's form. The Old and New Testaments that unpack the progression of covenants comprising the Adamic-Noahic, Abrahamic, Mosaic, Davidic, and new. (chap. 10)

Bible's frame. The kingdom of God; God's reign over God's people in God's land for God's glory. (chap. 10)

Bible's fulcrum. Christ Jesus as the one to whom all history points and from whom all fulfillment comes. (chap. 10)

Bible's message. The idea that God reigns, saves, and satisfies (God's kingdom) through covenant for his glory in Christ. (chap. 10)

biblical interpretation. The process of doing exegesis and then using it to do theology, which entails a personal encounter with the living God, resulting in a transformed life. See **exegesis** and **theology**. (intro.)

biblical theology. A method of studying how all of Scripture fits together and points to Christ; a way of analyzing and synthesizing what the Bible reveals about God and his relations with the world that makes organic salvation-historical and literary-canonical connections with the whole of Scripture on its own terms, especially with respect to how the Old and New Testaments progress, integrate, and climax in Christ. See **theology**. Cf. **practical theology** and **systematic theology**. (chap. 10)

canonical horizon. A view of the biblical text that considers how the placement and use of the text within the broader canon informs our understanding of God's intent for the passage. Here we keep in mind: (1) the progressive nature of revelation; (2) that all history is influenced by the defining work of Christ; and (3) that the divine authorship of Scripture allows for later texts to clarify, enhance, or deepen the meaning of earlier texts. (chap. 10)

casuistic laws. A formal category identifying laws that are situational, related to specific circumstances; often "if-then." Cf. **apodictic laws**. (chap. 1)

ceremonial law (theological category proposed by some). A category of laws with symbolic requirements related to Israel's religious ceremonies and cult worship that find their typological end in Christ and therefore are no longer applicable to Christians. Cf. **civil law** and **moral law**. (chap. 12)

Christotelic. Of or relating to the idea that all of the Old Testament's history (Matt. 2:15), laws (5:17–18), and prophecy (Acts 3:18) find their end or goal in Jesus (cf. Rom. 10:4). (chap. 10)

Christ's "fulfilling" the Old Testament. The idea that Jesus supplies the eschatological actualization of all Old Testament anticipation; the view that he is the goal and end of all Old Testament hopes and shadows, whether through direct or typological prophecy or through the overarching salvation-historical trajectories. (chap. 12)

civil law (content category). A category related to the *content* of certain laws—those governing private disputes between citizens or organizations in which the public authorities are appealed to for judgment or called on to intervene; the offended party is not the state or national community. Cf. **ceremonial law** and **moral law**. (chaps. 1, 12)

civil law (theological category proposed by some). A category of laws related to Israel's political and social structures that are time-bound and therefore no longer applicable in the new covenant age. Cf. **ceremonial law** and **moral law**. (chap. 12)

clause. A grammatical construction that can stand on its own, expressing a complete thought, and that in its most basic form is made up of a subject and its **predicate**; it may also include connecting words such as conjunctions and various modifiers. Clauses may be either **main** or **subordinate**. (chap. 5)

cognate. Similar vocabulary from a related language. (chap. 7)

cohortative. See ***yiqtol***.

compassion law (content category). A "law" dealing with charity, justice, and mercy toward others. It is not exactly the kind of law that can be enforced in court, but God knows the heart. (chaps. 1, 12)

concordance. A book that lists all instances of a word or phrase within a given Testament, usually followed by a sampling of its use in specific contexts. (chap. 7)

conjoined imperfect. See ***weyiqtol***.

conjoined perfect. See ***weqatal***.

contextualizing constituent. A form that orients the audience to the greater context by its unexpected placement at the front of a **clause**, thus altering base word order. Cf. **focus**. (chap. 5)

contrastive matching. The result when an **unmarked clause** and an adjacent **marked clause** are together treated as two contrasting parts of a single event or idea. This type of matching is often expressed when a default verb-first clause (i.e., ***wayyiqtol*** or ***weqatal*** = V_) is directly followed by a marked, non-verb-first clause (_V) resulting in the following pattern: V_ + _V. Cf. **identical matching**. (chap. 5)

coordinate relationships. Semantic relationships in which **propositions** or units of thought stand side by side and are equal in rank or prominence. Cf. **subordinate relationships**. (chap. 6)

criminal law (content category). A category of laws governing crimes or offenses that put the welfare of the whole community at risk. The offended party is the state or national community, and therefore the punishment is on behalf of the whole community in the name of the highest state authority, which in Israel meant YHWH. (chaps. 1, 12)

cultic/ceremonial law (content category). A category of laws governing the visible forms and rituals of Israel's religious life. (chaps. 1, 12)

Dead Sea Scrolls (DSS). Texts that were found in the region of Qumran at the Dead Sea in and soon after 1947. Because of their age and origin, they have taken on enormous importance in text-critical studies. (chap. 3)

diplomatic text. A critical edition of an ancient text by contemporary text critics that is drawn from a single ancient manuscript and does not include any reconstruction. Cf. **eclectic text**. (chap. 3)

directive discourse. The **text type** of commands or exhortations, at times in the form of progressive directions for a given task. The default pattern is the ***weqatal*** **clause**, usually after one or more initial **imperatives**. Cf. **anticipatory discourse** and **historical discourse**. (chap. 2)

direct speech. An actual utterance that is embedded through quotation in a discourse and that contains its own independent nature. (chap. 5)

discourse markers. Hebrew constructions whose chief purpose is to signal special structural features in a discourse rather than to convey semantic meaning. Some are not translated. (chap. 2)

DSS. See **Dead Sea Scrolls**.

dynamic verbs. Verbs that express actions, showing continued or progressive action on the part of a subject. Also called *fientive verbs*. Cf. **stative verbs**. (chap. 5)

eclectic text. A critical edition of an ancient text by contemporary text critics that includes their reconstructed text and does not align with any single text tradition. Cf. **diplomatic text**. (chap. 3)

embedded discourse units. Text blocks that interrupt a higher level of discourse. Almost always signaled by an initial asyndetic **clause**, embedded discourse most commonly takes the form of **direct speech**, but it may also provide other forms of digression from the primary line of discourse, whether to restate, clarify, or support. (chaps. 2, 5)

emendation. The process of altering a known text in an attempt to return it to its more original reading. (chap. 3)

episode. A literary unit within narrative that is shaped by multiple **scenes**. (chap. 2)

epochal horizon. A perspective on the biblical text relating to the place of the passage within **salvation history**; addresses where the text fits within the unfolding of God's kingdom purposes, ultimately culminating in Christ. (chap. 10)

exegesis. The personal discovery of what the biblical authors intended their texts to mean. See **biblical interpretation**. Cf. **theology**. (intro.)

external evidence. Factors such as the age and quality of a manuscript that help determine a text's original wording. Cf. **internal evidence**. (chap. 3)

family law (content category). A category of noncivil, domestic laws governing the Israelite household. (chaps. 1, 12)

fientive verbs. See **dynamic verbs**.

focus. A form that highlights prominent information by its unexpected placement at the front of a **clause**, thus altering base word order. Cf. **contextualizing constituent**. (chap. 5)

form criticism. See **genre analysis**.

form-equivalence. An approach to translation that retains correspondence of words, **grammar**, and history as much as possible between the original and receptor language. Cf. **idea-equivalence** and **sense-equivalence**. (chap. 4)

genre. An identifiable category of literary composition that usually demands its own exegetical rules. (chap. 1)

genre analysis. The examination of the shape, subject matter, and purpose of a particular text unit. Also called *form criticism*. (chap. 1)

gospel. The good news that the reigning God saves and satisfies believing sinners by Christ Jesus' life, death, and resurrection. (chap. 11)

grammar. The whole system and structure that a language uses for communicating effectively. (chap. 5)

grammatical correspondence. The measure of how closely word order and **syntax** in the original language is aligned with the word order and syntax in translation. Cf. **historical correspondence** and **lexical correspondence**. (chap. 4)

hapax legomenon (Greek "said only once"). A certain form that occurs only once in the biblical text, whether because the word itself is unique or because just its spelling is unique. (chap. 3)

historical context. Where a passage fits in space and time, and how this data informs one's reading of the passage. (chap. 8)

historical correspondence. The measure of how closely the translators retain the factual and cultural elements connected with the biblical times. Cf. **grammatical correspondence** and **lexical correspondence**. (chap. 4)

historical discourse. The **text type** of Old Testament narrative that conveys a succession of contingent events, usually in past **tense**. The default pattern is a ***wayyiqtol*** **clause**. Cf. **anticipatory discourse** and **directive discourse**. (chap. 2)

idea-equivalence. An approach to translation that seeks only to convey the concepts of Scripture, with little attempt to retain **lexical**, **grammatical**, or **historical correspondence**. Also called *paraphrase.* Cf. **form-equivalence** and **sense-equivalence**. (chap. 4)

identical matching. The result when a series of **marked clause**s describe two or more aligned elements of a single event. Here two or more marked, non-verb-first clauses stand adjacent, resulting in the following pattern: _V + _V. Cf. **contrastive matching**. (chap. 5)

imperative. A verb type used for giving a direct command. In Hebrew, it is always second person. (chaps. 2, 5)

imperfect. See ***yiqtol***.

imperfective aspect. The portrayal of an action as a process, as in "He was eating the apple." See **aspect**. Cf. **perfective aspect**. (chap. 5)

inerrant. Containing no error; relating to the view that the Bible (insofar as it aligns with its original form) is true and trustworthy in all its assertions—without error and completely reliable in its claims of fact (history, geology, chronology, science, etc.). (intro., chap. 1)

infallible. Incapable of error; relating to the view that the Bible (insofar as it aligns with its original form) is a sure and safe guide—faultless and completely reliable in its claims regarding faith (doctrine) and practice (ethics). (intro., chap. 1)

inference markers. Words that mark logical inference at a macro-level within discourse; לָכֵן and וְעַתָּה in Hebrew. (chap. 5)

intentional changes. Textual errors related to (1) deliberate alterations, (2) deliberate omission of words or phrases, or (3) explanatory glosses. (chap. 3)

internal evidence. Factors used in determining what an author most likely wrote and which variant readings are best explained as **unintentional** and **intentional changes** made by copyists—all of which help determine a text's original wording. Cf. **external evidence**. (chap. 3)

IOUS. An acronym that John Piper developed to help people know how to pray when approaching God's Word: "Incline my heart to your testimonies" (Ps. 119:36); "Open my eyes that I may behold wonderful things in your law" (119:18); "Unite my heart to fear your name" (86:11); and "Satisfy us this morning with your steadfast love, that we may rejoice and be glad all our days" (90:14). (intro.)

jussive. See ***yiqtol***.

Kethiv-Qere. Notes in the Hebrew Bible that alert the reader that the scribes believed a word in the body of the text is written one way (the *Kethiv*) but should be read another way (the *Qere*). Within the text the Kethiv consonants are written with the vowels of the Qere, and in the margin are the consonants of the Qere, which are to be combined with the vowel points written with the Kethiv found in the text. In printed texts, a small circle elevated above the Kethiv usually identifies a word as having a Qere; in electronic texts, the Kethiv is usually followed immediately in brackets by the Qere. (chap. 3)

KINGDOM. An acronym summarizing the redemptive flow of God's kingdom-building plan: (K) Kickoff and rebellion, (I) Instrument of blessing, (N) Nation redeemed and commissioned, (G) Government in the land, (D) Dispersion and return, (O) Overlap of the ages, (M) Mission accomplished. (chap. 10)

law of Christ. The makeup of God's law of love that is applicable to New Testament believers through **Christ's "fulfilling" the Old Testament** (1 Cor. 9:20–21; Gal. 6:2). Our obedience to this law is fueled by Jesus' unparalleled pattern in keeping the law and by the unparalleled power that he supplies for us to obey by means of his past pardon and future promise. Also called "the perfect law," "the law of liberty," and "the royal law" (James 1:25; 2:8, 12). (chap. 12)

lexical correspondence. The measure of how closely translators attempt to render single words in a source text into individual words in the target language. Cf. **grammatical correspondence** and **historical correspondence**. (chap. 4)

lexicon. A book that lists the words of a language, usually in alphabetical order, and gives their range of meaning through equivalent words in a different language. (chap. 7)

literary argument. The way in which an author structures his thoughts in order to communicate reality as he intends his audience to view it. Arguments seek to compel beliefs or actions, and they come in all **genres**, whether narrative plots, hortatory sermons, poetic prayers, or the like. (chap. 6)

literary-canonical connections. Biblical-theological links identified within the Bible's final-form composition and structure and its historical details. (chap. 10)

literary context. The literary setting in which a passage finds itself, and the way in which a passage contributes to the overall story or argument of its book. (chap. 9)

literary details. The particular features or aspects of a text that set it apart and that help identify its overall contribution. (chap. 9)

literary function. A passage's purpose and contribution within its book. (chap. 9)

literary placement. A passage's location in its book. (chap. 9)

literary unit. A discrete division of text with a clear beginning or end. The literary unit could be an entire **text block** or a paragraph within a text block marked by form and content. (chap. 2)

love principle. The lasting fundamental ethical truth taught in any given Old Testament law that clarifies how love for God or neighbor should manifest itself. (chap. 12)

LXX. See **Septuagint**.

main (*matrix* "mother") clause. A **clause** that is not grammatically subordinate to any other higher-level clause. In the construction "David, who is but a boy, slew Goliath," the words "David . . . slew Goliath" form the main clause. Cf. **subordinate clause**. (chap. 5)

marked clause. A **clause** containing any verb pattern other than the default, which signals literary features such as background, paragraph transition, and dramatic climax. Cf. **unmarked clause**. (chaps. 2, 5)

marked primary citation. Direct speech that (1) reports a single event, (2) has its characters speak individually, (3) is not retold from a previous conversation, (4) deals with full characters in a story, and/or (5) functions as a lively account of a direct conversation. Cf. **marked secondary citation**. (chap. 2)

marked secondary citation. Direct speech that (1) summarizes a more extended speech or speeches, (2) presents the statement of many as a single voice, (3) has one character cite a prior statement by another, (4) comes from a prop rather than full character or from someone not actually present and participating in the current conversation, and/or (5) functions as the official record of the principal points made by speakers. Cf. **marked primary citation**. (chap. 2)

markers of immediate significance. Clause modifiers that focus attention forward in a discourse; הִנֵּה and הֵן in Hebrew. (chap. 5)

Masorah parva. Small marginal comments found in the Hebrew Bible aimed at preserving an unaltered text. A small circle usually identifies a word as having a comment. The comments usually address statistical details regarding word counts, word placement, and spelling peculiarities. (chap. 3)

Masoretic Text (MT). The received, standard **text** of the Hebrew Scriptures. It is called *Masoretic* because it is the text tradition of the Masoretes, a Jewish scribal school that worked from A.D. 500–1000. (chap. 3)

modality. See **mood**.

mood. The expression of a verb that answers whether its action or state is actual or only possible. The indicative mood ("He studies Hebrew") contrasts with the subjunctive ("He should study Hebrew"). Hebrew does not inflect for mood but signals it by word order and context. Also called *modality*. (chap. 5)

moral law (theological category proposed by some). A category of fundamental ethical principles of the Mosaic law that some believe are eternally applicable, regardless of the time or covenant. Cf. **ceremonial law** and **civil law**. (chap. 12)

morphology. The study of how the smallest grammatical units (called *morphemes*) combine to form stems and words. (chap. 5)

MT. See **Masoretic Text**.

nominal clause. See **verbless clause**.

oracle. A divine pronouncement through a **prophet** that directs human action in the present or foretells future events. (chap. 1)

oracles of hope/salvation. Prophetic words affirming future hope or deliverance in accordance with the covenant restoration blessings. (chap. 1)

oracles of indictment. Prophetic words that identify specific covenantal violations or offenses against YHWH. (chap. 1)

oracles of instruction. Prophetic words that clarify God's expected response from the people in accordance with his covenant stipulations. (chap. 1)

oracles of warning/punishment. Prophetic words declaring the nature of God's punishment in accordance with the covenant curses. (chap. 1)

orthography. The study of an alphabet and of how its letters combine to represent sounds and to form words. (chap. 5)

paraphrase. See **idea-equivalence**.

perfect. See ***qatal***.

perfective aspect. The portrayal of an action as a complete whole (but not necessarily "completed action"), as in "He ate the apple" or "He eats the apple." See **aspect**. Cf. **imperfective aspect**. (chap. 5)

perspicuity of Scripture. The doctrine of Scripture's clarity—that while we cannot always know how much the authors assume of their readers, the very nature of God's Word demands that its message can be understood in any culture and in any age. The Bible is sufficiently clear, but not everything in it is equally clear. (chap. 8)

Peshitta. The Syriac translation of the Old Testament used by the Syrian church. Syriac is a later dialect of Aramaic. (chap. 3)

phonology. The study of a system of sounds (called *phonemes*) used in a given language. (chap. 5)

phrase. A group of words that fill a single slot in a **clause**. (chap. 5)

practical theology. The study and application of the biblical author's intended effect in a passage. See **theology**. Cf. **biblical theology** and **systematic theology**. (chap. 12)

predicate. The state, process, or action associated with the subject. The predicate may be a finite verb, or it may be another noun or an adjective without any explicit verb, thus creating a **verbless** (or nominal) **clause**. (chap. 5)

preterite. See ***wayyiqtol***.

principle of analogy. The higher-critical view that interpreters should limit what can qualify as "history" to present experience; in contrast, it is better to judge historical plausibility by the reasonableness of arguments made for belief in occurrences with which the historians may themselves have no personal connection. (chap. 1)

principle of correlation. The higher-critical view that interpreters should limit potential historical causation to natural forces or human agency; in contrast, it is better to broaden causation to include all *personal* forces (such as God) and not limit it to just natural or material forces. (chap. 1)

principle of criticism. The higher-critical view that interpreters should initially be skeptical about Scripture's truth claims until proved otherwise; in contrast, it is better to engage in thoughtful appraisal of the evidence in keeping with its source. (chap. 1)

prophet. A covenantal ambassador of the heavenly court, whom God commissioned to preach for God to the people and to pray for the people to God. (chap. 1)

proposition. The distinct thoughts in a passage. (chap. 6)

protasis. The contingent (or "if") portion of a two-part syntactic construction ("if-then," "when-then," "because-therefore"). Cf. **apodosis**. (chaps. 2, 5)

proverb. A succinct, memorable saying in common use that states a general truth or piece of advice. (chap. 1)

psalms of lament. Cries for help out of the midst of pain. (chap. 1)

psalms of praise. Hymns that celebrate who God is and what he has done, especially as Creator and Redeemer. (chap. 1)

psalms of thanksgiving. Expressions of gratitude for deliverance or provision after the pain. (chap. 1)

psalms of trust. Declarations of confidence out of the midst of pain. (chap. 1)

***qatal*.** A finite verb form in biblical Hebrew that generally expresses **perfective aspect** and past **tense**; also called the *perfect* or the *suffixed form* by scholars. *Perfect* refers to perfective aspect, not tense. (chaps. 2, 5)

royal psalms. Songs that focus on an unparalleled human king who would represent YHWH's reign on earth. (chap. 1)

salvation history. The progressive narrative unfolding of God's kingdom plan through the various covenants, events, people, and institutions, all climaxing in the person and work of Jesus. (chap. 10)

Samaritan Pentateuch. The Pentateuch of the Samaritan community, the semi-Jewish breakaway group that grew up after the exile of the northern kingdom. This group recognized only the Pentateuch as canonical. (chap. 3)

scene. A literary subunit within narrative that combines with other scenes to form an **episode**. (chap. 2)

sense-equivalence. An approach to translation that retains the historical-factual features of the text and captures the meaning of the Hebrew and Greek, while not hesitating to translate the words, **grammar**, and style into common words, structures, and idioms in the target language. Cf. **form-equivalence** and **idea-equivalence**. (chap. 4)

sentence. A **main clause** with all its **subordinate clauses**. (chap. 5)

Septuagint (LXX). The translation of the Old Testament into Greek that became the Bible of the early church. It is of great importance to **text criticism**, but very few scholars would regard it as superior to the MT, even though some of its readings are supported in the **DSS**. (chap. 3)

special revelation. Christian Scripture; God's disclosure of himself and his will in ways understandable to us through his written Word. (intro.)

stative verbs. Verbs that describe the condition of their subject rather than an action. They often relate to thoughts, emotions, relationships, senses, or state of being. Cf. **dynamic verbs**. (chap. 5)

study → do → teach. The three aspects of Ezra's **biblical interpretation** (Ezra 7:10). *Study* in order to *Do* in order to *Teach*. (intro.)

subordinate clause. A **clause** that serves as a modifier and is embedded in a higher-level clause, as in "who is but a boy" in "David, who is but a boy, slew Goliath." Cf. **main clause**. (chap. 5)

subordinate relationships. Semantic relationships in which **propositions** or units of thought supply support for those in higher rank or prominence. Subordinate relationships support by restatement, distinct statement, or contrasting statement. Cf. **coordinate relationships**. (chap. 6)

suffixed form. See *qatal*.

syntax. The way in which words combine to form **clauses** and **sentences** (micro-syntax) and larger text units (macro-syntax). (chap. 5)

systematic theology. The study of the Bible's doctrine designed to help us shape a proper worldview. See **theology**. Cf. **biblical theology** and **practical theology**. (chap. 11)

TaNaK. The threefold arrangement of Jesus' Bible into the Law (תּוֹרָה, *tôrâ*), the Prophets (נְבִיאִים, *nĕḇîʾîm*), and the Writings (or "the *other* Scriptures," כְּתוּבִים, *kĕṯûḇîm*). The acronym is derived from the first Hebrew letters of each of these three major section titles. (chap. 1)

Targum. An Aramaic translation of the Hebrew Scriptures made for postexilic Jews whose mother tongue was Aramaic. Targums tend to paraphrase freely. (chap. 3)

tense. Time (e.g., past, present, future). For example, English uses simple past ("He ate it") and future ("he will eat it"). Biblical Hebrew does not inflect for tense, so the time of an action is always context-determined. (chap. 5)

text block. A **clause** grouping intended to be read together as a single unit of discourse; text blocks usually begin with an asyndetic clause (Ø) and are carried on by a chain of וְ ("and") clauses but may include embedded units/text blocks initiated by asyndetic clauses or marked **subordinate clauses** that clarify or support the primary line of thought. (chap. 2)

text criticism. The discipline of restoring the biblical authors' original words by comparing and contrasting the various copies and translations of the Bible. (chap. 3)

text hierarchy. A way of visually displaying the thought flow of a text that indents all dependent material and aligns all related material. (chap. 2)

texts. Ancient manuscripts and fragments of the Hebrew Scriptures; one of the basic tools of **text criticism**. Cf. **versions**. (chap. 3)

text types. The various kinds of Hebrew discourse (i.e., **anticipatory**, **directive**, and **historical**), all of which utilize their own **predicate** patterns to distinguish unmarked from marked material. (chap. 2)

textual horizon. A view of the biblical text focusing on what the passage meant to its original author. It addresses the immediate **literary context**, accounting for both the words and the informing **theology** that may have influenced those words. (chap. 10)

theological triage. An assessment of doctrines into primary (essential to Christianity), secondary (reasonable boundaries), or tertiary (minor disagreements). (chap. 11)

theological wordbook. A book composed of articles that survey all major uses of many terms throughout Scripture and also often comment on their use outside the Bible. (chap. 7)

theology. The study of God. Specifically, it is used here to describe the synthesis and significance of **exegesis**. See **biblical interpretation**, **biblical theology**, **practical theology**, and **systematic theology**. (intro.)

TOCMA. An acronym summarizing DeRouchie's five broad steps of **biblical interpretation**: *Text*, *Observation*, *Context*, *Meaning*, and *Application*. (intro.)

transition/climax markers. וַיְהִי and וְהָיָה used as **discourse markers** that signal a transition and/or climax, often introducing a new paragraph or subparagraph. (chap. 2)

typology. The study of analogical correspondences among revealed truths about persons, events, institutions, and other things within the historical framework of God's **special revelation**, which are of a prophetic nature and are escalated in their meaning; at times typological relationships are identified only retrospectively. (chap. 10)

unintentional changes. Textual errors related to (1) the manuscript's being copied, (2) the scribe's fallibility, (3) dictation or faulty hearing, or (4) the scribe's judgment. (chap. 3)

unmarked clause. A **clause** that contains a verb pattern within a given **text type** that, by default, expresses continuity (i.e., temporal or logical succession), unless other factors guide otherwise. Cf. **marked clause**. (chaps. 2, 5)

verbless clause. A **clause** that has no explicit finite verb. The **predicate** is made up of an understood helping verb along with a noun, adjective, prepositional phrase, or some other nominal form. Also called *nominal clause*. (chap. 5)

versions. Translations of ancient **texts**; one of the basic tools of **text criticism**. (chap. 3)

voice. The expression of the relationship between the verb and its subject. Specifically, voice indicates whether the subject of the verb acts or is acted on. For voice, English has, for example, the active ("Bill hit the ball") and the passive ("The ball was hit by Bill"). (chap. 5)

Vulgate. The standard Bible of the Western church dating to the late fourth century A.D. The Old Testament portion is made up of Jerome's translation of the Hebrew text into Latin. (chap. 3)

waw*-consecutive imperfect.** See ***wayyiqtol.

***wayyiqtol*.** A finite verb form that is bound to a previous **clause** and perfective in **aspect**. It serves as the default **predicate** form in **historical discourse**, where it is almost always past **tense**. Also called *waw-consecutive imperfect* or *preterite*. (chaps. 2, 5)

weqatal. A finite verb form that is bound to a previous **clause** in certain **text types**. It is used, for example, as the default **predicate** pattern in **anticipatory discourse** and, after an initial **imperative**, in **directive discourse**. In form it is a simple וְ attached to a ***qatal***, but often with the accent shifted to the ultima. Also called *conjoined perfect*. (chaps. 2, 5)

weyiqtol. A finite verb form in certain **text types**. It is used, for example, to mark a purpose **clause** after a volitive. In form it is a simple וְ attached to a ***yiqtol***. Also called *conjoined imperfect*. (chaps. 2, 5)

whole counsel of God. The entirety of God's purposes in **salvation history** as revealed in Scripture (Acts 20:27). (intro.)

yiqtol. One of the forms of the Hebrew finite verb. The "long" form is often called the *prefixed* form or the *imperfect*, referring to its **imperfective aspect**, not **tense**; nonindicative occurrences are usually signaled by first position in a **clause**. The "short" *yiqtol* form usually functions volitionally in first position. The first-person form (often called the *cohortative*) expresses determination and often has the ָה suffix (paragogic ה), which draws the accent to itself (e.g., "Let us go"). The third-person volitive (often called the *jussive*) expresses the desire of the speaker (e.g., "May he go"). (chaps. 2, 5)

SELECTED BIBLIOGRAPHY

Abegg, Martin G., Jr., James E. Bowley, and Edward M. Cook, eds. *The Dead Sea Scrolls Concordance*. 3 vols. Leiden: Brill, 2003–9.

Abegg, Martin G., Jr., Peter Flint, and Eugene Ulrich. *The Dead Sea Scrolls Bible*. San Francisco: HarperSanFrancisco, 1999.

Accordance. http://www.accordancebible.com/.

Adam, Peter. "Preaching and Biblical Theology." *NDBT* 104–12.

Aharoni, Yohanan. *The Land of the Bible: A Historical Geography*. 2nd ed. Philadelphia: Westminster, 1979.

Aharoni, Yohanan, Michael Avi-Yonah, Anson F. Rainey, Ze'ev Safrai, and R. Steven Notley. *The Carta Bible Atlas*. 5th ed. Jerusalem: Carta, 2011.

Alcorn, Randy. "Prosperity Theology: The Gospel of Wealth." In *Money, Possessions, and Eternity*, 75–92. 2nd ed. Wheaton, IL: Tyndale House, 2003.

Alexander, Philip S. "Targum, Targumim." *ABD* 6:320–31.

Alexander, T. Desmond. *From Eden to the New Jerusalem: An Introduction to Biblical Theology*. Grand Rapids: Kregel, 2008.

———. *From Paradise to the Promised Land: An Introduction to the Pentateuch*. Grand Rapids: Baker Academic, 2012.

Alexander, T. Desmond, and David W. Baker, eds. *Dictionary of the Old Testament: Pentateuch*. Downers Grove, IL: InterVarsity Press, 2003.

Alexander, T. Desmond, and Brian S. Rosner, eds. *New Dictionary of Biblical Theology: Exploring the Unity and Diversity of Scripture*. Downers Grove, IL: InterVarsity Press, 2000.

Allison, Gregg R. *Sojourners and Strangers: The Doctrine of the Church*. Foundations of Evangelical Theology. Wheaton, IL: Crossway, 2012.

Alter, Robert. *The Art of Biblical Narrative*. 2nd ed. New York: Basic Books, 2011.

———. *The Art of Biblical Poetry*. 2nd ed. New York: Basic Books, 2011.

Andersen, Francis I. *The Hebrew Verbless Clause in the Pentateuch*. JBLMS 14. Nashville: Abingdon, 1970.

———. *The Sentence in Biblical Hebrew*. Janua Linguarum, Series Practica 231. The Hague: Mouton, 1974.

Anderson, Bernhard W., and Steven Bishop. *Out of the Depths: The Psalms Speak for Us Today*. 3rd ed. Louisville: Westminster John Knox, 2000.

The Aramaic Bible. 19 vols. Collegeville, MN: Liturgical Press, 1987–2007.

Arnold, Bill T., and Bryan Beyer, eds. *Readings from the Ancient Near East: Primary Sources for Old Testament Study*. Encountering Biblical Studies. Grand Rapids: Baker Academic, 2002.

Arnold, Bill T., and John H. Choi. *A Guide to Biblical Hebrew Syntax*. Cambridge: Cambridge University Press, 2003.

Arnold, Bill T., and Richard S. Hess, eds. *Ancient Israel's History: An Introduction to Issues and Sources*. Grand Rapids: Baker Academic, 2014.

Arnold, Bill T., and H. G. M. Williamson, eds. *Dictionary of the Old Testament: Historical Books*. Downers Grove, IL: InterVarsity Press, 2005.

Baker, David L. *Two Testaments, One Bible: The Theological Relationship between the Old and New Testaments*. 3rd ed. Downers Grove, IL: InterVarsity Press, 2010.

Baker, David W. "Israelite Prophets and Prophecy." In *The Face of Old Testament Studies: A Survey of Contemporary Approaches*, edited by David W. Baker and Bill T. Arnold, 266–94. Grand Rapids: Baker Academic, 2004.

Baker, David W., and Bill T. Arnold. *The Face of Old Testament Studies: A Survey of Contemporary Approaches*. Grand Rapids: Baker Academic, 2004.

Balla, Peter. "Challenges to Biblical Theology." *NDBT* 20–27.

Bandy, Alan S., and Bejamin L. Merkle. *Understanding Prophecy: A Biblical-Theological Approach*. Grand Rapids: Kregel, 2015.

Barker, William S., and W. Robert Godfrey, eds. *Theonomy: A Reformed Critique*. Grand Rapids: Zondervan, 1991.

Barr, James. *The Semantics of Biblical Language*. London: Oxford University Press, 1961; repr., Eugene, OR: Wipf & Stock, 2004.

Barrett, Matthew. "'Bigger Is Better': When the Prosperity Gospel Creeps into the Evangelical Church." *Credo* 4, 2 (2014): 27–29.

Barrett, Michael P. V. "Christ in the Covenants." In *Beginning at Moses: A Guide to Finding Christ in the Old Testament*, 109–44. Greenville, SC: Ambassador-Emerald International, 1999.

Barrick, William D. "Inter-Covenantal Truth and Relevance: Leviticus 26 and the Biblical Covenants." *MSJ* 21, 1 (2010): 81–102.

———. "The Kingdom of God in the Old Testament." *MSJ* 23, 2 (2012): 173–92.

———. "The Mosaic Covenant." *MSJ* 10, 2 (1999): 213–32.

———. "New Covenant Theology and the Old Testament Covenants." *MSJ* 18, 2 (2007): 165–80.

Barthélemy, Dominique. *Studies in the Text of the Old Testament: An Introduction to the Hebrew Old Testament Text Project*. Textual Criticism and the Translator 3. Winona Lake, IN: Eisenbrauns, 2012.

Barthélemy, Dominique, et al. *Preliminary and Interim Report of the Hebrew Old Testament Text Project*. 5 vols. New York: United Bible Societies, 1974–80.

Bartholomew, Craig, Mary Healy, Karl Möller, and Robin Parry, eds. *Out of Egypt: Biblical Theology and Biblical Interpretation*. Scripture and Hermeneutics 5. Grand Rapids: Zondervan, 2004.

Bateman, Herbert W., IV, ed. *Three Central Issues in Contemporary Dispensationalism: A Comparison of Traditional and Progressive Views*. Grand Rapids: Kregel, 1999.

Bateman, Herbert W., IV, Darrell L. Bock, and Gordon H. Johnston. *Jesus the Messiah: Tracing the Promises, Expectations, and Coming of Israel's King*. Grand Rapids: Kregel, 2012.

Bauer, Hans, and Pontus Leander. *Historische Grammatik der hebräischen Sprache des Alten Testamentes*. 2 vols. Halle: Niemeyer, 1918–22.

Bauer, Johannes B., ed. *Encyclopedia of Biblical Theology*. 3 vols. London: Sheed & Ward, 1970; repr., New York: Crossroad, 1981.

Bavinck, Herman. *Reformed Dogmatics*. Edited by John Bolt. Translated by John Vriend. 4 vols. Grand Rapids: Baker Academic, 2003–8.

Baylor *Handbooks on the Hebrew Bible*. Waco, TX: Baylor University Press, 2006–.

Beale, G. K. "The Cognitive Peripheral Vision of Biblical Authors." *WTJ* 76, 2 (2014): 263–93.

———. "Eschatology." *DLNT* 330–45.

———. *Handbook on the New Testament Use of the Old Testament: Exegesis and Interpretation*. Grand Rapids: Baker Academic, 2012.

———. *A New Testament Biblical Theology: The Unfolding of the Old Testament in the New*. Grand Rapids: Baker Academic, 2011.

———. "The Relevance of Jewish Backgrounds for the Study of the Old Testament in the New." In *Handbook on the New Testament Use of the Old Testament: Exegesis and Interpretation*, 103–32. Grand Rapids: Baker Academic, 2012.

———, ed. *The Right Doctrine from the Wrong Texts? Essays on the Use of the Old Testament in the New*. Grand Rapids: Baker Academic, 1994.

Beale, G. K., and D. A. Carson, eds. *Commentary on the New Testament Use of the Old Testament*. Grand Rapids: Baker Academic, 2007.

Beale, G. K., and Benjamin L. Gladd. *Hidden but Now Revealed: A Biblical Theology of Divine Mystery*. Downers Grove, IL: InterVarsity Press, 2014.

Beckwith, Roger T. "The Canon of Scripture." *NDBT* 27–34.

———. *The Old Testament Canon of the New Testament Church and Its Background in Early Judaism*. Grand Rapids: Eerdmans, 1985.

———. "The Unity and Diversity of God's Covenants." *TynBul* 38 (1987): 93–118.

Beekman, John, and John Callow. *Translating the Word of God*. Dallas: Summer Institute of Linguistics, 1974.

Beitzel, Barry J. *The New Moody Atlas of the Bible*. Chicago: Moody, 2009.

Bennett, Patrick R. *Comparative Semitic Linguistics: A Manual*. Winona Lake, IN: Eisenbrauns, 1998.

Ben-Tor, Amnon, ed. *The Archaeology of Ancient Israel*. Translated by R. Greenberg. New Haven, CT: Yale University Press, 1994.

Berding, Kenneth, and Jonathan Lunde, eds. *Three Views on the New Testament Use of the Old Testament*. Counterpoints. Grand Rapids: Zondervan, 2008.

Bergen, R. D., ed. *Biblical Hebrew and Discourse Linguistics*. Summer Institute of Linguistics. Winona Lake, IN: SIL, 1994.

Bergsträsser, Gotthelf. *Hebräische Grammatik*. 2 vols. in 1. Leipzig: Hinrichs, 1929; repr., Hildesheim: Olms, 1962.

Berkhof, Louis. *Systematic Theology*. 4th ed. Grand Rapids: Eerdmans, 1938.

Berlin, Adele. *The Dynamics of Biblical Parallelism*. 2nd ed. Grand Rapids: Eerdmans, 2009.

The Bethlehem Baptist Church *Elder Affirmation of Faith*. Minneapolis: Bethlehem Baptist Church, 2003. http://www.hopeingod.org/document/elder-affirmation-faith.

Beyerlin, Walter. *Near Eastern Religious Texts Relating to the Old Testament*. Philadelphia: Westminster, 1978.

Biblearc. http://www.Biblearc.com/.

BibleWorks. http://www.bibleworks.com/.

Biblia Hebraica Quinta: General Introduction and Megilloth. Stuttgart: Deutsche Bibelgesellschaft, 2004.

Bird, Michael F. *Evangelical Theology: A Biblical and Systematic Introduction*. Grand Rapids: Zondervan, 2013.

———. "New Testament Theology Re-Loaded: Integrating Biblical Theology and Christian Origins." *TynBul* 60, 2 (2008): 265–91.

Birdsall, J. Neville. "Versions, Ancient (Introduction)." *ABD* 6:787–93.

Blair, Thom, ed. *The Hebrew-English Interlinear ESV Old Testament: Biblia Hebraica Stuttgartensia (BHS) and English Standard Version (ESV)*. Wheaton, IL: Crossway, 2014.

Blaising, Craig A. "A Critique of Gentry and Wellum's *Kingdom through Covenant*: A Hermeneutical-Theological Response." *MSJ* 26, 1 (2015): 111–27.

Blaising, Craig A., and Darrell L. Bock, eds. *Dispensationalism, Israel and the Church: The Search for Definition*. Grand Rapids: Zondervan, 1992.

———. *Progressive Dispensationalism*. Grand Rapids: Baker, 1993.

Block, Daniel I., ed. *Israel: Ancient Kingdom or Late Invention?* Nashville: Broadman & Holman, 2008.

———. "Preaching Old Testament Law to New Testament Christians." In *The Gospel according to Moses: Theological and Ethical Reflections on the Book of Deuteronomy*, 104–46. Eugene, OR: Cascade, 2012. Originally published in *Hiphil (Scandinavian Evangelical E-Journal)* 3 (2006): 1–24. Subsequently published in three parts in *Ministry* 78, 5 (2006): 5–11; 78, 7 (2006): 12–16; 78, 9 (2006): 15–18.

———. "Tell Me the Old, Old Story: Preaching the Message of Old Testament Narrative." In *Giving the Sense: Understanding and Using Old Testament Historical Texts: Essays in Honor of Eugene Merrill*, edited by David M. Howard and Michael A. Grisanti, 409–38. Grand Rapids: Kregel, 2003.

Bloesch, Donald G. Christian Foundations. 7 vols. Downers Grove, IL: InterVarsity Press, 1992–2009.

Blomberg, Craig L. "The Unity and Diversity of Scripture." *NDBT* 64–72.

Bock, Darrell L. "A Critique of Gentry and Wellum's *Kingdom through Covenant*: A New Testament Perspective." *MSJ* 26, 1 (2015): 139–45.

———. "Single Meaning, Multiple Contexts and Referents: The New Testament's Legitimate, Accurate, and Multifaceted Use of the Old." In *Three Views on the New Testament Use of the Old*, edited by Kenneth Berdin and Jonathan Lunde, 105–51. Responses to other contributors on pp. 90–95, 226–31. Counterpoints. Grand Rapids: Zondervan, 2008.

Boda, Mark J., and J. Gordon McConville, eds. *Dictionary of the Old Testament: Prophets*. Downers Grove, IL: InterVarsity Press, 2012.

Bodine, Walter, R., ed. *Discourse Analysis of Biblical Literature: What It Is and What It Offers*. SBLSS. Atlanta: Scholars Press, 1995.

Bogaert, P.-M. "Bulletin de la Bible latine. VII. Première série." *RBén* 105 (1995): 200–38.

———. "Bulletin de la Bible latine. VII. Deuxième série." *RBén* 106 (1996): 386–412.

———. "Bulletin de la Bible latine. VII. Troisième série." *RBén* 108 (1998): 359–86.

———. "Versions, Ancient (Latin)." *ABD* 6:799–803.

Bond, Steve, ed. *Holman Concise Topical Concordance*. Nashville: Holman, 1998.

Botterweck, G. Johannes, Helmer Ringgren, and Heinz-Josef Fabry, eds. *Theological Dictionary of the Old Testament*. 15 vols. Grand Rapids: Eerdmans, 1974–2006.

Brand, Chad Owen, ed. *Perspectives on Israel and the Church: 4 Views*. Nashville: Broadman & Holman, 2015.

Bray, Gerald, ed. Contours of Christian Theology. 8 vols. Downers Grove, IL: InterVarsity Press, 1993–2002.

———. *The Doctrine of God*. Contours of Christian Theology. Downers Grove, IL: InterVarsity Press, 1993.

———. *God Is Love: A Biblical and Systematic Theology*. Wheaton, IL: Crossway, 2012.

Brenton, Lancelot C. *The Septuagint with Apocrypha: Greek and English*. 1844; repr., Peabody, MA: Hendrickson, 1986.

Bright, John. *A History of Israel*. 4th ed. Louisville: Westminster John Knox, 2000.

———. *The Kingdom of God: The Biblical Concept and Its Meaning for the Church*. New York: Abingdon, 1953.

Brock, S. P. "Versions, Ancient (Syriac)." *ABD* 6:794–99.

Bromiley, Geoffrey W., ed. *International Standard Bible Encyclopedia*. 4 vols. Grand Rapids: Zondervan, 1979–88.

Brooke, Alan E., Norman McLean, and Henry St. J. Thackeray, eds. *The Old Testament in Greek*. 3 vols. Cambridge: Cambridge University Press, 1906–40.

Brotzman, Ellis R., and Eric J. Tully. *Old Testament Textual Criticism: A Practical Introduction*. 2nd ed. Grand Rapids: Baker Academic, 2016.

Brown, A. Philip, II, and Bryan W. Smith. *A Reader's Hebrew Bible*. Grand Rapids: Zondervan, 2008.

Brown, Francis, S. R. Driver, and Charles A. Briggs. *The New Brown-Driver-Briggs Hebrew and English Lexicon*. Peabody, MA: Hendrickson, 1979.

Brueggemann, Walter. *Theology of the Old Testament: Testimony, Dispute, Advocacy.* Minneapolis: Fortress, 2005.

Brunn, Dave. *One Bible, Many Versions: Are All Translations Created Equal?* Downers Grove, IL: InterVarsity Press, 2013.

Bruno, Chris. *The Whole Story of the Bible in 16 Verses.* Wheaton, IL: Crossway, 2015.

Bullock, C. Hassell. *Encountering the Book of Psalms: A Literary and Theological Introduction.* Grand Rapids: Baker Academic, 2004.

Busby, Douglas L., Terry A. Armstrong, and Cyril F. Carr. *A Reader's Hebrew-English Lexicon of the Old Testament.* Grand Rapids: Zondervan, 1989.

Calvin, John. *Institutes of the Christian Religion.* Edited by John T. McNeill. Translated by Ford Lewis Battles. 2 vols. Library of Christian Classics. Philadelphia: Westminster, 1960.

Carson, D. A. "Approaching the Bible." In *New Bible Commentary: 21st Century Edition,* edited by D. A. Carson, R. T. France, J. A. Motyer, and G. J. Wenham, 1–19. 4th ed. Downers Grove, IL: InterVarsity Press, 1994.

———. "The Bible and Theology." In *NIV Zondervan Study Bible,* edited by D. A. Carson, 2633–36. Grand Rapids: Zondervan, 2015.

———. "Biblical Theology." *DBCI* 35–41.

———. *Christ and Culture Revisited.* Grand Rapids: Eerdmans, 2007.

———. "Current Issues in Biblical Theology: A New Testament Perspective." *BBR* 5 (1995): 17–41.

———, ed. *The Enduring Authority of the Christian Scriptures.* Grand Rapids: Eerdmans, 2016.

———. *Exegetical Fallacies.* 2nd ed. Grand Rapids: Baker Academic, 1996.

———. *The Gagging of God: Christianity Confronts Pluralism.* Grand Rapids: Zondervan, 1996.

———. *The God Who Is There: Finding Your Place in God's Story.* Grand Rapids: Baker, 2010.

———. "Grammatical Fallacies." In *Exegetical Fallacies,* 65–86. 2nd ed. Grand Rapids: Baker Academic, 1996.

———. *The Inclusive-Language Debate: A Plea for Realism.* Grand Rapids: Baker, 1998.

———. *The King James Version Debate: A Plea for Realism.* Grand Rapids: Baker, 1978.

———. "The Limits of Functional Equivalence in Bible Translation—and Other Limits, Too." In *The Challenge of Bible Translation: Communicating God's Word to the World; Understanding the Theory, History, and Practice: Essays in Honor of Ronald F. Youngblood,* edited by Glen G. Scorgie, Mark L. Strauss, and Steven M. Voth, 65–113. Grand Rapids: Zondervan, 2003.

———. "Logical Fallacies." In *Exegetical Fallacies,* 87–123. 2nd ed. Grand Rapids: Baker Academic, 1996.

———. "Mystery and Fulfillment: Toward a More Comprehensive Paradigm of Paul's Understanding of the Old and New." In *The Paradoxes of Paul,* 393–436. Vol. 2 of

Justification and Variegated Nomism, edited by D. A. Carson, Peter T. O'Brien, and Mark A. Seifrid. 2 vols. WUNT 181. Grand Rapids: Baker Academic, 2004.

———, ed. New Studies in Biblical Theology. Leicester: Apollos; Downers Grove, IL: InterVarsity Press, 1995–present. A master Scripture index for all the volumes in the series is available at http://www.theGospelCoalition.org/pages/nsbt.

———. "New Testament Theology." *DLNT* 796–814.

———, ed. *NIV Zondervan Study Bible*. Grand Rapids: Zondervan, 2015.

———, ed. *The Scriptures Testify about Me: Jesus and the Gospel in the Old Testament*. Wheaton, IL: Crossway, 2013.

———. "Systematic Theology and Biblical Theology." *NDBT* 89–104.

———. "Word-Study Fallacies." In *Exegetical Fallacies*, 27–64. 2nd ed. Grand Rapids: Baker Academic, 1996.

Carson, D. A., and Timothy Keller, eds. *The Gospel as Center: Renewing Our Faith and Reforming Our Ministry Practices*. Wheaton, IL: Crossway, 2012. Unpacks The Gospel Coalition's "Confessional Statement" (http://www.thegospelcoalition.org/about/foundation-documents/confessional-statement).

Carson, Thomas, ed. *New Catholic Encyclopedia*. 2nd ed. 15 vols. Washington, DC: Catholic University of America Press, 2003.

Carter, Charles W. *A Contemporary Wesleyan Theology: Biblical, Systematic, and Practical*. 2 vols. Grand Rapids: Francis Asbury, 1983.

Casillas, Ken. *Beyond Chapter and Verse: The Theology and Practice of Biblical Application*. Forthcoming.

———. *The Law and the Christian: God's Light within God's Limits*. Biblical Discernment for Difficult Issues. Greenville, SC: Bob Jones University Press, 2007.

Chafer, Lewis Sperry. *Systematic Theology*. 8 vols. Grand Rapids: Kregel, 1948.

Chalmers, Aaron. "The Importance of the Noahic Covenant to Biblical Theology." *TynBul* 60, 2 (2009): 206–16.

Chamberlain, Gary Alan. *The Greek of the Septuagint: A Supplemental Lexicon*. Peabody, MA: Hendrickson, 2011.

Chapell, Bryan. *Christ-Centered Preaching: Redeeming the Expository Sermon*. 2nd ed. Grand Rapids: Baker Academic, 2005.

———. *Christ-Centered Sermons: Models of Redemptive Preaching*. Grand Rapids: Baker Academic, 2013.

———, ed. *Gospel Transformation Bible: English Standard Version*. Wheaton, IL: Crossway, 2013.

Chavalas, Mark W., and Murray R. Adamthwaite. "Archaeological Light on the Old Testament." In *The Face of Old Testament Studies: A Survey of Contemporary Approaches*, edited by David W. Baker and Bill T. Arnold, 59–96. Grand Rapids: Baker Academic, 2004.

Chavalas, Mark W., and Edwin C. Hostetter. "Epigraphic Light on the Old Testament." In *The Face of Old Testament Studies: A Survey of Contemporary Approaches*, edited by David W. Baker and Bill T. Arnold, 38–58. Grand Rapids: Baker Academic, 2004.

Chavalas, Mark W., and K. Lawson Younger Jr., eds. *Mesopotamia and the Bible: Comparative Explorations*. Grand Rapids: Baker Academic, 2002.

Childs, Brevard S. *Biblical Theology of the Old and New Testaments: Theological Reflection on the Christian Bible*. Minneapolis: Fortress, 1993.

———. *Old Testament Theology in a Canonical Context*. Philadelphia: Fortress, 1990.

Chisholm, Robert B., Jr. *From Exegesis to Exposition: A Practical Guide to Using Biblical Hebrew*. Grand Rapids: Baker Academic, 1999.

———. *Interpreting the Historical Books: An Exegetical Handbook*. Handbooks for Old Testament Exegesis 2. Grand Rapids: Kregel, 2006.

Clark, David K. *To Know and Love God: Method for Theology*. Foundations of Evangelical Theology. Wheaton, IL: Crossway, 2003.

Clendenon, Ray, ed. NAC Studies in Bible and Theology. Nashville: Broadman & Holman, 2007–present.

Clines, David J. A., ed. *The Concise Dictionary of Classical Hebrew*. Sheffield, UK: Sheffield Phoenix, 2009.

———, ed. *The Dictionary of Classical Hebrew*. 9 vols. Sheffield, UK: Sheffield Phoenix, 1993–2014.

Clontz, T. E., and J. Clontz. *The Comprehensive Bible Cross References*. Castroville, TX: Cornerstone, 2011.

Clowney, Edmund P. *The Church*. Downers Grove, IL: InterVarsity Press, 1995.

———. *Preaching Christ in All of Scripture*. Wheaton, IL: Crossway, 2003.

———. *The Unfolding Mystery: Discovering Christ in the Old Testament*. Phillipsburg, NJ: Presbyterian and Reformed, 1988.

Cole, Graham A. *He Who Gives Life: The Doctrine of the Holy Spirit*. Foundations of Evangelical Theology. Wheaton, IL: Crossway, 2007.

Colunga, Alberto, and Laurentio Turrado, eds. *Biblia Vulgata*. Madrid: Biblioteca de Autores Cristianos, 1953; repr., 1977.

Combs, William W. "The History of the NIV Translation Controversy." *DBSJ* 17 (2012): 3–34.

———. "Paul, the Law, and Dispensationalism." *DBSJ* 18 (2013): 19–39.

"Commentary on the Critical Apparatus." In *BHQ*.

Comprehensive Aramaic Lexicon. http://cal1.cn.huc.edu/.

Compton, Jared M. "Shared Intentions? Reflections on Inspiration and Interpretation in Light of Scripture's Dual Authorship." *Themelios* 33, 3 (2008): 23–33.

Compton, R. Bruce. "Dispensationalism, the Church, and the New Covenant." *DBSJ* 8 (2003): 3–48.

Computer Assisted Tools for Septuagint/Scriptural Study. http://ccat.sas.upenn.edu/rs/rak/catss.html.

Coogan, Michael D., ed. *The Oxford History of the Biblical World*. Oxford: Oxford University Press, 1999.

Cook, John A. *Time and the Biblical Hebrew Verb: The Expression of Tense, Aspect, and Modality in Biblical Hebrew*. LSAWS 7. Winona Lake, IN: Eisenbrauns, 2012.

Cook, John A., and Robert D. Holmstedt. *Beginning Biblical Hebrew: A Grammar and Illustrated Reader.* Grand Rapids: Baker Academic, 2013.

Cowan, Christopher W. "The Warning Passages of Hebrews and the New Covenant Community." In *Progressive Covenantalism: Charting a Course between Dispensational and Covenant Theologies*, edited by Stephen J. Wellum and Brent E. Parker, 189–213. Nashville: Broadman & Holman, 2016.

Crown, Alan D., and Terry Giles. "Samaritan Pentateuch." *NIDB* 6:73–74.

Currid, John D. *Against the Gods: The Polemical Theology of the Old Testament.* Wheaton, IL: Crossway, 2013.

———. *Doing Archaeology in the Land of the Bible: A Basic Guide.* Grand Rapids: Baker, 1999.

Currid, John D., and David P. Barrett. *Crossway ESV Bible Atlas.* Wheaton, IL: Crossway, 2010.

Curtis, Adrian. *Oxford Bible Atlas.* 4th ed. Oxford: Oxford University Press, 2009.

Danker, Frederick W. *Multipurpose Tools for Bible Study.* 2nd ed. Minneapolis: Fortress, 2003.

Danker, Frederick W., et al. *Greek-English Lexicon of the New Testament and Other Early Christian Literature.* 3rd ed. Chicago: University of Chicago Press, 2000.

Davidson, Benjamin. *The Analytical Hebrew and Chaldee Lexicon.* 2nd ed. 1848; repr., Grand Rapids: Zondervan, 1993.

Davis, Dale Ralph. *The Word Became Fresh: How to Preach from Old Testament Narrative Texts.* Fearn, Scotland: Mentor, 2006.

Davis, John Jefferson. *Handbook of Basic Bible Texts: Every Key Passage for the Study of Doctrine and Theology.* Grand Rapids: Zondervan, 1984.

———. *Theology Primer: Resources for the Theological Student.* Grand Rapids: Baker, 1981.

Dawson, D. A. *Text-Linguistics and Biblical Hebrew.* JSOTSup 177. Sheffield, UK: Sheffield Academic, 1994.

Dean, David Andrew. "Covenant, Conditionality, and Consequence: New Terminology and a Case Study in the Abrahamic Covenant." *JETS* 57, 2 (2014): 281–308.

Decker, Rodney J. "The Church's Relationship to the New Covenant: Part 1." *BSac* 152 (1995): 290–305.

———. "The Church's Relationship to the New Covenant: Part 2." *BSac* 152 (1995): 431–56.

———. "An Evaluation of the 2011 Edition of the New International Version." *Themelios* 36, 3 (2011): 415–56.

Demarest, Bruce. *The Cross and Salvation: The Doctrine of Salvation.* Foundations of Evangelical Theology. Wheaton, IL: Crossway, 1997.

Dempster, Stephen G. *Dominion and Dynasty: A Biblical Theology of the Hebrew Bible.* NSBT 15. Downers Grove, IL: InterVarsity Press, 2003.

———. *Linguistic Features of Hebrew Narrative: A Discourse Analysis of Narrative from the Classical Period.* Ph.D. diss., University of Toronto, 1985.

Dennis, Lane T., and Wayne Grudem, eds. Cross-references in *ESV Study Bible*. Wheaton, IL: Crossway, 2008.

de Regt, L. J., J. de Waard, and J. P. Fokkelman, eds. *Literary Structure and Rhetorical Strategies in the Hebrew Bible*. Winona Lake, IN: Eisenbrauns, 1996.

DeRouchie, Jason S. "The Blessing-Commission, the Promised Offspring, and the *Toledot* Structure of Genesis." *JETS* 56, 2 (2013): 219–47.

———. *A Call to Covenant Love: Text-Grammar and Literary Structure in Deuteronomy 5–11*. Gorgias Dissertations 30/Biblical Studies 2. Piscataway, NJ: Gorgias, 2007.

———. "Confronting the Transgender Storm: New Covenant Reflections on Deuteronomy 22:5." *JBMW* 21, 1 (2016): 58–69.

———. "Counting Stars with Abraham and the Prophets: New Covenant Ecclesiology in OT Perspective." *JETS* 58, 3 (2015): 445–85.

———. "Counting the Ten: An Investigation into the Numbering of the Decalogue." In *For Our Good Always: Studies on the Message and Influence of Deuteronomy in Honor of Daniel I. Block*, edited by Jason S. DeRouchie, Jason Gile, and Kenneth J. Turner, 93–125. Winona Lake, IN: Eisenbrauns, 2013.

———. "Father of a Multitude of Nations: New Covenant Ecclesiology in OT Perspective." In *Progressive Covenantalism: Charting a Course between Dispensational and Covenant Theologies*, edited by Stephen J. Wellum and Brent E. Parker, 7–38. Nashville: Broadman & Holman, 2016.

———. "From Condemnation to Righteousness: A Christian Reading of Deuteronomy." *SBJT* 18, 3 (2014): 87–118.

———. "Making the Ten Count: Reflections on the Lasting Message of the Decalogue." In *For Our Good Always: Studies on the Message and Influence of Deuteronomy in Honor of Daniel I. Block*, edited by Jason S. DeRouchie, Jason Gile, and Kenneth J. Turner, 415–40. Winona Lake, IN: Eisenbrauns, 2013.

———. "The Profit of Employing the Biblical Languages: Scriptural and Historical Reflections." *Themelios* 37, 1 (2012): 32–50.

———. Review of *Kingdom through Covenant: A Biblical-Theological Understanding of the Covenants*, by Peter J. Gentry and Stephen J. Wellum. *BBR* 23 (2013): 110–13.

———, ed. *What the Old Testament Authors Really Cared About: A Survey of Jesus' Bible*. Grand Rapids: Kregel, 2013.

DeRouchie, Jason S., and Jason C. Meyer. "Christ or Family as the 'Seed' of Promise? An Evaluation of N. T. Wright on Galatians 3:16." *SBJT* 14, 3 (2010): 36–48.

"The Development and Use of Gender Language in Contemporary English: A Corpus Linguistic Analysis; Prepared for the Committee on Bible Translation by Collins Dictionaries." September 2010. http://www.thenivbible.com/wp-content/uploads/2015/02/Collins-Report-Final.pdf.

Dever, Mark. *The Message of the Old Testament: Promises Made*. Wheaton, IL: Crossway, 2006.

Dewey, David. *A User's Guide to Bible Translations: Making the Most of Different Versions*. Downers Grove, IL: InterVarsity Press, 2005.

DeYoung, Kevin. *The Biggest Story: How the Snake Crusher Brings Us Back to the Garden*. Wheaton, IL: Crossway, 2015.

Dines, Jennifer M. *The Septuagint*. Understanding the Bible and Its World. London: Bloomsbury, 2004.

Discoveries in the Judaean Desert. 32 vols. Oxford: Oxford University Press, 1951–2011.

Dockery, David S., Kenneth A. Mathews, and Robert B. Sloan, eds. *Foundations for Biblical Interpretation: A Complete Library of Tools and Resources*. Nashville: Broadman & Holman, 1994.

Doriani, Daniel M. *Putting the Truth to Work: The Theory and Practice of Biblical Application*. Phillipsburg, NJ: P&R Publishing, 2001.

———. "A Redemptive-Historical Model." In *Four Views on Moving beyond the Bible to Theology*, edited by Gary T. Meadors, 75–121. Responses to other contributors on pp. 51–56, 205–9, 255–61. Counterpoints. Grand Rapids: Zondervan, 2009.

Dorsey, David A. "The Law of Moses and the Christian: A Compromise." *JETS* 34, 3 (1991): 321–34.

———. *The Literary Structure of the Old Testament: A Commentary on Genesis–Malachi*. Grand Rapids: Baker, 1999.

———. "The Use of the OT Law in the Christian Life: A Theocentric Approach." *EJ* 17, 1 (1999): 1–18.

Duguid, Ian M. *Is Jesus in the Old Testament? Basics of the Faith*. Phillipsburg, NJ: P&R Publishing, 2013.

Dumbrell, William J. *Covenant and Creation: An Old Testament Covenant Theology*. 2nd ed. Milton Keynes, UK: Paternoster, 2013.

———. "The Prospect of Unconditionality in the Sinaitic Covenant." In *Israel's Apostasy and Restoration: Essays in Honor of Roland K. Harrison*, edited by Avraham Gileadi, 141–55. Grand Rapids: Baker Academic, 1988.

Duvall, J. Scott, and J. Daniel Hays. *Grasping God's Word: A Hands-On Approach to Reading, Interpreting, and Applying the Bible*. 3rd ed. Grand Rapids: Zondervan, 2012.

Duvall, J. Scott, and Verlyn D. Verbrugge, eds. *Devotions on the Greek New Testament: 52 Reflections to Inspire and Instruct*. Grand Rapids: Zondervan, 2012.

Dyer, John. *Best Commentaries: Reviews and Ratings of Biblical, Theological, and Practical Christian Works*. http://www.bestcommentaries.com/.

Edwards, Jonathan. "A History of the Work of Redemption." In vol. 1 of *The Works of Jonathan Edwards*, edited by Edward Hickman, 532–619. Bellingham, WA: Logos Bible Software, 2008.

Eichrodt, Walther. *Theology of the Old Testament*. Translated by J. A. Baker. 2 vols. OTL. Philadelphia: Westminster, 1961, 1967.

Einspahr, Bruce. *Index to Brown, Driver & Briggs Hebrew Lexicon*. 2nd ed. Chicago: Moody, 1976.

Eissfeldt, Otto. *The Old Testament: An Introduction*. New York: Harper & Row, 1965.

Elliger, Karl, et al., eds. *Biblia Hebraica Stuttgartensia*. 5th rev. ed. Stuttgart: Deutsche Bibelgesellschaft, 1983.

Elwell, Walter A., ed. *Evangelical Dictionary of Biblical Theology*. Grand Rapids: Baker, 1996.

———, ed. *Evangelical Dictionary of Theology*. 2nd ed. Grand Rapids: Baker Academic, 2001.

———, *Topical Analysis of the Bible: A Survey of Essential Christian Doctrines*. Peabody, MA: Hendrickson, 2012.

Emerson, Matthew Y. *Christ and the New Creation: A Canonical Approach to the Theology of the New Testament*. Eugene, OR: Wipf & Stock, 2013.

Eng, Milton, and Lee M. Fields, eds. *Devotions on the Hebrew Bible: 54 Reflections to Inspire and Instruct*. Grand Rapids: Zondervan, 2015.

Enns, Peter. "Apostolic Hermeneutics and an Evangelical Doctrine of Scripture: Moving beyond a Modernist Impasse." *WTJ* 65, 2 (2003): 263–87.

Erickson, Millard J. *Christian Theology*. 3rd ed. Grand Rapids: Baker Academic, 2013.

Estes, Daniel J. *Handbook on the Wisdom Books and Psalms*. Grand Rapids: Baker Academic, 2010.

"ESV Bible Translators Debate the Word 'Slave' at Tyndale House, Cambridge." https://www.youtube.com/watch?v=Mx06mtApu8k.

Etheridge, J. W. *The Targums of Onkelos and Jonathan ben Uzziel on the Pentateuch*. 2 vols. 1862–65; repr., Piscataway, NJ: Gorgias, 2005.

Evangelical Textual Criticism (blog). http://www.evangelicaltextualcriticism.blogspot.com/.

Evans, Craig A. "New Testament Use of the Old Testament." *NDBT* 72–80.

Evans, Craig A., and Stanley E. Porter, eds. *Dictionary of New Testament Background*. Downers Grove, IL: InterVarsity Press, 2000.

Evans, John F. *A Guide to Biblical Commentaries and Reference Works*. 10th ed. Grand Rapids: Zondervan, 2016.

Evans, Mary J. "Blessing/Curse." *NDBT* 397–401.

Evan-Shoshan, Abraham, ed. *A New Concordance of the Old Testament Using the Hebrew and Aramaic Text*. Grand Rapids: Baker Academic, 1989.

Exter Blockland, A. F. den. *In Search of Syntax: Towards a Syntactic Text-Segmentation Model for Biblical Hebrew*. Amsterdam: VU University Press, 1995.

Fee, Gordon D. *The Disease of the Health and Wealth Gospels*. Vancouver: Regent College, 2006.

Fee, Gordon D., and Mark L. Strauss. *How to Choose a Translation for All Its Worth: A Guide to Understanding and Using Bible Versions*. Grand Rapids: Zondervan, 2007.

Fee, Gordon D., and Douglas Stuart. *How to Read the Bible Book by Book: A Guided Tour*. Grand Rapids: Zondervan, 2002.

———. *How to Read the Bible for All Its Worth*. 4th ed. Grand Rapids: Zondervan, 2014.

Feinberg, John S., ed. *Continuity and Discontinuity: Perspectives on the Relationship between the Old and New Testaments: Essays in Honor of S. Lewis Johnson Jr.* Westchester, IL: Crossway, 1988.

———, ed. Foundations of Evangelical Theology. Wheaton, IL: Crossway, 1997–present.

———. *No One like Him: The Doctrine of God*. Foundations of Evangelical Theology. Wheaton, IL: Crossway, 2001.

Fensham, F. Charles. "The Covenant as Giving Expression to the Relationship between Old and New Testament." *TynBul* 22 (1971): 82–94.

Ferguson, Sinclair B. *The Holy Spirit*. Contours of Christian Theology. Downers Grove, IL: InterVarsity Press, 1996.

———. *Preaching Christ from the Old Testament*. Proclamation Trust Media Paper 2. London: Proclamation Trust Media, 2002.

———. *The Whole Christ: Legalism, Antinomianism, and Gospel Assurance—Why the Marrow Controversy Still Matters*. Wheaton, IL: Crossway, 2016.

Fields, Lee M. *Hebrew for the Rest of Us: Using Hebrew Tools without Mastering Biblical Hebrew*. Grand Rapids: Zondervan, 2008.

Fischer, David Hackett. *Historians' Fallacies: Toward a Logic of Historical Thought*. New York: Harper & Row, 1970.

Flint, Peter W., ed. *The Bible at Qumran: Text, Shape, and Interpretation*. Studies in the Dead Sea Scrolls and Related Literature. Grand Rapids: Eerdmans, 2001.

Fokkelman, J. P. *Reading Biblical Narrative: An Introductory Guide*. Louisville: Westminster John Knox, 2000.

———. *Reading Biblical Poetry: An Introductory Guide*. Louisville: Westminster John Knox, 2001.

Frame, John M. *Apologetics: A Justification of Christian Belief*. Edited by Joseph E. Torres. 2nd ed. Phillipsburg, NJ: P&R Publishing, 2015.

———. *Salvation Belongs to the Lord: An Introduction to Systematic Theology*. Phillipsburg, NJ: P&R Publishing, 2006.

———. *Systematic Theology: An Introduction to Christian Belief*. Phillipsburg, NJ: P&R Publishing, 2013.

France, R. T. *Jesus and the Old Testament: His Application of Old Testament Passages to Himself and His Mission*. Downers Grove, IL: InterVarsity Press, 1971.

———. "Relationship between the Testaments." *DTIB* 666–72.

Frankfort, Henri. *Kingship and the Gods: A Study of Ancient Near Eastern Religion as the Integration of Society and Nature*. Chicago: University of Chicago Press, 1978.

Freedman, David Noel, ed. *The Anchor Bible Dictionary*. 6 vols. New York: Doubleday, 1992.

Freedman, David Noel, A. Dean Forbes, and Francis I. Andersen, eds. *Studies in Hebrew and Aramaic Orthography*. Winona Lake, IN: Eisenbrauns, 1992.

Fuller, Daniel P. *Gospel and Law: Contrast or Continuum—The Hermeneutics of Dispensationalism and Covenant Theology*. Grand Rapids: Eerdmans, 1980.

———. *The Unity of the Bible: Unfolding God's Plan for Humanity*. Grand Rapids: Zondervan, 1992.

Fuller, Russell T., and Kyoungwon Choi. *An Invitation to Biblical Hebrew: A Beginning Grammar*. Grand Rapids: Kregel, 2006.

———. *An Invitation to Biblical Hebrew Syntax: An Intermediate Grammar.* Grand Rapids: Kregel, 2016.

Futato, Mark D. *Beginning Biblical Hebrew.* Winona Lake, IN: Eisenbrauns, 2003.

———. *Interpreting the Psalms: An Exegetical Handbook.* Handbooks for Old Testament Exegesis. Grand Rapids: Kregel, 2007.

Gaffin, Richard B. "Systematic Theology and Biblical Theology." *WTJ* 38, 3 (1976): 281–99.

Garrett, Duane A. "Type, Typology." *EDBT* 785–87.

Garrett, Duane A., and Jason S. DeRouchie. *A Modern Grammar for Biblical Hebrew* and *Workbook.* Nashville: Broadman & Holman, 2009.

Geisler, Norman L. *Systematic Theology: In One Volume.* Minneapolis: Bethany House, 2011.

Gentry, Peter J. *How to Read and Understand the Biblical Prophets.* Wheaton, IL: Crossway, 2017.

———. "The System of the Finite Verb in Classical Biblical Hebrew." *HS* 39 (1998): 7–39.

———. "The Text of the Old Testament." *JETS* 52, 1 (2009): 19–45.

Gentry, Peter J., and Stephen J. Wellum. *God's Kingdom through God's Covenants: A Concise Biblical Theology.* Wheaton, IL: Crossway, 2015.

———. *Kingdom through Covenant: A Biblical-Theological Understanding of the Covenants.* Wheaton, IL: Crossway, 2012.

Gibson, Arthur. *Biblical Semantic Logic: A Preliminary Analysis.* Sheffield, UK: Sheffield Academic, 2002.

Ginsburg, Christian D. *Massorah.* 4 vols. 1865–1905; repr., New York: Ktav, 1975.

Gladd, Benjamin L., and Matthew S. Harmon. *Making All Things New: Inaugurated Eschatology for the Life of the Church.* Grand Rapids: Baker Academic, 2016.

Glare, P. G. W., ed. *Oxford Latin Dictionary.* 2nd ed. 2 vols. Oxford: Oxford University Press, 2012.

Glenny, W. Edward. "Typology: A Summary of the Present Evangelical Discussion." *JETS* 40, 4 (1997): 627–38.

Glynn, John. *Commentary and Reference Survey: A Comprehensive Guide to Biblical and Theological Resources.* Grand Rapids: Kregel, 2007.

Goldenberg, Gideon. *Studies in Semitic Linguistics: Selected Writings.* Jerusalem: Magnes, 1998.

Goldingay, John. *Biblical Theology: The God of the Christian Scriptures.* Downers Grove, IL: InterVarsity Press, 2016.

———. *Israel's Faith.* Old Testament Theology 2. Downers Grove, IL: InterVarsity Press, 2006.

———. *Israel's Gospel.* Old Testament Theology 1. Downers Grove, IL: InterVarsity Press, 2003.

———. *Israel's Life.* Old Testament Theology 3. Downers Grove, IL: InterVarsity Press, 2009.

———. "Old Testament Theology and the Canon." *TynBul* 59, 1 (2008): 1–26.

Goldsworthy, Graeme. *According to Plan: The Unfolding Revelation of God in the Bible.* Downers Grove, IL: InterVarsity Press, 1991.

———. "Biblical Theology and Hermeneutics." *SBJT* 10, 2 (2006): 4–19.

———. *Christ-Centered Biblical Theology: Hermeneutical Foundations and Principles.* Downers Grove, IL: InterVarsity Press, 2012.

———. *The Goldsworthy Trilogy.* Exeter, UK: Paternoster, 2000.

———. *Gospel-Centered Hermeneutics: Foundations and Principles of Evangelical Biblical Interpretation.* Downers Grove, IL: InterVarsity Press, 2006.

———. "Kingdom of God." *NDBT* 615–20.

———. *Preaching the Whole Bible as Christian Scripture: The Application of Biblical Theology to Expository Preaching.* Grand Rapids: Eerdmans, 2000.

———. "Relationship of Old Testament and New Testament." *NDBT* 81–89.

Goodrick, Edward W. *Do It Yourself Hebrew and Greek: A Guide to Biblical Language Tools.* Grand Rapids: Zondervan, 1980.

Goppelt, Leonhard. *Theology of the New Testament.* Edited by Jürgen Roloff. Translated by John E. Alsup. 2 vols. Grand Rapids: Eerdmans, 1981.

Gowan, Donald E. *Theology of the Prophetic Books: The Death and Resurrection of Israel.* Louisville: Westminster John Knox, 1998.

Gray, Richard W. "A Comparison between the Old Covenant and the New Covenant." *WTJ* 4, 1 (1941): 1–30.

Green, Jay Patrick, ed. *The Interlinear Bible: Hebrew, Greek, English.* Peabody, MA: Hendrickson, 2005.

Green, Joel B., and Max Turner, eds. *Between Two Horizons: Spanning New Testament Studies and Systematic Theology.* Grand Rapids: Eerdmans, 2000.

Greenspahn, Frederick E. *An Introduction to Aramaic.* 2nd ed. Atlanta: SBL, 2003.

Greenspoon, Leonard J. "Versions, Ancient (Greek)." *ABD* 6:793–94.

Greidanus, Sidney. *Preaching Christ from the Old Testament.* Grand Rapids: Eerdmans, 1999.

Grisanti, Michael A. "A Critique of Gentry and Wellum's *Kingdom through Covenant*: An Old Testament Perspective." *MSJ* 26, 1 (2015): 129–37.

———. "The Davidic Covenant." *MSJ* 10 (1999): 234–50.

Grossfeld, Bernard, ed. *The Targum to the Five Megilloth.* New York: Hermon, 1973.

Grudem, Wayne A. *Bible Doctrine: Essential Teachings of the Christian Faith.* Edited by Jeff Purswell. Grand Rapids: Zondervan, 1999.

———. *Christian Beliefs: Twenty Basics Every Christian Should Know.* Edited by Elliot Grudem. Grand Rapids: Zondervan, 2005.

———, ed. *The ESV Study Bible.* Wheaton, IL: Crossway, 2008.

———. *Systematic Theology: An Introduction to Biblical Doctrine.* Grand Rapids: Zondervan, 1994.

Grudem, Wayne A., C. John Collins, and Thomas R. Schreiner, eds. *Understanding the Big Picture of the Bible: A Guide to Reading the Bible Well.* Wheaton, IL: Crossway, 2012.

Guthrie, Donald. *New Testament Theology.* Downers Grove, IL: InterVarsity Press, 1981.

Guthrie, George H. *Read the Bible for Life: Your Guide to Understanding and Living God's Word.* Nashville: Broadman & Holman, 2011.

Guthrie, Nancy. Seeing Jesus in the Old Testament. Wheaton, IL: Crossway, 2014–present.

Hackett, Jo Ann. *A Basic Introduction to Biblical Hebrew.* Peabody, MA: Hendrickson, 2010.

Hafemann, Scott J., ed. *Biblical Theology: Retrospect and Prospect.* Downers Grove, IL: InterVarsity Press, 2002.

———. "The Covenant Relationship." In *Central Themes in Biblical Theology: Mapping Unity in Diversity,* edited by Scott J. Hafemann and Paul R. House, 20–65. Grand Rapids: Baker Academic, 2007.

———. *The God of Promise and the Life of Faith: Understanding the Heart of the Bible.* Wheaton, IL: Crossway, 2001.

———. "The Kingdom of God as the Mission of God." In *For the Fame of God's Name: Essays in Honor of John Piper,* edited by Sam Storms and Justin Taylor, 235–52. Wheaton, IL: Crossway, 2010.

Hafemann, Scott J., and Paul R. House, eds. *Central Themes in Biblical Theology.* Downers Grove, IL: InterVarsity Press, 2006.

Hahn, Scott. "Covenant in the Old and New Testaments: Some Current Research (1994–2004)." *CurBR* 3, 2 (2005): 263–92.

———. *Kinship by Covenant: A Canonical Approach to the Fulfillment of God's Saving Promises.* Anchor Yale Bible Reference Library. New Haven, CT: Yale University Press, 2009.

Hallo, William W., and William Kelly Simpson. *The Ancient Near East: A History.* 2nd ed. New York: Harcourt, Brace, 1998.

Hallo, William W., and K. Lawson Younger Jr., eds. *The Context of Scripture.* Vol. 1, *Canonical Compositions from the Biblical World.* Leiden: Brill, 1997.

———, eds. *The Context of Scripture.* Vol. 2, *Monumental Inscriptions from the Biblical World.* Leiden: Brill, 2000.

———, eds. *The Context of Scripture.* Vol. 3, *Archival Documents from the Biblical World.* Leiden: Brill, 2002.

Hamilton, James M., Jr. *The Bible's Big Story: Salvation History for Kids.* Illustrated by Tessa Janes. Fearn, Scotland: Christian Focus, 2013.

———. "Biblical Theology and Preaching." In *Text Driven Preaching: God's Word at the Heart of Every Sermon,* edited by Daniel L. Akin, David L. Allen, and Ned L. Mathews, 193–218. Nashville: Broadman & Holman, 2010.

———. *God's Glory in Salvation through Judgment: A Biblical Theology.* Wheaton, IL: Crossway, 2010.

———. *What Is Biblical Theology? A Guide to the Bible's Story, Symbolism, and Patterns.* Wheaton, IL: Crossway, 2013.

Harris, R. Laird, Gleason L. Archer Jr., and Bruce K. Waltke. *Theological Wordbook of the Old Testament.* Rev. 1-vol. ed. Chicago: Moody, 2003.

Harris, W. Hall, III, and Michael H. Burer, eds. *The NET Bible*. Richardson, TX: Biblical Studies Press, 1996–2006. https://bible.org/netbible/.

Harrison, R. K. *Introduction to the Old Testament*. Grand Rapids: Eerdmans, 1969; repr., Peabody, MA: Hendrickson, 2016.

Harrison, R. K., and E. M. Blaiklock, eds. *The New International Dictionary of Biblical Archaeology*. Grand Rapids: Zondervan, 1983.

Hartman, L. F., B. M. Peebles, and M. Stevenson. "Vulgate." *NCE* 14:591–600.

Hasel, Gerhard F. *New Testament Theology: Basic Issues in the Current Debate*. Grand Rapids: Eerdmans, 1978.

———. *Old Testament Theology: Basic Issues in the Current Debate*. 4th ed. Grand Rapids: Eerdmans, 1991.

———. "The Relationship between Biblical Theology and Systematic Theology." *TJ* 5, 2 (1984): 113–27.

Hatch, Edwin, and Henry A. Redpath. *A Concordance to the Septuagint and the Other Greek Versions of the Old Testament*. 2nd ed. Grand Rapids: Baker Academic, 1998.

Hayes, John H., and Carl R. Holladay. "Literary Criticism: The Composition and Rhetorical Style of the Text." In *Biblical Exegesis: A Beginner's Handbook*, 90–103. 3rd ed. Louisville: Westminster John Knox, 2007.

Hays, Christopher B. *Hidden Riches: A Sourcebook for the Comparative Study of the Hebrew Bible and Ancient Near East*. Louisville: Westminster John Knox, 2014.

Hays, J. Daniel. "Applying the OT Law Today." *BSac* 158, 1 (2001): 21–35.

———. *The Message of the Prophets: A Survey of the Prophetic and Apocalyptic Books of the Old Testament*. Grand Rapids: Zondervan, 2010.

Hebrew University Bible Project. http://www.hum.huji.ac.il/english/units.php?cat=4980.

Heimerdinger, Jean-Marc. *Topic, Focus and Foreground in Ancient Hebrew Narratives*. JSOTSup 295. Sheffield, UK: Sheffield Academic, 1999.

Heller, Roy L. *Narrative Structure and Discourse Constellations: An Analysis of Clause Function in Biblical Hebrew Prose*. Harvard Semitic Studies 55. Winona Lake, IN: Eisenbrauns, 2004.

Helm, David. *The Big Picture Story Bible*. Wheaton, IL: Crossway, 2004.

Helm, Paul. *The Providence of God*. Contours of Christian Theology. Downers Grove, IL: InterVarsity Press, 1994.

Helyer, Larry R. *The Witness of Jesus, Paul, and John: An Exploration in Biblical Theology*. Downers Grove, IL: InterVarsity Press, 2008.

Hendel, Ronald, ed. The Hebrew Bible: A Critical Edition (HBCE). Formerly The Oxford Hebrew Bible Project. http://hbceonline.org/.

Henze, Matthias, ed. *Biblical Interpretation at Qumran*. Studies in the Dead Sea Scrolls and Related Literature. Grand Rapids: Eerdmans, 2004.

Hill, Andrew E., and John H. Walton. *A Survey of the Old Testament*. 2nd ed. Grand Rapids: Zondervan, 2000.

Hodge, Charles. *Systematic Theology*. 3 vols. New York: Scribner's, 1887; repr., Peabody, MA: Hendrickson, 1999.

Hoerth, Alfred J. *Archaeology and the Old Testament*. Grand Rapids: Baker Academic, 2009.

Hoerth, Alfred J., Gerald L. Mattingly, and Edwin M. Yamauchi, eds. *Peoples of the Old Testament World*. Grand Rapids: Baker, 1994.

Hoffmeier, James K. *The Archaeology of the Bible*. Oxford: Lion, 2008.

———. *Israel in Egypt: The Evidence for the Authenticity of the Exodus Tradition*. Oxford: Oxford University Press, 1996.

Hoffmeier, James K., and Dennis R. Magary, eds. *Do Historical Matters Matter to Faith? A Critical Appraisal of Modern and Postmodern Approaches to Scripture*. Wheaton, IL: Crossway, 2012.

Holladay, William L. *A Concise Hebrew and Aramaic Lexicon of the Old Testament*. Grand Rapids: Eerdmans, 1988.

Hollifield, Gregory K. "Does God Want You to Be Rich? A Practical Theologian's Response to the Gospel of Prosperity." *JMT* 15, 2 (2011): 25–53.

Hoppe, Leslie J. *A Guide to the Lands of the Bible*. Collegeville, MN: Glazier, 1999.

Horton, Michael. *The Christian Faith: A Systematic Theology for Pilgrims on the Way*. Grand Rapids: Zondervan, 2011.

———. *Covenant and Eschatology: The Divine Drama*. Louisville: Westminster John Knox, 2002.

———. *God of Promise: Introducing Covenant Theology*. Grand Rapids: Baker, 2006.

———. "Law, Gospel, and Covenant: Reassessing Some Emerging Antitheses." *WTJ* 64, 2 (2002): 279–87.

———. *People and Place: A Covenant Ecclesiology*. Louisville: Westminster John Knox, 2008.

———. *Pilgrim Theology: Core Doctrines for Christian Disciples*. Grand Rapids: Zondervan, 2013.

House, H. Wayne. "Creation and Redemption: A Study of Kingdom Interplay." *JETS* 35, 1 (1992): 3–17.

House, H. Wayne, and Thomas Ice. *Dominion Theology: Blessing or Curse? An Analysis of Christian Reconstructionism*. Portland, OR: Multnomah, 1988.

House, Paul R., ed. *Beyond Form Criticism: Essays on Old Testament Literary Criticism*. SBTS 2. Winona Lake, IN: Eisenbrauns, 1992.

———. *Old Testament Theology*. Downers Grove, IL: InterVarsity Press, 1998.

House, Paul R., and Eric Mitchell. *Old Testament Survey*. 2nd ed. Nashville: Broadman & Holman, 2007.

Howard, David M., Jr. "Recent Trends in Psalms Study." In *The Face of Old Testament Studies: A Survey of Contemporary Approaches*, edited by David W. Baker and Bill T. Arnold, 329–68. Grand Rapids: Baker Academic, 2004.

Hugenberger, Gordon P. *Marriage as a Covenant: Biblical Law and Ethics as Developed from Malachi*. Grand Rapids: Baker, 1998.

Janzen, Waldemar. *Old Testament Ethics: A Paradigmatic Approach*. Louisville: Westminster John Knox, 1994.

Jastrow, Marcus. *A Dictionary of the Targumim, the Talmud Babli and Yerushalmi, and the Midrashic Literature*. 2nd ed. 2 vols. in 1. 1926; repr., New York: Judaica, 1996. Available at http://www.tyndalearchive.com/tabs/jastrow/.

Jellicoe, Sidney. *The Septuagint and Modern Study*. Winona Lake, IN: Eisenbrauns, 1978; repr., 2014.

Jenni, Ernst, and Claus Westermann, eds. *Theological Lexicon of the Old Testament*. Translated by Mark E. Biddle. 3 vols. Peabody, MA: Hendrickson, 1994.

Jensen, Peter. *The Revelation of God*. Contours of Christian Theology. Downers Grove, IL: InterVarsity Press, 2002.

Jobes, Karen H., and Moisés Silva. *Invitation to the Septuagint*. 2nd ed. Grand Rapids: Baker Academic, 2015.

Johns, Alger F. *A Short Grammar of Biblical Aramaic*. 2nd ed. Berrien Springs, MI: Andrews University Press, 1982.

Johnson, Dennis E. *Him We Proclaim: Preaching Christ from All the Scriptures*. Phillipsburg, NJ: P&R Publishing, 2007.

———. *Walking with Jesus through His Word: Discovering Christ in All the Scriptures*. Phillipsburg, NJ: P&R Publishing, 2015.

Johnston, Philip S., and Peter W. L. Walker, eds. *The Land of Promise: Biblical, Theological and Contemporary Perspectives*. Downers Grove, IL: InterVarsity Press, 2000.

Jones, David W., and Russell S. Woodbridge. *Health, Wealth and Happiness: Has the Prosperity Gospel Overshadowed the Gospel of Christ?* Grand Rapids: Kregel, 2011.

Jones, Mark. *Antinomianism: Reformed Theology's Unwelcome Guest?* Phillipsburg, NJ: P&R Publishing, 2013.

Joüon, Paul, and T. Muraoka. *A Grammar of Biblical Hebrew*. 2nd ed. Subsidia Biblica 27. Rome: Gregorian & Biblical, 2011.

Joy, Charles R. *Harper's Topical Concordance of the Bible*. 2nd ed. San Francisco: Harper & Row, 1976.

Judaica Electronic Texts. http://www.library.upenn.edu/cajs/etexts.html.

Jumper, James N. *A Short Grammar of Biblical Aramaic: An Annotated Answer Key*. Berrien Springs, MI: Andrews University Press, 2003.

Kaiser, Walter C., Jr. *The Messiah in the Old Testament*. SOTBT. Grand Rapids: Zondervan, 1995.

———. "A Principlizing Model." In *Four Views on Moving beyond the Bible to Theology*, edited by Gary T. Meadors, 19–50. Responses to other contributors on pp. 121–25, 200–4, 249–54. Counterpoints. Grand Rapids: Zondervan, 2009.

———. *The Promise-Plan of God: A Biblical Theology of the Old and New Testaments*. Grand Rapids: Zondervan, 2008.

———. *Recovering the Unity of the Bible: One Continuous Story, Plan, and Purpose*. Grand Rapids: Zondervan, 2009.

———. "The Theology of the Old Testament." In *Introductory Articles*, edited by Frank E. Gaebelein, 283–305. Expositor's Bible Commentary 1. Grand Rapids: Eerdmans, 1979.

———. *Toward an Exegetical Theology: Biblical Exegesis for Preaching and Teaching*. Grand Rapids: Baker Academic, 1981.

———. *Toward an Old Testament Theology*. Grand Rapids: Zondervan, 1978.

———. *Toward Old Testament Ethics*. Grand Rapids: Zondervan, 1983.

———. *The Uses of the Old Testament in the New*. Chicago: Moody, 1985.

Kaiser, Walter C., Jr., and Duane A. Garrett, eds. *NIV Archaeological Study Bible*. Grand Rapids: Zondervan, 2005.

Kaiser, Walter C., Jr., and Moisés Silva. *Introduction to Biblical Hermeneutics: The Search for Meaning*. 2nd ed. Grand Rapids: Zondervan, 2007.

Kaiser, Walter C., Jr., and Paul D. Wegner. *A History of Israel: From the Bronze Age through the Jewish Wars*. 2nd ed. Broadman & Holman, 2016.

Kaminski, Carol M. *Casket Empty: God's Plan of Redemption through History—Old Testament Study Guide*. Salem, MA: Casket Empty Media, 2012.

———. *Casket Empty Old Testament Timeline*. www.CasketEmpty.com.

Kautzsch, E., ed. *Gesenius' Hebrew Grammar*. Translated by A. E. Cowley. 2nd ed. Oxford: Clarendon, 1910.

Kelby, Tom. *Psalms 1–19: A Preacher's Guide*. Webster, WI: Hands to the Plow, Inc., 2015.

Keller, Timothy. *Counterfeit Gods: The Empty Promises of Money, Sex, and Power, and the Only Hope That Matters*. New York: Dutton, 2009.

———. *Generous Justice: How God's Grace Makes Us Just*. New York: Dutton, 2010.

Kelley, Page H., Daniel S. Mynatt, and Timothy G. Crawford. *The Masorah of Biblia Hebraica Stuttgartensia: Introduction and Annotated Glossary*. Grand Rapids: Eerdmans, 1998.

Kim, Julius J. *Preaching the Whole Counsel of God: Design and Deliver Gospel-Centered Sermons*. Grand Rapids: Zondervan, 2015.

Kiraz, George A., ed. *The Antioch Bible: The Syriac Peshitta Bible with English Translation*. 35 vols. Piscataway, NJ: Gorgias, 2012–.

Kitchen, K. A. *The Bible in Its World: The Bible and Archaeology Today*. Downers Grove, IL: InterVarsity Press, 1977.

———. "The Fall and Rise of Covenant, Law, and Treaty." *TynBul* 40, 1 (1989): 118–35.

———. *On the Reliability of the Old Testament*. Grand Rapids: Eerdmans, 2003.

Kittel, Gerhard, and Gerhard Friedrich, eds. *Theological Dictionary of the New Testament*. Translated by Geoffrey W. Bromiley. 10 vols. Grand Rapids: Eerdmans, 1964–76.

Klein, William W., Craig L. Blomberg, and Robert L. Hubbard Jr. "Application." In *Introduction to Biblical Interpretation*, 477–504. 2nd ed. Dallas: Word, 2004.

Kline, Meredith G. *Kingdom Prologue: Genesis Foundations for a Covenantal Worldview*. Overland Park, KS: Two Age, 2000.

———. *The Structure of Biblical Authority*. 2nd ed. Eugene, OR: Wipf & Stock, 1997.

Klink, Edward W., III, and Darian R. Lockett. *Understanding Biblical Theology: A Comparison of Theory and Practice*. Grand Rapids: Zondervan, 2012.

Knoppers, Gary N. "Ancient Near Eastern Royal Grants and the Davidic Covenant: A Parallel?" *JAOS* 116, 4 (1996): 670–97.

Knox, Ronald Arbuthnott. *The Old Testament: Newly Translated from the Vulgate Latin*. 2 vols. New York: Sheed & Ward, 1950.

Koehler, Ludwig, Walter Baumgartner, and Johann Jakob Stamm, eds. *The Hebrew and Aramaic Lexicon of the Old Testament: Study Edition*. Translated by M. E. J. Richardson. 2 vols. Leiden: Brill, 2001.

Kofoed, Jens Bruun. *Text and History: Historiography and the Study of the Biblical Text*. Winona Lake, IN: Eisenbrauns, 2005.

Kohlenberger, John R., III, ed. *The Interlinear NIV Hebrew-English Old Testament*. Grand Rapids: Zondervan, 1993.

Kohlenberger, John R., III, and James A. Swanson. *The Hebrew-English Concordance to the Old Testament*. Grand Rapids: Zondervan, 1998.

Köstenberger, Andreas J. "The Present and Future of Biblical Theology." *Themelios* 37, 3 (2012): 445–64.

———. "Testament Relationships." *DBCI* 350–52.

Köstenberger, Andreas J., and David A. Croteau, eds. *Which Bible Translation Should I Use? A Comparison of 4 Major Recent Versions*. Nashville: Broadman & Holman, 2012.

Köstenberger, Andreas J., and Richard D. Patterson. *For the Love of God's Word: An Introduction to Biblical Interpretation*. Grand Rapids: Kregel, 2015.

———. *Invitation to Biblical Interpretation: Exploring the Hermeneutical Triad of History, Literature, and Theology*. Grand Rapids: Kregel, 2011.

Kruger, Michael J., ed. *A Biblical-Theological Introduction to the New Testament: The Gospel Realized*. Wheaton, IL: Crossway, 2016.

Kubo, Sakae, and Walter Specht. *So Many Versions?* Grand Rapids: Zondervan, 1975.

Kugel, James L. *The Idea of Biblical Poetry: Parallelism and Its History*. New Haven, CT: Yale University Press, 1981; repr., Baltimore: Johns Hopkins University Press, 1998.

Kunjummen, Raju D. "The Single Intent of Scripture—Critical Examination of a Theological Construct." *GTJ* 7, 1 (1986): 81–110.

Ladd, George Eldon. *Crucial Questions about the Kingdom of God*. Grand Rapids: Eerdmans, 1952.

———. *The Gospel of the Kingdom: Scriptural Studies in the Kingdom of God*. Grand Rapids: Eerdmans, 1959.

———. *The Presence of the Future: The Eschatology of Biblical Realism*. Grand Rapids: Eerdmans, 1974.

———. *A Theology of the New Testament*. Edited by Donald A. Hagner. 2nd ed. Grand Rapids: Eerdmans, 1993.

Lamsa, George M. *The Holy Bible from Ancient Eastern Manuscripts*. Philadelphia: Holman, 1957.

LaRondelle, Hans K. *The Israel of God in Prophecy: Principles of Prophetic Interpretation.* Andrews University Monographs; Studies in Religion 13. Berrien Springs, MI: Andrews University Press, 1983.

LaSor, William Sanford, David Allan Hubbard, and Frederic William Bush. *Old Testament Survey: The Message, Form, and Background of the Old Testament.* 2nd ed. Grand Rapids: Eerdmans, 1996.

Latin Vulgate. http://www.latinvulgate.com/.

Lawrence, Michael. *Biblical Theology in the Life of the Church: A Guide for Ministry.* 9Marks. Wheaton, IL: Crossway, 2010.

Leeman, Jonathan, ed. *9Marks Journal [Prosperity Gospel].* 2014. https://9marks.org/journal/prosperity-gospel/.

Leithart, Peter J. *A House for My Name: A Survey of the Old Testament.* Moscow, ID: Canon, 2000.

Letham, Robert. *The Work of Christ.* Contours of Christian Theology. Downers Grove, IL: InterVarsity Press, 1993.

Liddell, H. G., and R. Scott. *Greek-English Lexicon with a Revised Supplement.* 9th ed. Oxford: Clarendon, 1996.

Life Application Study Bible: NIV. Carol Stream, IL: Tyndale House, 2012.

Lints, Richard. *The Fabric of Theology: A Prolegomenon to Evangelical Theology.* Grand Rapids: Eerdmans, 1993.

Lioy, Dan. "The Heart of the Prosperity Gospel: Self or the Savior?" *Conspectus* 4 (2007): 41–64.

Lipiński, Edward. *Semitic Languages Outline of a Comparative Grammar.* 2nd ed. Orientalia Lovaniensia Analecta 80. Leuven: Peeters, 2000.

———. *Semitic Linguistics in Historical Perspective.* Orientalia Lovaniensia Analecta 230. Leuven: Peeters, 2014.

Livingston, G. Herbert. *The Pentateuch in Its Cultural Environment.* 2nd ed. Grand Rapids: Baker, 1987.

Lloyd-Jones, Sally. *The Jesus Storybook Bible: Every Story Whispers His Name.* Illustrated by Jago. Grand Rapids: Zonderkidz, 2007.

Logos Bible Software. https://www.logos.com/.

Long, V. Philips. *The Art of Biblical History.* Foundations of Biblical Interpretation. Grand Rapids: Zondervan, 1994.

———. "Historiography of the Old Testament." In *The Face of Old Testament Studies: A Survey of Contemporary Approaches,* edited by David W. Baker and Bill T. Arnold, 145–75. Grand Rapids: Baker Academic, 2004.

———, ed. *Israel's Past in Present Research: Essays on Ancient Israelite Historiography.* SBTS 7. Winona Lake, IN: Eisenbrauns, 1999.

Longacre, Robert E. *Joseph: A Story of Divine Providence—A Text Theoretical and Textlinguistic Analysis of Genesis 37 and 39–48.* 2nd ed. Winona Lake, IN: Eisenbrauns, 2003.

Longenecker, Bruce W. "New Testament Theology." *ZEB* 4:474–81.

Longman, Tremper, III. *How to Read Proverbs*. Downers Grove, IL: InterVarsity Press, 2002.

———. *How to Read the Psalms*. Downers Grove, IL: InterVarsity Press, 1988.

———. "Literary Approaches to the Old Testament." In *The Face of Old Testament Studies: A Survey of Contemporary Approaches*, edited by David W. Baker and Bill T. Arnold, 97–115. Grand Rapids: Baker Academic, 2004.

———. *Old Testament Commentary Survey*. 5th ed. Grand Rapids: Zondervan, 2013.

Longman, Tremper, III, and Raymond B. Dillard. *An Introduction to the Old Testament*. 2nd ed. Grand Rapids: Zondervan, 2006.

Longman, Tremper, III, and Peter Enns, eds. *Dictionary of the Old Testament: Wisdom, Poetry, and Writings*. Downers Grove, IL: InterVarsity Press, 2008.

Louw, Johannes P., and Eugene A. Nida, eds. *Greek-English Lexicon of the New Testament: Based on Semantic Domains*. 2nd ed. 2 vols. New York: United Bible Societies, 1989.

Lucas, Ernest C. *A Guide to the Psalms and Wisdom Literature*. Exploring the Old Testament 3. Downers Grove, IL: InterVarsity Press, 2003.

Lunn, Nicholas P. *Word-Order Variation in Biblical Hebrew Poetry: Differentiating Pragmatics and Poetics*. Paternoster Biblical Monographs. Eugene, OR: Wipf & Stock, 2006.

MacArthur, John, and Richard Mayhue, eds. *Biblical Doctrine: A Systematic Summary of Bible Truth*. Wheaton, IL: Crossway, 2017.

Macleod, Donald. *The Person of Christ*. Contours of Christian Theology. Downers Grove, IL: InterVarsity Press, 1998.

Marcos, Natalio Fernández. *The Septuagint in Context: Introduction to the Greek Version of the Bible*. Atlanta: SBL, 2009.

Marshall, I. Howard. *A Concise New Testament Theology*. Downers Grove, IL: InterVarsity Press, 2008.

———. "The Hope of a New Age: The Kingdom of God in the New Testament." *Themelios* 11, 1 (1985): 5–14.

———. "Jesus Christ." *NDBT* 592–602.

———. "Kingdom of God (of Heaven)." *ZEB* 3:911–22.

———. *New Testament Theology: Many Witnesses, One Gospel*. Downers Grove, IL: InterVarsity Press, 2004.

Martens, Elmer A. "The Flowering and Floundering of Old Testament Theology." *NIDOTTE* 1:172–84.

———. *God's Design: A Focus on Old Testament Theology*. 4th ed. Eugene, OR: Wipf & Stock, 2015.

———. "How Is the Christian to Construe Old Testament Law?" *BBR* 12, 2 (2002): 199–216.

———. "Old Testament Theology Since Walter C. Kaiser Jr." *JETS* 50, 4 (2007): 673–91.

———. "Tackling Old Testament Theology." *JETS* 20, 2 (1977): 123–32.

Martínez, Florentino García, and Eibert J. C. Tigchelaar. *The Dead Sea Scrolls Study Edition*. 2 vols. Grand Rapids: Eerdmans, 1997–98.

Mathis, David. *Habits of Grace: Enjoying Jesus through the Spiritual Disciplines*. Wheaton, IL: Crossway, 2016.

Matthews, Victor H. *Manners and Customs in the Bible: An Illustrated Guide to Daily Life in Bible Times*. 3rd ed. Peabody, MA: Hendrickson, 2006.

Matthews, Victor H., and Don C. Benjamin. *Old Testament Parallels: Laws and Stories from the Ancient Near East*. 3rd ed. New York: Paulist, 2006.

Matthews, Victor H., and James C. Moyer. *The Old Testament: Text and Context*. 3rd ed. Grand Rapids: Baker Academic, 2012.

Maura, Michael Otieno, Conrad Mbewe, Ken Mbugua, John Piper, and Wayne Grudem. *Prosperity? Seeking the True Gospel*. Nairobi: Africa Christian Textbooks Registered Trustees in partnership with The Gospel Coalition, 2015.

Mazar, Amihay, Ephraim Stern, Eric M. Meyers, and Mark A. Chancey. *Archaeology of the Land of the Bible*. 3 vols. New York: Doubleday, 1990.

McCall, Tom. *Sin*. Foundations of Evangelical Theology. Wheaton, IL: Crossway, forthcoming.

McCarter, P. Kyle, Jr. *Textual Criticism: Recovering the Text of the Hebrew Bible*. Guides to Biblical Scholarship, Old Testament. Minneapolis: Augsburg Fortress, 2001.

McCartney, Dan, and Charles Clayton. *Let the Reader Understand: A Guide to Interpreting and Applying the Bible*. 2nd ed. Phillipsburg, NJ: P&R Publishing, 2002.

McConville, J. G. *God and Earthly Power: An Old Testament Political Theology*. Edinburgh: T&T Clark, 2008.

———. *A Guide to the Prophets*. Exploring the Old Testament 4. Downers Grove, IL: InterVarsity Press, 2002.

McCune, Rolland. *A Systematic Theology of Biblical Christianity*. 3 vols. Allen Park, MI: Detroit Baptist Theological Seminary, 2009–10.

McGrath, Alister E. *Christian Theology: An Introduction*. 5th ed. Malden, MA: Wiley-Blackwell, 2011.

McRay, John, and Alfred Hoerth. *Bible Archaeology: An Exploration of the History and Culture of Early Civilizations*. Grand Rapids: Baker, 2006.

Meade, John D. "Circumcision of Flesh to Circumcision of Heart: The Typology of the Sign of the Abrahamic Covenant." In *Progressive Covenantalism: Charting a Course between Dispensational and Covenant Theologies*, edited by Stephen J. Wellum and Brent E. Parker, 127–58. Nashville: Broadman & Holman, 2016.

Meadors, Gary T., ed. *Four Views on Moving beyond the Bible to Theology*. Counterpoints. Grand Rapids: Zondervan, 2009: (1) Walter Kaiser, "A Principlizing Model," (2) Dan Doriani, "A Redemptive-Historical Model," (3) Kevin Vanhoozer, "A Drama-of-Redemption Model," and (4) Bill Webb, "A Redemptive-Movement Model."

Merrill, Eugene H. *Everlasting Dominion: A Theology of the Old Testament*. Nashville: Broadman & Holman, 2006.

———. *Kingdom of Priests: A History of Old Testament Israel*. 2nd ed. Grand Rapids: Baker, 2008.

Merrill, Eugene H., Mark F. Rooker, and Michael A. Grisanti. *The World and the Word: An Introduction to the Old Testament*. Nashville: Broadman & Holman, 2011.

Merwe, Christo H. J. van der, Jackie A. Naudé, and Jan H. Kroeze. *A Biblical Hebrew Reference Grammar*. Biblical Languages: Hebrew 3. Sheffield, UK: Sheffield Academic, 2002.

Metzger, Bruce M. *The Bible in Translation: Ancient and English Versions*. Grand Rapids: Baker Academic, 2001.

Meyer, Jason C. *The End of the Law: Mosaic Covenant in Pauline Theology*. NAC Studies in Bible and Theology 7. Nashville: Broadman & Holman, 2009.

———. "The Mosaic Law, Theological Systems, and the Glory of Christ." In *Progressive Covenantalism: Charting a Course between Dispensational and Covenant Theologies*, edited by Stephen J. Wellum and Brent E. Parker, 66–99. Nashville: Broadman & Holman, 2016.

———. *Preaching: A Biblical Theology*. Wheaton, IL: Crossway, 2013.

Meyers, Eric M., ed. *The Oxford Encyclopedia of Archaeology in the Near East*. 5 vols. New York: Oxford University Press, 1997.

Millard, A. R., James K. Hoffmeier, and David W. Baker, eds. *Faith, Tradition, and History: Old Testament Historiography in Its Near Eastern Context*. Winona Lake, IN: Eisenbrauns, 1994.

Miller, Cynthia L. *The Representation of Speech in Biblical Hebrew Narrative: A Linguistic Analysis*. HSM 55. Winona Lake, IN: Eisenbrauns, 1999.

———, ed. *The Verbless Clause in Biblical Hebrew: Linguistic Approaches*. LSAWS 1. Winona Lake, IN: Eisenbrauns, 1999.

Miller, J. Maxwell, and John H. Hayes. *A History of Ancient Israel and Judah*. Philadelphia: Westminster, 1986.

Miqraot Gedolot HaKeter. http://www1.biu.ac.il/indexE.php?id=6261&pt=1&pid=43&level=3&cPath=6261.

Moberly, R. W. L. *The Old Testament of the Old Testament: Patriarchal Narratives and Mosaic Yahwism*. Eugene, OR: Wipf & Stock, 2001.

———. *Old Testament Theology: Reading the Old Testament as Christian Scripture*. Grand Rapids: Baker Academic, 2013.

———. "Theology of the Old Testament." In *The Face of Old Testament Studies: A Survey of Contemporary Approaches*, edited by David W. Baker and Bill T. Arnold, 452–78. Grand Rapids: Baker Academic, 2004.

Monson, James M. *The Land Between: A Regional Study Guide to the Land of the Bible*. Highland Park, IL: Institute of Holy Land Studies, 1983.

Moo, Douglas J. "The Law of Christ as the Fulfillment of the Law of Moses: A Modified Lutheran View." In *Five Views on Law and Gospel*, edited by Wayne G. Strickland, 319–76. Responses to other contributors on pp. 83–90, 165–73, 218–25, 309–15. Counterpoints. Grand Rapids: Zondervan, 1999.

———. "The Law of Moses or the Law of Christ." In *Continuity and Discontinuity: Perspectives on the Relationship between the Old and New Testaments: Essays in Honor of S. Lewis Johnson Jr.*, edited by John S. Feinberg, 203–18, 373–76. Westchester, IL: Crossway, 1988.

———, ed. "Updating the New International Version of the Bible: Notes from the Committee on Bible Translation." August 2010. Available at http://www.thenivbible.com/wp-content/uploads/2014/11/2011-Translation-Notes.pdf.

———. *We Still Don't Get It: Evangelicals and Bible Translation Fifty Years after James Barr.* Grand Rapids: Zondervan, 2014. Available at http://www.thenivbible.com/wp-content/uploads/2014/11/We-Still-Dont-Get-It.pdf.

Moo, Douglas J., and Andrew David Naselli. "The Problem of the New Testament's Use of the Old Testament." In *The Enduring Authority of the Christian Scriptures*, edited by D. A. Carson, 702–46. Grand Rapids: Eerdmans, 2016.

Morgan, Christopher W., and Robert A. Peterson, eds. *The Kingdom of God*. Theology in Community. Wheaton, IL: Crossway, 2012.

Morrish, George. *A Handy Concordance of the Septuagint: Giving Various Readings from Codices Vaticanus, Alexandrinus, Sinaiticus, and Ephraemi*. London: Bagster, 1887; repr., Eugene, OR: Wipf & Stock, 2008.

Morwood, James, ed. *The Oxford Latin Desk Dictionary*. Oxford: Oxford University Press, 2005.

Motyer, J. Alec. *Look to the Rock: An Old Testament Background to Our Understanding of Christ*. Downers Grove, IL: InterVarsity Press, 1996.

Moulton, Harold K., ed. *The Analytical Greek Lexicon Revised*. 1852; repr., Grand Rapids: Zondervan, 1979.

Mounce, William D., ed. *Mounce's Complete Expository Dictionary of Old and New Testament Words*. Grand Rapids: Zondervan, 2006.

Muck, Terry C., ed. NIV Application Commentary. 42 vols. Grand Rapids, Zondervan, 1994–2012.

Muraoka, T. *A Greek-English Lexicon of the Septuagint*. Leuven: Peeters, 2010.

———. *Greek-Hebrew/Aramaic Two-Way Index to the Septuagint*. Leuven: Peeters, 2010.

———. *Hebrew/Aramaic Index to the Septuagint Keyed to the Hatch-Redpath Concordance*. Grand Rapids: Baker Academic, 1998.

Murray, David. *Jesus on Every Page: 10 Simple Ways to Seek and Find Christ in the Old Testament*. Nashville: Thomas Nelson, 2013.

Naselli, Andrew David. "D. A. Carson's Theological Method." *SBET* 29, 2 (2011): 245–74.

Nave, Orville J. *Nave's Topical Bible*. Peabody, MA: Hendrickson, 2002.

Nida, Eugene A. "The Sociolinguistics of Translating Canonical Religious Texts." *Traduction, Terminologie, Rédaction* 7, 1 (1994): 191–217.

———. "Theories of Translation." *ABD* 6:512–15.

Nida, Eugene A., and Charles R. Taber. *The Theory and Practice of Translation*. Leiden: Brill, 1969; repr., 2003.

Nida, Eugene A., and Jan de Waard. *From One Language to Another: Functional Equivalence in Bible Translation*. Nashville: Thomas Nelson, 1986.

Niehaus, Jeffrey J. *Ancient Near Eastern Themes in Biblical Theology*. Grand Rapids: Kregel, 2008.

———. "An Argument against Theologically Constructed Covenants." *JETS* 50, 2 (2007): 259–73.

———. *Biblical Theology*. Vol. 1, *The Common Grace Covenants*. Wooster, OH: Weaver, 2014.

———. "Covenant and Narrative, God and Time." *JETS* 53, 3 (2010): 535–59.

———. "Covenant: An Idea in the Mind of God." *JETS* 52, 2 (2009): 225–46.

———. *God at Sinai: Covenant and Theophany in the Bible and Ancient Near East*. SOTBT. Grand Rapids: Zondervan, 1995.

———. "God's Covenant with Abraham." *JETS* 56, 2 (2013): 249–71.

O'Connor, Michael Patrick. *Hebrew Verse Structure*. 2nd ed. Winona Lake, IN: Eisenbrauns, 1997.

Oden, Thomas C. *Classic Christianity: A Systematic Theology*. 2nd ed. New York: HarperOne, 2009.

O'Leary, De Lacy. *Comparative Grammar of the Semitic Languages*. London: Routledge, 2001.

Ollenberger, Ben C., ed. *Old Testament Theology: Flowering and Future*. 2nd ed. SBTS 1. Winona Lake, IN: Eisenbrauns, 2004.

Orion Center for the Study of the Dead Sea Scrolls and Associated Literature at Hebrew University of Jerusalem. http://orion.mscc.huji.ac.il/.

Ortlund, Dane C., and Miles V. Van Pelt, eds. Short Studies in Biblical Theology. Wheaton, IL: Crossway, 2015–present.

Ortlund, Dane C., Erika Allen, and Bill Deckard, eds. *ESV Women's Devotional Bible*. Wheaton, IL: Crossway, 2014.

Osborne, Grant R. *The Hermeneutical Spiral: A Comprehensive Introduction to Biblical Interpretation*. 2nd ed. Downers Grove, IL: InterVarsity Press, 2006.

———. "Type, Typology." *EDT* 1222–23.

———. "Typology." *ZEB* 5:952–54.

Oswalt, John N. "Recent Studies in Old Testament Apocalyptic." In *The Face of Old Testament Studies: A Survey of Contemporary Approaches*, edited by David W. Baker and Bill T. Arnold, 369–90. Grand Rapids: Baker Academic, 2004.

Owens, John Joseph. *Analytical Key to the Old Testament*. 4 vols. Grand Rapids: Baker Academic, 1989.

Oxford English Dictionary. http://www.oed.com/.

Packer, J. I. *Concise Theology: A Guide to Historic Christian Beliefs*. Wheaton, IL: Tyndale House, 1995.

Palmer, David L. *Casket Empty: God's Plan of Redemption through History—Old Testament Study Guide*. Salem, MA: Casket Empty Media, 2016.

———. *Casket Empty New Testament Timeline*. www.CasketEmpty.com.

Payne, J. Barton. "Covenant (NT)." *ZEB* 1:1063–69.

———. "Covenant (OT)." *ZEB* 1:1051–63.

———. "Covenant, the New." *ZEB* 1:1071–76.

Payne, J. Barton, and R. Alan Cole. "Old Testament Theology." *ZEB* 4:581–94.

Payne, Philip B. "The Fallacy of Equating Meaning with the Human Author's Intention." *JETS* 20, 3 (1977): 243–52.

Pentecost, J. Dwight. *Thy Kingdom Come: Tracing God's Kingdom Program and Covenant Promises throughout History*. Grand Rapids: Kregel, 1995.

Peshitta Institute of Leiden, ed. *The Old Testament in Syriac*. Leiden: Brill, 1972–.

Pietersma, Albert, and Benjamin G. Wright. *A New English Translation of the Septuagint*. Oxford: Oxford University Press, 2007.

Piper, John. *Desiring God: Meditations of a Christian Hedonist*. 4th ed. Colorado Springs: Multnomah, 2011.

———. *Future Grace: The Purifying Power of the Promises of God*. 2nd ed. Colorado Springs: Multnomah, 2012.

———. "The Goal of God in Redemptive History." In *Desiring God: Meditations of a Christian Hedonist*, 308–21. 3rd ed. Sisters, OR: Multnomah, 2003.

———. "Introduction to the Third Edition: New Realities in World Christianity and Twelve Appeals to Prosperity Preachers." In *Let the Nations Be Glad! The Supremacy of God in Missions*, 15–34. 3rd ed. Grand Rapids: Baker, 2010.

———. *The Pleasures of God: Meditations on God's Delight in Being God*. 2nd ed. Sisters, OR: Multnomah, 2000.

———. *Reading the Bible Supernaturally: Seeing and Savoring the Glory of God in Scripture*. Wheaton, IL: Crossway, 2017.

———. *Seeing and Savoring Jesus Christ*. Wheaton, IL: Crossway, 2004.

Plummer, Robert L. *40 Questions about Interpreting the Bible*. 40 Questions. Grand Rapids: Kregel, 2010.

———. "Righteousness and Peace Kiss: The Reconciliation of Authorial Intent and Biblical Typology." *SBJT* 14, 2 (2010): 54–61.

Porter, Stanley E., and Richard S. Hess, eds. *Translating the Bible: Problems and Prospects*. Sheffield, UK: Sheffield Academic, 1999.

Poythress, Vern S. "Dispensing with Merely Human Meaning: Gains and Losses from Focusing on the Human Author, Illustrated by Zephaniah 1:2–3." *JETS* 57, 3 (2014): 481–99.

———. "Kinds of Biblical Theology." *WTJ* 70, 1 (2008): 129–41.

———. "The Presence of God Qualifying Our Notions of Grammatical-Historical Interpretation: Genesis 3:15 as a Test Case." *JETS* 50, 1 (2007): 87–103.

———. *Reading the Word of God in the Presence of God: A Handbook for Biblical Interpretation*. Wheaton, IL: Crossway, 2016.

———. *The Shadow of Christ in the Law of Moses*. Phillipsburg, NJ: Presbyterian and Reformed, 1991.

Poythress, Vern S., and Wayne A. Grudem. *The TNIV and the Gender-Neutral Bible Controversy*. Nashville: Broadman & Holman, 2004.

Pratico, Gary D., and Miles V. Van Pelt. *Basics of Biblical Hebrew: Grammar* and *Workbook*. 2nd ed. Grand Rapids: Zondervan, 2007.

Pratt, Richard L., Jr. *He Gave Us Stories: The Bible Student's Guide to Interpreting Old Testament Narratives.* Phillipsburg, NJ: P&R Publishing, 1993.

Preuss, Horst Dietrich. *Old Testament Theology.* 2 vols. OTL. Louisville: Westminster John Knox, 1995.

Pritchard, James B., ed. *The Ancient Near East: An Anthology of Texts and Pictures.* Foreword by Daniel E. Flemming. Princeton, NJ: Princeton University Press, 2011. Reprinted from 2 vols. in 1958, 1975.

———, ed. *Ancient Near Eastern Texts Relating to the Old Testament.* 3rd ed. Princeton, NJ: Princeton University Press, 1969.

———, ed. *The Ancient Near East in Pictures Relating to the Old Testament.* 2nd ed. Princeton, NJ: Princeton University Press, 1994.

Provan, Iain W., V. Philips Long, and Tremper Longman III. *A Biblical History of Israel.* 2nd ed. Louisville: Westminster John Knox, 2015.

Rad, Gerhard von. *Old Testament Theology.* 2 vols. OTL. Louisville: Westminster John Knox, 2001.

Rahlfs, Alfred, and Robert Hanhart, eds. *Septuaginta.* Stuttgart: Deutsche Bibelgesellschaft, 2007.

Rainey, Anson F., and R. Steven Notley. *The Sacred Bridge: Carta's Atlas of the Biblical World.* 2nd ed. Jerusalem: Carta, 2015.

Rasmussen, Carl. *Zondervan Atlas of the Bible.* 2nd ed. Grand Rapids: Zondervan, 2010.

Reader's Edition. Logos Bible Software.

Rendtorff, Rolf. *The Canonical Hebrew Bible: A Theology of the Old Testament.* Leiden: Deo, 2005.

Reviews of Peshitta and Targum scholarship. http://www.targum.info/biblio/reviews.htm.

Ridderbos, Herman N. *When the Time Had Fully Come: Studies in New Testament Theology.* Grand Rapids: Eerdmans, 1957.

Robar, Elizabeth. *The Verb and the Paragraph in Biblical Hebrew: A Cognitive-Linguistic Approach.* Studies in Semitic Languages and Linguistics 78. Leiden: Brill, 2014.

Roberts, Vaughan. *God's Big Picture: Tracing the Storyline of the Bible.* Downers Grove, IL: InterVarsity Press, 2002.

Robertson, David A. *Linguistic Evidence in Dating Early Hebrew Poetry.* Missoula, MT: Scholars Press, 1973.

Robertson, O. Palmer. *The Christ of the Covenants.* Phillipsburg, NJ: Presbyterian and Reformed, 1987.

———. *The Israel of God: Yesterday, Today, and Tomorrow.* Phillipsburg, NJ: P&R Publishing, 2000.

Rosenthal, Franz. *A Grammar of Biblical Aramaic.* Index of Biblical Citations compiled by Daniel M. Gurtner. 7th ed. Leipzig: Harrassowitz, 2006.

Rosner, Brian S. "Biblical Theology." *NDBT* 3–11.

———. *Paul and the Law: Keeping the Commandments of God.* NSBT 31. Downers Grove, IL: InterVarsity Press, 2013.

———. "Salvation, History of." *DTIB* 714–17.

Ross, Allen P. *Introducing Biblical Hebrew*. Grand Rapids: Baker Academic, 2001.

Runge, Steven E., and Joshua R. Westbury. *High Definition Old Testament: ESV Edition*. Bellingham, WA: Lexham, 2012. Available from Logos Bible Software.

———. *Lexham Discourse Hebrew Bible*. Bellingham, WA: Lexham, 2012. Available from Logos Bible Software.

Rydelnik, Michael. *The Messianic Hope: Is the Hebrew Bible Really Messianic?* NAC Studies in Bible and Theology 9. Nashville: Broadman & Holman, 2010.

Ryken, Leland. *The ESV and the English Bible Legacy*. Wheaton, IL: Crossway, 2011.

———. *How to Read the Bible as Literature*. Grand Rapids: Zondervan, 1984.

———. *The Literature of the Bible*. Grand Rapids: Zondervan, 1974.

Ryken, Leland, and Tremper Longman III, eds. *A Complete Literary Guide to the Bible*. 2nd ed. Grand Rapids: Zondervan, 1993.

Ryrie, Charles C. *Basic Theology: A Popular Systematic Guide to Understanding Biblical Truth*. 2nd ed. Chicago: Moody, 1999.

———. *Biblical Theology of the New Testament*. Chicago: Moody, 1959.

Sailhamer, John H. *Introduction to Old Testament Theology: A Canonical Approach*. Grand Rapids: Zondervan, 1995.

———. *The Meaning of the Pentateuch: Revelation, Composition, and Interpretation*. Downers Grove, IL: InterVarsity Press, 2009.

———. "The Messiah and the Hebrew Bible." *JETS* 44, 1 (2001): 5–23.

Sakenfeld, Katharine Doob, ed. *The New Interpreter's Dictionary of the Bible*. 5 vols. Nashville: Abingdon, 2009.

Sandy, D. Brent, and Ronald L. Giese, eds. *Cracking Old Testament Codes: A Guide to Interpreting Literary Genres of the Old Testament*. Nashville: Broadman & Holman, 1995.

Sarles, Ken L. "A Theological Evaluation of the Prosperity Gospel." *BSac* 143 (1986): 329–50.

Sasson, Jack M., ed. *Civilizations of the Ancient Near East*. 2 vols. Peabody, MA: Hendrickson, 2001.

Satterthwaite, Philip E. *A Guide to the Historical Books*. Exploring the Old Testament 2. Downers Grove, IL: InterVarsity Press, 2012.

Satterthwaite, Philip E., Richard S. Hess, and Gordon J. Wenham, eds. *The Lord's Anointed: Interpretation of Old Testament Messianic Texts*. Exeter, UK: Paternoster, 1995.

SBL Writings from the Ancient World. Atlanta: SBL, 1990–.

Schenker, Adrian, et al., eds. *Biblia Hebraica Quinta*. Stuttgart: Deutsche Bibelgesellschaft, 2004–.

Schiffman, Lawrence H., and James C. VanderKam, eds. *Encyclopedia of the Dead Sea Scrolls*. 2 vols. New York: Oxford University Press, 2000.

Schlegel, William. *The Land and the Bible: A Historical Geographical Companion to the Satellite Bible Atlas*. Available at http://www.bibleplaces.com/wp-content/uploads/2015/08/The-Land-and-the-Bible.pdf.

———. *Satellite Bible Atlas*. Israel: William Schlegel, 2013.

Schnittjer, Gary Edward. *The Torah Story: An Apprenticeship on the Pentateuch*. Grand Rapids: Zondervan, 2006.

Schreiner, Thomas R. *40 Questions about Christians and Biblical Law*. 40 Questions. Grand Rapids: Kregel, 2010.

———. *Interpreting the Pauline Epistles*. 2nd ed. Grand Rapids: Baker Academic, 2011.

———. *The King in His Beauty: A Biblical Theology of the Old and New Testaments*. Grand Rapids: Baker Academic, 2013.

———. *Magnifying God in Christ: A Summary of New Testament Theology*. Grand Rapids: Baker Academic, 2010.

———. *New Testament Theology: Magnifying God in Christ*. Grand Rapids: Baker Academic, 2008.

———. "Preaching and Biblical Theology." *SBJT* 10, 2 (2006): 20–29.

Schreiner, Thomas R., and Ardel B. Caneday. *The Race Set before Us: A Biblical Theology of Perseverance and Assurance*. Downers Grove, IL: InterVarsity Press, 2001.

Schultz, Richard L. "Integrating Old Testament Theology and Exegesis: Literary, Thematic, and Canonical Issues." *NIDOTTE* 1:185–205.

Scobie, Charles H. H. "History of Biblical Theology." *NDBT* 11–20.

Scorgie, Glen G., Mark L. Stauss, and Steven M. Voth, eds. *The Challenge of Bible Translation: Communicating God's Word to the World*. Grand Rapids: Zondervan, 2003.

Scott, William R., Harold Scanlin, and Hans Peter Rüger. *A Simplified Guide to BHS: Critical Apparatus, Masora, Accents, Unusual Letters and Other Markings*. 4th ed. N. Richland Hills, TX: D&F Scott Publishing, 2007.

Scripture 4 All: Hebrew Interlinear Bible (OT). http://www.scripture4all.org/OnlineInterlinear/Hebrew_Index.htm.

Septuaginta: Vetus Testamentum Graecum Auctoritate Societatis Litterarum Gottingensis Editum. 24 vols. Göttingen: Vandenhoeck & Ruprecht, 1931–2006.

Septuagint Online. http://www.kalvesmaki.com/LXX/.

Sherlock, Charles. *The Doctrine of Humanity*. Contours of Christian Theology. Downers Grove, IL: InterVarsity Press, 1996.

Silva, Moisés. *Biblical Words and Their Meaning: An Introduction to Lexical Semantics*. 2nd ed. Grand Rapids: Zondervan, 1994.

———. "God, Language, and Scripture: Reading the Bible in the Light of General Linguistics." In *Foundations of Contemporary Interpretation*, edited by Moisés Silva, 193–280. Grand Rapids: Zondervan, 1996.

———, ed. *New International Dictionary of New Testament Theology and Exegesis*. 2nd ed. 5 vols. Grand Rapids: Zondervan, 2014.

Simpson, D. P., ed. *Cassell's Latin Dictionary*. New York: Macmillan, 1968.

Smith, Gary V. *Interpreting the Prophetic Books: An Exegetical Handbook*. Handbooks for Old Testament Exegesis. Grand Rapids: Kregel, 2014.

Smith, George Adam. *The Historical Geography of the Holy Land*. London: Hodder and Stoughton, 1894; repr., New York: Harper & Row, 1966.

Smith, Jerome H., ed. *The New Treasury of Scripture Knowledge*. 2nd ed. Nashville: Thomas Nelson, 1992.

Smith, Ralph L. *Old Testament Theology: Its History, Method, and Message*. Nashville: Broadman & Holman, 1994.

Smith, R. Payne, ed. *A Compendious Syriac Dictionary*. Oxford: Clarendon, 1903; repr., Eugene, OR: Wipf & Stock, 1999.

Snell, Daniel C. *Life in the Ancient Near East, 3100–332 B.C.E.* New Haven, CT: Yale University Press, 1998.

Snoeberger, Mark A. "A Review Article: *Kingdom through Covenant: A Biblical-Theological Understanding of the Covenants*." *DBSJ* 17 (2012): 99–103.

Soden, Wolfram von. *The Ancient Orient: An Introduction to the Study of the Ancient Near East*. Translated by Donald G. Schley. Grand Rapids: Eerdmans, 1994.

Soderland, S. K. "Text and MSS of the OT." *ISBE* 4:798–814.

Sokoloff, Michael. *A Dictionary of Jewish Babylonian Aramaic*. Baltimore: Johns Hopkins University Press, 2003.

———. *A Dictionary of Jewish Palestinian Aramaic of the Byzantine Period*. 2nd ed. Baltimore: Johns Hopkins University Press, 2002.

Soulen, Richard N., and R. Kendall Soulen. *Handbook of Biblical Criticism*. 4th ed. Louisville: Westminster John Knox, 2011.

Sparks, Kenton L. *Ancient Texts for the Study of the Hebrew Bible: A Guide to the Background Literature*. Peabody, MA: Hendrickson, 2005.

Sperber, Alexander, ed. *The Bible in Aramaic*. 4 vols. Leiden: Brill, 1959–73.

———. *A Historical Grammar of Biblical Hebrew*. Leiden: Brill, 1966.

Spicq, Ceslas, ed. *Theological Lexicon of the New Testament*. Translated by James D. Ernest. 3 vols. Peabody, MA: Hendrickson, 1993.

Stallard, Mike, ed. *Dispensational Understanding of the New Covenant: 3 Views*. Schaumburg, IL: Regular Baptist, 2012.

Stein, Robert H. *A Basic Guide to Interpreting the Bible: Playing by the Rules*. 2nd ed. Grand Rapids: Baker Academic, 2011.

———. "Kingdom of God." *EDBT* 451–54.

Steinmann, Andrew E. *From Abraham to Paul: A Biblical Chronology*. St. Louis: Concordia, 2011.

Stern, Ephraim, Ayelet Leyinzon-Gilbo'a, and Joseph Aviram, eds. *The New Encyclopedia of Archaeological Excavations in the Holy Land*. 4 vols. New York: Simon & Schuster, 1993–2008.

Sternberg, Meir. *The Poetics of Biblical Narrative: Ideological Literature and the Drama of Reading*. Indiana Studies in Biblical Literature. Bloomington, IN: Indiana University Press, 1985.

Stevenson, William B. *Grammar of Palestinian Jewish Aramaic*. Oxford: Clarendon, 1962; repr., Eugene, OR: Wipf & Stock, 2000.

Storms, Sam, and Dane C. Ortlund, eds. *ESV Men's Devotional Bible*. Wheaton, IL: Crossway, 2015.

Strauss, Mark L. *How to Read the Bible in Changing Times: Understanding and Applying God's Word Today*. Grand Rapids: Baker, 2011.

———. "Why the English Standard Version (ESV) Should Not Become the Standard English Version: How to Make a Good Translation Much Better." Paper presented at the National Meeting of the Evangelical Theological Society, Providence, RI, November 21, 2008. Available at http://zondervan.typepad.com/files/improvingesv2.pdf.

Strecker, Georg. *Theology of the New Testament*. Louisville: Westminster John Knox, 2000.

Strickland, Wayne G., ed. *Five Views on Law and Gospel*. Grand Rapids: Zondervan, 1999.

———. "Preunderstanding and Daniel Fuller's Law-Gospel Continuum." *BSac* 144 (1987): 181–93.

Stuart, Douglas. *Old Testament Exegesis: A Handbook for Students and Pastors*. 4th ed. Louisville: Westminster John Knox, 2009.

Swete, Henry Barclay. *An Introduction to the Old Testament in Greek*. 2nd ed. Cambridge: Cambridge University Press, 1914; repr., Eugene, OR: Wipf & Stock, 2003.

Tal, Abraham, ed. *The Samaritan Pentateuch: Edited according to MS 6 of the Shekem Synagogue*. Tel-Aviv: Tel-Aviv University Press, 1994.

Taylor, Bernard A. *Analytical Lexicon to the Septuagint*. 2nd ed. Peabody, MA: Hendrickson, 2009.

Taylor, Willard H. "Biblical Theology." *ZEB* 1:622–30.

Tenney, Merrill C., and Moisés Silva, eds. *The Zondervan Encyclopedia of the Bible*. 2nd ed. 5 vols. Grand Rapids: Zondervan, 2009.

Theological and Academic Resources for the Septuagint. http://www.kalvesmaki.com/.

Thesaurus Linguae Graecae. http://stephanus.tlg.uci.edu/.

Thiele, Edwin R. *The Mysterious Numbers of the Hebrew Kings*. 2nd ed. Grand Rapids: Zondervan, 1983.

Thielman, Frank. *Theology of the New Testament: A Canonical and Synthetic Approach*. Grand Rapids: Zondervan, 2005.

Thiselton, Anthony C. *Systematic Theology*. Grand Rapids: Eerdmans, 2015.

Thompson, Frank Charles, ed. *Thompson Chain-Reference Bible: New International Version*. Grand Rapids: Zondervan, 1983.

Todd, James M., III. *Sinai and the Saints: Reading Old Covenant Laws for the New Covenant Community*. Downers Grove, IL: InterVarsity Press, 2017.

Topical concordances at the following websites:

- http://www.crosswalk.com/.
- http://www.biblestudytools.com/.
- http://www.studylight.org/.
- https://www.biblegateway.com/.

Torrey, R. A., and Timothy S. Morton. *The Treasury of Scripture Knowledge*. 3rd ed. Peabody, MA: Hendrickson, 2010.

Tov, Emanuel, ed. *Electronic Resources Relevant to the Textual Criticism of Hebrew Scripture*. http://rosetta.reltech.org/TC/vol08/Tov2003.html.

———. *Scribal Practices and Approaches Reflected in the Texts Found in the Judean Desert.* Studies on the Texts of the Desert of Judah 54. Atlanta: SBL, 2009.

———. *The Text-Critical Use of the Septuagint in Biblical Research.* 3rd ed. Winona Lake, IN: Eisenbrauns, 2015.

———, ed. *The Texts from the Judaean Desert: Indices and an Introduction to the Discoveries in the Judaean Desert Series.* DJD 39. Oxford: Clarendon, 2002.

———. "Textual Criticism (OT)." *ABD* 4:393–412.

———. *Textual Criticism of the Hebrew Bible.* 3rd ed. Minneapolis: Fortress, 2011.

Ulrich, Eugene. *The Dead Sea Scrolls and the Origins of the Bible.* Studies in the Dead Sea Scrolls and Related Literature. Grand Rapids: Eerdmans, 1999.

United Bible Societies. *Septuagint Bibliography.* http://www.ubs-translations.org/cgi-bin/dbman/db.cgi?db=lxxbib&uid=default.

Vance, Donald A., George Athas, and Yael Avrahami, eds. *Biblia Hebraica Stuttgartensia: A Reader's Edition.* Peabody, MA: Hendrickson, 2015.

VanderKam, James C. *The Dead Sea Scrolls and the Bible.* Grand Rapids: Eerdmans, 2012.

VanGemeren, Willem A. *Eschatology.* Foundations of Evangelical Theology. Wheaton, IL: Crossway, forthcoming.

———. *Interpreting the Prophetic Word: An Introduction to the Prophetic Literature of the Old Testament.* Grand Rapids: Zondervan, 1996.

———, ed. *New International Dictionary of Old Testament Theology and Exegesis.* 5 vols. Grand Rapids: Zondervan, 1997.

———. *The Progress of Redemption: The Story of Salvation from Creation to the New Jerusalem.* Grand Rapids: Baker Academic, 1996.

Vanhoozer, Kevin J. "Exegesis and Hermeneutics." *NDBT* 52–64.

Van Pelt, Miles V. *Basics of Biblical Aramaic: Complete Grammar, Lexicon, and Annotated Text.* Grand Rapids: Zondervan, 2011.

———, ed. *A Biblical-Theological Introduction to the Old Testament: The Gospel Promised.* Wheaton, IL: Crossway, 2016.

———. "Introduction." In A *Biblical-Theological Introduction to the Old Testament: The Gospel Promised*, edited by Miles V. Van Pelt, 23–42. Wheaton, IL: Crossway, 2016.

van Wolde, Ellen, ed. *Narrative Syntax and the Hebrew Bible: Papers of the Tilburg Conference 1996.* Biblical Interpretation 29. Leiden: Brill, 1997.

Vaux, Roland de. *Ancient Israel: Its Life and Institutions.* Grand Rapids: Eerdmans, 1997.

Vermes, Geza. *The Complete Dead Sea Scrolls in English.* 7th ed. London: Penguin Books, 2012.

Vetus latina: Die Reste der altlateinischen Bibel nach Petrus Sabatier neu gesammelt und in Verbindung mit der Heidelberger Akademie der Wissenschaften herausgegeben von der Erzabtei Beuron. Freiburg: Herder, 1949–.

Vetus Testamentum Syriace et Neosyriace. 1852; repr., London: Trinitarian Bible Society, 1954.

Viening, Edward. *The Zondervan Topical Bible.* Grand Rapids: Zondervan, 1969.

Vine, W. E., Merrill F. Unger, and William White Jr. *Vine's Complete Expository Dictionary of Old and New Testament Words*. London: Oliphants, 1939; repr., Nashville: Thomas Nelson, 1996.

Vlach, Michael J. *Has the Church Replaced Israel? A Theological Evaluation*. Nashville: Broadman & Holman, 2010.

———. "Have They Found a Better Way? An Analysis of Gentry and Wellum's *Kingdom through Covenant*." *MSJ* 24, 1 (2013): 5–24.

———. "The Kingdom of God and the Millennium." *MSJ* 23, 2 (2012): 225–54.

———. "New Covenant Theology Compared with Covenantalism." *MSJ* 18 (2007): 201–19.

———. "What Does Christ as 'True Israel' Mean for the Nation Israel? A Critique of the Non-Dispensational Understanding." *MSJ* 23, 1 (2012): 43–54.

Vogt, Ernesto. *Lexicon Linguae Aramaicae Veteris Testamenti Documentis Antiquis Illustratum*. Rome: Pontifical Biblical Institute, 1991.

Vogt, Peter T. *Interpreting the Pentateuch: An Exegetical Handbook*. Handbooks for Old Testament Exegesis. Grand Rapids: Kregel, 2009.

Von Gall, August, ed. *Der hebräische Pentateuch der Samaritaner: Genesis–Deuteronomy*. 5 vols. in 1. Giessen: Töpelmann, 1918; repr., Berlin: de Gruyter, 1965.

Vos, Geerhardus. *Biblical Theology: Old and New Testaments*. Grand Rapids: Eerdmans, 1948.

Waltke, Bruce. K. "Old Testament Textual Criticism." In *Foundations for Biblical Interpretation*, edited by David S. Dockery, Kenneth A. Mathews, and Robert B. Sloan, 156–86. Nashville: Broadman & Holman, 1994.

———. "The Phenomenon of Conditionality within Unconditional Covenants." In *Israel's Apostasy and Restoration: Essays in Honor of Roland K. Harrison*, edited by Avraham Gileadi, 123–39. Grand Rapids: Baker Academic, 1988.

———. "Samaritan Pentateuch." *ABD* 5:932–40.

———. "Textual Criticism of the Old Testament." In *Introductory Articles*, vol. 1 of Expositor's Bible Commentary, edited by Frank E. Gaebelein, 211–28. Grand Rapids: Zondervan, 1979.

Waltke, Bruce K., and David Diewert. "Wisdom Literature." In *The Face of Old Testament Studies: A Survey of Contemporary Approaches*, edited by David W. Baker and Bill T. Arnold, 295–328. Grand Rapids: Baker Academic, 2004.

Waltke, Bruce K., and M. O'Connor. *An Introduction to Biblical Hebrew Syntax*. Winona Lake, IN: Eisenbrauns, 1990.

Waltke, Bruce K., and Charles Yu. *An Old Testament Theology: A Canonical and Thematic Approach*. Grand Rapids: Zondervan, 2006.

Walton, John H. *Ancient Israelite Literature in Its Cultural Context*. Grand Rapids: Zondervan, 1994.

———. *Ancient Near Eastern Thought and the Old Testament: Introducing the Conceptual World of the Hebrew Bible*. Grand Rapids: Baker Academic, 2006.

———. *Chronological and Background Charts of the Old Testament*. 2nd ed. Grand Rapids: Zondervan, 1994.

———. "Principles for Productive Word Study." *NIDOTTE* 1:161–70.

———, ed. Zondervan Illustrated Bible Backgrounds Commentary: Old Testament. 5 vols. Grand Rapids: Zondervan, 2009.

Walton, John H., and Craig S. Keener, eds. *NIV Cultural Backgrounds Study Bible*. Grand Rapids: Zondervan, 2016.

Walton, John H., Victor H. Matthews, and Mark W. Chavalas, eds. The IVP Bible Background Commentary: Old Testament. Downers Grove, IL: InterVarsity Press, 2000.

Weber, Robert, and Roger Gryson, eds. *Biblia sacra: Iuxta Vulgatam versionem*. 4th ed. Stuttgart: Deutsche Bibelgesellschaft, 1994.

Webster, Brian L. *The Cambridge Introduction to Biblical Hebrew*. Cambridge: Cambridge University Press, 2009.

Wegner, Paul D. *The Journey from Texts to Translations: The Origin and Development of the Bible*. Grand Rapids: Baker, 2004.

———. *A Student's Guide to Textual Criticism of the Bible: Its Methods and Results*. Downers Grove, IL: InterVarsity Press, 2006.

Wells, Tom, and Fred G. Zaspel. *New Covenant Theology: Description, Definition, Defense*. Frederick, MD: New Covenant Media, 2002.

Wellum, Stephen J. "Baptism and the Relationship between the Covenants." In *Believer's Baptism: Sign of the New Covenant in Christ*, edited by Thomas R. Schreiner and Shawn D. Wright, 97–161. NAC Studies in Bible and Theology. Nashville: Broadman & Holman, 2007.

———. *Christology*. Foundations of Evangelical Theology. Wheaton, IL: Crossway, forthcoming.

———. "Progressive Covenantalism and Doing Ethics." In *Progressive Covenantalism: Charting a Course between Dispensational and Covenant Theologies*, edited by Stephen J. Wellum and Brent E. Parker, 215–33. Nashville: Broadman & Holman, 2016.

Wellum, Stephen J., and Brent E. Parker, eds. *Progressive Covenantalism: Charting a Course between Dispensational and Covenant Theologies*. Nashville: Broadman & Holman, 2016.

Wenham, Gordon J. *A Guide to the Pentateuch*. Exploring the Old Testament 1. Downers Grove, IL: InterVarsity Press, 2003.

Weston, Anthony. *A Rulebook for Arguments*. 4th ed. Indianapolis: Hackett, 2008.

White, James R. *The King James Only Controversy: Can You Trust Modern Translations?* 2nd ed. Minneapolis: Bethany House, 2009.

———. "The Newness of the New Covenant: Better Covenant, Better Mediator, Better Sacrifice, Better Ministry, Better Hope, Better Promises (Part 1)." *RBTR* 1, 2 (2004): 144–68.

———. "The Newness of the New Covenant: Better Covenant, Better Mediator, Better Sacrifice, Better Ministry, Better Hope, Better Promises (Part 2)." *RBTR* 2, 1 (2005): 83–104.

Whitney, Donald S. *Spiritual Disciplines for the Christian Life*. 2nd ed. Colorado Springs: NavPress, 2014.

Wiley, H. Orton. *Christian Theology*. 5th ed. 3 vols. Kansas City: Beacon Hill, 1940.

Williams, Michael. *How to Read the Bible through the Jesus Lens: A Guide to Christ-Focused Reading of Scripture*. Grand Rapids: Zondervan, 2012.

Williams, Ronald J., and John C. Beckman. *Williams' Hebrew Syntax*. 3rd ed. Toronto: University of Toronto Press, 2007.

Williamson, Paul R. "Covenant." *NDBT* 419–29.

———. *Sealed with an Oath: Covenant in God's Unfolding Purpose*. NSBT 23. Downers Grove, IL: InterVarsity Press, 2007.

Wise, Michael, Martin Abegg Jr., and Edward Cook. *The Dead Sea Scrolls: A New Translation*. San Francisco: HarperSanFrancisco, 2005.

Witherington, Ben, III. *The Indelible Image: The Theological and Ethical Thought World of the New Testament*. 2 vols. Downers Grove, IL: InterVarsity Press, 2009.

Wolters, Al. "The Text of the Old Testament." In *The Face of Old Testament Studies: A Survey of Contemporary Approaches*, edited by David W. Baker and Bill T. Arnold, 19–37. Grand Rapids: Baker Academic, 2004.

Wonneberger, Reinhard. *Understanding BHS: A Manual for the Users of Biblia Hebraica Stuttgartensia*. 2nd ed. Rome: Pontifical Biblical Institute, 1990.

Wright, Christopher J. H. *How to Preach and Teach the Old Testament for All Its Worth*. Grand Rapids: Zondervan, 2016.

———. *Knowing Jesus through the Old Testament*. 2nd ed. Downers Grove, IL: InterVarsity Press, 2014.

———. *The Mission of God: Unlocking the Bible's Grand Narrative*. Downers Grove, IL: InterVarsity Press, 2006.

———. *Old Testament Ethics for the People of God*. Downers Grove, IL: InterVarsity Press, 2004.

Wright, N. T. *The Climax of the Covenant: Christ and the Law in Pauline Theology*. Minneapolis: Fortress, 1993.

———. *Jesus and the Victory of God*. Minneapolis: Fortress, 1997.

———. *The New Testament and the People of God*. Minneapolis: Fortress, 1992.

———. *Paul and the Faithfulness of God*. 2 vols. Minneapolis: Fortress, 2013.

———. *The Resurrection of the Son of God*. Minneapolis: Fortress, 2003.

Würthwein, Ernst, and Alexander Achilles Fisher. *The Text of the Old Testament: An Introduction to the Biblia Hebraica*. Translated by Errol F. Rhodes. 3rd ed. Grand Rapids: Eerdmans, 2014.

Yamauchi, Edwin M. *Persia and the Bible*. Grand Rapids: Baker, 1990.

Yamauchi, Edwin M., and Marvin R. Wilson. *Dictionary of Daily Life in Biblical and Post-Biblical Antiquity*. 4 vols. Peabody, MA: Hendrickson, 2014–16.

Yarbrough, Robert W. "Biblical Theology." *EDBT* 61–66.

———. "The Practice and Promise of Biblical Theology: A Response to Hamilton and Goldsworthy." *SBJT* 12, 4 (2008): 78–87.

Young, Ian, Robert Rezetko, and Martin Ehrensvärd. *Linguistic Dating of Biblical Texts: An Introduction to Approaches and Problems*. 2 vols. London: Routledge, 2014.

Young, Rodger C. All his published essays found at http://www.rcyoung.org/papers.html.

Younger, K. Lawson, Jr., ed. *The Context of Scripture*. Vol. 4, *Supplements*. Leiden: Brill, 2016.

Zaspel, Fred G. *The New Covenant and New Covenant Theology*. Frederick, MD: New Covenant Media, 2011.

Zimmerli, Walther. *Old Testament Theology in Outline*. Atlanta: John Knox, 1978.

Zondervan Exegetical Commentary on the Old Testament. Grand Rapids: Zondervan, 2015–.

Zuck, Roy B., ed. *A Biblical Theology of the New Testament*. Chicago: Moody, 1994.

———, ed. *A Biblical Theology of the Old Testament*. Chicago: Moody, 1991.

INDEX OF SCRIPTURE

Exodus

Leviticus

Numbers

Deuteronomy

Joshua

Song of Solomon

Isaiah

Jeremiah

Romans

INDEX OF SUBJECTS AND NAMES

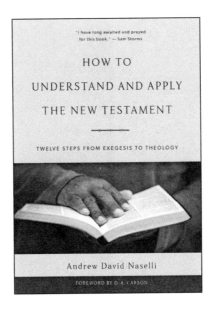

Also from P&R

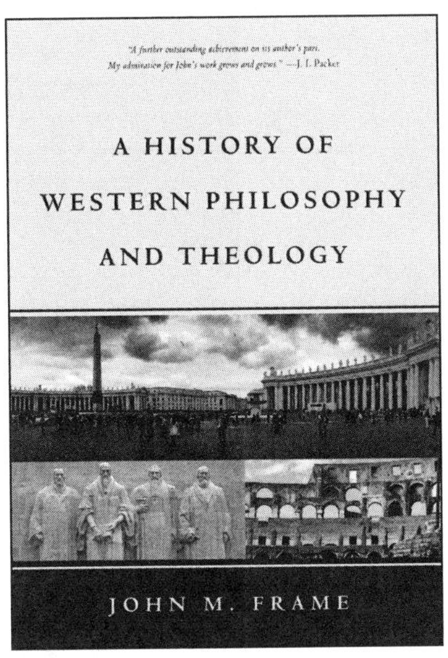

A History of Western Philosophy and Theology is the fruit of John Frame's forty-five years of teaching philosophical subjects. No other survey of the history of Western thought offers the same invigorating blend of expositional clarity, critical insight, and biblical wisdom. The supplemental study questions, bibliographies, links to audio lectures, quotes from influential thinkers, twenty appendices, and indexed glossary make this an excellent main textbook choice for seminary- and college-level courses and for personal study.

"I have never read a history of Western thought quite like John Frame's. Professor Frame unabashedly tries to think through sources and movements out of the framework (bad pun intended) of deep-seated Christian commitments, and invites his readers to do the same. These commitments, combined with the format of a seminary or college textbook, will make this work invaluable to students and pastors who tire of ostensible neutrality that is no more neutral than the next volume. Agree or disagree with some of his arguments, but John Frame will teach you how to *think* in theological and philosophical categories."

—**D. A. Carson**, Research Professor, Trinity Evangelical Divinity School